At war

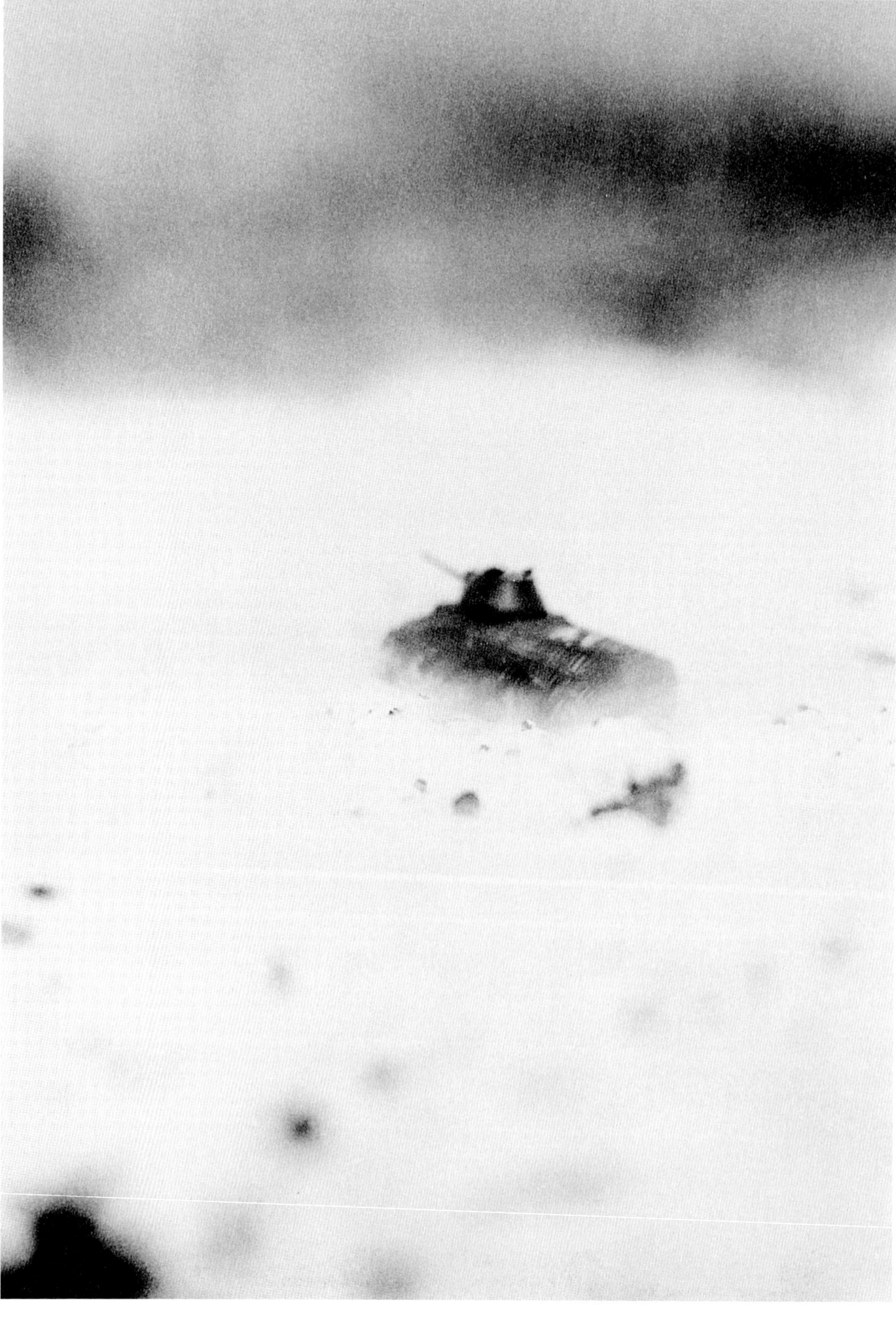

At war

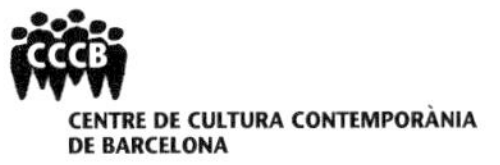
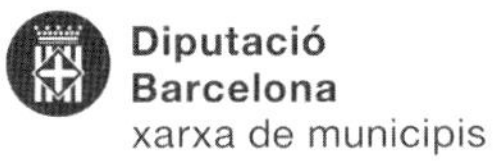
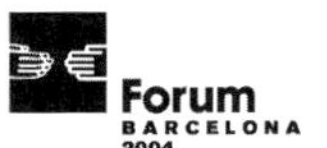
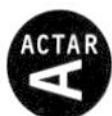

EXHIBITION
"At War" has been co-produced by the
Centre de Cultura Contemporània de
Barcelona and the Forum Barcelona 2004.
It is on show at the CCCB between
May 17 and September 26, 2004.

CURATORS
Antonio Monegal
Francesc Torres
José María Ridao

COORDINATION
CCCB Exhibition Department

DOCUMENTATION
CCCB Exhibition Department
with the collaboration of Sònia Aran,
Natalia Beneditchouk, Anna Fabra
and Íngrid Guardiola

MONTAGE DESIGN AND DIRECTION
F-451 arquitectura

EXHIBITION GRAPHIC DESIGN
Mont Marsà

INDUSTRIAL MONTAGE
Relluc, Decostyle
and Moquetas Santos Martínez

INSTALLATION OF ORIGINAL PIECES
Montajes Livi and CCCB Registration
and Conservation Unit

AUDIOVISUAL DOCUMENTATION
Lisa Berger
with the collaboration of Tania Ramos
and Parthiv Shah

AUDIOVISUAL PRODUCTION /
AUDIOVISUALS EDITOR
CCCB Audiovisuals Department

AUDIOVISUAL INSTALLATIONS
CCCB Audiovisuals Department

LIGHTING
Maria Domènech
with the collaboration of the CCCB
Production Unit

ELECTRICAL INSTALLATION
AND SPECIAL MONTAGES
CCCB Production Unit

REGISTRATION
CCCB Registration and Conservation Unit

TRANSPORT
SIT Transportes Internacionales

PRESS AND COMMUNICATION
CCCB Communication Unit

And the collaboration of the
Documentation Centre, the Adminis-
trative Services and the Technical
and General Services of the CCCB.

CATALOGUE
DIRECTION
Antonio Monegal
Francesc Torres

COORDINATION
CCCB Publications

TEXT COORDINATION
Rosa Puig

PHOTOGRAPHIC DOCUMENTATION
Judith Rovira

GRAPHIC DESIGN
Max Weber

TRANSLATIONS AND PROOFREADING
Paul Hammond
Mark Waudby

PUBLISHED BY
Centre de Cultura Contemporània de
Barcelona, Institut d'Edicions de la
Diputació de Barcelona, Forum Barcelona
2004 and Actar

PRINTING
Ingoprint

© Diputació de Barcelona, 2004
© Centre de Cultura Contemporània de
  Barcelona, 2004
  Montalegre, 5 - 08001 Barcelona
  www.cccb.org
© Fòrum Barcelona 2004

ISBN: 84-95951-69-X
D.L.: B-824584-04

p. 2 and 10
David Levinthal, Two works from
"Hitler moves East" series, 1975-1977
Kodalith Film, 23.5 x 18.4, 19 x 23.5 cm
Courtesy of the artist and Galerie Xippas,
Paris

The exhibition *At War*, a co-production of the Centre de Cultura Contemporània de Barcelona and the Universal Forum of Cultures – Barcelona 2004, reflects on the experience of war. In addition to examining historical evidence, emphasis is placed on the everyday experience of conflict. The exhibition also takes a look at the postwar experience, a period strongly characterized by latent violence that is often more drawn-out and just as tragic as war itself. *At War* brings together works of art, objects and documents—elements that together evoke the memory of an experience whose imprint on the minds of those affected can never be erased. Conflict is as much a part of the contemporary world as ever, and we are all, to one extent or another, the children of war.

Yet it is by coming to terms with this tragic experience and the scars and shattered lives it leaves behind that we can begin to build peace. We must recognize that the approaches used at the end of the twentieth century to deal with conflict are not valid for the twenty-first century. We must create a new world order based not on power and conquest but on the subtlety of intelligence and on an understanding of the motives of others. John Hume, winner of the Nobel Peace Prize for his contribution to achieving reconciliation in Northern Ireland, sums this up succinctly when he affirms that it is agreement and not victory that leads to peace.

The four major exhibitions at the Forum Site, along with some 20 organized by museums and cultural centers in the city of Barcelona, pose two main questions: how do we relate to each other as human beings, and how should we relate to each other? What circumstances have we placed ourselves in on the Earth? Our survival as a species depends on the answers we give to these and related questions. These exhibitions show us both our capacity for destruction and the boundless human capacity for creation, self-expression and love; art in all its forms and humanity's great creation—the city—a focal point for coexistence, exchange and peace; the twin strands that define human existence.

The Universal Forum of Cultures, an event to be held for the first time in Barcelona, focuses on reflection and experience centering on three core themes whose bearing on our future cannot be overstated: the process of building peace, sustainable development and respect for cultural diversity. The Forum is a new kind of international event that brings together people rather than states. Its central aim is to provide a platform for global civil society to make itself heard and a framework for reflection, dialogue, experience, festivity, and celebration of all the arts.

Today more than ever, such a process of reflection is both timely and essential. First and foremost, though, the Forum is a unique experience: a tangible demonstration of the fact that we are many and that we are diverse, but that if we combine our energies and our wills, we can build a better and more just future for generations to come.

JOAN CLOS
Mayor of Barcelona
President of Forum Barcelona 2004

How often has it been said, after a war, that the errors and actions which led to it and the horror and the violence experienced during it ought to help to prevent it from ever happening again? Unfortunately, we have to admit that, however paradoxical it may seem, civilisations have often been built on the back of waging war. Both for those who have lived it personally and for those who only know it through stories, idealisations or fictional imagery, war is an experience of us all, an integral part of our culture, of our relationship to life, to other people, to the world.

The actuality of war is, then, permanent. At times it is claimed that the never-ending bombardment of images of the wars of our time by the media manages, due to the deadening effect of repetition, to efface or attenuate the real perception we have of this form of violence. If this is so, the valiant and profound reflection that the Centre de Cultura Contemporània de Barcelona offers with the exhibition *At War* will help the spectator to become aware of the background of a number of images which, despite everything, are impossible to confuse with those in the movies.

At War is an account of the remembering and the experience of war, a raw and direct reminder of the dark side of our culture. In this exhibition our vision cannot help but identify with that of its protagonists, both real and fictional, because their account calls on our own experience, it is directed to each and every one of us, irrespective of whether we have lived the experience of a war or not.

It is essential for us not to forget that war forms a part of us all. There will always be moments in which we inevitably drop our guard, but our weaknesses are there to be confronted and overcome. The more we bear in mind what a war represents, the further away we shall be from repeating the nightmarish experience of it.

CELESTINO CORBACHO
President of the Diputació de Barcelona and of the CCCB Consortium

War and civilisation

I remember a video by Heimo Zobering which shows a sniper in action. The camera is located inside the room where he has taken up position, so we never see the target he is aiming at. With mechanical spontaneity, the sniper repeats the same gestures: he loads, waits and shoots; he reloads, waits again, and shoots again. The scene appears insignificant. But, there is a life at the end of each bullet. A life which is ebbing away.

War around the world is an everyday activity that kills millions of people. We talk about war when the United States spring into action and all the media follow in their wake. But war is found in many places. Although we do not even know about some of them because there is also a class system in war. Africa is scarred by wars. Three million people died in the Congo over a five-year period. How many First-World citizens have this war in their thoughts? The last genocide of the twentieth century took place in Rwanda, while the rest of the world looked passively on, beginning with the UN which, once again, showed its powerlessness to act. They say that an international peacekeeping force of 6,500 soldiers would have sufficed to prevent the genocide. And, at the present time, in the Sudan, there are 700,000 people trapped in the region of Darfur without any access to healthcare, and the world fails to show concern about them. And Uganda, and Chechenia and Kashmir and many other conflicts.

Violence is a component of human experience, with this difference in potential that determines all relationships between people —which Michel Foucault called power— running through it. Ritual and word have been the two traditional instruments against violence. Ritual helps sublimate it, although at times tension spills over and becomes a catalyst. The word is the best antidote to violence, until demagogy erupts to work in favour of the expansion of violence. No matter how much Jean-Jacques Rousseau branded man as completely irresponsible, condemning social relation-ships as being to blame for all evils, something profound links man and violence. After all, the desire to survive compelled him to give over part of his freedom to the State (Hobbes) and to control his urges in the process of civilisation (Freud), even at the cost of an undeniable unease which provokes recurrent outbreaks of a violence which never diminishes.

Among the forms of human violence are the wars which, since time immemorial, have pitted tribes, communities, cities, nations and empires (us against others) against one another in a fight for land, water, wealth or simply the desire for power. War has had several manifestations throughout history according to the technological potential and the macrophysics of power of each moment. War entered the modern age as an extension of politics by other means and, in the twentieth century, wars on a massive scale were waged, which mobilised the entire citizenry and led to the growing involvement of the rearguard in the conflict. Besides mass warfare, the century has contributed crimes of logic (Albert Camus), wars of mass destruction (and as a —positive— consequence, the nuclear deterrent) and, in its final period, the privatisation of war (with an appreciable loss of the State's monopoly of violence) and the spread of weapons of mass destruction.

According to Ramón Lobo in *El País* an ancient from the Acholi tribe in the devastated country of Uganda said, "Peace occurs when a man is only afraid of snakes". However, in order to build peace you have to look war in the face. Only then, by ceasing to rely on the good conscience of the fine pacifist spirit, will humanity be able to make war a permanent taboo one day.

At War is an exhibition which seeks to show the imagery of twentieth century warfare. It is not an attempt to issue a moral sanction, or to stage a militant exhibition. Quite simply, it aims to set out the mental construction process which leads a society to war and mobilises its citizens around it, the cultural constructions which go with it, and the marks it leaves on the experience and memory of peoples.

The exhibition has not been prompted by recent events. It was devised and planned before society's mass mobilisations against the war in Iraq. Although it is to be hoped that this return to politics will have repercussions on the exhibition, resulting in the more active and motivated attitude of the visitors. At the end of the day, an exhibition, like all work involving creation, is what it is and what its recipients make it.

JOSEP RAMONEDA
Director of the CCCB

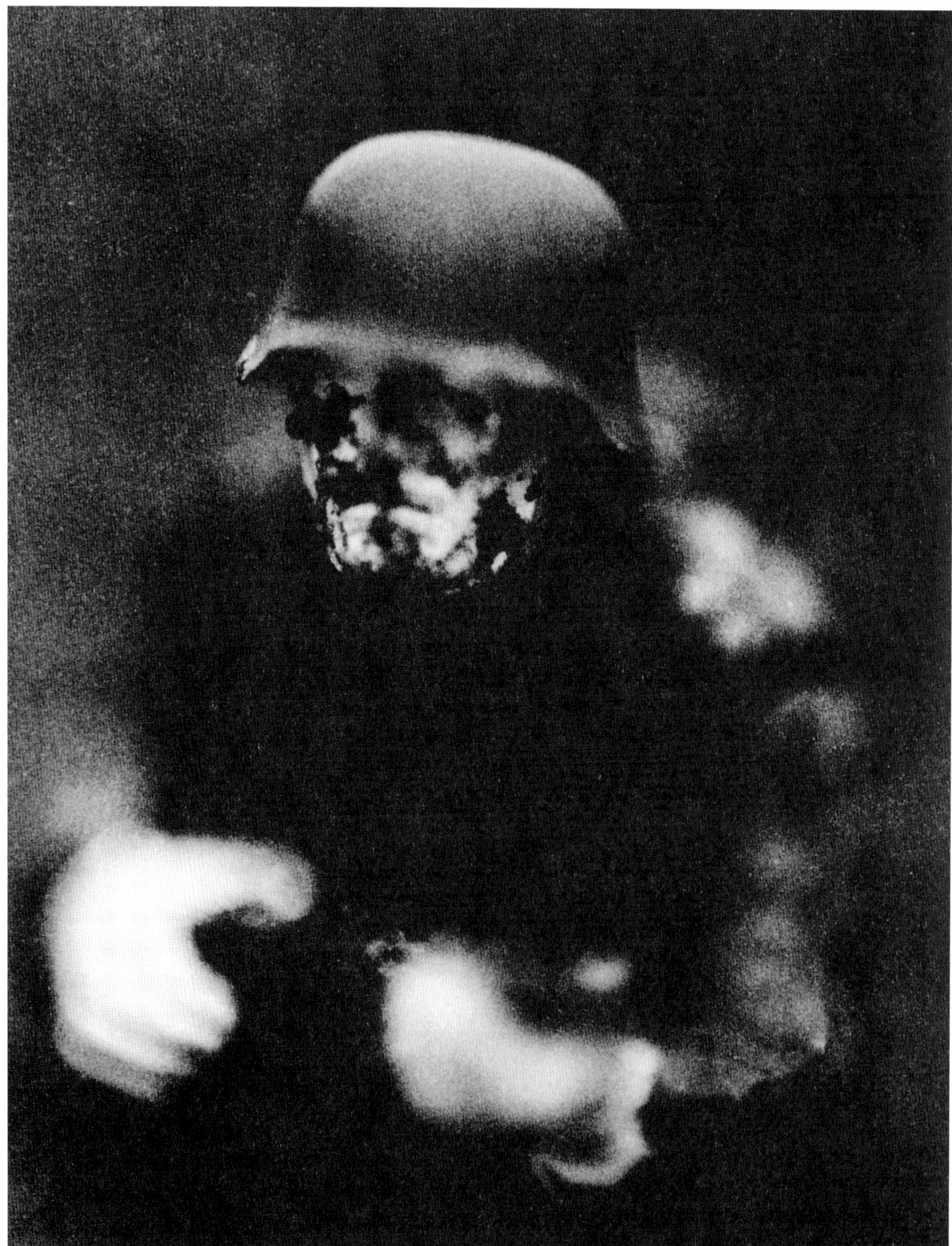

Introduction

At war
Antonio Monegal and Francesc Torres

I. The culture of war

"War is always an expression of culture, often a determinant of cultural forms, in some societies the culture itself."
JOHN KEEGAN

"If we are describing a war, we shall first of all mention the preliminaries such as the general's speeches, the outlay of both sides, and their fears; next, the attacks, the slaughter, and the dead; finally, the victory trophy, the triumphal songs of the victors, the tears and enslavement of the victims."
HERMOGENES

In March 2002 the Massachusetts Institute of Technology announced that it had been awarded a $50M grant by the Pentagon to design the high-tech equipment of the "soldier of the future." A scandal broke out when Ray and Ben Lai, creators of the comic *Radix*, accused MIT scientists of having copied a drawing of one of their characters, Valerie Fiores, to illustrate the proposal with which they'd competed for the research money. Looking at the two drawings, the similarities are obvious. The director of MIT's military nanotechnology lab apologised in public to the comic artists for the plagiarism, but the fact that a scientific project might illustrate its virtues and possibilities by using a drawing of an S-F woman warrior seems to have passed people by. The proof that there's nothing problematic about this association emerged months later when in a presentation of the project to the press the scientific head of the US Army, Michael Andrews, explained that in order to understand what the uniform they're designing involves we ought to think of the extraterrestrial in the movie *Predator*. When we talk about how the wars of the future will be, then, we find that these projections are not only informed by how wars are fought right now, but by something that's present in peacetime culture, and which in this instance belongs to the sphere of leisure and entertainment.

This exhibition sets out to identify both the changes wrought in the evolution of warfare from the beginning of the twentieth century until now and the invariable aspects which define the phenomenon of war as such, aspects that are manifested in the majority of conflicts and in the processes prior to their violent materialisation. We've attempted to bring the point of view of the fighters face to face with that of the victims, the vision of those who believe they are struggling for a noble cause with that of those who oppose war and radically reject it. In that sense, this isn't an exhibition in favour of or against war, but rather one about what war is, about different facets of the experience of war, about its direct impact on individuals and communities, and about its representation as formalised in cultural products.

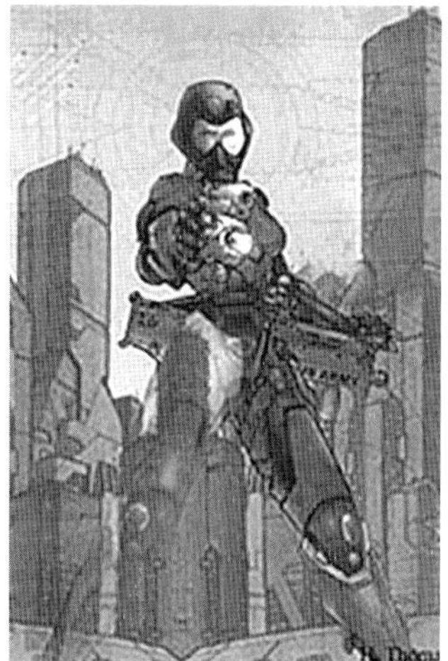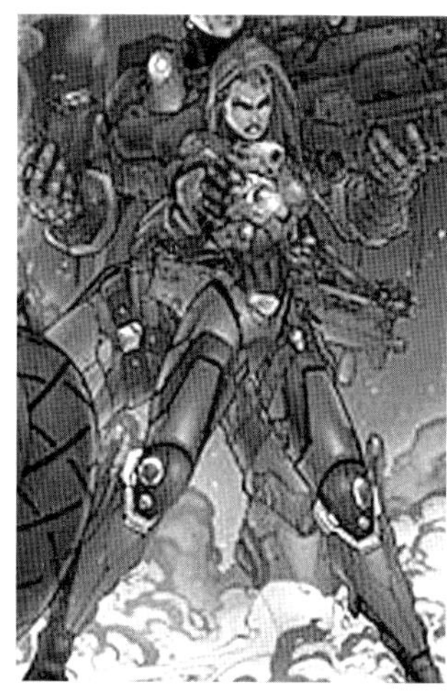

There are many ways of organising a discourse about war. It can be done from the perspective of history or, more specifically, of military history. Or by choosing the geo-strategic or political aspects. Or by restricting it to one type of conflict: wars between states, civil wars, guerrilla wars, the nuclear deterrent. Or by considering the problematic of a particular group: refugees, reporters, violated women, kid soldiers. In the traditional epic, and in such recent variants as the war movie, the subject matter is usually heroes and military achievements. Most views of, and shows about, war focus on a particular conflict: the two World Wars, the Spanish Civil War, the Cold War, Vietnam, Iraq, et cetera. Or on a single form of representation: photography, cinema, painting, television. And it's logical that this is so, because wars are distinctive and the variety of contexts, moments and even images is limitless. The specific difference of *At War* is that it isn't subject to such limits, since its aims demand that the inexhaustible complexity of the phenomenon of war and the multiplicity of its expressions be recognised. It's not an historical exhibition, but neither does it renounce historical referentiality and neither have its exhibits been chosen for their artistic value alone. It is not about bringing a miscellany together, a heterogeneous compendium of representations, but about elaborating a unified discourse about the phenomenon of war as a whole. In order to do this the criterion has been not to speak of all that war is, nor of all wars, but rather of war as it is experienced by individuals, by those who are or have been in the front line, the beleaguered city, the concentration or refugee camp, as well as those of us who are far away in time or space and who experience it through representations of it.

The concept of experience and the challenge of representing said experience are the axes that articulate the exhibition as a whole.
Two forms of experience come together, then, in the show: represented experience and experienced representation. Those who have been there have borne witness, have registered the images, have left us their account. Those of us who haven't lived it accede via these representations to a mediated experience, yet one that is nevertheless a form of knowledge. What each of us knows, or thinks they know, about what a war is, comes from somewhere: from actual experience or from the media, history books, blockbuster movies, video games, the stories told by fathers and grandfathers. Even those who've never been in the middle of a war zone live in an environment in which war is present in one way or another. The exhibition, then, isn't just about reflecting on what happens when and where a war is effectively going on, but also embraces those aspects of the phenomenon of war which impinge on the social space that is seemingly at peace, such as the one in which this exhibition takes place. There is no society which is not "at war" in one way or another. The exhibition aims to make visitors think about war's place in the culture and to invite them to convert their tour through such a place into an experience of their own everyday position in this space "at war."

Our approach emphasises the culture of war understood as the nexus of context, behaviour, logic and the values that war produces at its very heart, and its inscription in cultural terms: its historical legacy interwoven in the collective memory and deposited in cultural artefacts, its role in configuring the identity of nations, its potential for preparing us for future wars and for justifying their necessity. It presupposes understanding culture not as a collection of more or less canonic works but as a series of processes configuring a vision of the world which determines our options for behaviour and even our political decisions.

Instead of following the chronological sequence of historical conflicts, the exhibition is divided up thematically, deploying a narrative that reproduces and synthesises the different planes of the process: what happens before, during and after each war. Unlike those discourses which only focus on the time of the fighting, the violence and destruction, we recognise a number of latent cultural conditions that precede the conflict, and certain sequels which are also established in the culture. We proceed from the position that it is impossible to be exhaustive since the impact of war touches every aspect of human experience, and that what must be emphasised is that war doesn't begin when the first shot is fired or end with the signing of a communiqué or the raising of a flag. We are "at war" long before hostilities begin and their echo resounds long after the last soldier returns home.
The exhibition begins with the socialisation of violence: how we human

beings become familiar as children with the idea of the possibility of
war and the existence of institutions like armies and the arms industry
in which this potential is realised. From there we move on to the
construction of the image of the enemy and of the causes of the conflict:
the means by which a society is divided into irreconcilable groups or how
two established collectives end up perceiving that their interests or their
worldviews are not negotiable and can only be resolved by violence.
The next section enters into the hostilities per se, what would customarily
be thought of as the object of an exhibition about war. This central part
of the exhibition, the most ample, has in turn various sections and
addresses the experience of soldiers and that of the civilian population,
the flight of refugees, the destruction of cities, and genocide. The military
sphere is covered first of all: the mobilising of the troops and the protests
against the war mark its beginning; it takes in the idleness of the soldiers
prior to the fighting, before going into the fighting proper and then into
its effects (the dead, the wounded, the prisoners).

No vision of war in the twentieth century can be reduced to the
viewpoint of the combatants, because it is the civilian population which
increasingly suffers its consequences. And so the exhibition devotes one
section to various themes relating to the repercussions of the war for the
non-combatants: the bombing and besieging of cities, the use of nuclear
weapons and their threat during the Cold War, the Holocaust. Next comes
the outcome of the war: victory and defeat (when these occur), the signing
of the documents of surrender or ceasefire (when these occur), reprisals
against collaborators, celebration, war-crimes trials. Finally, the narrative
concentrates on the remembering of the war, and on its forgetting:
monuments, history books, the testimony of survivors as part of oral
history, the current state of famous battlefields, now empty, reclaimed by
nature, or in some instances erased by the expansion of real estate.

This narrative sequence is largely a discursive artifice, since it is
obvious that not all wars have the same characteristics or go through
each of the phases outlined here, but it enables us to consider a number
of constants. The thesis to which it implicitly leads is that the process
described is cyclical: the remembering of wars, the way they are
monumentalised, taught to children and youngsters, registered within the
social fabric of a community—all this is part of the system of socialisation
that war perpetuates as a defining feature, at least up until now, of human
culture. Circumstances, causes and technologies change, but the impulse
and process that this generates is historically reproduced in forms that
are different, but which partake of common elements. While the general
categories that organise the discourse of the exhibition underline the
recurring, more universal aspects, each of the pieces on display invokes
the particularity of the historical event to which it refers; it brings the

mark of a specific conflict with it, thus representing the diversity of
the phenomenon of war.

In that sense war is similar to art: as a human activity it responds to a
permanent impulse but is determined by historical change and by the social
context, and adopts a practically inexhaustible variety of forms. This is
one of the reasons why we've given the arts a central role in the implementation of the exhibition narrative. A second reason is our recognition of the
impossibility of taking on board the real experience of war if not indirectly,
as representation, via the functioning of a mediating device.

This is an exhibition about war that flees from the military in a
way. There are almost no weapons, medals and uniforms. And yet there
are meaningful objects from many of the wars of the twentieth and
twenty-first centuries, objects which due to their particular capacity for
bearing witness to an event are not presented as relics or fetishes but as
documents. All these authentic objects were there, they were part of an
experience we don't have direct access to, and they therefore constitute a
resource for imagining it, for representing it through metonymic figuration.
Next to the objects, the iconographical representations and works of art
whose message relates to the phenomenon of war furnish the raw material
with which this experience is narrated for the vast majority of a public
which has had no direct knowledge of combat or of being the civilian
victims of an armed conflict. Along with their phenomenological proximity
to all that is transformable into myth, the use of the different arts as
a narrative tool enables us to fully enter the territory of representation, a
highly malleable, elusive context subject to ideological factors like warfare
itself and its subsequent sedimentation into written history, account being
taken of the fact that this understanding, however artificial or artful it
may be, is what drives the decisions and judgements that lead to the
justification of war or its rejection, and influence our way of behaving in it
once it's been declared.

II. Before the conflict

"You'll pretend you were men instead of babies, and you'll be played in the movies by
Frank Sinatra and John Wayne or some of those other glamorous, war-loving, dirty old men.
And war will look just wonderful, so we'll have a lot more of them. And they'll be fought
by babies like the babies upstairs."
KURT VONNEGUT

"War is inconceivable without a clear picture of the enemy."
KARL VON CLAUSEWITZ

Generally speaking, there's a tendency in social and anthropological
studies of war to forego its behavioural aspects either as a sediment
inherited from our prehuman past or as a mere consequence of environmental pressures or political, ideological and economic imperatives.
Only recently have people begun to consider the ritual aspects of the
violence organised by the State or by the unified social group as the result
of a process of culturalisation of biological components of an evident
evolutionary import that have needed to pass to the world of the symbolic
in order to go on being useful; put another way, evolution is not now
dictated by biology but by culture instead. It's important to bear in mind
that when a model of regulated behaviour as atavistic as aggression in all
its facets is temporally maintained as a transcultural and transhistorical
expression, it has to be for some very powerful reasons, reasons which,
if they were first of a biologico-evolutionary kind, were later progressively
culturalised and crystallised through religion, nationalism, philosophy,
political ideology, economy and science.

Within the expository framework of *At War*, the biological, evolutionary
and adaptive bases of human violence—its roots outside of history—are
taken as read and give way to an exploration of the phenomenon of war in
its contemporary cultural form. The narrative material of the exhibition
is confined to the twentieth century and its more recent sequels since
this is our own period, necessarily leaving aside other highly significant
historical periods from a bellicose point of view. As a result, the exhibition
proceeds from an ellipsis by means of which one attempts to suggest the
moment, in fact a process lasting millions of years, in which biology is
transmuted into culture. Biologically conditioned aggression in itself is
of no use to us as a basic explanation for the ritualised, rationalised and
socially ratified act of mutual collective murder, executed with the clear
intention of attaining tangible, although not always material, gains for the
victor, gains that are perceived as being unattainable by other means.
This is culture, a culture that for better or worse has largely defined the
human being ever since the onset of his humanity. This leap in time
enables us, in short, to frame the exhibition within the current historical
moment, since at the same time as we situate the narrative in history we

call on the constant, ahistorical and recurring aspects found in any human expression articulated in terms of myth, such as art, religion or sexuality.

The need for us to refer to cultural origins in order to explain the phenomenon of war has also led us to seek its bases in the social structures, processes and practices present all around us. In the field of entertainment, fashion and advertising we can find frequent examples of how the theme of war invades the terrain of civil society. It is present in the cinema and in video games, in recruiting ads and camouflage clothing, but also under a less obvious guise: sports events. Like certain festivals, competitions are ways of ritualising collective confrontation and, although in principle they should be inoffensive, we know that they may acquire a violent character. We find these connections synthesised in the works of the film-maker Leni Riefenstahl. It's easy to forget that what we see in *Triumph of the Will* is not an army marching past but the congress of a political party: this militarisation of civil society anticipates the war ahead. The aesthetic of *Olympiad* reflects the same ideology of strength, will and action, except that here international rivalries are sublimated as sporting ritual. And many years later her photo essays about the ceremonial struggles between the Nuba warriors of the Sudan again demonstrate the confluence between ritualised warfare, festival and the sports contest. To be sure, Nazism is an extreme and particularly pernicious example of the militarisation of a society, but the fact that two of these three works by Riefenstahl refer us to activities not determined by the Nazi mindset should enable us to dissociate the historical conjuncture and the ideological connotations of this particular iconography from the cultural processes depicted. Neither the Olympic Games as such nor the combats of the Nubas come out of a totalitarian ideology: they are simply different cultural expressions of an ancestral form of conduct, symbolically linked to the drive that leads people to make war, but which must not be confused with it.

Nazism also provides the most terrifying example of another process that leads to war: the construction of the idea of the other as an enemy, which is the subject of the next part of the exhibition. The shift from sports uniforms to military ones which we've seen in Riefenstahl's cinema brings with it another form of uniformity that is constituted by means of the segregation and exclusion of the other. Ethnic, racial, religious or national identities are defined via systems of differentiation that may or may not give rise to conflicts. The existence of conflicts between human groups is inevitable, but the ways in which they are resolved are something else, and history as well as anthropology and archaeology tell us that, whether we like it or not, violence is one of them.

Wars have many possible causes, and this exhibition cannot claim to embrace them all. It is possible, however, to demonstrate the diversity of

causes which, for example, differentiate civil conflicts from those involving
states, and to note a condition common to them all: without an enemy
there's no war. Whatever the pretext or the genuine cause may be, it has
to serve for justifying a violent confrontation with another collective,
on which the blame is put for the conflict and for the impossibility of
a peaceful solution. The dehumanisation or demonisation of the enemy
forms part of the processes by which the conditions for the use of force
are consolidated. And these mechanisms of discrediting the other are
repeatedly based on culturally ordained perceptions and prejudices.
The processes of strengthening cultural identity, which serve to promote
social cohesion, are the other side of the system that identifies the other
as an enemy. Through the speeches of the leaders and through propaganda,
through the memory of past grievances or the threat of future dangers,
and often with the collaboration of the media, the cultural framework
is gradually set up which transfers the notion of the necessity and
legitimacy of war to the social milieu. In this way culture, understood as
that conception of the world which determines the options of behaviour
available, incorporates within it the image of the enemy who has to be
yielded to or destroyed.

III. The literal vanguard

War has been a privileged theme throughout art history. The most
ancient representations of armed conflict between rival groups (executions
included) are found in eastern Spain, in the Neolithic caves of Roure,
Molino de las Fuentes, Les Dogues, La Vieja and Los Trepadores. Since
then we've never ceased depicting war. There is, however, a significant
qualitative difference between the representation of war by the artist
who's an eyewitness of what he depicts and the idealised reconstruction
of the historical event based on versions told or written by others and
elaborated at a temporal or physical remove from the event represented.
This desire for authenticity is nothing new. In the seventeenth century
Willem Van de Velde the Younger, although famous, was but one more
within a numerous group of artists who participated as eyewitnesses at
battles on land and sea. Whether on his own account and at his own risk or
as an assignment, he painted the action and sold the results. Francisco
de Goya, to take an obvious example, is perhaps the paradigmatic example
of the frontline reporter armed with a pencil instead of a camera.

The first war in history to be photographed, shortly after the death of
Goya, was the Crimean War. All we can see in the photos of Roger Fenton,
sent by the British government, are static images registered by cameras
too slow to capture any type of movement. As H. Avery Chenoweth
explains in his book *The Art of War*, due to this limitation the *Illustrated
London News* dispatched artists to the front to document the feats of
war. The sketches done on the battlefield were redrawn for being printed
alongside the text. The problem persisted during the War of Secession
in the States, with the result that the newspapers (which had realised by
then that action sells papers) sent journalists who knew how to draw to
the front with the same idea in mind. Winslow Homer was one of the more
famous, and some, like James O'Neal, died at the front.

In *The Warrior's Honour* Michael Ignatieff states:
"With the first machine-gun—the Gatling—being used in the American
Civil War there began a process of mechanisation of death that was
to culminate in Verdun and on the Somme. At the same time the
photographs of Brady and the recent inventions of Morse and the telegraph
brought the public that was reading the news at home ever closer to
the horror of the battlefield. The new technological possibilities created
a new moral agent—the war-correspondent—and a new genre—the
war report—whose heroic stories fomented, from the 1860s onwards, the
typically modern contradiction between myth and reality."

The speed and immediacy of the war, with the nearness to events that these brought with them, also shaped the languages and functions of the visual arts.

As a result of this process the British and American armies ended up having an artists' corp, in the same way as in their own time an artillery or medical corps had been set up, through which they henceforth documented their campaigns. They weren't the only ones, although perhaps some of the finest representatives of the genre are found therein. These corps remained active, despite the fact that from the First World War onwards there now existed still and movie cameras sufficiently rapid, lenses sufficiently luminous and films sufficiently sensitive to register the action. Chenoweth himself is a retired colonel from the US Marine Corps, a Korean War veteran who has served as a war artist in Vietnam and the Gulf, and his book documents the history of this practice, which continues into the present, although without the recognition and the calibre of other eras. The works presented in this exhibition focus on the First and Second World Wars, Korea and Vietnam, with English, French, American, Russian, German, Australian and Vietnamese examples. The British Armed Forces continue sending contemporary artists to their wars under the auspices of the Imperial War Museum in London, albeit on condition that they aren't exposed to the dangers of battle, which is something of a contradiction as far as documenting a war is concerned.

All this constitutes a collection as extraordinary as it is unknown of war art ostensibly generated from first-hand experience, and of a very different kind to the epic easel painting which has always adorned the world's military, history or art museums. The artistic quality of these obscure works is often very high, which poses an interesting question about the criteria that determine what a work of unquestionable relevance is. Physical proximity to the horror and danger of the battlefield gives these artists a moral authority that is scarcely comparable with that of other artists who explore the same content without having lived it.

The clearest way of explaining this is through a photographic analogy: it's impossible to photograph the fighting without being there. As Robert Capa once said, "If the photo ain't good enough, you weren't close enough." In fact this is an essentially military way of understanding the issue: whatever the intelligent missiles launched from a safe distance, whatever the marvellous telephoto lenses capable of snatching an image from miles away, the aims are only attained at ground level in intimate proximity between both the photographer's lens and its subject and the infantryman and the objective of his action.

The art of the twentieth century thought of itself as the vanguard of a movement with a direct impact on reality, with the radical intent of changing it. This change has been sought via direct confrontation, in the

likeness of the revolutionary, militarised political vanguards. We often
use the word "avant-garde" without taking these military connotations
into account, and without recognising the influence the First World War
had on the revolution in aesthetic languages and in the formation of these
movements. We've tried in the exhibition to emphasise that a number
of these avant-gardistes—Otto Dix, George Grosz, Gino Severini, Fernand
Léger, Oskar Kokoschka and Mikhail F. Larionov, for example—also
formed part of that other vanguard, the frontline one, and their personal
experience in the war conditioned their aesthetic language or its future
content. In the output of Paul Nash and Christopher Nevinson, who covered
the First World War as members of the British war artist scheme, it is
easy to perceive the tensions between the experiments typical of the time
and the documentary exigencies resolved in more realistic terms.
The 49-year-old Félix Vallotton tried in vain to enlist in the French army,
but did manage to get official authorisation to visit the front and paint
works like *Verdun* based on that experience. For many avant-gardistes
war was the occasion to tackle the formal problems posed by movement,
explosive energy, destructive violence and dehumanisation.

Many of the changes in the history of the art of the twentieth century
can be traced through its dialoguing with armed conflicts and its
successive responses to the challenge that representing the experience
of war presupposed. The works of American artists from the First World
War like George Harding and Harvey Dunn, from the Second like Kerr Eby
and Tom Lea, or of the Australian Ivor Hele in Korea, deserve to be re-
examined in the light of the rehabilitation of figurative painting. We are
exhibiting Captain Dunn's drawing box, an ingenious waterproofed system
that has a roll of paper passing over the central support. This allows
the artist to draw sequentially, as if creating a movie storyboard. Dunn
invented his system at the very moment in which, to quote Paul Virilio,
the use of cinematography in both the aerial reconnoitring of the theatre
of operations and the registering of the armed action transformed the
battlefield into a movie set. Dunn's gadgetry weds two kinds of historical
register, a wedding that eloquently illustrates the transitional moment
between two eras represented by the Great War.

It is striking to observe that the basic feature of any war is the
anonymity of the great majority of its protagonists. That a very significant
part of the art that has most directly reflected modern warfare is also
the most unknown, like the proverbial soldier who lies beneath so many
commemorative monuments, while the historic avant-gardes—with the
exception of those members of it who fought—have largely been so from the
rear, plainly shows that, without being mutually exclusive, physical courage
and intellectual courage are two different forms of extreme radicalness, one
of which, however, is more dangerous to the health than the other.

Included in this section are the other technologies of frontline visual testimony that dominate contemporary culture: photography, cinematography and the TV news item. Also in the vanguard, literally so, are all those reporters who risk their lives in order to show us the violence and horror from close to; so that we might see the conflict from a distance. It's unnecessary to insist on the danger of a job that has seen many of them off: a long list including, among others, Capa himself, Larry Burrows, John Hoagland, Miguel Gil and José Couso. James Nachtwey was wounded in Baghdad in December, while the exhibition was being prepared. Regular armies have their own corps of photographers and cameramen, like the team with video cameras which participated in the capture of Saddam Hussein (the twin capture of a physical person and of a media icon). Nevertheless, it's indisputable that the representation of wars today is mainly in the hands of reporters, who've been converted into our chief mediators because even the testimony of the combatants and the victims almost always reaches us via them. Photographers like Gilles Pérez and Gervasio Sánchez have turned their work into an insistent discourse of denunciation. We depend on them to a great degree in order to find out what's happening in different wars, with the constant conflict between independence and kowtowing to the media that this brings in its wake. And with growing interference from governments and armies, who've been aware ever since Vietnam that public opinion is an indispensable battlefront not only for being able to go to war but also for winning it. The images we don't see are as decisive as the ones we do. There are many photographers and cameramen who've experienced the frustration of shooting images that don't get publicised because the conflict isn't topical or because it's politically undesirable. Information doesn't reach us of some wars because few are interested in going there to seek it. Another exhibition could be mounted on the subject of "invisible" wars, an exhibition that would be necessarily different because the cultural experience of representation could not be covered. The study Susan Sontag has undertaken in *Regarding the Pain of Others* of the moral sense of images of war is aimed precisely at our involvement in and responsibility towards the effect the visual document has to have in those of us who don't participate in the actual experience of war but in its representation. For that very reason our focus has been to bring together a selection of images that owe their ability to move us to both their aesthetic quality and the circumstances of their production, to the fact of testifying from a position literally in the vanguard.

IV. Urbicides

"I don't know how the Third World War will be fought,
but the fourth will be with sticks and stones." ALBERT EINSTEIN

There have been many changes in the ways of making war. Some have to
do with technological developments. The invention of nuclear weapons
has largely determined the military history of the twentieth century and
their consequences continue to condition strategic decision-making.
With the Cold War over, the nuclear threat subsists under new forms that
no longer fashion a necessarily deterrent system. Moreover, it coexists
with the danger of other weapons of mass destruction, chemical and
bacteriological ones. Recent events like the terrorist attack on the Twin
Towers and the Pentagon have placed the debate about new kinds of
warfare on the agenda, a debate actively exploited by the official discourse
of the Bush administration, yet one which has long exercised the theorists.
The studies of Martin Van Creveld, Mary Kaldor, Philippe Delmas, Jeremy
Black and Chris Gray, to name but a few, are all prior to that ill-fated 11
September, because the lessons had begun to be learnt in other wars, in
the Middle East, in the dissolution of Yugoslavia, in Kuwait, in Somalia,
when analysing the consequences of the fall of the Berlin Wall and the
actual dynamics of armed groups. As the example of the research at MIT
shows, for the armies of the great powers the future has to do with high
technology and investments that sustain a huge industrial network.
The development of so-called intelligent weaponry forms part of a process
initiated in the 1970s, long before the end of the Cold War, and directed
at the production of new conventional weapons which might be utilised.
The logic of mutually assured destruction (MAD) which governed the
nuclear deterrent has been replaced by what is known in specialised
circles as RMA, revolution in military affairs, which, as Ignatieff explains
in *Virtual War*, has as its goal to be able to make war again, to restore
to it "its position as a continuation of politics by other means," because
the ability to make war, which is what gives power to any nation, doesn't
function if it can't be used.

The end of a Cold War that has lasted for almost half a century is,
therefore, the point of inflection that defines the conceptions of war in
which we move and the projections that might be made as to the future.
The main transformation, however, doesn't come from the introduction of
new technologies, nor is it centred on the performance of regular armies,
because rarely do we find the latter confronting each other. It is evidenced
in the civil conflicts which originate in the instability and weakness of
certain states, and in the growing participation of irregular combatants
who do not obey the traditional codes of the military institutions. With the

incorporation of women into active combat posts and the recruitment of
children in wars in the so-called Third World, the act of war can no longer
be considered as something contained within the old system of military
castes. As Van Creveld points out, each society makes war by taking to the
limit what its culture allows it to, and in that sense each form of making
war is a portrait of its protagonist.

The use of sophisticated weaponry in the bombings of Belgrade or
Baghdad is no more representative of the new modalities of war than
the car bomb or the machetes of the massacres in Rwanda. All have
something in common, however, with other contemporary conflicts: for the
most part it's the civilian population which suffers their effects. This is
the trait that typifies war right now, and it's not particularly new, because
it was the bane of the twentieth century. In other epochs the experience
of war was mainly reserved for the combatants: volunteers, professionals,
mercenaries or press-ganged recruits, but fighters all the same. And
until the First World War the greater part of the casualties were soldiers:
being at the front was mortally dangerous. Since then, however, it's been
the civilians who've come off worse—as victims or as hostages, since
they've been the latter in besieged cities and throughout the Cold War.
In *A History of Bombing* Sven Lindqvist convincingly demonstrates the
point to which contemporary war has been conducted at the expense
of and against non-combatants by transgressing the most basic principles
of international law. Among other things, the possession of nuclear
weapons is meaningless if their use on the civilian population is excluded,
because selective precision is not one of their main features, which has
meant that nuclear weapons have a treatment apart in jurisprudence
in order to side-step their total prohibition. And the practice of genocide
has to be added to this legacy.

Today, approximately 75% of the dead in any war are civilians—
following the trend of the century it is calculated, for example, that of the
almost 27 million dead the Soviet Union suffered in the Second World
War three-quarters were civilians. This is only an estimate, since although
the armed forces and guerrilla groups are accustomed to knowing their
own casualty figures, in many wars there is no organisation or agency
that counts the civilian dead. The exhibition attempts to reflect this fact
and to avoid a uniquely military perspective of what the hostilities and
the experience of war consist of. As a result it gives the same amount of
attention to the impact of war on the civilian population as to the fighting.
And it does this by primarily concentrating on how the space of cities and
the great population centres have been converted into military targets: the
concept of *urbicide* articulates the display material on the experience of
war for a civilian population through a selection of examples of bombed or
besieged cities. Such experiences as those of Leningrad, Dresden, Beirut,

Sarajevo or Kabul speak to us of another facet of the culture of war: the traumatic turning upside-down of every aspect of daily life. And they remind us that war isn't all that remote, something confined to the front, but comes to call on citizens in their homes. Without going further afield, the bombings suffered by Barcelona on 16, 17 and 18 March 1938 and the organisation of the passive defence of the city and its network of shelters inspired the English writer John Langdon-Davies to write *Air Raid* and served as a model when preparing the civil resistance of London to the German bombings. While these disasters of war may seem remote in time and space, and specific to the historical past or to other geographies, the aim of this section of the exhibition is that we doubly recognise ourselves in them: in the way they affect non-combatants and in the way they've left their mark on the culture we move around in.

Nuclear weapons are made in order to hang over our cities as permanent threats and they're the most extreme expression of what the logic of total war signifies. The reference to the bombing of Hiroshima is treated in the exhibition as one more example of urbicide and at the same time as the starting point of an important technological discovery that ushers in a different culture of war. In terms of the number of dead it is not one of the cities that has suffered the most, but the instantaneous scope of the destruction and its identity as an exercise in apocalyptic horror make it a symbol whose legacy is ever-present. In addition to the strategic consequences, which persist in any discussion about weapons of mass destruction, the event in itself has remained inscribed in the annals of those acts which invite moral reflection on human nature. And war is the context in which the majority of these inconceivable disasters are produced. Without seeking to explore all their implications, the exhibition could not fail to address those events which, like the Holocaust, have marked the contemporary conscience and which, although they oughtn't to be confused with war per se, have found in war their condition of possibility. Genocide is founded on a conception of the enemy present in the origin of different wars, with the particularity that in this instance the objective is the extermination of the other.

By looking at the process from the point of view of the extending of war to non-combatants, the echoes and connections with the part of the exhibition devoted to the construction of the enemy are more clearly perceived: in order to justify hostilities against civilians, beyond resorting to the euphemism of collateral damage, it is necessary for a certain cultural founding of antagonism to have come about and for it to be able to define every member of that other collective, and not just a government or soldiers taking up arms, as an enemy. This cultural dimension is clearly present in civil conflicts, embodied in ethnic, ideological or religious differences, but it also forms part of the supposed confrontation between civilisations to which some of today's international conflicts are attributed.

V. Remembrance

"Many heroes lived before Agamemnon, but all are oppressed in unending night,
unwept, unknown, because they lack a dedicated poet."
HORACE

"Only the dead have seen the end of war."
GEORGE SANTAYANA

Remembrance is almost all there is in the exhibition. The images and objects evoke past events, however near in time they may be. There's an insuperable distance between each of these exhibits and the experience to which they allude, an experience that's presented to us in a deferred manner. The function and even the mission a good part of these cultural products fulfil, the very reason for which many of these things have been preserved, is to cause us to remember, to bear witness. But this doesn't prevent us from distinguishing that there's a type of concrete experience which is not the remembering of the experience of war, but the experience of the remembering of war, the way one lives, not war as such, but its recollection. And the exhibition pays special attention to the way in which war is present in the culture, in the form of remembrance, during the last part of its itinerary.

To begin with, it has to be recognised that before being able to speak of remembering you'd have to be certain a war was over, and that wars don't always end in a clear and decisive manner. The opposite, rather—in the majority of contemporary wars it's very difficult, not to say impossible, to pinpoint the once and for all end point. Rather than talk about finalised wars, analyses of the current situation exist which refer to wars in suspension. Peace, therefore, would be no more than a state of tension that has yet to be activated in violent form. When it comes to sustaining the artifice of narrative continuity, however, the exhibition has recourse to underlining some of the cases in which the cut-off point is more obvious and, by means of the categories of victory and defeat, to highlighting the moment from which to describe the effects that follow a war.

The more immediate ones have to do with surrender and treaty signings, celebrations and parades, reprisals and suicides, exiles and returns, and trials for war crimes. Not only do people die in wars, there are also idle periods, periods of waiting, which doesn't refer here to the possibility of combat, but to hoping for the return of a loved one from the front, from the prisoner-of-war, refugee or concentration camp: someone who may or may not come back alive, because at times it's news of a missing person that is awaited. Or someone hopes to recover a body that's maybe buried somewhere nobody knows. Or someone hopes to get back home. Or someone hopes to be able to know, to be able to say, to be able to recall.

And so that time of respite, of waiting, introduces us fully into the time
of remembering, which is also that of forgetting.
The remembering of wars, of the victories as well as the defeats, is one
of the privileged acts of a nation's collective affirmation. Monuments,
cemeteries, accounts are constructed and by means of these commemorative processes identity is too. An exhibition about war couldn't end
without reflecting on the function of remembrance, because the final goal
is to present a cycle that's complete: the discourse about war inscribed in
the collective memory in the shape of monuments and commemorations,
and of the history books used in school, is an integral part of the system
of socialisation that turns war into a constant feature in human culture as
we know it. And the signs of identity linked to the remembering of past
conflict frequently contribute to identification of the enemy. Wars often
have their origin and justification in earlier wars, and the very possibility
of making war stems from this archaic memory, from the awareness that
it's an activity that has always existed.

An exhibition as full as this of historical evocations, as replete with
images of war, which attempts to show and to explain so many different
aspects of the phenomenon of war, has also to make the limits of representation clear and to allow for the space of the unsayable and that which
cannot be shown. To deal with the experience of war obliges us to peer
into the depths of human tragedy, the memory of war is also the memory of
death, and so this section covers different ways, some classic and others
specific to contemporary art, of approaching this extreme experience.
Alfredo Jaar's installation about the massacres in Rwanda, for example,
has been chosen not only for its inherent power and the magnitude of the
horror, but also for its being a counterpoint to the exhibition as a whole,
qua negation of iconic representation, and for its dialoguing with the
tradition of funerary memorials.

In an exhibition chiefly guided by the criterion of being reliant on
the straight participants' point of view, the act of letting the eyewitness
speak could not be lacking. Notwithstanding the many depictions of war,
until the very end of the exhibition one doesn't hear any voice relating a
personal experience. When it comes to referring to the role of the history
of warfare in this section on memory, we've chosen to fall back on oral
history. Instead of including the discourse of institutional historiography,
we open up a space for the spoken word and for personal testimony.
This is the other side of the history books, the side of the usually
anonymous individual. We might have found another lesson in the books,
seeing how by and large different versions of the same events are taught to
pupils in different countries or in different epochs. In oral testimony
we come face to face with someone specific who has lived a war the way
most human beings, combatants or victims, live it, without his or her

experience extending beyond their immediate surroundings, often without
knowing very well why people are fighting. It's only possible to present
a selection of testimonies: they speak of a series of conflicts in different
places and times, but most of all they personify the infinite variety of
individual experiences of war.

At the end of the itinerary, the narration the exhibition elaborates about
the successive stages of the phenomenon of war, taking in the socialisation
of violence, the construction of the enemy, the hostilities, victory and
defeat and remembrance, can also be read as an analogy of the ages of man:
from the child who plays, to the young man who fights and the family which
suffers in the city, to the old folk who reminisce, and finally the grave.
In the last analysis the cycle is condensed in a name, of a person or of a
place, written in a book or carved in stone, or cast into oblivion. Like those
memorable names of battlefields whose emptiness the camera of María
Bleda and José María Rosa portrays. It may be that these names, which are
themselves monuments but which designate empty places, don't have to
be filled with meaning, and that those other ones which maybe mean
nothing to us, yet in which an elusive experience is hidden to which we can
only accede indirectly by means of their representations, do have to be.

The socialisation of violence

Violence and natural selection:
a Darwinist reading of war

Robert Sala and Eudald Carbonell

There is a stark, affecting and harrowing passage in the book *Through a Window* by the chimpanzee specialist Jane Goodall, in which the author describes the confrontation between communities of these primates. The introduction of a group of male chimpanzees to the territory of another community ended in an extreme show of strength and agitation, with attacks on a female and her young. Only by reading these detailed descriptions of the circumstances surrounding these attacks, generally directed at females and geared to controlling areas with resources, can we see how similar this behaviour is among humans.

The chimpanzees in the Gombe reserve, in West Africa, open the doors to understanding human aggressiveness and its origins. They also show us that we are not alone in our custom of pursuing and destroying others. Violence is inherent in evolution and biology. The father of the theory of evolution, the British naturalist Charles Darwin, defined this very clearly in *The Origin of the Species*: "As more individuals are produced than can possibly survive, there must in every case be a struggle for existence, either one individual with another of the same species, or with the individuals of distinct species".

The scientific theory which explains biological evolution on Earth is precisely founded on the consideration that the basis for change, adaptability and survival is the fight for existence. The chimpanzees of Gombe were only fighting for their survival, while seeking to gain new spaces where their offspring could grow and be fed, if necessary, to the detriment of another community. Their war, during the fifties, ended in the extermination of one of the two communities of chimpanzees. A terrible ending which illustrates that the fight for survival, far from being just a concept, and often a metaphor, is, in many cases, a real and violent fact.

Violence is, and has been, the key to survival for populations and species. We can assume, therefore, that humans maintain and develop the fight for survival. However, by adding to this universal norm the refinement of techniques which are applied to aggression and the complexity of its causes, given that our resources are not just food-related, humans cross a qualitatively different threshold. Technology makes warfare much more complex, however it does not create it, but *only* boosts its effects. It is a fact that, in our present-day world, the West confronts the East in an endeavour to gain control of energy resources, and the East responds with extremely well-planned attacks; the North plunders the natural resources of the South, while exacerbating the living conditions of those populations suffering this treatment; and the peoples of the North fight amongst themselves to gain absolute control of resources. The technological differential between both sides facilitates action and aggression, geared, among other things, to maintaining precisely that supremacy. This is what we call *technological selection*, when a technological differential, rather than a difference in biological adaptation, comes into play.

The most dramatic aspect of this consideration, due to the lack of ethical scruples and justice it represents, is the realisation that, according to the WHO, mankind's current technological know-how would enable us to feed a greater number of individuals than currently exists on the planet. In spite of this, the fight between groups of humans is maintained and exacerbated, in an escalation of complexity which distances us from the behaviour of other species, in spite of them being identified as the origin of aggressiveness. Although violence is a law of nature, we must consider that, at the present time, in the human environment, it is in no way justified by the reasons which explain aggression in the natural world.

The analysis of human evolution offers us numerous examples of critical episodes in which some populations have confronted others. The causes have been manifold, from the development of new technological systems which give improved capacity, to the establishment of more powerful social relationships which will favour their founding groups. Among the consequences, we find the need for emigration or the extinction of entire species.

The dawn
Technology introduces a gradient of sophistication to violence which brings more disastrous consequences, as we have seen. It is, however, the use of instruments which saves the genus *Homo* from evolutionary disaster. Over two and a half million years ago, when our most distant ancestors were embarking on the *arms race,* no other animal, not even a primate, had this capability. Having access to tools capable of flaying large herbivores put us on the same level as the great carnivores. Pick-shaped blocks of hewn stone made it possible to cultivate underground tubers. With such a varied diet, man was able to face competition from carnivores and herbivores and make his way in a world completely new to woodland animals: open grassland. Suddenly man was the animal with the greatest ability to look for new foodstuffs.

The technological differential one and a half million years ago
Two million years ago, all the human populations in Africa had the same types of technology and, therefore, the same capacities for intervention on the environment, and there was no technological differential among them. It was the only moment in history when mankind was technologically

uniform. Nevertheless, just a little over one and a half million years ago,
in the Great African Lakes region, some populations of the species *Homo
ergaster* created a new technological form: the Mode 2, or Acheulean.
We find traces of this technology 1.6 million years ago at archaeological
sites in Ethiopia and Tanzania, such as the famous Olduvai Gorge.

The last generation of tools enabled their users to control broader
territories, to obtain greater and more varied resources. By making
standardised tools, they saved themselves time and increased efficiency.
Some of their objects were versatile, such as a Swiss knife, which could be
used for different purposes, a quality which enabled them to set out
in search of food with the right kind of tools at the ready. This enabled
them to increase their mobility and gain control of a broader territory, and
also to occupy new ecological zones.

We could consider that such a situation stemmed from the
demographic growth of the populations which developed the Mode 2,
to the detriment of the groups who continued to produce technology
according to the old Mode 1, resulting in the loss of land and the ability
to survive. When these latter populations travelled across this land, they
found it impossible to gain access to the resources in the traditional way
because other communities were making use of them.

It is a very similar process to the one established by the European
newcomers on the American continent with a railway line running
across it and organised systematically from a far-off capital city; or
to Africa today, where the West is attempting to put a stop to illegal
trading in order to protect wild fauna, but also prevents the indigenous
population from gaining access to the resources they have traditionally
enjoyed without providing them with an alternative which does not
involve cultural deracination.

The competitiveness generated by the technological differential
has only one outcome: the emigration of disadvantaged populations.
One and a half million years ago, only Africa was occupied by humans,
and, as a consequence, there were vast regions of Asia and Europe with
no competitors. Of course, the climate and ecology of Southern Asia
and Mediterranean Europe were very different to those hitherto
experienced by man, but he had the advantage because, initially, Eurasian
animals were not used to this small predator with minuscule teeth who
was not skilled at running or jumping on his victims. Thus, just like
many African animals, there were human populations who set out on a
migration path for the first time.

This was a true migration, which took entire populations across vast
territories with the aim of finding zones with enough resources to survive.
The fight for survival had a new form: the technological pressure of
some communities on others. There is no evidence of war and we cannot

refer to weapons in the strict sense of the word: all the tools available to these populations were created in order to obtain food, not for violent purposes. However, there must have been frequent confrontations as examples from contemporary history show us.

Demographic density and cannibalism

The following episode is a clear example of a well-documented act of direct violence. This event took place on the Atapuerca Ridge, 800,000 years ago. At that time, the Earth was recovering from profound cooling and entering a more temperate period which was nevertheless cooler than the present day. We do not know if this event was caused by the extreme climate, the excess of human populations in the area, or a sharp decline in the number of herbivores. The fact is, the remains of at least six humans survive from that period. They had been flayed by other humans and were found in one of the caves on the ridge: the Gran Dolina. Once they had been defleshed and eaten, their bones were left at the same place where the animal remains, which had been consumed in exactly the same way, were found.

The fact that the human bones had been mixed with those of other animals, leads us to think that no ritual was involved, as this would have taken place in a specially designated place, and not at a settlement which would have been the setting for all kinds of domestic activities. We can only surmise it was an act of gastronomic cannibalism. However, having ascertained this, an important part of the story is still missing: how did these settlers obtain these six individuals? There were two children, aged between four and six, two adolescents, aged about eleven, and two young adults aged eighteen or under. Were they captured in a clash with another group? Or were they humans who had been killed previously?

We can assess other data available to us in order to ascertain what happened. There are 10 geological levels at the Gran Dolina, only five of which contain the remains of human activity. Among these five levels, level TD6, with the cannibalised remains, and level TD10, are particularly important due to their wealth of remains indicating two periods when mankind had a strong impact on the ridge. An impact such as this must be correlated with high demographic density. With this data to hand, and given the climatic and environmental conditions mentioned above, the hypothesis of a confrontation between two human communities fighting for a space and its resources, just like the chimpanzees at Gombe, takes shape and seems highly likely.

Extinction of the Neanderthals

The Neanderthals were the only species to originate in Europe. No other group of humans had been born in this region due to its inhospitable climatic and environmental conditions. Furthermore, 100,000 years ago,

the species *Homo neanderthalensis* had spread for the first time to the
Near and Middle East. This was the great expansion of the Neanderthal
period. During these early stages of his evolution, Neanderthal man
successfully confronted other populations and occupied exceptionally arid
and harsh zones. One of the best examples is the easternmost Neanderthal
cave: Teshik-Tash, near Samarkand, in Uzbekistan, Central Asia. It stands
1,800 metres above sea level, is 44,000 years old, and was the centre
of the last glaciation, when the climate was colder than it is at present.
The colonisation of these spaces bears witness to Neanderthal man's
ability to adapt. Teshik-Tash provides another important piece of
information: the bone remains of a child aged eight or nine, buried in a
tomb with chamois antlers, the favourite animal of this community.

What made such an advanced and capable species disappear?
Despite the technological and economic advances they achieved and
the development of their symbolic and artistic skills, the Neanderthals
failed to overcome the first large-scale confrontation known to us.

When Neanderthal man spread as far as the Near East, it seems
he coexisted with, and was a direct competitor of the species *Homo
sapiens.* At that time, the Neanderthals survived and even managed
to form settlements in the region. They had won their first battle but,
50,000 years later, they were to lose the war. Forty thousand years ago,
when the Earth was undergoing major cooling following a slight climato-
logical improvement, groups of *Homo sapiens* entered an unknown
land for the first time: Europe. They entered from the East and relics of
their settlements can be found there, but also, and most importantly,
in Catalonia and over the rest of the Iberian Peninsula: L'Abric Romaní
(Capellades, Anoia), L'Arbreda (Serinyà, Pla de l'Estany) and El Castillo
(Puente Viesgo, Cantabria).

The caves mentioned above contain the oldest remains indicating the
presence of our species in Europe, some 40,000 years ago. Under the refuse
man left behind, at lower levels, predating this period, all three contain
remains denoting occupation by the Neanderthals. Once these newcomers
had established their settlements, the former occupants never returned,
although they were to be found elsewhere. The last Neanderthals were
found in cul-de-sacs such as the Iberian Peninsula or the valleys of
the Alta Garrotxa region, on infertile land, such as Banyoles lake, far from
the great valleys, hemmed in as a result of pressure from our species.

The data are clear, but the thing that is missing is a hypothesis
explaining what happened. There are no remains of a single battlefield.
Ecologists assert that there is a norm in biology according to which
the species which encroaches on another species' territory always ends
up eradicating this species. Some biologists point to the possible
introduction of new diseases from Africa which the Neanderthals were

unable to survive. However, we archaeologists have another type of data.

In the cave of L'Arbreda, the Neanderthals, who had used flint at L'Abric Romaní because it was the local rock, had to use harder rocks such as porphyry, quartz and quartzite because there were no good sources of flint in north-east Catalonia. However, when modern humans arrived they always used flint. Where did they get it from? Studies indicate that they brought it from the other side of the Pyrenees. Long-distance trade 40,000 years ago? This seems to have been the case.

Trade bears out the existence of a good social and economic network, a trans-Pyrenean relationship which linked geographically distant populations. These links made it possible to control and better exploit the land. The Neanderthals had never done this, and it seems that the same applies to our species before it arrived in Europe. However, when modern humans established themselves on the new continent, the strong ties gave them an advantage over the other species who became increasingly cut off until they were so small in number, and so isolated, they could no longer reproduce adequately and died out.

This is the first historical example of widespread confrontation, on a very broad geographical scale, including the whole of Europe, between two groups, as a result of which one of them died out without leaving any trace. Although there has been a great deal of speculation about the issue, there are no clear data about the intermixing of both species.

This historic event bears too much of a resemblance to the current organisation of the entire planet from the West, which is looking for resources, even in territories beyond the Earth. First of all, we controlled resources directly by organising commercial colonies until we were able to establish ourselves permanently and govern territories and all their inhabitants, both indigenous and newcomers, with a pronounced difference in their welfare. In the era of decolonisation, the Europeans abandoned the seats of government in colonised countries. However, the heads of state have continued to control them, to such an extent that they can be established and destroyed at whim. We have seen a good example of this process over the past year: the war in Iraq and the removal from office and arrest of Saddam Hussein, a governor appointed by the West.

Eastern farmers who brought us culture

At the end of the last glaciation, 10,000 years ago, many populations from around the world exchanged the hunter-gatherer economy for a new form of food-management: agriculture and stockbreeding. Our European continent was not among the first to make this breakthrough.

The rise in sea level 8,000 years ago, after the glacial period had ended, caused the level of the Mediterranean to rise spectacularly above the Strait of the Bosphorus, which was dry land at the time. This led to

immense flooding of a basin bathed by the waters of a small lake, which
preceded the Black Sea. Its shores were inhabited by large communities of
farmers and herdsmen who were obliged to search for new lands. Perhaps
this, and the typical demographic growth among Neolithic populations,
who were able to obtain new foods, triggered the emigration of many
communities to the West. A new population change for Europe caused by
natural selection. This time, a number of scattered groups from the old
communities who were established prior to this change remained across
Europe, such as the Basques.

Modern times

Throughout history, there have been many cases of violence among
humans. We have introduced only some of the most primitive ones. In the
recent memory of all the peoples involved, there is still a clear image of
the European occupation of America 500 years ago. An occupation which
still continues with the plundering of resources, without any consideration
for the needs of the inhabitants of the region, as we saw in 2003 in the
case of Bolivia. Although this plundering has been widely criticised and
reported, the authorities and businesses will not back down.

The twentieth century experienced the most brutal violence in history,
including the methodical elimination of opponents and obstacles in Nazi
Germany, such as the Jews, Gypsies and communists. These acts return
us to the base instincts which Sigmund Freud discovered and condemned
during the War, as Stefan Zweig says: "[...] he saw the terrible confirmation
of [...] his opinion that savagery, the basic instinct for destruction, could
not be eradicated from the human spirit."

The need of Africans and Maghrebis to look for a decent life has very
recently spread to our country. They are the descendants of the people
who settled on the Iberian Peninsula 1,300 years ago in a vast expansive
movement. The rejection that this is causing, together with the satani-
sation of the other, is reported daily, without remembrance of the time
when we were immigrants. The opposition of the West creates a strong
response from the immigrants, who remain entrenched in their culture,
marginalised and unable to advance in a globalised world. This set of
circumstances does not allow the cross-pollination which so many people,
such as Juan Goytisolo, have defended. A cross-pollination which can
obviously not use force. The force of the person who claims to want to
spread democracy around the world, whether we like it or not. Nowadays it
is done through the ballot box, whereas it used to be done by the cross.

Chiaroscuros

While natural selection provided us with the technology to survive, it
also brought us the ability to rationalise. Moreover, the remains of a giant

animal, a hippopotamus, were found for the first time on a site in Kenya dating back 1.8 million years, together with stone tools made by humans. Many archaeologists like us believe this represents a great leap forward for mankind, who was looking for large animals to feed more numerous groups. This is the first example of solidarity, because instead of continuing to look for food individually and eating alone, man chose to look for food for his entire group.

Solidarity emerged through selection and opened the doors to a new form of behaviour. It also created ambivalence among humans, a typical contradiction: solidary people subsisted two million years ago but what about now? We must be aware of what our natural reality is.

Future without violence

In the review we have just carried out we have seen how new forms of confrontation, of the refinement of former biological competitiveness, have emerged through evolution and we have seen this competitiveness act in the most modern environments, in those places where we would never have said that it may be a natural law. The confrontation between states and cultures is a very modern form of concealed biological competitiveness. Concealed, above all, by a supposed desire to emancipate and culturalise. The West does not want to eliminate the imbalances in the Third World, what it does want to do is impose its way of seeing things, a single line of thought, which is supposedly better and more beneficial: initially by painting it with a spirituality which is now openly economic. Many of us have refused to categorise the so-called Social Darwinism (the explanation of the social order through the fight for survival) as a natural law. However, it is difficult for us to maintain this posture when so many people are striving to enforce it and make it a true universal social law in favour of the strongest.

The biological competitiveness specified by Darwin in *The Origin of the Species* and the discovery of the instinct made by Freud in his works, brings humans closer to their deepest reality: their condition as indistinct animals. The implementation of competitiveness over our two and a half million years of existence has allowed us to survive as a species by imposing ourselves on highly capable competitors and at the expense of the extinction of a great many relations whom we have left by the wayside. Technological specialisation, an evolutionary breakthrough, has made us particularly competitive.

It has also enabled us to solve internal imbalances among the human species and our relationship with the ecological environment, allowing greater prospects for the survival and rescue of endangered species and ecological systems in those places where we have made the decision to do so. Today, in the third millennium, this ability makes competitiveness

totally unnecessary because the technological level makes life easier for
many more millions of humans than there are at present, without the
need to damage the ecological spaces which have been retained and,
even more importantly, without violence. In many places, we have asserted
that humans are surpassing natural selection by applying medicine
and food-production technology. If this is really the case, why are we still
unable to eschew that tool of natural selection: violence? Why don't we
apply more widely the more strictly human capacities such as solidarity
and rationality? Today, the answer is clear: in the West we wish to
maintain the technological differential and we do not want equal welfare
levels between us and the peoples on the rest of the planet.

When these people arrive in our Western world we do everything
possible to show them who is in charge here and cause their cultural
annihilation, dressed up as democratic and enlightened culture when it
is precisely the contrary: the maintenance of the old imposition by force.
We have not changed all that much and we must condemn the fact that
this aggressive behaviour is not only unjustified, but is also completely
unnecessary for us to survive. However, if it is a question of achieving
greater supremacy and spreading ourselves across the planet, it will be
necessary in order to maintain the status of the Rogue States condemned
by Noam Chomsky. Then, we must say so bluntly and without false and
hypocritical disguises.

The solution to the problem of violence of the Western states against
the East and South must be a question for the future. A question which
cannot be resolved through natural selection, because we have already
stopped it with our technology: a new, more solidary species will not
emerge. It must be resolved through our rational, technological, economic
and social behaviour, through more effective control of the organised
conduits which provoke violence and through the socialisation of
technology. However, this will only be possible when we become aware
of two things: firstly, that we fall into the category of animals, without
subterfuge or nuances, and, secondly, that confrontation and natural
selection are no longer necessary for us to survive, due to the technological
level we have attained. We cannot hide or take refuge behind the mask of
the natural state.

Symbolic wars:
struggle, play, festival

Manuel Delgado

Battles that bring people together

What we understand by war today involves, among other things, a reconducting of that process of conciliation between identities, interests and conceptions of the world on which any form of coexistence is based, a coexistence whose components never cease to allude to the precariousness of the links between them and the chronic, but latent, disagreement in which they exist. If peaceful coexistence is possible it is because the jointly present but never fully convergent segments of any society—namely, the individuals, groups or nations who coexist, but whose interests are antagonistic—accept certain forms of arbitration in the resolution of their conflicts and avail themselves of segregated spatio-temporal spheres in which to state their differences without resorting to harmful confrontation; that is, without damaging the body, property or identity of the adversary. Within these special frameworks, social sectors that remain united by what separates them can re-enact their differences and obtain symbolic satisfaction of their aspirations. These competing elements—persons, families, corporations, territories—thus encounter a way of avoiding the shock at the same time as they hit upon a formula enabling it to be institutionalised and borne in mind as a possibility. It is a question of the minor relatives of war that may emerge as festivals or games whose subject is the conflict involving one or other modality of hand-to-hand fighting and in which ritual aggression stands in for the physical kind. These are symbolic wars and they only differ from the real ones in their intensity and their destructive effects, although they fulfil both with the mission of keeping the sectors virtually or literally in conflict united.

The consensus obtained through the mediation and symbolic expression of the warring factions may be interrupted by the irruption of harmful violence as a mechanism by which to solve conflicts among the permanently confronted segments within a society. This recourse to force is often produced as a result of the breakdown of the role that allegorical, non-harmful violence assumes as a device for draining social tensions. The use of harmful violence, lived by those who enact it as inevitable, takes the social interrelation to a level of insurmountable paroxysm, in which the terms of the peaceful social pact are cancelled and the instances of arbitral control ignored or disobeyed, and this to the point that certain serious disagreements are resolved by victory elimination, expulsion or submission of one or other of the factions in conflict re-negotiation or reconciliation.

This was precisely the premise, remember, on which Norbert Elias and Eric Dunning built their genealogy of modern sport, a consequence of the ambition of eighteenth-century English society to seek out structures for re-enacting and peacefully resolving conflict, structures that would enable them to overcome what had been a long, drawn-out period marked by devastating and continuous civil wars, and one of the self-disciplines with which, on the personal level, to proceed to that pacification of bodies that was to have such importance in the process of modernisation.[1] Elias and Dunning were surely right in establishing modern sport as one means of avoiding civil war, based on turning the existence of warring factions within society and their pseudo-violent resolution into spectacle, and guaranteeing that the State will be able to administer a right to use force to which it has exclusive rights. Yet the formula England encountered in the formation of clubs and in the controlled disciplining of disagreement would be, in effect, just one more variety of the kinds of mechanism with which any society confronts conflicts between the groups inhabiting it. Anthropology has provided endless bits of proof that, as Mary Douglas pointed out in *Purity and Danger*, "perhaps all social systems are built on contradiction, [and are] in some sense at war with themselves."[2]

In effect, any society from that constituted by an individual on his own to the community of nations is made up of sectors that are never fully in agreement, sectors which remain in tension vis-à-vis each other, and which coexist with the permanent threat of a dissolution of their ties which would only be avoided, in the extreme, by recourse to physical violence. This theoretical premise relating to the cohesive function of all confrontation has two sources. On the one hand, the functionalism of Émile Durkheim and Marcel Mauss is part of a major line structuring all European social anthropology, based on which many exotic cases of armed conflict within a single society have been studied.[3] On the other, Georg Simmel, to whom we owe a sociology which sees any struggle as having a structuring power.[4] The basic premise of both contributions is that war is but one of the strategies social cohesion employs in order to overcome the centripetal and dissolutive tendencies it continually experiences. This prior notion deems it that the fractions submit the terms of their co-presence in the framework of a single society to continual negotiation.

Never for a moment do such often mutually hostile and unassimilable constitutive units of the social cease generating tensions which might provoke the irreversible severing of their ties. Violent conflict between portions of a society is produced precisely so that such an extreme eventuality cannot come about. The latter reading would coincide in turn with the Marxist one, in that it turns the idea of war into a vehicle for resolving contradictions within a society, in this case a definitive overcoming of the class struggle.

This task of assembling the heterogeneous and contrary, which confrontation performs, is fundamental, but one understands that the consequences involved in taking it to its more expeditious expressions are not desirable. The cohesive quality of combat is thus maintained through mechanisms that simultaneously avoid and institutionalise it. In this way conflict has the possibility of existing in delimited realms, without its *mise en scène* having an effect on the minimum amounts of stability in the system. The accumulation of rancour that the functioning of the machinery of coexistence cannot help but exude has at its disposition settings in which to become explicit, doing so, what's more, in the only way it accepts: by means of violence. It is a question, however, of a virtual violence exhibited in ritual battles in which the opposed sectors make do with metaphors of victory of one side over another and whose minimum expressions would be the burlesque relationships or singing or poetry competitions we find in many mutually remote cultures. It must be added that such realms of controlled shock are not just reservoirs of aggressiveness in a raw state; they teach an authentic pedagogy of the culturally available styles of violence to the social elements involved. What is re-enacted in rites in which symbolic harm is done are not catharses involving the psychological de-inhibition of tensions, but authentic models of and for violence, as Clifford Geertz demonstrated in his famous article on cockfighting in Bali —"each nation loves its own form of violence"—[5] or as Joseba Zulaika subsequently applied to the case of the festive-ritual paradigms which inspire ETA's armed activities in the Basque Country at the present time.[6]

All societies, then, have ordinary technologies at their disposal for regulating disagreements, by means of which pacific societal ties prevail over the logic of traumatic confrontation, albeit without losing sight of this completely. Their mission is of the same kind as that which war undertook to guarantee as a final recourse: the welding together of social antagonisms. In our world those expedients are organised, in the first instance, around judicial systems, while in societies that are, politically speaking, partly or totally non-centralised, arbitration is entrusted to ritual personalities. Further to or aside from such regulatory mechanisms, societies are endowed with ambits in which a controlled dosage of violence is permitted and can be exercised in a planned way. Festive rites of which the sports spectacle continues being a modern version suppose this same democratisation or inoffensive trivialising of the right to aggression, whose instrumental dimension political power claims exclusive right to in state-controlled societies.

From festival to warfare

We know that war implies that things which wouldn't be acceptable
under normal conditions —homicide, rape, pillage— turn out not only to
be permitted but are obligatory, even. Herein lies the first proof of the
direct kinship of war and festival, which reproduces this same generalised
inversion of the values of everyday life, with one difference that of degree.
The most important thing, however, is that festival, like war, allows the
recourse to violence to be present in one way or another in the communication between opposed social groups and individuals coexisting beneath
a single social umbrella. In that sense the festival would find its lesser
parallel in the role played in face-to-face interaction by humour, jokes or
certain games based on parodic confrontation, institutionally envisaged
formulas of pseudo-aggression in which the public exhibition is tolerated
of certain more or less veiled interpersonal hostilities.

The rapport between war and festival was insistently underlined by the
theorists who radicalised the sociological thinking of Durkheim and Mauss
Roger Caillois, Georges Bataille, Michel Leiris—who saw in struggle the
most efficacious way of guaranteeing in the case of an extreme risk of
dissolution the maintenance at any price of the social link. It was Caillois,
in fact, who most clearly explained the nexus between these two forms of
excess, devoting the conclusion of his theory of festival in *Man and the
Sacred* to the interchangeability between the exacerbating of the social
specific to the festive dimension and the one the collective experience
of war is privy to. In saying of the festival —"we live remembering one
and waiting for another,"—[7] Caillois affirmed the same about war as
Simmel: "In any state of peace the conditions are shaped for the future
combat and in any combat the conditions are shaped for the future peace."[8]
For his part, in his *Theory of Religion* Bataille included ritual violence
in the distribution of intrasocial kinds of violence: "As a matter of fact,
external violence is antithetical to sacrifice or the festival, whose violence
works havoc within."[9]

Both cultural history and anthropology have afforded many examples
of how grand festive celebrations frequently simulate genuine, bloodless
civil wars. Experts have corroborated the presence in the traditional
African societies studied by them of festive mechanisms consisting of
simulated violence between bands from a single society, and whose main
task seemed to be that of keeping the cycle of aggression and counter-
aggression under control, of providing compensations and of reducing the
dissolutive effects of antagonism.[10] Things are thus to the point that one
of the best-known cases, that of the Incwala of the Swazis of Southeast
Africa, has been repeatedly cited as a model for the many versions that
have been encountered right across the continent.[11] Rites of rebellion
are an all but universal phenomenon and we have around us in our own

cultural context all kinds of celebrations based on festive revolt, of which
Carnival is undoubtedly the paradigm. We would be able to find to hand
all kinds of expression within traditional culture based on a confrontation between rival bands —the festivals of Moors and Christians, for
instance— not to mention countless festive combats involving vegetables,
tomatoes, sweets, etc. No less numerous, in turn, are the popular rituals in
our environment based on exhibitions "of sound and fury", such as those
involving the intense use of pyrotechnic materials, or festivals incorpo-
rating real or simulated acts of aggression against living creatures, be
they disguised humans or flesh-and-blood animals which are ceremonially
goaded. The examples could also be ones closer to home. Cases in which
there emerges the amount of literal violence that symbolic violence cannot
dodge are innumerable and many of them exceedingly close at hand.
Apropos of this, Henri Lefebvre was given to ask: "But then is there not
always something cruel, wild and violent in festivals?"[12]

Moreover, we have the frequency with which festivals end all but
naturally in acts of real violence. The historical and ethnographically
proven coincidence between periods of carnival and insurrections or
revolts would extend in this direction, with examples drawn from all places
and all periods. In point of fact, and by way of example, we have a classic
study that focuses precisely on one such episode, *Le Carnaval de Romans*,
in which Emmanuel Le Roy Ladurie recounts how in February 1580 the
inhabitants of that Dauphiné town shifted from the pseudo-violent theatri-
calisation of their disputes to a huge explosion of bloody violence between
contradictory social forces.[13] Likewise, the way in which today's popular
celebrations often end in acts of harmful violence and real destruction,
which would also include those sports-inspired meetings that have
involved tragic events on the terraces or in the street.[14] Also numerous
and close to hand would be the cases in which popular celebration ends in
disturbance or altercation of a very real kind, in the same way as the youth
revolts of recent decades —from May 68 in France to today's anti-globali-
sation movements— have not hidden their formal debt to the festive world
and have often been organised as genuine performances.

It has to be said that we're speaking of harmful violence in order to
refer to the fracture of consensus and the super-acceleration of social
interaction of which war is the most durable and generalised expression.
We do this so as to distinguish such violence from the symbolic violence
deployed in all the substitutes for struggle which collective life employs
so as to in fact avoid the catastrophic consequences that would be
produced in the event of the tensions they exorcise managing to affect the
plane of reality. But this doesn't mean that over and above its functional
role this harmful violence is not just as metaphorical as the other kind.
It is so, without a doubt, in as much as both forms of violence —harmful

and symbolic— dramatise social ideas and emit coded messages. It is
essential, then, that acts of violence are not viewed as mere formulas
meant to cause physical or moral damage to others —in the case of verbal
or psychological violence— and still less as the savage and spasmodic
kinds of energy that irrationalist theories defend. On the contrary, they
are also forms —perhaps the most energetic that exist— of representation
and communication, texts bearing semantic contents which the actors,
and often their victims too, are capable of interpreting and whose hidden
grammar the experts have to try and re-establish.

Thus we may say that harmful violence adds to its properly metonymic
and instrumental function —that of suppressing or giving in to the
adversary, not just symbolically but in the actual social structure— that of
constituting itself as the vehicle of a particular expressiveness. And this
so as to lead to an important consideration, already implicit in what's been
said: violence and warfare are not the outcome of opposed parties having
given up on their ability to communicate, but of them having decided to
intensify the efficacy of their messages to the maximum. Contrary to what
is usually thought, armed conflicts are not a consequence of the "failure
of dialogue," but of its exacerbation. Measures taken towards peace do
not in fact depend on the contending parties "maintaining conversations,"
but rather on them stopping doing this in that particular tone. Likewise,
peace doesn't imply a definitive disavowal of violence in itself, but a
provisional renunciation of its empirical scope, which is always present
as a potentially available recourse in the communication between human
beings and groups.

In the beginning was the war
It is very possible that no world was ever conceived or generated for
something that wasn't going to last. Consequently, all societies strive to
cultivate not only the illusion of an impossible equilibrium, as we've just
seen, but also a loyalty to what is imagined to be their own founding.
Even such a society as the modern one strives to overcome the uneasiness
the continuous changes it experiences produce by generating its own
chimera of continuity vis-à-vis an often invented past or one that is a
consequence of manipulation. Thus, those same domains in which social
life staged the ritual resolution of its contradictions, its unreal coherence,
are usually also the ones that are constituted as a proscenium of the
splendour of its first step forward in time.

Almost all societies consider themselves to be the result of an
outbreak of inaugurating violence and they keep themselves alive by
periodically taking pains to recreate this so as to render the forgetting
of it impossible. Georges Balandier's approach to a general anthropology
of violence and warfare proceeds in fact from this belief in a founding

violence[15] responsible for the onset of the era in which each society considers it lives and of a conservative violence "of memory" that the festive punctuation of social time takes charge of distributing in small inoffensive doses. In modern societies, those which find a source of meaning in the accumulation of certain events that institutional historians take it upon themselves to put into some kind of order, such beginnings usually coincide with a traumatic and fortunate shock, that moment held to be magnificent which enabled the invaders and their internal allies to be expelled, which wiped out the perfidious or obliged them to give up their evil ways, or which forced those who were different and therefore inferior to yield to a supposedly legitimate authority. One speaks, then, of the Liberation, the Proclamation of..., the Revolution, the Uprising, Independence, etc. In traditional societies, which do not promote their own history, this inaugural war was the one that in mythic times established an absolute segregation between human and other beings, namely demons, animals, monsters and actual strangers. This occurred in the form of an imaginary explosion of generalised violence which had the pre-society as its setting, a struggle between those who wished to found the world and those who wished to remain faithful to their ancient subhuman condition. Thus it was that a creative chaos could give rise to a created cosmos.

This is the moment that festivals usually re-enact at the end and at the beginning of each of their calendar cycles. Reproduced in them is that conflagration which in the annals of sanctified history or in mythic narration made the birth of the known world possible. Just as ritualised violence enabled society to conceal from itself the evidence of the incompatibilities, imbalances and unstable features of which it was made, so festive enervation aims to negate the future, to depict the given social order as consequence and protagonist of a continuity preserved from the deterioration that the action of time and men brings about. It is recognised, then, that violence was indispensable at a given moment in order to rectify an unjust or undesirable situation, so as to re-establish a lost equilibrium or to constitute another, desired one, and that it may, therefore, be so again at any moment. If the festival deploys a false violence it is because it is hoped that social matters continue as they are, since, if the violence were real, modifications would indeed be produced in the actual state of the world. If, on the other hand, it is thought that the social structure must be corrected or recast, then it is understood that recourse to violence is necessary, albeit a violence whose sacred condition was known at all times, since the ceremonial order is based on it and it is that very condition, preserved and cyclically reanimated, which those who rendered our world order possible used in their day. Festivals like jokes or games have been entrusted with keeping the sacred flame of potential violence alive.

If we've seen how ritualised forms of pseudo-violence behave rather like a thermostat which keeps the tensions deriving from the coercion society submits its constituent elements to at an acceptable level, obliging them to get along with each other, any intensified violence which is damaging would imply that the elements of the system have reached the conclusion that a profound readjustment in their correlation is necessary. Put another way: that which, maintained at a certain level, behaved rather like negative feedback, namely as an attenuating of the divergence which keeps the system in equilibrium, is converted, beyond that level, into positive feedback, namely a process that once triggered becomes ever rapider and is only brought to a halt when it reaches a new level of equilibrium or definitive collapse. What sets off such an apparatus of violent regulation is not that it is understood that society must change, but rather the exact opposite: it is perceived that undesirable changes have been produced which have separated the state of social affairs from their ideal situation, namely the one that existed at the time of their founding. At the end of the day, it is a question of propitiating a return to the pristine moment in which things were as they should be, and which can be traced back to a more or less recent historical event, or further back to lay claim, for instance, to the Second Coming of Christ or the return to primitive communism, in the case of the prophetic or apocalyptic movements we know about. Violent intervention in history doesn't operate so that the world may change, but because it is thought that the world has changed too much. War is embarked on in order to thwart mutations in a social order imagined as whole and which, of course, only exists in the impossible remembrance of some more or less epic beginnings, those which traditional myths or the mystique of historic deeds are called upon to relate.

In that festive condition there is also found the justification for the oft-claimed sacral nature of acts of aggression, for the conviction that whosoever uses violence must be being faithful to some design of the gods, the mythical ancestors or founders of the fatherland, and for the manner in which a reference is always bandied about to a redolent past which lived reality has betrayed. It would be necessary to consider the point to which a similarly millenarian act is or isn't harmful violence, in the sense of something refounding an order experienced as alienating, perverted or contaminated and whose restoration is lived as pressing. Even in micro-social cases—the bar-room brawl, the family row; even, on the personal level, the psychosomatic symptom which expresses the war with oneself—the act of violence is executed in order to redress something which is experienced as disorder, which is perceived as an impurity that only the damage inflicted on another person or on oneself perceived as an other can cleanse.

The violence of wars implies, therefore, a going back to a beginning identical to that of the festival, except that, because the purificatory violence used is not an imitation but the real thing, its effects strategically modify the hierarchy and the functioning of a society in which there are those who feel it to be the victim of intruders or corrupters who have betrayed or sullied its founding principles. Founding violence, then, is used not, as in the festival, to preserve the consensus relative to the already founded, but to re-instate what is thought to be disordered by the malevolent action of internal or external enemies. It ought not to be thought fortuitous that Mauss, Durkheim's nephew and foremost disciple, was the first to draw attention to how easy it was to pass from the festival to warfare, or that such an assessment is situated right at the end of one of his masterworks, *The Gift*. In the last few lines of his book Mauss evokes the case of the Melanesian chiefs Bobal and Buleau —"more friends than rivals"— whose followers passed a "sleepless night of song and dance" together.[16] The next morning one side took to killing the other. Claude Lefort managed to grasp the terrible implications of such an episode: "The premonitory human communion is proclaimed with frenzy; however minor the threat, only killing may avoid the breakdown."[17]

The wheel of violence

To sum up, we have tried to emphasise that war and its near relative, festival, is not one of the demands of the exchange principle but one of its expressions, or, indeed, one of its requisites. This is the conclusion that would be drawn were we to abandon any consideration of violence as a substance in order to treat it as what it is: a relation, which would consign the terms of its analysis to those of any other form of communication. Violence would thus seem to be involved in the production of meaning, not so much as a vehicle, however, but as a sign. The same could be said in terms of the quality one might allot to violent action as value. And, because it is sign and value, the act of aggression cannot exist except in order to be communicated or transferred; that is, in order to be an object of circulation. Violence, it can be established, does nothing more than function as a form of free currency for all sorts of uses, with which to pay or with which to collect debts.

This in turn could be placed in a relationship with the role of harmful violence in retaliation and the restorative virtue urged on the latter, which may be brought to bear in the resolution of conflicts. An anthropology of violence, and of warfare as its maximum expression, can only be a variant of an anthropology which would study the technologies of compen-sation which culture has available to it for the regulation of prestations and symmetrical counter-prestations, and in particular of one of its most expeditious modalities: retaliation. Human relations are not only based on the ongoing exchange of prestations and gifts, but also on the no less inevitable exchange of grievances. Goods are exchanged, but also, so to speak, are evils. Any contravened offence implies a pending debt—"you'll pay me them all together," people say—whose satisfaction may accept the free currency which is violence as a payment. Like objects given as presents, insults and injustices also seem possessed, in turn, of an intensity which calls for their devolution, a spirit which in the manner of the Melanesian Hau in Mauss' theory of gifts always wishes to return to where it started out. Consequently, all aggression intended to cause damage presupposes a "settling of scores" in one way or another, the regularising of an inequality in the interplay of reciprocities.

It is here that we might come upon some explanation about the singular ill-feeling, so heavy with atrocities, with which wars are usually conducted, especially we might add civil wars: this would be the outcome of the largely deferred status of the business of moral or physical damages waiting to be resolved, the accumulated volume of the debt and therefore of the reparation required in order to re-establish equilibrium, the cancellation of debts permitting both parties to be even, to be "in peace." This is also what causes the violence that is meted out without there existing an account due for settlement to infuriate people so much, which renders such violence deserving of the disqualifying epithet it receives: "gratuitous." Lastly, the key would equally be found here to the shift from invisible forms of violence—shouts, insults, humiliation, coercion—to those others which have things and bodies as an object of aggression: the devolution of the insult/gift is always made with interest. In these instances the gift is returned with usury.

In its maximum expression, warfare unleashed violence involves another road by which to return to a primitive situation of paroxysm of communication and generalised reciprocal giving. The model is the potlatch of the Indians of Northwest America, to which anthropology from Franz Boas onwards has paid so much attention and to which Mauss would devote part of in his already cited study *The Gift*. The potlatch is, like war, a perfect example of a total social fact—economic, mythical, religious, juridical, commercial, aesthetic, domestic—the main feature of the celebration being that in it the participants end up in a fever of ostentation, consumption and expenditure in which competition is established in terms of what each individual is in a position to squander. This logic of destruction, then, erupts out of the dynamic of challenges or counter-challenges. It has an effect on the rival, of course, since it is a question of overwhelming him by giving things to him—which in the case of war are damaging things—but, as in the potlatch, it also has an effect on those who give him everything so as to come out winners in the struggle. The warrior, and with him the people at war, gives everything,

but benefit is not always obtained from his victory. In wars all lose loved ones and possessions, but the victor gains, as in the potlatch, status, prestige, authority, power, the privileges
he wrests from the other. And that is valid for all the modalities of struggle, from world conflagration to the domestic or street altercation. In them the fractions —international coalitions, nations, classes, races, religious groups, neighbours, fellow countrymen, relatives— give in wholeheartedly to the atrocious game of reciprocity in aggression and offence, to the wheel of violence, in order to settle once and for all just "who gives the orders around here."

Such a perspective has an importance when it comes to remarking the singularity of certain types of war, in particular those we call, not in vain, "domestic" or "fratricidal," in order to make it clear that they are produced in the bosom of a single organism, be it the body itself or a society that recognises itself as possessing an identity. We speak of civil wars. Wars waged by States against other States or societies are actions in which it may indeed come about that material gains are sought after and obtained, at least for the socially or politically hegemonic classes of the winning side. In the event of triumph, territories, spoils, slaves, raw materials, dependencies, submissions, sources of wealth and economic benefits are obtained. Yet no civil war enriches the society undergoing it but impoverishes it instead, whoever wins. Unlike the international war of today, both the historic civil war and primitive warfare between tribal segments or between sorely vexed fellow citizens are essentially anti-surplus wars, in the sense that they don't seek the accumulation of riches but their elimination by means of the most generous of expenditures.[18]

We arrive, here, at the conclusion of our argument. A certain wish to be positive would invite one to deduce from all of this the possibility, or otherwise, of expelling war from the life between peoples and from that of peoples coexisting with themselves, of suppressing the violence —exceptional violence, but the everyday kind too— from the existence of human beings forever. Contrary to what many of us might like, though, it is more than likely that war and violence exist inasmuch as their near relatives —festivals, jokes, games— turn out to be insufficient for resolving the disputes between incompatible identities and interests by symbolic means. Likewise, the perennial nature of violence and war would be that of those same principles of exchange of signs and of goods or evils of those it participates in, and which are those that distinguish human from animal society. And, to end, one might offer the diagnosis that violence and war will only disappear in the moment in which human beings cease being convinced that in order to communicate hate —like love— bodies can usually do more than words.

Notes

1. ELIAS, Norbert & DUNNING, Eric, *The Quest for Excitement: Sport and Leisure in the Civilizing Process*, Blackwell, Oxford-New York 1986.

2. DOUGLAS, Mary, *Purity and Danger*, Routledge & Kegan Paul, London 1966, p. 140.

3. On the integrating role of vengeful violence in African segmentary and lineal societies, see Edward Evan Evans-Pritchard's classic *The Nuer* (1940). As a complement to this, cf. Bazin, Jean & Terray, Emmanuel, *Guerres de lignages et guerres d'États en Afrique*, Éditions des Archives Contemporaines, Paris 1982.

4. SIMMEL, Georg, «La lluita», *Sociologia 1, Edicions 62/La Caixa,* Barcelona 1984.

5. GEERTZ, Clifford, «Deep Play: Notes on the Balinese Cockfight", in *The Interpretation of Cultures*, Basic Books, New York 2000, pp. 412 ff.

6. ZULAIKA, Joseba, *Basque Violence: Metaphor and Sacrament*, University of Nevada Press, Reno 1988.

7. CAILLOIS, Roger, *Man and the Sacred*, University of Illinois Press, Champaign 2001.

8. SIMMEL, *op. cit.,* p. 306.

9. BATAILLE, Georges, *Theory of Religion*, Zone Books, New York 1989, p. 57.

10. As an introduction to the subject of "primitive wars", cf., for example, ADLER, Alexander, «La guerre et l'état primitif», in ABENSOUR, M. (ed.), *L'Esprit des lois sauvages*, Seuil, Paris 1987, pp. 95-114.

11. *Cf.* BALANDIER, Georges, *Le désordre. Éloge du mouvement*, Fayard, Paris 1988.

12. LEFEBVRE, Henri, *Everyday Life in the Modern World*, Harper & Row, New York 1971, p. 36.

13. LE ROY LADURIE, Emmanuel, *Le Carnaval de Romans*, Gallimard, Paris 1979.

14. As occurs with micro-physical expressions of personal violence, domestic strife, bar-room brawling in these cases, too, the relation between real violence deriving from an unforeseen intensification of false festive violence can be direct and explicit. It's worth remembering, here, that the first episode in the civil war in ex-Yugoslavia occurred on Sunday 13 May 1990, when the followers of Dynamo, Croats, and those of Red Star, Serbs, violently confronted each other in the Maksmis stadium and then in the streets of Zagreb. A local proof of how it is when one perceives the insufficiency of the strategies of false or limited damage for maintaining the cohesion which can be stepped up in that activation of the most radical forms of socialising energy, whose culmination is generalised armed violence.

[15] BALANDIER, Georges, «La violence et la guerre: une anthropologie», Revue Internationale des Sciences Sociales, 110 (December 1986).

16. MAUSS, Marcel, *The Gift*, Routledge & Kegan Paul, London 1970, p. 80.

17. LEFORT, Claude, «L'échange ou la lutte des hommes", in *Les formes de l'histoire*, Gallimard, col. Bibliothèque des Sciences Humaines, Paris 1978, pp. 15-30.

18. Hans Magnus Enzensberger attributes this relinquishment to the autism of the combatant in the new civil wars laying waste to contemporary societies, "his complete lack of egoism, a loss of self so total and radical that even the regulating principle of survival itself doesn't function" *(Aussichten auf den Bürgerkrieg, Suhrkamp, Frankfurt am Main 1996).*

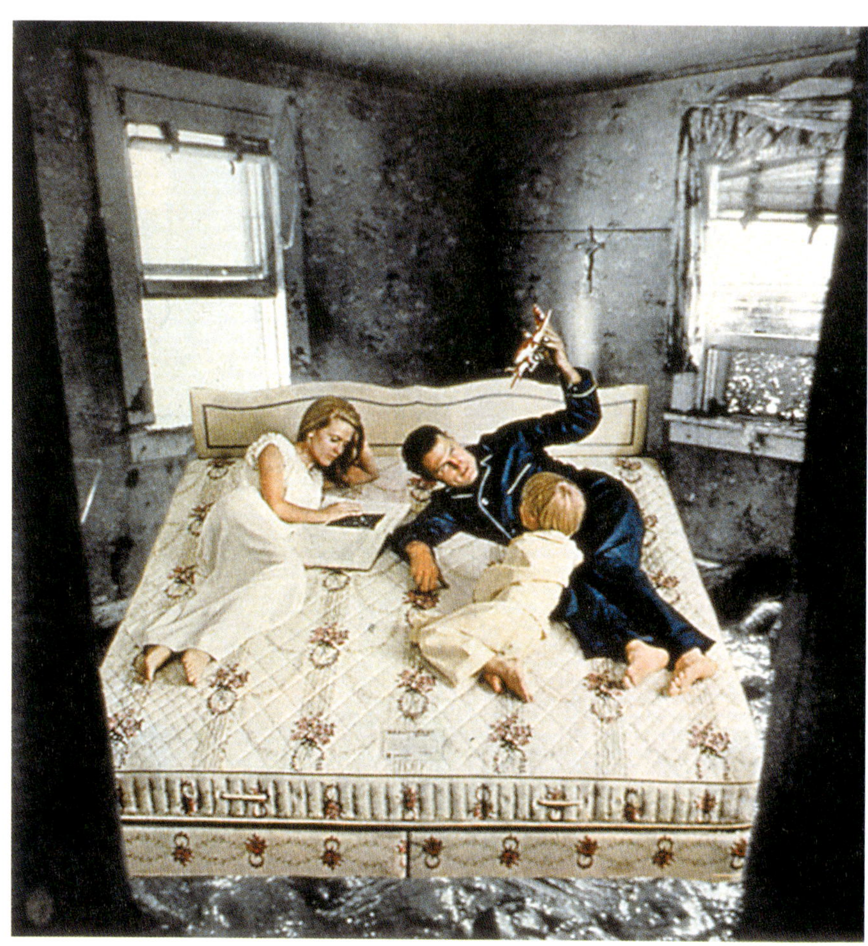

MARTHA ROSLER, Beauty rest, from the series
"Bringing the war home: House beautiful", 1967-1972
Photocollage printed on top of a colour photograph,
60 x 50 cm
Courtesy of Galerie Anne de Villepoix, Paris

LARRY BURROWS, "As the bombing stops-This girl Tron",
Life magazine cover, 8 November 1968
35 x 26.5 cm

MARTHA ROSLER, Tron (amputee), from the series
"Bringing the war home: House beautiful", 1967-1972
Photocollage printed on top of a colour photograph, 60 x 50 cm
Courtesy of Galerie Anne de Villepoix, Paris

MARTHA ROSLER, Giacometti, from the series "Bringing
the war home: House beautiful", 1967-1972
Photocollage printed on top of a colour photograph, 60 x 50 cm
Courtesy of Galerie Anne de Villepoix, Paris

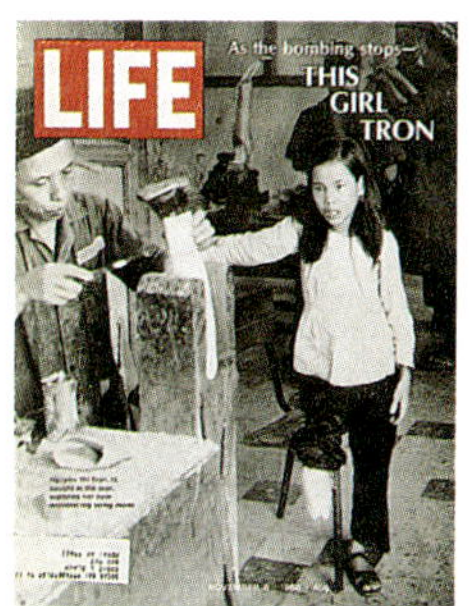

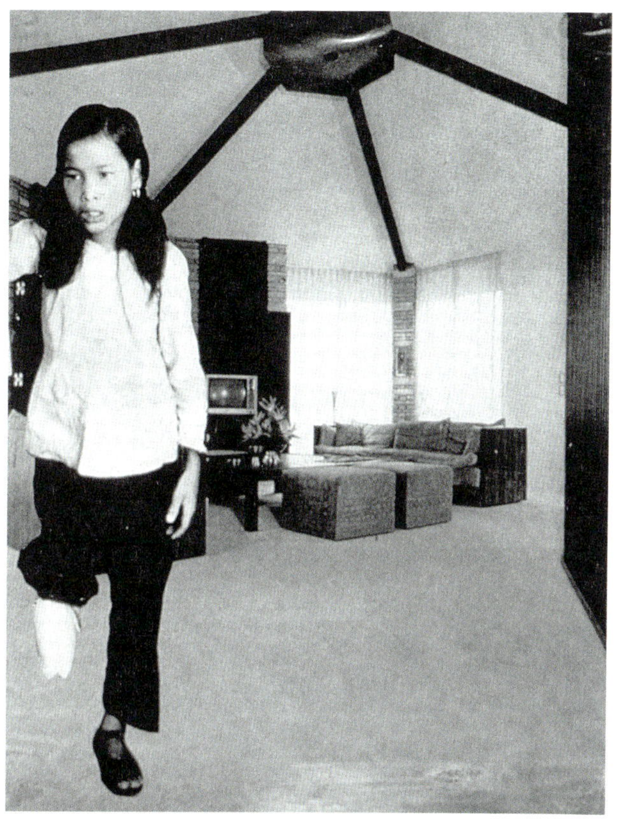

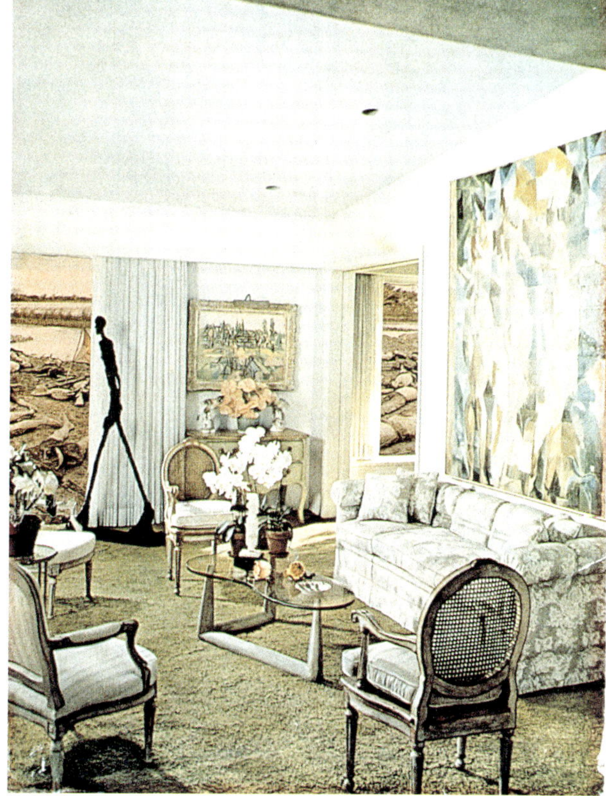

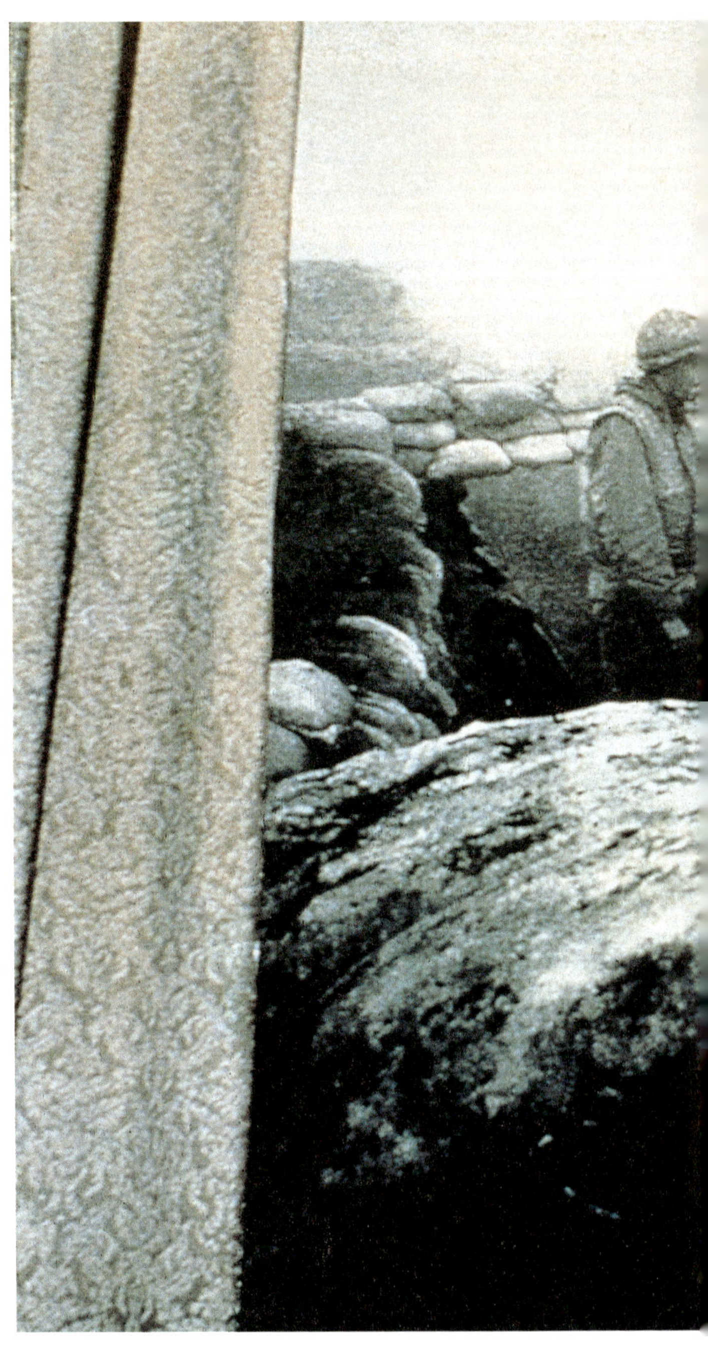

MARTHA ROSLER, Cleaning the drapes, from the series
"Bringing the war home: House beautiful", 1967-1972
Photocollage printed on top of a colour photograph, 60 x 50 cm
Courtesy of Galerie Anne de Villepoix, Paris

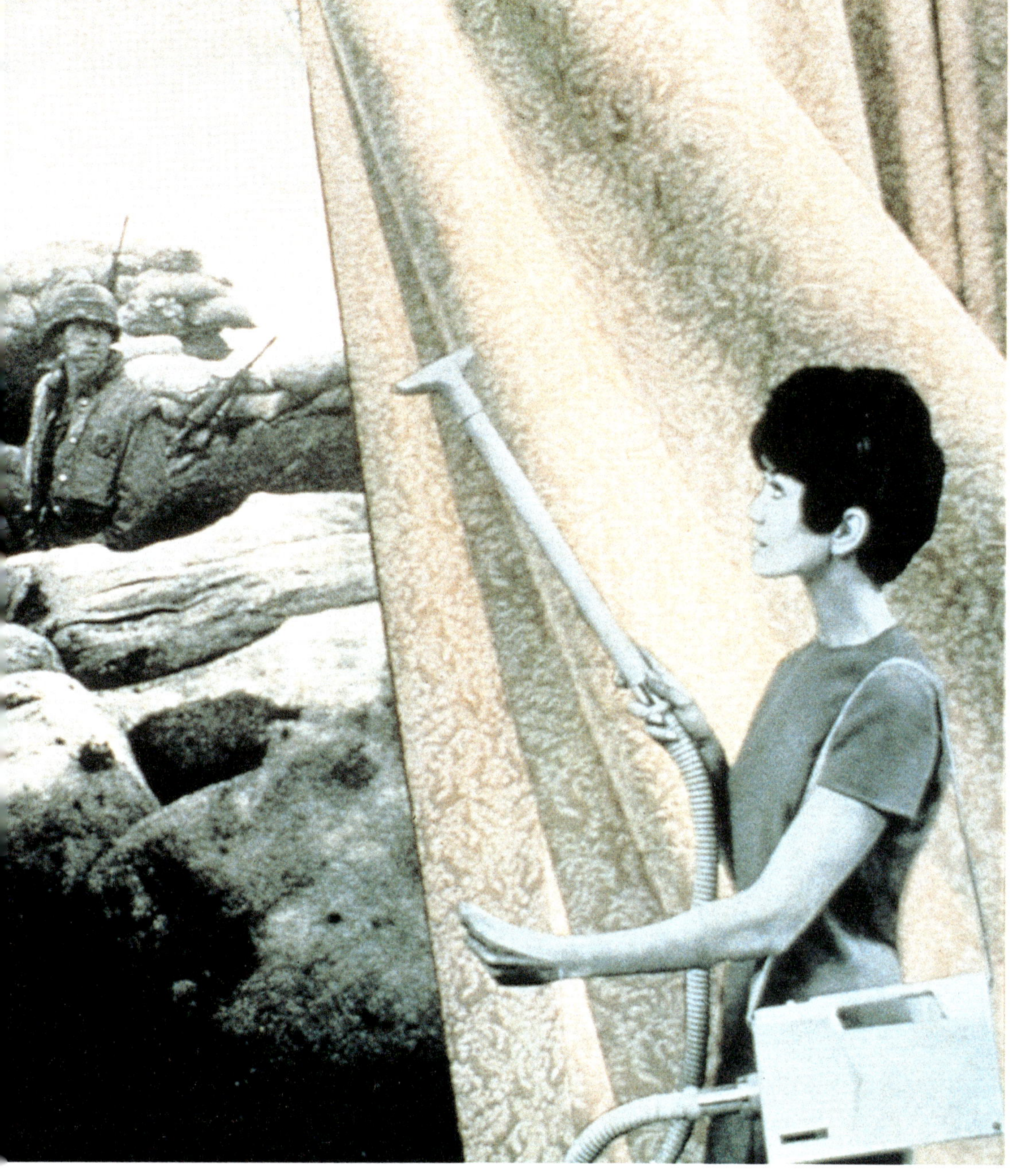

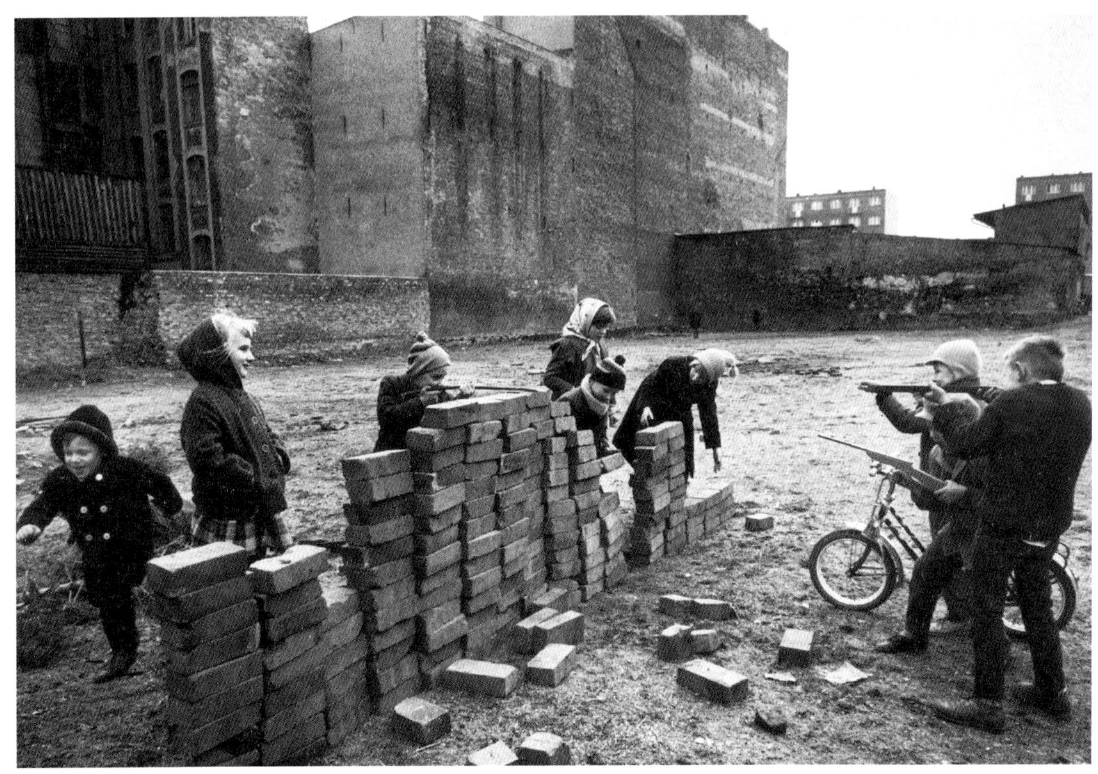

Children play war games, even in countries at war.
Sometimes, they play with real weapons and, at other times,
they train as real soldiers with toy weapons. In many wars,
they are soldiers with weapons that can kill.

RAYMOND DEPARDON, Children playing at "building the wall",
West Berlin, 1962
Raymond Depardon / Magnum Photos / Contacto

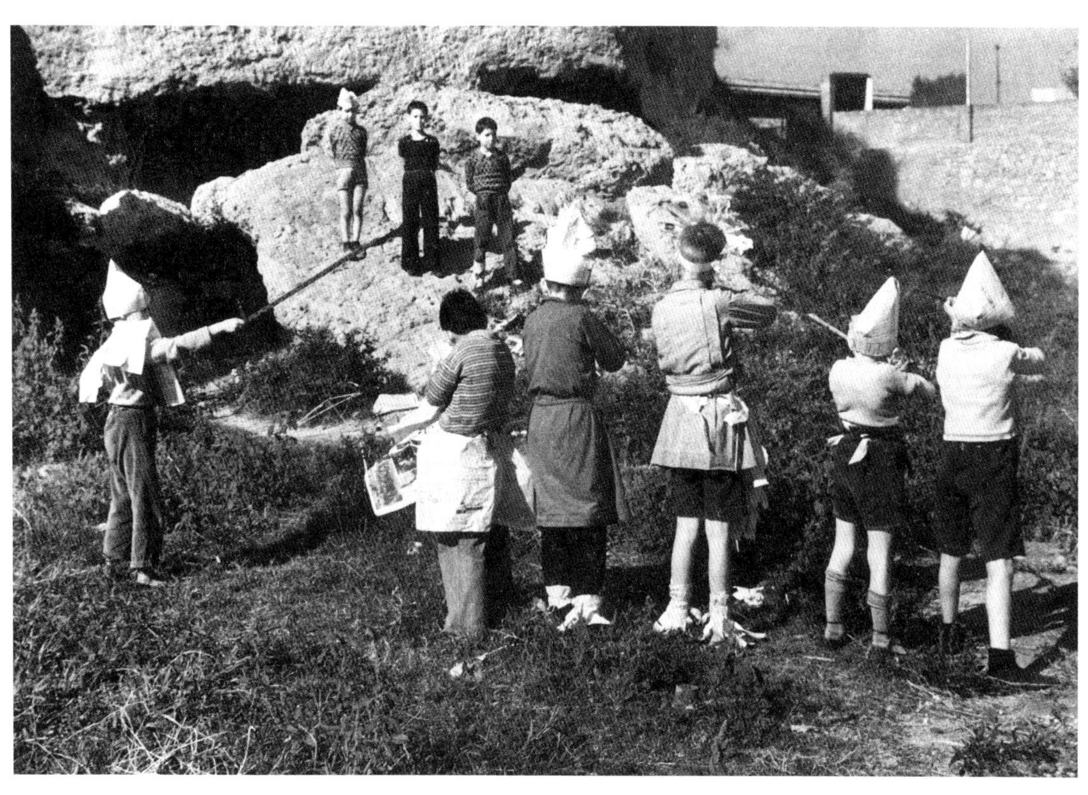

AGUSTÍ CENTELLES, Children playing war games,
Montjuïc, Barcelona, 1936
Silver gelatine print, 30 x 40 cm
Arxiu Agustí Centelles, Barcelona

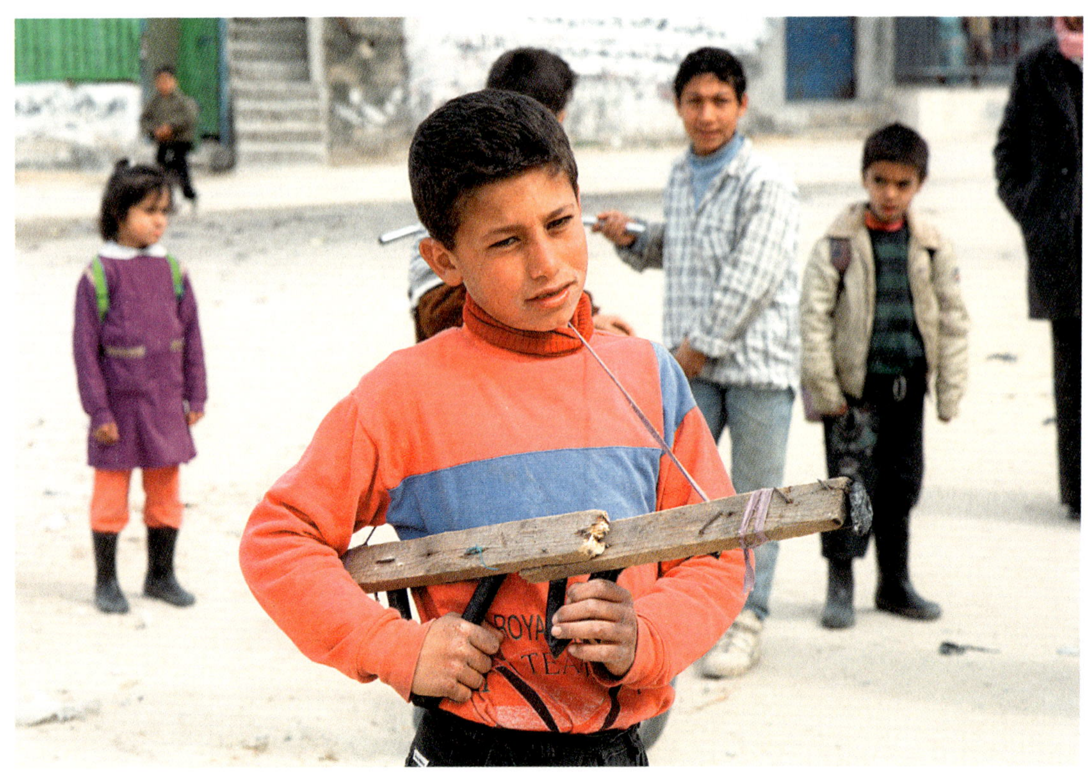

PETER TURNLEY,
Boy holding home-made toy gun,
Gaza, 1993
Corbis / Cover Barcelona

DANIEL REEVES with JON L. HILTON,
Smothering dreams, 1981
Video, 22´05´´
Courtesy of Electronic Arts Intermix,
New York

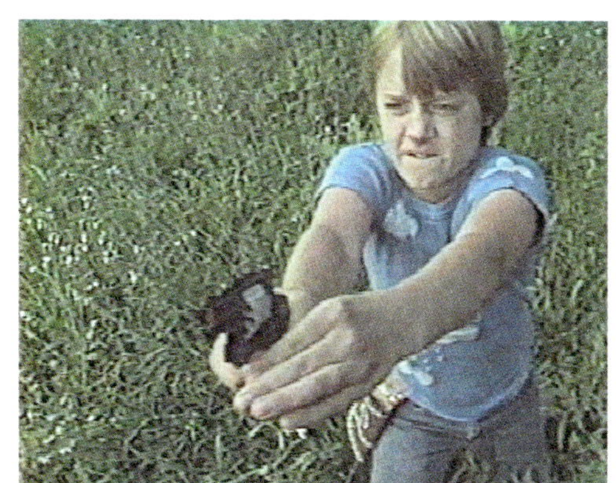

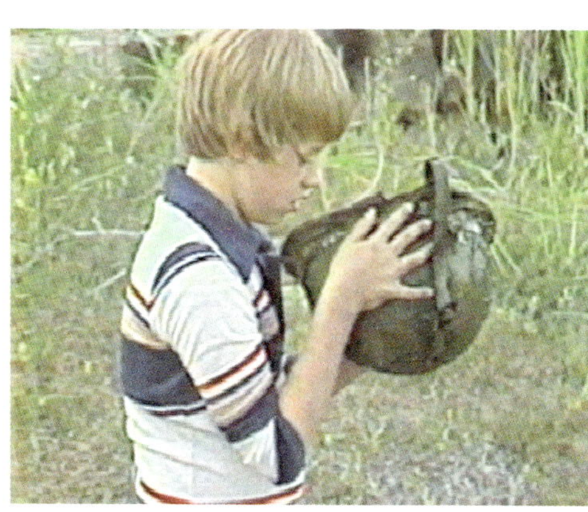

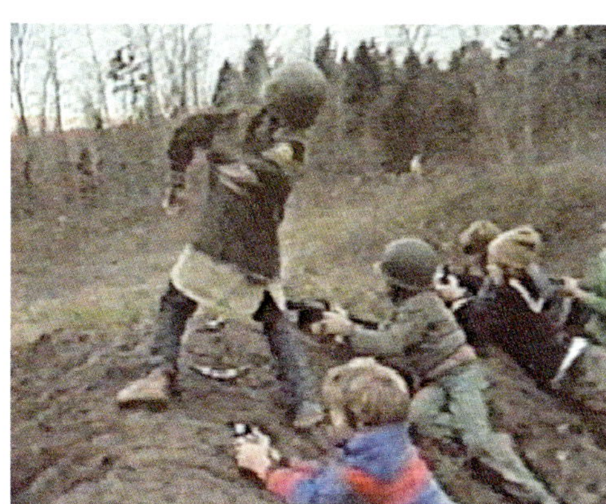

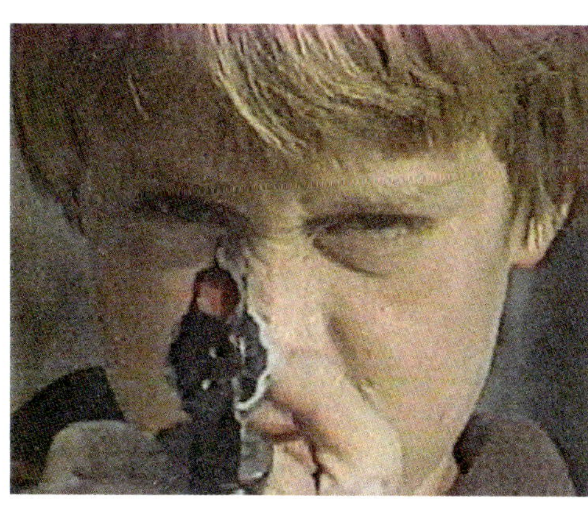

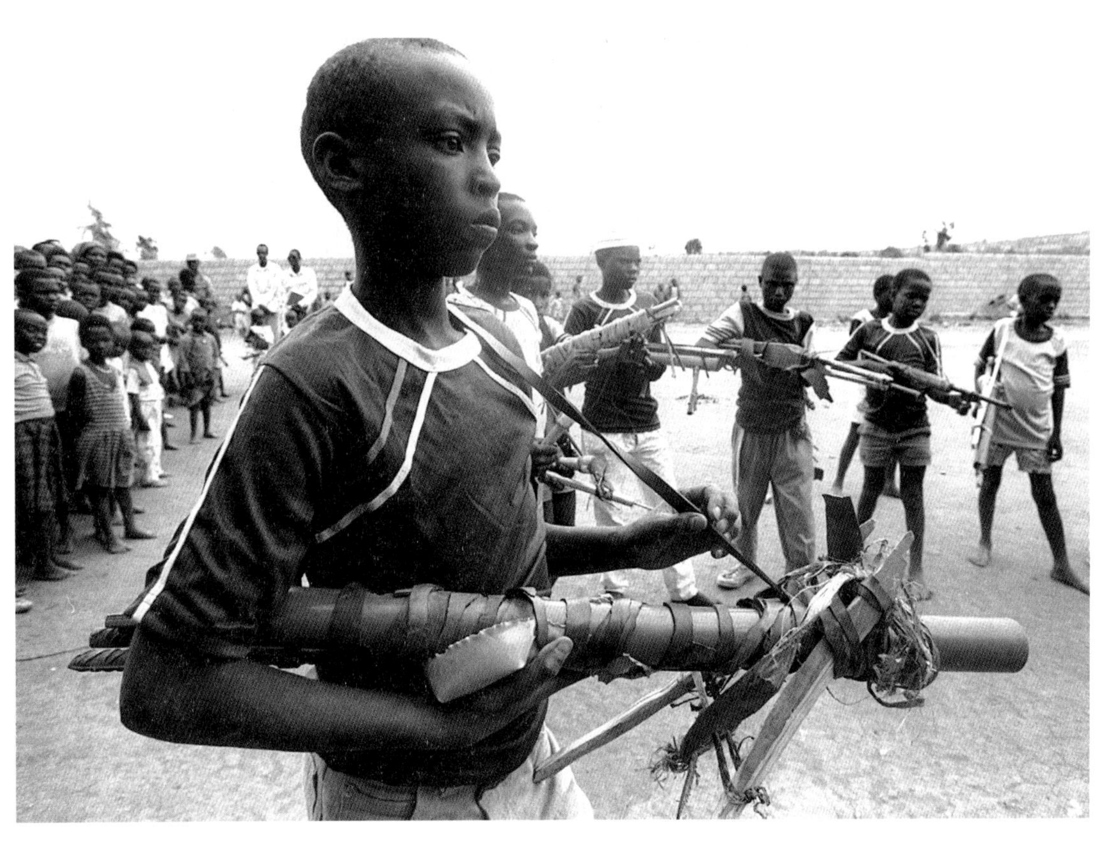

BETTY PRESS, Boys stand ready to perform a "psycho-drama",
Rwanda, 1994
UNICEF

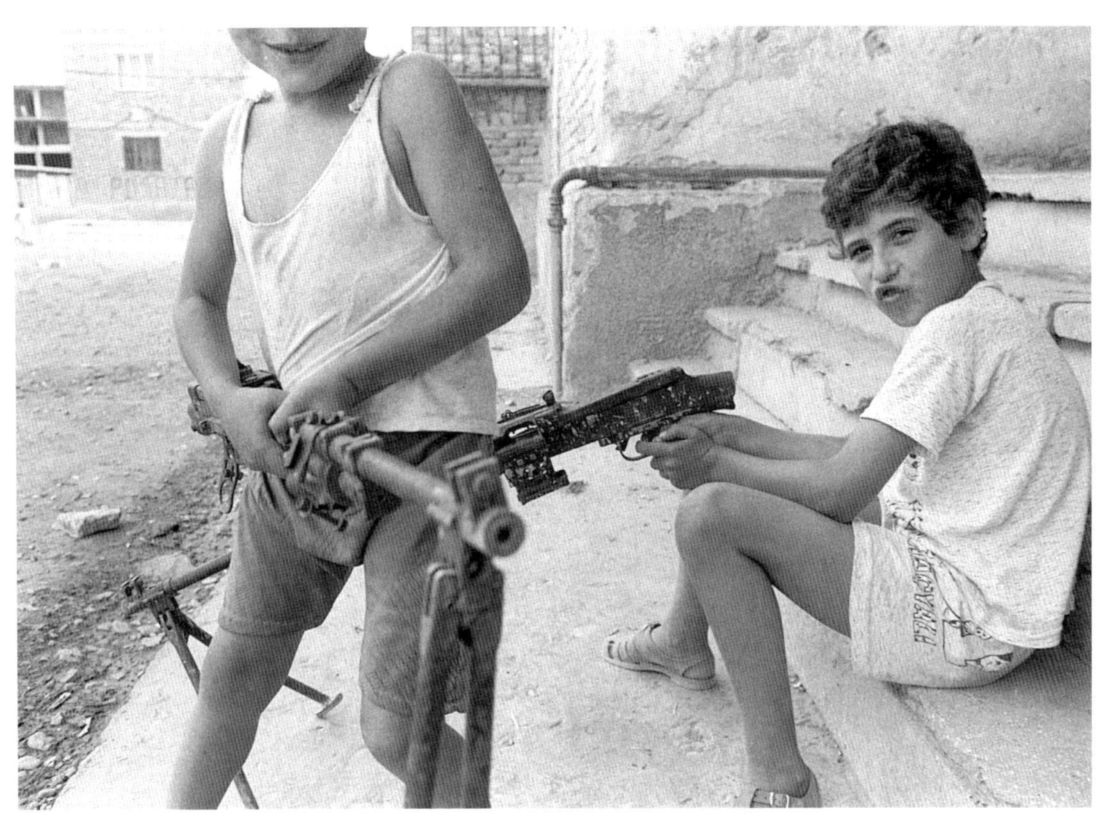

ROGER LEMOYNE, Two boys play with gun parts
on the steps of a building in the southern town of Berat,
Albania, 1990s
UNICEF

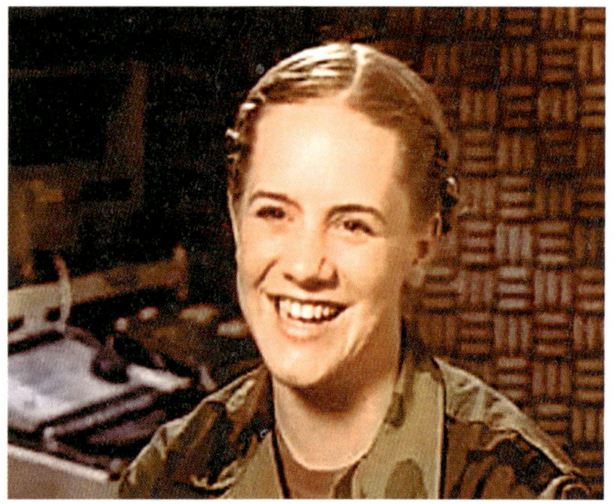
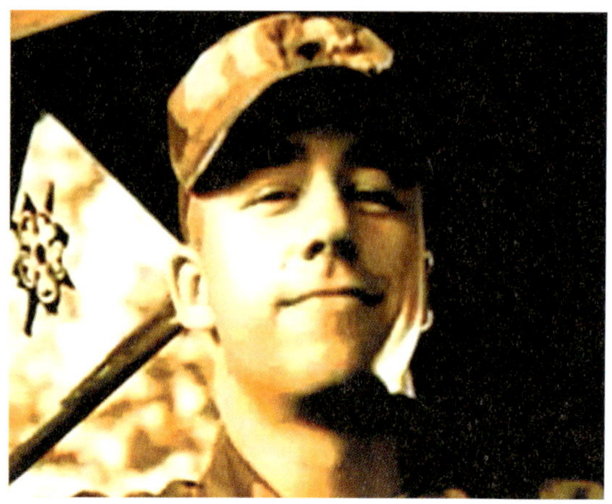
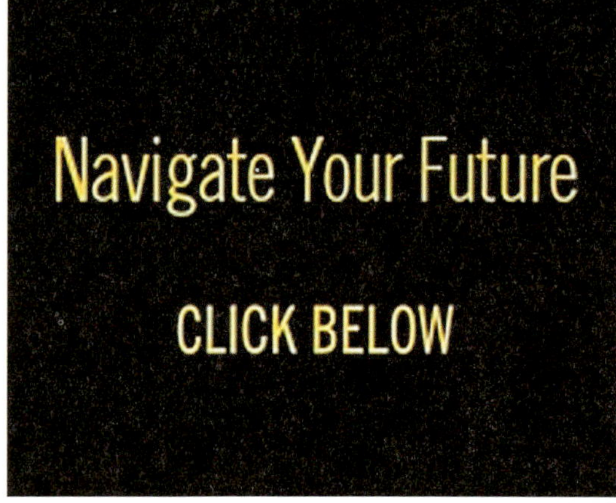

www.goarmy.com

The field of advertising makes visible the economy of war in peacetime:
in the production of technology as well as in the recruitment of
human resources. Video games are not just a form of entertainment through
which war is assimilated as a possibility in culture; technological
sophistication also makes them an instrument simulating war for training,
planning and monitoring combat.

Abu-Ali / retroyou, Arxius Babilonia [.mil.com.gov], 1999-2003
2 videos of images captured on the Internet, 22' 51'' and 20' 55''
Arxius de l'Observatori – OVNI, Barcelona

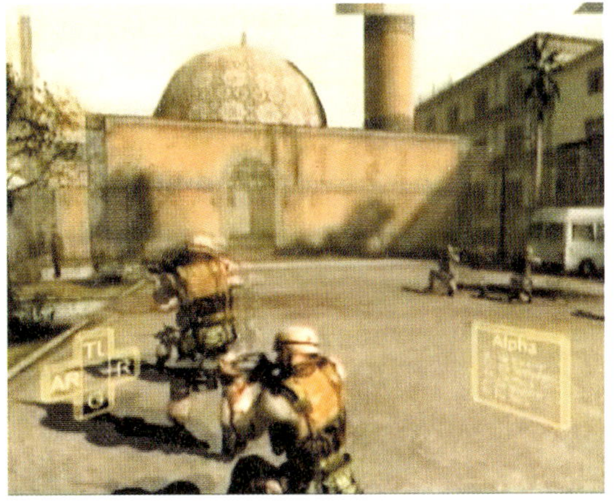

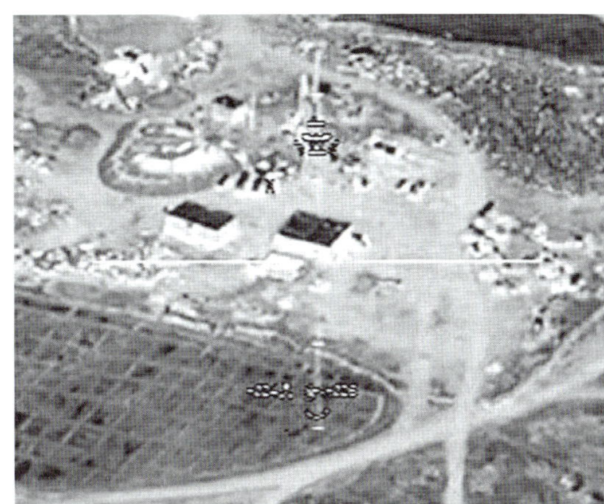

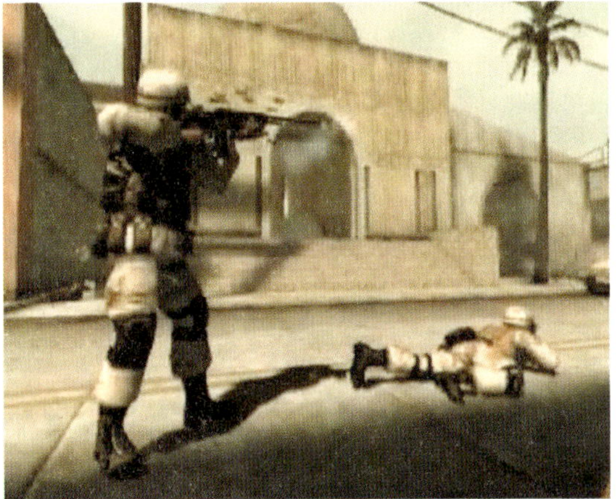

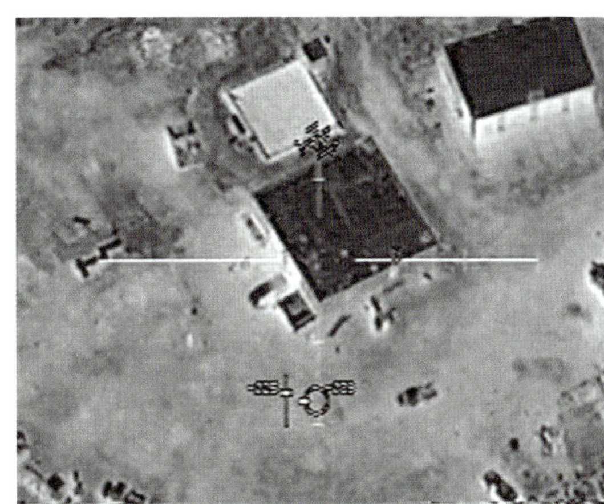

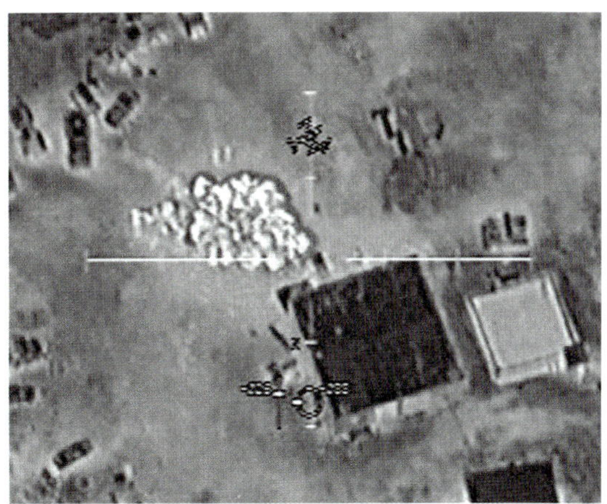

www.fullspectrumwarrior.com

Anaconda Operation, 2002

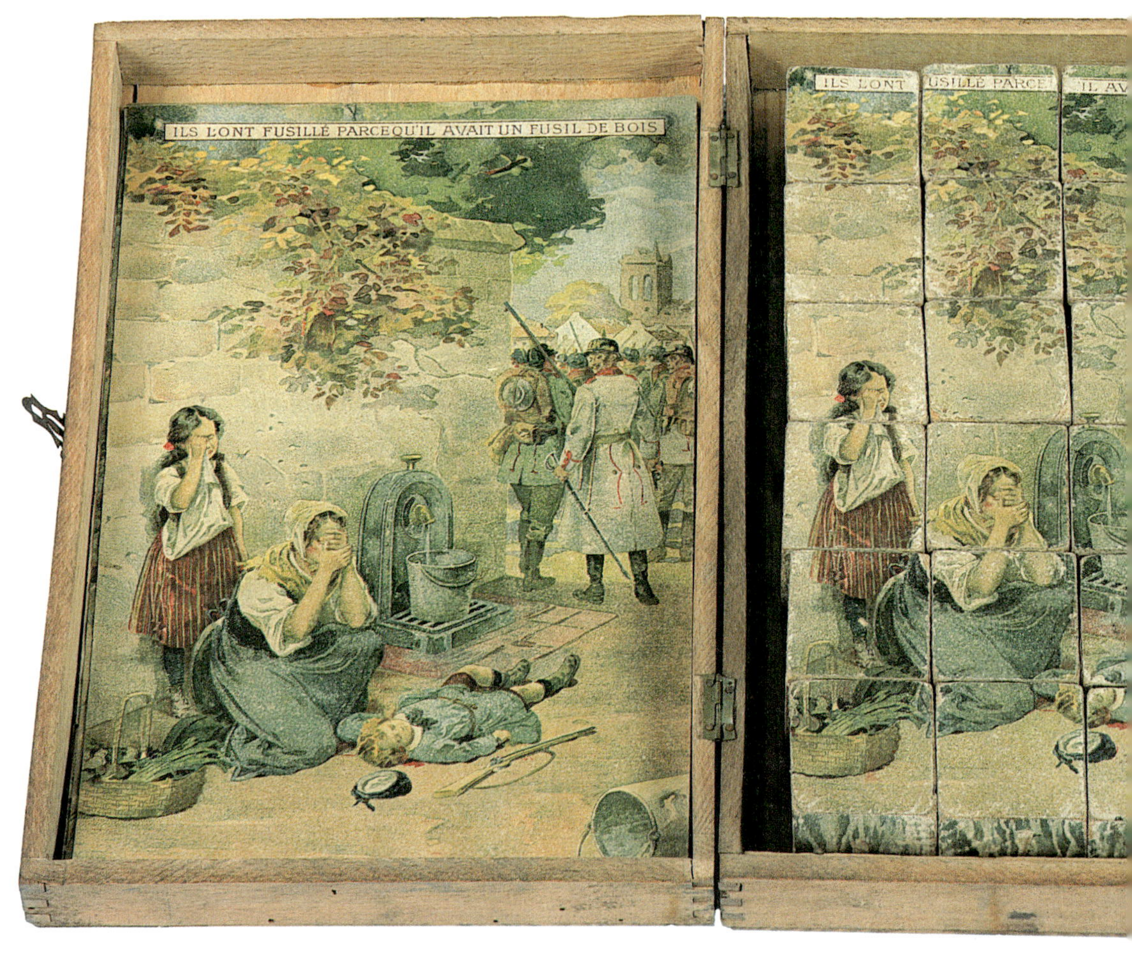

Set of 24 cubes depicting German atrocities
combining typical childhood objects
and extremely violent contents, 1915-1919
Wood and paper, 29 x 19.7 cm
Historial de la Grande Guerre, Péronne (Somme)

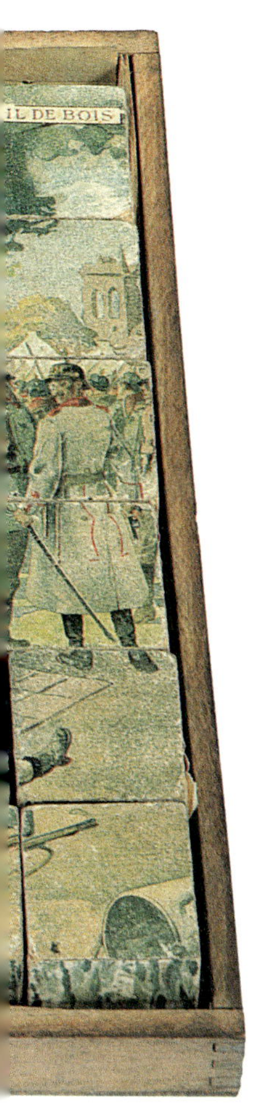

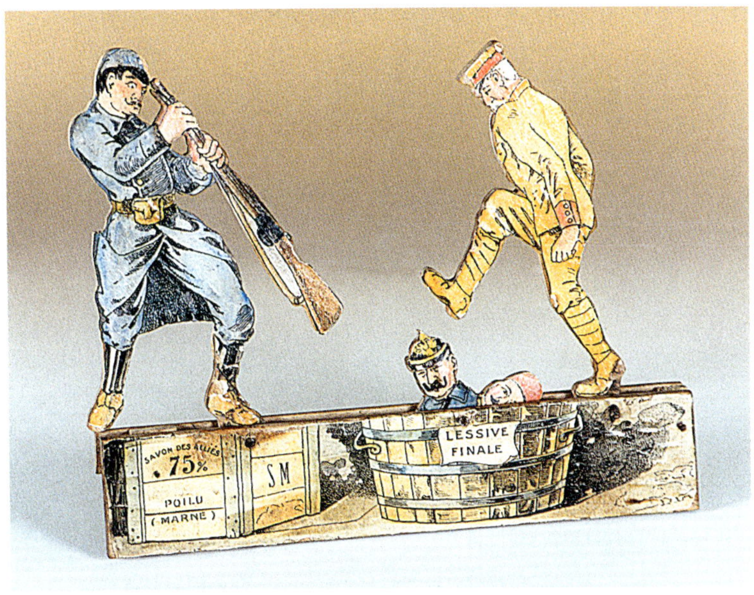

"Final wash". Animated wooden toy: a French soldier on the left and a British
soldier on the right dunk the heads of Wilhelm II, Franz-Joseph I and Mustapha
Kemal in a washtub during the "final wash", 1914-1915
Wood and printed paper, 18.5 x 23 x 3.5 cm
Historial de la Grande Guerre, Péronne (Somme)

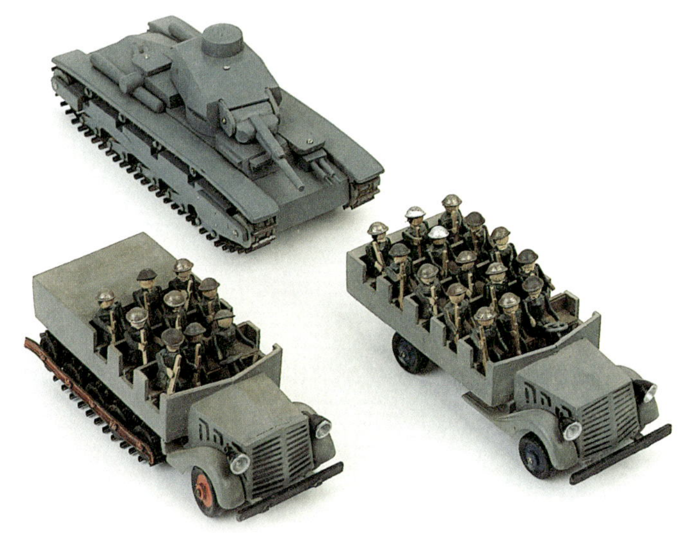

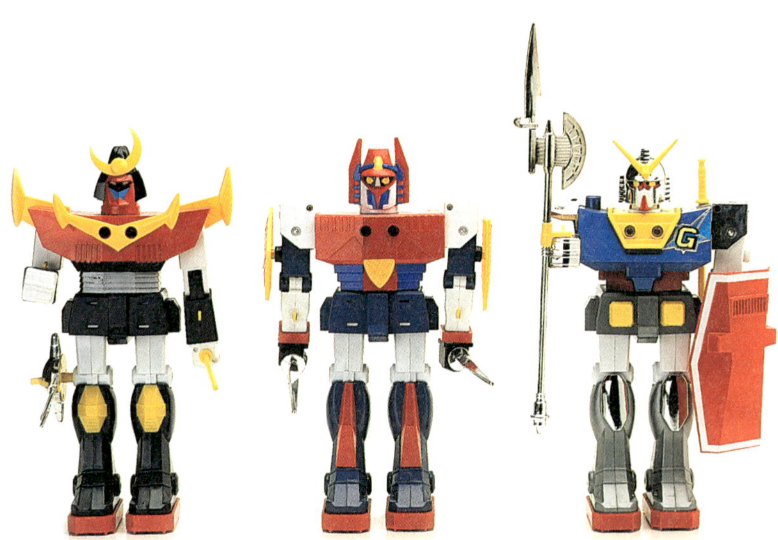

Military tanks and trucks
Museu del Joguet de Catalunya, Figueres

Robots "Zanbot, Duncan and..."
Museu del Joguet de Catalunya, Figueres

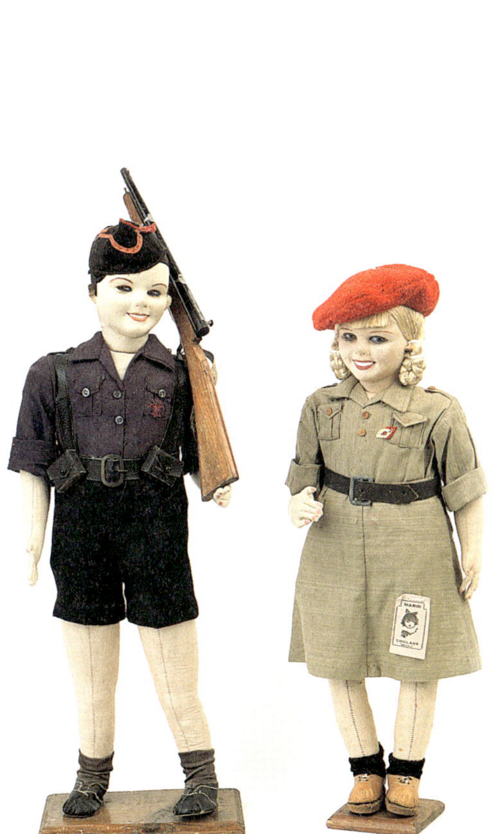

Toy soldiers
Museu del Joguet de Catalunya, Figueres

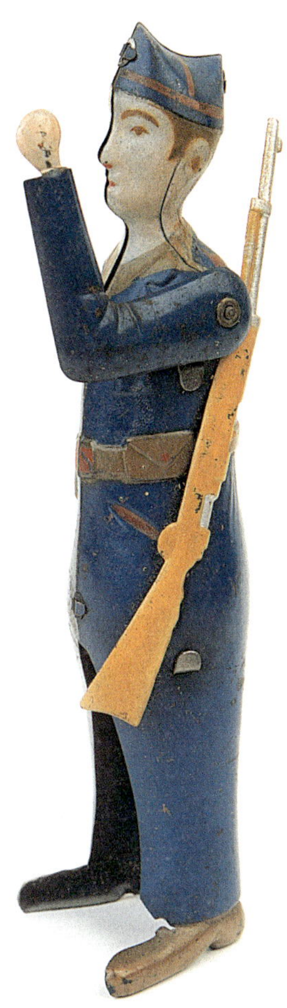

Militiaman, 1936
Tin toy, 45 x 10 cm
Museu del Joguet de Catalunya, Figueres

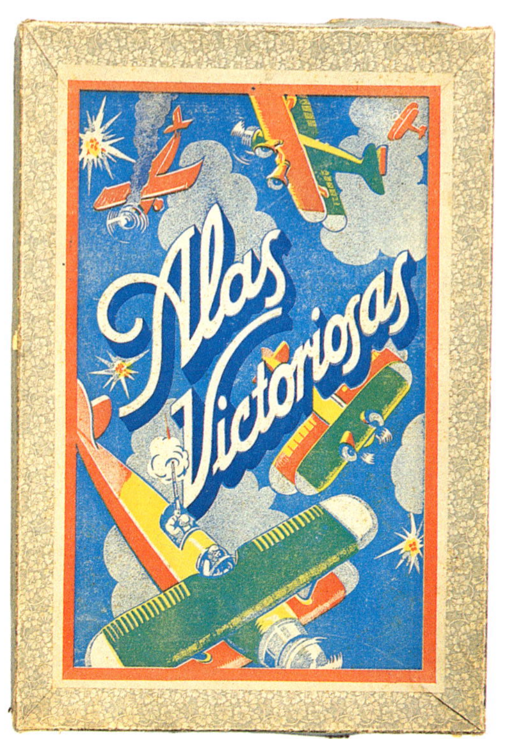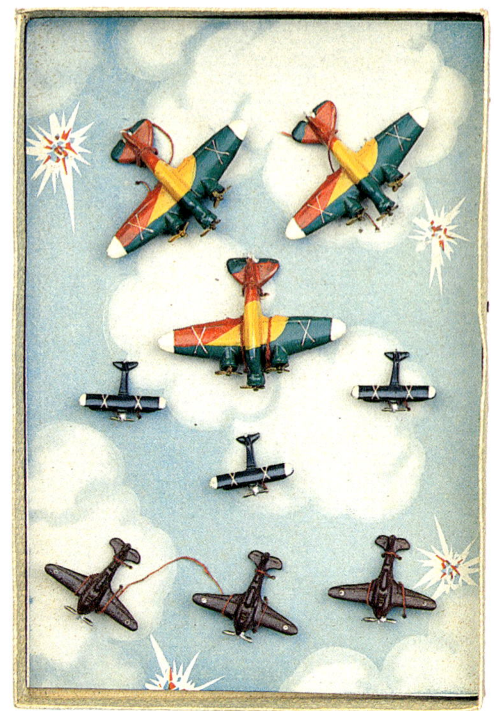

"Air raid: a game of calculation
and luck which tests your aim.
Victorious wings"
22.2 x 31.5 x 2.8 cm
Museu del Joguet de Catalunya, Figueres

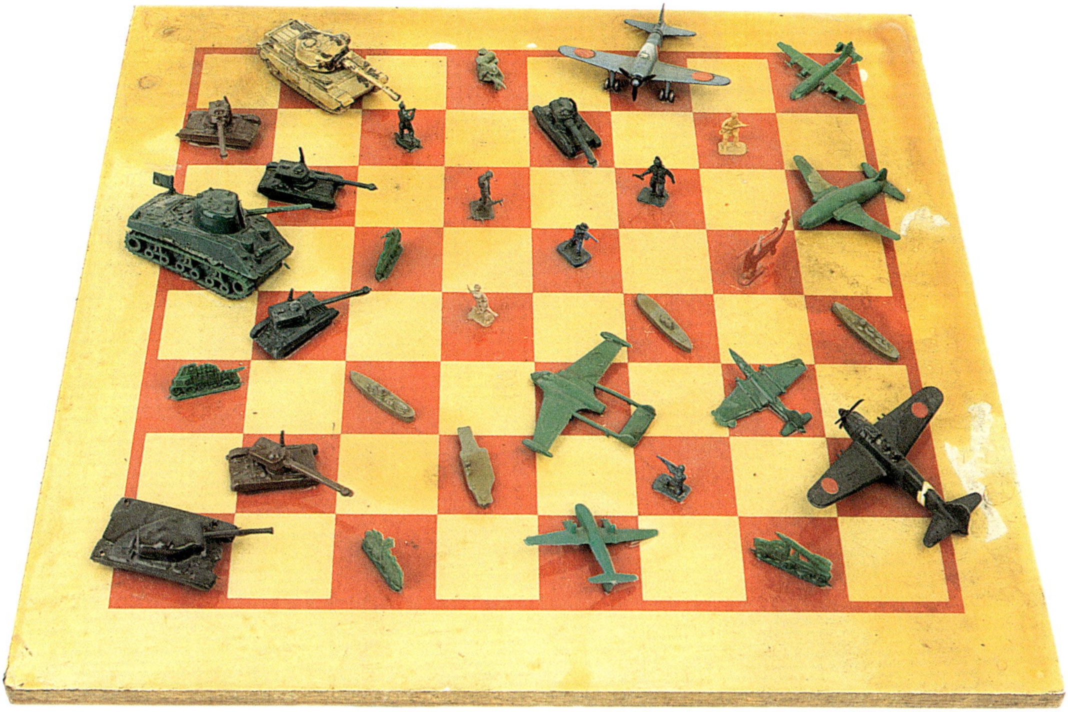

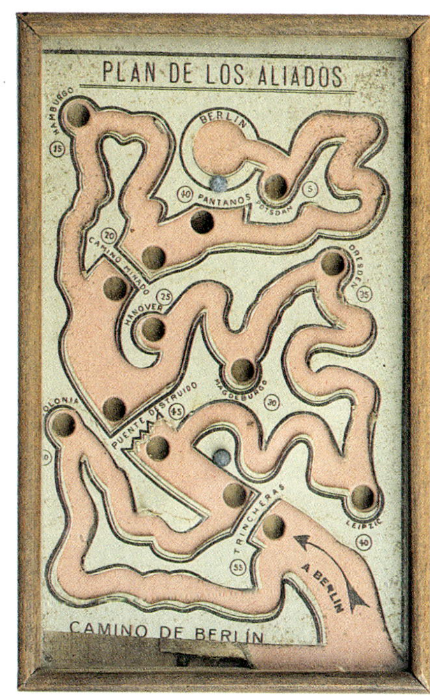

FRANCESC ABAD, Chess set
40 x 40 x 2.8 cm
Museu del Joguet de Catalunya, Figueres

"Allied plan" game
19 x 19 x 2.8 cm
Museu del Joguet de Catalunya, Figueres

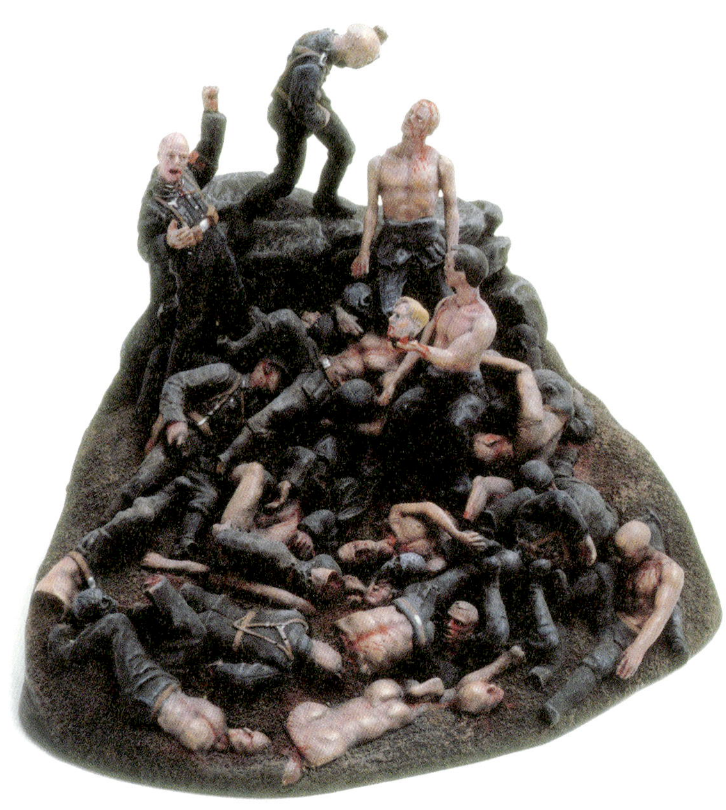

JAKE AND DINOS CHAPMAN, I spit on your grave III, 2000
Polyester resin and enamel paint, 7 x 12 x 10 cm
Courtesy of the artists and Jay Jopling / White Cube, London

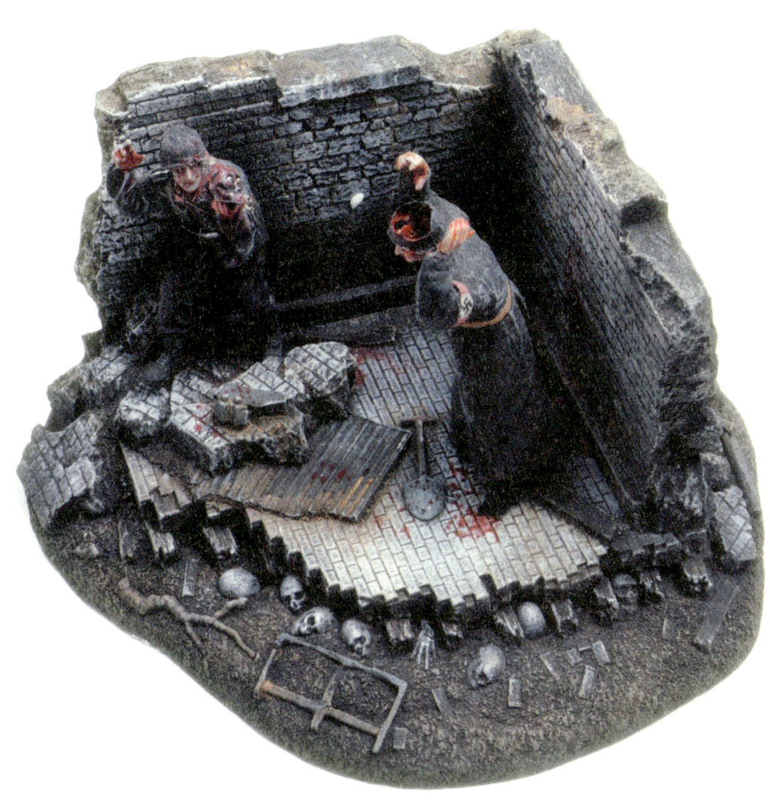

JAKE AND DINOS CHAPMAN, Cannibal holocaust II, 2000
Polyester, lacquer, 7 x 11 x 10.8 cm
Courtesy of the artists and Jay Jopling / White Cube, London

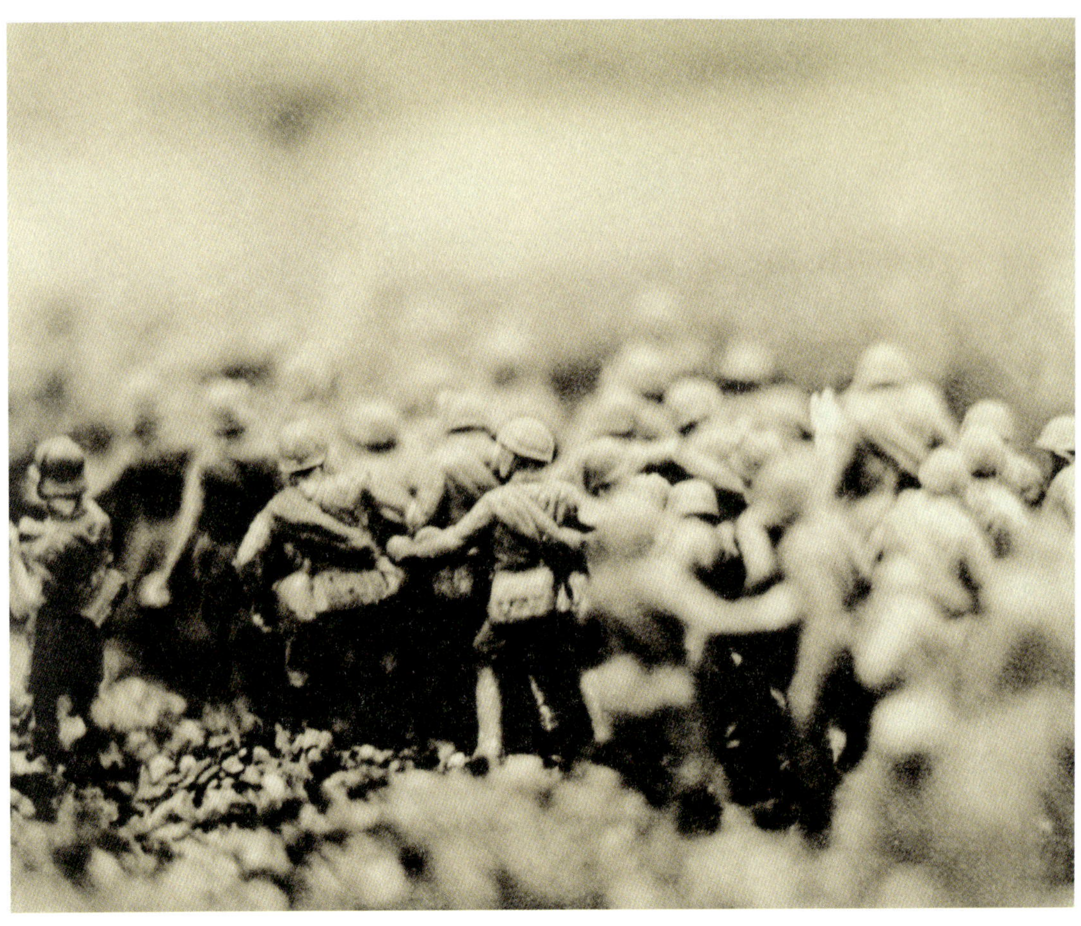

DAVID LEVINTHAL, Four works from "Hitler moves East" series, 1975-1977
Kodalith Film, 20.3 x 29.2 cm, 26.7 x 31.7 cm, 19 x 23.5 cm, 18.4 x 24.1 cm
Courtesy of the artist and Galerie Xippas, Paris

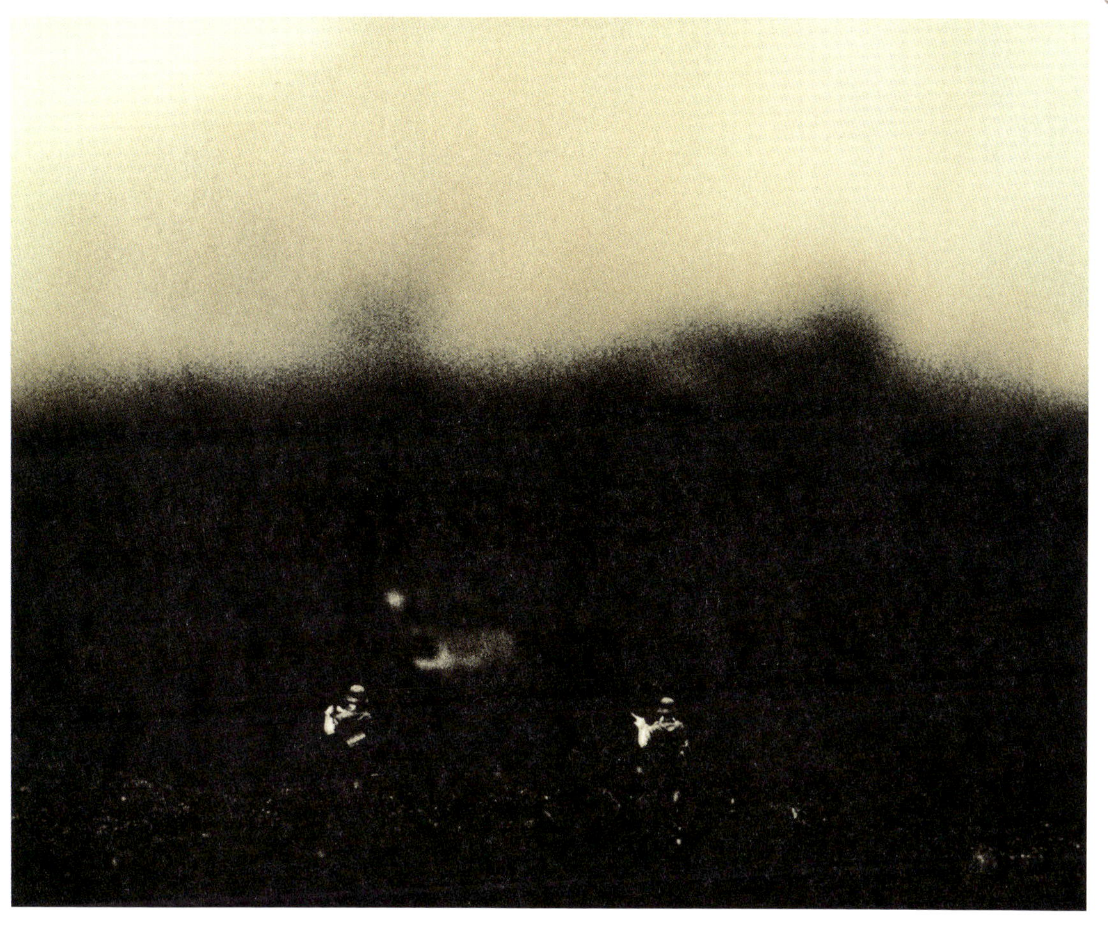

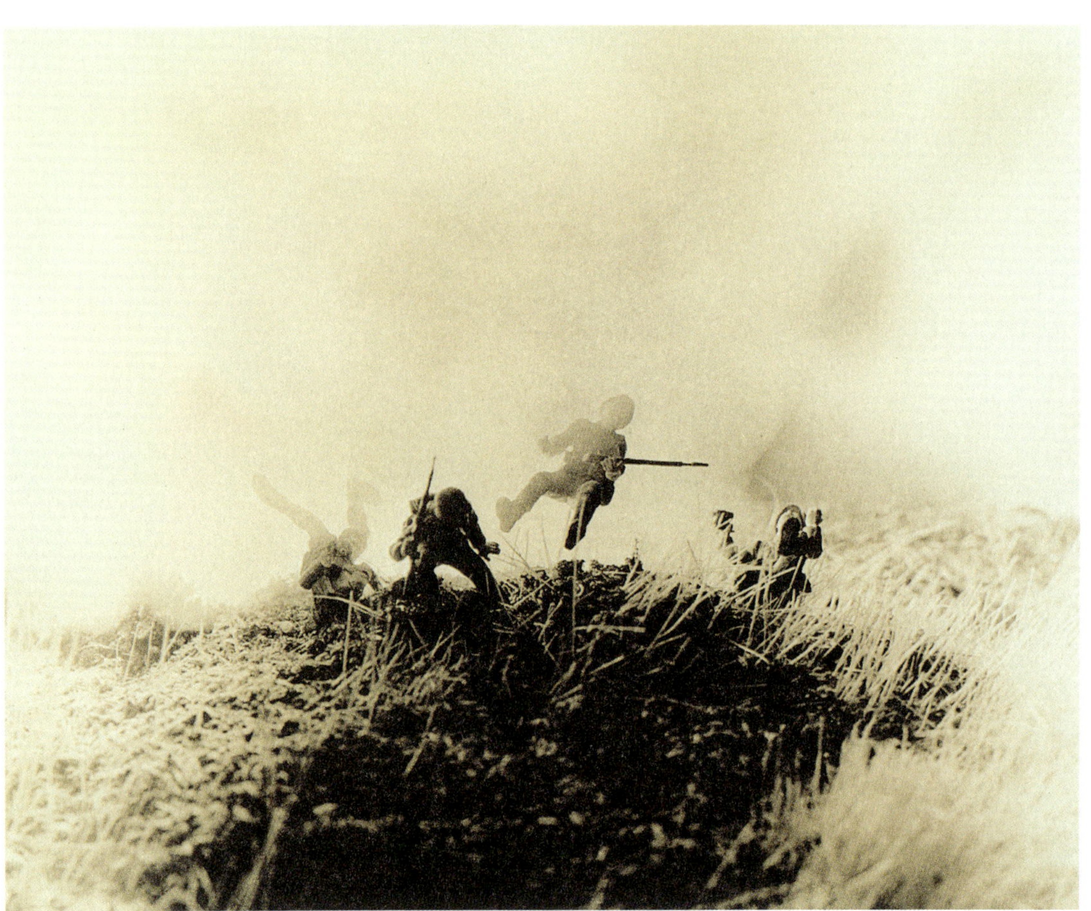

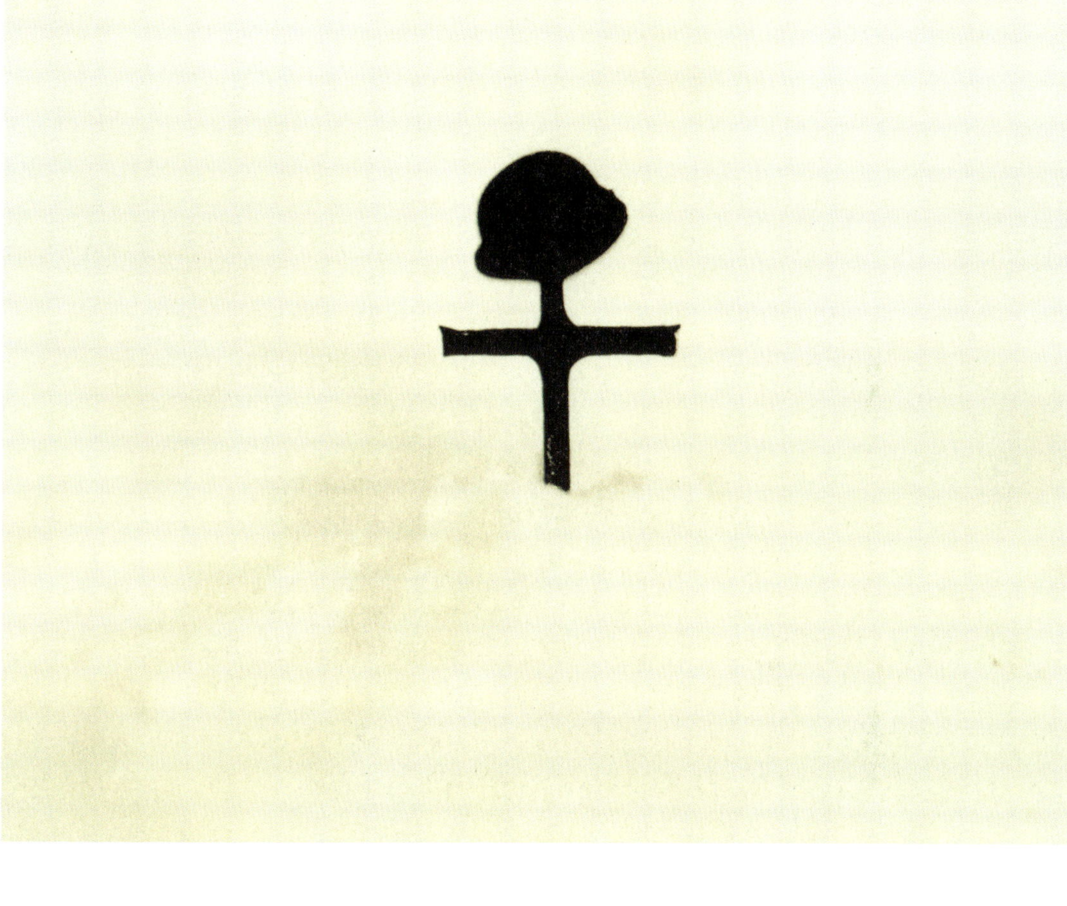

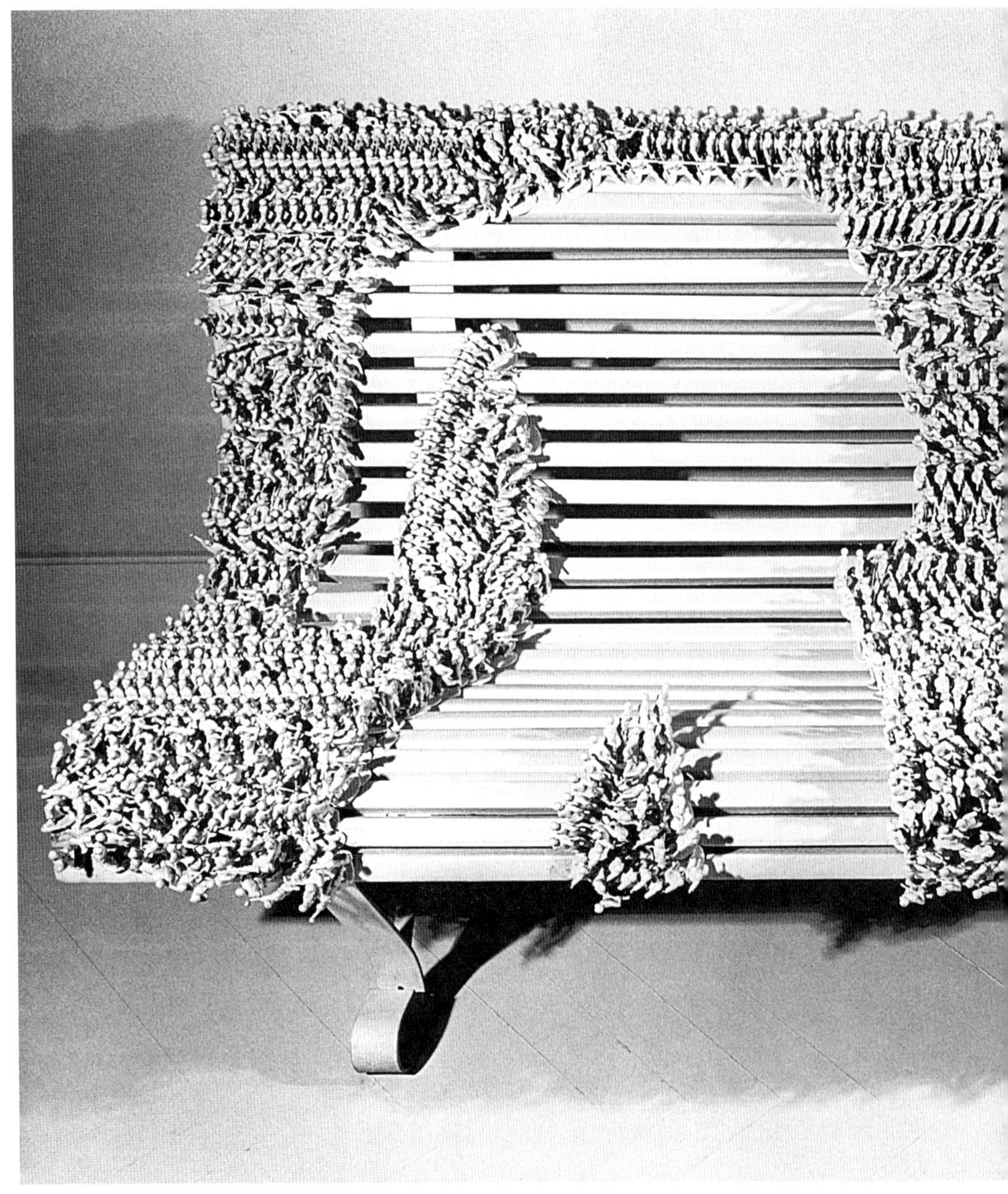

ANTONI MIRALDA, Bench, 1968
Plaster and plastic, 80 x 200 x 80 cm
Collection Durand-Ruel, Paris

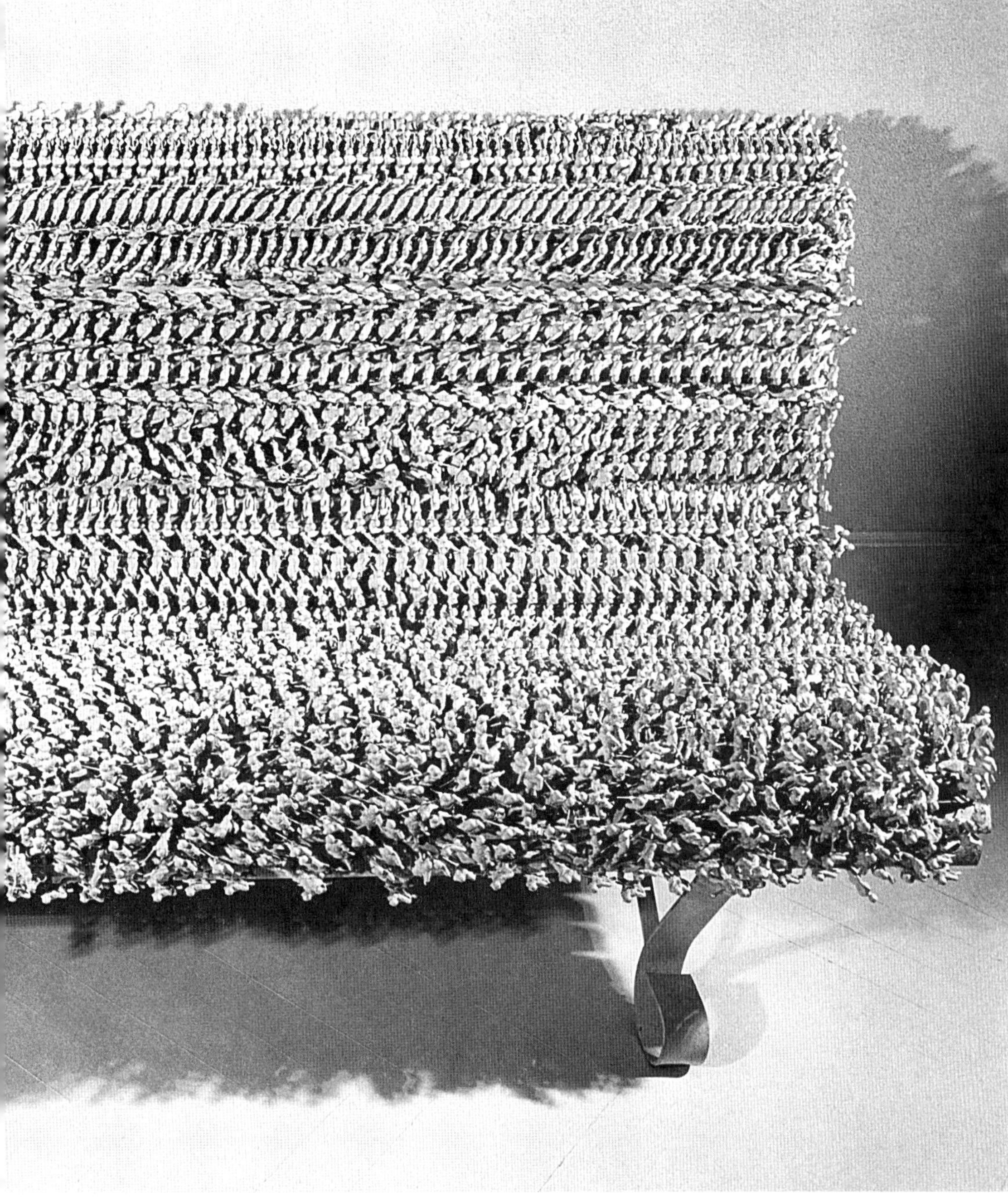

The construction of the enemy

The enemy in the mirror

José María Ridao

The dramatic repetition of warlike incidents throughout history is undoubtedly at the origin of one of the most devastating perceptions concerning the human condition: that violence forms part of the set of instincts each individual is born with, to the extent that, however terrifying and even monstrous this may turn out to be, it forms one of the species' inexorable traits. Any look at the past, even a rapid and succinct one, seems to offer reliable confirmation of the notion that if men and women have always existed side by side with the exercise of brute force this is due, finally, to nothing more than that the interminable succession of tortures, crimes, ritual sacrifices, outbreaks of individual or collective hatred, fields of ruins and corpses are a product of some link in the genetic code from which one cannot escape unless it be through civilisation. When civilisation declines or capitulates —it's usually shored up immediately afterwards— the more hidden and therefore more authentic drives of the individual find their way clear and the disaster, the tragedy, then takes place.

In fact, and despite what history seems to suggest, it is difficult to tell if violence forms part of human instinct. Alongside the countless examples of individuals who, somnambules, their eyes bloodshot, seem to find a stimulus and not an obstacle in the suffering they cause, there exist others whose behaviour is exactly the opposite: a ready compassion for whoever is completely at the mercy of one of their gestures or decisions. In one of his texts on the Spanish Civil War, George Orwell describes an incident in which some insuperable scruples assailed him at the moment of firing at an enemy soldier who, surprised by the onset of the fighting, was trying to take cover while pulling up his trousers. Similarly, one might ask oneself about the existence of such an instinct when observing the numerous procedures consecrated by a tradition as long as that of violence and aimed at concealing its ravages, or at least disguising the responsibility of he who exercises it. The mask the executioner hides behind during the execution would obey a scruple, then, which is not that different from the one which encourages the individuality of soldiers to be done away with beneath the rigorous anonymity of their uniforms, or the one that causes a jargon to be elaborated which cloaks, or even dignifies, the act of killing itself, be this in the context of the battlefield or in that of the extermination camp. Finally, the reverential distaste with which people contemplate the remains of their fellow men, the mixture of rejection and anguish in the presence of the vision of death, might also be an indication that in opposition to the instinct of violence, or at least along with it, there exists that of compassion.

This is an old controversy, defined and redefined around two opposed positions: one which defends the individual's original ferocious inclinations, Thomas Hobbes's *homo homini lupus*, and the other which defends, by way of contrast, the innate goodness of the human being, according to the Rousseauesque vision of the native or the savage. While opting for one or the other calls, in the last analysis, for a curtailing of reason in benefit of faith, superstition or simple preference —that's to say, an impetuous leap into the void— the role that might be reserved to civilisation in the development of each of these alternatives seems, instead, to meet the requirements of an unswerving logic. Set within the perspective of Hobbes, civilisation has of necessity to assume a positive connotation insofar as it is the sum of the system of controls that makes good fellowship possible between individuals programmed for self-destruction. Outbreaks of violence would therefore invite one to identify the precise point at which the system has broken down, perhaps the motive or motives why it has done so, even the expedients employed by one side or the other in order to deliberately evade the requirements essential for keeping the peace.

However paradoxical it may seem, it has been the experience of the twentieth century, and in particular that deriving from some of its more dramatic episodes, which has helped underline the insufficiencies of the Hobbesian approach, not because it defends the individual's original inclination towards violence, but because in defending it, it places civilisation, in an implicit yet irrevocable way, on the side of good. Crimes like those of Nazism, perpetrated—as has been said so many times— in the midst of an exquisitely educated country, emphasise the fact that, just as it can come down on one side, civilisation can launch itself towards the opposite one, and instead of reining in a violence which is innate, according to Hobbes's version, can encourage crime among a few individuals who, according to Jean-Jacques Rousseau's, ought to be peace-loving by nature. Far from encapsulating any system of controls, civilisation would thus become a deadly instrument. An instrument which, in reducing conjectures about the congenital status or otherwise of violence in the human being to the point of irrelevance, would mainly focus on the fact that in order to exercise this violence it is necessary to have an enemy; and that in order to have an enemy it is, in turn, necessary to identify one; and that even before identifying one it is essential to construct one.

Controversies about pacifism are as old as those to do with the true nature of the individual, perhaps because they are nothing but variations on arguments concomitant with those employed by Hobbes and Rousseau. In opposition to voices like Erasmus's which condemn war without exception, there usually appear, with disturbing regularity, calls for realism sheltering behind the well-founded obviousness of the practical instance: nobody in his right mind can be in favour of war —it is said— but the fact that whoever suffers an act of aggression refuses in advance to resist it belongs to the realm of pure fantasy, if not to that of complete stupidity. From Erasmus's point of view, and generally speaking that of the pacifism which situates itself consciously or unconsciously in its wake, this objection seems consistent provided that an important detail is overlooked: that it isn't the person being attacked who is required to reject war, but the person doing the attacking. For his part the person being attacked exercises his right to self-defence, one of the most indisputable of assumptions, maybe the only indisputable one, in which violence would be able to count on the endorsement of morality provided that it was exercised within certain fixed limits. When all is said and done, whoever resists cannot be held responsible for having made that sombre leap from the world of reason to that of the facts, of having transgressed Sebastian Castellio's unanswerable maxim, according to which "to kill a man is not to defend a doctrine, it's to kill a man." From this angle it isn't a doctrine the person being attacked is defending when he resists his attacker; what he defends is what the person doing the attacking tries to wrest from him, be it his life, freedom, opinions, goods, independence.

Civilisation, conceived not as a system of controls intended to avoid the outbreak of violence but as an instrument for constructing the enemy against which it is permissible, even necessary, to exercise violence, is wont to proceed from the point at which Erasmus's type of pacifism is called into question. If instead of using reason to identify the procedures for keeping the peace it is used to define the exceptions to the prohibition on having recourse to violence, then the meaning of the search is completely transformed, installing it inevitably in the sphere of war. The arguments which will come up from then on do not obey, cannot obey, any other design than that of legitimising the recourse to brute force. The distinction may be subtle, but not theoretical: if, as a few of today's powers would like, the United Nations were to replace the ultimate objective of preserving peace by that of guaranteeing security, or worse still, that of combating terrorism, the main content of its deliberations would become the establishing of adequate levels of armament and the perfecting of the art of war; a war which ought not to be lost, but which nobody would propose to avoid.

Naturally, the terminology employed to encourage this momentous, determinant alteration of the meaning of the search to which reason is applied is not at odds with the objective of masking it, to the extent that today it is almost a cliché to ascertain the perversion of language which usually precedes moments of crisis. Words in current use suffer a radical manipulation of their meaning to the extent of expressing one thing and its opposite; newly coined expressions are good for rebaptising rejected realities and putting them in circulation again as if they were hitherto unheard-of; concepts built out of refined ideological requirements are taken, moreover, for instant realities, accessible without any intermediation to the senses: these and similar phenomena have been regularly observed, their ability being emphasised to cause one of the principal antidotes to violence—the word—to deteriorate to the point of being invalidated, almost. Yet it may be that the perversion of language is no more than the symptom of another perversion with profounder implications: that of the frame of reference. Thus, the use of formulas like "guaranteeing security" or "combating terrorism" —to mention but a few of those that are making their mark on our own time— implies that one has a definition to hand of the concepts of security and terrorism, elaborated or otherwise from naive criteria, who knows? Yet it implies, furthermore, that whoever employs these formulas implicitly places himself in the condition of the person being attacked; that's to say, of someone who has the right to self-defence.

To demonstrate that, in effect, one has such a right —although the aggression to which one theoretically responds may go back to remotest Antiquity or be imperceptible to any unwitting observer— is the task allotted to some of the more consolidated ideological discourses, and which extend from the most diverse variants of determinist theory to the recent strategic formula of preventive attack, without forgetting, of course, the historiographical account. With regard to the first of these discourses —determinist theory— it suffices to verify that from the moment in which it is accepted that a people, race or class has an immutable essence, and it is admitted, furthermore, that among the particular traits that essence has is that of being hostile to other peoples, outbreaks of violence are more than a possibility, are a duty imposed by virtue of a few reasons presented as common sense or as realism.

To this end it is surprising to observe the temporal as well as spatial transmigration of stereotypes upon which death and destruction are wont to thrive: the representation of the pre-Columbian Indian coincides with that of today's Moslem, and that of today's Moslem with that of the Congolese native from the time of King Leopold, and that of the Congolese native with the persecuted Jew, and that of the persecuted Jew with that of Leo Tolstoy's Chechenian, and that of Tolstoy's Chechenian with the Chechenian the more recent Moscow press depicts. For each and every one of these figures, and for so many others, simple names on an interminable list which would include poor and gypsies alike, Hutus as well as Tutsis, Serbs as well as Bosnians, the stigma is always identical and operates in either direction: people who've been resolute for as long as anyone can remember, who are envious of other people's prosperity, lax and disruptive unless met with a threatening display of the knout, of inflexibility, resolve, force.

For as long as anyone can remember: that is the exact moment in which historiographical accounts take over from determinism with the intention of establishing the right to self-defence; with the intention of recalling or shedding light on a previous, albeit remote, bout of aggression through which to excuse an immediate resorting to brute force in the here and now. The procedures that historiography is in the habit of using are numerous, particularly a certain historiography which is conscious that, as Richard Rorty points out, the struggle for political leadership is a struggle for the narrative of the past, so as to offer alibis for the destruction and barbarism:

as many procedures as the art of storytelling has, from the most virtuoso
to the most truculent and implausible. The oft-repeated platitude that it's
in novels and not in the manuals that one learns about history contains
more meaning than is usually accorded it, since, if one looks closely, history
is at times no more than a bad novel. Unlike more successful literary
works, none of its chapters contains the least surprise since it is limited to
repeating, in prose which leaves something to be desired, what has been
repeated time and again to the point of sending the sensitive critic to sleep.

Even so, the historiography which sets out to safeguard the impres-
criptible validity of old debts, real or invented, never appears to lose an
ability to dazzle with the same artifices, as if under certain circumstances
entire peoples or nations recover that childlike pleasure of listening to
the same unvaried tale. How many times has the ground been prepared
for a massacre by resorting to the story that the mother country was lost
through the fault of a race of traitors whose descendants continue to exist
without reneging on their scheming in the same ancestral home they have
lived in for centuries? How many times, prior to any period of obscurantism
and terror, has one denounced with a fanatical zeal the hatred that those
must feel against who, in reality, one directs one's own hatred, the dubious
intrigues of those at whom, when all is said and done, more dubious
intrigues are aimed? The invariable score kept to by the chorus of figures
which roams through historiographical accounts of this ilk, in which the
only thing that changes are the names, the nationality or the obsession,
has no other meaning than that of exchanging the condition of the person
doing the attacking for that of the person being attacked, in such a way that
it appears that the person who is doing the attacking is defending himself,
thereby eluding all moral responsibility, all scruples.

If some novelty is to be found in the strategy of the preventive attack,
the hitherto latest ideological discourse aimed at presenting as self-defence
what self-defence would avail itself of with difficulty, it is that it situates
the aggression not in the past but in the future. It would thus respond not to
what has happened but to what runs the risk of happening. But then
which instance would evaluate that risk and according to which guidelines?
And descending to the terrain of execution, who would decide, and how,
the proportionality between the attack realised and the risk it was
necessary to ward off? Before whom would the responsibilities be purged
for the mistakes, even the abuses, when deciding on the attack? Under
the semblance of a formula which the international community would be
in a position to assume through a simple act of will, like the one a handful
of governments created in the Azores, the doctrine of preventive attack
conceals, to be sure, an invitation to dispense with a concrete idea of
the law, which links it to the interests of the weak in the face of the strong,
as Robert Kagan noted in a scandalous essay.

But maybe it conceals much more. In particular a drift towards what, on

the internal plane, would be equivalent to the criminal law of the perpetrator;
that is, to the law devised not to persecute the crime, but to persecute the
criminal, as a long tradition of authoritarian regimes have done throughout
the last century. Each time that, on the international level, one speaks of
rogue states or, with greater reason, of that Axis of Evil counterposed to a
beneficent coalition of governments for which the law doesn't obtain, seeing
as they have a cause that demands one act without paying attention to
procedure, one moves in the direction of a characterisation of subjects in
terms of invariable essences about which no compromise is possible.
From this angle a rogue state or a member of the Axis of Evil will be able to
remain inactive and therefore to maintain its threat as something latent;
in the last analysis it won't be able to escape the destiny to which it is, alas,
fated. This is precisely the idea insisted upon in the abundant literature
about Islam that has appeared as a result of the outrages against the Twin
Towers and the Pentagon, in which Moslem religious precepts lead inexorably
to violence, and, furthermore, any person educated in those precepts remains
marked by them for life, independently of whether or not he or she respects
them, of whether or not he or she repudiates them.

Transformed into a foundation of this new determinism, the heir of those
others which in the past imagined that the individual remained a prisoner
of geography or of race, Islam ceases to be a religious creed as pacifist or
as obscurantist as all the others in order to all of a sudden become a single,
unlikely geo-strategic actor endorsed by hundreds of thousands of believers
who under the guise of peace-loving citizens going about their business would
nevertheless be prepared, should the opportunity arise, to convert themselves
into the militants of a single, monstrous cause. Next, knowledge and erudition
place themselves at the service of prejudice, perhaps by virtue of the same
mechanism by which civilisation occasionally changed into an instrument of
barbarism: knowledge of history, of the vicissitudes that took place in the past,
doesn't work as a magic charm against fear, but as a guarantee.

The historian Tom Segev relates an episode he heard Gabriel Stern,
one of the most prestigious Israeli journalists and an old family friend,
recount in Tel Aviv. During the 1948 war Stern was sent to guard what had
been the Italian Hospital not far from the line that would divide Jerusalem.
As he did every day, Stern began patrolling through the deserted corridors
of the building and suddenly found himself face to face with a uniformed
man armed with a rifle, on whose face he read the same expression of panic
that there must have been on his own. A few awful seconds passed between
Stern being conscious of the imminent danger and the gesture of raising
his rifle to his shoulder. When the shot rang out his enemy didn't collapse
in a heap, instead his image shattered into a thousand bits: Stern had
opened fire against himself reflected in a mirror. Segev points out that the
experience made a permanent mark on the attitude of the journalist, who
never again fired a gun. Although the morals of the episode are many,
and it is difficult to know which one moved Stern the most, one thing is
certain: he'd fired first against the enemy his fear had constructed.

The essence of conflict

Joan Esteban

We live in a world in which conflict invades our daily lives. Wars, neo-imperialist invasions, rebellions and civil strife, ethnic and religious pogroms, strikes, disturbances and all kinds of social tension are depicted daily in the press. Their presence is so normal that we no longer ask ourselves about why they are produced.

Serious reflection on conflict is practically non-existent. Analysts and politicians refer to conflict as if it were like the daily weather forecast: unstoppable and inscrutable.

They inform us that "a wave of terrorism is spreading," that there are "perverse leaders," "extremist" movements, "fanatical" organisations… It doesn't seem to interest them in the least to try and understand why people, maybe young, in love, with dreams, risking their lives, become terrorists, perverse leaders, extremists, fanatics.

Why bother about something that can be crushed? Mosquitoes are a nuisance so we wipe them out. Why go any further?

The mosquitoes undoubtedly have a very different point of view, however. They know they're powerless, but perhaps they dream of a massive suicide attack that wipes out the human race and allows them to live in the same kind of equilibrium as they do with other warm-blooded animals. Maybe they too are basically eminent terrorists that deserve the destiny we've allotted to them.

War and conflict are presented to us as the antithesis of society and culture. In war and open conflict we discover that the norms, the morality and the basic ingredients of the education that define our modern societies disappear beneath the frenzy of passion and hate.

War and conflict appear, then, as something incompatible with reason.

On the other hand conflict, violence and war have been and are humanity's inseparable companions. Notwithstanding this, the reality of them continues to seem impenetrable and their causes complex, almost incomprehensible. Each case is a one-off. Even on a single continent, Africa for instance, wars of national liberation have nothing in common with ethnic conflicts or religious and tribal ones. In today's India revolutionary, religious and independence conflicts coexist with one another. It appears that all these realities do not follow a pattern or share common characteristics that might enable us to outline a rational explanation of conflict. Perhaps this is because they boil down to the triumph of irrationality.

Having said that, beneath the dense verbiage of these diverse and seemingly unrelated realities a common foundation exists that we can conceptualise and express as a mathematical model. To do this we must focus on the essential elements, leaving secondary, accidental problems to one side. After all, the decision to initiate a conflict and the conduct of both sides during its evolution are the outcome of rational calculation.

In any conflict situation the breaking of an earlier agreement which had formed the basis of coexistence is produced. This occurs between countries, social groups, races or religions. Such a break comes about because at least one side considers that a better end result can be reached in this way. The revolutionaries believe they will be able to establish the new ideal society; the nationalists, independence with regard to those who were their neighbours, perhaps for centuries; the religious extremists, or tribal or ethnic fanatics, to arrive at total superiority and the expulsion of "the others." When the social pact is broken, those who were formerly living together take divergent paths and each group rushes headlong in pursuit of its dreams.

Once unleashed, the conflict subsists until it is resolved in favour of one of the two sides and a new pact is established (probably with winners and losers).

So, while the conflict situation persists:

• each group pursues its own interests and attempts to impose them on the others;

• success is uncertain and all admit that there is some possibility of being defeated; and

• the participating groups are prepared to make sacrifices —including their own lives— in order to increase their chances of victory.

These are the ingredients that will enable us to express conflict as an abstract model in which the decision to participate and the intensity with which one fights are the product of rational calculation as to the value conceded to each of the alternatives.

We shall designate each group by a letter: $a, b, c, \ldots, g$.

The size of each group obviously plays an essential role. We shall represent the relative size of each group with the symbol $n_a, n_b, n_c, \ldots, n_g$. And so n_d, for example, is the percentage of the population that is a member of group d. As percentages are involved, their sum is equal to the unit.

For each group, managing to attain their objectives is their ideal outcome. We will utilise the symbol u_{dd}, for example, to signify the value that group d gives to fully attaining its objectives, If it doesn't manage this, if other groups triumph, it will clearly be worse off. For group d, the value that group a might triumph will be u_{da}. And so u_{dd} will be better than u_{da}, namely $u_{dd} > u_{da}$. Perhaps we may be worse off with some groups than with others. That is to say, it may come about that $u_{dc} > u_{da}$. In this case, although the best for it is its own victory, group d prefers group c to win rather than group a. Thus, $u_{aa}, u_{ab}, u_{ac}, \ldots, u_{ag}$ represents the value that the victory of each of the groups in the struggle has for group a. Likewise, we will have another similar collection of numbers for each of the other groups, $b, c, \ldots, g$.

We have said that in a situation of conflict the outcome is uncertain. All the groups that actively participate in the struggle have some probability of winning, although for some this may be slight. It is obvious that if one group is absolutely certain of not having any probability of winning, it is going to decide not to participate in the struggle. We shall call p_a, p_b, p_c, ..., p_g the probability that each group may triumph. The sum of the probabilities of the different possible outcomes of the conflict situation has to be the unit.

Given that the outcome of a conflict is uncertain, group d has to weigh up the value it gives to the victory of any other group, c for example, u_{dc} for the probability that this may occur, p_c, namely $p_c u_{dc}$. Consequently, for group d, faced with a given situation of conflict with evaluations u_{da}, u_{db}, u_{dc}, ..., u_{dg} and with probabilities p_a, p_b, p_c, ..., p_g, its overall evaluation, w_d will be

$$w_d = p_a u_{da} + p_b u_{db} + p_c u_{dc} + ... + p_g u_{dg}.$$

The groups can increase their probabilities of success by means of greater activism. Activism is, however costly. One has to devote time and money to it, maybe put one's life in danger.

In general terms, we will say that each person in group d contributes a number of resources, x_d, to his group's cause. Thus, the sum total of resources mobilised by group d will be the quantity that each person contributes, multiplied by the number of members in the group; that is to say, $x_d n_d$.

If $x_d n_d$ is the effort made by group d in defence of its interests, the total effort X will be the sum of the resources mobilised by each of the groups. That is,

$$X = x_a n_a + x_b n_b + x_c n_c + ... + x_g n_g.$$

The variable X will indicate the total resources that the members of this society are prepared to destroy with the aim of offsetting the efforts of the others and attempting to secure victory over the rest. We may, then, measure the intensity of a conflict through X ; that is to say, of those who are prepared to sacrifice all so as to avoid the opponent's victory. The probability of victory depends on the intensity of the effort of each group in relation to the sum total of resources, X, which are being mobilised. To sum up, it seems reasonable to suppose that

$$p_d = \frac{x_d\, n_d}{X}.$$

That is, the probability of each group's victory is equal to the proportion of the effort said group makes in relation to the total.

The resources sacrificed by each person have a cost for him in terms of the wellbeing, c_d, he is renouncing in exchange for contributing to the victory of his group. This cost will become increasingly burdensome. In fact, it seems appropriate to suppose that, if we already contribute a great deal, any additional effort has to be increasingly costly. In short, we will suppose that

$$c_d = \frac{1}{2} x_d^2.$$

The result of the effort made by a group depends on what the other groups do.

So, in a conflict situation each group d is going to take into consideration the evaluation it makes of the victory of each group, u_{da}, u_{db}, u_{dc}, ..., u_{dg}, and of the effort each group is making, $x_a n_a$, $x_b n_b$, $x_c n_c$, ..., $x_g n_g$, since such efforts determine the probability of victory.

Given a conflict situation, then, the total value for group d if each group member contributes x_d will be represented by

$$W_d = \frac{x_a n_a}{X} u_{da} + \frac{x_b n_b}{X} u_{db} + \frac{x_c n_c}{X} u_{dc} + \frac{x_d n_d}{X} u_{dd} + \ldots + \frac{x_g n_g}{X} u_{dg} - \frac{1}{2} x_d^2.$$

This expression determines the value for group d that the contribution to the conflict of resources x_d has, in knowing that the other groups are contributing x_a, x_b, x_c, ..., x_g, and that their size is n_a, n_b, n_c, ..., n_g.

The best response of group d to a given conflict situation consists of choosing value x_d, of maximum value. In fact the greater our effort, the greater our probability of victory and the lesser that of the others (because through our effort we increase X). However, the greater our effort the more costly it is for us. Thus, the best response is the level of effort that best combines the additional gain in our probabilities of victory with the additional cost we will have to support.

The best response of group d in terms of effort contributed to the conflict depends on the effort the other groups contribute. An increase in the mobilisation of another group will provoke a response on the part of the contrary groups in also opposing more mobilisation. These readjustments of action and reaction may continue until the conflict situation is in a state of equilibrium. That is, until we find ourselves faced with a series of decisions about mobilisation that no group now wishes to alter.

As a consequence a state of equilibrium will be a situation in which efforts x_a, x_b, x_c, ..., x_g, are each group's best response in terms of what the others do. In other words, each of these actions is that of maximum value for each group, given the actions of the others. In fact, a unique state of equilibrium is all that exists.

What occurs in a state of equilibrium? What are the probabilities of success p and what level X will the conflict attain? How will these values depend on the degree of radicalism of the groups and on their size?

The data we rely on are the evaluations that the groups and their sizes realise. With them we will obtain the values of equilibrium of the resources that each group will contribute to the conflict x_a, x_b, x_c, ..., x_g, the total resources used X, and the probabilities different groups have of winning, p_a, p_b, p_c, ..., p_g.

It is possible to demonstrate the following mathematical outcome:[1]

Let us calculate, first of all, the loss group d experiences if group c wins in terms of its ideal solution in which it is the group itself that wins. This loss is $u_{dd} - u_{dc}$. If we multiply it by the square of the size of the actual group n_d we obtain the variable $y_{dc} = (u_{dd} - u_{dc})n_d^2$. For each group d we can calculate y_{da}, y_{db}, y_{dc}, ..., y_{dg}. Note that $y_{dd} = 0$, always. If we order this information by lining up the g numbers corresponding to group a, y_{aa}, y_{ab}, y_{ac}, ..., y_{ag}, in a second row the g numbers y of each group b, and so on until reaching a last row with the numbers of group g, we will obtain a matrix with g rows each of g numbers. This will be matrix Y. A matrix like the one we've constructed has a single specific value (in the unitary root) and a single specific vector. The simplest mathematical programmes calculate the values and vectors specific to matrixes with up to three/four lines. Well, the g numbers making up the specific vector of this matrix are the probabilities each of the groups has of winning and the square root of the specific value is the conflict level in equilibrium, X.

In effect, the probabilities of winning p and the level of conflict in equilibrium X are the solution of the following linear system of equations:

$$\begin{pmatrix} p_a \\ p_b \\ p_c \\ \dots \\ p_g \end{pmatrix} \begin{pmatrix} 0 & y_{ab} & y_{ac} & \dots & y_{ag} \\ y_{ba} & 0 & y_{bc} & \dots & y_{bg} \\ y_{ca} & y_{bc} & 0 & \dots & y_{cg} \\ \dots & \dots & \dots & 0 & \dots \\ y_{ga} & y_{gb} & y_{gc} & \dots & 0 \end{pmatrix} = \begin{pmatrix} p_a \\ p_b \\ p_c \\ \dots \\ p_g \end{pmatrix} X^2$$

If we can calculate the distantiation the groups may sense between each other ($u_{dd} - u_{dc}$) and the size of the different groups, we can calculate the different values y_{dc}. Introduce these into the computer and any basic mathematics programme will give us the probability each group has of winning and the total level of conflict that we will witness.

There is a highly relevant case that is simple to calculate. It involves the situation in which all the groups sense the same distance between each other, for example $u_{dd} - u_{dc} = 1$ for any two of groups d and c. Ethnic and religious conflicts appear to fit this example. In general terms this case corresponds to situations in which, if the actual group doesn't win, it makes no difference which of the others has won. Here, $y_{dc} = n_d^2$.

What can we do with this information? We can get to know how the level of conflict X depends on the number of groups existing and on their relative sizes. We can also get to know which groups are going to behave in an extremist way in a conflict situation.

In this respect we may observe that the conflict is more intense when the number of groups involved is smaller and that the maximum X is obtained when the conflict is between two groups of equal size.

We may also verify that the slogan "divide and rule" turns out to be true. In effect, in a conflict between two groups, one of which is divided up into minor groups with mutually opposed interests, the probability increases of the group that has remained united winning. A simple way of verifying this is to take the above case in which $y_{dc} = n_d^2$ for two groups a and b, $y_{ab} = n_a^2$ and $y_{ba} = n_b^2$. (supposing that $n_a > 1/3$). We take one of the two groups, group b, for instance, and divide it in two. Now we will have three groups with n_a, $n_b/2$ and $n_b/2$. We may ascertain that p_a—namely the first term of the vector specific to the new matrix of three row—is greater than before.

Finally, we may also verify with our computer the role of the centre party in fomenting extremist behaviour or not. This situation is reflected in the hypothesis that if the extremists experience a loss of 1 if the centre wins, they consider they lose 2 if the group that is at the other extreme of the political spectrum wins. In exchange the centre people only experience a loss of 1 if either of the two extremist groups wins. Let us call n_c the size of the centre group and n_d and n_i the size of the right and the left. In order to simplify things, we will suppose that the size of the two extremes is the same.

We will observe extremist behaviour when right and left put more resources into the conflict than the centre people, and consequently have probabilities of winning greater than their simple weight within the overall population. Well then, we will be able to verify with the computer that as the size of the centre group is reduced, the extremes go from putting less to putting more resources into the conflict than the centre individuals.

In conclusion, we simply wish to underline how a problem as complex and passionate as conflict is capable of being reduced to a set of equations that can be resolved by the programmes any home computer has.

Note

1. ESTEBAN, Joan and RAY, Debraj, «Conflict and Distribution», *Journal of Economic Theory*, no. 87, 1999, pp. 379-415.

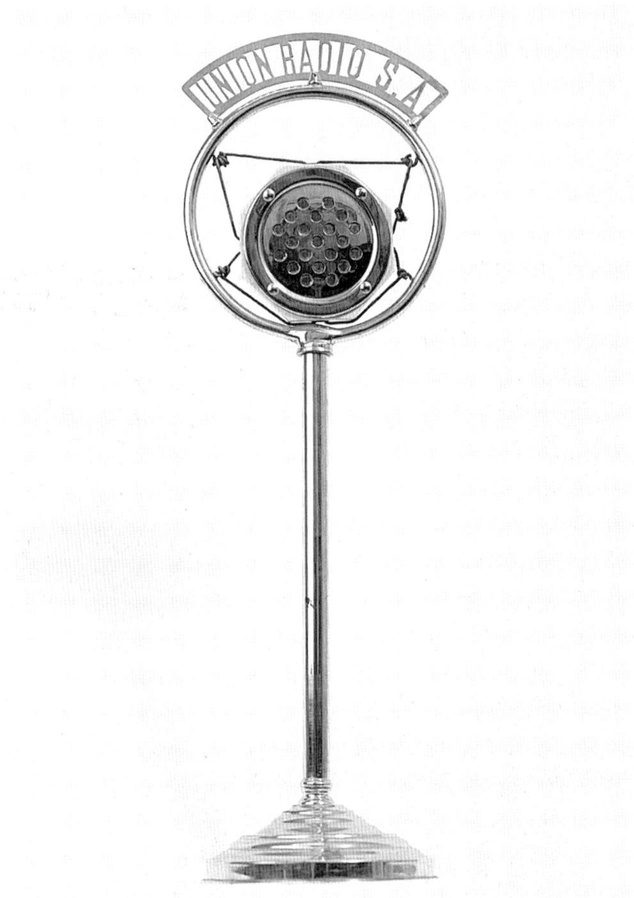

The radio broadcasts by General Queipo de Llano
during the Spanish Civil War are one of the first
examples of the way in which the media were used
as a weapon of war.

Microphone used by General Queipo de Llano, 1910-1936
Metal, plastic, rope and cable, 58 x 20 x 16 cm
Museo del Ejército, Madrid

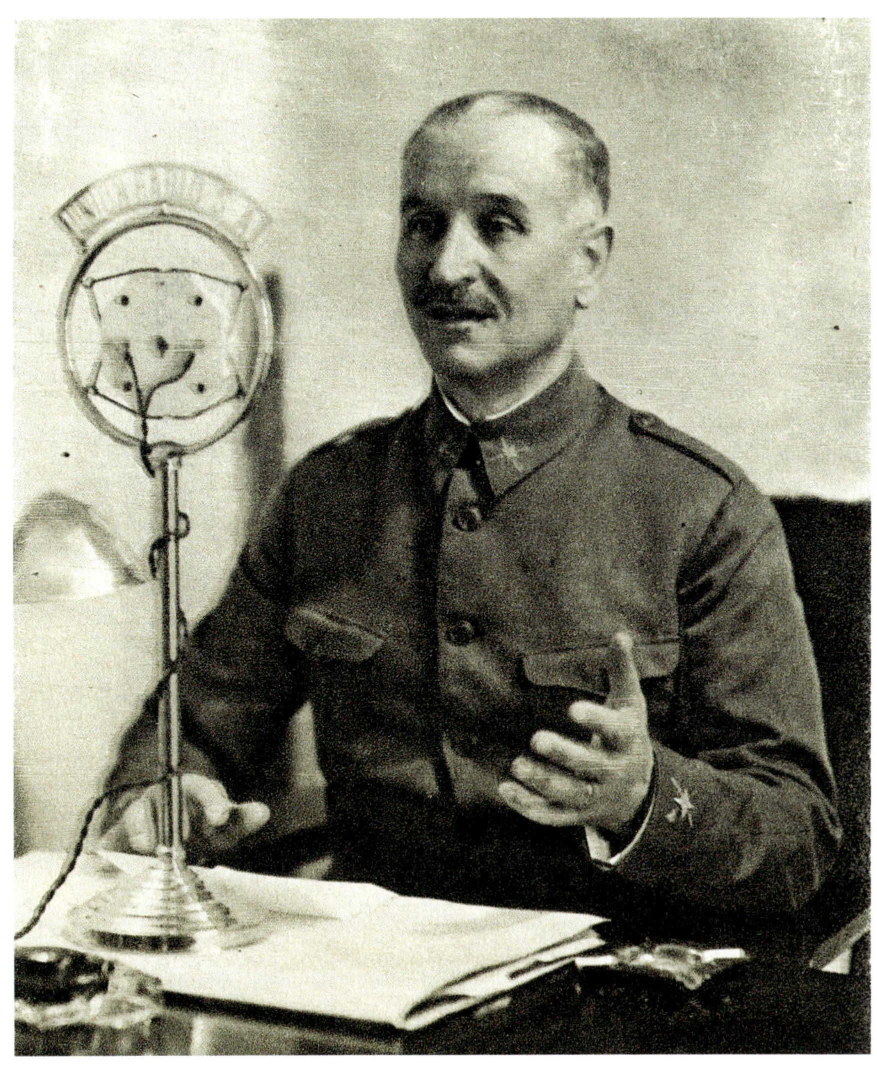

"Our brave legionnaires and regular soldiers have taught the
Reds what it means to be a man. At the same time, they have
taught what it means to the wives of the Reds who have,
at last, known real men, not castrated militiamen. They won't
be saved by yelling and stamping their feet."
QUEIPO DE LLANO, Seville, summer 1936

JALÓN ÁNGEL, Portrait of Gonzalo Queipo de Llano y Sierra,
Forjadores del imperio, Imprenta Arte, Bilbao, c. 1937
Biblioteca Nacional de España, Madrid

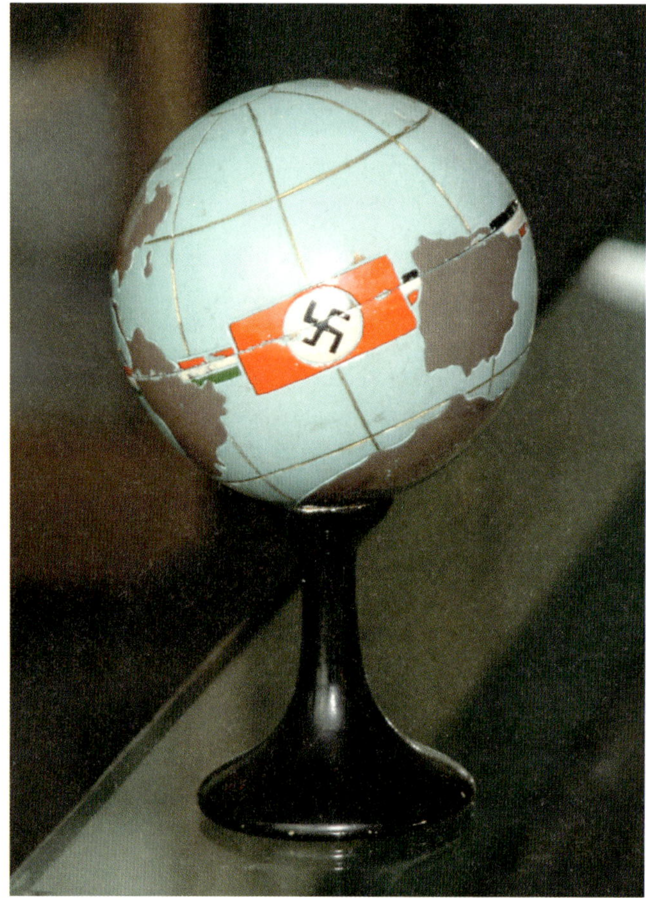

This globe was a gift to Hitler and was found in his office
by the Soviet troops. The areas shaded in the same
colour represent all the territories which were to be part
of the Third Reich.

Globe with the areas to be occupied by Germany
coloured brown. From Hitler's office, c. 1939-1945
Wood (ball) and black plastic (base), 22.8 x 15.5 x 31 cm
Central Armed Forces Museum, Moscow

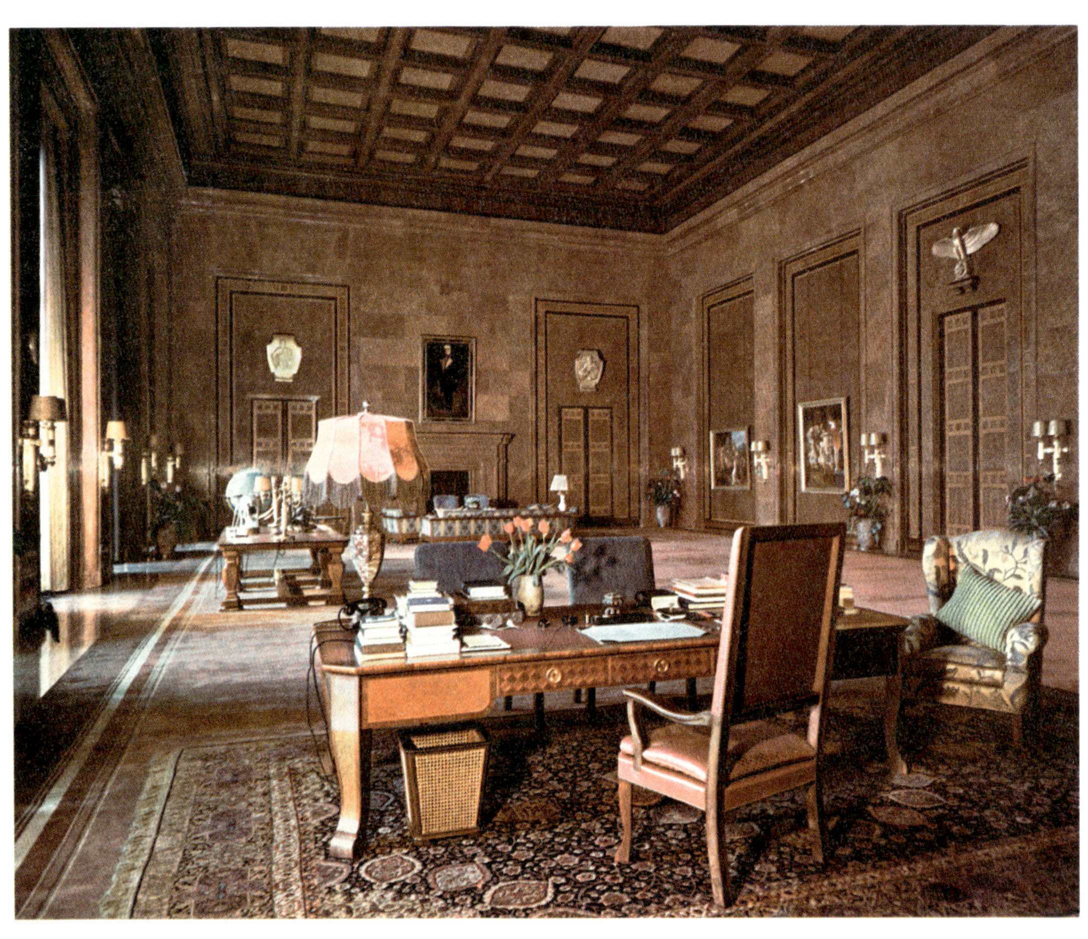

Adolf Hitler's office
Bildarchiv Preussischer Kulturbesitz, Berlin

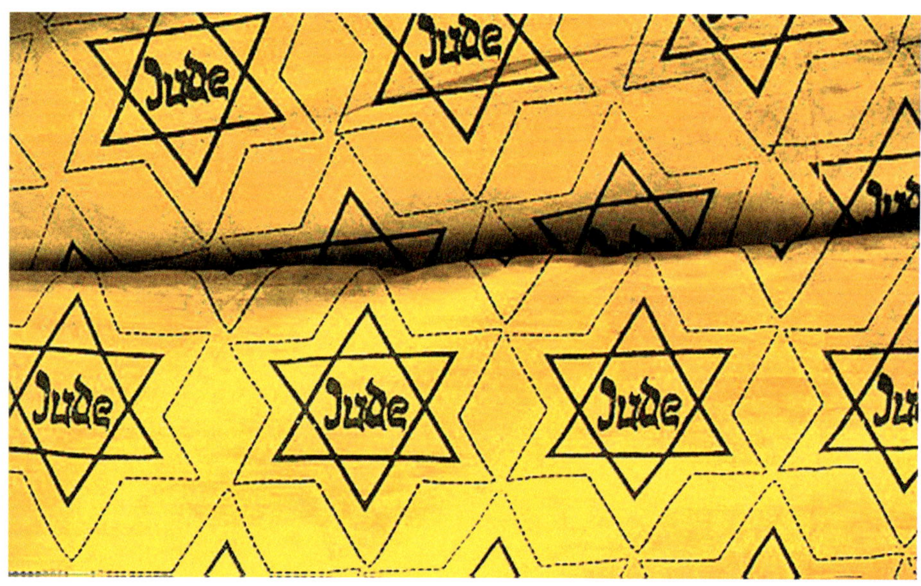

"May the bright flame of our enthusiasm never fade. It alone gives light and warmth
to the creative art of modern political propaganda. It rises from the depths of the
people, and must always return to the people to find its roots and strength. It may be
good to have power based on weapons. It is better and longer lasting, however,
to win and hold the heart of a nation."
JOSEPH GOEBBELS, Nazi Party Congress, Nuremberg, 1934

Piece of fabric with the shape of the "Jewish star"
stamped on to it, 1940-1943
Cotton, 152 x 328 cm
Haus der Geschichte der Bundesrepublik Deutschland, Bonn

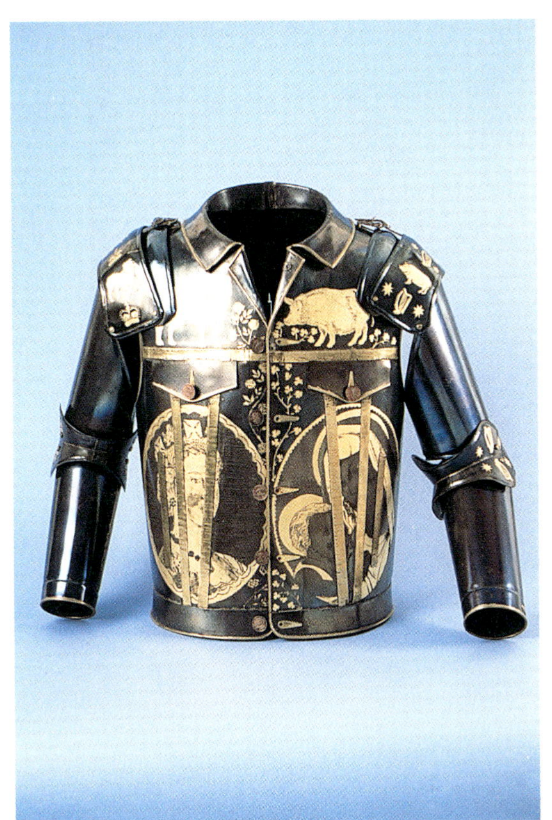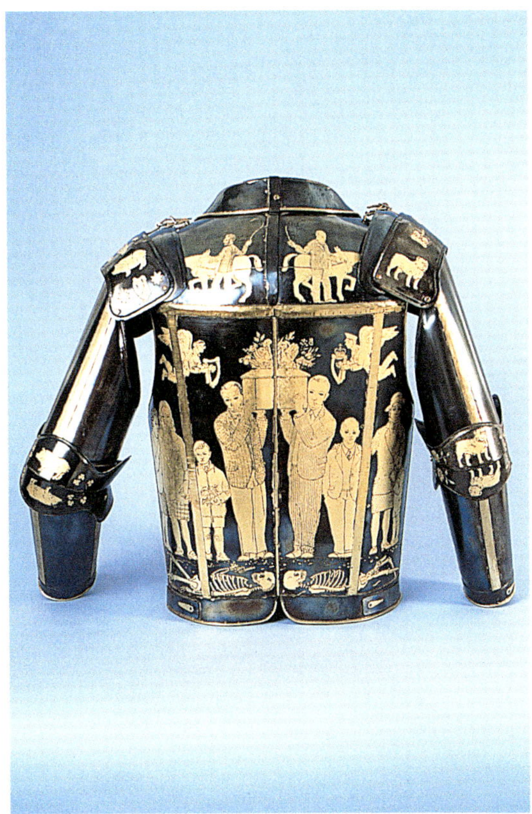

This work is a criticism of the confrontations between communities during the
troubles in Northern Ireland. The emblems
engraved on the armour/flak jacket
symbolise the two factions.

JOHN KINDNESS, Sectarian armour, 1994
Etched, gilded steel and brass, 60 x 50 x 26 cm
Imperial War Museum, London

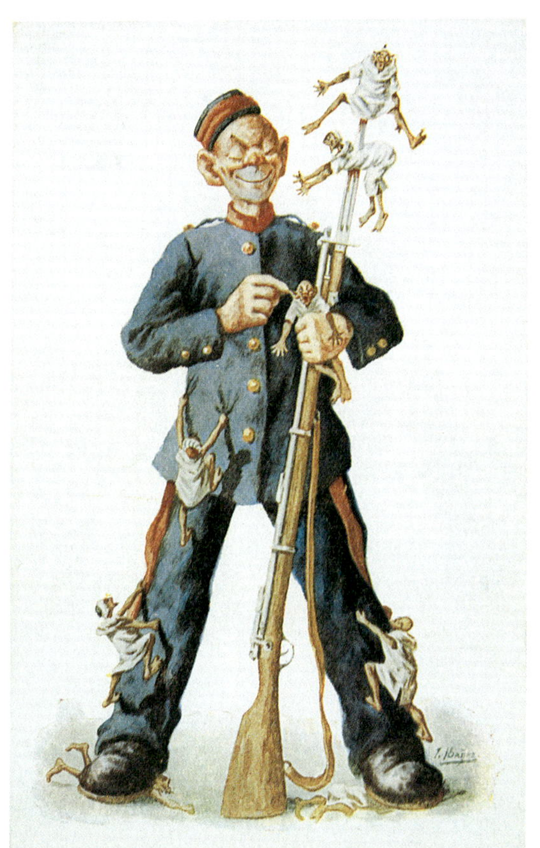 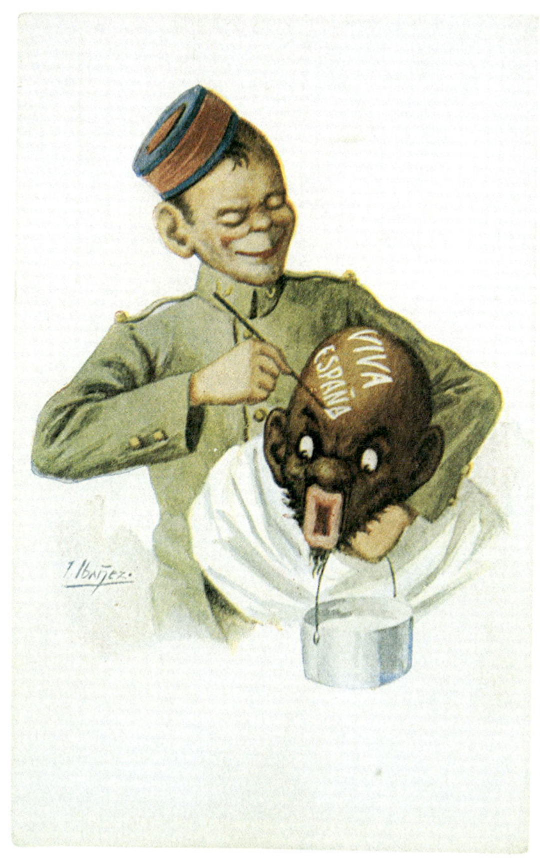

These caricatures show how deeply rooted racial prejudice against the Moors was in Spanish culture during the colonial period, and to what extent it was openly displayed.

J. IBÁÑEZ, Infantryman,
Ed. Victòria, N. Coll Salieti, 1920s
Printed postcard, 13.7 x 8.7 cm
Pedro Parra Collection, Barcelona

J. IBÁÑEZ, Soldier painter,
Ed. Victòria, N. Coll Salieti, 1920s
Printed postcard, 13.7 x 8.7 cm
Pedro Parra Collection, Barcelona

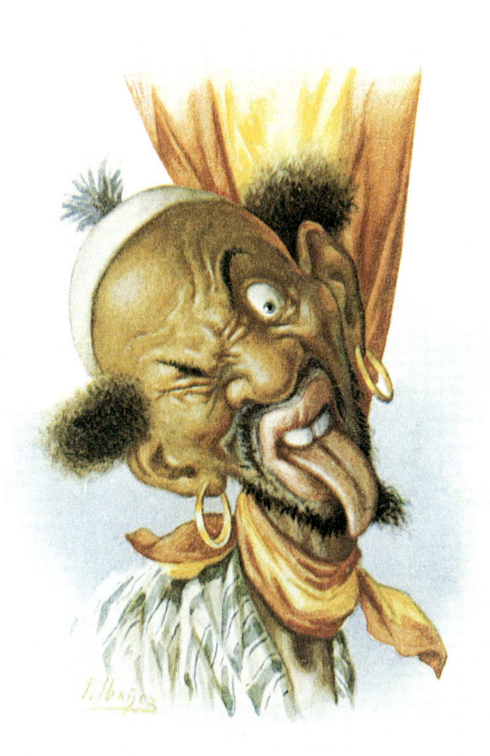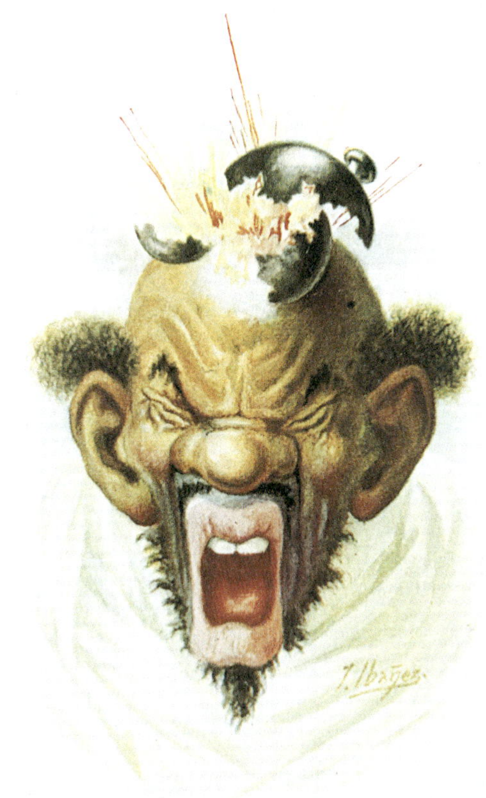

"Set up road blocks and weed out the spies of the Rwandese Patriotic Front. Leave the heads of the Tutsis by the wayside."

"The Rwandese Patriotic Front are posing as villagers. Beware of your Tutsi neighbors. Now's the time to be brave. Go out with your sickles and machetes. Show them how strong you are!"

"The Tutsis once dominated us. They want power. The roaches are working us as slaves and hogging all the wealth."
Radio Mille Collines broadcast, Rwanda, 1994

J. IBÁÑEZ, Moor head,
Ed. Victòria, N. Coll Salieti, 1920s
Printed postcard, 13.7 x 8.7 cm
Pedro Parra Collection, Barcelona

J. IBÁÑEZ, Untitled,
Ed. Victòria, N. Coll Salieti, 1920s
Printed postcard, 13.7 x 8.7 cm
Pedro Parra Collection, Barcelona

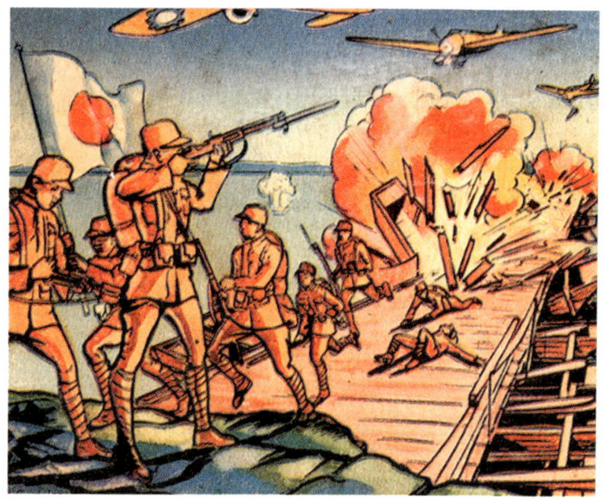 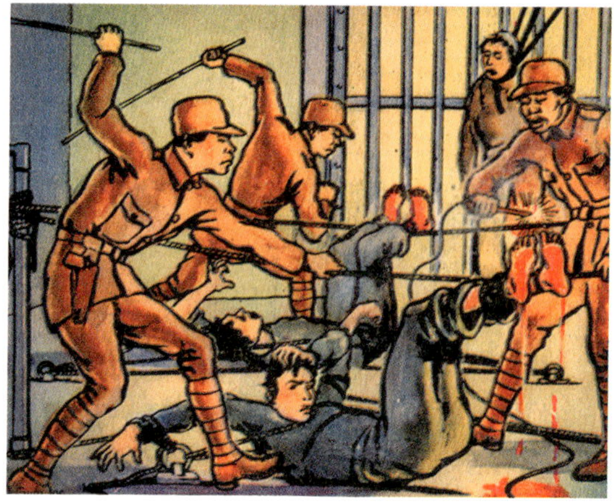

Before the United States entered the war with Japan
in 1941, the perception of the Japanese as a ruthless
enemy was already circulating. These picture cards show
the atrocities committed in China by the Japanese.

Airmen destroy pontoon bridge to trap Japs
Bubble-gum cards collection "The horrors of war",
no. 147, 1938
Printed on card, 5 x 8 cm
Carl H. Scheele Collection, Arlington

Japs torture Reds after armistice,
Bubble-gum cards collection "The horrors of war",
no. 265, 1938
Printed on card, 5 x 8 cm
Carl H. Scheele Collection, Arlington

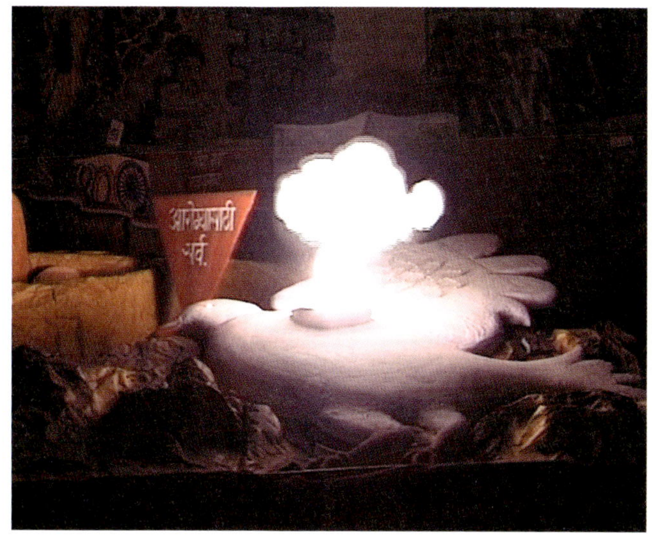

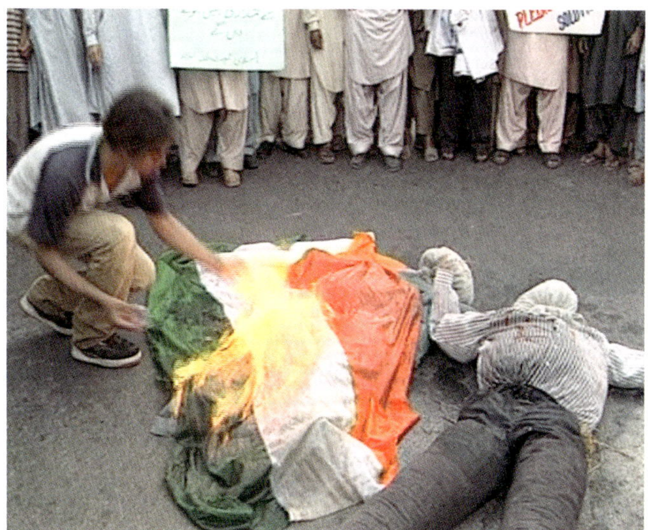

ANAND PATWARDHAN, *Jang aur aman / War and Peace*,
Mumbai, India, 2002
Video, 170'

Hostilities

The experience of combat
Joanna Bourke

There is horror inscribed on the body at war. Otto Dix's *War Triptych*
(1932) and Pablo Picasso's *Guernica* (1937) present us with the mutilated,
agonized and contorted flesh of combat. There is no glory here, no hypnotic
beating of drums, no braying horses, no clash of sword against sword.
Instead, combat has become mechanical slaughter, a silent scream.
Even the body has lost its boundaries: guns are "arms" and radar are
"eyes." Nature's landscape is churned inside-out by tanks, torn apart by
artillery shells, and blasted by bomber-planes, until it resembles Otto
Dix's *Meadows of Langemark, February 1918 or Paul Nash's A Night
Bombardment.* The roar of these killing machines attempts to render us
deaf to the human cries of battle —that hubble of sounds, screeches and
stutterings that are the language of emotion. Time and again we hear
the stammerings of combatants who cannot "take it" any more. These are
men whose starkly emotional sentences attest to how "The sights cannot
be explained in writing. Writing is not my line. No fighting either For
them that wants to let them fight Because I will never like it no no
never" and, as another terrorised private put it, "I admit I am a coward.
A bloody, bleeding coward, and I want to be a live Coward than a dead
blasted Hero."[1] There are many such accounts, including more poignant
descriptions of fear like the one a Private sent to his mother after the
Battle of the Somme, simply saying: "It makes my head jump to think about
it."[2] The Second World War poet and combatant, Shawn O'Leary, put it
best in his poem of 1941 when he wrote:

"And I –
I mow and gibber like an ape.
But what can I say, what do? –
There is no saying and no doing."[3]

For politicians, military strategists and many historians war may be
about the conquest of territory or the struggle to recover a sense of national
honour, but for servicemen warfare is more brutal, more bloody, than this.
In the austere words of the American combat artist Kerr Eby: "War is Hell"

The most obvious point of all is that combat alters bodies: muscles
elbowed out fat, scars appeared, limbs disappeared. Phallic-like weapons
attached themselves to men's bodies. For the survivors, combat was one of
the major rites of manliness, a rite of passage from boyhood to manhood.
Despite the popularity of this myth of manly virility, even the heroic
bodies of "strong, silent men" carrying out their duty to their nation lasted
only a short period in contact with battle in the trenches. Disillusionment

rapidly set in. Lieutenant A. B. Scott started his front-line horror all too conscious of his physical vulnerability. His terror is audible in his diary for 17 July 1918 when he admitted that he was "going all to pieces". He confessed that:

"My imagination is killing me. Last night I was alone inspecting the wire when for some hellish reason I saw a picture of myself disabled by a bullet and lying for hours until I bled to death – days it would have been for my vitality is tremendous. For several minutes I couldn't move, covered with a clammy sweat and paralysed with fear."

It only took a month in the front lines for him to change his tune. He had just experienced some extremely heavy fighting when on 18 August 1918 he wrote:

"Slowly and surely I am breaking up, and now I am so far gone that it is too much trouble to go sick. I am just carrying on like an automaton, mechanically putting up wire and digging trenches while I wait, wait, wait for something to happen — relief, death, wounds, anything, anything in earth or hell to put an end to this, but preferably death — I am becoming hypnotised with the idea of Nirvana — sweet, eternal nothingness."[4]

Fear had killed off his imagination, transforming him into just one further "automaton" of war.

Even men who started the war with grandiose ideas of acting like warriors were quickly disenchanted. James C. Farley was a Lance Corporal in the U.S. Marine Corps during the Vietnam War. In 1963 he was the crew chief on a chopper called Yankee Papa 13 when it came under fire. His comrade, 25-year-old James E. Magel, was killed in front of him while another comrade was shot in the face about 60 feet away. For Farley, that wasn't what war was supposed to be about. "I wanted to be a professional soldier," he admitted later, "And I probably would have been if it hadn't been for Vietnam. Vietnam wrecked it." The photograph of Farley crying in base camp immediately after returning from that traumatic mission was plastered on the cover of *Life* magazine (see p. 239). Farley was embarrassed by his display of grief. "It embarrassed me for years," he admitted, "I guess because, well, it's not what a Marine is supposed to do. I guess it still bothers me... That I didn't hold it in."[5] Fantasies of heroism and invincibility never survived the confrontation of battle.

Few men could maintain a zest for warfare for long periods in active service. Men unable to maintain such a philosophy often took a more dramatic route to oblivion. The strain of battle could cause men to commit suicide. Others feigned illness or incapacity, or found other ways to evade exposure to the horrific physical risks.[6] Forging signatures to ensure that they were miles away at zero-hour, getting another man to answer their name at roll call, dodging parades, and slipping out of camp were habitual activities for many servicemen. In the words of an American soldier during the Second World War: "These combat situations are so confusing that it's very easy to go in the other direction. Say you get lost, get sick, get hurt. By the time you get back to your outfit, a couple of days have passed."[7]

It was the power of fear and panic that posed the greatest challenge to the military. Indisputably, the emotions had to be disciplined. Teaching men to respond automatically to orders, to ignore rumours, to focus on their leaders and comrades, and to become accustomed to the fog and noise of battle were crucial.[8] Coercion was often used in the front lines to get a man or group of men to fight. "Panic may be checked by officers firing on their own men," opined an article in 1914 published in the *American Review of Reviews*.[9]

Men who exhibited signs of fear were typically punished, not to steel *their* nerves but to provide an example to others.[10] Men had to be prepared to give not only their limbs or life for their country, but their "guts" and "nerves" as well.[11] Human sympathy took second place to the rational discipline of the emotion of fear.

But most combatants simply "got on with the job." The threat of physical devastation was endured by stoicism, shortening one's view of time, and resolutely ignoring the threatening environment. Trooper William Clarke of the 1st Cavalry Division summarized this attitude:

"You became hardened in the trenches, you got fed up with being frightened and hungry, cold, wet and miserable and often you just didn't care whether you survived. Seeing so many corpses became just another sight. Often when you moved in the trenches you trod and slipped on rotting flesh. Your feelings only came to the fore when it was a special mate who had been killed or wounded and then it would go quickly away. Because what you really wanted to do was to go to sleep, get warm, get clean and have a good hot meal."[12]

Stoicism was bolstered by other factors. The "rightness of the cause" could be a powerful motivating force. It worked very well in getting people to enlist, and it shored up people behind the lines. But in the front lines it had limited usefulness. More effective was the appeal to the sufferings of "innocents." The lightly clad corpses of women drowned from the *Lusitanian* in May 1915 gave C. A. Brett "a bitter dislike for all Germans and a desire to kill as many as possible."[13] The extermination camps of the Second World War had an even great impact.

In 1945, the unit of Timuel Black, a Chicago schoolteacher, arrived at Buchenwald and, appalled by the stench, he roared: "Let's kill all the son-of-a-bitches. Kill all the goddam Germans. Anyone who would do this to people, they're not worth living."[14]

More than any other experience, though, witnessing the death of a comrade was guaranteed to cause a welling-up of murderous hatred. W. R. Kirkby was one such soldier. During the Battle of Cambrai in 1917 he saw his closest friend killed. As he put it:

Finally, the rage that came with the realisation that "they" were trying to kill "me" stung men out of their lethargy. The Rev. Harold Augustine Thomas recalled one man who had been wounded "in a tender part of the body" while visiting the latrine. This wounding transformed a man who had been extremely mild and one who could "wax elequently [sic] on the brotherhood of man and the iniquity of an appeal to Arms" into a "revengeful militarist." He wanted "blood, rivers of blood, the blood of every Turk on the Peninsular, but particularly the blood of that sniper, his ancestors and progeny to sanguinarily [sic] specified generations."[16]

Apart from these rationalisations, there was one further element that enabled combatants to kill: dehumanisation. This took two forms. On the one hand, "we" were transformed into something less than fully human in the course of battle and, on the other hand, the enemy was not any sort of human either. The first point is often ignored, but in many first-hand accounts of battle, it was essential that perpetrators described themselves as having lost control. Over and over again, killing narratives insisted that they were not "really" killing: they had been "taken over" by "primitive blood-lust," and only returned to their "real selves" afterwards. Killing was popularly conceptualised as being part of human heredity, but exceptional circumstances resulted in this instinct overpowering the "civilised" man. Men were transformed into animals "for the duration," and this enabled them to return to their "normal selves" afterwards, unbrutalised and often living next to their former victims.

Even more centrally, it was important to encourage the fiction that the people being killed were not "really" human. "It was a strange impersonal feeling; they were merely targets," admitted artilleryman Kenneth H. Cousland.[17] Euphemisms proliferated. During the genocidal attacks on the Armenians, the Turks had a word for the Armenians: "dog-food." Dr Mehmed Reshid, Governor of Diyarbekir in 1915 and nicknamed the "Executioner Governor" in honour of the numerous tortures and murders he oversaw, explained his actions by saying, "I am a physician… Armenian traitors had found a niche for themselves in the bosom of the fatherland; they were dangerous microbes. Isn't it the duty of a doctor to destroy these microbes?"[18] Nearly 80 years later in Rwanda, Tutsis were described as "cockroaches," with the Hutus simply engaged in "bush-clearing." Hutus were ordered to "remove tall weeds" (adults) as well as the "shoots" (children). "Innocence" was simply not a recognised concept. This is what the cartoon *How the War Started* portrays: a Hutu perpetrator shouts, "You can kill everyone! Don't even spare the fetuses." Similar language was used during the massacre at My Lai in Vietnam on 16 March 1969, "Rusty" Calley having no doubt that even babies could be "the enemy": "The old men, the women, the children — the *babies* — were all VC or would be VC in about three years," he asserted, continuing, "And inside of VC women, I guess there were a thousand little VC now."[19] Dehumanisation enabled desensitisation.

During the Second World War a similar process took place. The virulent racism of all the participating countries was crucial in explaining the viciousness of the war. For instance, Shir Azuma was a Japanese soldier who participated in the murders and rapes in Nanjing (China) in 1937. He recalled:

"While the women were fucked, they were considered human, but when we killed them, they were just pigs. We felt no shame about it. No guilt. If we had, we couldn't have done it. When we entered a village, the first thing we'd do was steal food, then we'd take the women and rape them, and finally we'd kill all the men, women, and children to make sure they couldn't slip away and tell the Chinese troops where we were. Otherwise, we wouldn't have been able to sleep at night."[20]

Racist attitudes were not the preserve of the Axis forces during the Second World War. For many British, American and Australian servicemen and women the Japanese were a brutish population and Allied troops were engaged in exterminating "slant-eyed gophers" (in Admiral William F. Halsey's words).[21] As the historian John W. Dower has shown in his classic *War Without Mercy: Race and Power in the Pacific War* (1986), this was particularly true when the enemy was a racial "other."[22] Jo Gullett, for example, fought with the Australian army during the Second World War. For him the Japanese soldiers were "clever animals with certain human characteristics, but by no means the full range."[23] Such attitudes were deliberately fostered by senior officers keen to stimulate the "offensive spirit" in their men.

By classifying the Japanese or Vietnamese as inhuman, they all became fair game. Furthermore, it tied into ideas in common circulation about human nature and warfare: it was in man's instincts to kill. There was no point in feeling guilty for what was inherent in human nature.

As all this implies, language moulds the experience of violence. Through language and symbols, "the Other" is defined. In war and even more potently in genocidal conflicts, language became characterised by polysemy (the same word had different, even contradictory, meanings). Killing was "action," "severe measures," "reprisal action," "rendering harmless," "evacuating," or "giving special treatment." A separation of "act" from "idea" took place.

In other words, in the face of mass killing, language itself comes under threat and is perverted. Words, which used to connect people, break down. As Jan Gross argues, totalitarianism is not about mass organisation, but about the *prevention* of all association.[24] Speech becomes ritualised and the distinction between what is and what ought to be fractures. Syntax, grammar, figure of speech are all distorted. Under genocide, language becomes divorced from experience — it is simply ideology. Thus, in the case of Rwanda, many Hutu perpetrators knew that their Tutsi neighbours were innocent of the charges — but still insisted in killing them. In the words of one 74-year-old perpetrator who admitted that he knew the stories on Radio RTLM were lies but still killed: "I regret what I did.... I am ashamed, but what would you have done if you had been in my place?... I defended the members of my tribe against the Tutsis."[25] Connections between people suddenly dissolve. Military personnel as well as some historians have over-emphasised the importance of comradeship in enabling people to engage in mass killing. Rather, instead of comradeship, atrocity becomes possible when individual perpetrators become disorientated and alienated from each other. The result is moral confusion.

This was one reason why Vietnam was so susceptible to atrocity — ties of comradeship broke down, combatants barely knew the men they were serving alongside and, if they did, tended to hate them second only to their hatred of the Vietnamese.

But it would be very wrong to assume that combat was only about trauma. Fear, anxiety, pain: these are the familiar stories of combat. But there could also be excitement, joy, and satisfaction. Traditionally, military historians have been very wary about admitting that many combatants found battle exciting. But the letters and diaries of these men testify to the fact that, on certain occasions, combat was an exhilarating adventure. The enthusiastic glee expressed by many recruits to the idea of shedding human blood can be understood by looking at the multiple and complex ways in which martial combat has become an integral part of the modern imagination. Prior to battle — indeed, years before war might be anticipated — literature and films provided scripts more exotic and thrilling than everyday scenarios. Once our gaze is turned from a narrow canon represented by Wilfred Owen, Siegfried Sassoon and Edmund Blunden, "high diction" with its stock phrases (baptisms of fire, transfigured youth, and gallant warriors) emerges as the dominant grammar of war.[26] There is also the glorious flesh of the imagination: the chiselled features of airmen, the muscular bulk of sailors, and the fertile curves of mothers, creators of life in the midst of terrible carnage. These representations of the body at war inspire military fervour. Walter Raleigh, Francis Drake, Robert Clive, Charles Gordon, David Livingstone and T. E. Lawrence are the romantic symbols which preoccupy boys' magazines. Flying aces such as Germany's Erich Hartmann (who scored 352 hits during the Second World War), are dreamt about. War's emblems include the female sex. Florence Nightingale's nursing zeal in the Crimea, Harriet Tubman's underground railroad during the American Civil War, and female partisans during the Spanish Civil War, in Yugoslavia, Greece and Russia during the Second World War, and in Vietnam throughout the later half of the century have encouraged women to participate more fully in armed struggles. Although such narratives might not directly stimulate enaction, the excitement they generated created an imaginary arena crowded with murderous potential and provided a linguistic structure within which aggressive behaviour might legitimately be fantasised.

Did actual combat dent the pleasures of imaginative violence? The philosopher, J. Glenn Gray reflected that the attractions of war included "the delight in seeing, the delight in comradeship, the delight in destruction".[27] Even Otto Dix, artist of some of the most traumatic images of war, admitted after serving for three years in the trenches during the First World War that:

"War is a horrible thing, but there was something tremendous about it, too. I didn't want to miss it at any price. You have to have seen human beings in this unleashed state to know what human nature is.... I need to experience all the depths of life for myself, that's why I go out, and that's why I volunteered."[28]

Such sentiments are repeated time and again in the writings of combatants. For instance, Flora Sandes, daughter of a rural English vicar, fought with the Serbian Army during the First World War. She admitted to feelings of joy when the savage explosion of her bombs was followed by a "few groans and then silence," since a "tremendous hullabaloo" signalled that she had inflicted "only a few scratches, or the top of someone's finger... taken off." She described her seven years' of war service as being a time of "romance, adventure and comradeship." Another First World War soldier recounted that the first time he stuck a German with his bayonet was "gorgeously satisfying... exultant satisfaction."[29] Second Lieutenant F. R. Darrow found that bayonetting Prussians was "beautiful work."[30] "Sickening yet exhilarating butchery" was reported to be "joy unspeakable" by another sapper.[31]

Nowhere was this more the case than in aerial combat. For instance, Roderick Chisholm was a night fighter in the Royal Air Force during the Second World War. On 13 March 1941 he destroyed two enemy aircraft. The experience (he wrote) could "never be equalled": "For the rest of that night it was impossible to sleep; there was nothing else I could talk about for days after; there was nothing else I could think about for weeks after... it was sweet and very intoxicating."[32] Equally, Spitfire pilot Flight-

Lieutenant D. M. Crook, described the "moments just before the clash"
as "the most gloriously exciting moments of life." He was "absolutely
fascinated" by the sight of a plane going down and could not pull his
eyes away from the sight. The day after shooting down his first plane, he
bragged about it to his wife ("she was delighted") and "with considerable
pride" also informed his family of his success.[33] Kenneth Hemingway dive-
bombed Japanese soldiers on the ground: "Oh, boy... Og [sic], Boooyy!"
he yelled, describing his "exhilaration" as similar to the joy of drinking
champagne on a sunny spring morning. He felt "ruthlessly happy — quite
an atavistic orgy!"[34] After a "kill," pilots admitted that they "all felt much
better" and there would be "a good deal of smacking on the back and
screaming of delight."[35] Shooting down a plane made the crew "frightfully
excited" so that they recited the phrase, "it was wizard," repeatedly.[36]

What was it about the language of killing from the air that could
aestheticise killing? George Mosse argued that air warfare was conceptualised as being in line with certain chivalrous codes (or recognised
formalities, ceremonies and courtesies) involving honourable exchange,
compassion and altruism at the same time as invoking reckless adventure
and a high-minded disdain of death.[37] Alexan Deineka's iconic painting,
A Shot-Down Ace (see p. 183) epitomises the individual, romanticised
fighter pilot in war. Combatants manipulated knightly grammar to
describe their actions. Aerial combat linked modernity with old-fashioned
chivalry. Fighter pilots were the "knighthood of this war."[38] The airman
was equated with the cavalry of old: he was the "glorious Horseman of the
clouds" roaming amongst the clouds and speeding through fields of space.
The fight was "mount against mount" and airmen drove "steeds of steel
and wire." Once again there was "single combat," a "romantic adventure,"
a duel in which the true warrior either conquered or died.[39]

Of course, it must be remembered that this truly was "myth." After
all, there was little that was really chivalrous about war from the air.
By the Second World War flying machines had been transformed into the
chief agents of death. The fact that 65% of deaths in the 1939-1945 war
involved civilians is largely due to the advances in the technology of
flying and killing from the skies. The age of "total war" was heralded by
the flying machine.

Whether or not men admitted to enjoying the slaughter, their status as
men as well as combatants was enhanced by the number of enemy troops
they were able to kill. This emphasis on the *number* of enemy personnel
slaughtered is frequently assumed to be characteristic of the Vietnam War.
It is clear, however, that the phenomenon of "body counts" in Vietnam
was the perverse, militaristic equivalent of what was a very real goal for
many combatants during all the wars of the century. In all conflict, soldiers
boasted about killing and they multiplied the scale of their murderous

zeal. And there was a flourishing trade in souvenirs such as helmets, bent
bayonets, and rifles for troops to take home to bolster wild stories of
killing that they had told loved ones.[40] Weapons were even domesticated,
a souvenir bearing witness to a man's status as an ex-combatant.

Of course wars are not the creation of combatants: wars are the result
of calculated strategy or just plain failed statescraft. War is collective
cultural practice. But if we are to understand why civilians — men, and
sometimes women, who are more comfortable on the shop-floor than the
rifle range — cope with the demand that they kill and risk being killed
in wartime, we need to recognise the dual nature of emotions in war.
There is excitement as well as terror in war. Individual action in battle is
not "banal." Quite the contrary: it has infused every subtle nuance of the
society from which it was born. This is why there is such a large degree
of complicity in the waging of war. Violent fantasies are widespread: the
John Wayne Syndrome has a robust counterpart in the GI Jane Syndrome.
But this exhibition can't help but remind us of one terrible fact: in modern
times, civilians have become the victims-of-choice. In 1914, for the first
time in modern warfare, civilians in countries that were not invaded had
bombs rained down upon them. In occupied countries, new, long-distant
technologies of war (such as machine guns, artillery, aerial bombers
and atom bombs) could not discriminate between combatants and non-
combatants. At Buchenwald, Hiroshima and My Lai the chief victims
were civilians. "Body counts" exemplify this sense that individuals are
expendable, valueless. Battered and bruised, the corporeal self has become
the central target of battle: humanity's entire wrath focuses upon our
puny skeletons.

Notes

1. Unnamed soldier in convalescent hospital, in SCHOLES, Dorothy, "Papers of Miss Dorothy Scholes", unpaginated, Wigan Archives Service D/DZ.EHC and BOURKE, Joanna (ed.), *The Misfit Soldier*, Cork University Press, Cork 1999, p. 32. In both, punctuation and capitalisation as in original.

2. Private HUBBARD, Arthur H., "Letters Written May – November 1916", in Imperial War Museum archives (hereafter IWM).

3. O'LEARY, Shawn, "Shell Shock", in *Spikenard and Bayonet. Verse of the Front Line*, Melbourne 1941, p. 20.

4. Diary entries for 17 July 1918 and 18 August 1918, in Lieutenant SCOTT, A. B., "The Diary," in *32nd Division, Artillery and Trench Mortar Memories*, London 1933, pp. 66 and 96.

5. Farley cited in HENDRICKSON, Paul, *The Living and the Dead. Robert McNamara and Five Lives of a Lost War*, Alfred A. Knopf, New York 1996, pp. 132-133.

6. For a detailed analysis, see BOURKE, Joanna, *Dismembering the Male: Men's Bodies, Britain and the Great War*, Reaktion, London 1996.

7. Robert Rasmus, interviewed by Terkel, Studs, in *"The Good War": An Oral History of World War II*, Pantheon, New York 1984, p. 44. For many examples, see BOURKE, Joanna, *Dismembering the Male: Men's Bodies, Britain, and the Great War*, op. cit.

8. These are discussed in depth in BOURKE, Joanna, *An Intimate History of Killing*, Granta Press, London 1999.

9. "The Psychology of Panic in War," *American Review of Reviews*, 50 (October 1914), p. 629.

10. Brigadier-General JACK, James L., *General Jack's Diary*, 1914-1918, Eyre and Spottiswoode, London 1964, p. 111, diary entry for 19 September 1915.

11. Major PALMER, H. A., "The Problem of the P & N Casualty – A Study of 12,000 Cases", 1944, 3, p. 11, in Contemporary Medical Archives Center RAMC 466/49.

12. Trooper CLARKE, William, "Memoir", p. 6, IWM.

13. BRETT, C. A., "Recollections", p. 3, IWM.

14. Interview with Timuel Black, in TERKEL, Studs *"The Good War". An Oral History of World War II*, Pantheon, New York 1984, p. 281.

15. KIRKBY, W. R., "The Battle of Cambrai, 1917. I was There", p. 104, IWM.

16. Rev. THOMAS, Harold Augustine, "A Parson – Private with an Aspect of Gallipoli", p. 43, IWM.

17. COUSLAND, Kenneth H., "The Great War", p. 61, Liddell Hart Centre for Military Archives.

18. Dr. MEHMED RESHID, cited in DADRIAN, Vahakn N., *The Role of Turkish Physicians in the World War I Genocide of Ottoman Armenians*, Pergamon, Oxford 1986, p. 175.

19. CALLEY, William L., *Body Count*, Hutchinson and Co., London 1971, p. 8.

20. SCHMIDT, David Andrew, *Ianfu. The Comfort Women of the Japanese Imperial Army of the Pacific War. Broken Silence*, The Edwin Mellen Press, Lewiston 2000, p. 87.

21. CAMERON, Craig M., *American Samurai: Myth, Imagination and the Conduct of Battle in the First Marine Division*, 1941-1951, Cambridge University Press, Cambridge 1994, p. 1.

22. DOWER, John W., *War Without Mercy: Race and Power in the Pacific War*, Pantheon Books, New York 1986.

23. GULLETT, Henry ("Jo"), *Not as a Duty Only. An Infantryman's War*, The Melbourne University Press, Melbourne 1976, p. 127.

24. GROSS, Jan T., *Revolution from Abroad: The Soviet Conquest of Poland's Western Ukraine and Western Belorussia*, The Princeton University Press, Princeton (NJ) 1988.

25. PRUNIER, Gérard, *The Rwanda Crisis*, Hurst & Co., London 1998, p. 247.

26. The best discussion of this remains BOGACZ, Ted, "'A Tyranny of Words': Language, Poetry, and Antimodernism in the First World War", *Journal of Modern History*, 58 (September 1986), pp. 643-68.

27. GRAY, J. Glenn, *The Warriors. Reflections on Men in Battle* , Harper & Row, New York 1970, pp. 28-29.

28. Cited in EBERLE, Matthias, *World War I and the Weimar Artists*, Yale University Press, New Haven (CT) 1985, p. 22.

29. Captain COLYER, Wilfred Thomas, "Memoirs", no page numbers, part 5, chapter 18 [labelled Chapter 2 but located between chapters 17 and 19], IWM.

30. Letter by Second Lieutenant F. R. Darrow describing the offensive of August 1917 at Hill 70 near Lens, in *Letters from the Front. Being a Record of the Part Played by Officers of the Bank in the Great War 1914-1919*, vol. 1, Canadian Bank of Commerce, Toronto 1920, p. 241.

31. "ANZAC", *On the Anzac Trail. Being Extracts from the Diary of a New Zealand Sapper*, William Heinemann, London 1916, p. 121, entry for 28 April 1915.

32. CHISHOLM, Roderick, *Cover of Darkness*, Chatto & Windus, London 1953, p. 71.

33. Flight-Lieutenant CROOK, D. M., *Spitfire Pilot*, Faber & Faber, London 1942, pp. 28, 30-31 and 75.

34. HEMINGWAY, Kenneth, *Wings over Burma*, Quality, London 1944, pp. 41-42 and 68-69.

35. See the interview of K. O. Moore and Alec Gibb, in Squadron Leader BOLITHO, Hector "Two in Twenty-Two Minutes", in *Slipstream. A Royal Air Force Anthology*, Eyre and Spottiswoode, London 1946, pp. 10-11.

36. *Ibid.*, quoting from a letter from the pilot "John", no date but probably January 1940.

37. MOSSE, George L., "The Knights of the Sky and the Myth of the War Experience", in HINDE, Robert A. and WATSON, Helen E. (eds.), *War: A Cruel Necessity? The Bases of Institutional Violence*, Tauris Academic Studies, London 1995.

38. GEORGE, David Lloyd, "A Nation's Thanks", 29 October 1917, in GEORGE, David Lloyd, *The Great Crusade. Extracts from Speeches Delivered During the War*, Hodder and Stoughton, London 1918, pp. 148-149.

39. "The Revival of Knighthood", in COBBOLD, W. N., *Poems on the War. March 21st to November 11th, 1918 and After the Armistice*, Cambridge 1919, pp. 10-11.

40. SLEDGE, E. B. "Sledgehammer", *With the Old Breed at Peleliu and Okinawa*, Cambridge University Press, New York 1990, p. 120; and WOLFF, Tobias. *In Pharaoh's Army. Memories of a Lost War*, Bloomsbury, London 1994, pp. 15-16.

Reasons to kill
Jon Lee Anderson

In the summer of 1989 I spent several weeks with Afghan *mujahedin*—
holy warriors, as they called themselves—who had laid siege to the eastern
city of Jalalabad, in Afghanistan. The city was being defended by the
entrenched soldiers of President Najibullah's Soviet-backed regime.
The Soviets, who had occupied the country and fought a 10-year losing war
to occupy it, had finally withdrawn their troops some months earlier, but
they were still supporting Najibullah. The principal *mujahedin* factions,
backed mainly by Pakistan, Saudi Arabia and the United States, had come
together for the assault on Jalalabad. Their assumption was that if the city
fell, Kabul, the capital, would be theirs for the taking.

To bolster their ranks the *mujahedin* had recruited hundreds of young
boys directly from their *madrasah* schools in the Afghan refugee camps
of nearby Pakistan. Sent to Jalalabad's frontlines they died like flies. One
morning, at a *mujahedin* bunker outside the besieged city, I watched as
several government MiG jets suddenly appeared overhead. My companions
were several adult gunmen and two young boys. Together, we watched as
the MiGs began to dive, coming in low and roaring and then ripping past.
As they pulled up again, they loosed their bombs and large smoke puffs
rose from the spots where the bombs struck, on the flanks of a nearby hill.

As the MiGs disappeared again, a woman concealed in a *burkha*—the
traditional head-to-toe garments of Afghan women—appeared on the path
outside the bunker. She was sobbing and yelling hysterically, her arms
outstretched. The older of the two young Afghan boys standing near me
tried to hide. The woman was his mother, and she had come to fetch him,
I discovered. He was only 13-year-old, it turned out, and he had run away
from home a few days earlier to join the *mujahedin*. She begged the older
men standing there to let him come home. "Please," she pleaded with
them. "He is too young for war, and we need him at home." The *mujahedin*
stared back at her, smiling disinterestedly. They turned away, ignoring
her, fixing their gazes on the smoke columns rising from the bomb
explosions. The woman was clearly frightened, and she did not come any
closer, nor say anything else. Her son did not show himself, but stayed
hidden inside the bunker. After a few moments, when it was obvious that
she had failed in her mission, the woman stumbled away again, wailing
disconsolately. I asked the younger boy who had remained in sight how
old he was and what he was doing there. He was 11, he said, and had been
brought to the war front by one of his uncles. "Why?" I asked him. "To kill
kafirs," he replied, scowling manfully and staring out determinedly at the
landscape beyond us.

In those days, in Afghanistan, the definition of a *kafir* shifted according to whom you met. Formally an "unbeliever," an infidel, I knew that the term also included foreigners—people like me—who were killable because they did not share the faith of Islam, or merely because they looked different. Although I was standing right next to him, the Afghan boy was too young and unaware to realize that I could easily have fitted the bill.

A day or two after my encounter with the boy, my *mujahedin* escorts evacuated me urgently from the frontline after a group of "Arab *jihadis*" sent a scout to sniff around the hilltop fortress where I was staying. The *jihadis* were religious volunteers from other Muslim countries who had come to fight alongside the Afghans. I had not sought out contacts with them, even though they operated out of a nearby camp, because they were said to be unfriendly to Westerners.

The *jihadis'* scout spoke with our sentry and told him that he and his fellow Arabs were looking for *kafirs* to kill, and thought they had seen one—*me*—with the *mujahedin* in the fortress. The sentry lied to the Arab, telling him that he was mistaken. There were no *kafirs* there, he said, only Afghan *mujahedin*. The Arab went away, but according to the sentry, who came inside immediately to warn us, he had looked unconvinced.

At this news my Afghan companions became extremely alarmed and said that it was only a matter of time before the Arabs sent back a larger force of armed men to find me. Moving quickly, they made me conceal myself with a turban and a wraparound Afghan patou blanket, and then they placed me between them, all heavily-armed, in the back seat of a jeep. We set off within minutes. The only track that led out to safety passed directly in front of the Arabs' bivouac. As we drove by, the *jihadis* stared at the jeep with expressions of open hostility. They did not open fire, apparently, because I was under the protection of their local allies.

It was years later before I ever heard the name Osama Bin Laden, but I eventually learned that he was in Jalalabad that summer, and that those *jihadis* had been his men. A whole lot of history has happened in the years since then, and many things in the world have changed. But there are some things, it seems, that just go on and on and acquire a life of their own. Somewhere, probably not too far from where he was in the summer of 1989, Osama and his fellow *jihadis* are still hunting *kafirs*, but now their battlefield has expanded to encompass the whole world.

I was born in the late fifties and I grew up on the tales told by my father about *his* war, which had been World War Two. He had been present at Pearl Harbour, an eyewitness of the deadly Japanese aerial attack which had provoked America's belated entry into the war. Many times, I heard stories of the cruel Japanese mistreatment of Allied POWs, of the unfathomable phenomenon of the Kamikaze pilots, which seemed to bear proof, nonetheless, of a peculiarly Japanese penchant for death. I harbored no doubts that Japanese and German fascism had represented the epitome of human evil, and that with the Allied Victory in 1945 good had finally emerged triumphant. I found President Truman's decision to drop atomic bombs on Hiroshima and Nagasaki more difficult to comprehend, but I accepted the explanation this had been a tragic necessity of war, because millions more would have died if the conflict had been allowed to continue.

When I was seven or eight years old I often played a game called "war" with my friends. We spent many hours happily running and hiding, ambushing and shooting one another with toy guns. Before each game we flipped coins to decide who would be the "goodies"—the Americans— or the "baddies," which meant "Krauts" or "Japs." No one ever wanted to be a baddie, but once the game of war began it didn't matter anymore; you tried to kill as many as you could of the boys on the other side and not end up dead yourself. Somehow or other, no matter who "died," the goodies always managed to win.

The American involvement in Vietnam radically altered my boyhood perceptions about war, and about my own country, as I began to comprehend that Americans were as capable as the Germans and the Japanese of committing atrocities, of massacring women and children, of slaughtering entire communities with guns and with bombs. I became skeptical of American foreign policy specifically, and distrustful of authority in general. I was not alone. The bitter Vietnam experience caused many Americans to question and actively oppose the actions of our government, both at home and abroad. After its Vietnam debacle, and for a few short years, during the soul-searching Carter Administration, Americans exhibited little desire to be directly involved in new foreign military adventures, and the Pentagon's clout was in remission.

When as a young journalist in the early eighties I made my way into the world, I found myself drawn to the battlegrounds of El Salvador and Nicaragua, places where the United States had finally emerged from its shell to intervene again in the name of anticommunism. Under President Reagan the old Cold War language of Vietnam had been revived and Americans were informed that these new conflicts were vital to their national security, battles between democracy and communism, freedom and totalitarianism. America's powerful entertainment culture also began to reflect the change in attitudes. The war-weary cynicism of the films of the late seventies like *Apocalypse Now* and *The Deer Hunter* gave way to a spate of patriotic "'feel-good" movies about Vietnam, like Rambo: *First Blood*. The Vietnam War had not produced any nationally acclaimed real-life action heroes, but Hollywood soon concocted them for a new generation of Americans. In the virtual world of cinema, Sylvester Stallone and Chuck Norris ventured back into the jungles of Indochina to single-handedly rescue MIA's who had supposedly been left behind and who, years later, were still being held secretly captive in appalling conditions. Their Asian captors were invariably depicted as sadistic fanatics and they died like flies under the righteous fury of the all-American heroes.

That none of these narratives were actually *true* did not matter so much as the message they transmitted. The message was that all the American hand-wringing over Vietnam had been unjustified and that the United States had been right, after all, to wage war in Southeast Asia, just as it was now right to wage war in Central America and elsewhere in order to contain expansionism by the Soviet Union, which Reagan had dubbed "the Evil Empire" (cribbing the moniker from another Hollywood film, *Star Wars*). Wars were only bad if you lost them, it seemed; war itself was not bad. If the battle at hand was a choice between good and evil, then the end justified the means. Atrocities committed in the name of this battle, therefore, were tragic necessities of the struggle, the "collateral damage" of the wars in which freedom would be won. Ultimately, if the West prevailed the world could be made a better place for all.

Throughout the eighties would-be liberators from around the world swanned through Washington, being fêted as heroes at the White House and receiving generous covert American patronage for their wars. The new battles were being fought by proxy on America's behalf, rather than with US troops. To the American public, the fact that their own soldiers were not dying in faraway lands made the new policy much more palatable. For a time, even Jonas Savimbi, that venal old battle-axe of a tribal warrior, boasted swank offices in the US capital, his murderous Angolan guerrilla campaign having been refashioned as a frontline battle against the advance of Soviet and Cuban tyranny. The Nicaraguan *contras*, meanwhile, who were armed and financed by the CIA so as to bring down the left-wing Sandinista government, were Washington's ultimate darlings, their leaders hailed by Ronald Reagan as "the moral equivalents of our Founding Fathers." I once spent several days in the jungle with the *contras'* military leader, who went by the code name of Three Eighty. His real name was Enrique Bermúdez, and he had formerly been a senior official in the regime of the late Nicaraguan dictator, Anastasio Somoza, and so I had few illusions about his democratic credentials. But I had expected him, at the very least, to have patriotic feelings towards his homeland. One afternoon, though, standing next to me and looking out over the miserable jungle encampment where his men were bivouacked, Three Eighty confessed to me that he felt more at home in Bethesda—a suburb of Washington, D.C., where he owned a home—than he did in his homeland.

During the eighties the US once more began to deploy its military forces openly, and with varying degrees of failure and success it did so in Lebanon, in Grenada, in Panama, and in the skies over Tripoli. By the time the Cold War ended and the breakup of the Soviet Union left the United States as the world's sole remaining superpower, America had acquired a new set of enemies to replace the Communist bloc. Anti-Western Muslim extremists had begun making their appearance, stage left, a few years earlier.

After the overthrow of the Shah in the Iranian Revolution of 1979, and the long, traumatic US embassy hostage crisis, which had contributed to Carter's electoral defeat, Americans had a new International Public Enemy to fear and despise: Ayatollah Khomeini. I recall seeing dart boards sold in Washington, D.C. with Khomeini's baleful visage on them, instead of the usual bull's eye. A bestselling book and the eponymous B-movie, *Not Without My Daughter,* (the heavily-dramatized account of an American woman who marries an Iranian man, has a daughter by him and ends up as a hostage to him and his family before finally escaping with her child to freedom, attracted an important cult following in the United States. Until his death in 1989, whereupon Saddam Hussein replaced him as the ultimate Western bogeymen, I can think of no international figure as unanimously hated by Americans as was Ayatollah Khomeini. In a sense, the irascible old cleric had become the living manifestation of America's frustrated international ambitions in the post-Vietnam era.

It was this hatred of Khomeini, and the fear that his revolution might destabilize the oil-rich Persian Gulf, which led the United States to temporize with, and to assist, Saddam Hussein during his military buildup in the eighties. The United States looked the other way as Saddam ethnically cleansed his country, executing tens of thousands of Iraqis of Persian descent and expelling hundreds of thousands more to Iran. It looked the other way, again, as Saddam repeatedly used poison gas in the Iran-Iraq War, even as it supplied him with satellite images giving him the precise locations of the Iranian troop concentrations. Following the Iran-Iraq War, the United States looked away again as Saddam waged his genocidal "Anfal" campaign against the independence-minded Kurds, during which he again used poison gas; this time against entire communities of civilians. It was not until he invaded Kuwait that the United States finally resolved to check Saddam's bellicosity and expel his army from there in the 1991 Gulf War. But afterwards it was once again the American fear of Iran which led to the decision by President George Bush *père* not to intervene as Saddam quelled the Shiite uprising against his rule, in which he slaughtered tens of thousands more Iraqi civilians.

It was a few years before Hollywood came up with a movie which made Americans feel good about *that* experience, but it finally did with the 1999 *Three Kings,* starring George Clooney and Mark Wahlberg. It is a remake of another popular action movie, *Kelly's Heroes,* which had been set in Germany at the end of World War II. In *Three Kings,* a band of errant GIs goes into the Iraqi desert at the end of the Gulf War in search of one of Saddam's hidden caches of gold bullion. The Americans find their treasure, but along the way they must confront their own consciences as they come up against graphic examples of Saddam's brutality—despite their orders not to intervene. The movie climaxes with the American scalliwags doing "the right thing," giving up their hard-won loot in order to save the lives of some Iraqi civilians.

Naturally enough, outside the United States there are alternative narratives to all this bad mutual history. I spent the month of January 2003 in Iran, talking with people about the coming war in Iraq. I discovered that many Iranians were less than jubilant about the prospect of a new conflict next door. Their reticence had nothing to do with feelings of sympathy for Saddam Hussein; on the contrary. It had to do with their own intimate knowledge of war and their fear that after the Americans invaded Iraq they would make war on Iran. The Iranians suffered terribly during the eight long years of the Iran-Iraq war, in which as many as a million Iranians died. Most of the men I met with who were over 30 years old had participated in the war themselves as soldiers and I met several who had been wounded, gassed or served years in Iraq's prisons as POWs.

One day I asked Mehrdad, a war veteran who is now a university lecturer, about the famous battlefield "human wave" assaults by the young religious volunteers known as the *basiji.* Countless thousands of them had died in the minefields of the war armed with nothing more than the "keys to paradise" they wore around their necks, talismans given to them by their *imams* as they marched praying off to their deaths. I had read many articles about the *basiji,* and had remained horrified and fascinated by the phenomenon—seemingly a latter-day version of the World War II kamikazes— ever since. Wearily, Mehrdad acknowledged that he had seen many such young boys go off to their deaths. I insisted that he tell me how he had felt about that. Hadn't the use of these boys in the war been shocking to him? Hadn't the human wave assaults been a criminal waste of young lives?

Mehrdad looked at me with a look of great pain in his eyes and, nodding, he replied: "Yes, it was very tragic. But you must understand that we needed our *flesh wall* to withstand Saddam's attacks. He had all of this superior technology which American and other Western countries had given him, but we had only human beings. Our flesh wall was all we had; it was our final line of defence."

It was a chastening moment. Until then, I realized, most of my knowledge of that war had come almost entirely from a Western, and rather contemptuous, perspective. Mehrdad's use of the term "flesh wall"—what a ghastly pairing of words—allowed me to see that Iran's use of children in the war had been a tactic of sheer desperation, one which he and many other Iranians remembered as a great national tragedy. This also made me reflect upon on the fact that it had only been three generations since millions of young Europeans, and Americans, had been sent to their deaths in the killing fields of World War One, similarly borne by noble thoughts of glory and honor and sacrifice at the service of their respective gods, kings and countries.

It seems that we are not so different, after all.

Ever since the attacks of September eleven, there has been a great deal of soul-searching by Americans over the horrific events of that day. Americans have been alarmed and bewildered by the global rise in anti-American feeling which those attacks, and the US government's reaction to them—the "War on Terror"—seems to have sparked off. Asking "Why do *they* hate us so much?" many people have concluded that the blame lies with the perfidies of US foreign policy, past and present, and with the inequities of American cultural and economic hegemony. Many others have closed ranks behind the official doctrine of the US government, which is that September 11th, 2001, was a watershed event which called upon a division of the world between those people who are good, and those who are evil. The evil ones, of course, are the terrorists, but also, to a certain extent, anyone who opposes or even criticizes the Western system. As George W. Bush emphasized: "Either you are with us or against us; civilization against barbarism..." Everything is so much easier when it is black and white—like it was in my games of war as a boy. But reality is never entirely black and white, naturally, because nothing occurs in a vacuum. The fact is that the United States would do well to engage in some corrective measures in its behavior towards other nations, and as a people Americans would greatly benefit from an increased awareness of, and respect for, other cultures. The obliviousness of many Americans to their own power and influence is galling to many people around the world and has fomented much of the resentment. At the same time there are endemic social injustices and savage wars for which the United States bears no historic or moral responsibilities, conflicts fuelled by disputes over natural resources, or by racial, tribal or religious hatreds which go back hundreds of years.

Islamic fundamentalism has emerged as the greatest source of
terrorism in the world today and while US foreign policy, especially as
regards Israel, may have provided the trigger for it, the root cause of the
problem of Islamic terrorism lies within Islam itself. Unlike the adherents
of the other great monotheistic religions, Judaism and Christianity,
Muslims believe that their holy book, the Koran, is literally the transcribed
word of God. Within Islam there are different schools of thought, and
some allow room for more tolerant views than others, but the social and
cultural isolation of the majority of Muslims has allowed the most severe
and xenophobic versions of Islam to survive and to grow in strength.
It may be that this has occurred as a consequence of the great transfor-
mations that have taken place in Western society since the Renaissance.
With the undeniable triumph of secular projects in all aspects of human
society—philosophy, science, literature and modern technology—and
with their spread through the sweeping process of economic globalization
spearheaded by the West, the devout Muslim finds himself alienated
and seeks divine sustenance—his only means of support—to overcome
his loss of control.

To its most ardent believers Islam is not just a religion but a way of life.
To the devout it offers a blueprint to achieving an earthly Utopia and at the
same time the prospect of an afterlife in Paradise. This all-encompassing
quality of Islam is its great strength, but also its main problem. As long as
Muslims believe in the Koran *absolutely*, many will never surrender their
intolerance of other faiths or other lifestyles, because of their deep-seated
conviction that Islam is the one true religion which should be spread over
the world through a *jihad* or holy war.

I used to travel quite a bit to the Palestinian territory of Gaza, where
I became well acquainted with a devout young Muslim man named
Hisham. Over the course of several years, during my visits, his religious
convictions deepened and radicalized. During several overnight stays at
his home we would stay up until the wee hours discussing philosophy
and religion, and especially Islam. On my last visit I challenged Hisham
to convince me that Islam was, as he claimed, a "religion of peace."
I asked him to tell me what would happen to minorities like Christians
and Jews in the future independent Palestinian *Islamic* state, which
was his ultimate dream. "There would be no problem," Hisham assured
me, adding quickly, "Their beliefs would be respected." I was not
convinced by Hisham's reply, however, and told him so. We argued this
point for some time and, at length, Hisham acknowledged that eventually
those people of other faiths would have to convert to Islam. "And if
they didn't?" I asked him. "Then they will be killed," he replied.

We stared hard at one another and as our eyes met I understood that Hisham was my enemy. He was saying, to all intents and purposes, that there were circumstances under which he would feel no compunction about taking *my* life. He had convinced himself that he and his fellow believers had all that was right on their side. At that instant I also realized that, were it ever to go that far, I was prepared to take *his* life in order to stop him. For the first time in my life I knew that I was capable of killing another man, consciously, and with a clear mind. For years I had wandered through conflicts, trying to recognize the impulses which made other men kill one another, and now I had found it in myself.

I slept safely in Hisham's house that night as his guest but when I left the next morning, and we said goodbye to one another, I knew that I would never return.

The arts and war:
a solid couple

Hélène Puiseux

War punctuates the history of humanity, it marks our notion of time, our dates often make reference to it. "Before the war," "during the war," "after the war," "in the interwar period" are all phrases in our current vocabulary. Sometimes we are "in war," caught up in war, called up like soldiers, struck down like victims, displaced like refugees. We establish a lived rapport with it which we call reality: our point of view is sentient, carnal, narrow and biased, like Fabrice del Dongo's of the Battle of Waterloo in *La Chartreuse de Parme*:[1] stunned by the noise, the lack of visibility, Fabrice isn't even sure of being in a battle because what he sees doesn't remotely resemble the grandly framed and composed war engravings that have lulled his childhood. So different from reality, these engravings are nevertheless at the origin of his desire to go and fight, they have dictated his attitudes, influenced his life. While he lives the greatest battle of the nineteenth century, which has left so many traces in people's minds and in literature from Victor Hugo[2] to Stendhal, by way of François-René de Chateaubriand or William Makepeace Thackeray,[3] and which has inspired so many paintings,[4] at the centre of the event Fabrice witnesses only disorder, noise and enjoyment.
It's only much later that his questions, and ours too, are heard.
Do we best understand war from a distance? Recounted by others? Years later? What's the point of representing it? How do art, artefacts, the *mise en scène* and literature function to construct that venerable couple consisting of man and war? A host of questions and answers which the exhibition presented at the Centre de Cultura Contemporània de Barcelona addresses.

"The idea of a battle"

Chateaubriand writes the account of this same Battle of Waterloo years after the war. His memoirs are involved, not a journal: 18 June 1815, around midday, he was walking along the road from Ghent, where he was a refugee during the Hundred Days:

"I'd brought *Caesar's Commentaries* and was strolling along, immersed in my reading [...] I hadn't gone 30 paces when the rumbling began, now brief, now long, and at unsteady intervals; sometimes it was only perceptible by a vibration of the air, which was communicated to the earth on these immense plains, so far off was it. These less vast, less undulating reports, less linked together than those of the thunderstorm, awakened the idea of a battle in my mind [...] A southerly wind getting up brought the noise of the artillery more distinctly to me. This great battle, as yet nameless, the echoes of which I was hearing at the foot of a poplar and of which the village clock had just sounded the unknown death knell, was the Battle of Waterloo. A silent, solitary listener to the formidable stilling of destinies, I would have been less moved had I found myself in the mêlée: the danger, the firing, the ubiquity of death would not have left me time to meditate, but alone beneath a tree, in the Ghent countryside, like the shepherd of the flocks which were passing around me, the weight of my reflections crushed me. What was this battle? Was it definitive? Was Napoleon there in person? Was the world, like the robe of Christ, in the balance? A victory or otherwise of one or the other army what would the consequence of this be for the different peoples, liberty or slavery?"[5]

This text affirms the value of distance and of displacement: distantiation in space (Chateaubriand only hears "the idea of a battle"), the temporal distance it is necessary to bring about between the act and its understanding, distantiation through giving form, here literary, to something as others give it stage presence via works of art or of theatre. Sonorities open up the space of memory; metaphors, transpositions, the play of memory, of emotion and imagination, are embedded, reinforced by the reading of Caesar, in the long shared past of man and war.

Instant shock

Let's leap foward 186 years. On Tuesday 11 September 2001, at 8.48, a Boeing 767 crashes into the North Tower of the World Trade Center, which immediately catches fire; CNN's automatic cameras on Manhattan film the inconceivable and at 9.06 they record the impact of a second Boeing against the South Tower. We all still have in our heads, in our eyes, the planes hitting the giant towers crammed with people, the fires and later the collapse of the buildings in an enormous cloud of yellow dust. For an instant we think it's a shot from a science-fiction movie. The whole planet, glued to the screen, participates live in a new form of warfare, terrorism on a grand scale. The 9.06 image is brandished by the United States as a piece of evidence for establishing the identity, in this twin shock, of an "act of war," a legal term which permits a riposte; UN Resolution 1368 grants the USA "the right to individual or collective self-defence," which will bring about the war in Afghanistan. The fulgurating image becomes a sign, a pious image, annulling in itself cause, time and space, and thereby giving rise to an inability to think it, the image, through. Carol Gluck of Columbia University had deservedly titled a reflection on this saturated image *What's Wrong with This Picture*,[6] an image which has seized hold of "reality," cast it without mediation into our homes, where, witnesses *à distance*, we see it without seeing it. We don't understand. The violence of this hitherto unknown type of conflict and the radical newness of the enemy, invisible and all but unlocalisable, momentarily escape the construction of a meaning, the acceptable memorising of such an event. What is my place, our place, in all this?

A thousand faces

Between Chateaubriand meditating beneath his poplar tree and us
shocked in front of our TV sets, between Waterloo and the World Trade
Center, countless conflicts stretch forth, colonial conquests, European
rivalries, two World Wars, independence struggles and, of late, terrorism.
War is to have a thousand faces: from guerrilla warfare to the Cold War,
from civil war to the Resistance, from revolutions to outrages, it takes over
every space: air, land and sea. The techniques of war and the enriching
of artistic techniques have, in offering it new approaches, new framings,
moulded new sensibilities, formulated new questions, that of responsibility
among others. War has drawn much nearer to the individual, whereas the
art of past centuries dispatched it into the epic heavens thanks to visions
organised through great masses. A double awareness is elaborated:
war is institutionalised violence, codified and ideologically justified,
but on the individual level it remains a temporal space subtended by
the problem of responsibility and in which uncontrollable upheavals are
produced. In both cases it remains the encounter, brusquely flattened,
recto verso, of life and death, in which guilt, responsibility and their
opposites are indistinctly mixed together. This awareness is accomplished
under the avalanche of the particularly murderous conflicts of the century
that has just ended, doubled by an avalanche of images, without one
medium ever substituting for the other.

The long nineteenth century had progressively set in place the
different techniques for representing war, painting, sculpture, photos, and
had paved the way for the as yet rudimentary cinema, pre-1914. These
arts had explored the whole range of tonalities in which the musical score
of war is played: heroism, the heroising of loss, aestheticism, the macabre.
When the First World War begins one can see and read everywhere, outside
as well as in the home, bits of conflict, fragments of space, images of
victors and of victims, en masse or isolated, in the great disorder of events.
Certain arts will be particularly suitable for underlining this disorder of
the state of war. Photography is in part responsible for this development
since it has enabled space to be fragmented, to encompass the wretched
bodies, the ruins, the idle periods, the ephemeral life that is set up around
the mess rooms, the waiting, the brutal nature of the corpses. Painting has
come down from the easel; it too frames more tightly. Films themselves are
to travail at giving meaning, in a discourse of approbation and disappro-
bation, according to the director's point of view.

The cinema: replaying, ruminating, familiarising

The great cinema industry is set up during the First World War
(in Germany and in Hollywood), with its dual system, information

(the Newsreels) and works of fiction: thousands of films utilising the war, inspired by history or straightforwardly imaginary, are to stage it with techniques that often link up once more with the practises of the epic. Cinema is to put forward many individualised imaginary versions of a great event that is hard to understand or to live. Alongside other forms of discourse the cinema comes on the scene in order to render the unacceptable acceptable to us and to suggest we have our places there.[7]

Let's take the example of the sudden shock produced by the use of the atom bomb in Japan in 1945: long before the World Trade Center towers, the mushroom clouds of Hiroshima and Nagasaki struck us dumb. The anguish of the possible destruction of humanity has been diffused, brooded over, reworked by the cinema, less by recourse to documents (often classified top secret) than by hundreds of science-fiction films. The latter show the eventual future ravages to our world brought on by imaginary conflicts, with the possibilities of survival and of refurbishment that a reducing to zero of the conditions of life offers. Fiction films on nuclear issues have performed a task of familiarisation, have elaborated a *modus vivendi* by creating imaginary societies in the image of our own and by having them survive, aside from a few rare exceptions, the atomic apocalypse. Corresponding to the era of the Cold War, they constitute one face of it, a counterpoint to the ambient anguish. Better yet, some of them even took the trouble of entrusting the solution to contemporary problems to nuclear weapons: the USA's racial problems are resolved in the cinema, then, thanks to a nuclear war, before being politically resolved in the real world by the Civil Rights movement: such is the scenario of *The World, the Flesh and the Devil* in 1959.[8]

It is perhaps on the question of American responsibility in the creation of a world in thrall to nuclear weapons that films have played the clearest role. In the largely American corpus most of them are presumed to take place in the United States, inviolate in reality, but which scenarios elect as a victim of bombardments or of radiation due to scientists, to Cold War enemies, named or otherwise, to the carelessness of American society. Everything takes place as if this imaginary, pitiless destruction of America was in payment for the bombings of Hiroshima and of Nagasaki yet in images alone. We see the profitable outcome of the operation, which is the maintenance of America's good conscience.

By way of contrast, on the extermination camps, the announcement of which, ratified by images shot by the forces of occupation, had horrified the world, the work of elaboration and rumination is far from being finished, each new film opening up a whole range of protests. This fact of the camps still escapes fictional construction, for having posed the question of the most profound of problems, that of the presence of evil in

we ourselves, and not something conveniently situated outside or placed
in the hands of a few mad scientists and military men or a threatening
"other." The questions raised by the 11 September outrage undoubtedly
pertain to this confused register, in which hidden beneath the violence of
terrorist aggression there are inevitably Western responsibilities in play.
Wars are not transparent.

The cinema has adopted the hues and the devices which, prior to it,
the oral or literary epic and history painting partook of. Films manoeuvre
between two forms: the first is dependent on the aestheticising and
heroising epic composition built around the destiny of a soldier or a group
of soldiers caught up in a cause, in a quest for self-knowledge and of
victory over oneself, for want of victory *tout court*. Or the films incline,
rather, towards a pathos-filled vision which boils down to the aestheticising, not now of destiny and its risks, but solely of loss, suffering and
death, extreme disorder. Whether they end well or badly, whether they
condemn the idea of war and the misfortune of the individual who is its
victim, or whether they celebrate its formative aspect, the films go to form
in our imaginary a repertoire of shots, of situations, of types of landscapes,
of combats, of expectations. They create a sort of encyclopaedia of war
consisting of systems, of mythologies about people at war, which in turn
serve ideologies and utopias in real life: for or against war, for or against
glory, for or against this or that belligerent. These images even serve
as a reference to the real, in making it unreal: soldiers serving in the Gulf
War have frequently said "you'd have thought you were in a war film," or
even "in a bad war film."

From *The Iliad* to the collective film 11'09''01,[9] verbal or filmed images
play their part in the distribution of responsibility and of guilt, they
construct war as a power, at once destructive and creative, and they
determine the moral position, with regard to suffering and domination,
that each person accepts or finds himself obliged to take. They propose,
and even impose, due to their system of echoes and reverberations, figures
and attitudes, they suggest glaring and invisible responsibilities,
which evolve with the readings that are made of it. In short, they permit
humanity to live in its own activity, war, in attempting to understand it.

The fragment as discourse of the absurd: objects, photos, television
Beginning in the second half of the twentieth century, at the same time as
the image of war invades the cinema screen, composition-wise, it becomes
more and more fragmented, intimate, almost obsessive. In painting as
in photography, fragmentation, the individualisation of subjects, the
accentuation of details and caricature form and deform the world (cf. Otto
Dix, George Grosz, Don McCullin, et cetera), the absurd is linked to war,

becomes its woof and weft. It is imbedded in objects born of the fighting: helmets, weapons, bits of uniform, sculptures made by soldiers in periods of idleness, letters from the front.

The conquest of private space prepared by the family snapshot and the press photo is magnified by television, which causes bits of it to enter our homes every day, to invite itself to our meals, occupy our evenings. It behaves like a self-service, offering daily news footage of the real world, films, arts broadcasts and commemorative documents on war or to do with it. In this self-service the viewer moves about on terms of absolute familiarity with war, with its souvenirs, its stories and even its portable film mythology; in short, everything that goes to form its imaginary, which is going to be confronted, mobilised, with daily bits of information or those of fiction. Television is still the greatest purveyor of images of war, it offers a constantly enriched catalogue of it. It is easily organised by propaganda and ideology, but the mass of images supplied and their contradictory discourse makes them the bearer of a critical power capable of disarticulating the meaning sought after by the institutions which produce them and of insisting on the absurdity created by the dominant disconnectedness of current images.

If the loss of meaning, the leaching of war by the absurd, are multiplied tenfold by television, then its jerky tempo, its short, always urgent, images are things the major networks are conscious of. They attempt to remedy this by different stylistic devices: CNN, for instance, gave a meaning to the Gulf War, the images of which, weighed down by the customary censorship, offered none. Inserts and captions played the role of linkages and framings for constructing an ideological discourse. The techniques of inculcating viewer loyalty were taken over from the devices of TV soap operas. Rarefied and monotonous spaces, speeded-up time, recurring characters: American dramaturgy of the Gulf War installed in the viewer's imagination a diverting, majestic composition in the service of law and order. In 1990-1991 the real character of this ensemble of images was War and, in tune with the political commentaries, just war, an ancient and questionable asset taken up once again by the Americans during the recent Iraq War. Now and then mythic characters rapidly assert themselves, like Bin Laden in Winter 2001-2002 with his rare appearances in orchestrated settings, a figure from a time outside of time, or at least giving this to be understood, a figure from a time immemorial at the service of another facet of war, Holy War.

Nevertheless most of the conflicts televised retain that disconnected look, mutilated by the censors, pushed right and left by other current events. The war in Afghanistan showed this recently. War in the TV newscasts is always like Fabrice at Waterloo, nose pressed up against the event.

The constantly evolving image of war, shocking, explanatory or anaesthe-
tising, conveys everything and its opposite. The next avatar will
doubtless arise from the role of Internet, which liberates a multitude of
fragments issuing from all the media possible, from painting to writing,
from cinema to photography or to television, organised or otherwise
at the level of web sites, but in any event mutually inarticulated for
the moment, apart from by the desire and randomness animating the
internaut. Part of our idea of war is edified here, and of our place in it,
of our feelings of guilt and our responsibilities, present and future,
which are the actual thread of any questioning, a thread deriving from
the intellectual and affective need to combat and overcome the absurd.
We cannot live in a world deprived of meaning.

The imagined war and the imaged war nourish the idea of real war
and are nourished by it in turn. Our cohabitation with this human activity
of which we are never rid is situated between a necessarily partial lived
reality and the affective or rational construction that a society's artists
offer the world. Works of art become so many elucidations, propositions,
that depict the different facets of war and inscribe it in an evolutive
system of resonances, a great ascending funnel which expands with time,
full of contradictions and cross references. In the nineteenth century
artists had shown war's pathetic and painful side without stripping it
of its heroic, epic character. Those of the twentieth century have smashed
it to smithereens, revealing its other visages, absurdity, the extreme
disorder it creates, out of which innovations, good or bad, may arise in
the contradictions of humanity. For better or worse, men and war —art
and war— form an inseparable couple.

Notes

1. STENDHAL, *La Chartreuse de Parme* (1839), Gallimard, Collection La Pléiade, Romans et nouvelles, T. II, 1952, pp. 56-94.

2. HUGO, Victor, *Les Misérables*, Part II, Book One, Gallimard, Collection Folio Classique, pp. 403-471.

3. THACKERAY, William Makepeace, *Vanity Fair* (1847-48).

4. LARGEAUD, Jean-Marc, "L'ombre portée du 18 juin 1815: iconographie et mémoire", in BURTON, Philippe (ed.), *La Guerre imaginée*, Seli Arslan, Paris 2002.

5. CHATEAUBRIAND, François-René de, *Mémoires d'Outre-tombe*, Gallimard, Collection La Pléiade, T. I, pp. 962 ff.

6. *Between War and Media* (a colloquium), the Maison Franco-Japonaise and Tokyo University, Tokyo, 25-27 March 2002.

7. It's the same for all the groupings formed around a conflict: the Spanish Civil War, the Vietnam War, the conquest of the American West, the two World Wars, etc.

8. *The World, the Flesh and the Devil*, Ranald MacDougall, USA, 1959.

9. *11'09''01*, a collective film by 11 directors about the World Trade Center outrage, France, 2002.

The art of war in the twentieth century
David D. Perlmutter

The humanity of war and pictures

Human beings can be distinguished from all other animals by several attributes: among them are that we make war with manufactured weapons and we create pictures on artificial or natural media. Both qualities are best studied—as is done in this exhibit—as combined rather than as separate phenomena.

First, war, as the philosopher Heraclitus asserted, is the father of all things. Few national borders were determined by compassion and altruism; most people live on land that their ancestors seized from others by violence. Many of our technologies, including the Internet, were created for the purposes of war or "defense"; some of our cherished political ideals, such as those of democracy and the "welfare state," are traced to the demands and outcomes of war.

At the same time human beings are visually oriented. Ninety percent of the data we process about the world arrives through our eyes. Not coincidentally do we associate the first manufactured visual pictures, revealed in the cave paintings of Franco-Cantabria (*c.* 20-30,000 years ago), with the rise to dominance on the earth of anatomically modern humans. Since then we have always made images to glorify, record, decry, explain and honor war.

So can we speak of a distinctive art of war of the twentieth century? Marc Bloch, the French historian murdered by the Nazis, warned against "hecto-history," the artificial dividing of great human processes into 100-year blocks. Yet the previous century did contain or culminate in some of the most important developments in both the history of war and its portrayal in images.

Primarily, war and images became in the twentieth century—unlike in any other era of human existence—both products and reflections of mass industrial mechanization. Perhaps other centuries saw more people die in war, but no century produced as many *pictured* deaths of people killed by machines and their masters. Unsurprisingly, historians have variously called the twentieth a "century of blood," a "stinking" century, the "Black Century," and the century of "total war." There were two "hot" world wars and one "cold" one. In addition hundreds of lesser conflicts—relatively so, since millions have died in them—have raged and still do in every part of the globe. The scale of death from war from 1901 to 2000 is hard to visualize in our mind's eye. It would take at least 4,000 monuments like the present-day Vietnam Memorial in Washington, D.C. to inscribe the names of each victim.

In addition the twentieth century allowed us to witness war "from our living rooms," as the saying went during America's war in Vietnam. In the 1880s the illustrator Albert Robida startlingly predicted this phenomenon, showing a bourgeois European family watching on some sort of home visual film screen far-off battling horse- and camel-riding tribesmen. In the twentieth century such scenes became a mass communication product (the still photos, films, video, and digital pictures of photojournalism) delivered by cameras, print media, televisions and computers to mass audiences. The time it took for such visions to arrive in our houses decreased over the course of the century. During World War II, for example, film was shipped home for editing and publication, a process that might take months. Joe Rosenthal, the photographer who took the famous *Raising the Flag at Iwo Jima* image, did not see his final print until many weeks later. In Vietnam it required about a day to get "film in the can" back to New York or Paris for development and onto the evening news or the front page. Satellites and video and then digital technology and web cams now allow transfer of "live from Ground Zero" imagery as it happens to the home-front viewer. Being "first" (even by seconds) with the most sensational images of war became the holy grail of modern photojournalism.

Lastly, war art was not wiped out by the machine gun. Despite the mass industrial nature of war and of picture-making, the traditional arts (painting, drawing, carving, sculpture) still retained the ability to critique war, though in novel ways and to different audiences. They no longer sought the utmost fidelity of scene, as did the oil paintings of previous eras: instead they aimed to interpret war through emotion and fragmentation. Simultaneously, the new electro-mechanical and digital images of war did not remain simply commodities: many entered the museum as venerated and profitable art objects or "icons." As artists of the war image, war photographers became as respected as any Renaissance master.

Picturing war before the twentieth century
In the Neolithic, we have the first definite images of interhuman combat and warriors: tribesmen with spears and arrows engaged in battles and personal duels. Spain, notably, boasts some of the best depictions of the "new" war art, such as that of the Gasulla Gorge in Castellon. But similar incarnations are found in India, Africa and Australia. At these early dates we recognize "leaders" distinguished by body size, headdress, and different positions and equipment. Familiar tactics are here too, such as encirclement, flanking, charges, skirmish lines and ambush. Violence is omnipresent.

For our purposes, the entire pre-photographic "civilized" era of warfare (from the pharaohs to Waterloo) can be compressed to a few observations. Generally, images of war were servants of state power and the vanity of warlords—again, often in contradiction to the truth. Ramses II adorned his mausoleum with images of himself as a giant, smiting miniaturized Hittites at Kadesh (c. 1300 BCE). Yet, we know that the battle was a draw, at best. Assyrian kings would portray themselves as ever-victorious, even in times of defeat, in their bas-reliefs, and decorate their palaces with scenes of massacre to intimidate potential rivals and foreign ambassadors. Roman generals, given a triumphal parade, would ride their chariots into the Eternal City flanked by slaves holding up paintings depicting the battles that brought them fame. It is generally not until the Renaissance that we have the first secular critiques of war—horrors of war as disgrace, not boast—and also the exalting of the common soldiers.

But the imperial impulse persisted. In a famous exchange, Napoleon, the hard-headed emperor, castigated his favorite artist, Jacques-Louis David, for ennobling the vanquished Spartans of Thermopylae. His argument: "David, you will tire yourself out painting the defeated." Napoleon, like all the god-kings before him, insisted on *La Gloire* in paint and stone and bronze.

The era of prints and painting was not wholly a "Romantic" period in the depiction of war. Certainly there were innumerable pictures of dashing cavalry charges, handsome portraits of long-mustached hussar officers, and noble "death of" scenes. Yet Jacques Callot and then Francisco de Goya and others showed the useless, ignoble and dirty facets of the enterprise.

By the mid-nineteenth century the invention of photography had arrived, allowing the artist to stand near the warrior and "capture" the vista of war and, with the later innovation of the "negative," produce innumerable copies of that image for the masses.

However, old restrictions applied here too. For the first war photographed, the Crimean War (1854), we have mainly sittings and posings—that was all the generals would encourage or tolerate. The American Civil War provided the initial real images of battlefield death and horror. In a famous 1863 essay, jurist and philosopher Oliver Wendell Holmes wrote in the *Atlantic Monthly* of his reaction to photographs of the dead at Antietam: "Let him who wishes to know what war is look at this series of illustrations." The public, however, could at first view actual photographs only at exhibitions or in *cartes de visite*. Newspapers could only print engravings or woodcuts inspired by photographs, which were then often highly edited. Neither could the early cameras capture motion; battles could not be shot in progress.

New technologies contributed to what we recognize as film photography and photojournalism. The Second Boer War (1899-1902) did yield some films for the home-front British audiences. The short films

Skirmish Round the Flag and *The Sneaky Boer,* though, were fakes filmed in England. It was not until the early part of the twentieth century that mass publics would see still photography and films from the battlefronts.

The twentieth century revolution: war and pictures mechanized
We may mark the twentieth century's distinctive features in war and war pictures as commencing with the guns of August of 1914. World War I seemed to survivors of its fury to be a culmination of all war technology: fleets of steel battleships; combat in the air and under the sea; the triumph of the machine gun; railroads as arteries of mobilization and deployment; metal monsters roving the land (curiously called "tanks," in a British subterfuge to make the enemy think their new secret weapon was a storage device for water). The colossal scale, too, seemed unsurpassable: entire nations mobilized; armies in the tens of millions; battles in far-off corners of the world.

The art of war was profoundly affected. Many thought that the mass slaughter and the mass imagery had not only killed off the optimistic spirit of Western civilization, but had also murdered the idea of "war art" itself. Battles fought at twilight on moonscapes with machine guns and artillery did not lend themselves to the sensibility and tactility of realistic oil painting. The subjects themselves were drabber and shabbier: modern armies dressed for cover, not color. The cavalry charge—indeed the mass charge of soldiery itself—was suicide. Heroes were invisible in the mud and blood and fog. Lady Butler, the general's wife who was famous for her heroic canvases, was appalled by the butcher's bill of the Western front in the first months of the war and immediately understood that her era was dead. "Who will look at my *Waterloo* now?" was her rhetorical question. Realism was the order of the day.

But what kind of realism? The photos and films of the war were unremarkable except for their blandness. The discordance that was often presented between the realities of war shown to the public and those suffered in the field was made more stark and more widely known. Censorship—total and stifling—was the practice among all belligerents. The public saw camp scenes, men going "over-the-top," tidy marches, generals pointing at maps, politicians shaking hands, and little else in the newspapers, magazines, and movie reels of the time. Few battles were shown in any detail: little suffering and death, only some material devastation. The rot-trenched hell that an entire generation of European youth died in was snipped or boxed out of visual culture.

The exceptions were propaganda pictures of enemy atrocities: some based on reality, others wholly faked. After the war, of course, Hollywood, in tune with the times, began to make "anti-war" films like *All Quiet on the Western Front* that fixed the image of the trenches as abattoirs.

But most important for the genre of war art itself, the photograph and the film (news, documentary, and fiction) were now the main definers of the "reality" of war. True, production of "oil art" and statuary of the war did not slacken. (It persists, officially and unofficially, to this day.) "Last gunner firing" painting groups and the bronze of *Canada's Golgotha* won public admiration. Also, traditional arts have remained dominant in the memorials of war. Every village in France, for example, has a statue group or obelisk commemorating its World War I dead.

But in truth the non-specialist can name only a handful of post-1914 images of war that are within the traditional media of canvas, metal or stone. This writer's students, when pressed, could name only one painting of war for the entire century: *Guernica*. No wonder that non-photographic artists have essentially surrendered the old right of painting, that of the "realism of oil," to the new media. The painters (and many sculptors) of the new century sought novel ways of rendering and interpreting the ideas and emotions of war.

We may now speak of the twentieth century as the era of the industrialization of war, warriors and art. Interestingly, the mass audience found new appreciation of the mass-mobilized warriors. The common soldier became a protagonist in story and art. No twentieth-century general could refer to his men, as did Wellington in the previous century, as the "scum of the earth." The ordinary soldier, still cannon fodder in practice, was treated as a hero and was a common subject for the camera, from the frontlines of Verdun to Stalingrad, to Hue, and to Kuwait City and innumerable Hollywood films. Indeed, the picturing of the death of the individual soldier, once a genre only accorded to warlords, is now the subject of concentrated media attention, at least in the West.

For example, in February 1969 *Life* magazine published 217 portrait photographs of Americans who had been killed in one week of fighting in Vietnam. The faces startle us with their incongruity of setting and visage: most of the soldiers are posing in clean and pressed military uniform, smiling, resolute, the incarnation of the strength of our youth. No surprise then that Western publics now chafe at the number of casualties in war that a Napoleon or a World War I general would think inconsequential. Perhaps the heroicization of the noncommissioned man (and woman) through close-up photography has increased the value of individual life—if not for an enemy, at least for our own warriors.

The truth of war images
Another recurring feature of twentieth century war imagery is the debate over "truth." The camera mimics some of the natural processes of the

human eye—thus we perceive that a photograph is more realistic than, say, a Cubist drawing. Yet realism has its codes, too. Makers of "nonfiction" films, for example, regularly insert stock footage to substitute for specific references in the narration without informing audiences of the difference. As the great American photographer Albert Streichen said, "Photographs can't lie but liars can photograph." Perhaps it is better to state, as did the art historian Ernst Gombrich, that *pictures cannot lie in the same way that words can.* We do not say, for instance, that great fiction-based-on-fact war films like *The Longest Day* are lies because they show John Wayne fighting on a Normandy beach. On the other hand, we would judge it a lie if we were told that the movie was the original battle captured on film of the time. Or, if a picture of a corpse-filled ditch, captioned "Dead Hutus Killed by Tutsis in Burundi," is recaptioned "Dead Tutsis Killed by Hutus in Rwanda," one or both sets of words may be partly or wholly false. The photographed human beings, however, remain just as dead. The picture, too, is the same; it is only the context of interpretation that has changed.

Yet truth mattered in the previous century as much as in this one. This was and is seen in controversies about famous war icons. During the Spanish Civil War, Robert Capa, the century's most celebrated war photographer, shot his *Dying Spanish Militiaman.* Although the world would see many "dying soldier" images in the years and wars to come, this is the one most widely known. Immediately, however, there were allegations that the event was staged—a stunt for the camera. But subsequent scholarship, in tracing records of the events and looking at Capa's original negative roll, proves that it was an authentic "captured moment of death." Faking, of course, was common: all armies in World War II, for example, staged propaganda images. Many of the famous "war shots" repeated today in collections and history books were enactments.

Photo manipulation was, of course, not unique to the twentieth century. From the early days of photography, its founders discovered that one could "tidy up" an image. Some neatening could take place before the picture was taken. Many photos of the American Civil War included props and re-arrangements of the scenes—even of the dead bodies. Then further changes were made in the transition to newspaper- and magazine-printed engravings and woodcuts.

Today we face a greater challenge in ascertaining what is authentic: most war photographs are shot digitally. There is no negative for some future detective or historian to "check." In the most recent Gulf War a *Los Angeles Times* reporter was fired for being too creative with his Photoshop software; questions were raised about many other images, video and still. The future is ominous in this regard, as the digital "editing" techniques common in Hollywood films become ubiquitous, cheap and simple.

In the century to come, who will be able to detect the difference between photo fact and fantasy?

Perhaps these techno-fantasies point to the continuing need for visual artistry about war. The anti-sloganeered posters created by Barbara Kruger, for example, demand that we stop and think about what we supposedly can see with our eyes. Earlier in the century, painters Gino Severini and Christopher Nevinson reacted to the technologicalization of death in World War I by focusing on the iconoclasm of the machine itself. Is the steel killing mechanism the message of modern war imagery—not the men at all, who are simply its servants or slaves? Félix Vallotton, in his 1917 oil, *Verdun, tableau de guerre interprété*, tried to answer the question, "What can I depict out of all that?", after actually seeing the field of the war's costliest battle. In the painting, man is a nearly invisible bystander; the flashes, smoke and guns are the star players.

Limited visions of war

How much we should be allowed to see is always a controversy. World War II, for example, was visually different to World War I. Censorship during the former was due less to coercion than cooperation. In most cases war photographers voluntarily complied with government requests; they believed that home-front audiences had no interest in seeing their sons lying headless on South Seas beaches. On the other hand, research on public opinion found that many civilians wanted to see more of the sacrifice of the combatants. Paul Fussell, cultural critic and World War II combat veteran, argued that his comrades held "the conviction that optimistic publicity and euphemism had rendered their experience so falsely that it would never be readily communicable...[and was] systematically sanitized and Norman Rockwellized, not to mention Disneyfied." The rules for the American press were "no dead or badly wounded GIs." (It was acceptable, as in a famous *Life* magazine photo, to show incinerated Japanese soldiers.) Near the end of the war this situation changed slightly: Americans saw some dead from the island battles against Japan and a dead American from street fighting in Germany. In the Third Reich the rules were similar, but in desperation in the last years, and in sufferance to Goebbels's policy of "total war," many grim pictures trickled home. Russians saw atrocity pictures featuring civilians killed by the Germans. In many belligerent countries like Japan, however, censorship was heavy-handed. Generally, it was allowable to show the death of the enemy or of people other than one's own countrymen. Despite all this, the war confirmed that battlefront news photographers could be "artists" as well as industrial workers. As in the American Civil War, the best of such images merited museum display as well as becoming popular icons.

In the next half century of picturing war in Africa, Asia, central and eastern-Europe, and the Middle East, another issue arose. Why were we being shown certain wars and not others? The attentive can cite some famous wars of the post-Korea era, from the American War in Vietnam to the Arab-Israeli wars, and the well-known and well-reported genocides, such as those in Biafra and Rwanda. Yet, there have been hundreds of wars since World War II and dozens of major genocides. During the time of this exhibition at least 40 wars rage around the world, although the most informed of us may be hard-pressed to name but a few. Why, we might ask, is the slaughter of one people covered by thousands of cameras, while another people expires in non-televisual and unphotogenic obscurity? It follows that the camera defines the war: you, the reader, can conjure an image in your mind of the slaughter pits of Rwanda but not of those in Tibet. In the Sudan over a million are dead from the civil war between the "Arab" Muslim north and the "Black" Christian south, yet the Sudan has been a minor sideshow to Western lenses. The inequality of war and death in the camera's eye, and thus in the mind of the public, is considerable.

There are no simple answers. Certainly, some countries are the centers of the attention of major-power political leaders; the cameras logically follow their gaze and their deployment of troops. Geography and resources matter. Vietnam was the great "domino"; Biafra was mineral-rich; Somalia was on the horn of Africa controlling the main oil shipping routes; Bosnia was in central Europe; Iraq has oil. Such nations are deemed "strategically" important. But accessibility is another variable. A war on the fringes of Europe can be covered easily (albeit not without danger) but the Chinese government has never allowed foreign cameras to view its conquest and subjugation of Tibet (estimated dead: two million plus). When the government of Syria crushed a Muslim uprising in the city of Hama (20-40,000 dead) only a few still pictures were smuggled to the West. Of course, political factors seem to dominate. To wit, Saddam Hussein killed his own people in droves, but because he was a useful ally against the Ayatollah's Iran, America and the West pointedly ignored atrocity images from Iraq of slaughtered Kurdish babies.

The twentieth century was also the time when the creation and dissemination of pictures of war became a giant industry. Simply put, the maw of news must be fed, and striking photos of war and violence are a lucrative commodity. Indeed, a rarely studied feature of war photojournalism icons is their significant monetary value. Picture rights alone will accrue hundreds of thousands of dollars over time. Careers are made, too, for the picture shooter who bags the icon. The premium put on "getting the money shot" or "shooting the Pulitzer" makes for unappetizing off-camera anecdotes. Rakiya Omaar, a Somali and the former executive director of Africa Watch, noted: "Anyone who has watched a Western film crew in an African famine will know just how much effort it takes to compose the 'right' image…they rush through crowded corridors, leaping over stretchers, dashing to film the agony before it passes…When the Italian actress Sophia Loren visited Somalia last month, the paparazzi trampled on children as they scrambled to film her feeding a little girl." Hers is a common observation, although in fairness one must concede that many news journalists feel their duty is to help, not to hurt or to shoot and run.

How did pictures of war affect war?

For the student of the art World War II raised of war another question that we still struggle with today. If we are allowed to see the horrors of war, how do they affect us? Do they desensitize us, excite us, dull us to inaction or spur our outrage? Does their propagation, as war leaders worry, undermine support for war? Research on this subject provides an ambiguous and sobering answer: it all depends on who is watching what is done to whom.

It is often stated that, for example, the Hitler regime, like Stalin's henchmen, kept their mass killings of Jews, Poles and others off-camera, and thus secret. This was true in formal terms: there were severe proscriptions that no films or pictures were to be made of death camps or mass shootings of civilians. Yet, these images were made anyway, some by officials. Ironically, many images of the Holocaust that today appear in museum exhibitions and memorializing picture books were, in fact, mementos taken by German soldiers and even, incredibly, concentration and death camp guards. These pictures were sent home and circulated. The Japanese depredations in China were thus documented as well. (There are many other such cases: in Cambodia, for example, the Khmer Rouge genocide was recorded only by the perpetrators' own pictures of their victims.) Sympathy, it seems, is in the eye of the beholder, and one man's atrocity photo is another's delightful tourist souvenir or bureaucratic notation.

We may make the same point about the "effects" of the war image, even famous ones. Consider *Guernica*. Perhaps the picture affected individual minds. It is also argued that its return to Spain was a symbol for national reconciliation. But did the twentieth century's most famous "anti-war" artwork do anything to impact the war from which it arose? Did any army's fortune wax or wane; did any nation change its policies; was a Basque life spared from the inferno? Research on the influences of icons of war suggest that they may have many powers, from the aesthetic to the economic to the political, but these may not conflate. A picture may be "powerful" as a picture alone but not in any way affect the course of a war.

This is a troubling thought. Today it is commonly stated that "if there had been cameras at Auschwitz, there would have been no Holocaust." The psychological assumption in such a premise is that we are all equally outraged by horrors perpetrated against other human beings. Study and experience prove this to be a fantastical notion. Certainly the camera can expose a horror that no other medium of art could in the past as quickly or as realistically. Yet, as said, there were cameras at Auschwitz—those of the killers. It is now known that both Western governments and the press were aware that a great slaughter was occurring but chose to ignore it. Anti-Semitism was a factor, but also there was a backlash by many, especially in America, to heavy-handed and sometimes false British atrocity propaganda in World War I.

The Soviet slaughters of their own people, and then the mass rapes in Germany and in Eastern Europe by the Russian armies, were even more off-camera. The president of the United States insisted that all images of "Uncle Joe" Stalin's realm be favorable, whether in newsprint or in Hollywood films. Alexander Solzhenitsyn writes of a gulag guard taunting the prisoners, "You think Europe cares about you?" Well, Europe didn't see the gulags, but we may wonder if Europe (and America) in the thirties and during World War II *wanted* to see them. Likewise, war-weary America had no interest in the killing fields of Cambodia in the late seventies, even if camera crews had been allowed to cover them. Gilles Peress, in another example, may go to Rwanda and capture the charnel pits, and his photographs may make it to the breakfast tables of statesmen and the living rooms of Houston, Tokyo and Pamplona, but the reaction may be, as the title of his book of pictures suggests: *The Silence.* There is much evidence, then, that publics are not spurred to action by watching the slaughter of alien peoples: we go about our daily routine, numbed to such "infotainment."

Conclusion: war and images reconciled

Now we have entered another century. The events of just its first three years offer small hope that the genre of the war image will expire for want of subjects or become a topic too antiquarian for a museum of *contemporary* culture. Governments worry about how to control pictures of war, others seek to profit from them, others suffer as their subjects, and a few try through images to struggle against war. Most of us are silent witnesses to the mass carnage and the mass imagery that political elites and the news industry allow us to see. Some images of war become famous; many are mass commodities; artists with camera and pens and computer keyboards struggle to show what they see of war in front of their faces and in their mind's eye.

Does this past and present allow us to predict the future? We note that humans are very adaptable: we can eat hamburgers, honey, and crickets; we can live in the jungle, ghettos, and the Arctic; we can also love our neighbor and cooperate with him, or we can kill him and steal his goods. All these activities are within our capacity: they include the ability to make war and to make pictures. These are not opposites and are often composites. We are, as Shakespeare put it, angels and killers; but we can also be soldiers and poets, death-camp guards and painters. The future, then, is unwritten; the survival of our species is not guaranteed; but we can be certain that unto the last days we will make pictures to elucidate for ourselves the experience of war.

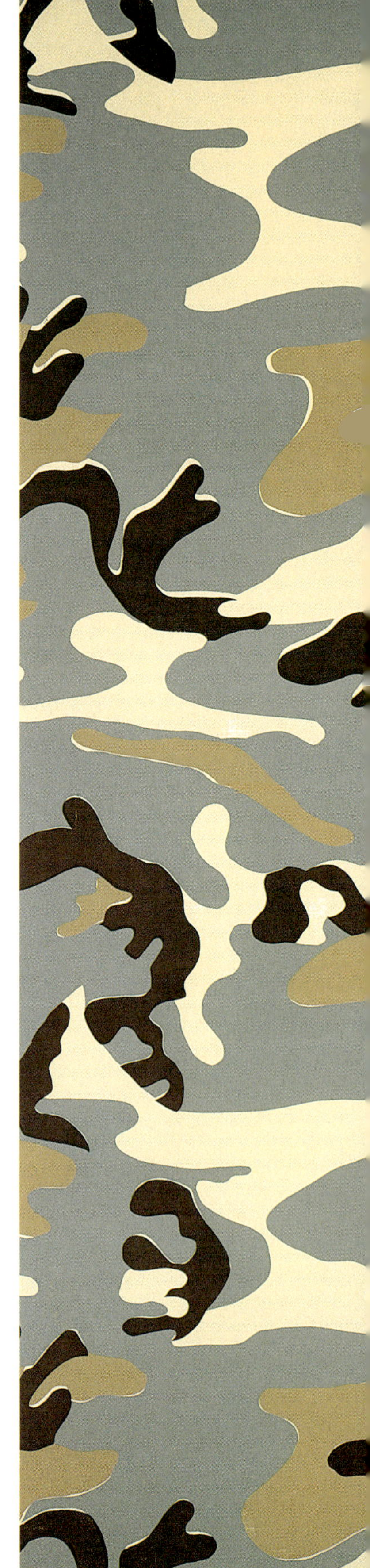

ANDY WARHOL, Camouflage, 1986
Acrylic and silkscreen on canvas, 203.2 x 203.2 cm
Founding Collection, The Andy Warhol Museum, Pittsburgh

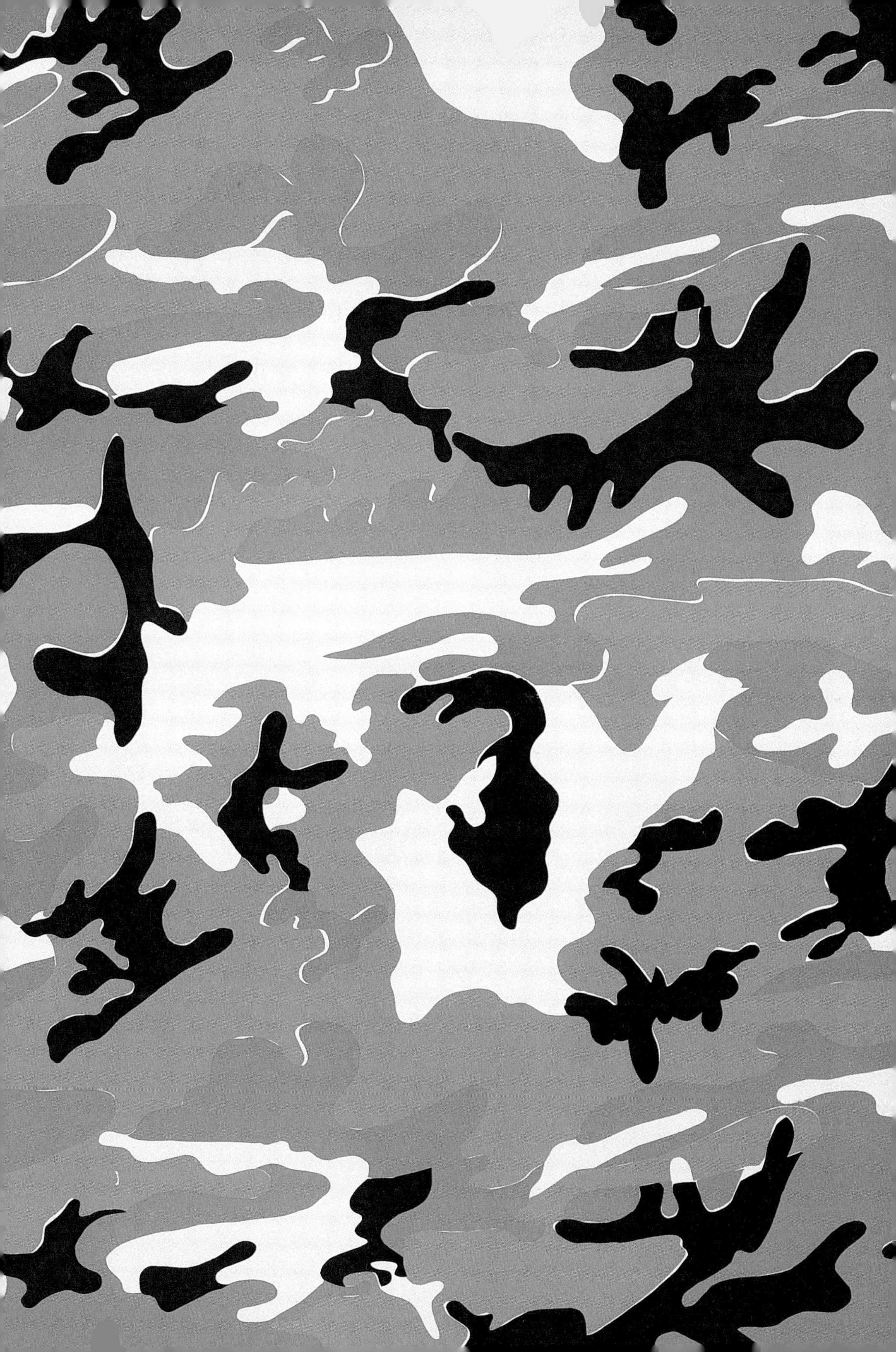

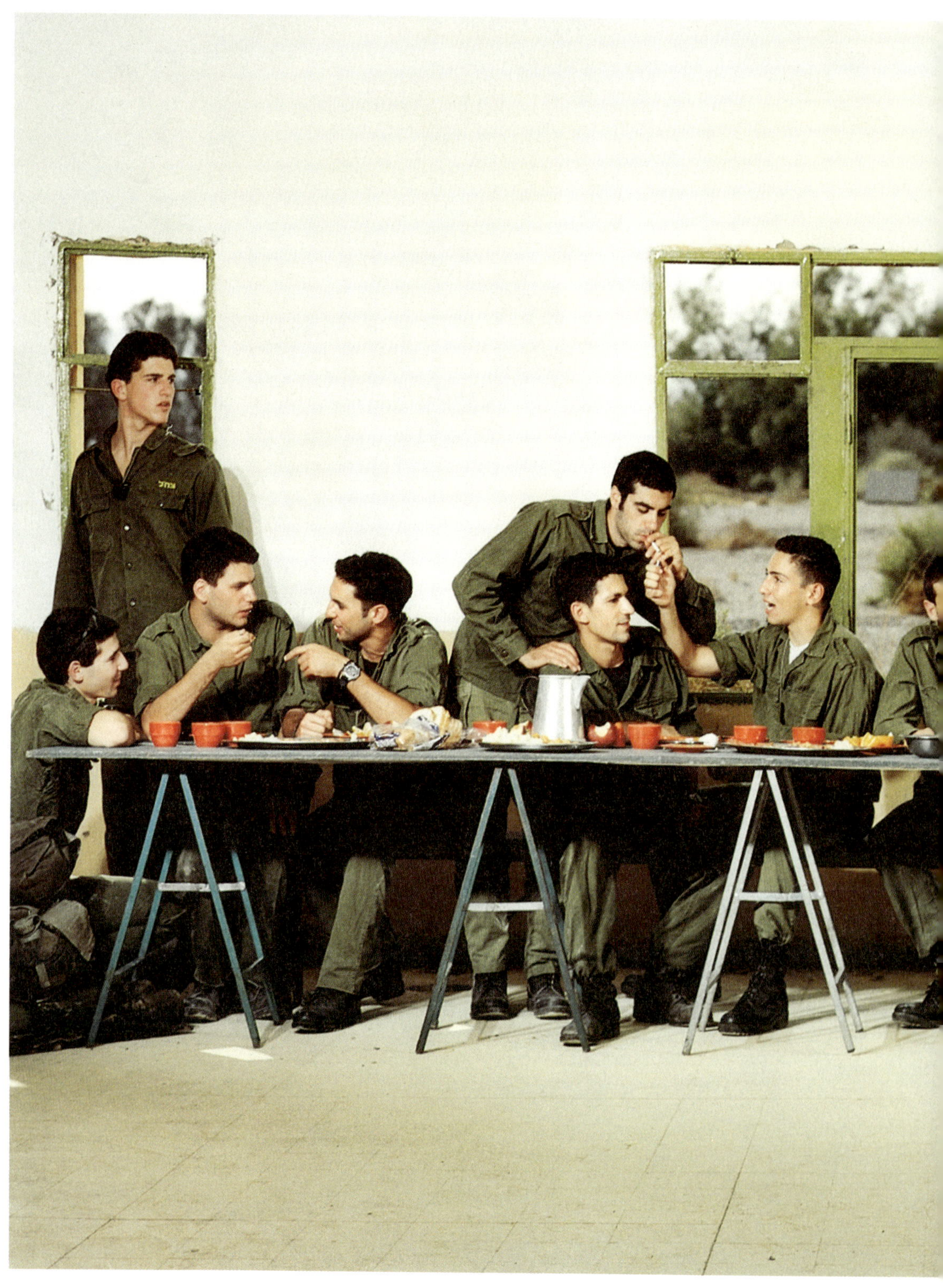

ADI NES, Untitled, 1999
90 x 148 cm
Courtesy of Dvir Gallery, Tel Aviv

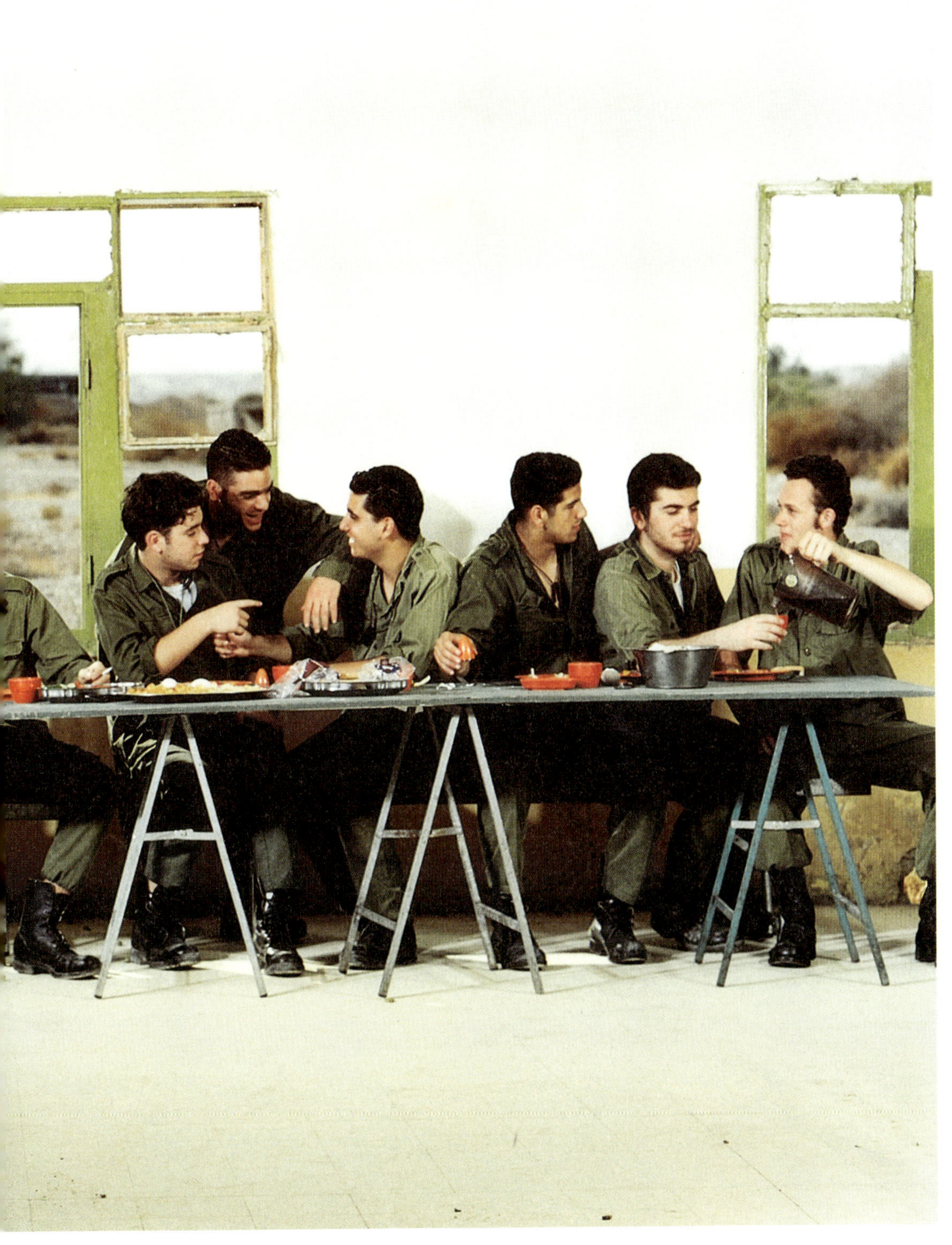

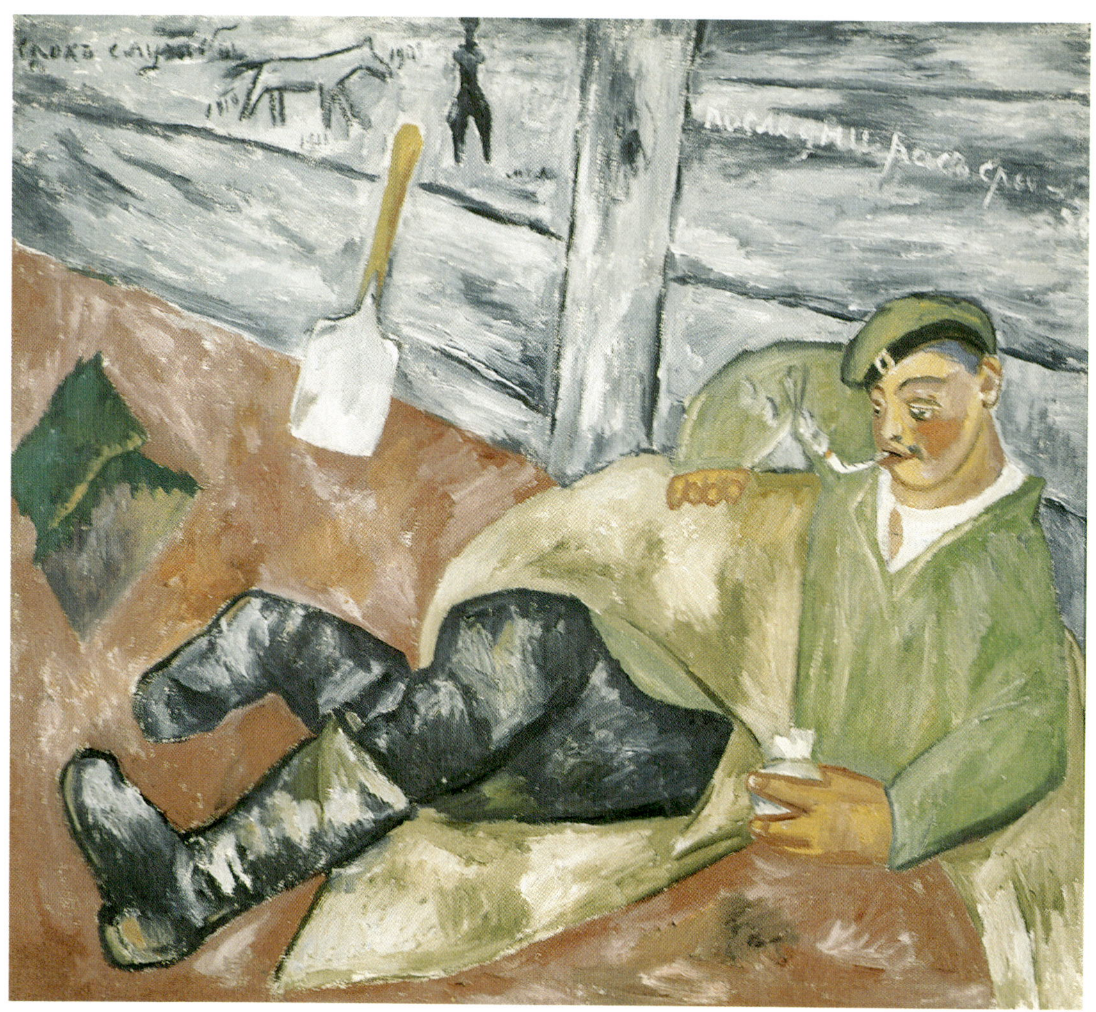

Larionov was a sergeant in the Russian army during the
invasion of Eastern Prussia, when he was seriously wounded.
His happy scenes of soldiers resting, inspired by his military
service, date from a period before the war.

MIKHAIL FIODOROVICH LARIONOV, Soldier at rest, 1911
Oil on canvas, 119 x 122 cm
Tretyakov Gallery, Moscow

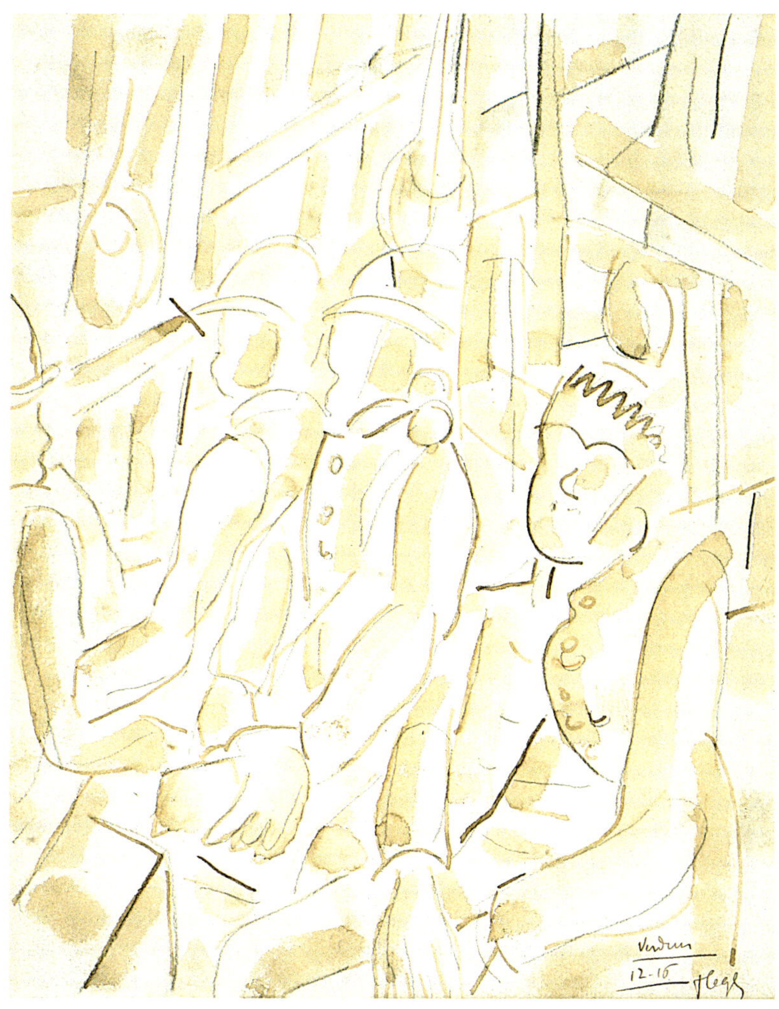

Léger was a sapper and stretcher-bearer during the First World War; he took part in several battles, including the Battle of the Marne and the Battle of Verdun, where he was gassed. In a letter from 1915, he described the war as: "pure abstraction, far purer than cubist painting itself".

FERNAND LÉGER, Foot soldiers waiting for the time to attack in their
cave-shelter in Bazile below Douaumont, 1916
Pencil, pen and wash, 29 x 23 cm
Musée d'Histoire Contemporaine – BDIC, Paris

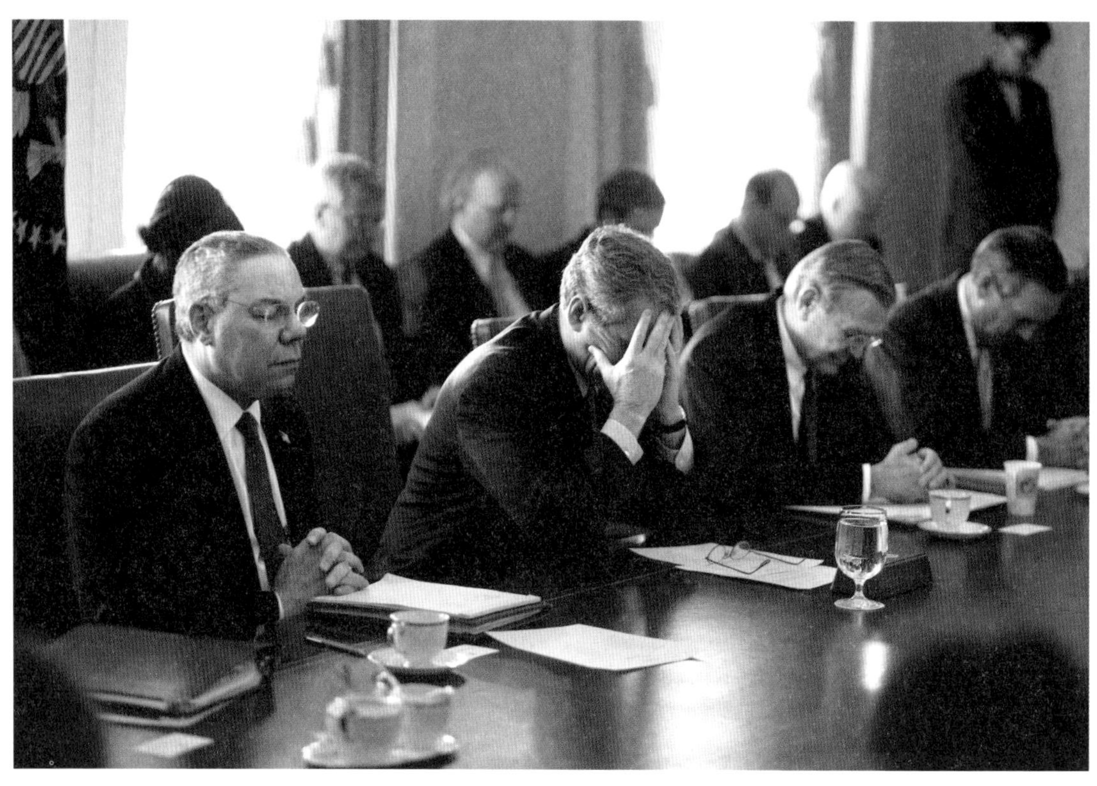

BROOKS KRAFT PHOTOGRAPHY, Bush cabinet prayer,
23 March 2003
Brooks Kraft Photography, Washington

DON MELL, An Iraqi soldier steps outside his dug-out
to pray during Ramadan, on the southern front near
Majnoon island, Irak-Iran War, 1984
AP / Radial Press

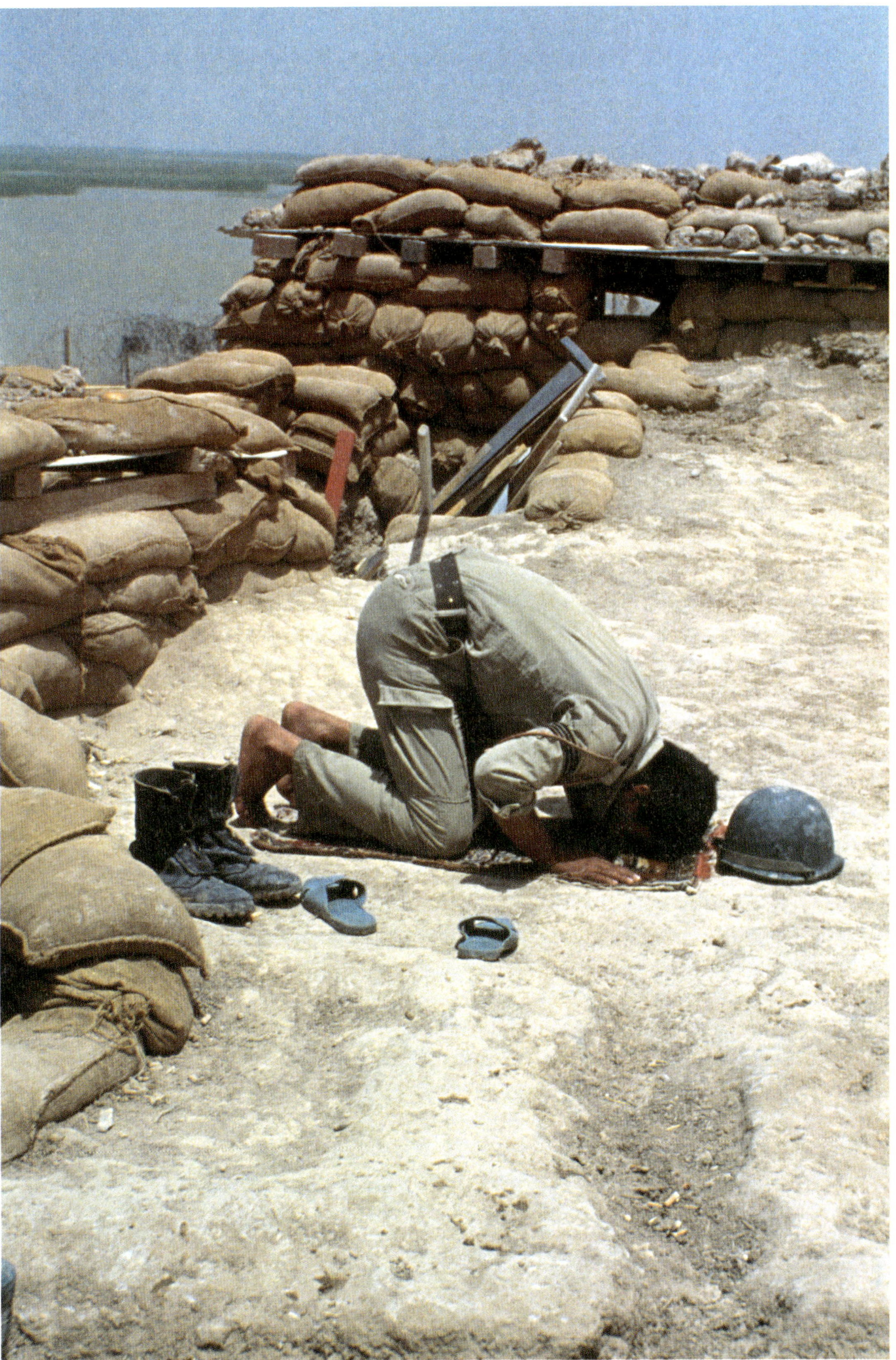

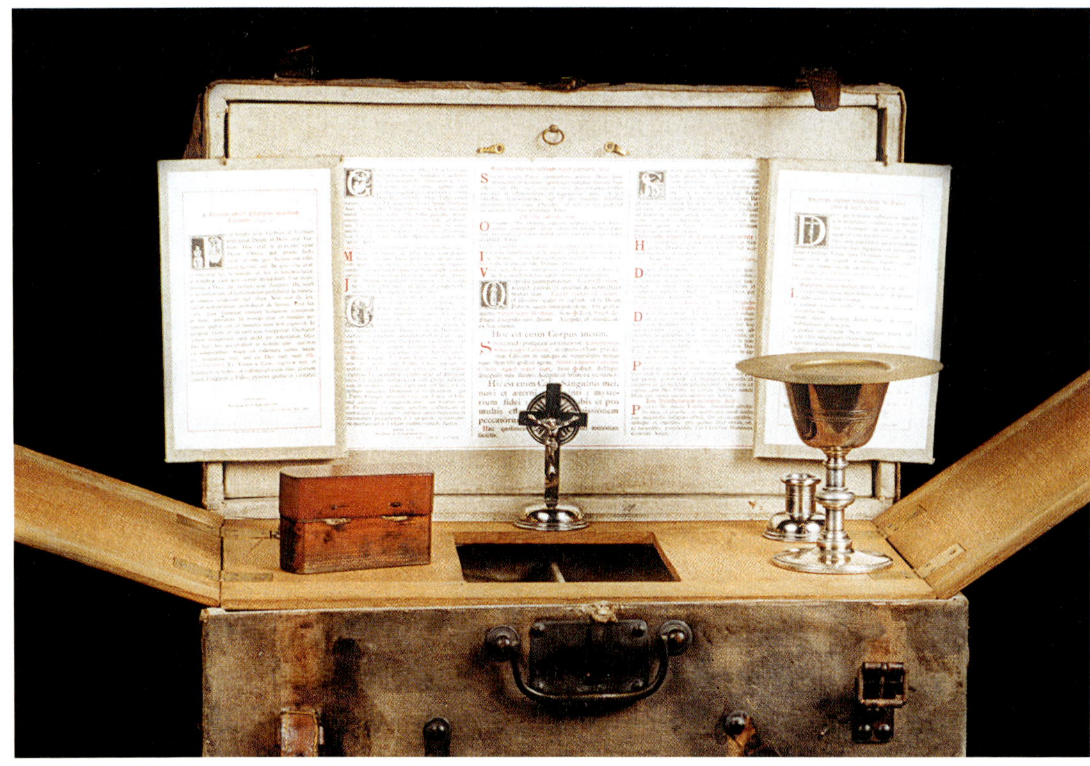

Religions are often a basic ideological component of the baggage which accompanies soldiers during wartime. This travelling case contains all the objects required for an altar used at the front during the First World War.

Travelling case containing a folding altar, a crucifix, two candle holders, a ciborium and a box, c. 1915
Cardboard, jute and wood, 53.5 x 31.5 x 24 cm
Historial de la Grande Guerre, Péronne (Somme)

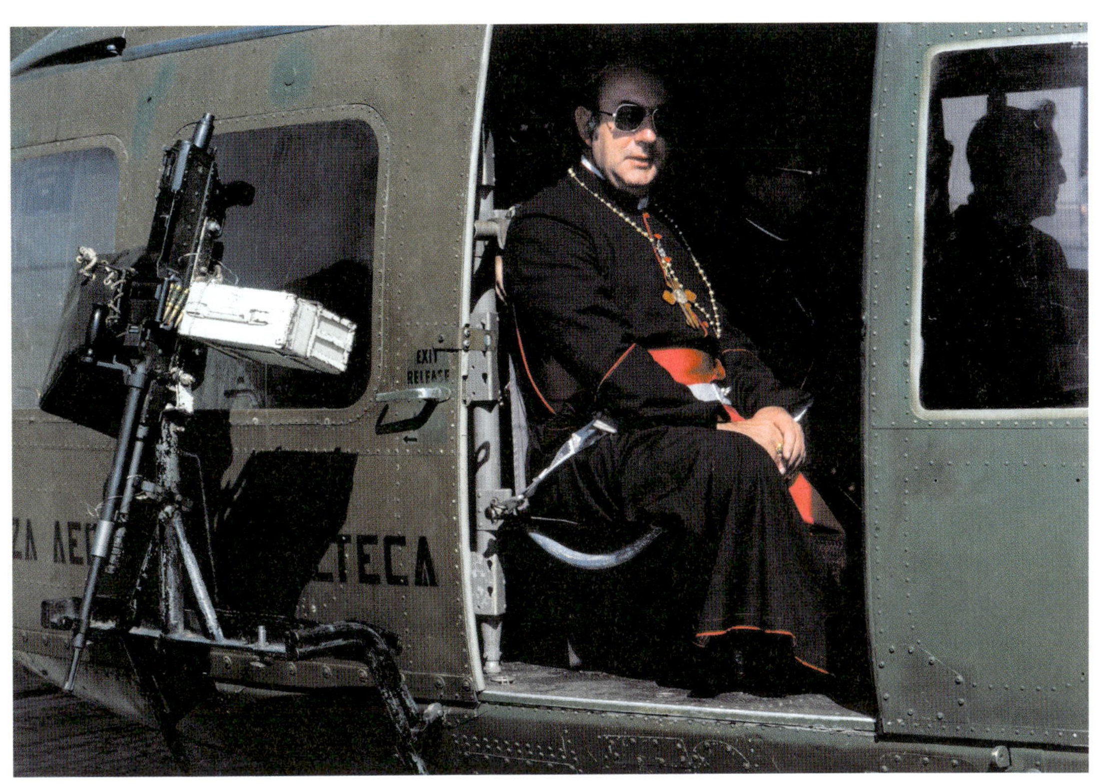

JAMES NACHTWEY, Guatemala, 1983
Collection of the artist, New York

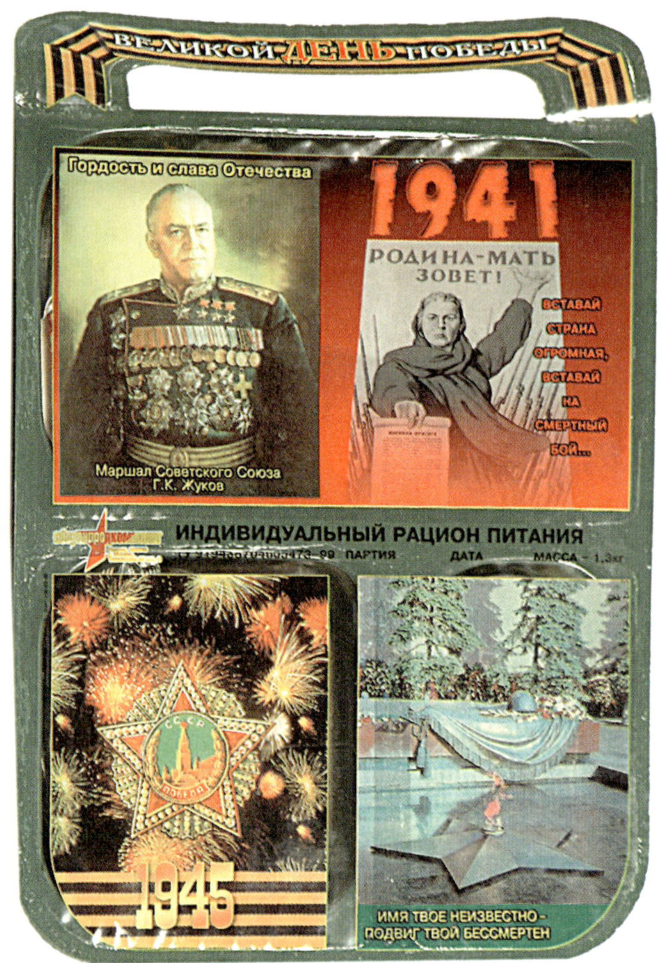

The memory of former wars is part of the ideological background which boosted the soldiers' morale, as shown by this food parcel prepared for the present-day Russian army, decorated with some of the most famous epic events in Soviet history.

Individual ration of food in Armed Forces of the Russian Federation. Images on the cover: Marshal of the USSR Georgi Zhukov, Motherland calls you, Order of victory, Tomb of unknown soldier, Memorial place, 2003-2004
Plastic, 37 x 24 x 7 cm
Central Armed Forces Museum, Moscow

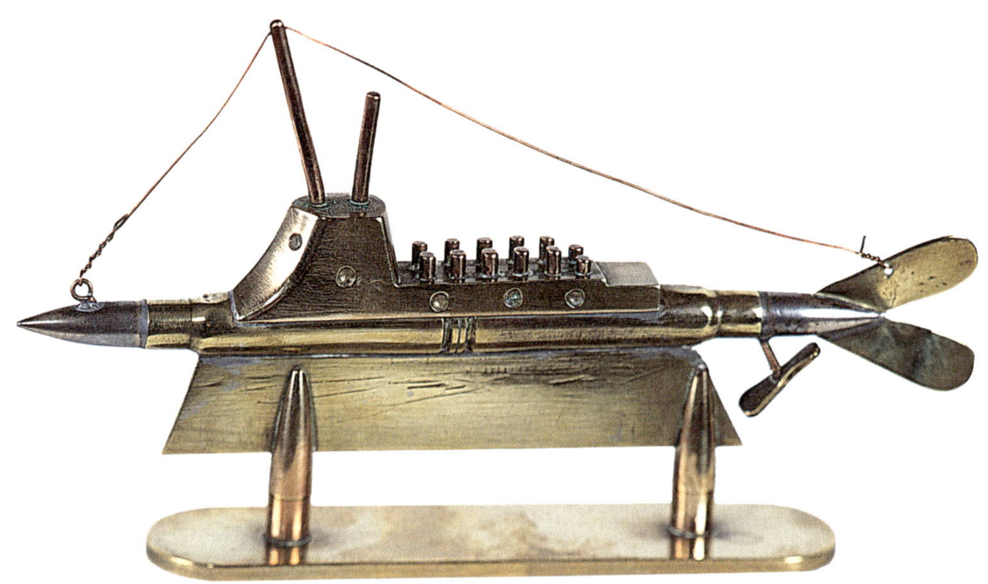

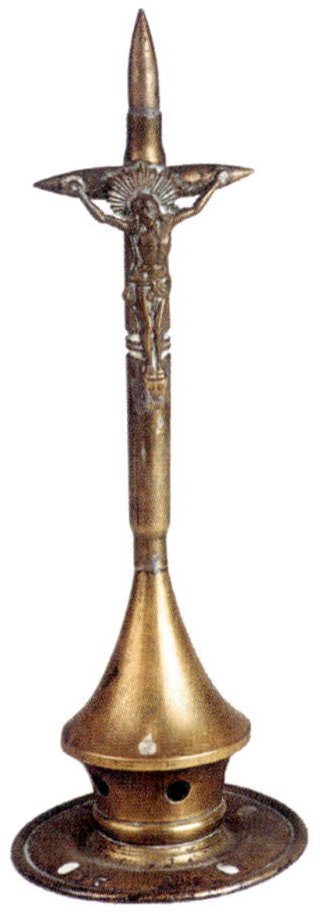

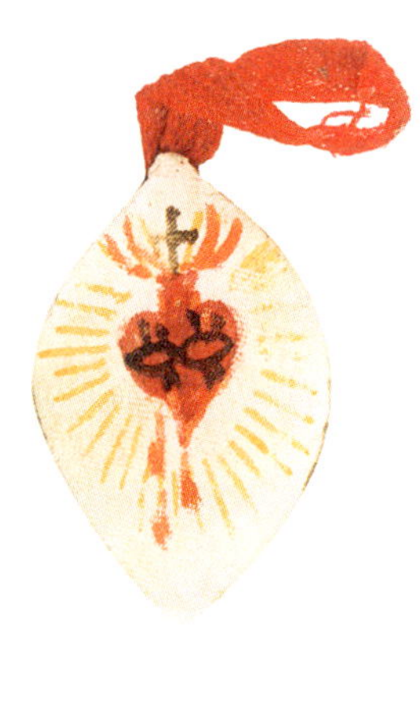

Submarine made from bullets and recovered
elements, 1916-1920
Metal, 18 x 10 x 3 cm
Historial de la Grande Guerre, Péronne (Somme)

Crucifix made in a trench from bullets on
the spike of a German helmet, 1915
Copper, 22 x 7 cm diameter
Historial de la Grande Guerre, Péronne (Somme)

Detente in the shape of a tear with the bleeding
heart of Jesus, c. 1940
Drawing and painting on wool, 6.8 x 3 cm
Museo del Ejército, Madrid

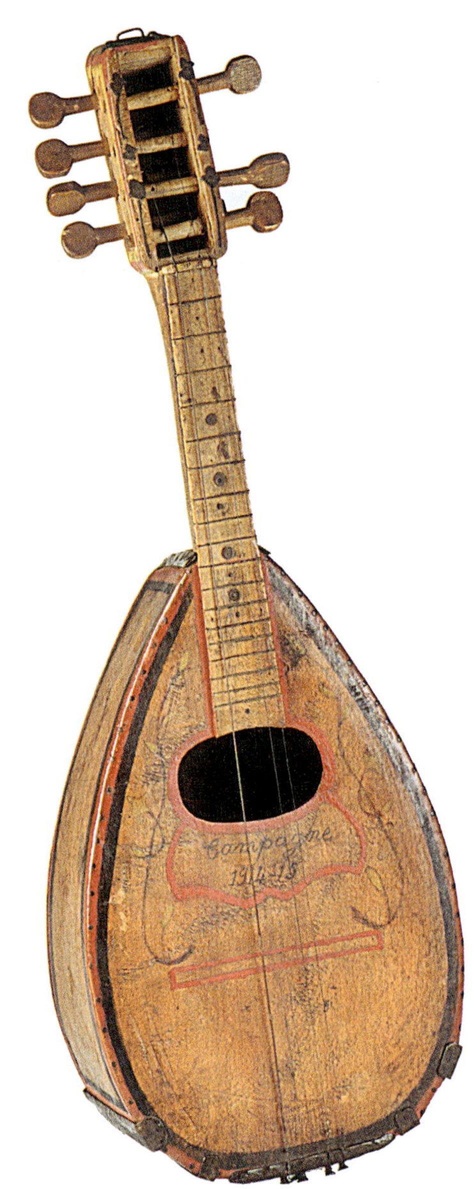

Mandolin (trench art), 1915
Painted wood, 11 x 19 x 55 cm
Historial de la Grande Guerre, Péronne (Somme)

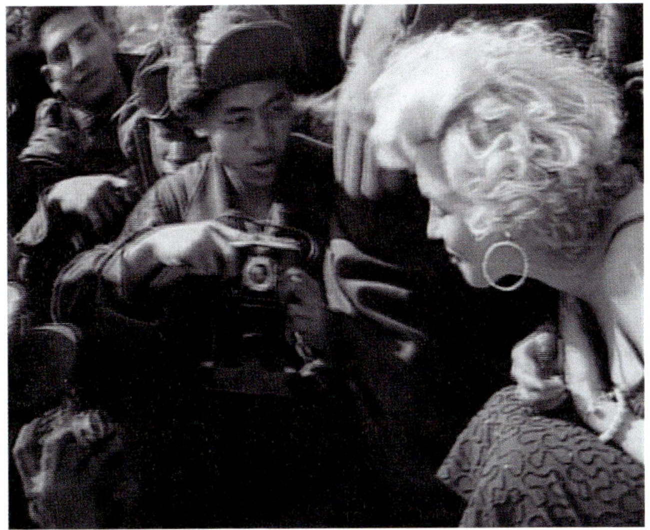

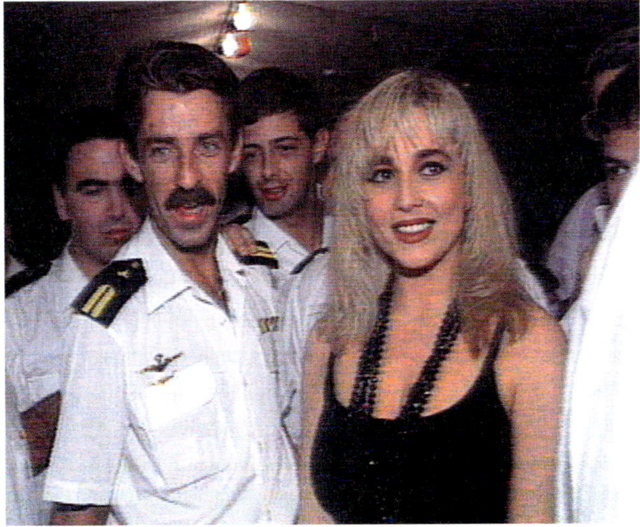

Many regular armies send performers to entertain the
troops while they are at the front, in order to alleviate
the tension, sense of disorientation and boredom, and take
their minds off the drama which is to unfold.

Marilyn Monroe performing for the United States' troops in Korea, 1954
Pictures from Footage Farm, London

Marta Sánchez performing for the Spanish troops stationed in Iraq during the first
Gulf War, 1991
Televisió de Catalunya, Sant Joan Despí

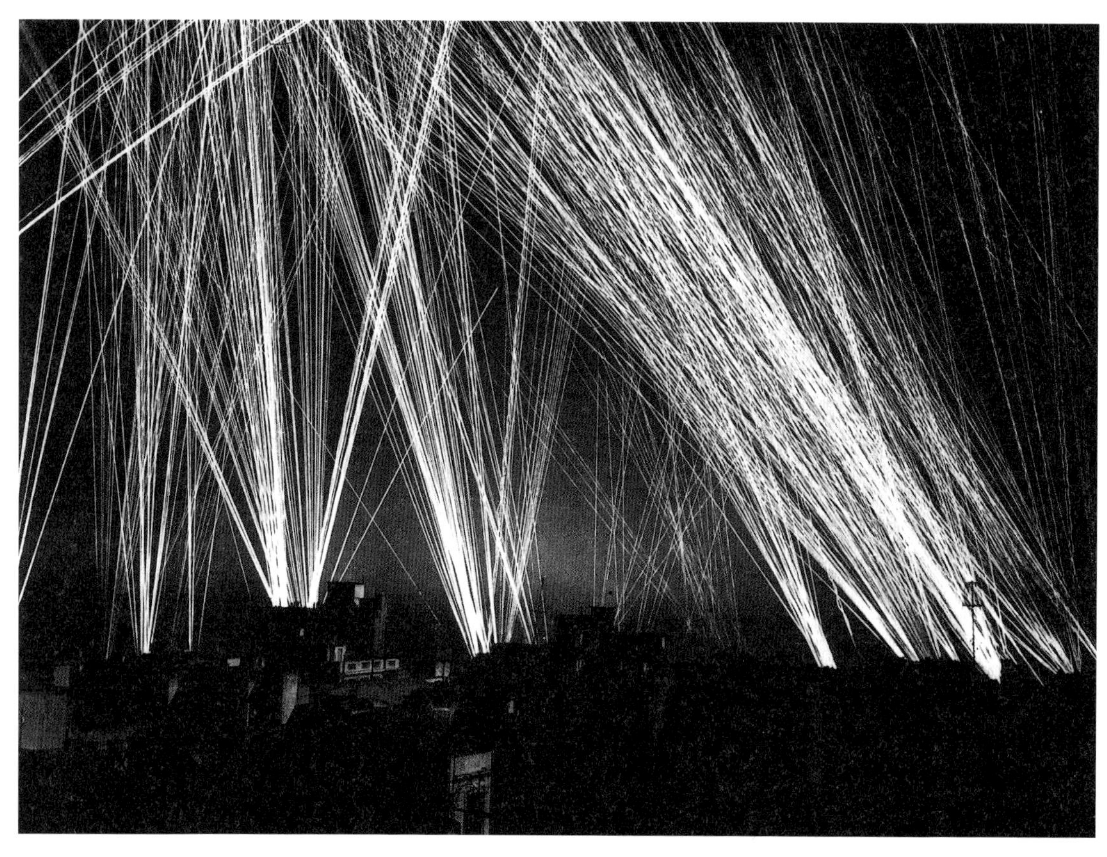

W. R. WILSON, Ack-ack fire during an air raid
on Algiers by the Nazis, 1943
National Archives, Washington

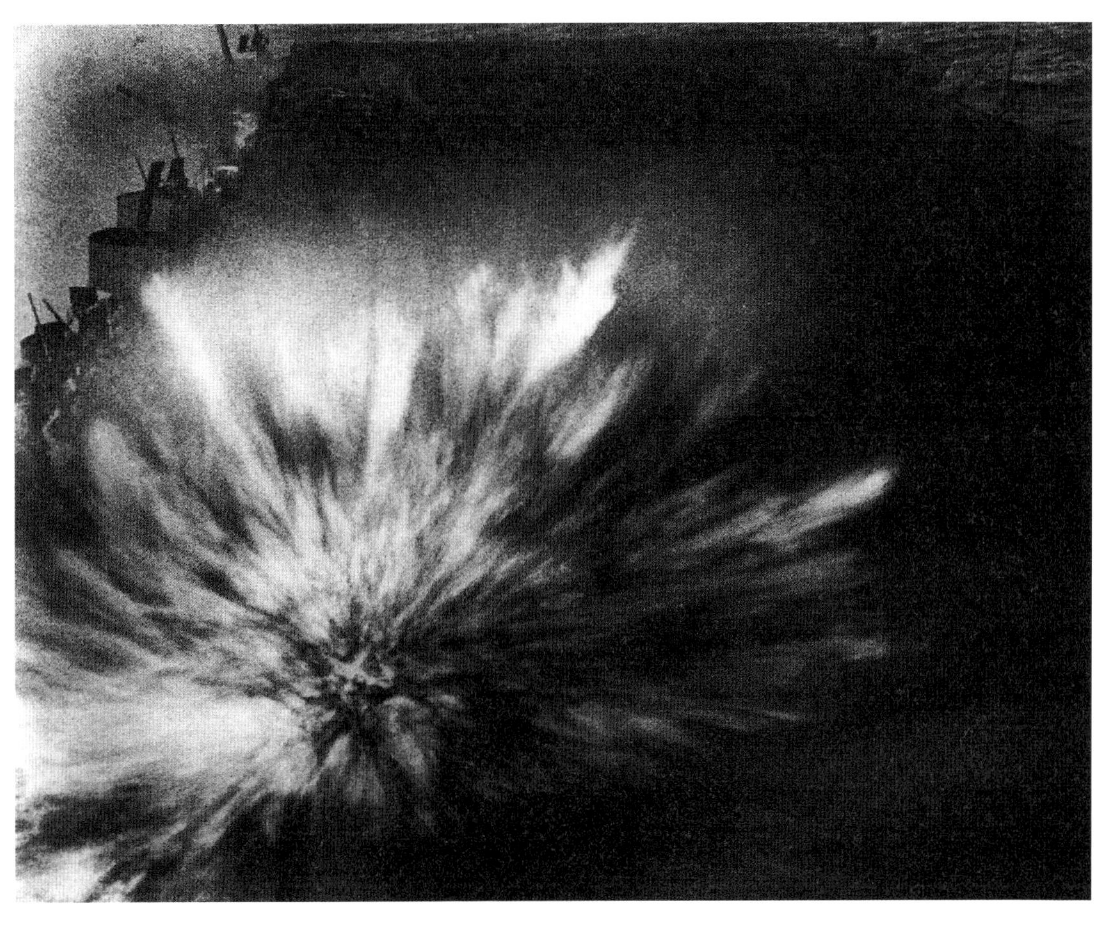

ROBERT FREDERICK, Japanese attack on the USS
Enterprise, the photographer lost his life while taking the
picture, afternoon of 24 August 1942
National Archives, Washington

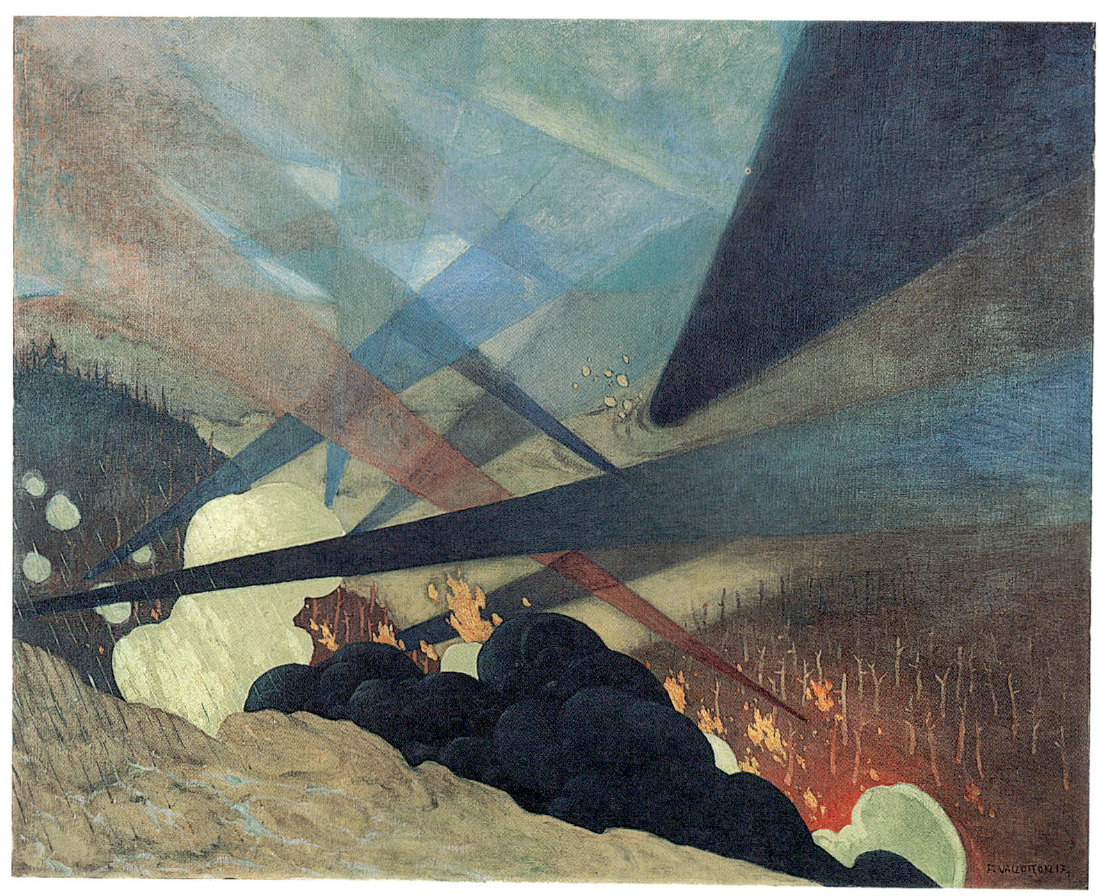

Vallotton said that "war always seeks its own image, its plastic expression".
He was not allowed to enlist in the French army and go to war because he
was 49 years old. However, he obtained official permission to visit the front
and painted this picture based on his experience, in which he combines
imagery with avant-garde experimentation.

FÉLIX VALLOTTON, Verdun, interpreted war painting,
coloured black, red and blue projections, destroyed lands,
clouds of gas, 1917
Oil on canvas, 114 x 146 cm
Musée de l'Armée, Paris

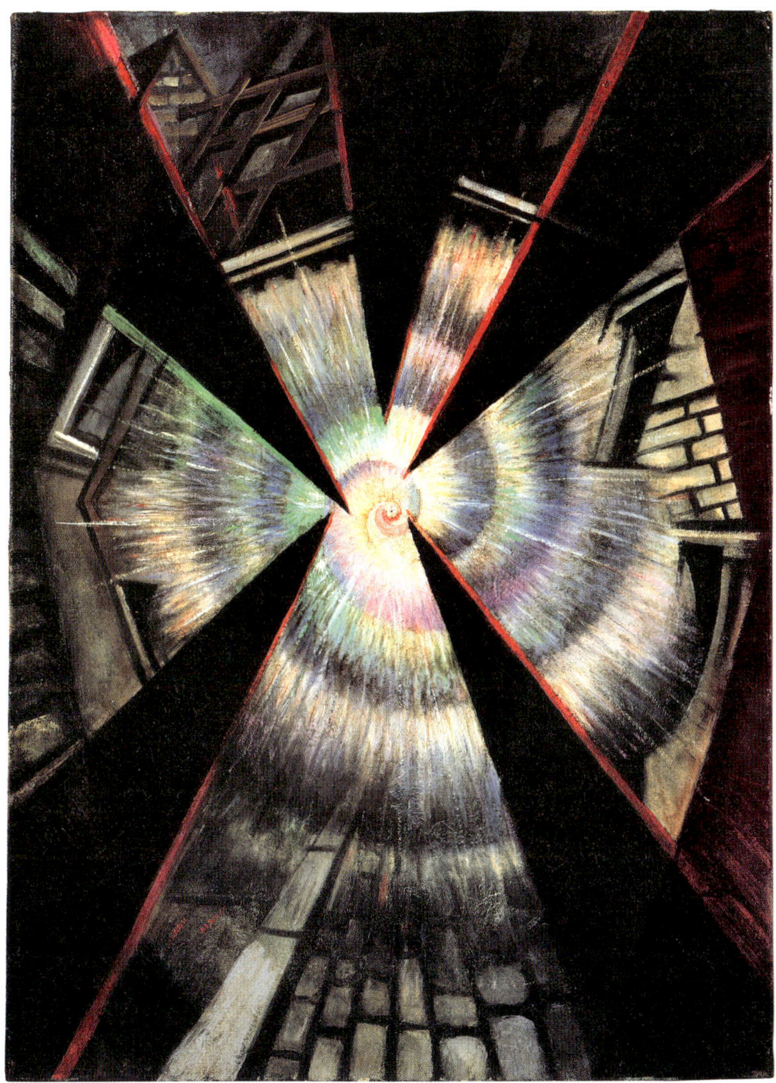

Nevinson, the only English follower of Marinetti, started out as a futurist.
He was an ambulance driver for the Red Cross and named official
war artist in 1917. The works prior to this appointment mainly focused on
the destruction and suffering of war. This is the last painting to use a
language akin to that of futurism.

CHRISTOPHER RICHARD WYNNE NEVINSON, Bursting shell, 1915
Oil on canvas, 76 x 56 cm
Tate Gallery, London

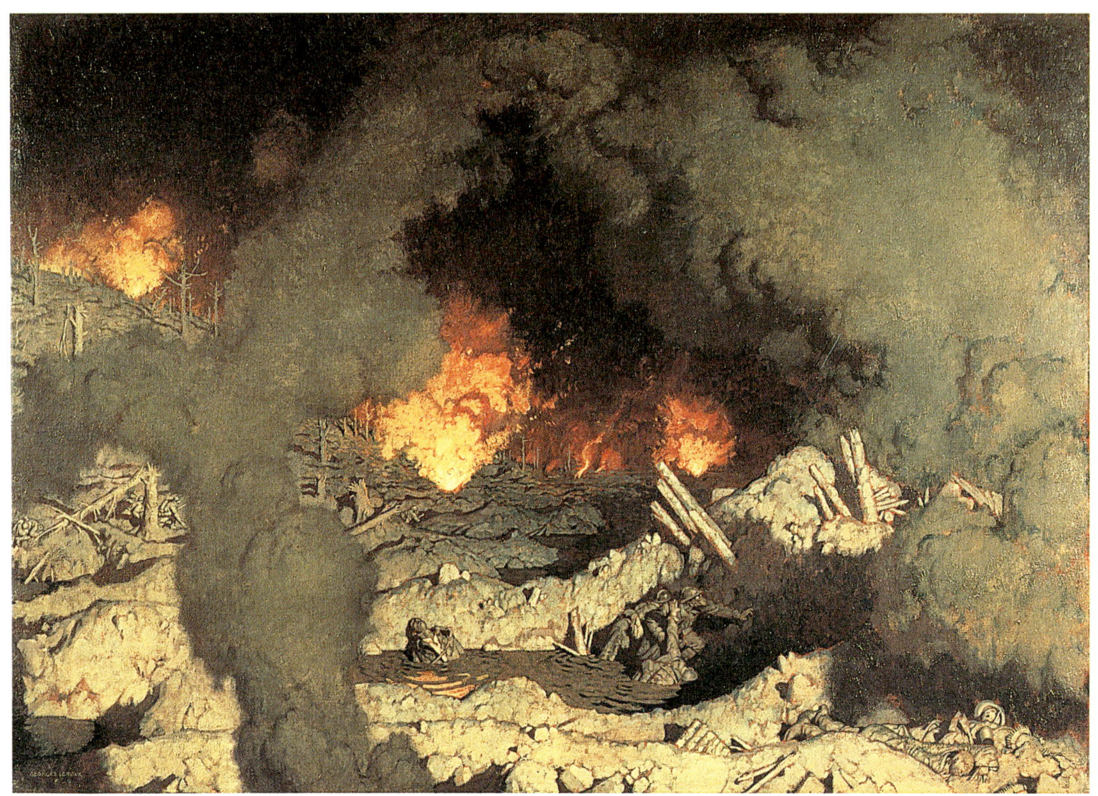

Leroux served in a camouflage unit in Northern France and Belgium during the First World War. On his way back from a reconnaissance mission he saw "a group of French soldiers sheltering in an enormous waterlogged shell crater". That same evening, he drew the sketch which he later used for this painting.

GEORGES LEROUX, Hell, 1916
Oil on canvas, 114.3 x 162 cm
Imperial War Museum, London

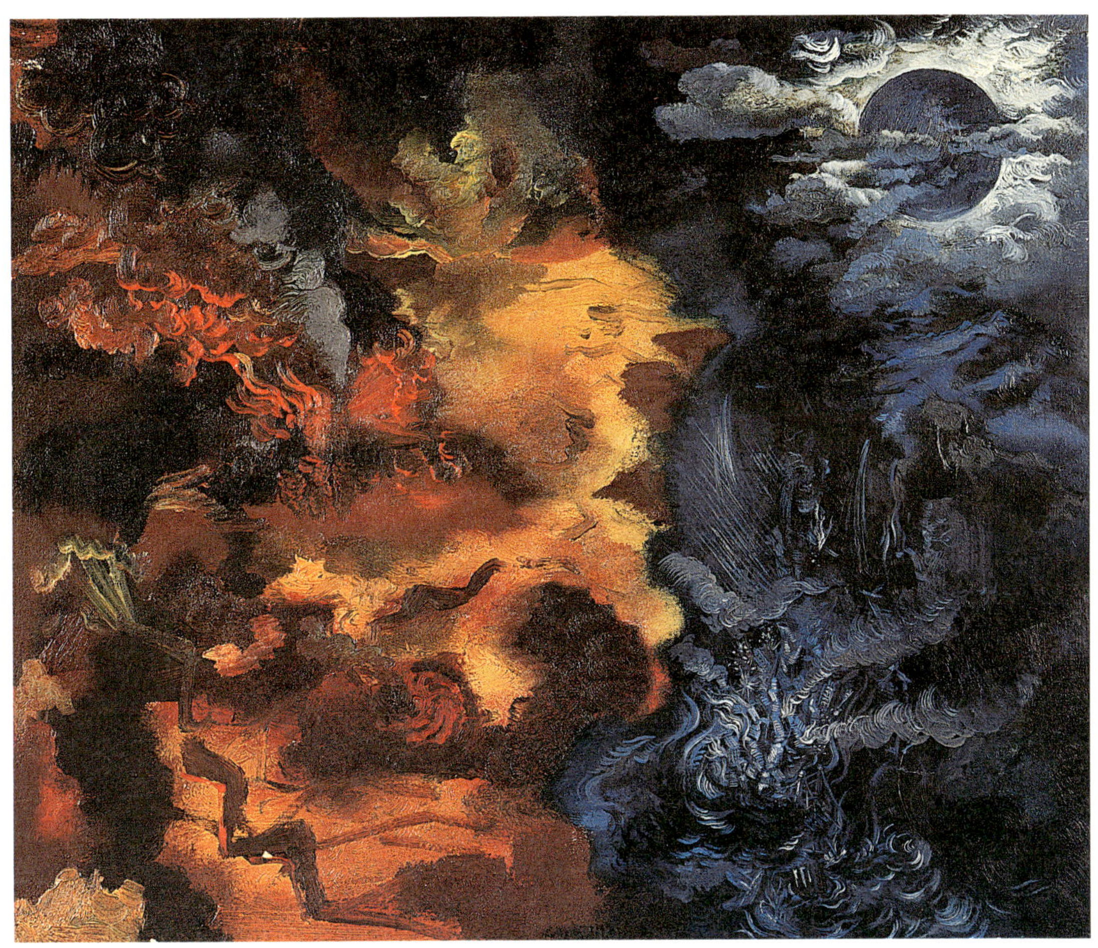

Groz's experiences of the First World War led him to predict
another imminent conflict during the period between the Wars.
This work was painted after he left for the United States.
One half shows fire and destruction and, the other half, a flood
with New York skyscrapers collapsing.

GEORGE GROSZ, Apocalyptic landscape, 1936
Oil on board, 50.5 x 61 cm
George Grosz Estate, Courtesy of Ralph
Jentsch, Capri

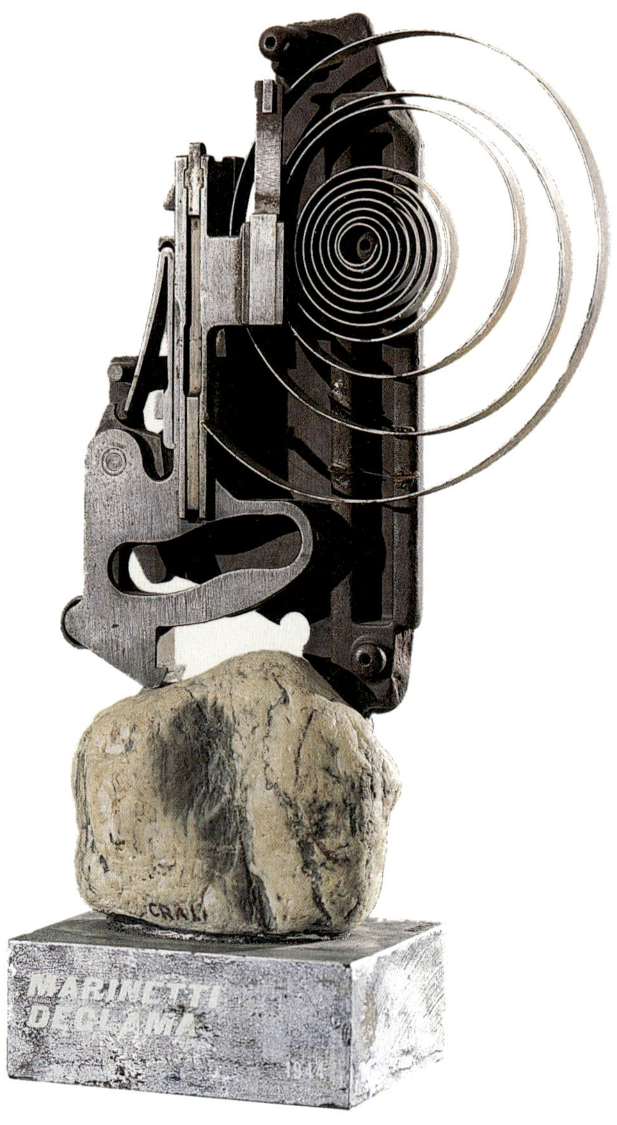

The futurists viewed war as the greatest manifestation of restorative energy. Crali is particularly well known for his works of *aeropittura*, or aeropainting, which focused on the theme of aviation. This work pays tribute to the founder of futurism and his glorification of war.

TULLIO CRALI, Marinetti declaiming the war, 1944
Stone and metal, 38 x 23 x 10.5 cm
Museo di Arte Moderna e Contemporanea di Trento e
Rovereto, VAF Foundation, Rovereto

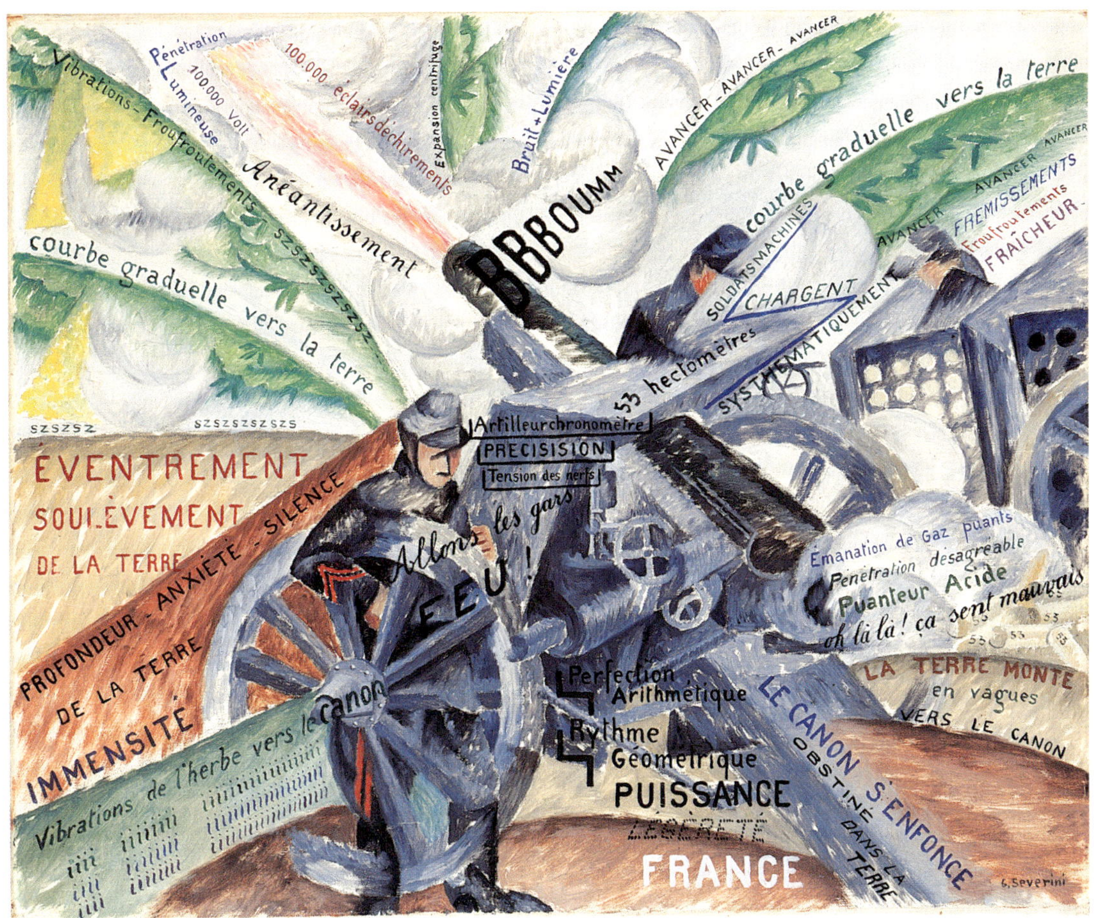

The futurists' interest in action and machinery
made warfare into one of their core themes.
In this emblematic work, Severini uses words to
depict dynamism and noise.

GINO SEVERINI, Gun in action, 1915
Oil on canvas, 50 x 60 cm
Museo di Arte Moderna e Contemporanea di
Trento e Rovereto, VAF Foundation, Rovereto

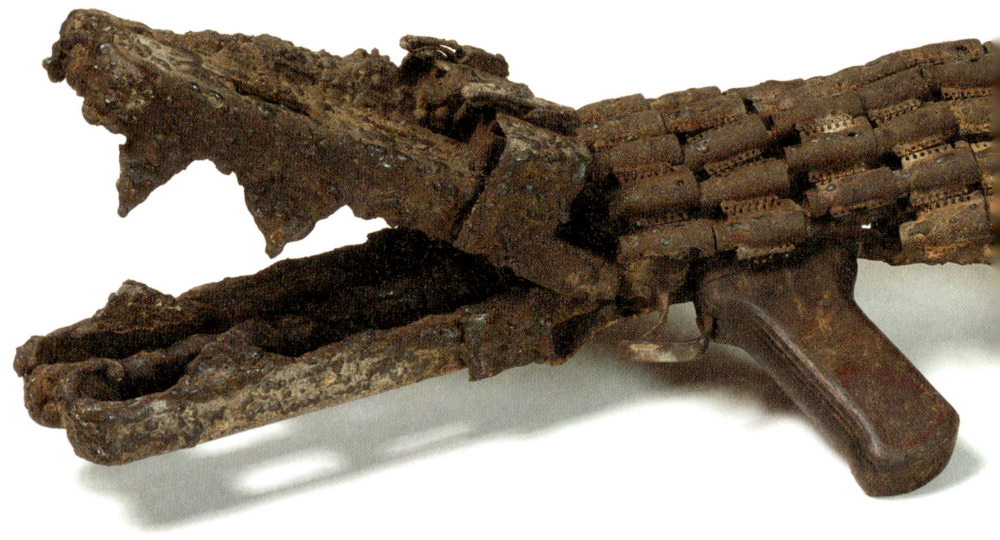

The project "Transforming Arms into Ploughshares", launched
by the Christian Council of Mozambique, has withdrawn over
200,000 weapons from circulation in exchange for tools since the
1992 peace agreement, following 16 years of civil war. Delgado's
work was first shown at the Christian Aid exhibition "Swords into
ploughshares: Transforming arms into art", held in London from
18th January to 3rd February 2002.

HUMBERTO DELGADO, Crocodile, c. 2000
Wood and metal, 18 x 20 x 70 cm
Imperial War Museum, London

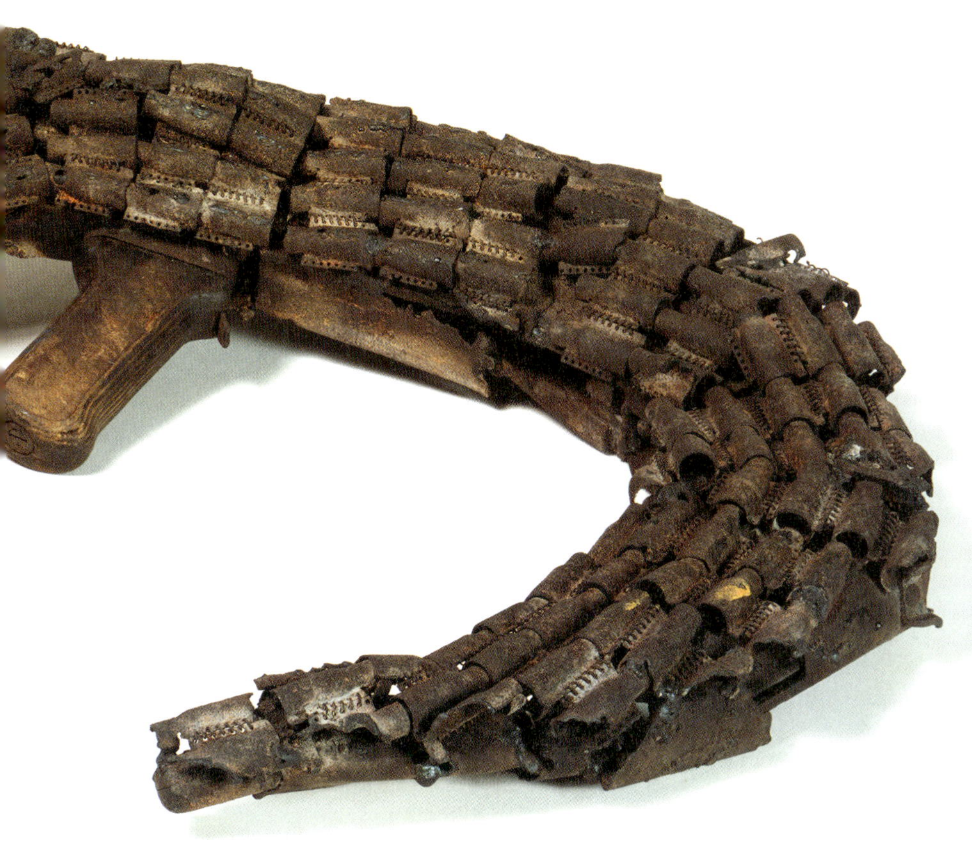

The success of the weapon collection scheme inspired
the initiative of raising funds for the programme through
the works produced by the artists from the Mozambique
Núcleo de Arte group using pieces of recycled weapons.
In this way, these instruments of battle, which bear
witness to the experience of war, have been fashioned
into art for peace.

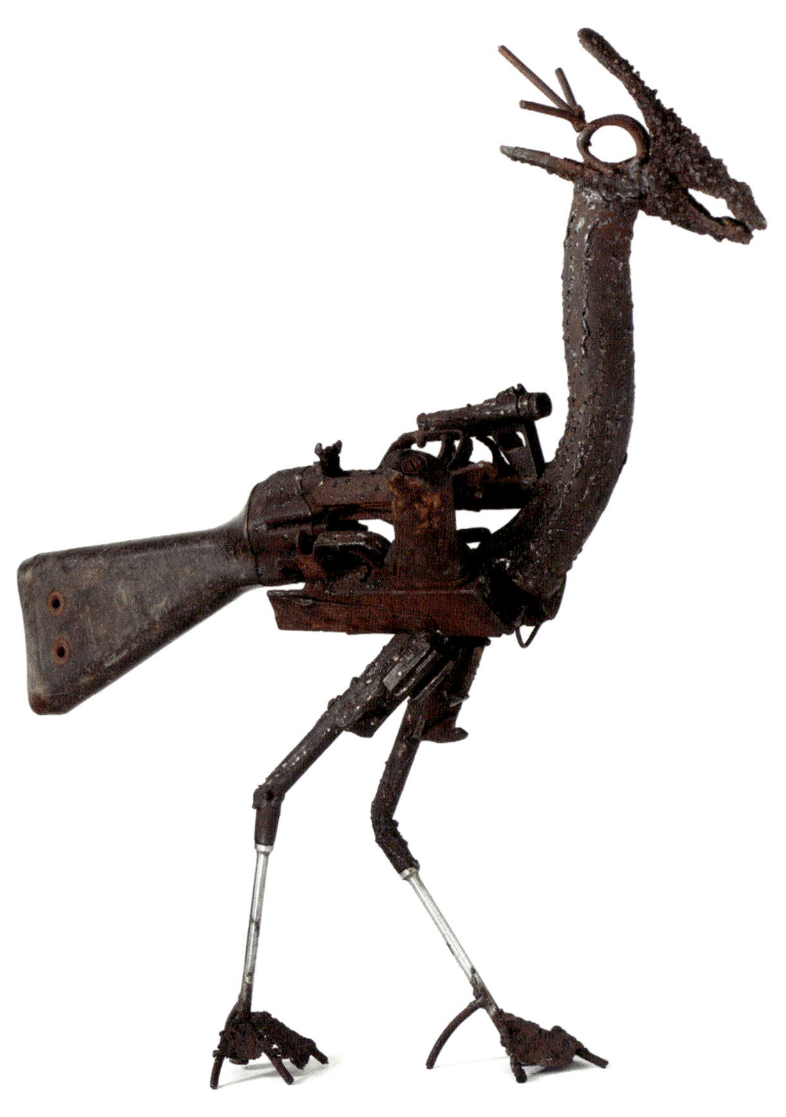

FIEL DOS SANTOS, Bird that wants to survive, *c.* 2000
Made from dismantled weapons, 67 x 28 x 65 cm
Royal Armouries Museum, Leeds

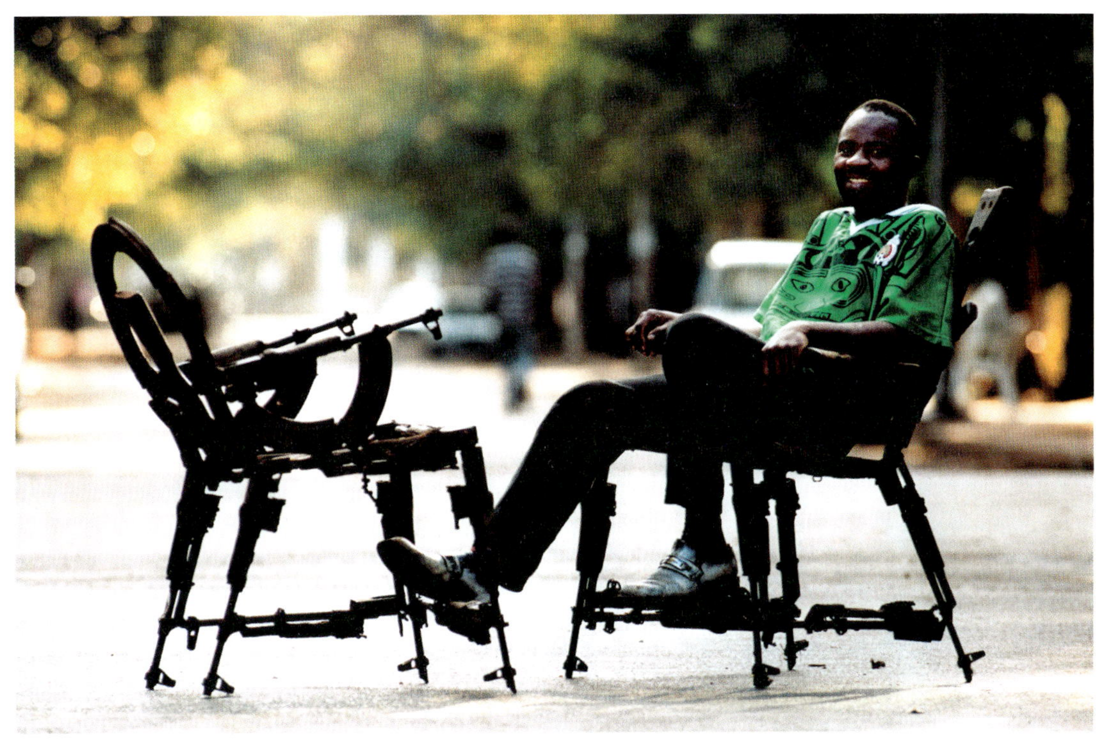

Although this use of weapons is a symbol of the peace
which follows civil war, the Mozambican artist Kester evokes
the tradition of African thrones and chairs, which are often
decorated with the images of weapons as symbols of power.

KESTER, Chair / throne of weapons, *c.* 2000
Three Kalashnikov AKMs, four AK-47 weapons
and 14 pattern magazines, 92 x 53 x 74 cm
Royal Armouries Museum, Leeds

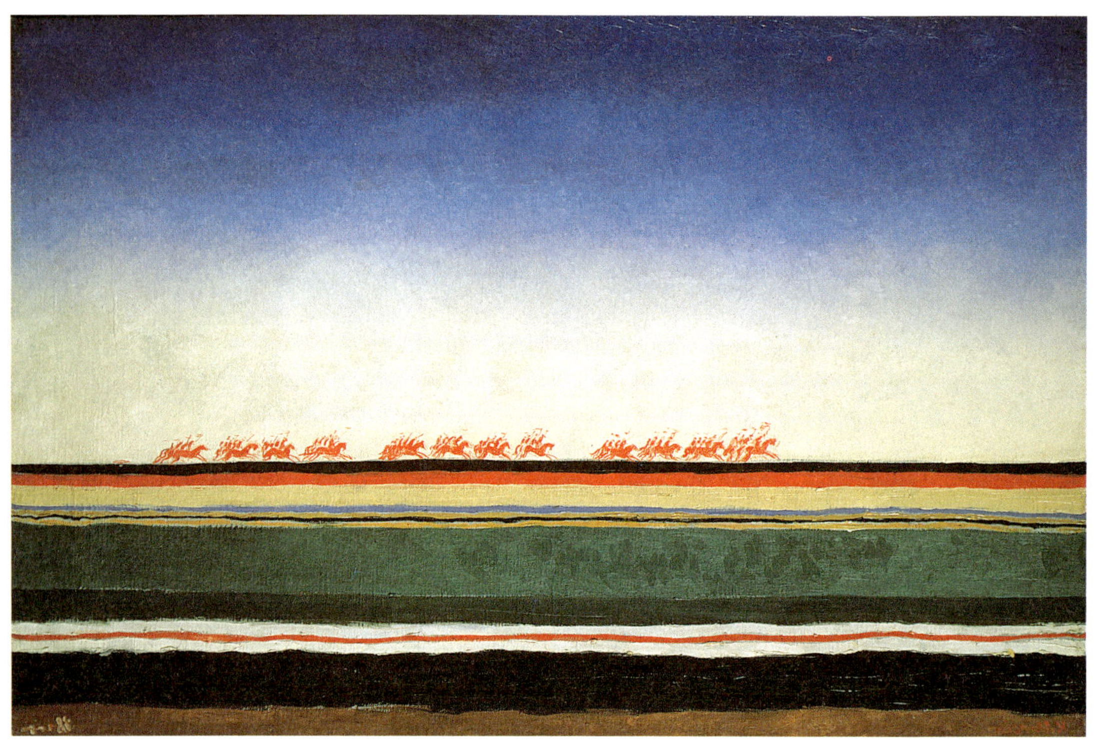

Under the hegemony of socialist realism, during
the last phase of his career, Malevich felt
compelled to imbue his works with referential
elements, which in this painting are condensed
into a lightly sketched epic motif.

KAZIMIR MALEVICH, Red cavalry, c. 1932
Oil on canvas, 91 x 140 cm
The State Russian Museum, Saint Petersburg

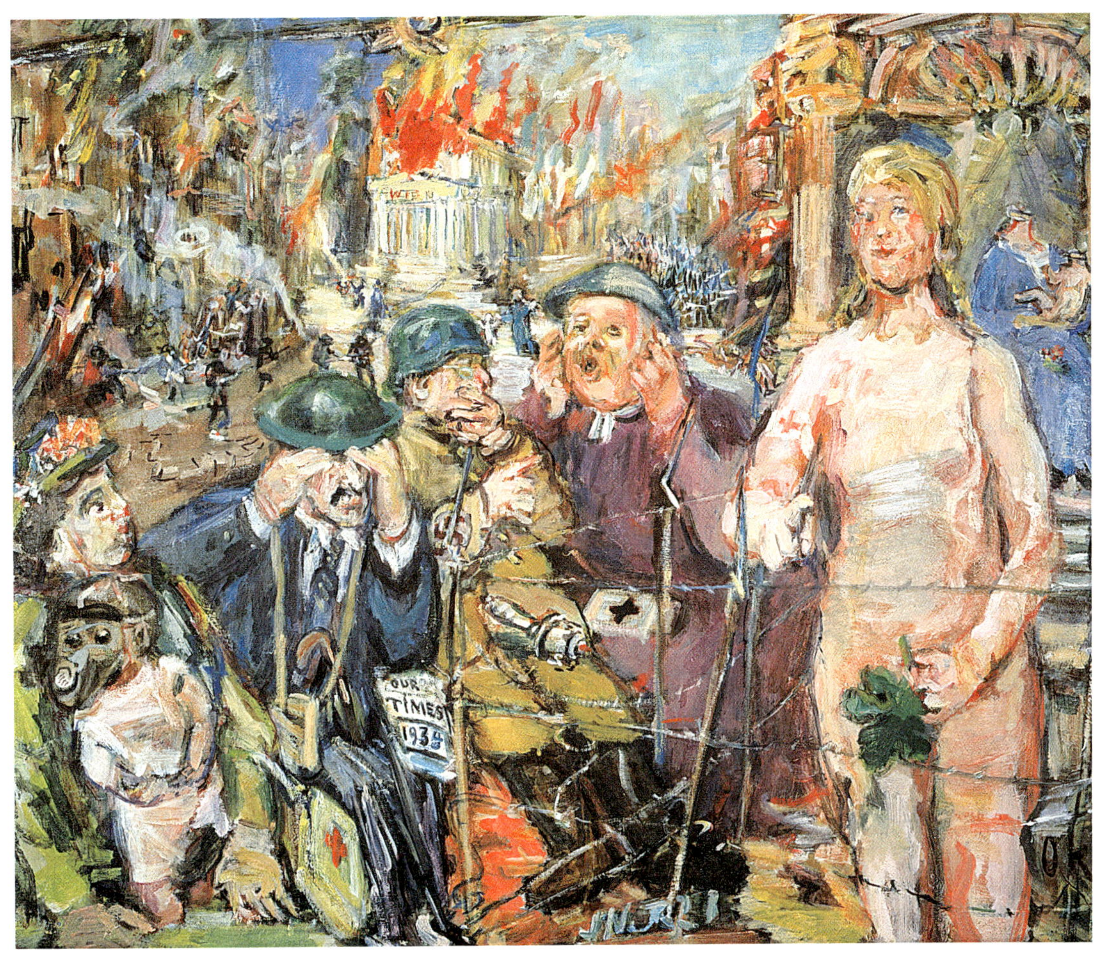

Kokoschka served in the Austrian cavalry during the First World War and was seriously wounded on the Russian front and in Italy, although he hardly ever depicted this experience in his works. The Nazis considered him an exponent of "degenerate art" and he went into exile in London, where he painted this condemnation of war as a protest against the annexation of Austria by Germany.

OSKAR KOKOSCHKA, Anschluss -
Alice in Wonderland, 1942
Oil on canvas, 63.5 x 76.5 cm
Wiener Städtische Allgemeine Versicherung
Aktiengesellschaft, Vienna

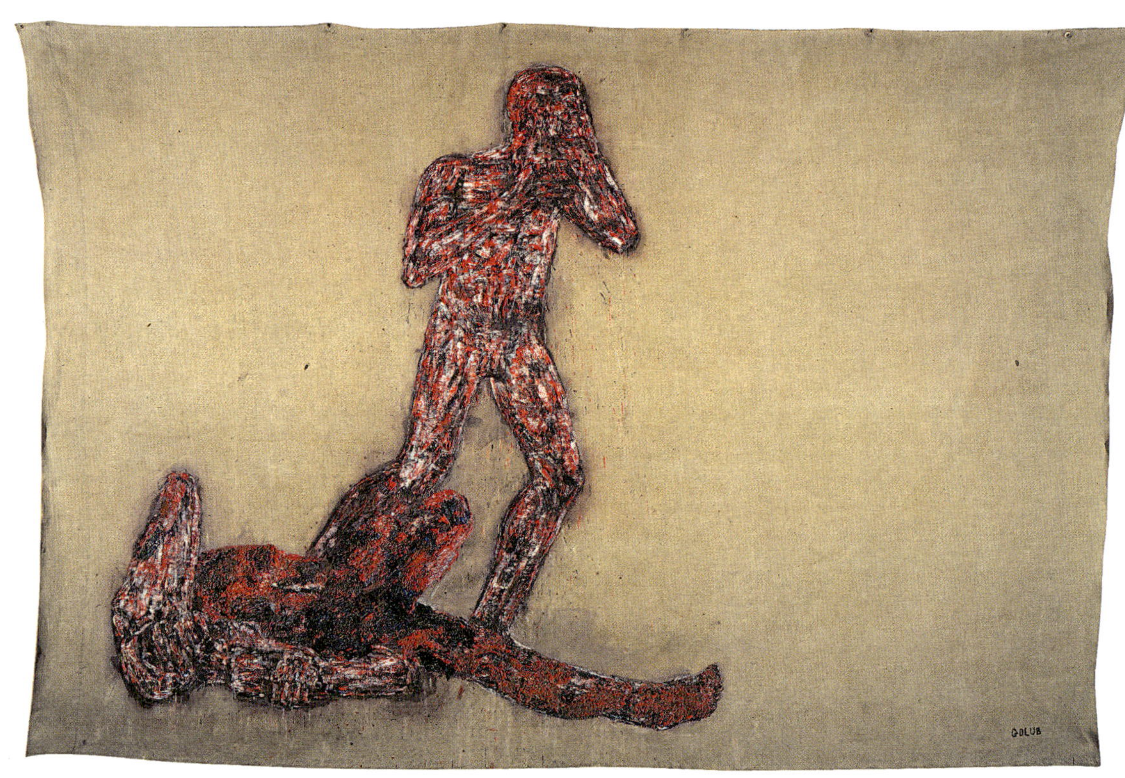

Golub is a figurative and activist painter who has challenged the dominant trends of abstract expressionism and pop art. His response to the Vietnam War was the series "Napalm" and "Vietnam": the latter a mural painting. The theme of violence reappears in his works of the eighties, devoted to terrorism and torture, and in the series "Mercenaries".

LEON GOLUB, Napalm III, 1969
Acrylic on canvas, 281 x 396 cm
Courtesy of Ronald Feldman Fine Arts, New York

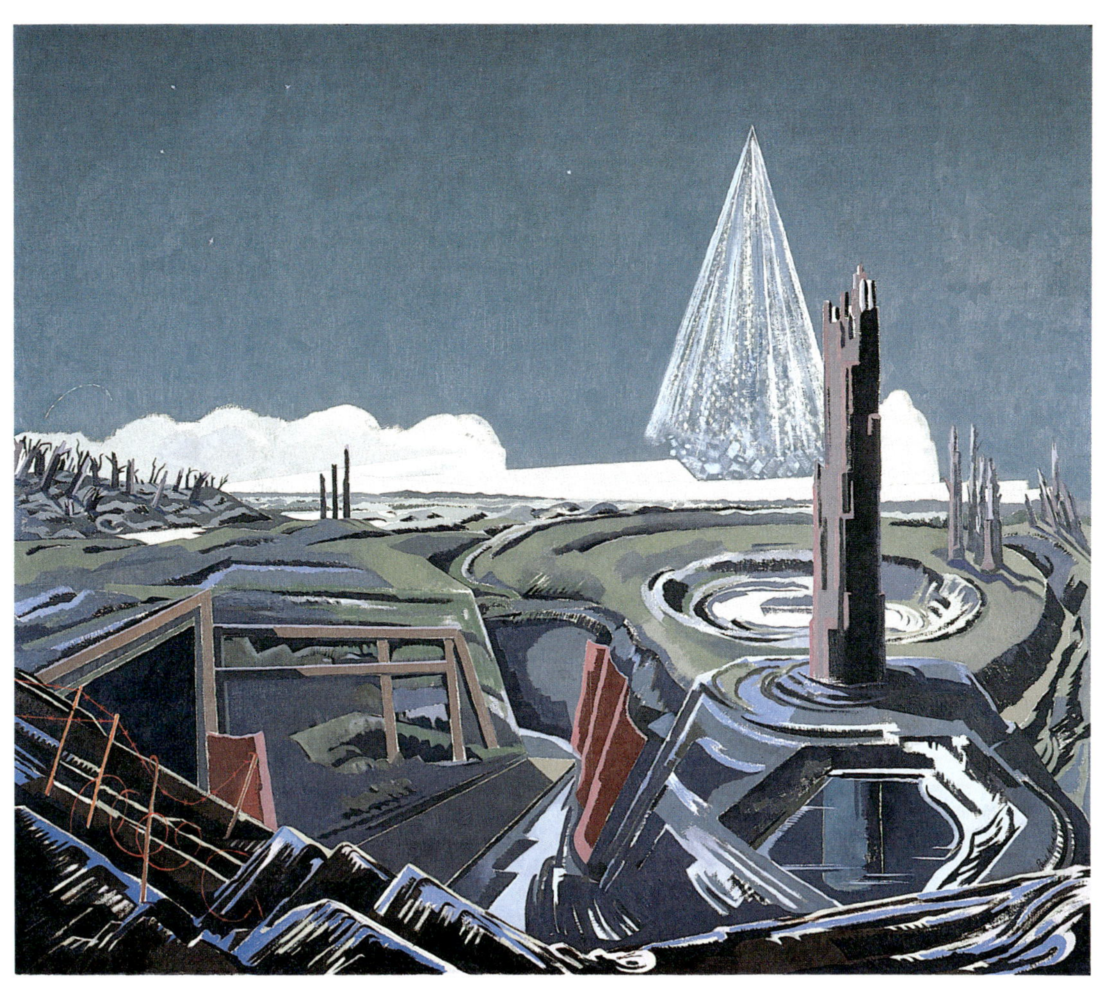

PAUL NASH, A night bombardment, 1919-1920
Oil on canvas, 182.9 x 214.4 x 4.4 cm
National Gallery of Canada, Ottawa.
Transfer from the Canadian War Memorials, 1921

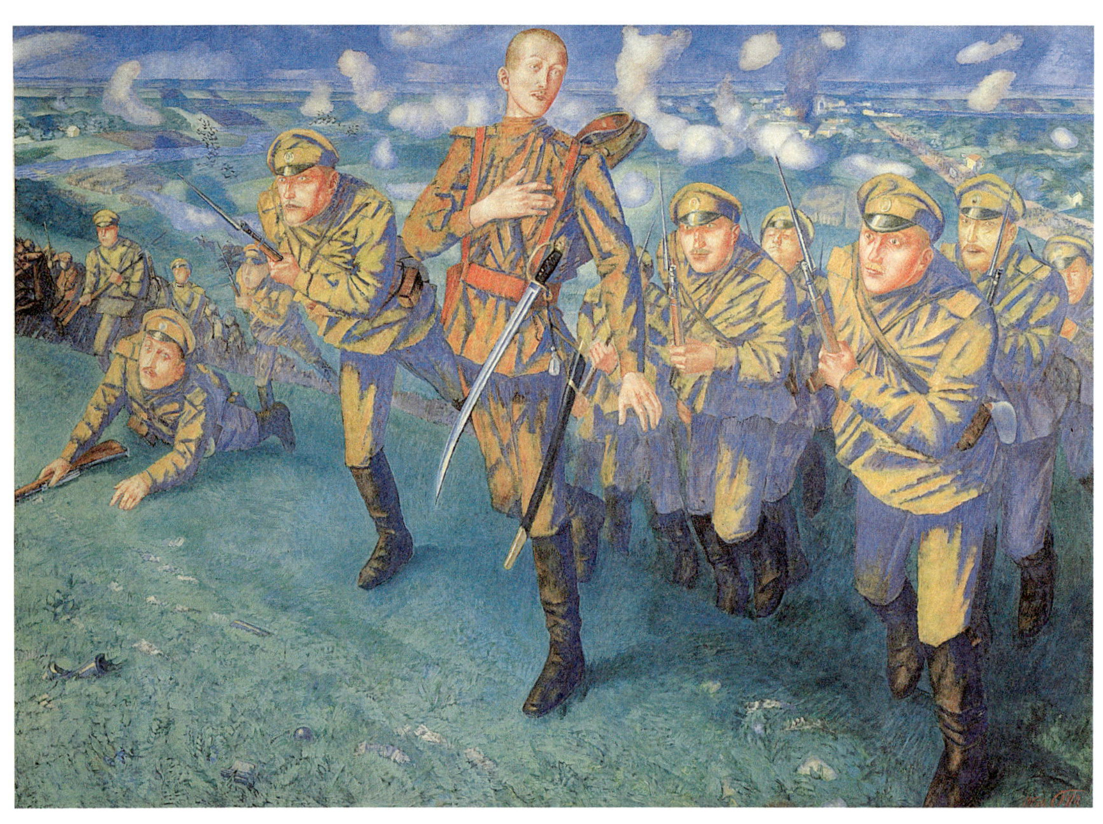

KUZMA PETROV-VODKIN, On the firing line, 1916
Oil on canvas, 196 x 275 cm
The State Russian Museum, Saint Petersburg

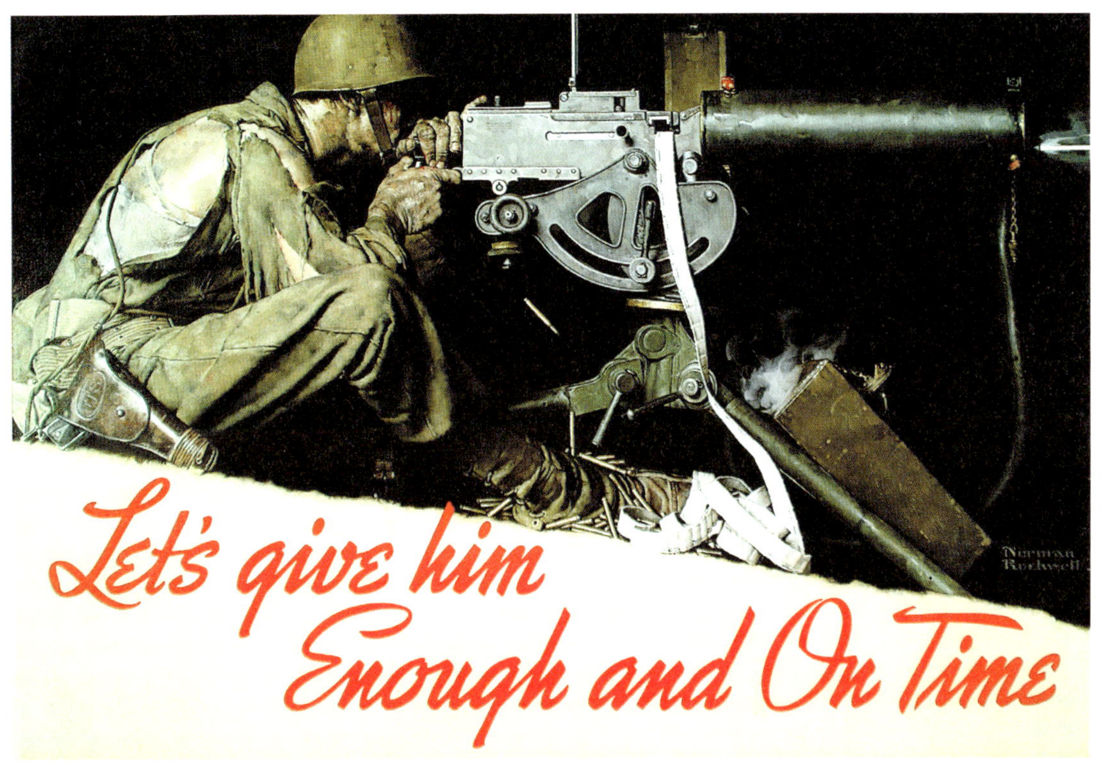

Known as an illustrator of traditional scenes from
American life, Rockwell was a marine during the First
World War and painted aircraft in camouflage colours.
During the Second World War, he played an active role
in the propaganda campaign with his posters.

NORMAN ROCKWELL, Let's give him enough and on time, 1942
Oil on canvas, 96.5 x 142.2 cm
National Museum of the US Army, Army Art Collection, Washington

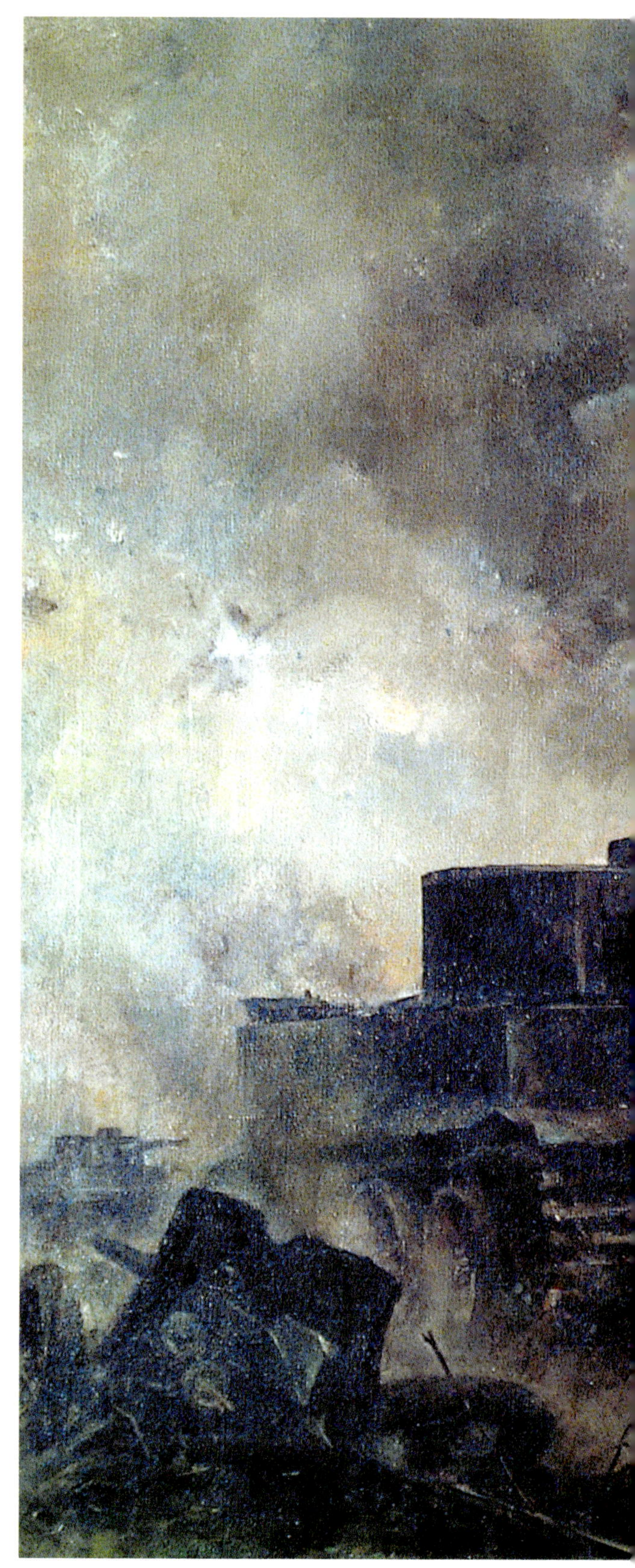

RUDOLF LIPUS, Panzer attack - East front, 1944
Oil on canvas, 78.1 x 89 cm
National Museum of the US Army, Army Art
Collection, Washington

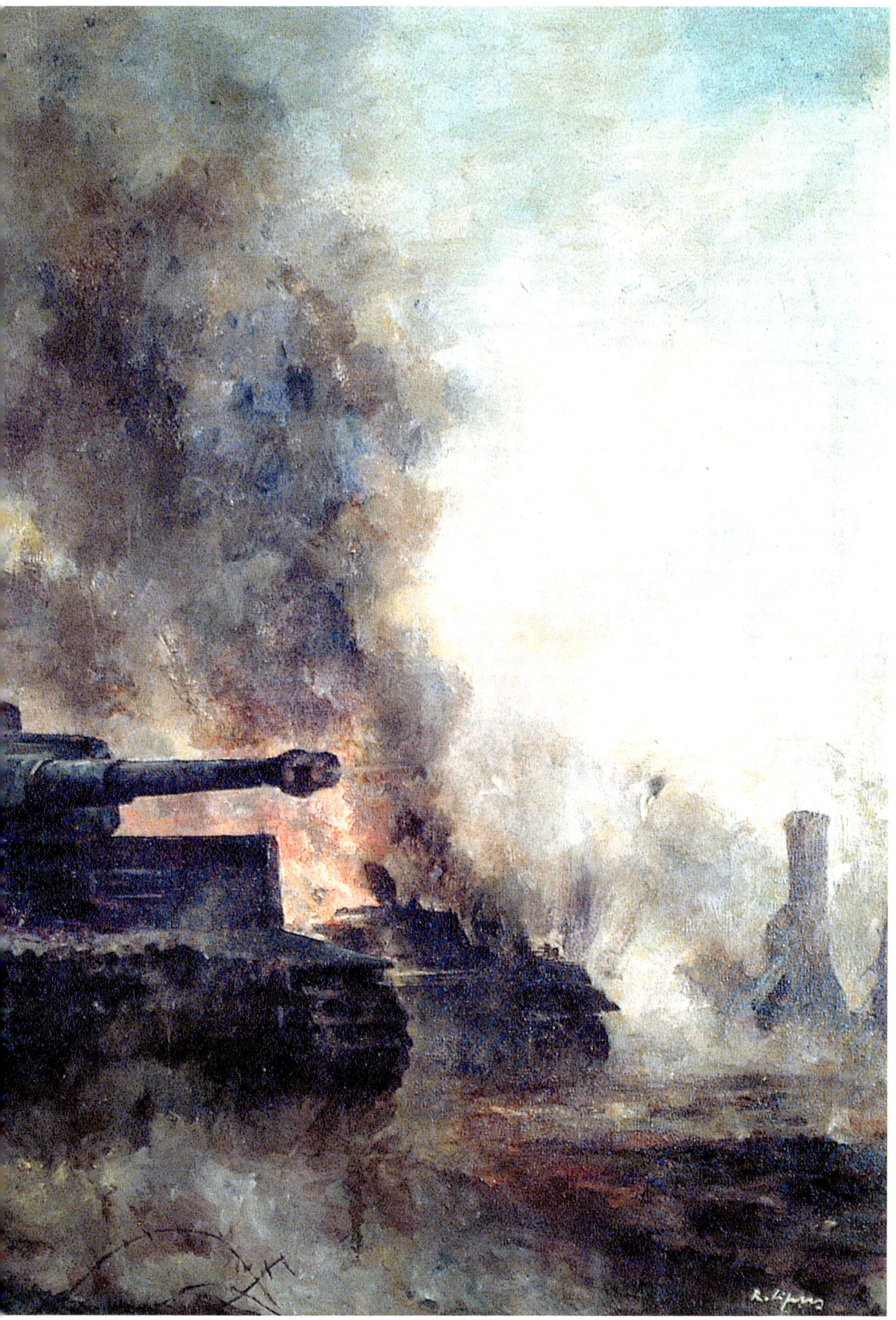

ALEXANDER ALEXANDROVICH DEINEKA, A shot-down ace, 1943
Oil on canvas, 283 x 188 cm
The State Russian Museum, Saint Petersburg

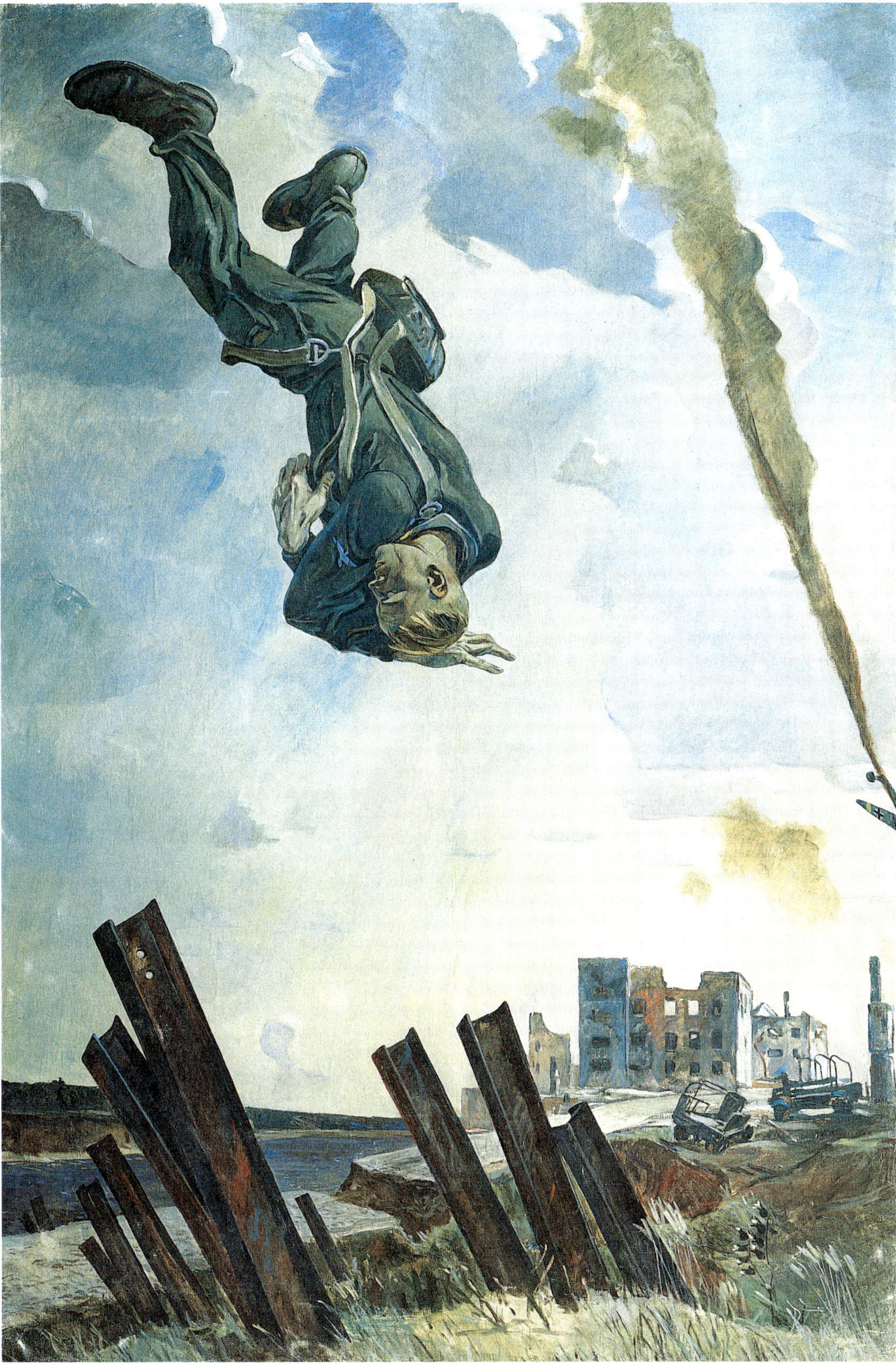

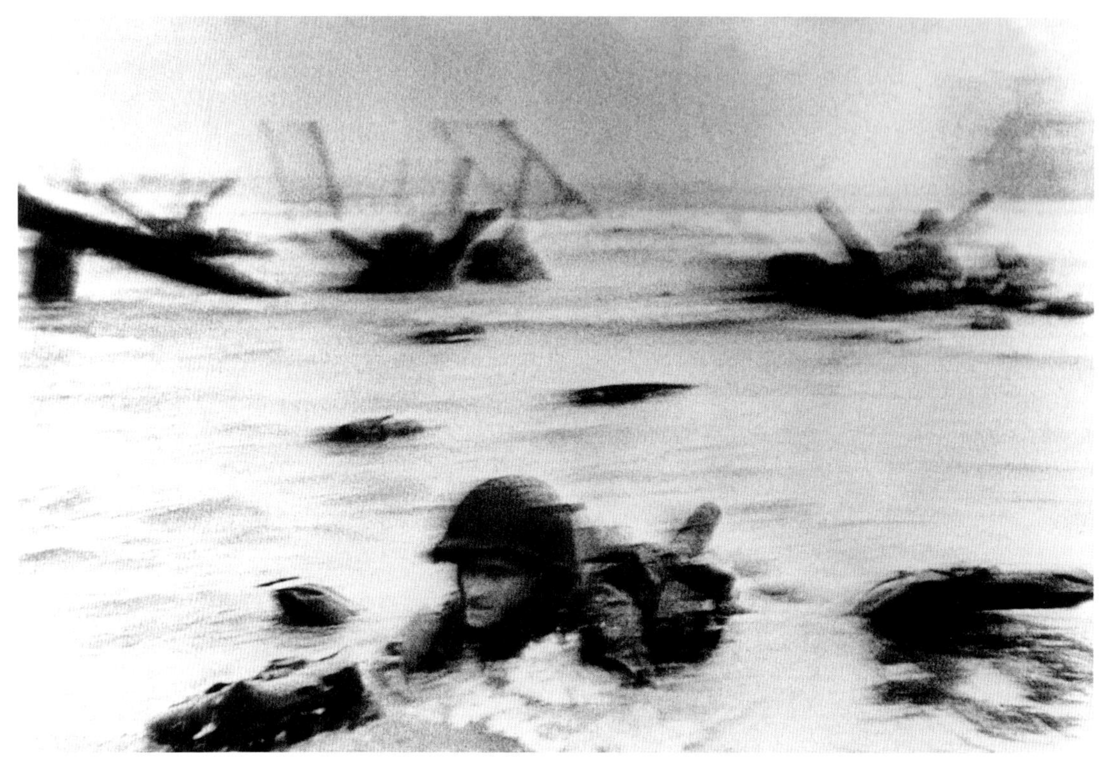

Capa was with the first soldiers to land on the Normandy beaches on D-Day. After shooting the rolls of film on his two cameras, his hands were shaking so much that he was unable to reload them, and he had to be taken from the beach on a hospital barge. Back in London, there was such a rush to send the material to *Life* magazine, that the negatives were overheated during the drying process and only nine of the 72 photographs survived. The person responsible was Larry Burrows, who later became a photographer in Vietnam.

Capa said that these photographs were "a cut-out of the whole event which will show more of the real truth of the affair to someone who was not there than the whole scene".

ROBERT CAPA, The first wave of American troops lands at dawn,
Omaha Beach, Normandy, 6 June 1944
Robert Capa / Magnum Photos / Contacto

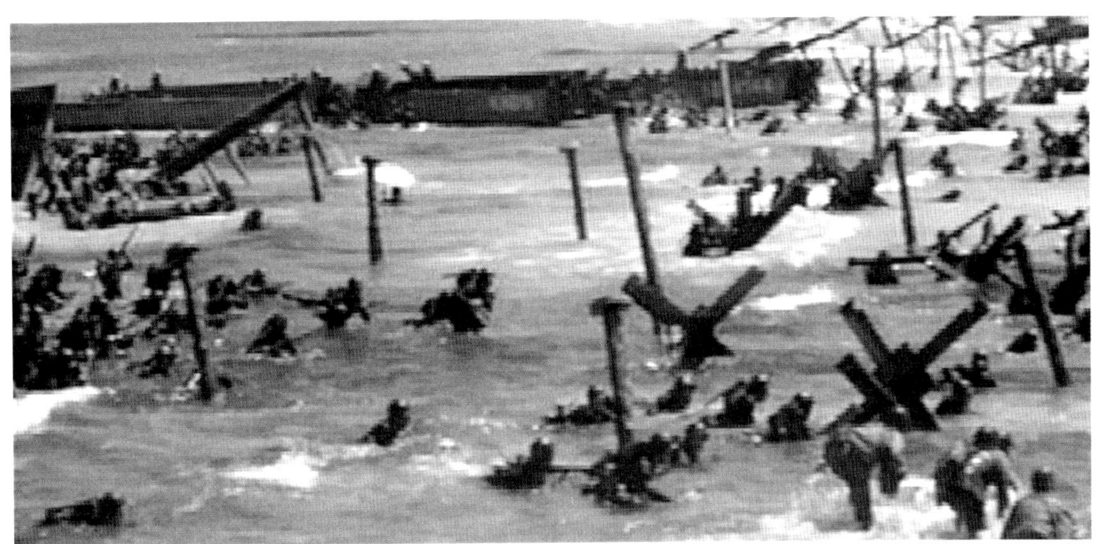

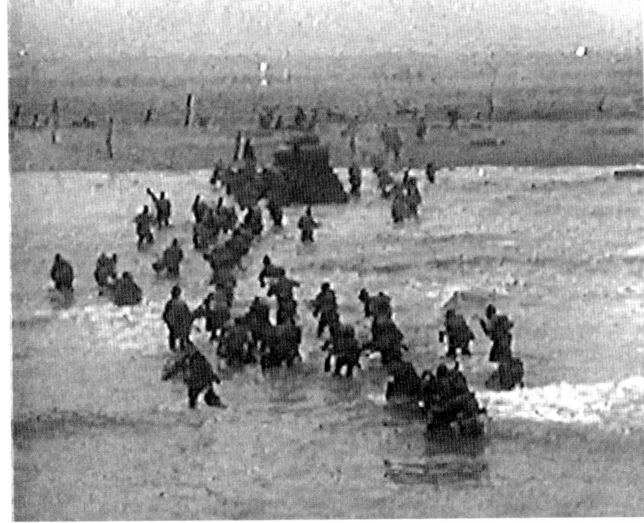

DARRYL F. ZANUCK, *The longest day*, USA, 1962
Film, 178'

Allies land in France, USA, June 1944
Documentary
Fox Movietone News, New York

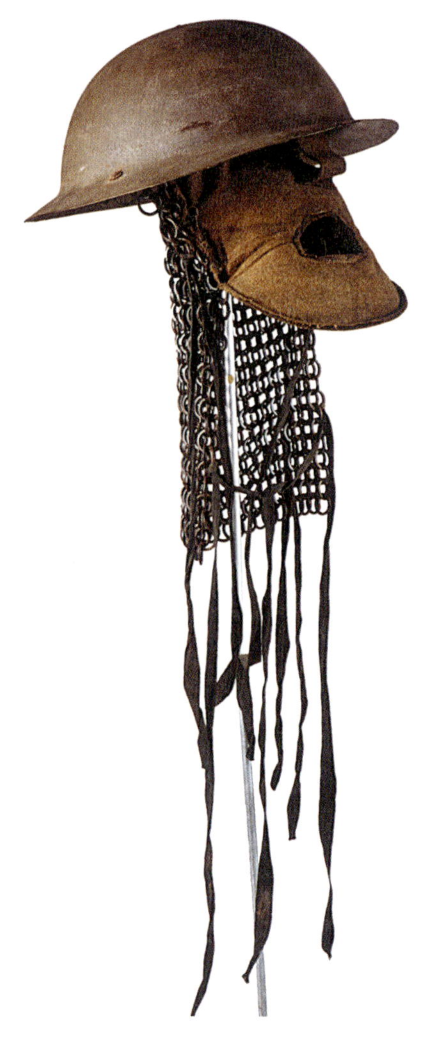

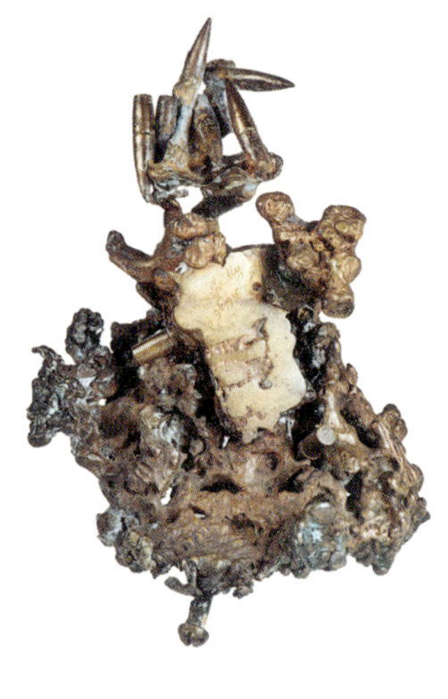

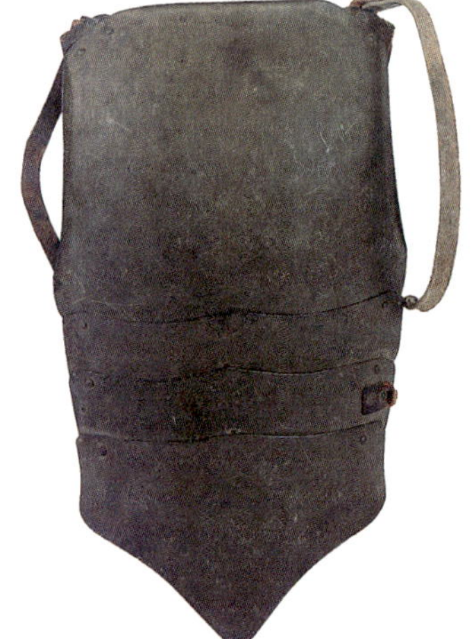

Some objects associated with the violence of war have an unusual
appearance which, seen out of context, invites us to appreciate
their almost sculptural nature, despite the fact that our recognition
of their function or past remains disturbing.

British machine gunners' helmet, 1916-1918
Steel, fabric, 52 x 39 cm diameter
Historial de la Grande Guerre, Péronne (Somme)

Solidified mass of melted rifle bullets, remains
of the explosion of a munitions train in Cerisy-Gailly
station (Somme), 6 September 1916
Copper, 14 x 17 x 13 cm
Historial de la Grande Guerre, Péronne (Somme)

US Army abdominal shield used by sentries and
comprising three movable plates, 1917
Iron and leather straps, 56 x 37 x 7.5 cm, 6 kg
Historial de la Grande Guerre, Péronne (Somme)

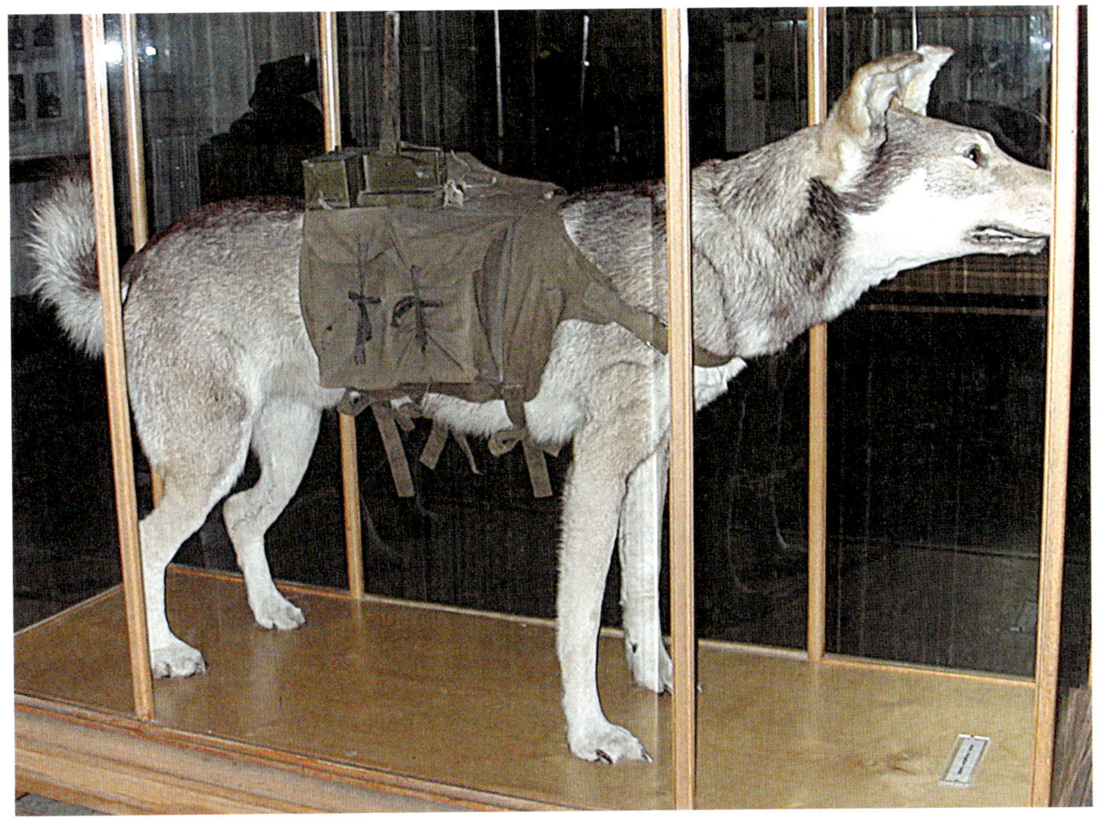

These dogs were trained to eat under army
tanks, the idea being that they would later
be fitted with backpack bombs and then be
concealed under enemy tanks.

Bomb dog, 1939-1945
Military Historical Museum, Saint Petersburg

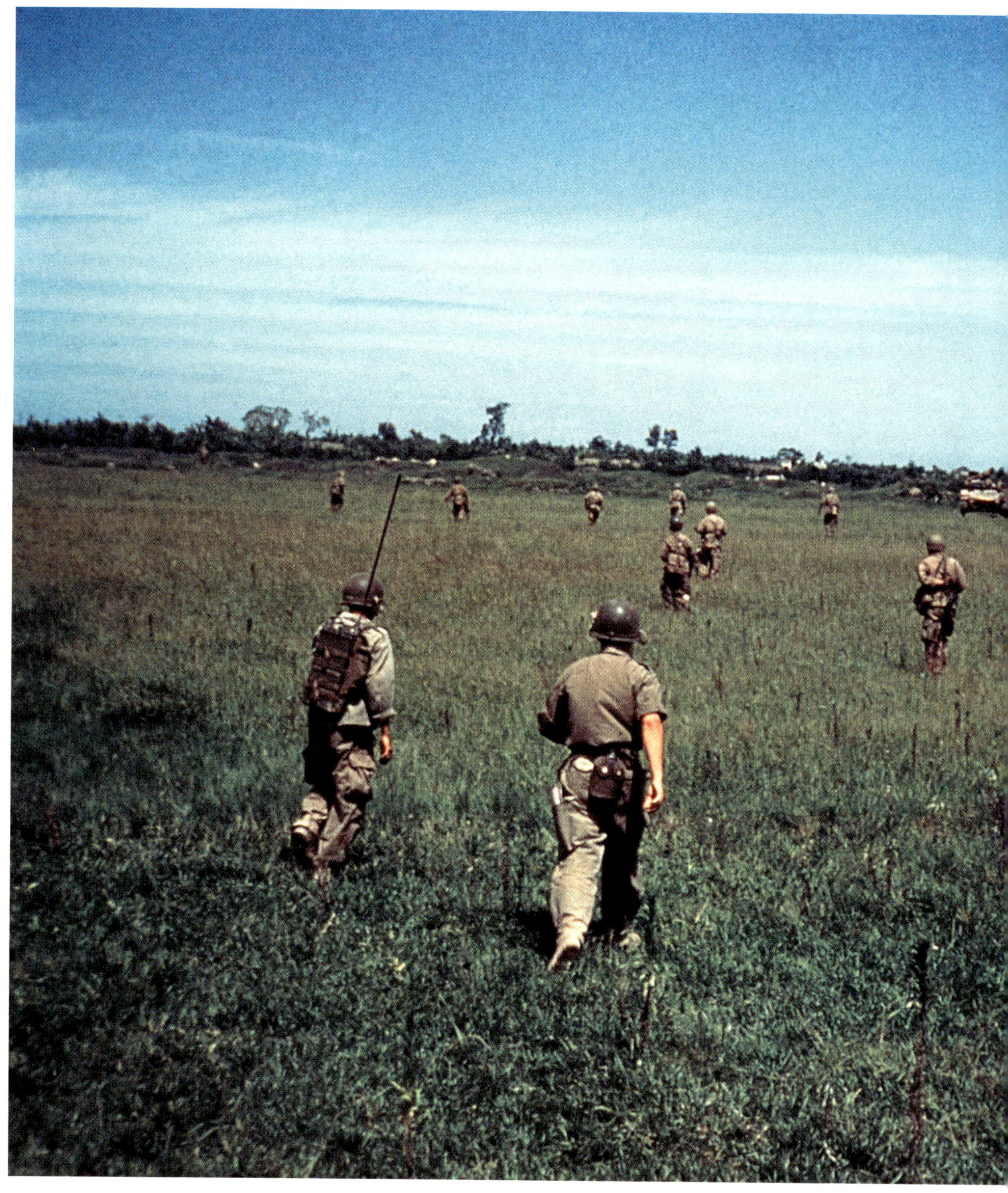

Capa bore witness to many wars with his camera, from
the Spanish Civil War and the Second World War, to the war
in Indochina, in which he died when he stepped on a mine.
This is the last photograph he took before he died.

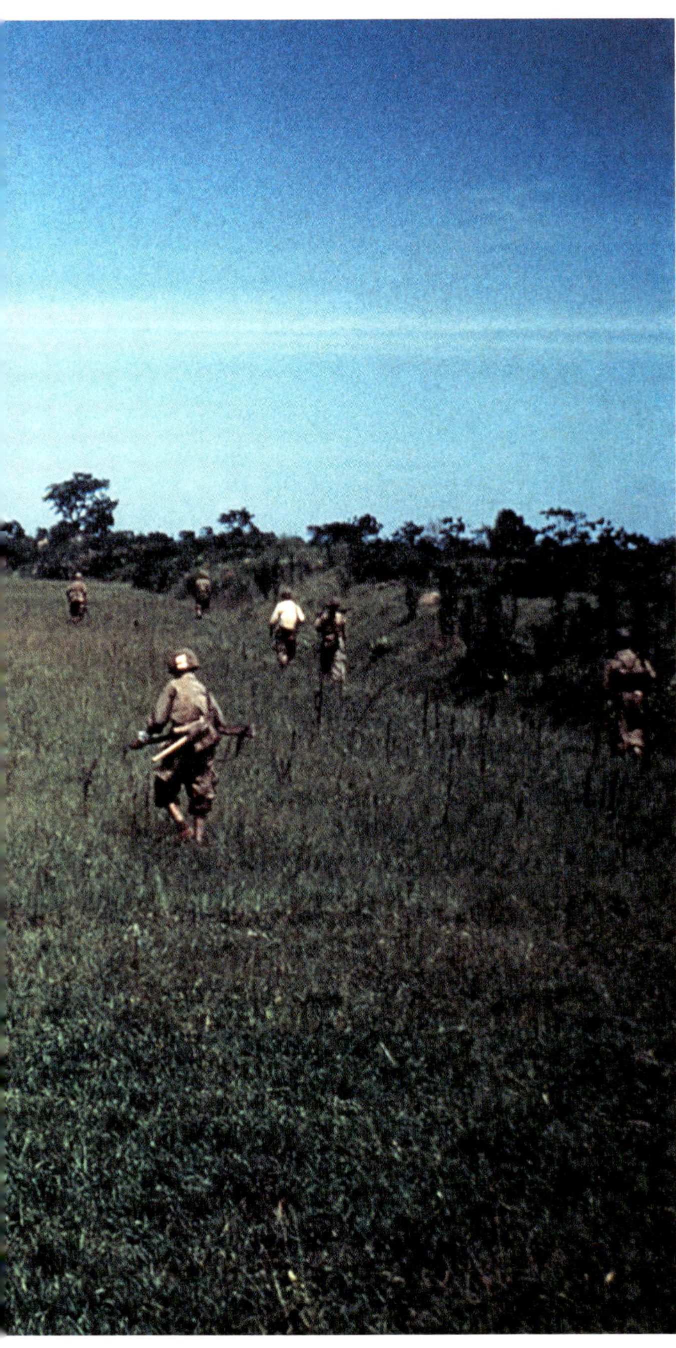

ROBERT CAPA, Vietnamese troops advancing between
Namdinh and Thaibinh, Indochina, 25 May 1954
Robert Capa / Magnum Photos / Contacto

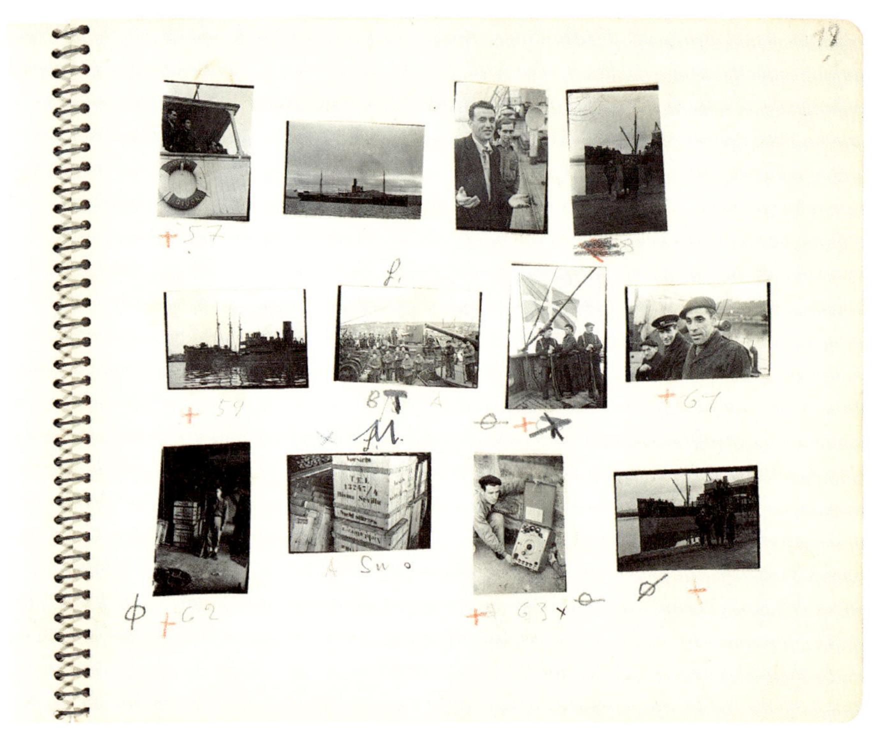

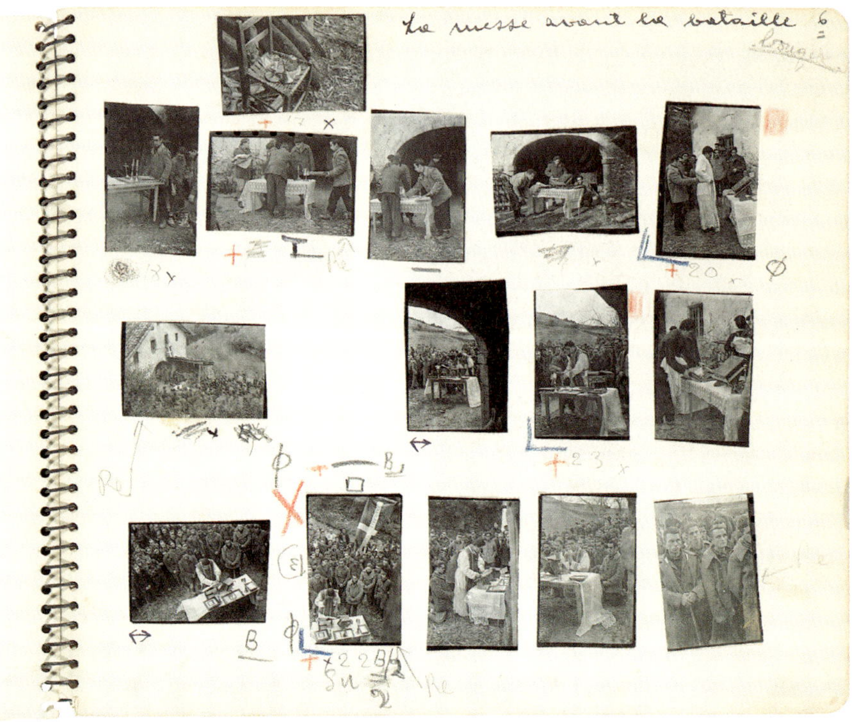

The original notebook with the contacts for Capa's
reports in Spain (1937). It was one of the books seized
by the French police, probably in 1940.

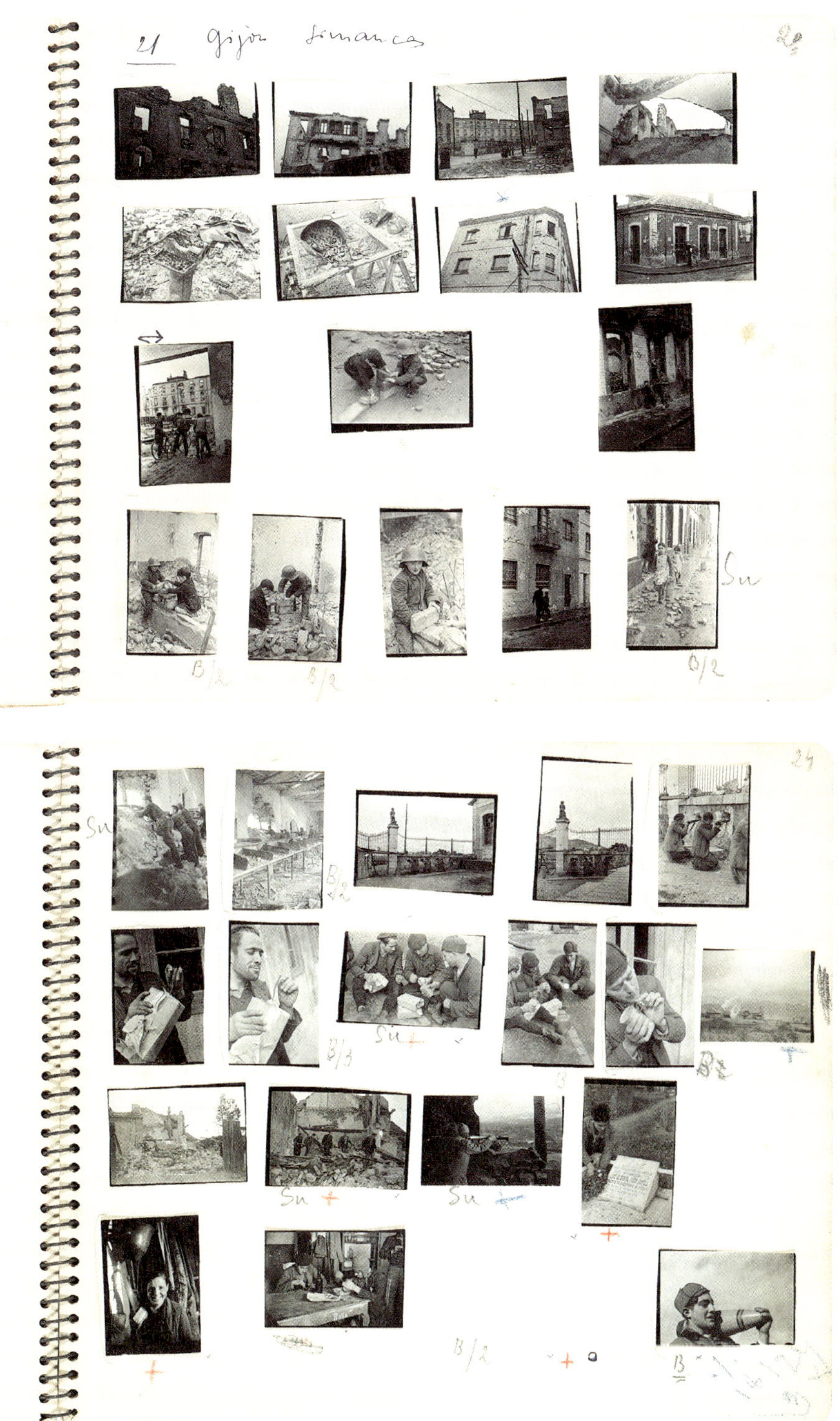

ROBERT CAPA, Selection of photos from one of the eight
albums "Capa. Espagne", 1937
Archives nationales, Centre historique, Paris

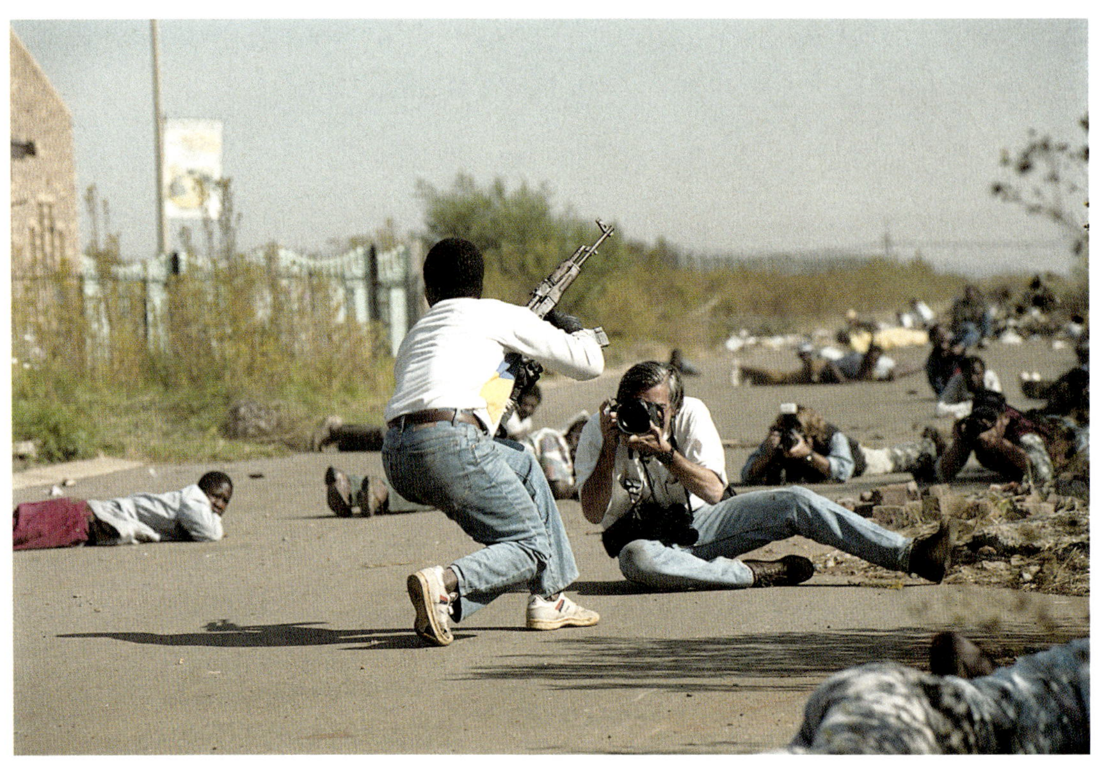

Peter Turnley photographed one of his colleagues, James Natchwey, in action. This image shows the other, more dangerous and committed side of the media treatment of wars, illustrated by Alex Webb's photo in Haiti.

PETER TURNLEY, Fighting on a South African street,
East Rand, South Africa, 1994
Corbis / Cover Barcelona

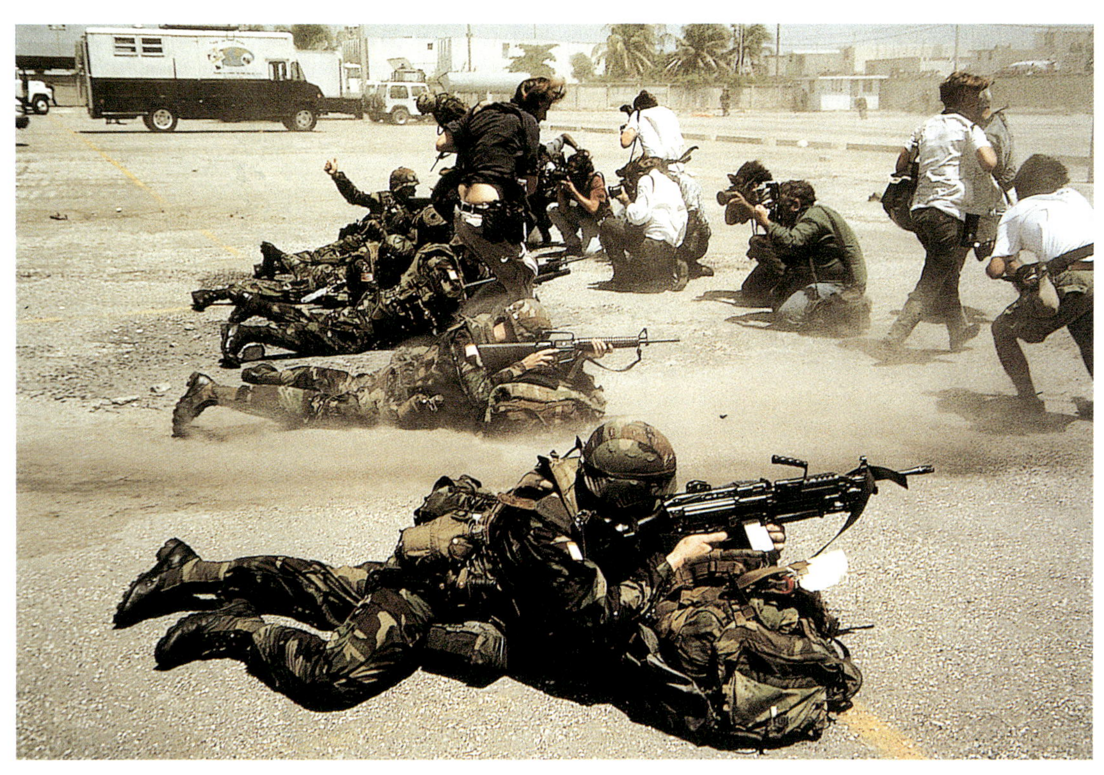

ALEX WEBB, US troops land as the press
awaits, Port-au-Prince, Haiti, 1994
Alex Webb / Magnum Photos / Contacto

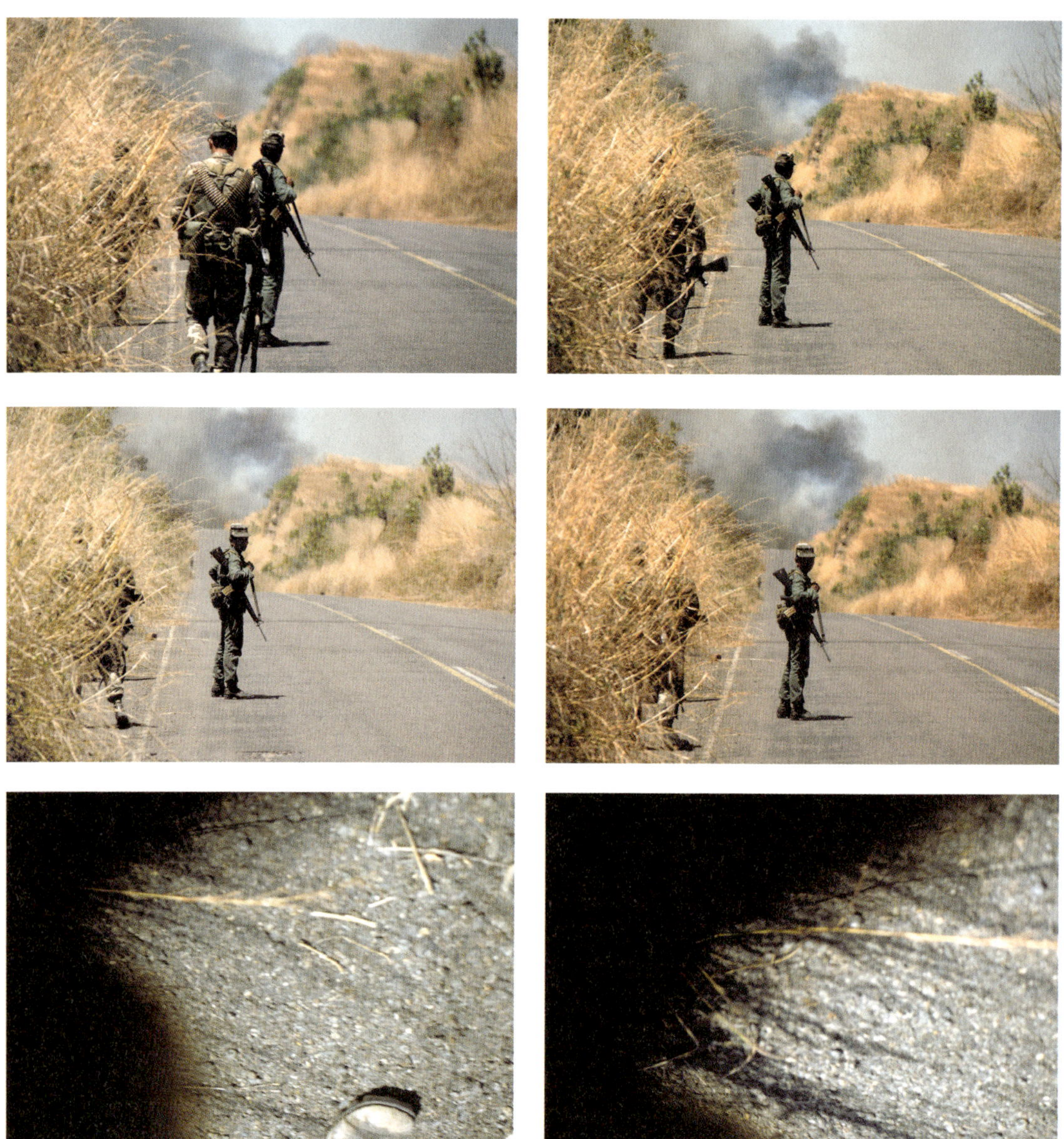

The last frames from Hoagland's roll of film which record the moment of his own death in El Salvador.

JOHN HOAGLAND, War at El Salvador, 1984
Courtesy of Eros Hoagland

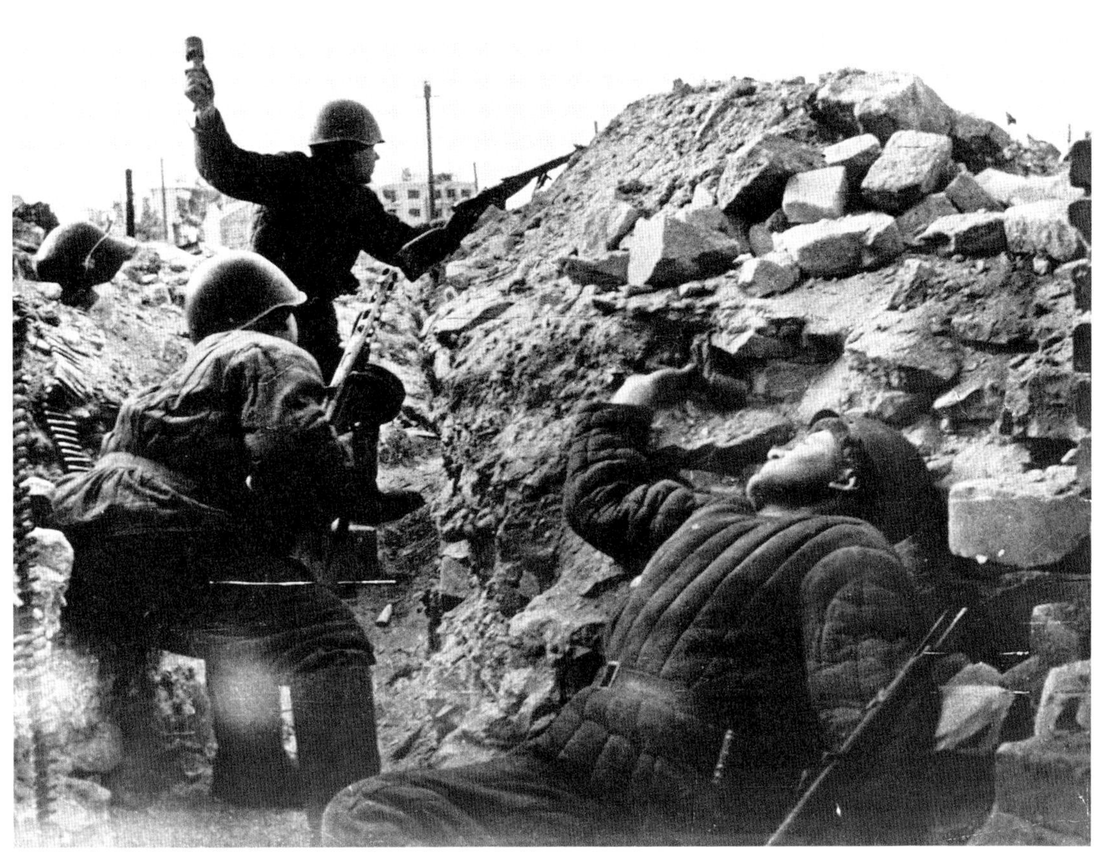

Charge! Battle of Stalingrad, 1942-1943
Musée d'Histoire Contemporaine - BDIC, Paris

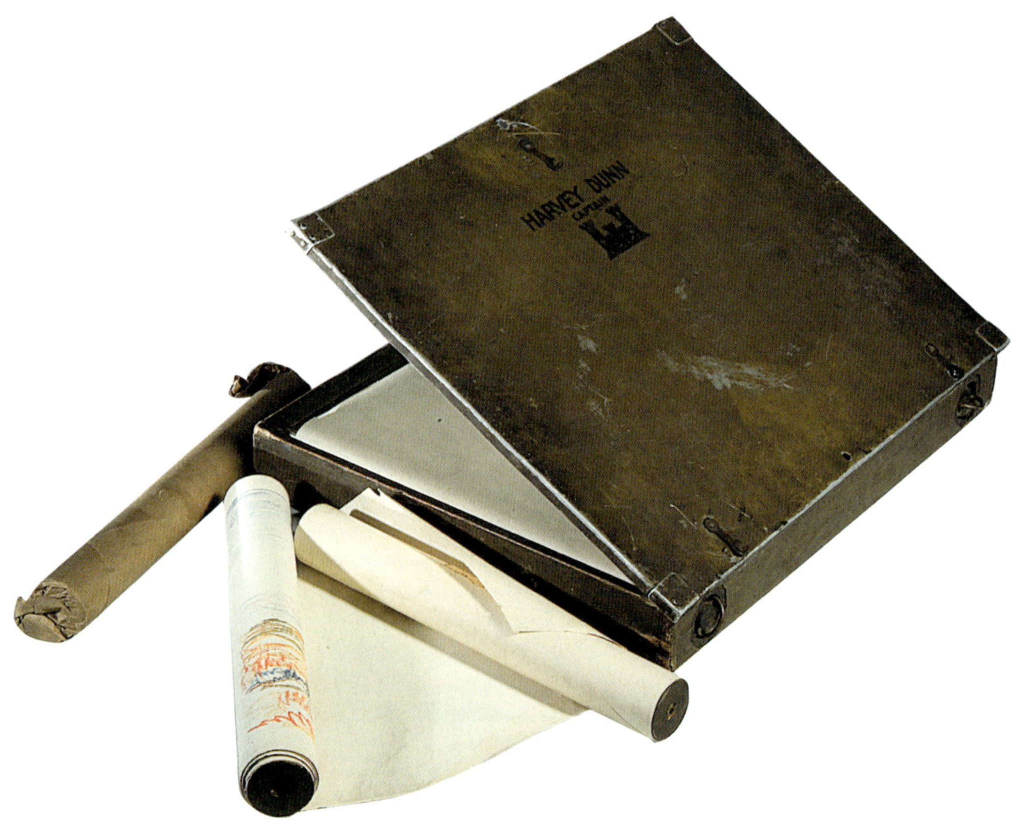

Captain Dunn's sketch box, which he took with him to the front during the
First World War, consists of an ingenious waterproofed system which allows a
roll of paper to be pulled down over a central support. It makes it possible to
draw in sequence —like a film storyboard— the action on a battlefield, which
had already become the biggest film set in history through the use of the film
camera as a documentary tool.

HARVEY DUNN, Artist's sketch box, c. 1914-1918
Box, 5.1 x 43.2 x 36.2 cm
Smithsonian Institution, National Museum of American History,
Behring Center, Washington

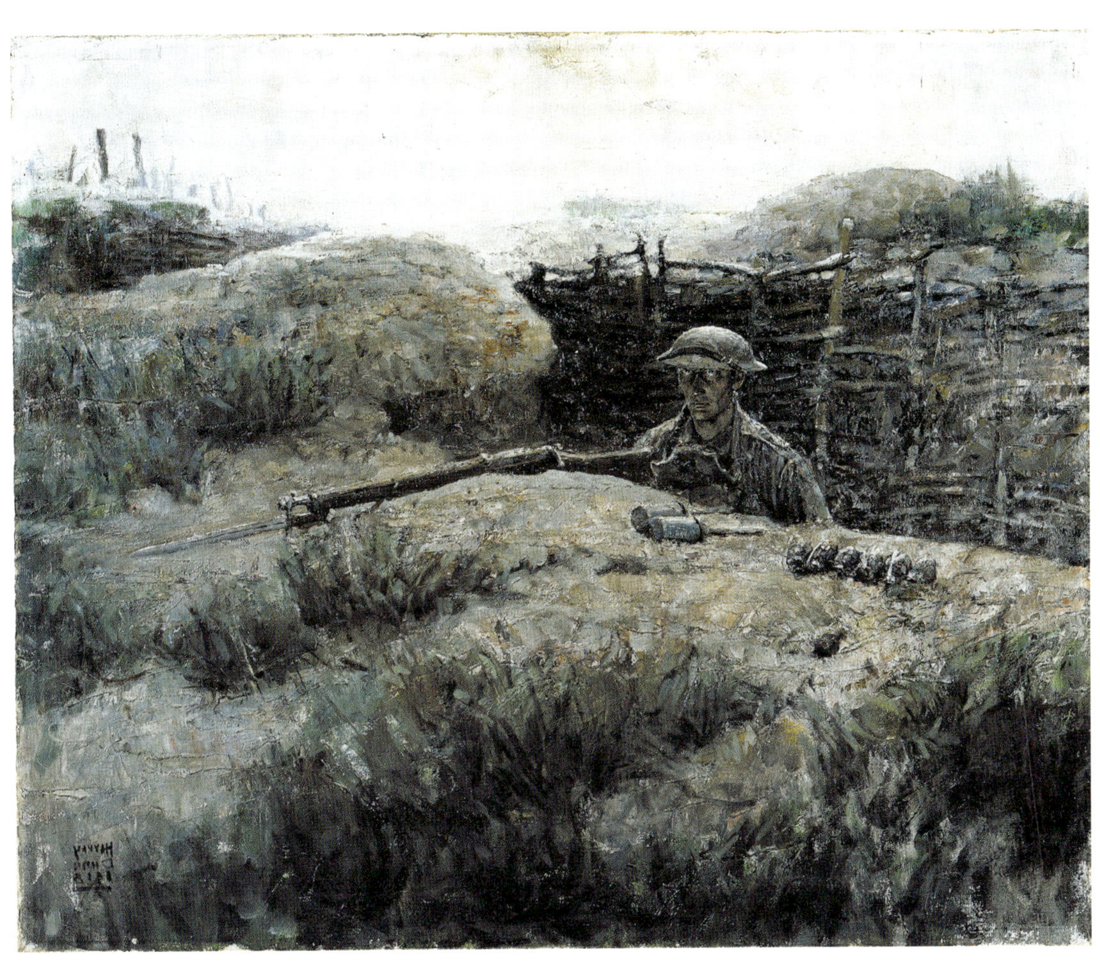

HARVEY DUNN, The sentry, 31st January, 1920
Oil, 72.5 x 60.3 cm
Smithsonian Institution, National Museum of American History,
Behring Center, Washington

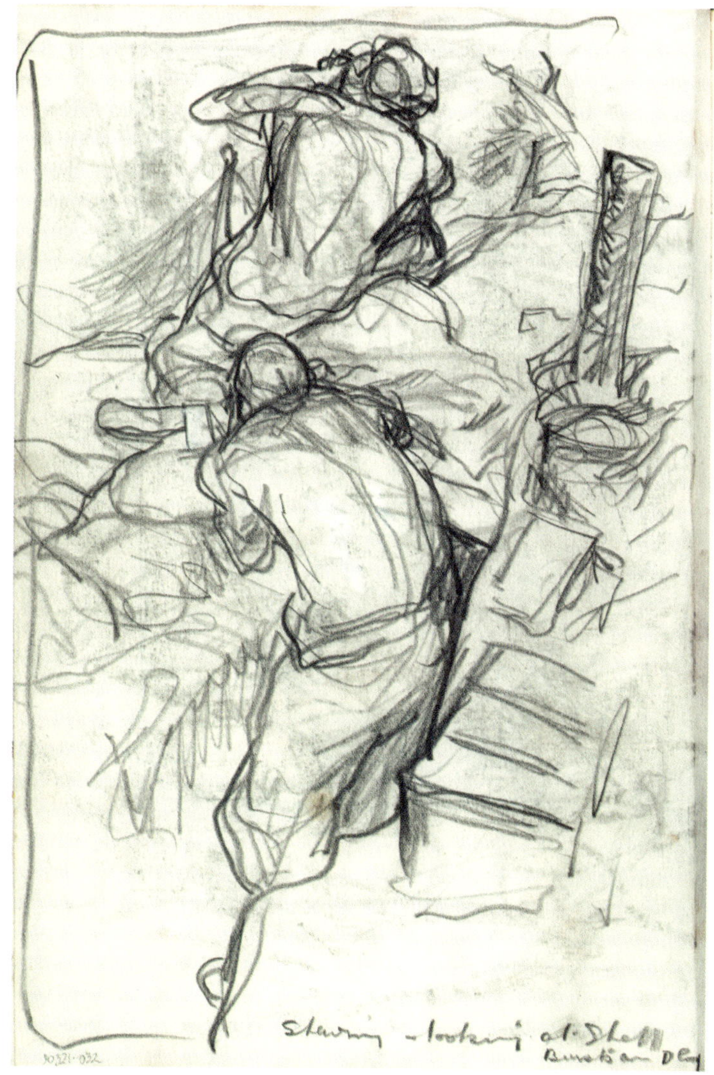

Hele was the longest serving, official Australian war artist.
He was in North Africa and New Guinea during the Second World
War and re-enlisted as a major to go to Korea. His technically
accomplished drawings from the front were the source for the
historic paintings he produced at his studio.

IVOR HENRY THOMAS HELE, Page of artist's sketchbook containing
drawings of servicemen and activities during the Korean War, 1952
Carbon pencil and white gouache highlights on paper, 30.1 x 21 cm
Australian War Memorial, Canberra

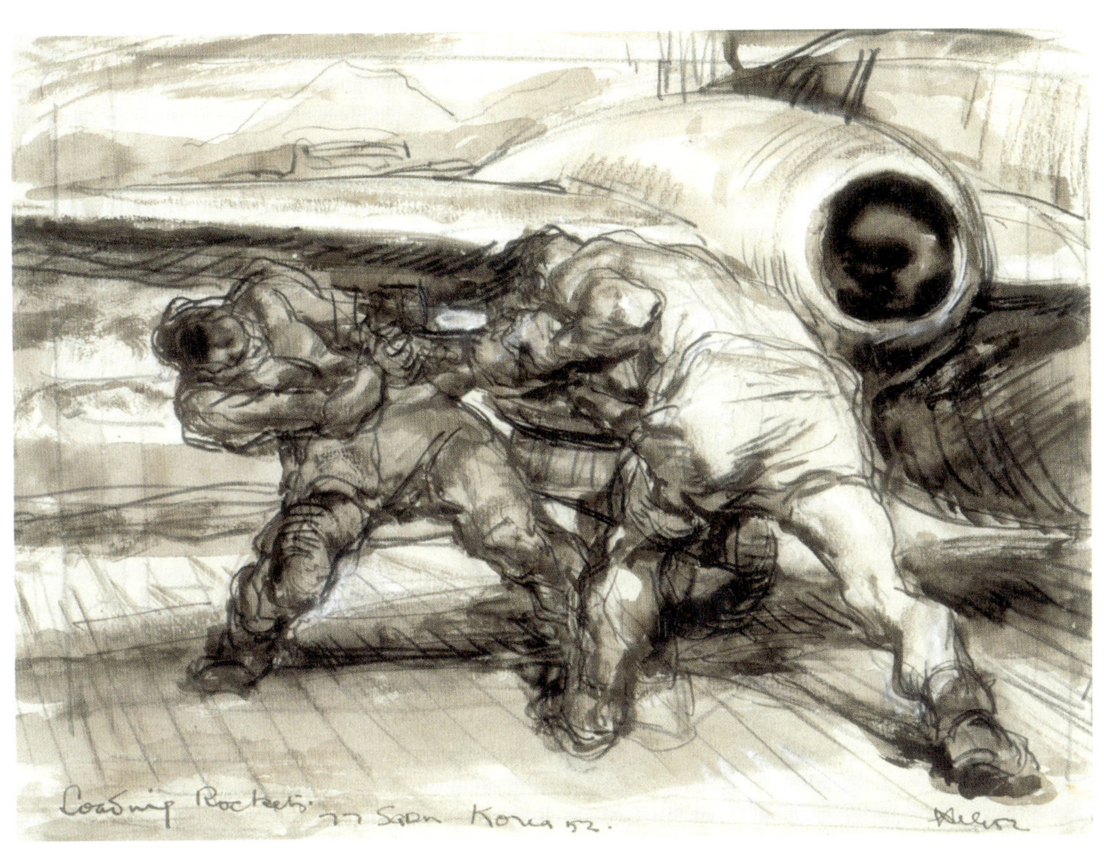

IVOR HENRY THOMAS HELE, Adjusting rockets on jets, Korea, 1952
Pencil and pen, brush and sepia ink with wash, heightened with white,
with crayon on paper, 28.3 x 38.7 cm
Australian War Memorial, Canberra

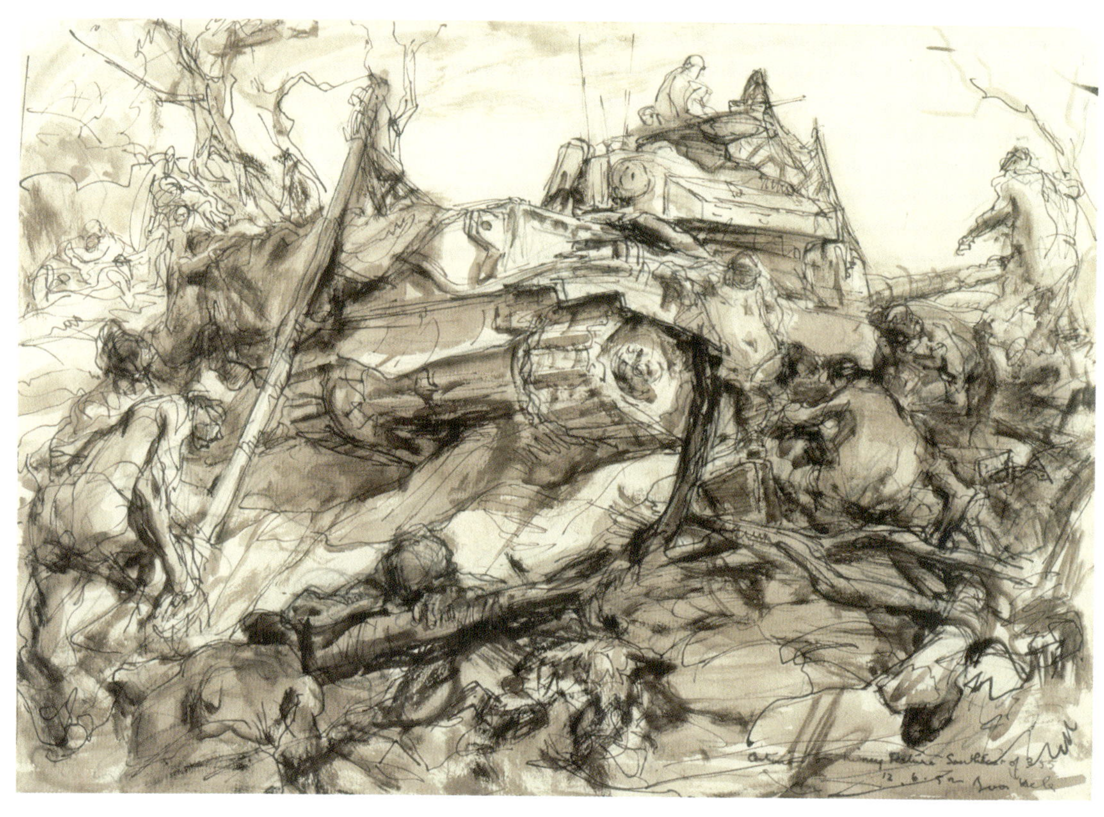

IVOR HENRY THOMAS HELE, Study for Centurion tank, Korea, 1952
Brush and sepia ink with wash, with pencil on paper, 37.8 x 53.8 cm
Australian War Memorial, Canberra

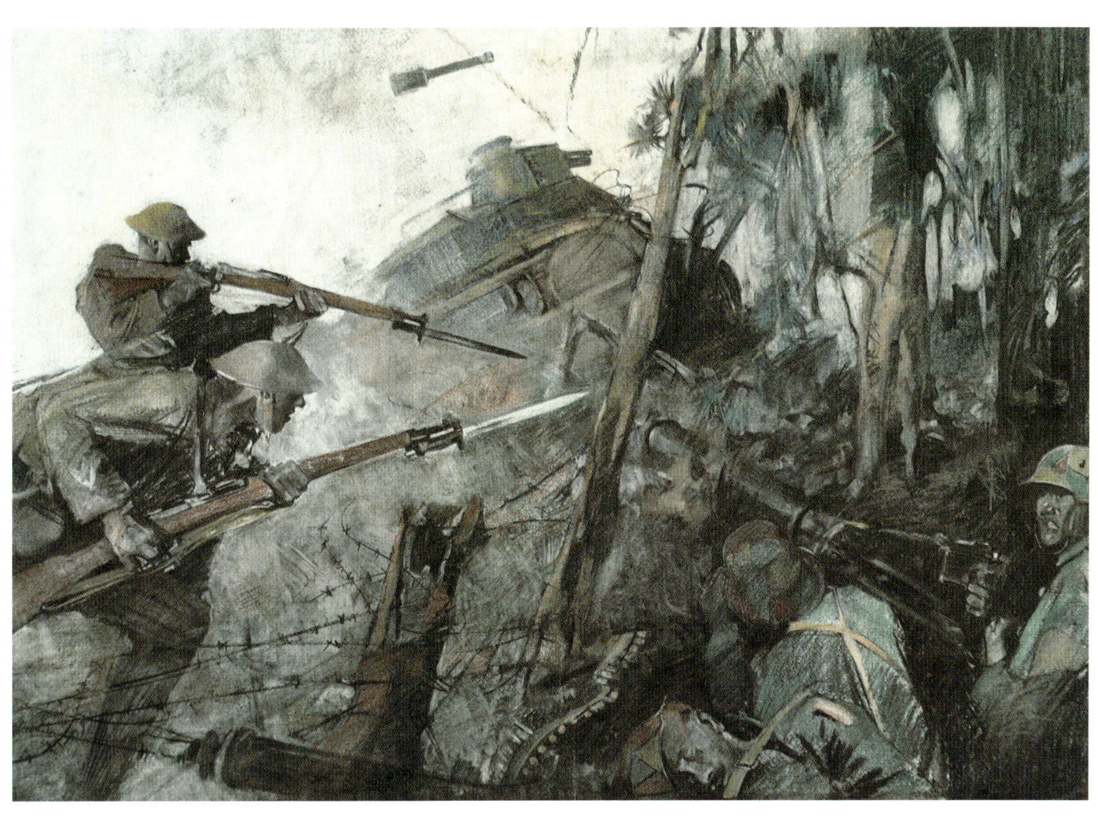

GEORGE HARDING, Storming machine gun, 1918
Charcoal on paper, 48.2 x 68.5 cm
National Museum of the US Army, Army Art
Collection, Washington

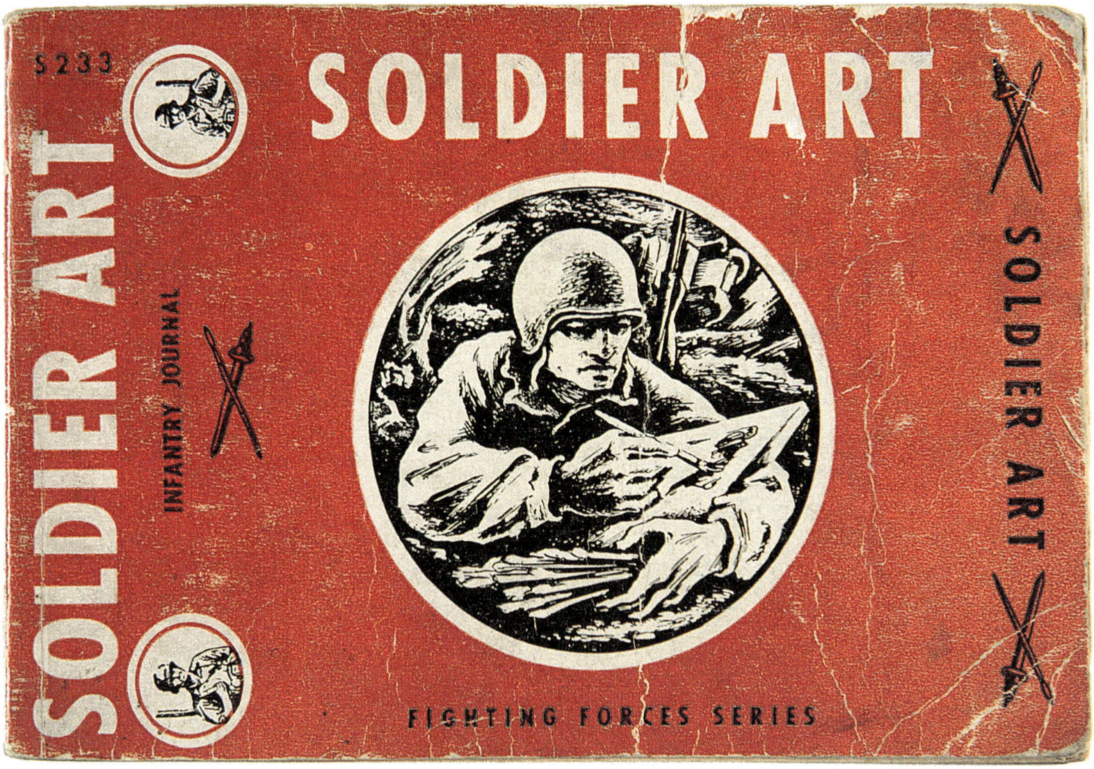

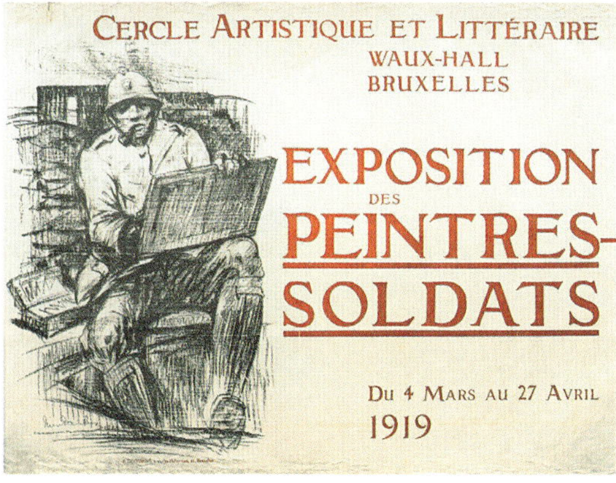

SEVERAL ARTISTS, "Soldier art. Fighting forces series" National Gallery of Art, Washington, 1945
11 x 16.2 x 1.2 cm
Francesc Torres Collection, Barcelona

A. PAULUS, Poster from the exhibition "Peintres-Soldats", Brussels, 1919
Lithograph, 65 x 89.7 cm
Imperial War Museum, London

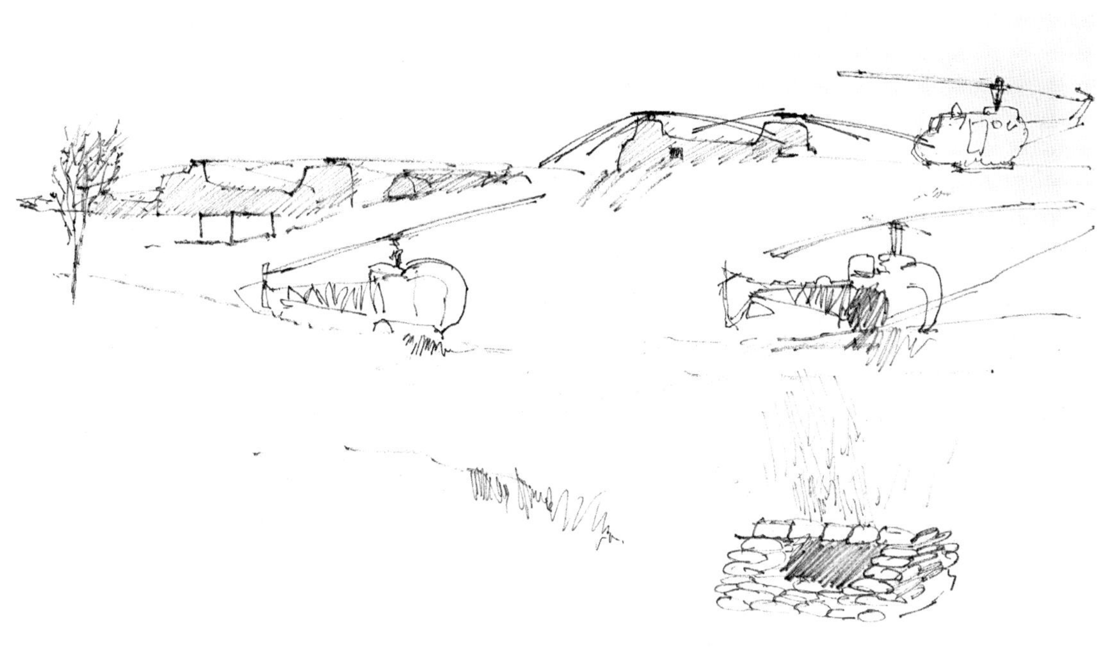

Wehrle — GOLF COURSE

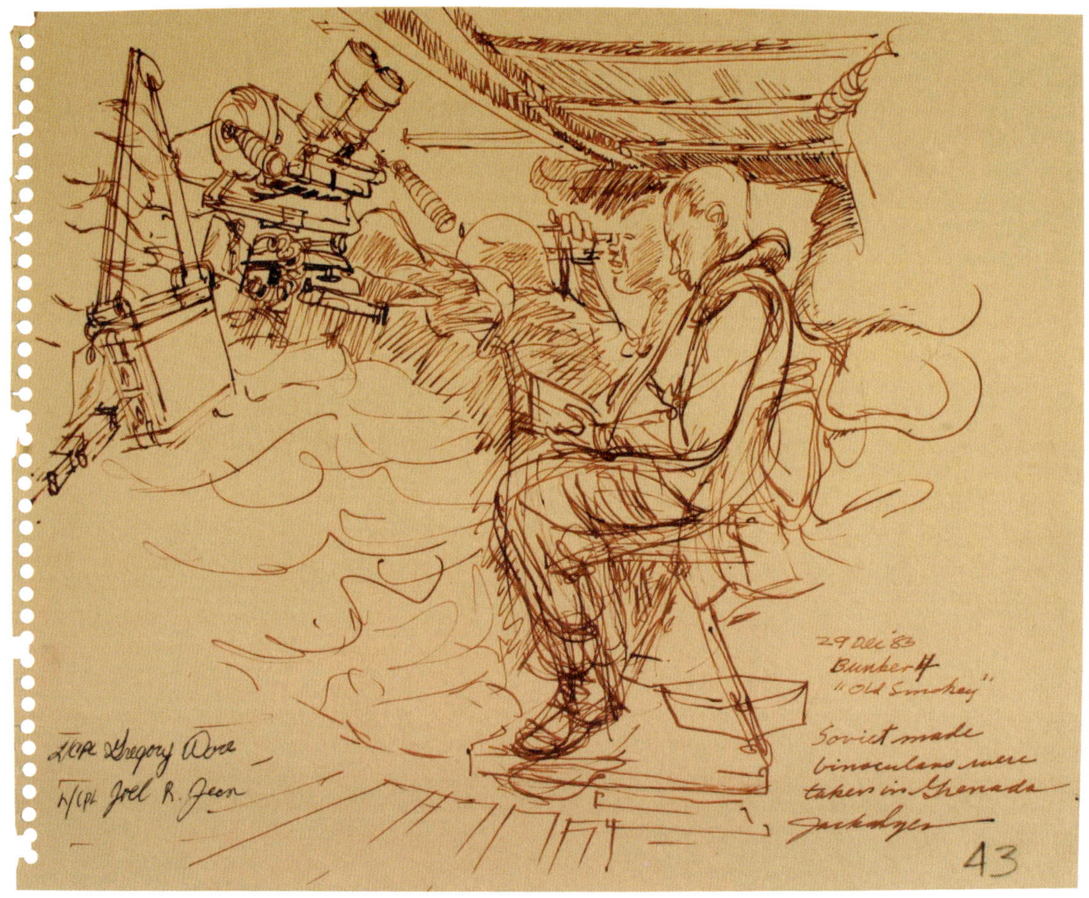

This selection of sketchbooks featuring drawings made at the front
during both world wars, in Korea, Vietnam and Lebanon, exemplifies
the way in which the work of war artists has borne witness to, and
provided a first-hand record of warfare throughout the century.

MAJOR JOHN T. DYER, USMC, retired, Bunker Four, "Old
Smokey", Beirut, 29 December 1983
Brown ink on white paper, 20.3 x 25.4 cm
Marine Corps History and Museums Division, Washington

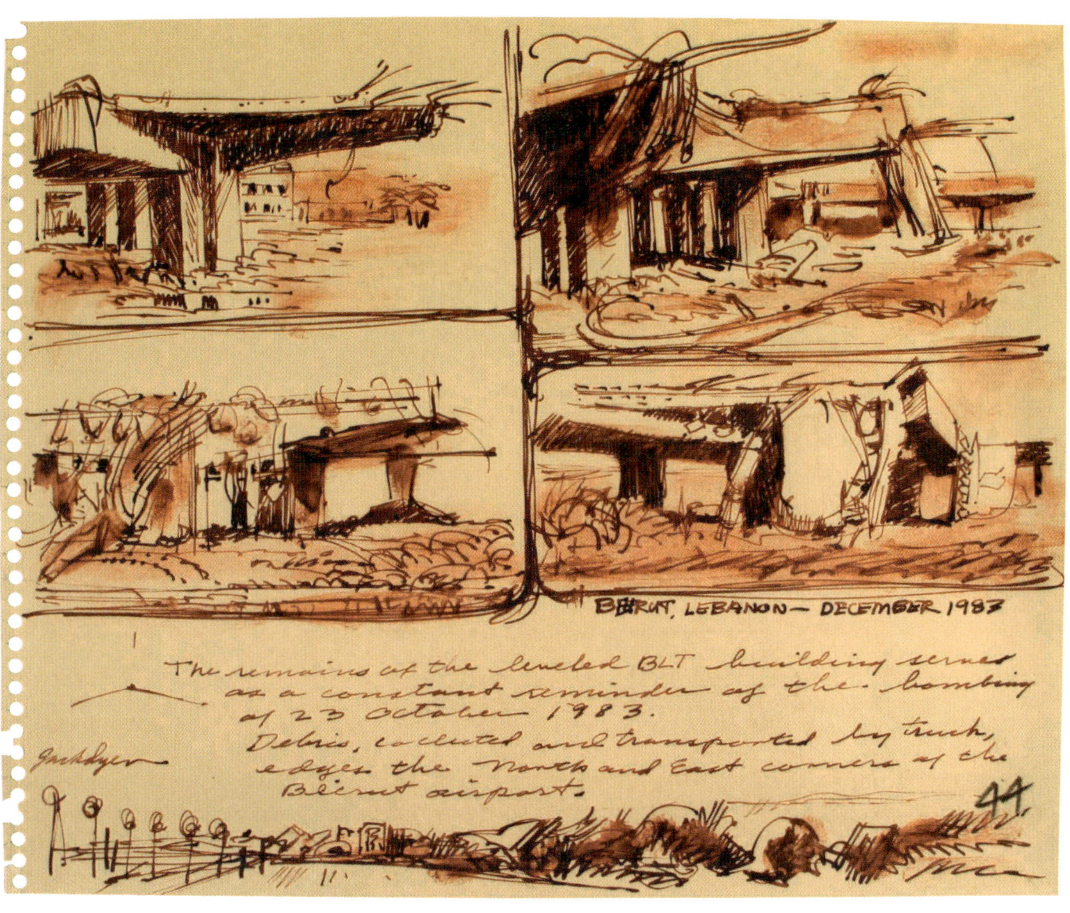

MAJOR JOHN T. DYER, USMC, retired, Four compositions, Debris of the Battalion
Leading Team who suffered a car bomb attack, Beirut, 25 December 1983
Brown ink on white paper, 20.3 x 25.4 cm
Marine Corps History and Museums Division, Washington

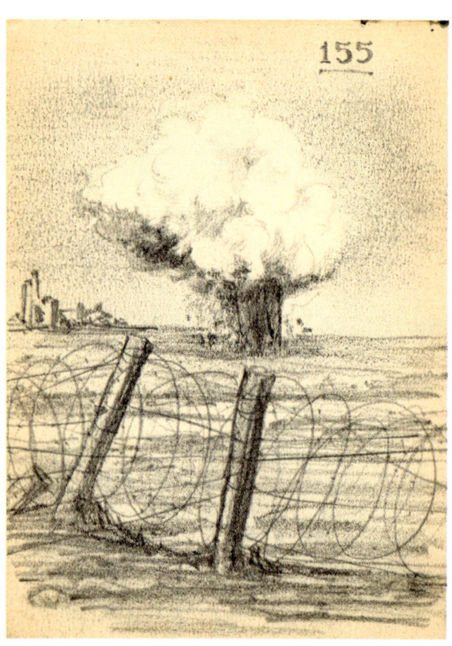

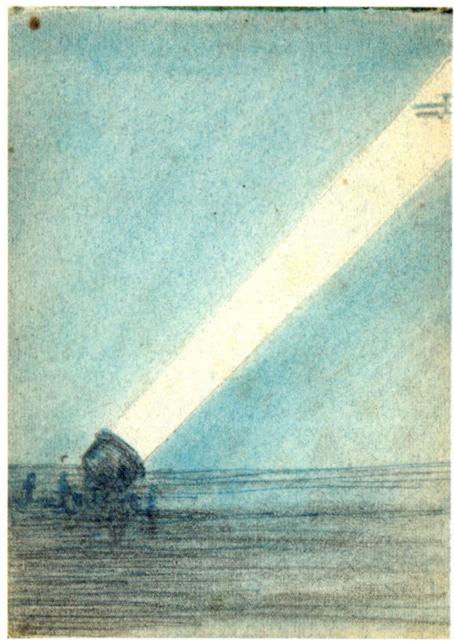

CHARLES BASKERVILLE, Sketchbook, 1918
Pencil on paper, 11 x 8.2 cm
National Museum of the US Army, Army Art Collection,
Washington

P. A. KRIVONÓGOV, Towards the Rumanian borders, 1944
Paper and pastel, 24 x 35 cm
Central Armed Forces Museum, Moscow

P. A. KRIVONÓGOV, Crossing the Dniester, 1944
Paper and charcoal, 30 x 39 cm
Central Armed Forces Museum, Moscow

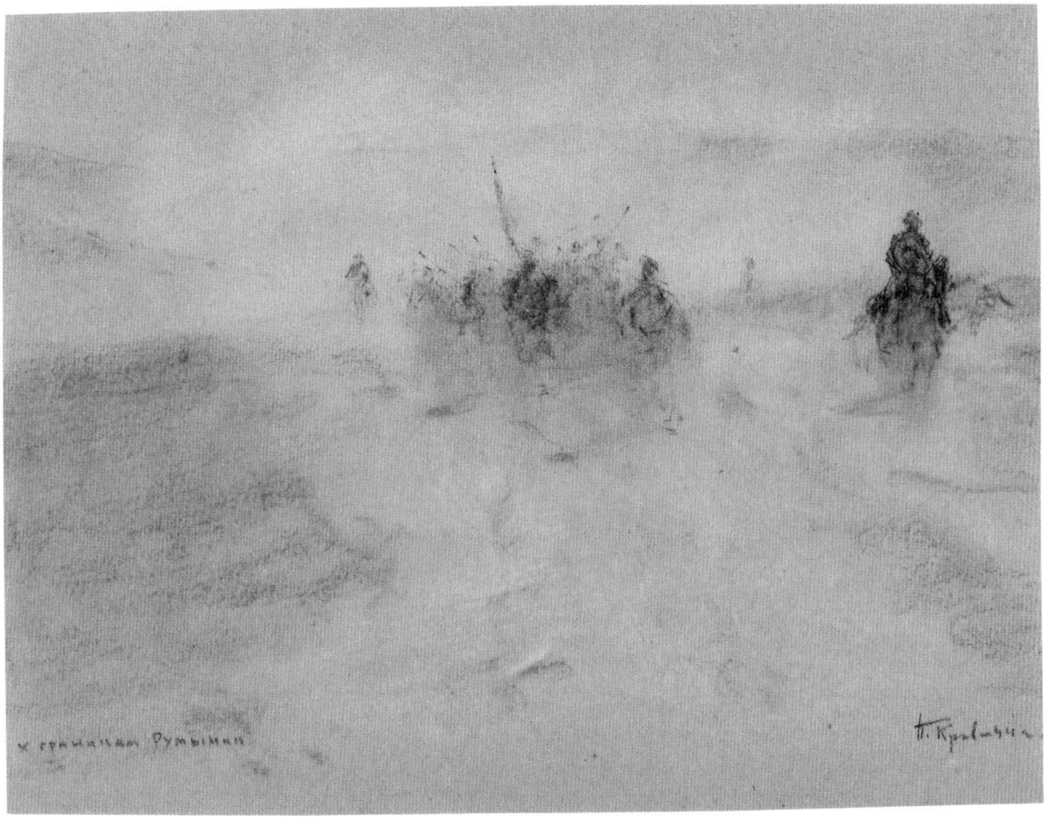

к границам Румынии

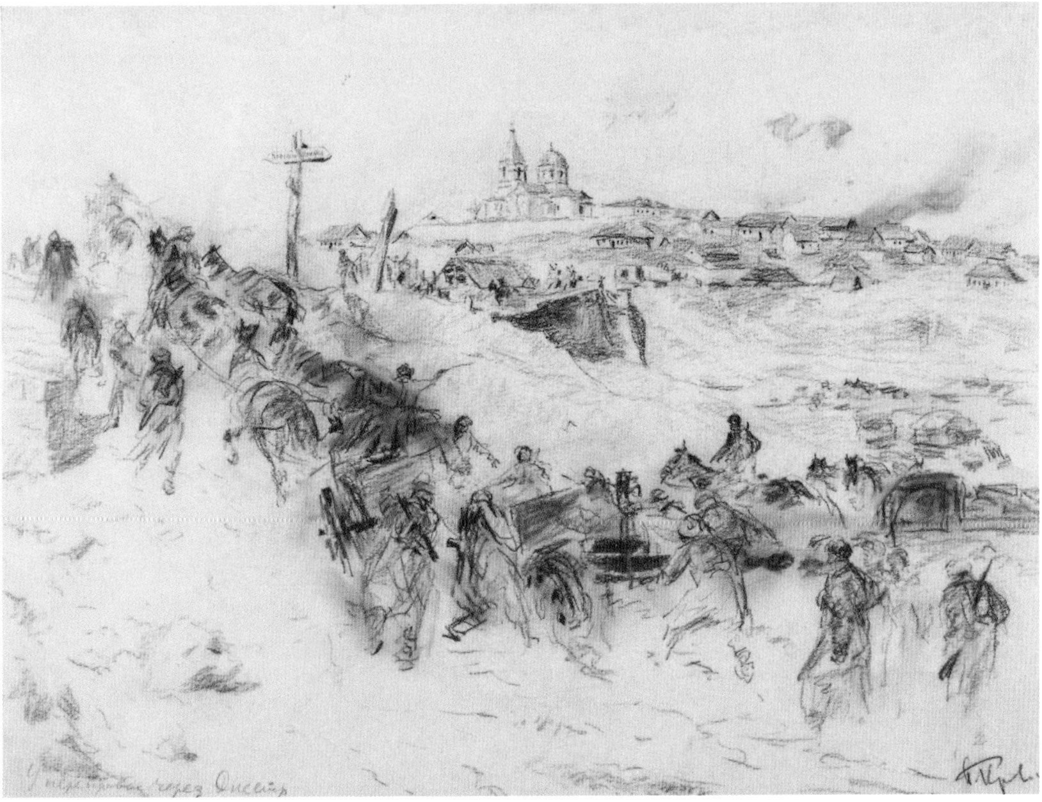

...через Днепр

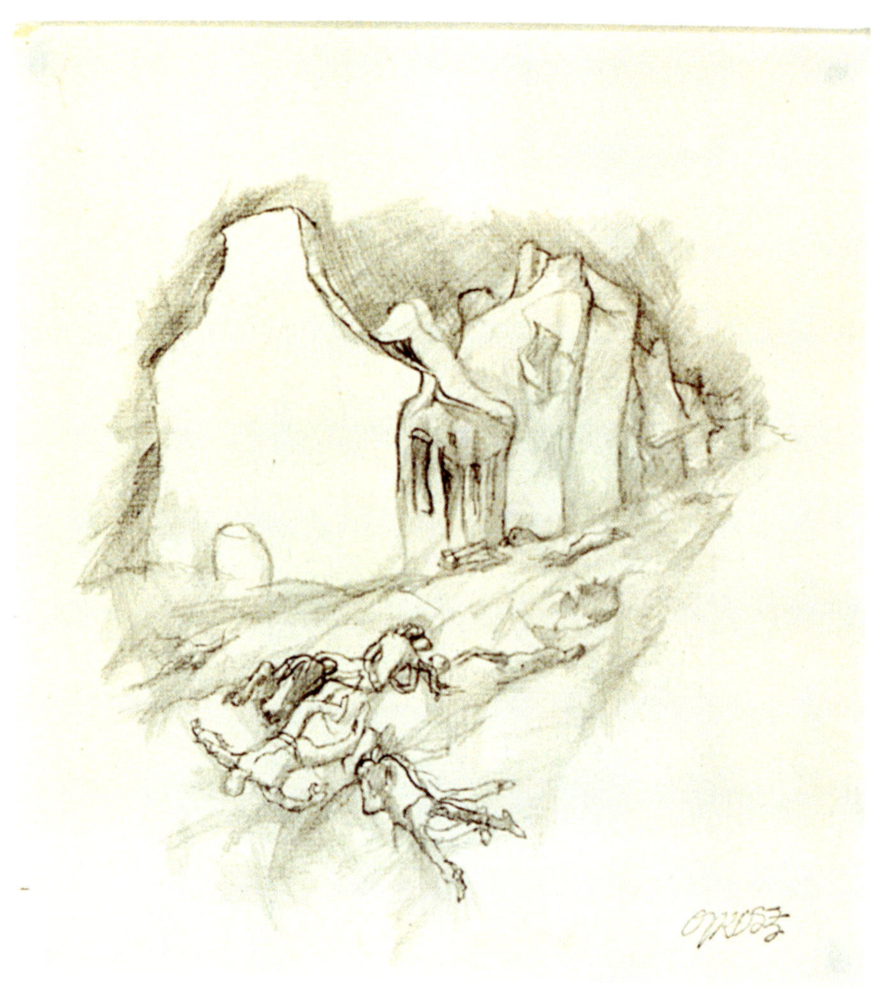

Grosz joined up as a volunteer in Berlin in November 1914.
At the beginning of 1915, he was moved to a reserve battalion and,
the same year, became actively involved in the resistance movement
against the war, at the height of militarism. His many pictures
of the front and the rearguard, and the effects of battle, show his
rejection and condemnation of war.

GEORGE GROSZ, Drawing no. 4-157-1, 1915
Pen and ink, 20 x 20 cm
George Grosz Estate, Courtesy of Ralph Jentsch, Capri

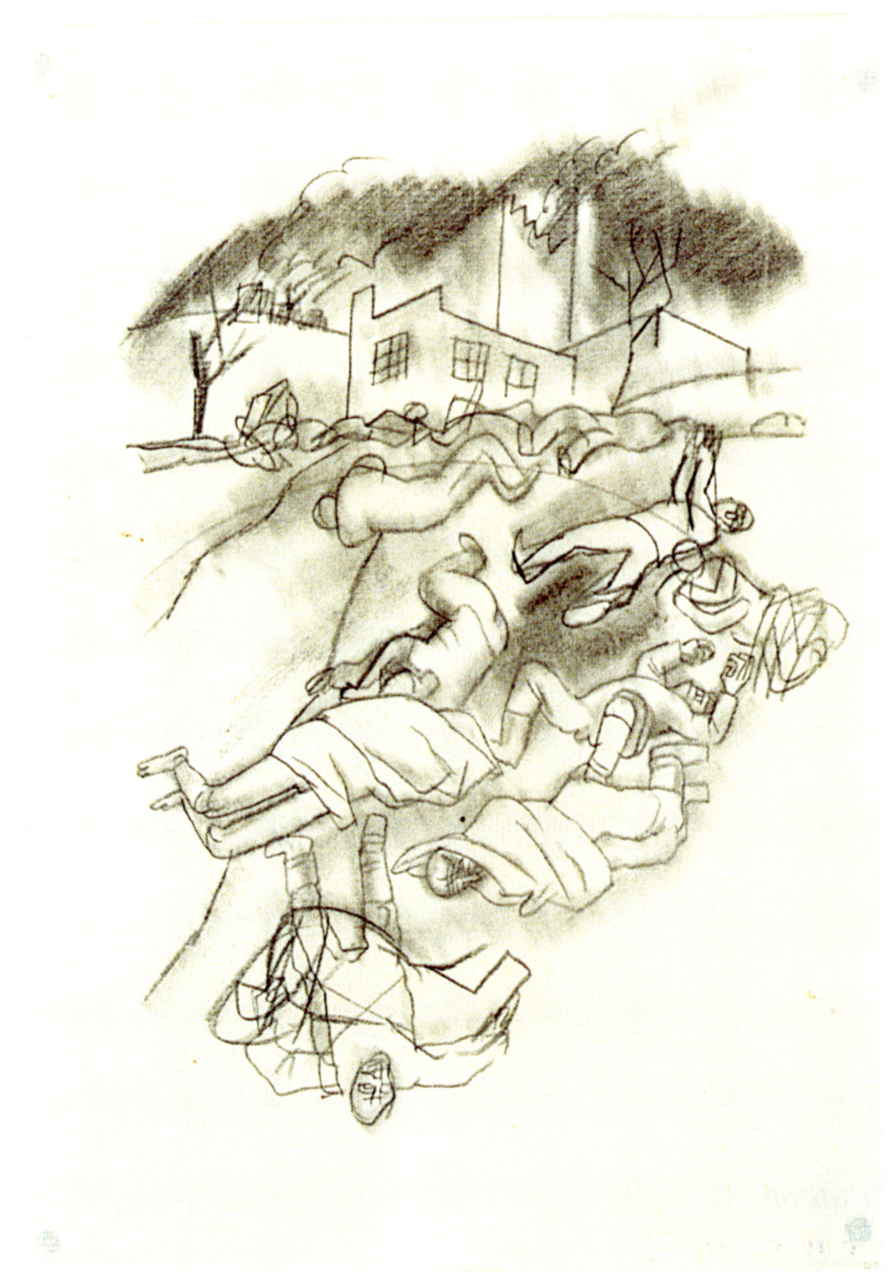

GEORGE GROSZ, Drawing no. 5-183-5, 1915
Pen and ink, 24 x 20 cm
George Grosz Estate, Courtesy of Ralph Jentsch, Capri

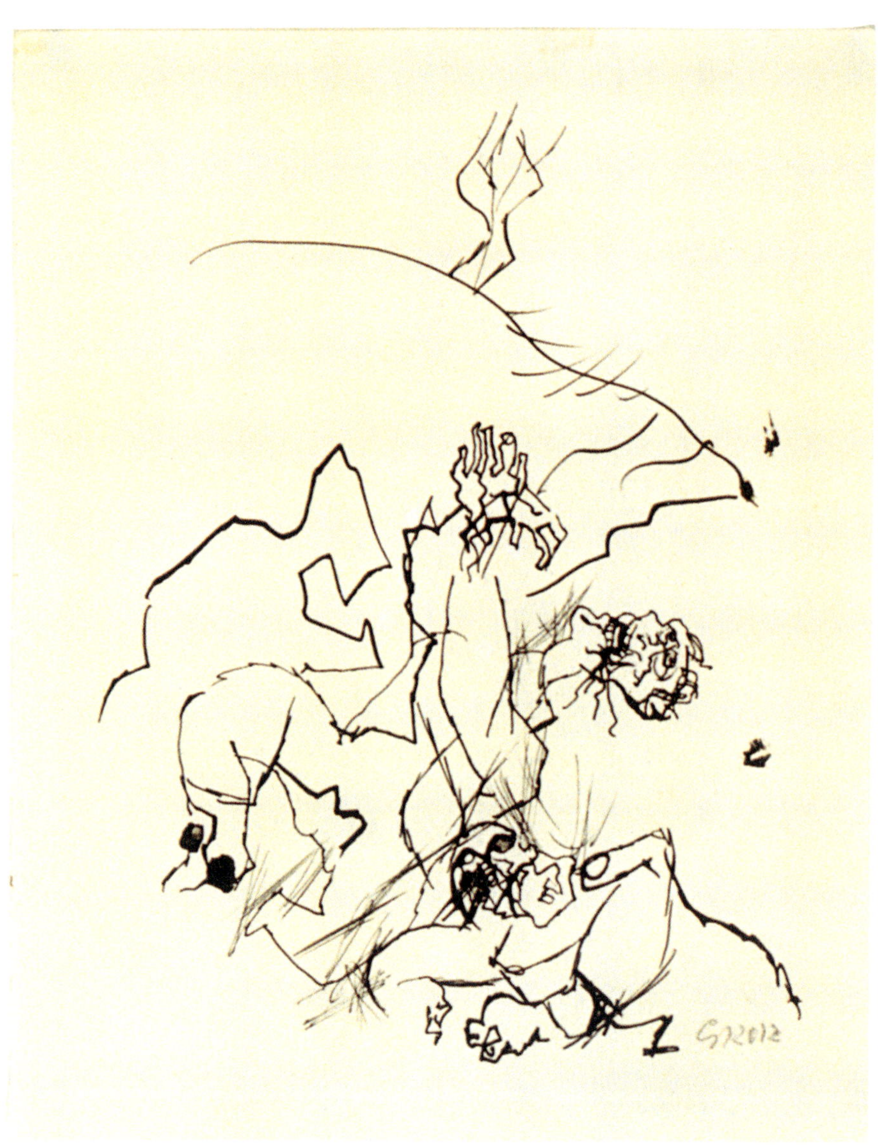

GEORGE GROSZ, Drawing no. 3-2-3, 1914
Pen and ink, 22 x 19 cm
George Grosz Estate, Courtesy of Ralph Jentsch, Capri

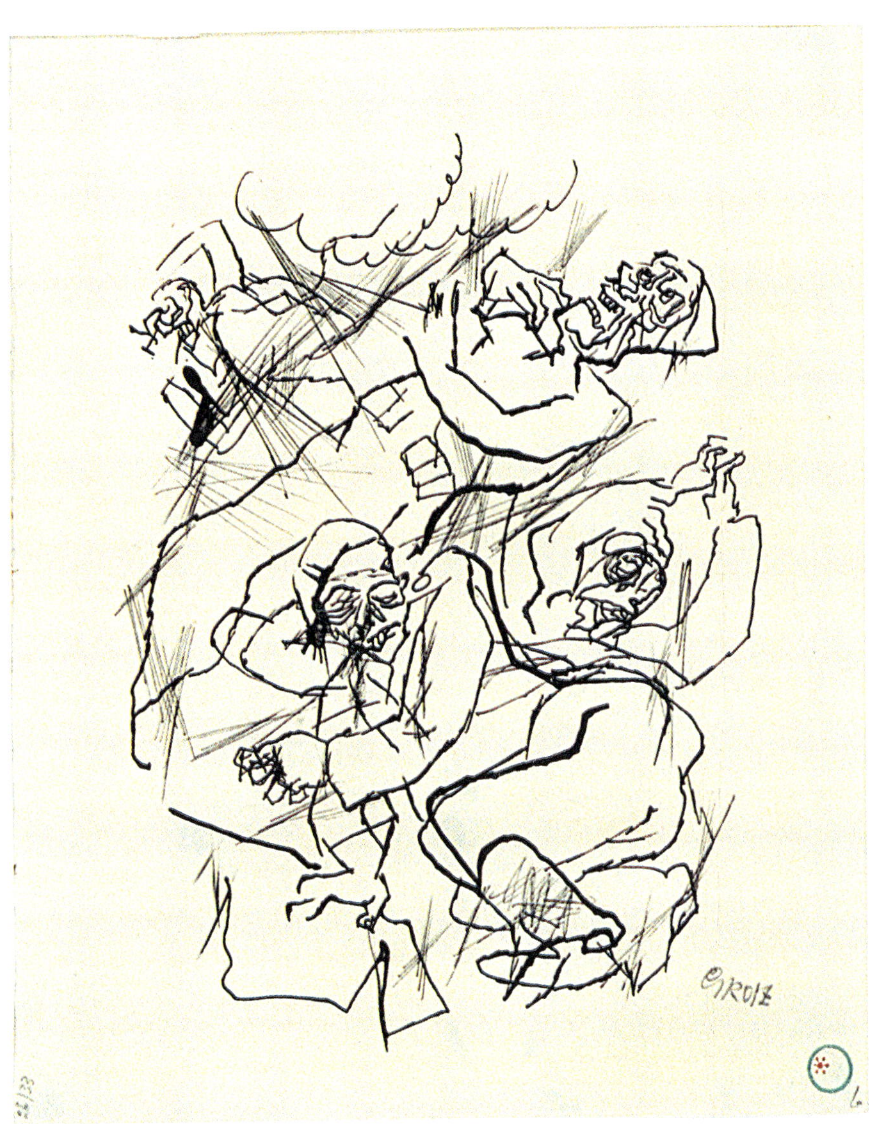

GEORGE GROSZ, Drawing no. 3-38-10, 1914
Pen and ink, 23 x 19 cm
George Grosz Estate, Courtesy of Ralph Jentsch, Capri

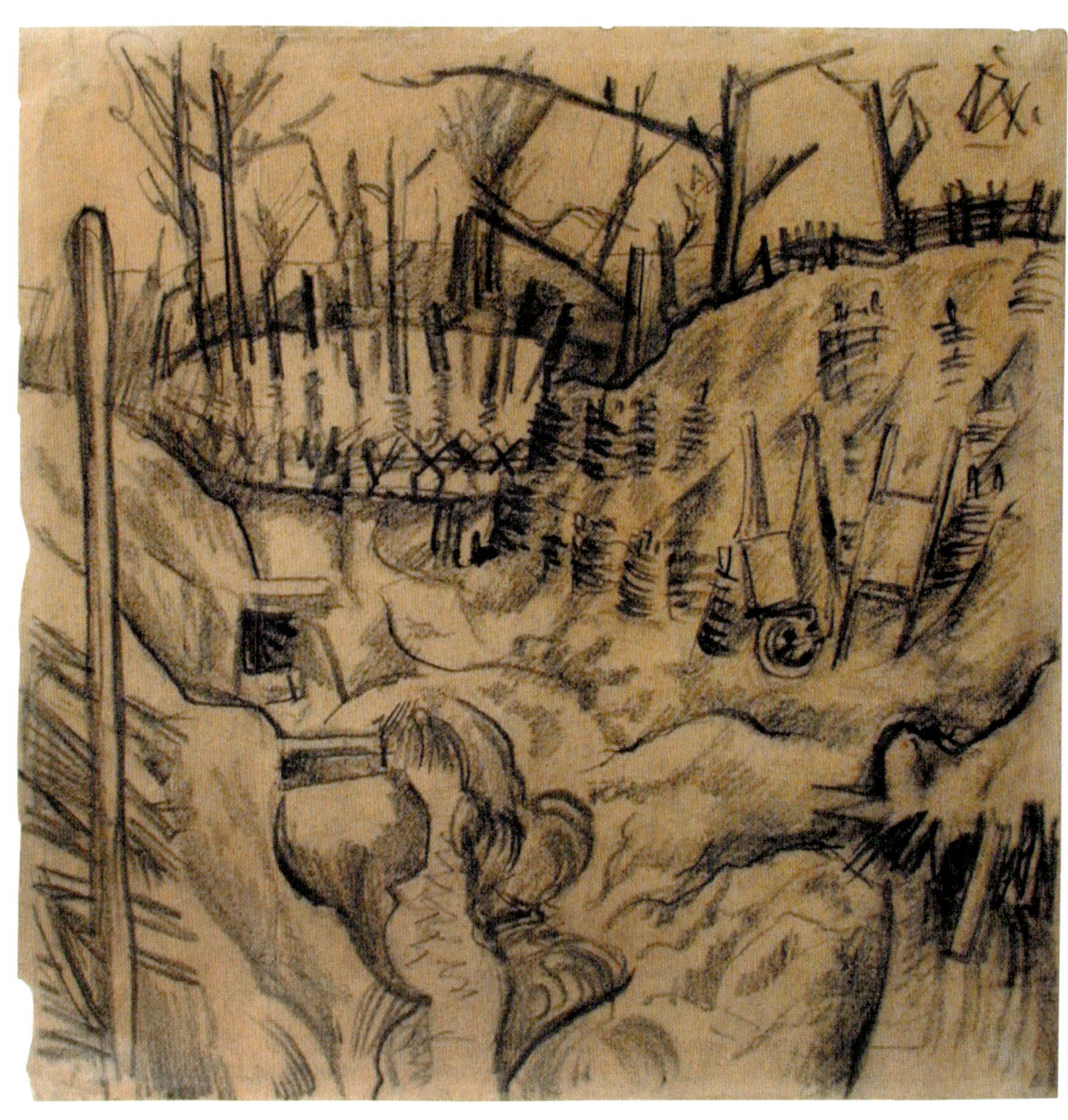

OTTO DIX, In the stream at Souchez, 1915
Black charcoal and pencil on strong, heavily sized,
brown paper, 28.4 x 28.4 cm
Galerie Albstadt-Städtische Kunstsammlungen,
Sammlung Walther Groz, Albstadt

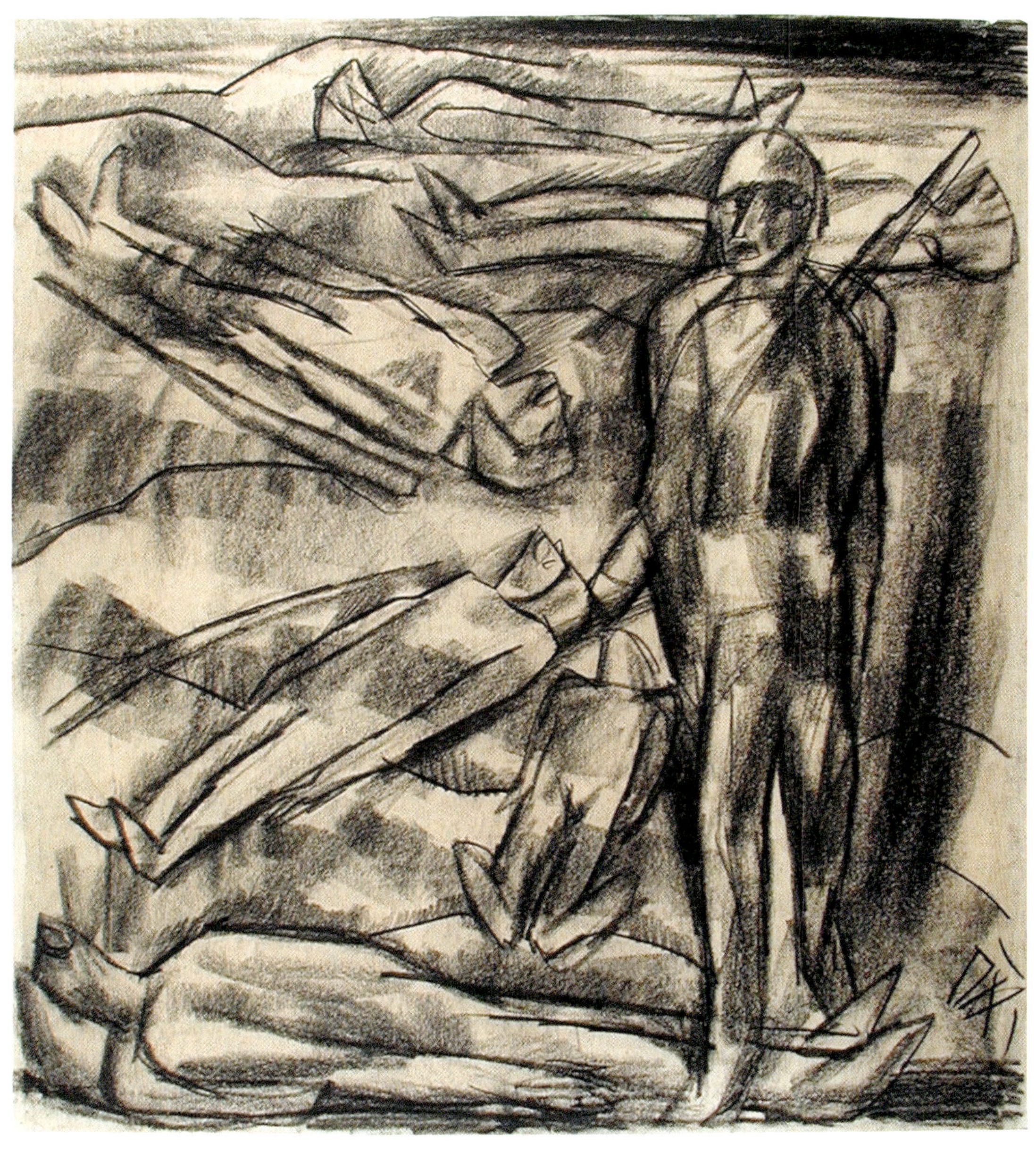

OTTO DIX, Soldier, 1918
Charcoal drawing on strong, beige drawing paper,
41.2 x 38.7 cm
Galerie Albstadt-Städtische Kunstsammlungen,
Sammlung Walther Groz, Albstadt

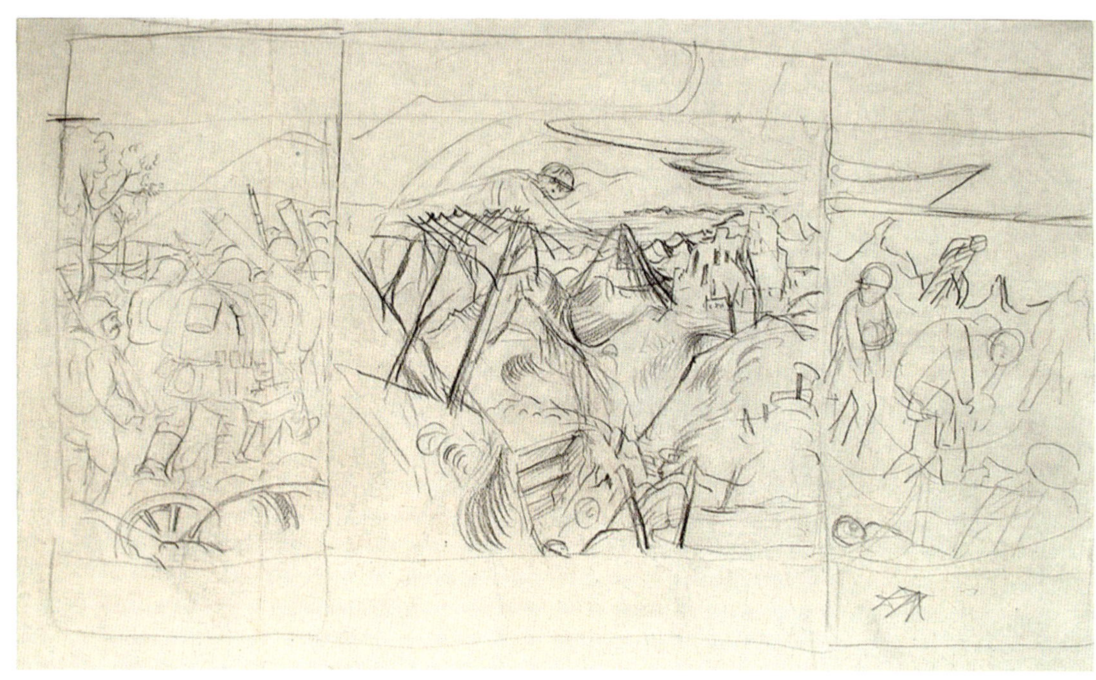

Preparatory drawing for the major triptych "The War", one of the most brutal expressions of the horrors of war in the history of art. Constructed like an altarpiece, the memory of the past war serves to denounce the resurgence of warmongering in Germany. The work was condemned by the Nazis and led to Dix being sacked from his post as an art lecturer.

OTTO DIX, First sketch for "War" triptych, 1929
Pencil on strong handmade cardboard, 44.8 x 85.2 cm
Galerie Albstadt-Städtische Kunstsammlungen, Albstadt

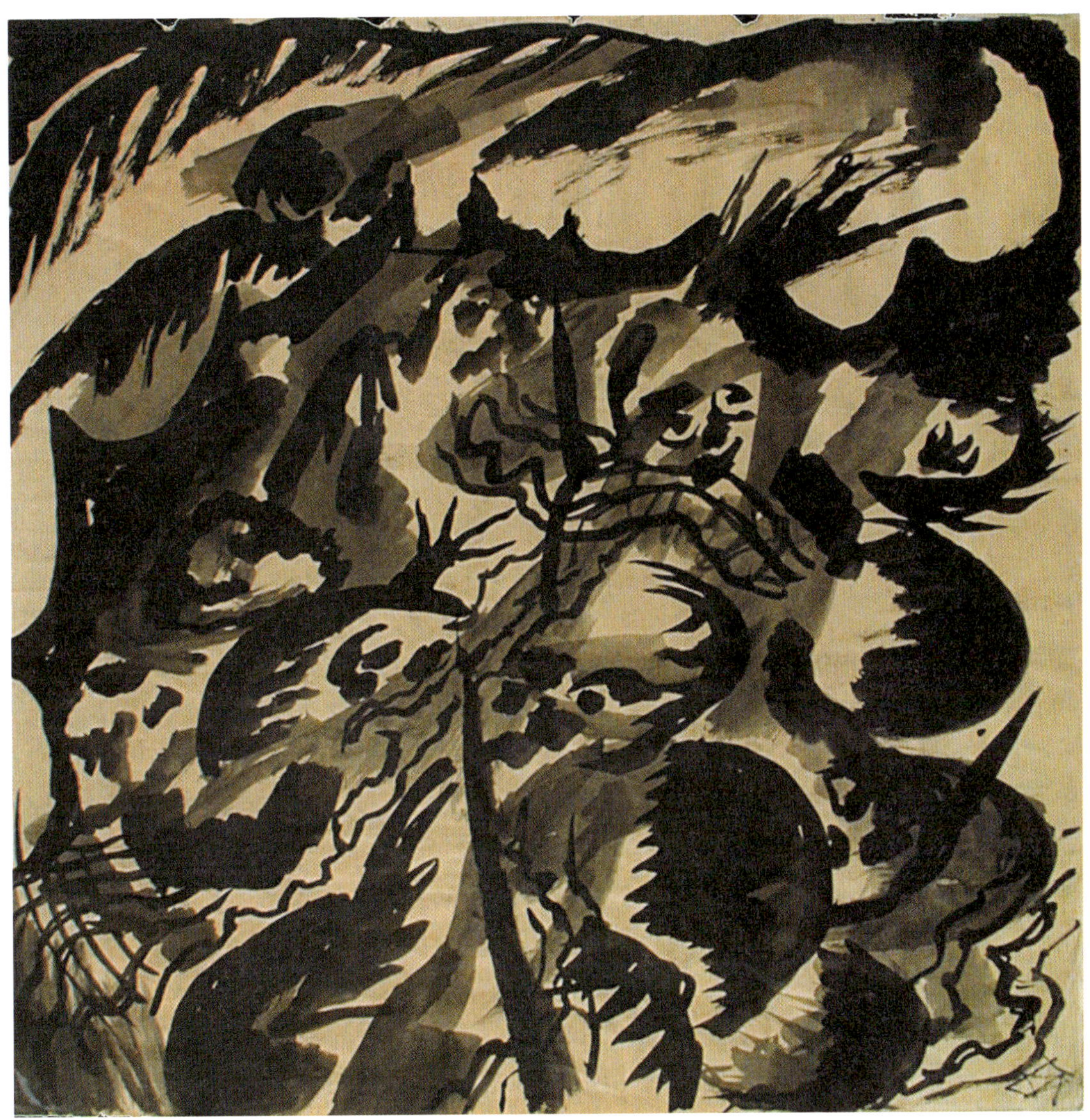

Dix joined the artillery in August 1914. He later said of his youthful enthusiasm: "War is a horrible thing, but there was also something tremendous about it, too. I didn't want to miss it at any price". He produced these drawings while on active service at the front and they begin to reveal his ambivalence to war and served as the basis for his disillusioned post-war works.

OTTO DIX, The thick mud, 1918
Black Indian ink, brushed on brownish paper, 38.2 x 39.6 cm
Galerie Albstadt-Städtische Kunstsammlungen, Albstadt

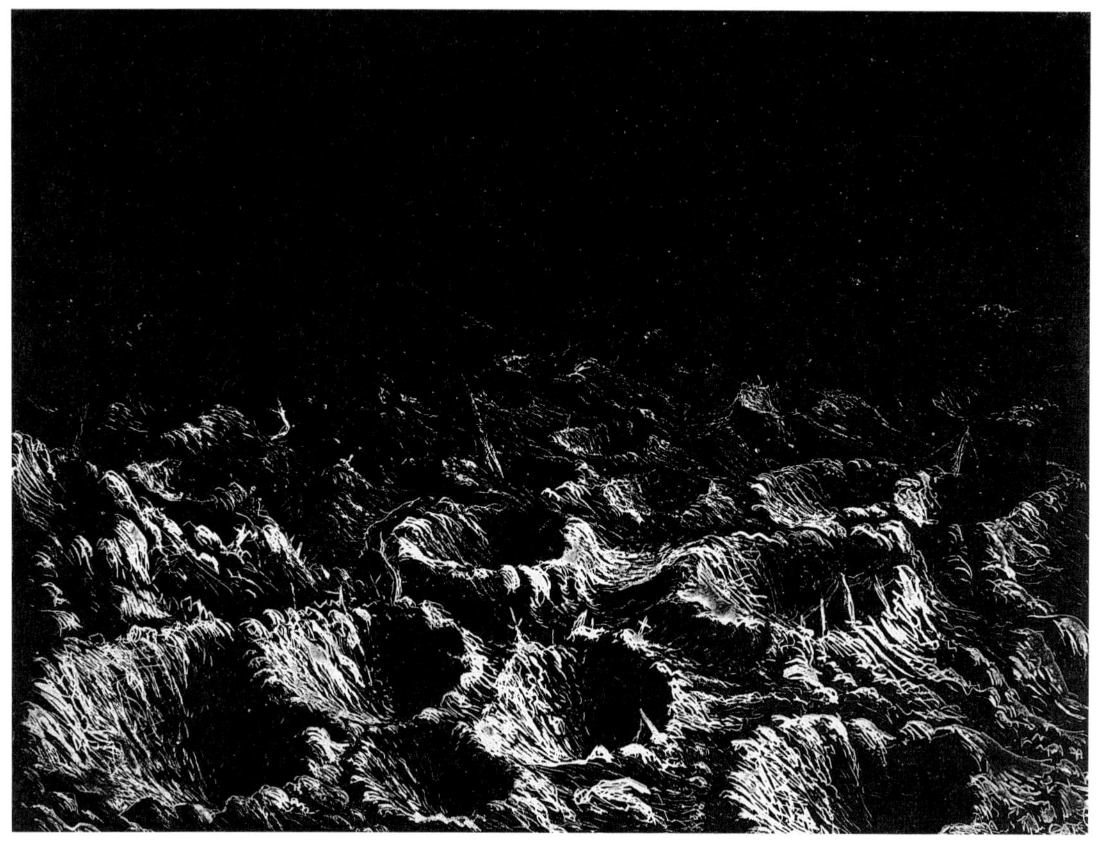

The disappointment which follows defeat and the disaster of war is evidenced
in this dramatic series of 50 prints inspired not just by Dix's own experience,
which is brought together in his drawings, but also by Goya and Callot and
the anti-war book by Ernst Friedrich, *Krieg dem Kriege*.

OTTO DIX, Shell holes illuminated by flares near
Dontrien, from the portfolio "War", 1924
Aquatint on Ingres paper, 19.2 x 25.5 cm
The British Museum, London

OTTO DIX, Caved-in trench, from the portfolio "War",
1924
Etching, drypoint, aquatint, 29.2 x 24 cm
The British Museum, London

OTTO DIX, Body on the wire fence, from the portfolio
"War", Flanders, 1924
Etching, 29 x 24.3 cm
The British Museum, London

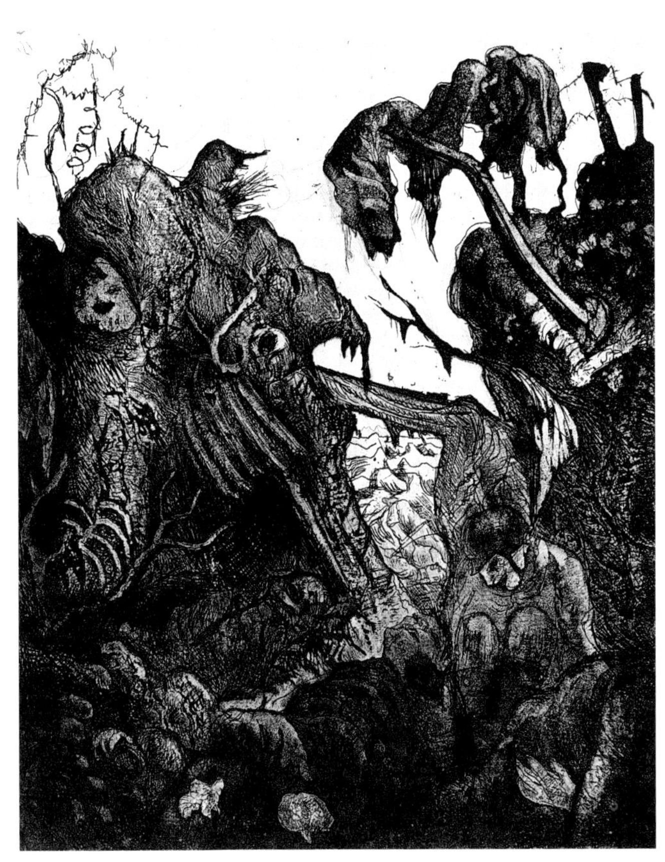

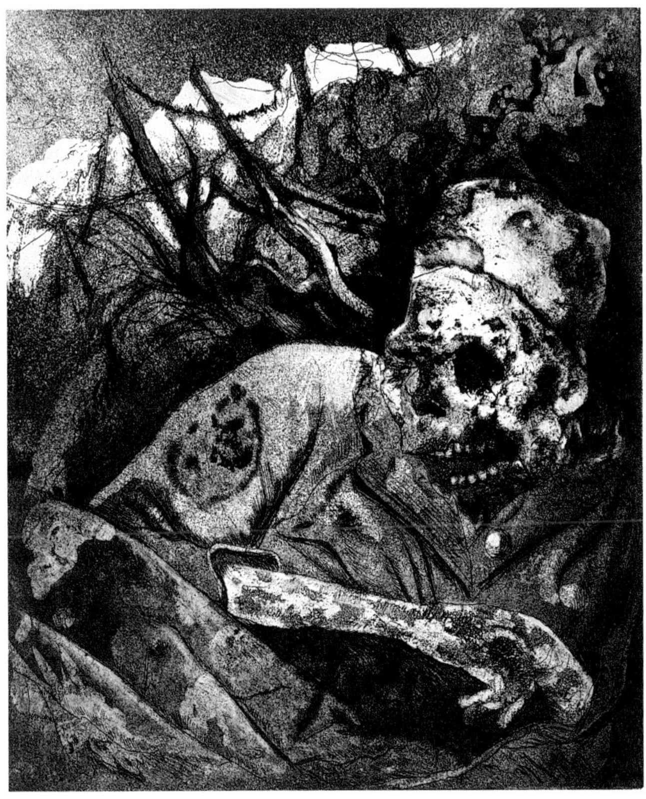

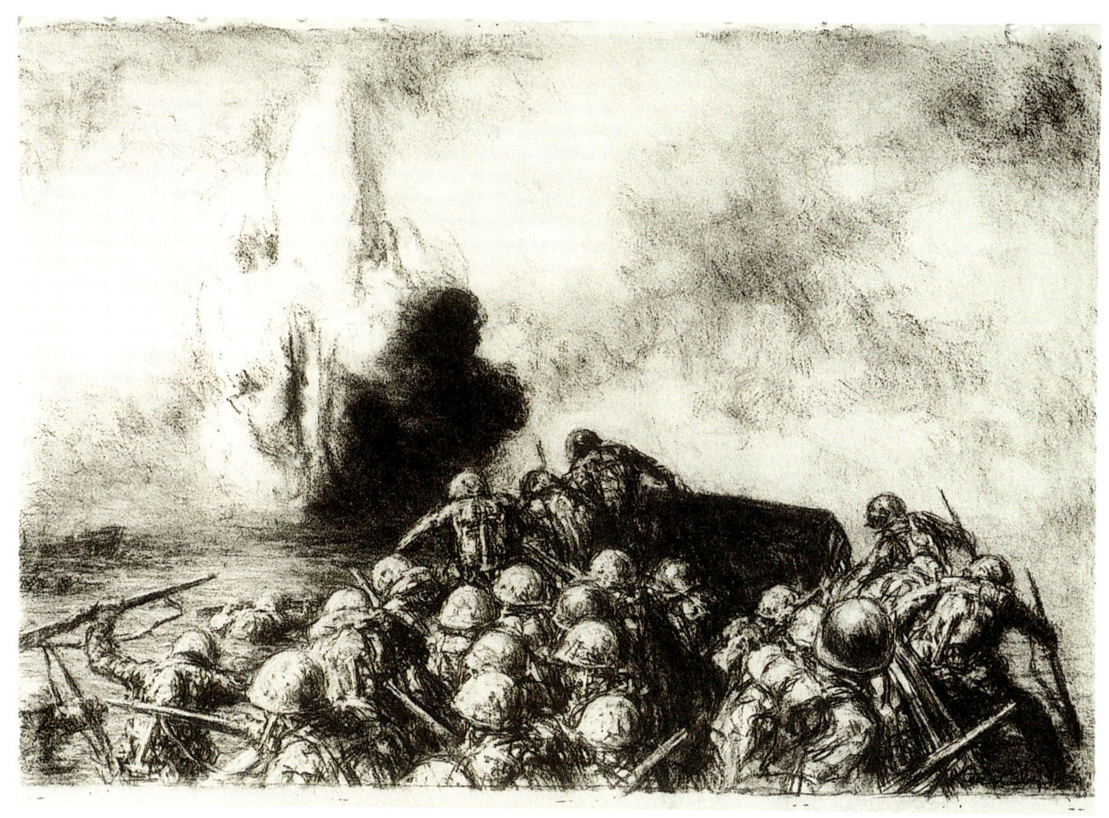

A veteran of the First World War, Eby later produced a number of
works about his experience. In 1941 he tried to join up but was
rejected on the grounds of age. He joined the war artists' scheme
organised by Abbot Laboratories, and in 1943 and 1944 took part
in the harsh combats in the South Pacific with the US marines,
where he contracted malaria. He died of its after-effects in 1946.

KERR EBY, The wave breaks on the reef, 1944
Charcoal, 52.7 x 76.2 cm
Navy Art Collection, Naval Historical Center, Washington

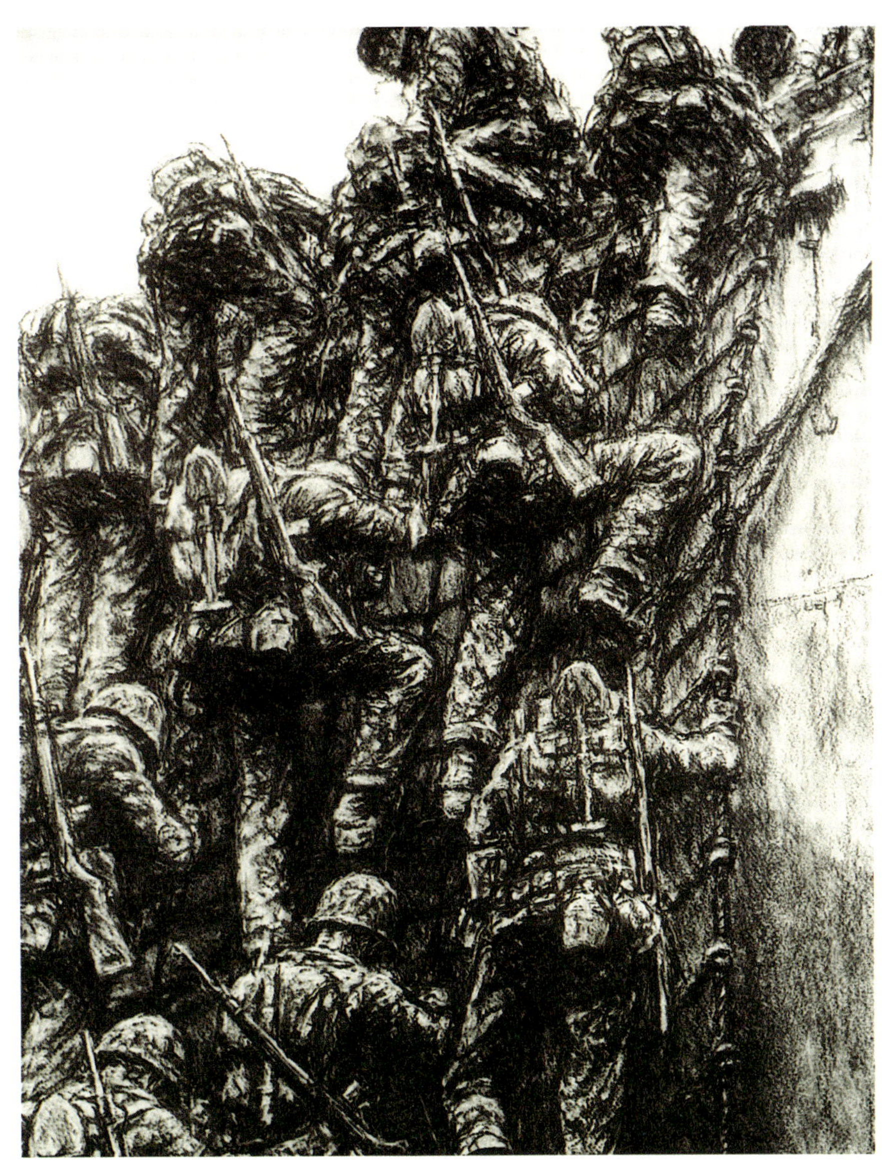

KERR EBY, Down the net, 1944
Charcoal, 86.3 x 66 cm
Navy Art Collection, Naval Historical Center, Washington

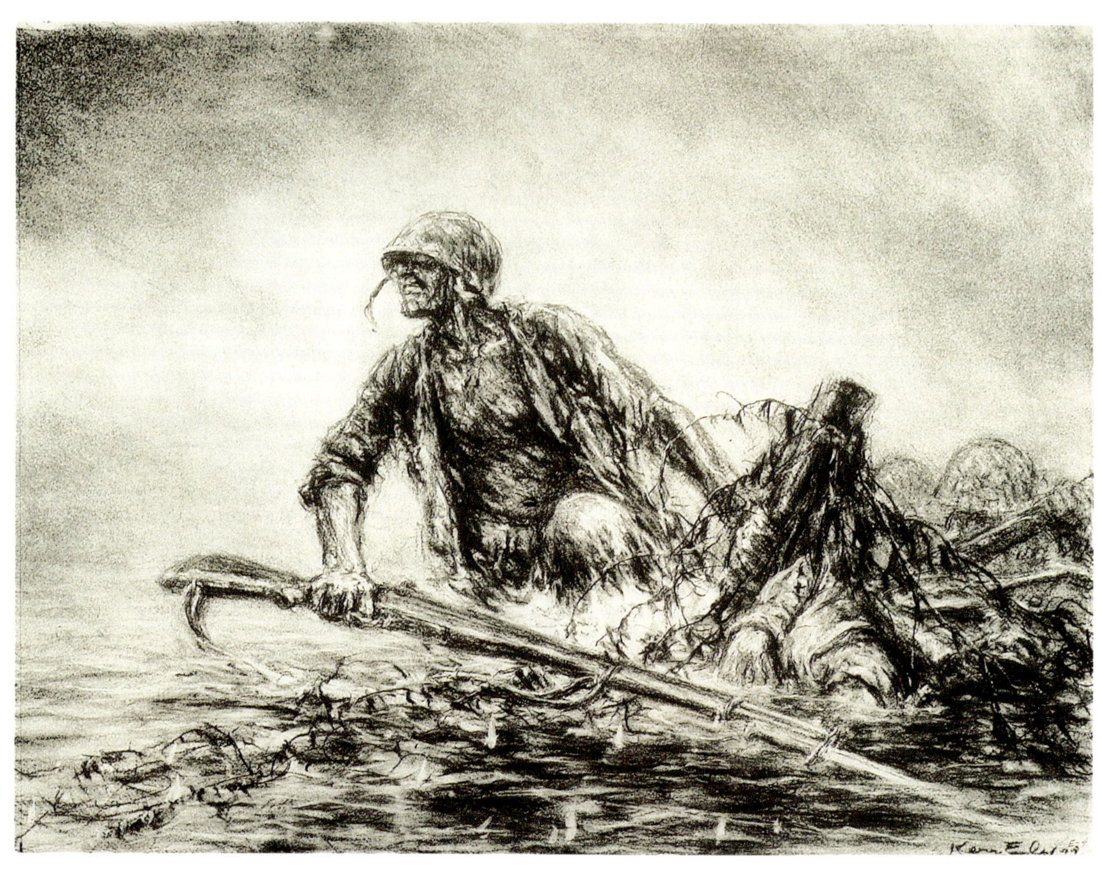

KERR EBY, Bullets and barbed wire, 1944
Charcoal, 53.3 x 73.6 cm
Navy Art Collection, Naval Historical Center, Washington

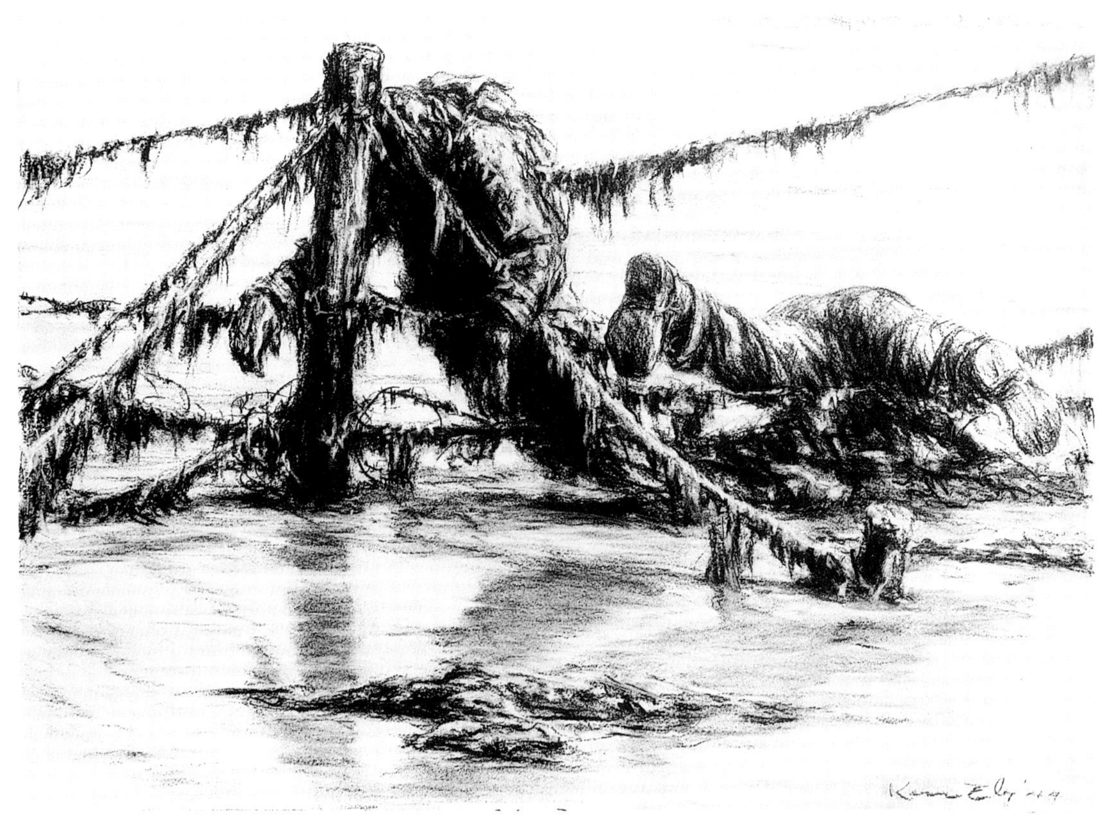

KERR EBY, Ebb tide, Tarawa, 1944
Charcoal, 54.6 x 73.6 cm
Navy Art Collection, Naval Historical Center, Washington

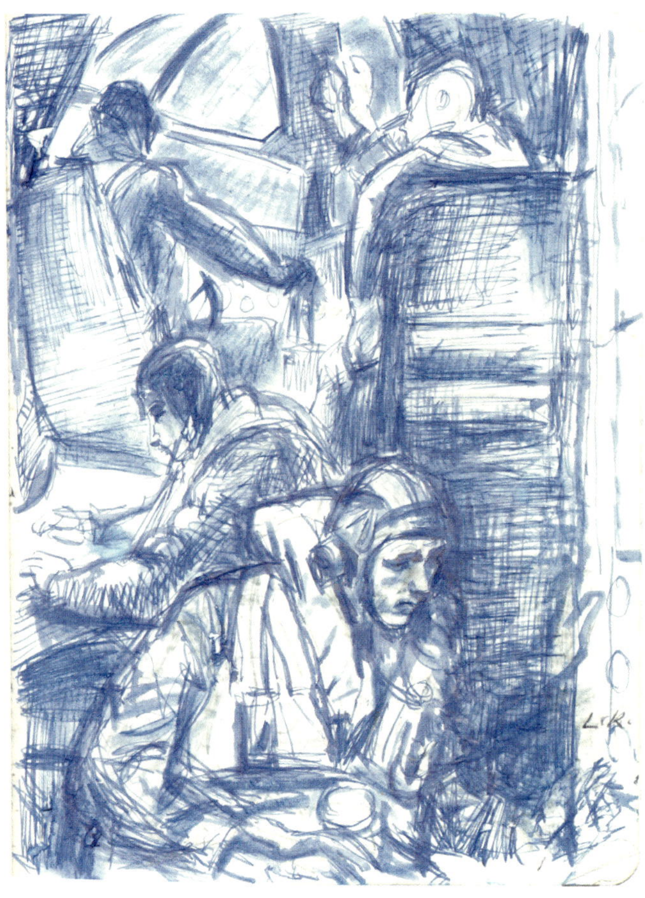

The first elected woman Royal Academician, Laura Knight
was part of the British official war artists' scheme and
was later commissioned to produce a pictorial record of the
participants at the Nuremberg Trials.

DAME LAURA KNIGHT, R.A.F. subjects, Sketchbook of
Second World War, n.d.
Pen, ink, watercolour and charcoal, 26.3 x 20.8 cm
Imperial War Museum, London

DAME LAURA KNIGHT, Take-off, interior of a
bomber aircraft, n.d.
Oil on canvas, 182.8 x 152.4 cm
Imperial War Museum, London

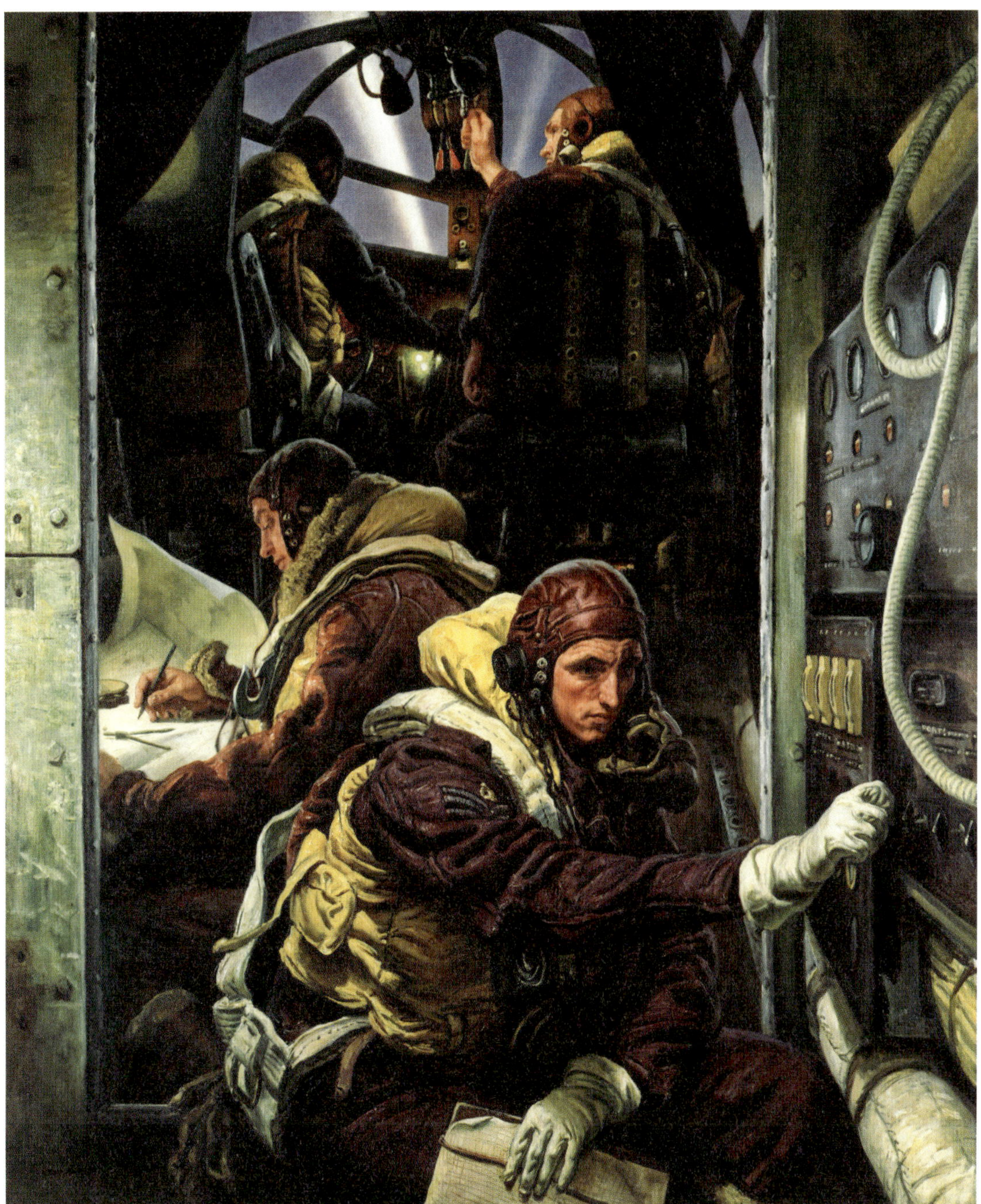

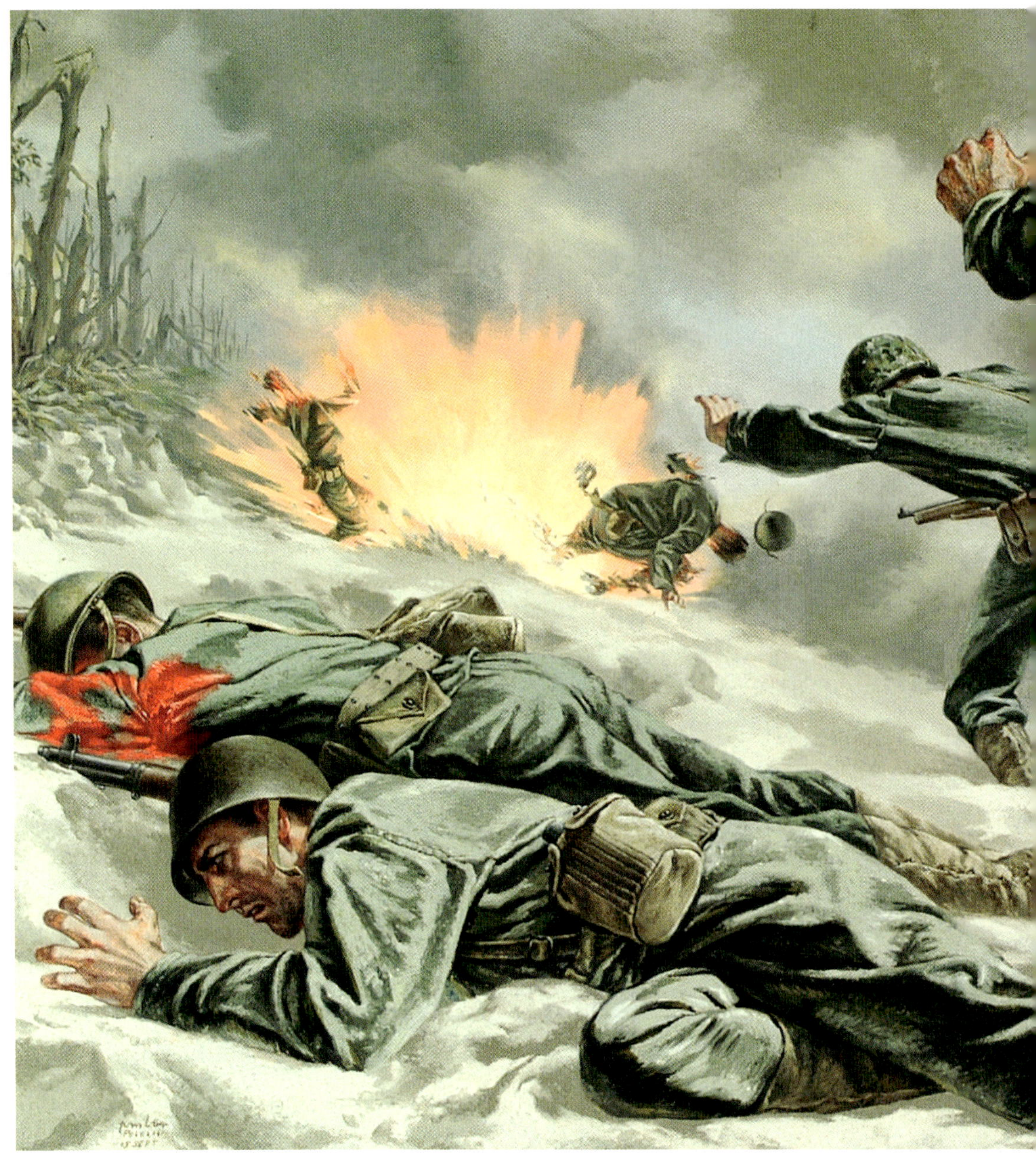

Before the United States entered the war in 1941, Lea had already embarked for the North Atlantic on an assignment for *Life* magazine, which he continued to work for throughout the conflict. He was in the Mediterranean, India, China and the Pacific, where he took part in the landings on Peleliu Island, the site of a bloody battle lasting 26 days. His paintings are based on the sketches he made during the battle.

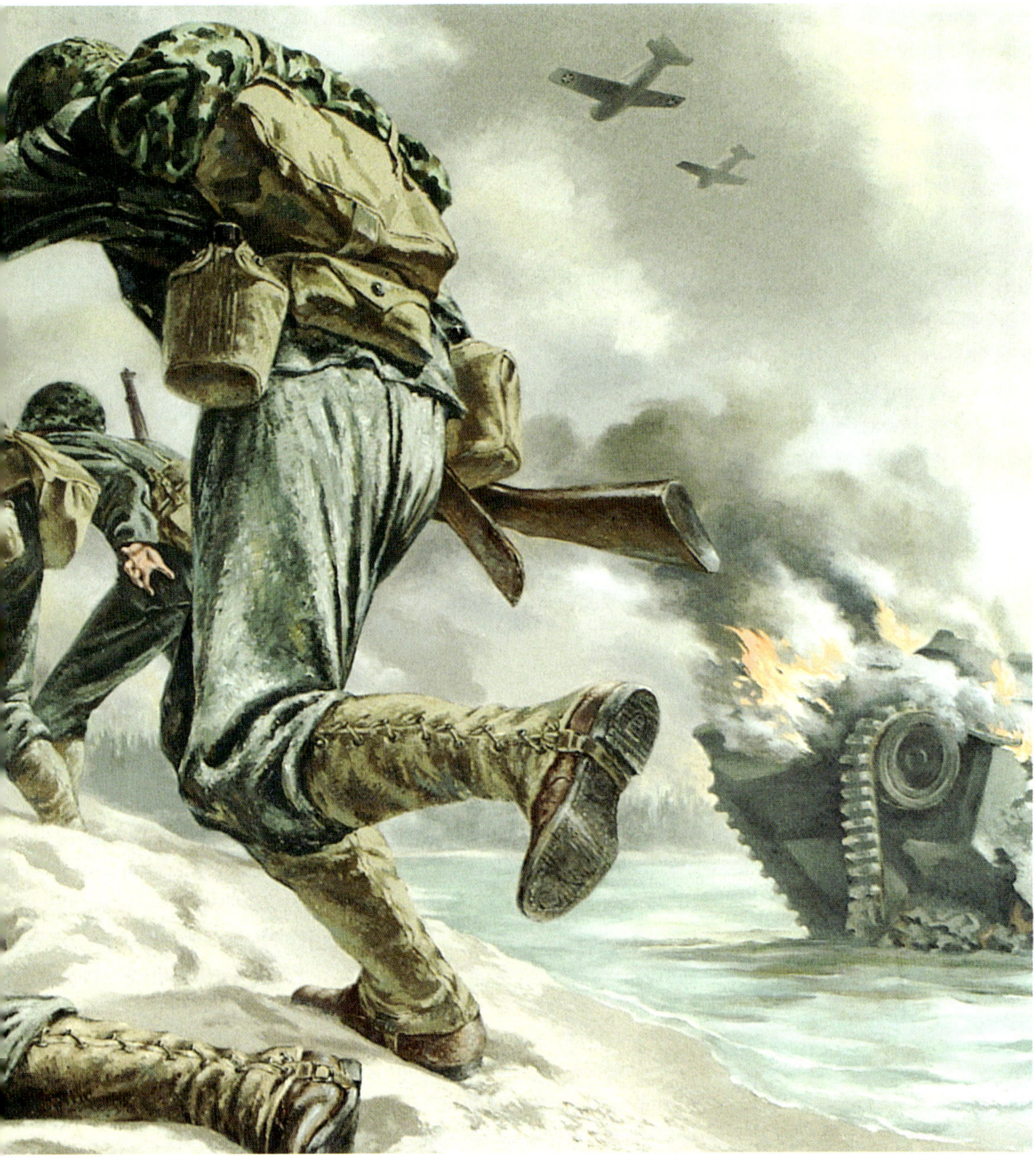

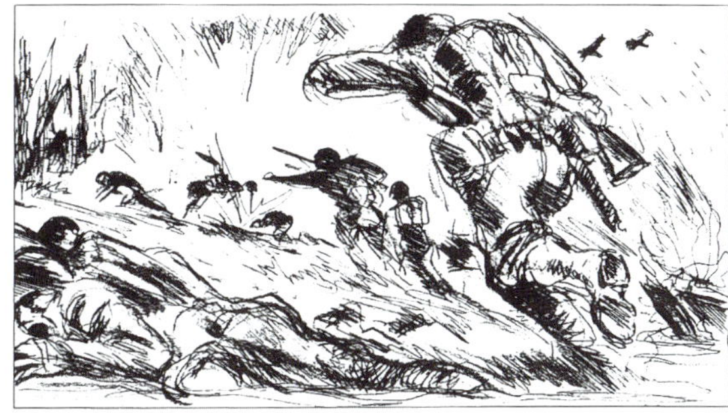

TOM LEA, The beach, 1944
Oil on canvas, 55.8 x 106.6 cm
National Museum of the US Army,
Army Art Collection, Washington

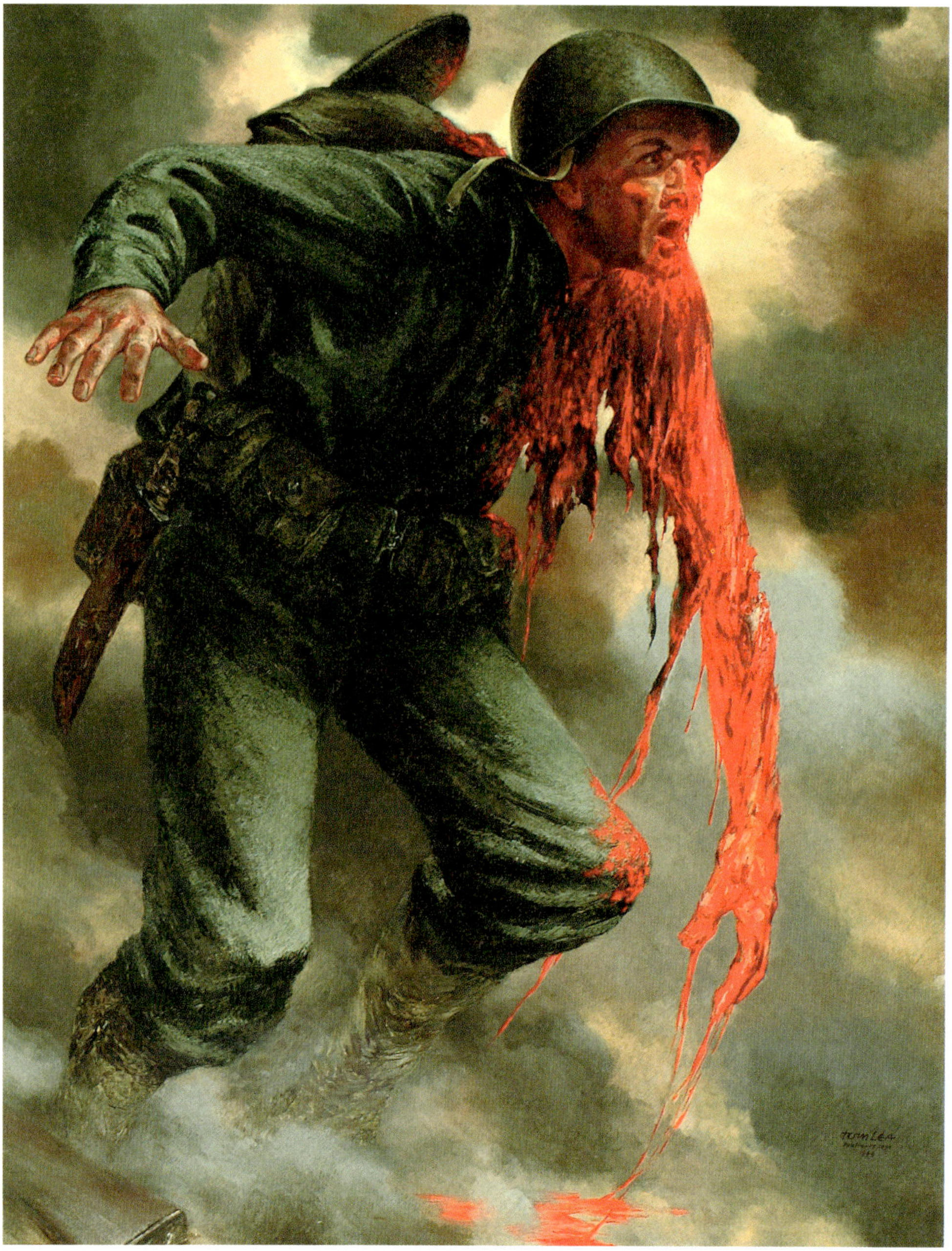

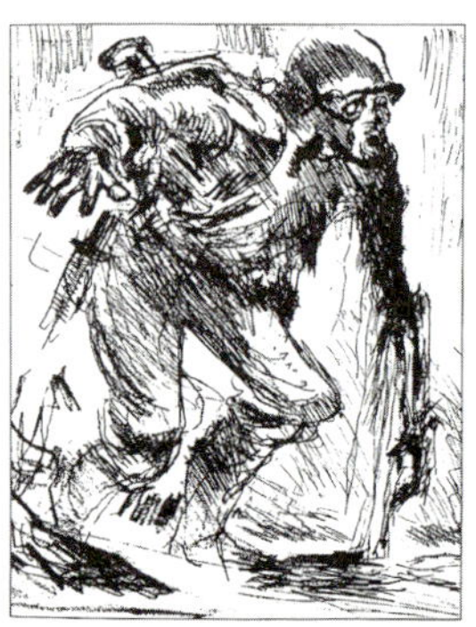

TOM LEA, The prize, 1944
Oil on canvas, 92.7 x 71.1 cm
National Museum of the US Army,
Army Art Collection, Washington

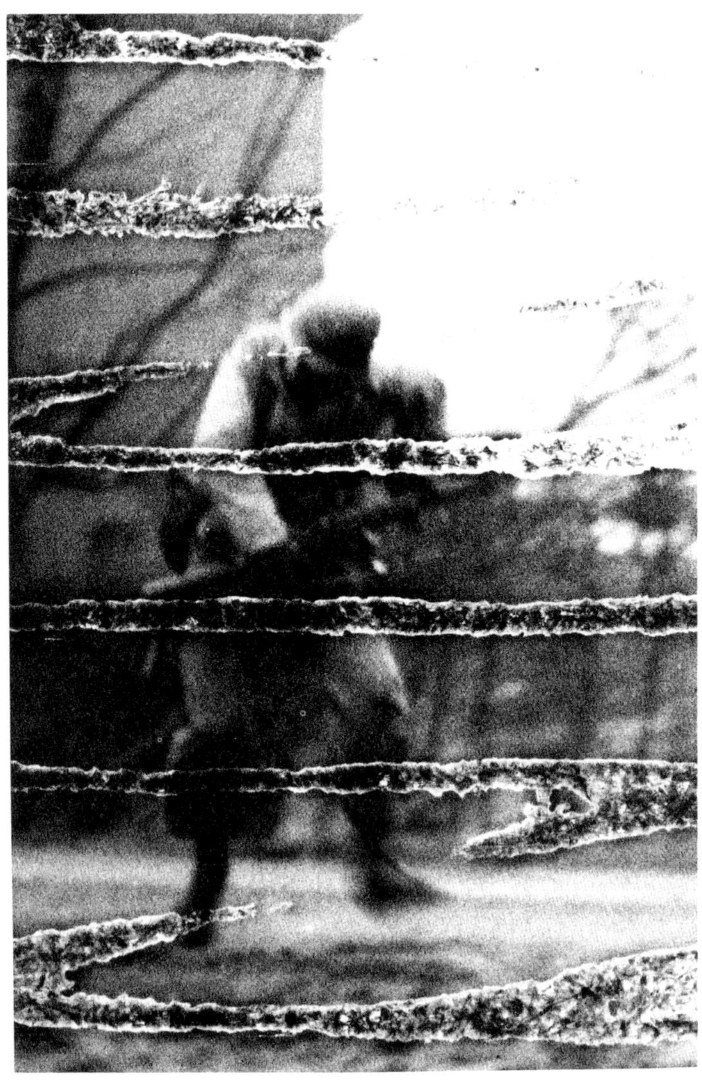

Vaccaro was a soldier in the Second World War. He took
part in the Normandy landings in 1944 and covered the
advance on Germany carrying his camera alongside his gun.
This photograph clearly shows the difficult conditions
under which he produced this record of events.

TONY VACCARO, American reporter, taken in
action, France, 1944
Musée d'Histoire Contemporaine - BDIC, Paris

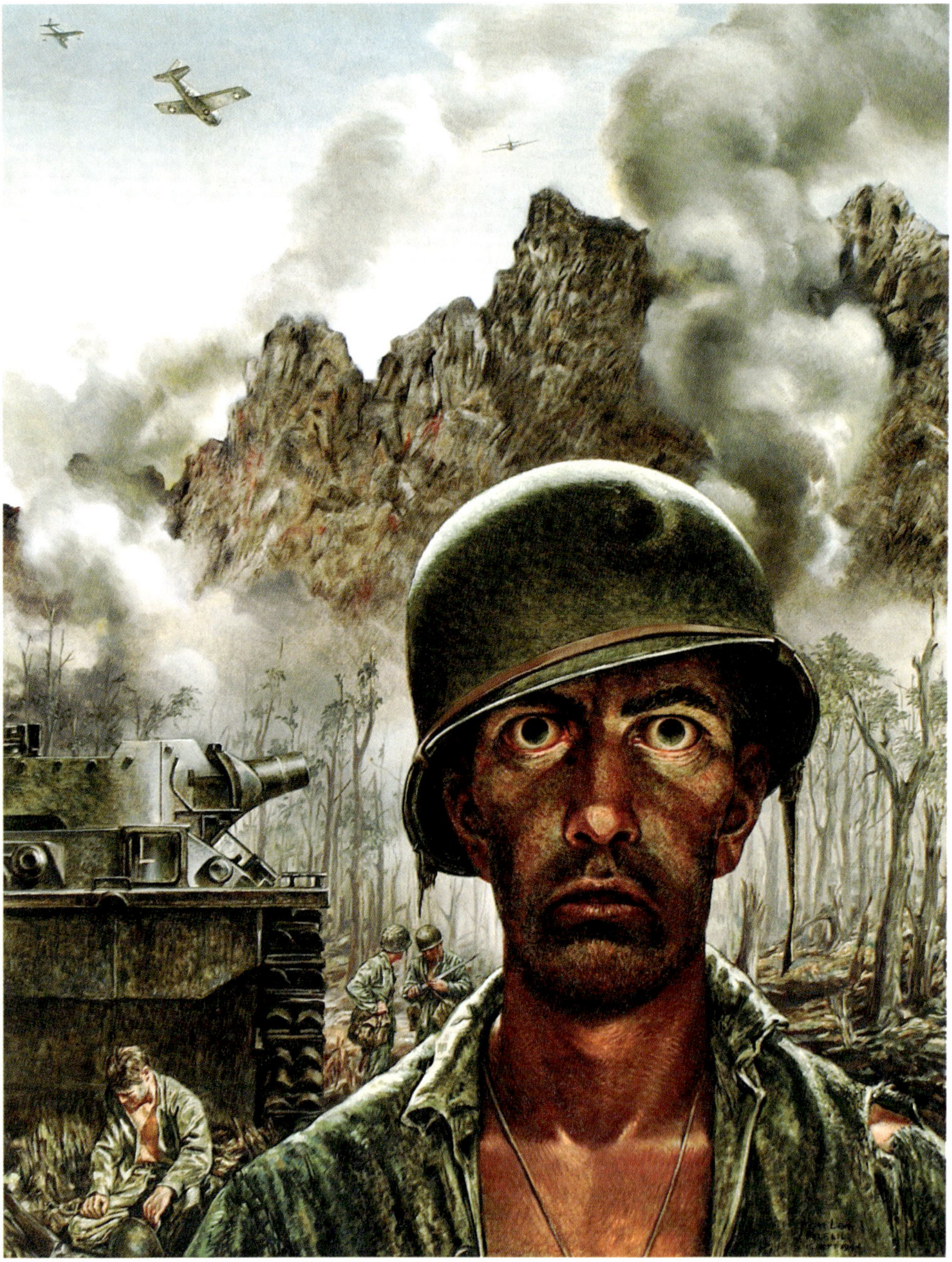

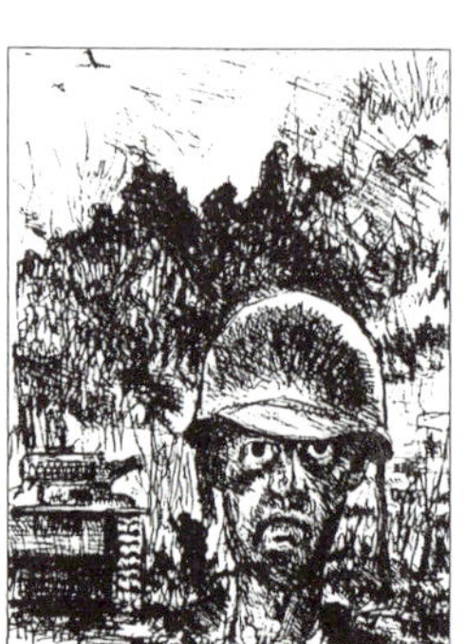

TOM LEA, Marines call it that 2,000
yard stare, 1944
Oil on canvas, 91.4 x 71.1 cm
National Museum of the US Army,
Army Art Collection, Washington

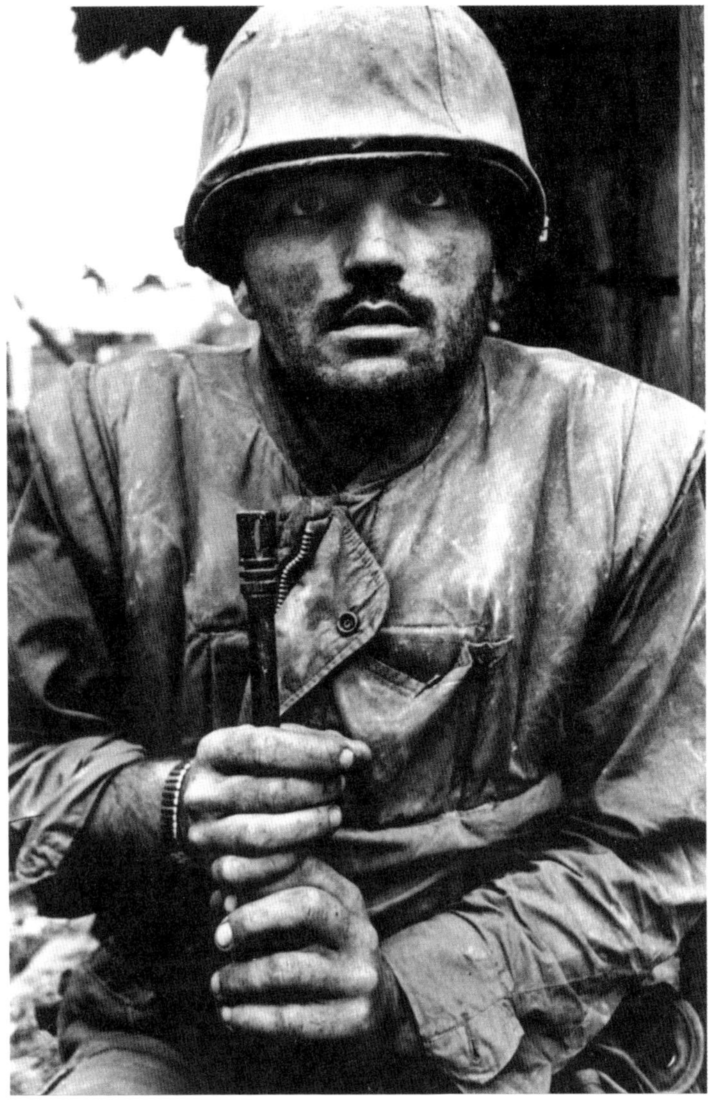

The vacant expression on the face of this marine
waiting to be evacuated after the Battle of Hue,
in February 1968, evinces the shock caused by
what he has seen.

DON MCCULLIN, Portrait of marine during the Battle of Hue, 1968
Don McCullin / Contact Press Images / Contacto

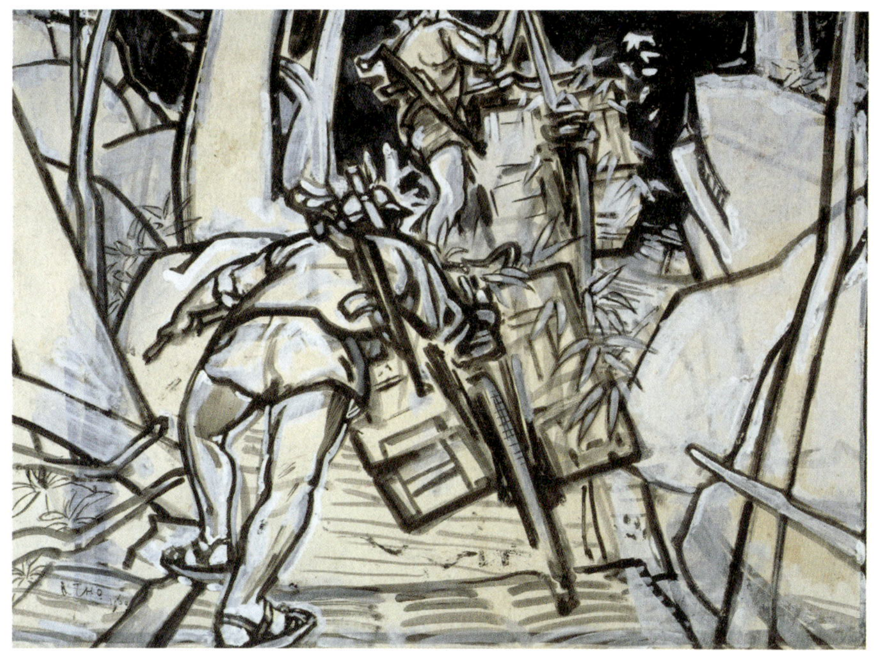

Few armies can afford to take official war artists on board. In Vietnam they were all needed to fight. Nevertheless, among the veterans, there were artists who drew and painted what they saw. This peaceful vision comes as a surprise. The Vietnamese seldom depict the most brutal part of the battle, the reason for this being that the soldiers have witnessed so much horror that they prefer to remember other aspects of the experience of war.

QUANG THO, Ho Chi Minh Trail, 1969
Gouache on machine-made paper, 39 x 54 cm
The British Museum, London

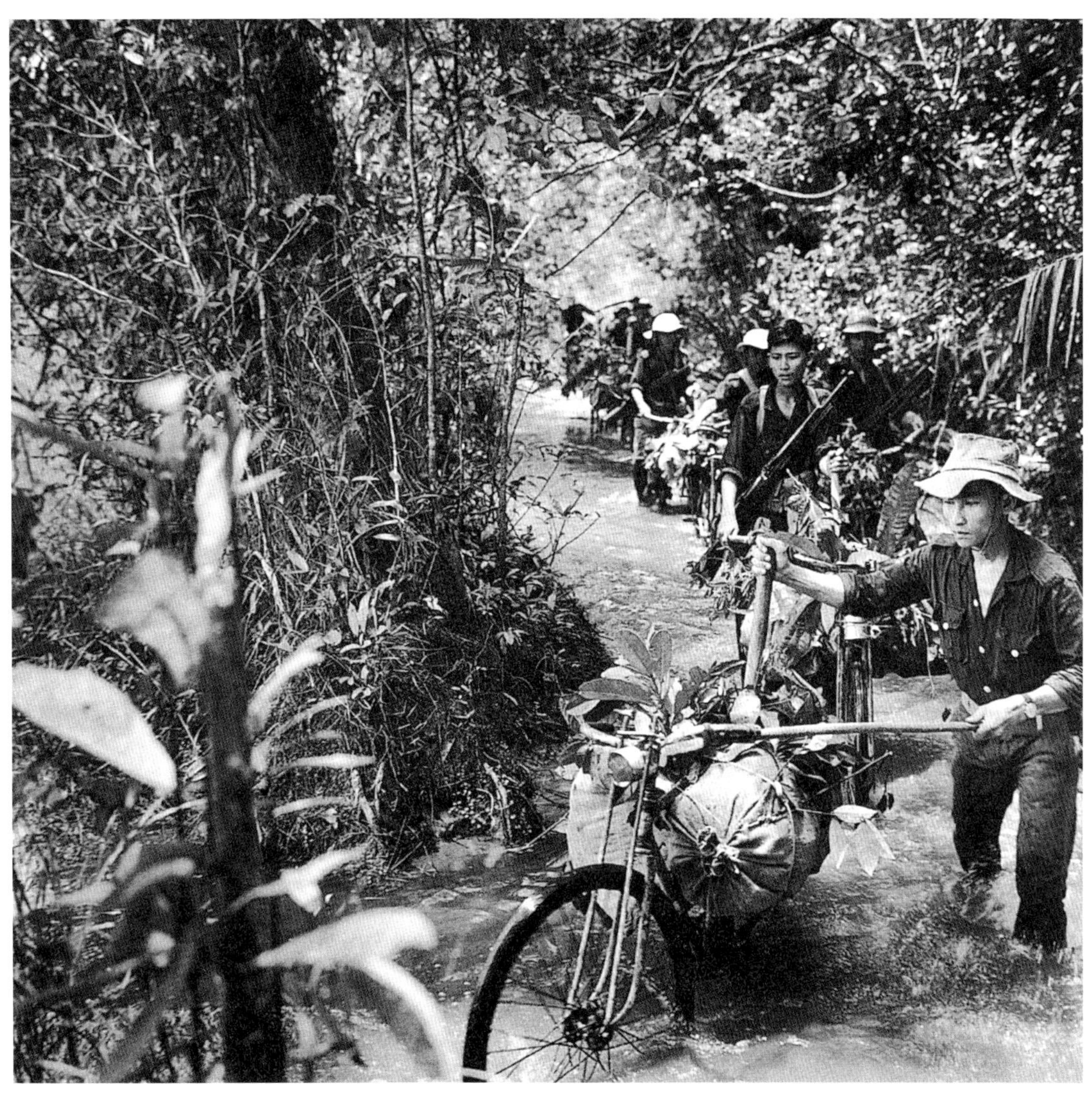

DINH THUY, South Vietnam, 1966
Courtesy of Another Vietnam (National Geographic), Washington

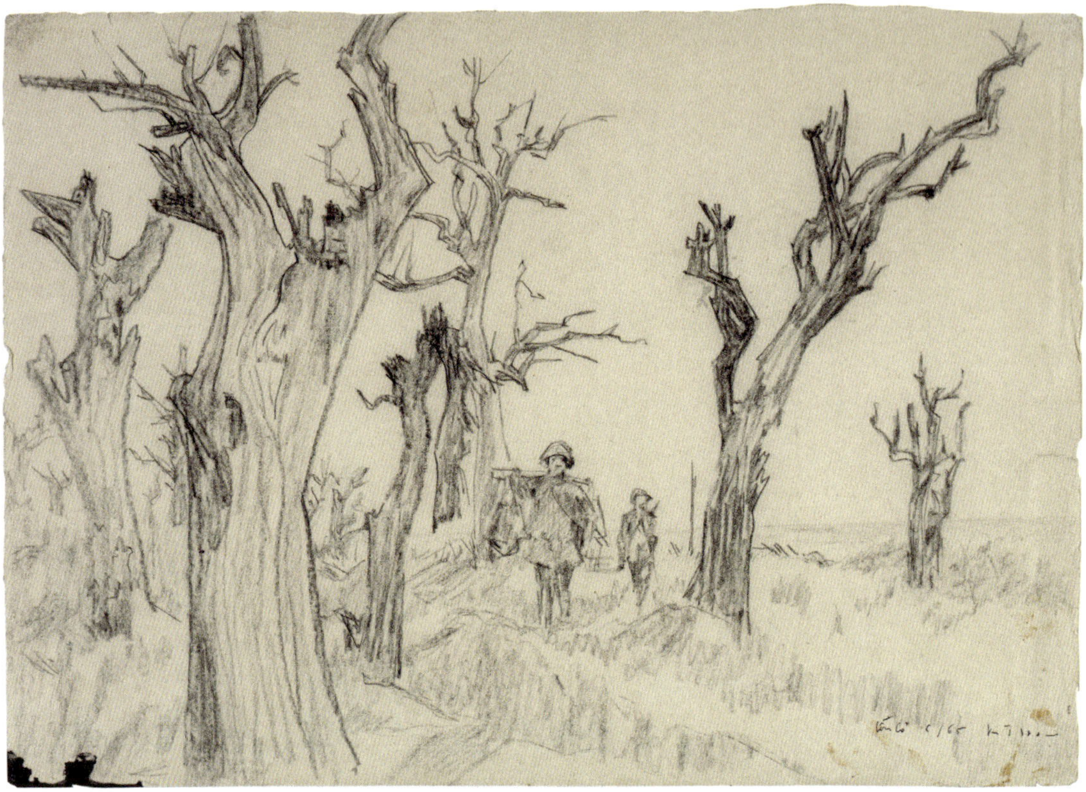

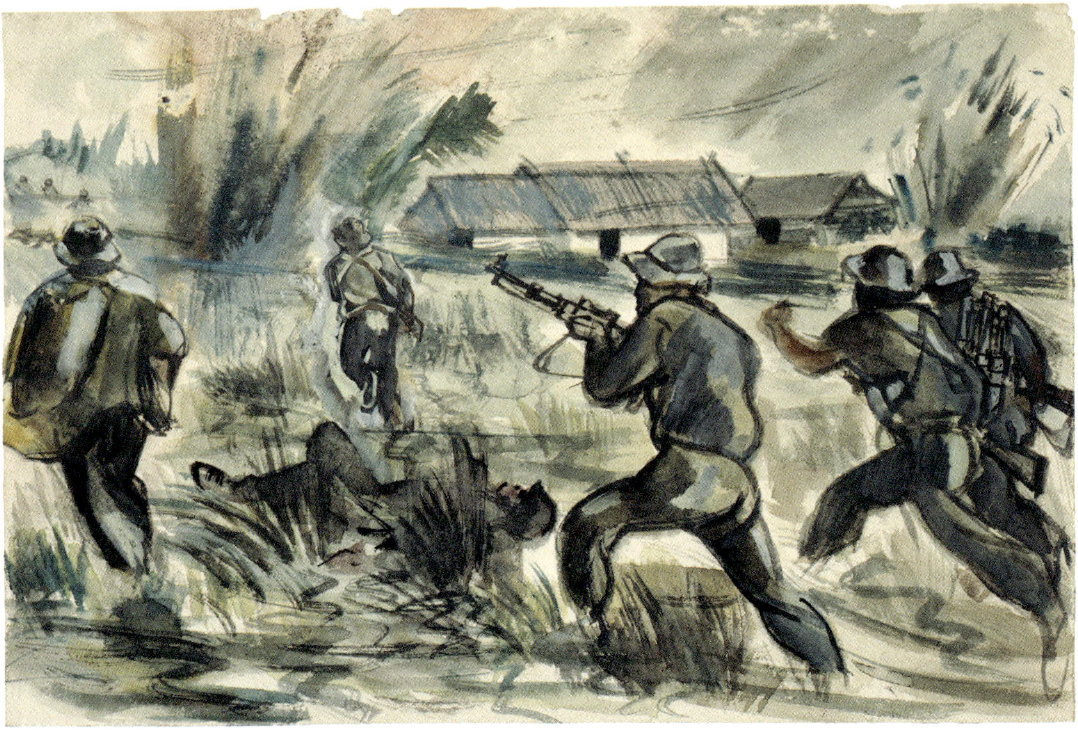

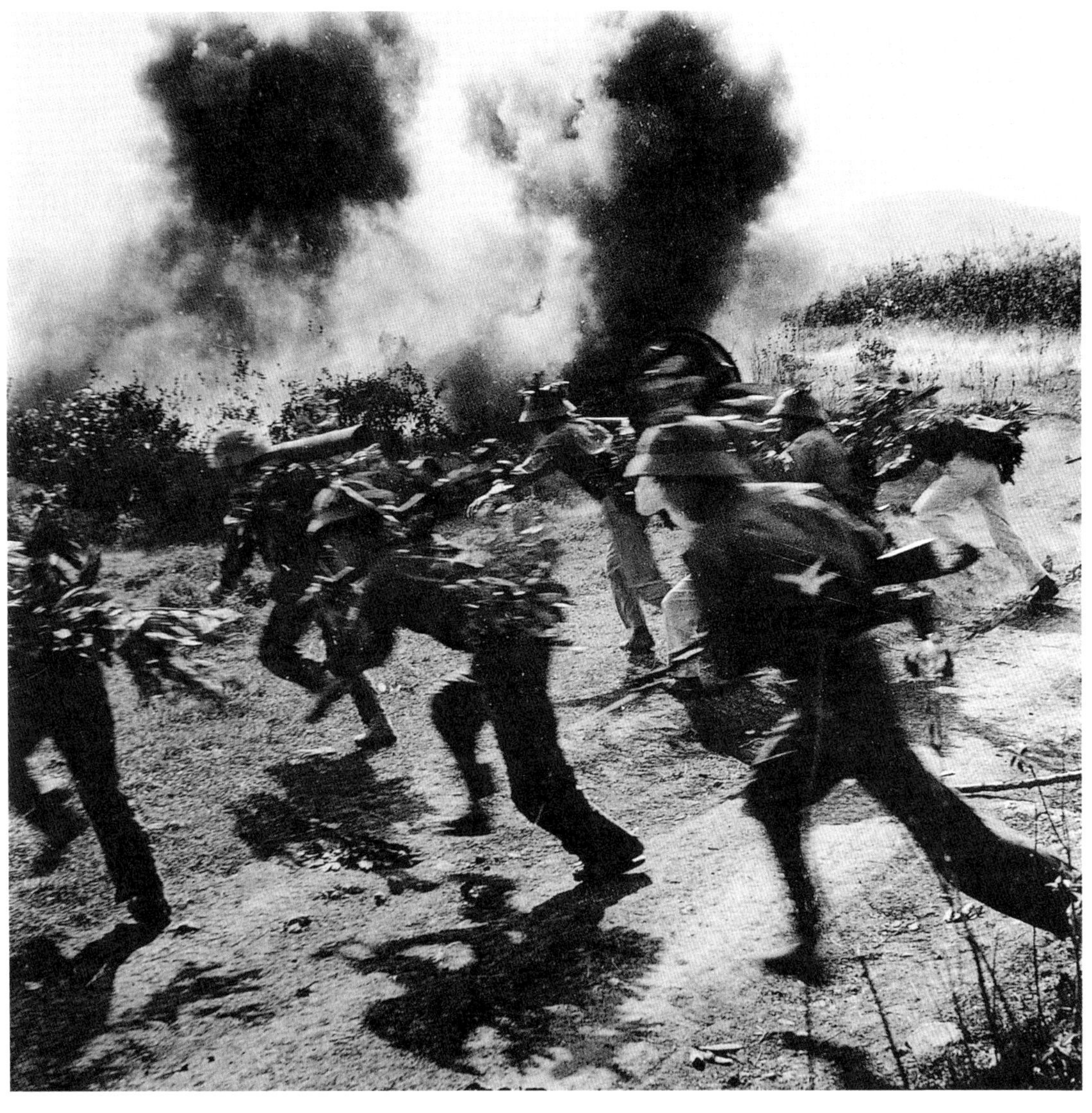

VAN DA AND NGUYEN THU, Walking in a war-torn
landscape, 1965
Charcoal on paper, 27.5 x 39.5 cm
The British Museum, London

TRUONG HIEU, Battle scene, c. 1965-1975
Gouache on machine-made paper, 16 x 25 cm
The British Museum, London

NGUYEN DINH UU, Southern Laos, 1972
Courtesy of Another Vietnam (National Geographic),
Washington

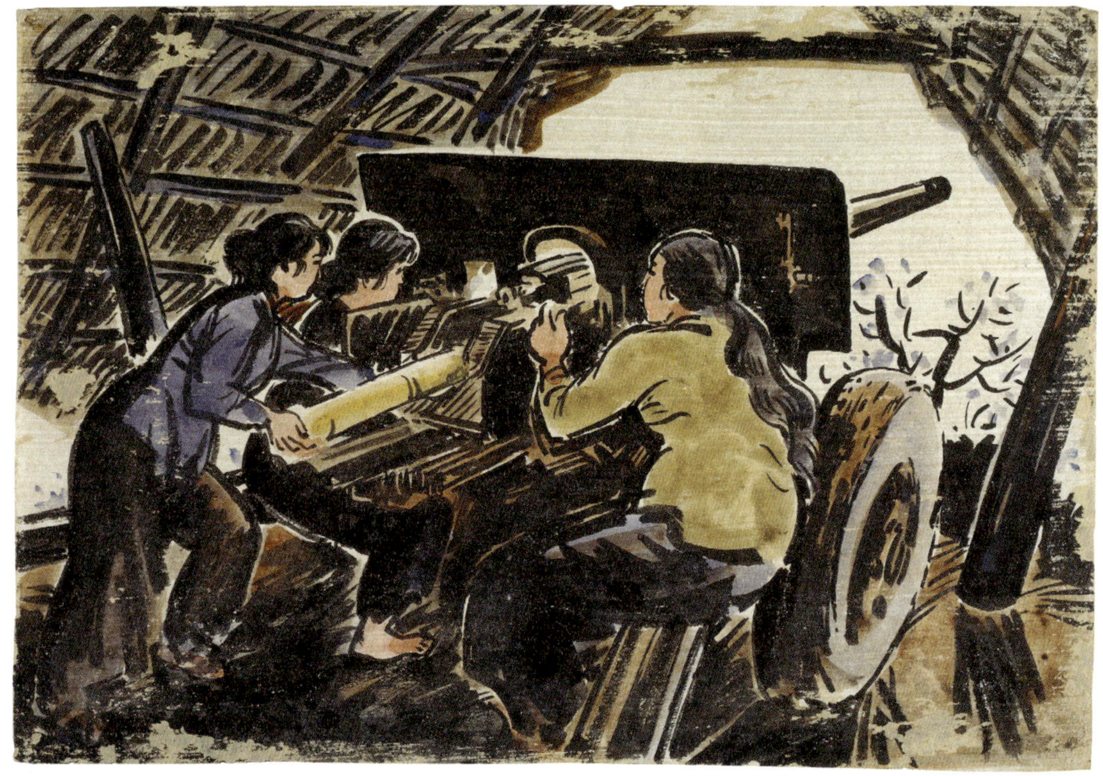

Pictures showing the role of Vietnamese women
during the war are one of the many examples
of the ways women have fought in many conflicts,
in militias and guerrilla groups (Spain, Eritrea,
Nicaragua, etc.), and their growing numbers in
many regular armies.

QUANG THO, Three women with a field gun, 1965
Black ink with watercolour on shell-coated hand-made
paper, 26 x 28 cm
The British Museum, London

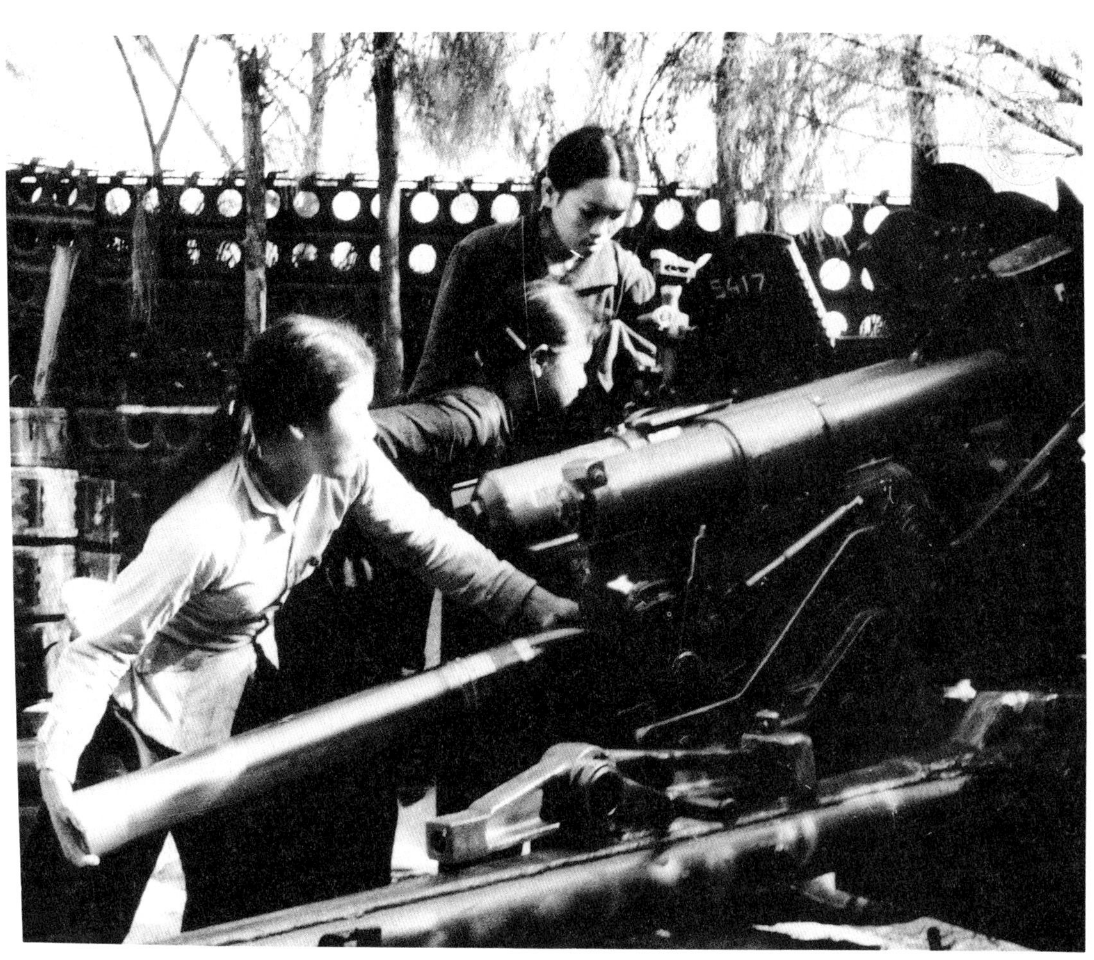

ANONYMOUS VIETNAMESE, Women in combat, 1969
Musée d'Histoire Contemporaine - BDIC, Paris

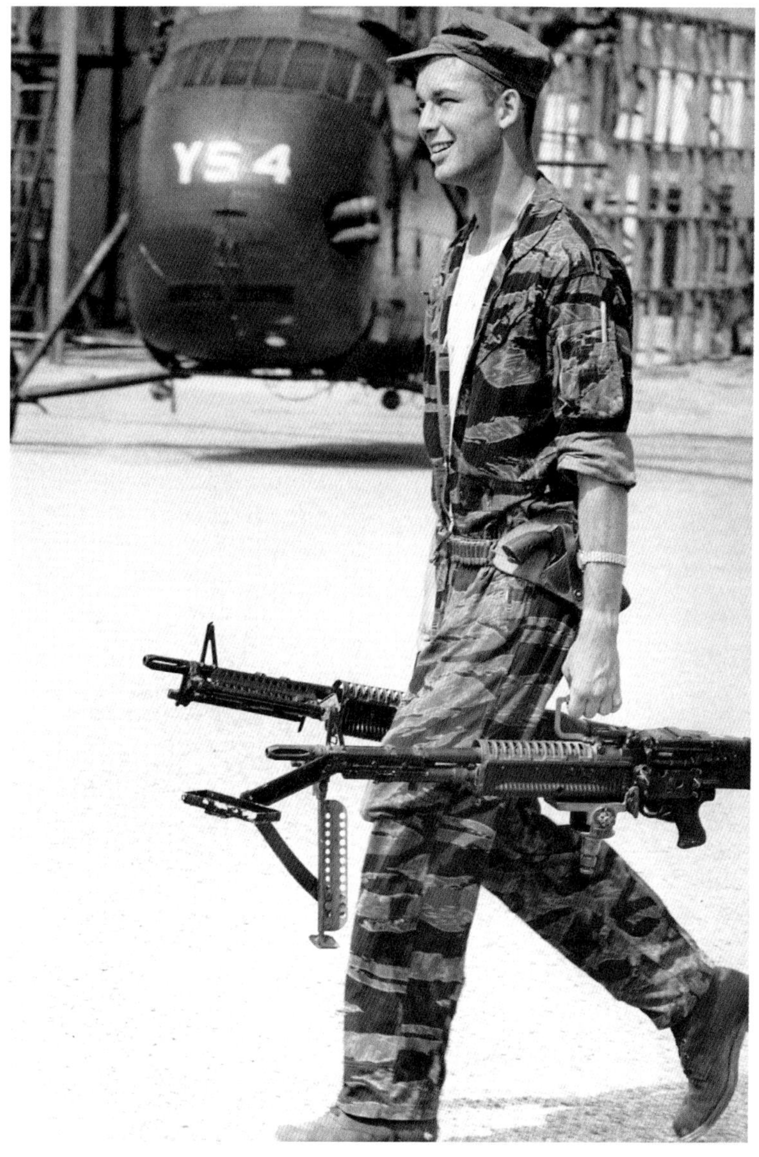

LARRY BURROWS, Before the mission, Yankee Papa 13 crew chief James Farley carries two M-60s to his helicopter, Da Nang, South Vietnam, March 1965
Courtesy of James and Sarah Burrows

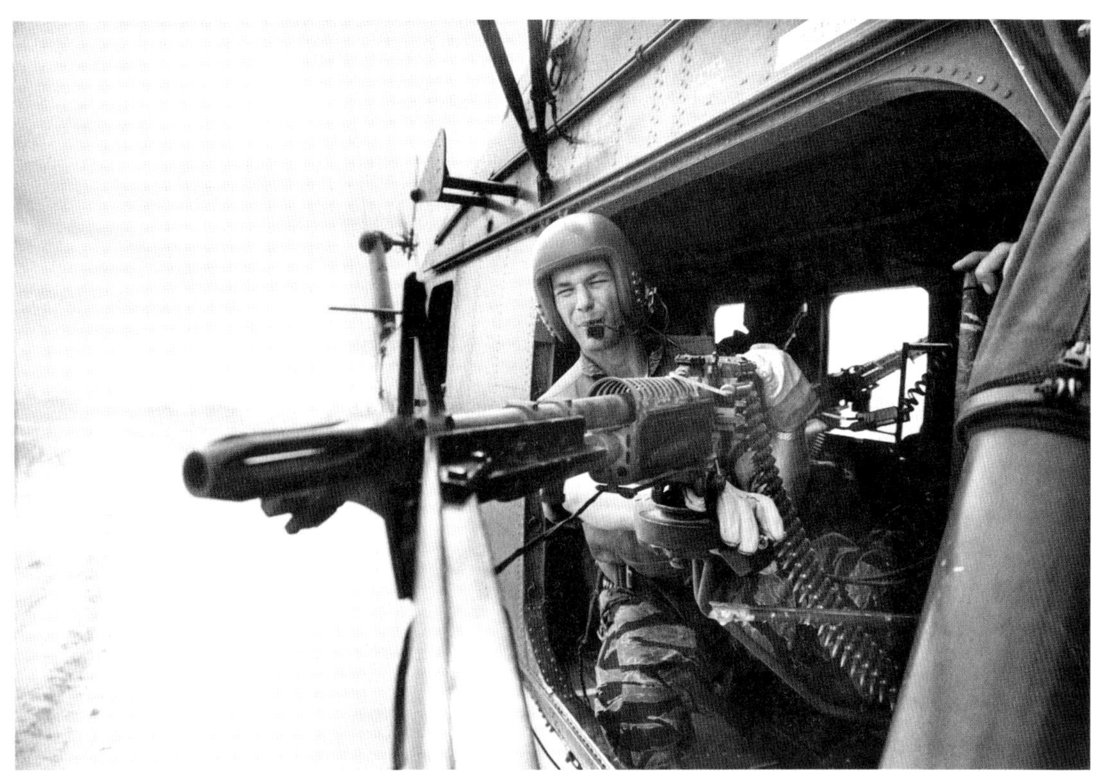

For his famous report, published in *Life* magazine, the photographer was travelling with the crew of the Yankee Papa 13 when another helicopter in the fleet was shot down. Burrows died in a helicopter in Vietnam with fellow photographers Henri Huet, Kent Potter and Keisaburo Shimamoto.

LARRY BURROWS, Coming into the landing zone. Yankee Papa 13 crew chief James Farley returns fire, South Vietnam, March 1965
Courtesy of James and Sarah Burrows

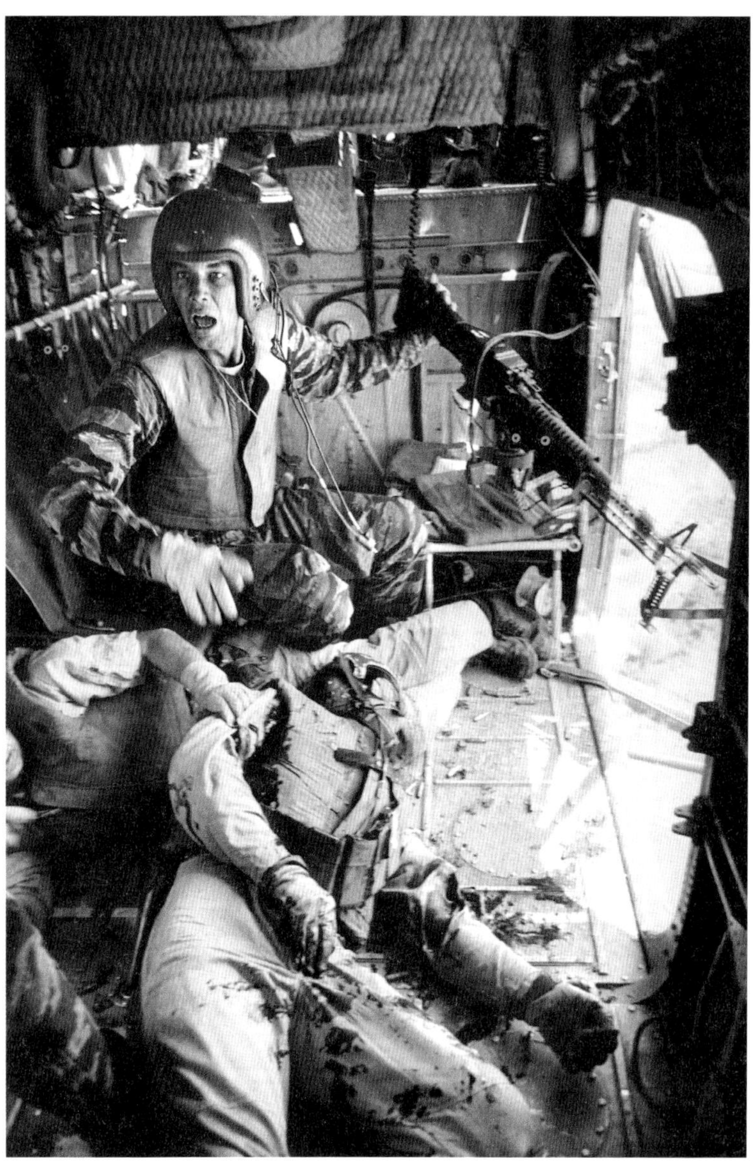

LARRY BURROWS, Yankee Papa 13 crew chief James Farley, his
gun jammed and with two wounded comrades aboard, shouts
to his gunner, South Vietnam, March 1965
Courtesy of James and Sarah Burrows

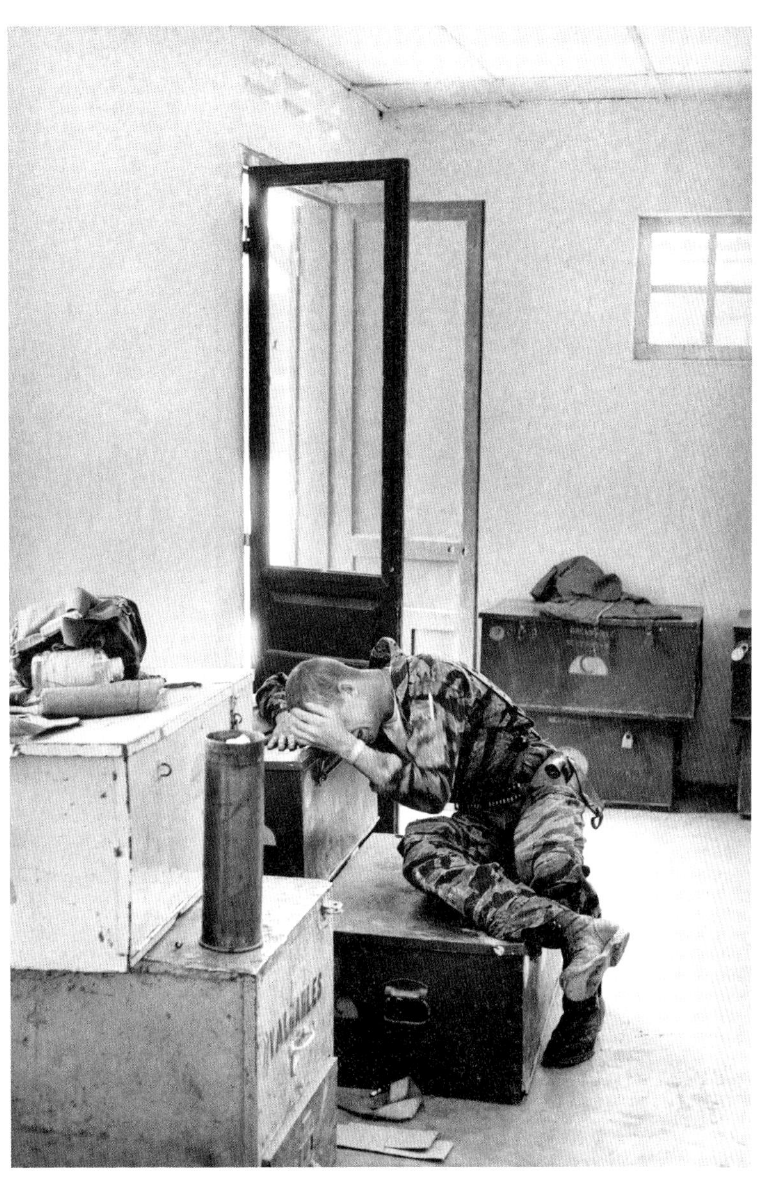

LARRY BURROWS, In a supply shack, the tragic and frustrating
mission over, crew chief James Farley weeps, Da Nang, South
Vietnam, March 1965
Courtesy of James and Sarah Burrows

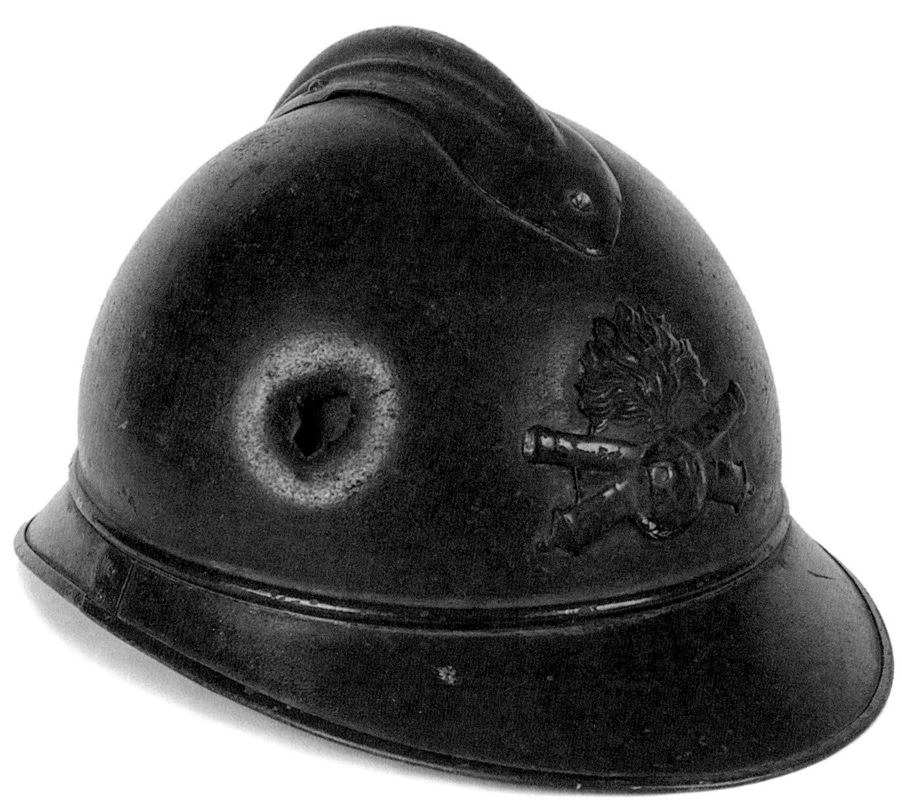

On 17th March 1916, Wilhelm Apollinaris de Kostrowitsky, alias Guillaume Apollinaire, was wounded in the head by a shell burst while reading a newspaper in a trench. His injuries led him to suffer emotional and behavioural disorders, although his death in 1918 was a result of the "Spanish flu" epidemic.

Apollinaire's military helmet, showing the hole made by the shell burst
which caused him serious head injuries, 17 March 1916
16 x 24 x 30 cm
Bibliothèque historique de la Ville de Paris, Fonds Apollinaire, Paris

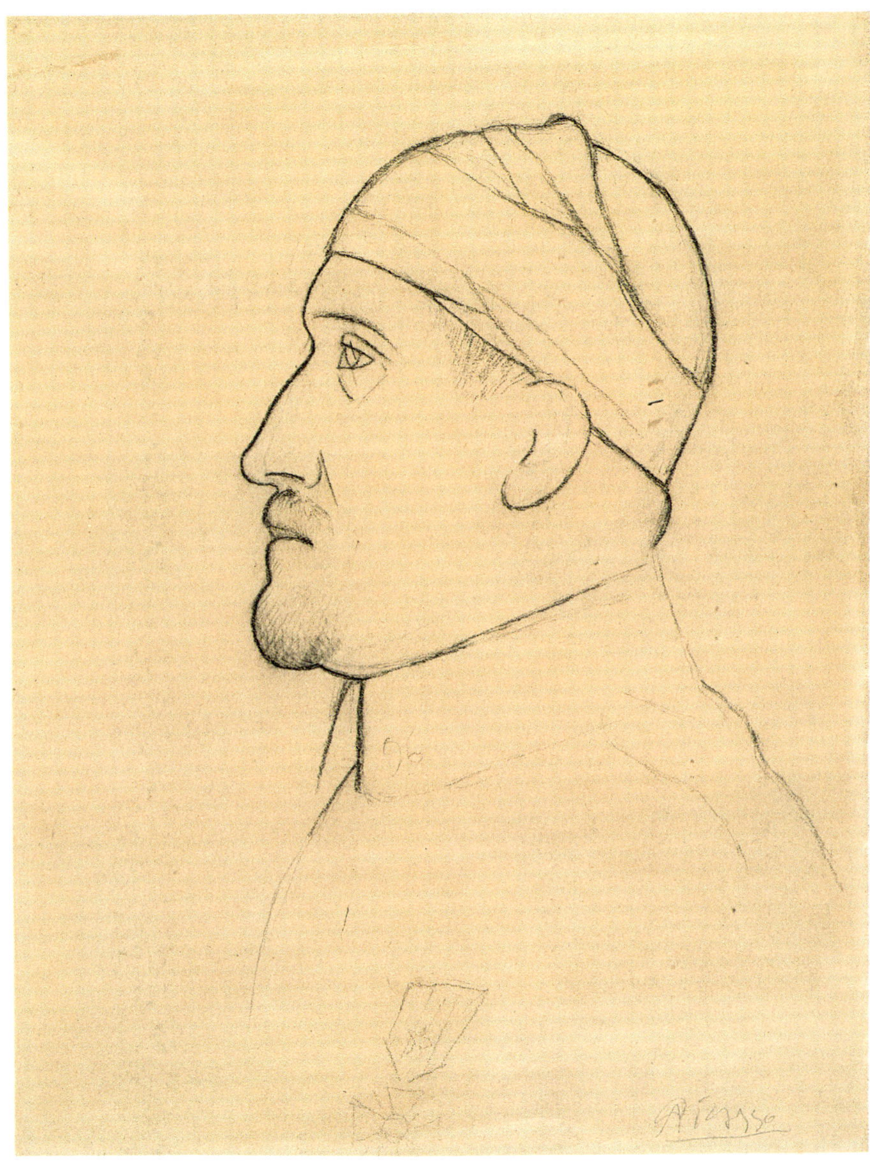

Picasso, who had painted Apollinaire wearing his gunner's
uniform in 1914, painted him in 1916 after he had been
wounded. He did the same with his other friends such as
André Rouveyre, Jean Cocteau and Jean Hugo.

PABLO PICASSO, Portrait of Guillaume Apollinaire with
bandaged head, 1916
Pencil on paper, 45 x 60 cm
Musée Picasso, Paris

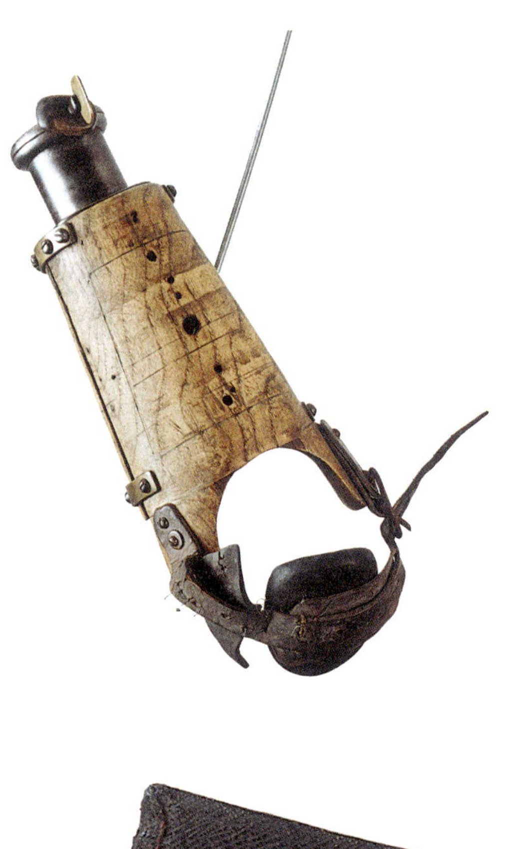

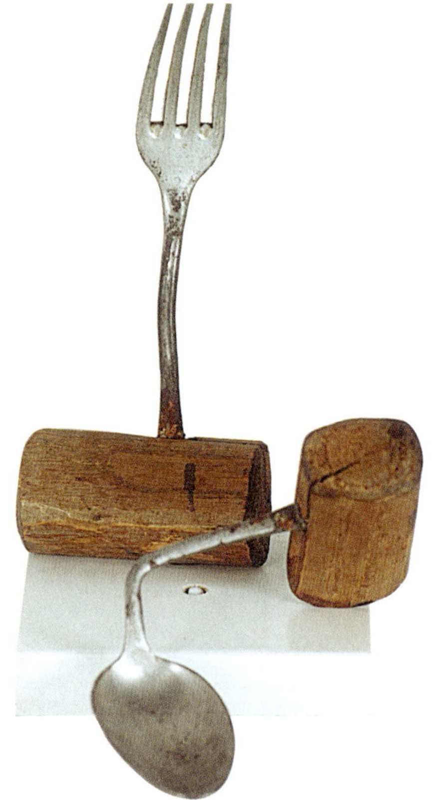

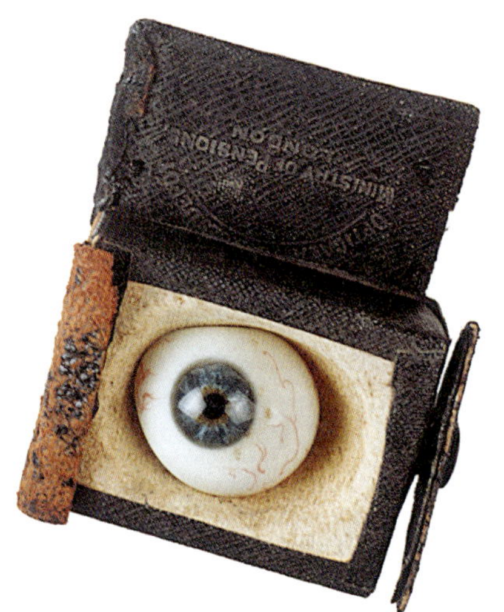

Hôpital Gratry, Clapping device for one-armed serviceman to applaud the entertainments at the Franco-American festival, 30 June and 1st July 1917
Wood, metal and paper, 20.2 x 10.4 x 0.8 cm
Historial de la Grande Guerre, Péronne (Somme)

Glass eye in its original box, early twentieth century
Glass and black cardboard, 1.4 x 2.5 x 2.7 cm (eye);
3 x 5.5 x 4 cm (box)
Historial de la Grande Guerre, Péronne (Somme)

Set of two pieces of cutlery for a disabled serviceman, adapted to his disability, First World War
Wood and iron handle, 18 x 8 x 4.5 cm (spoon); 15 x 7 x 11 cm (fork)
Historial de la Grande Guerre, Péronne (Somme)

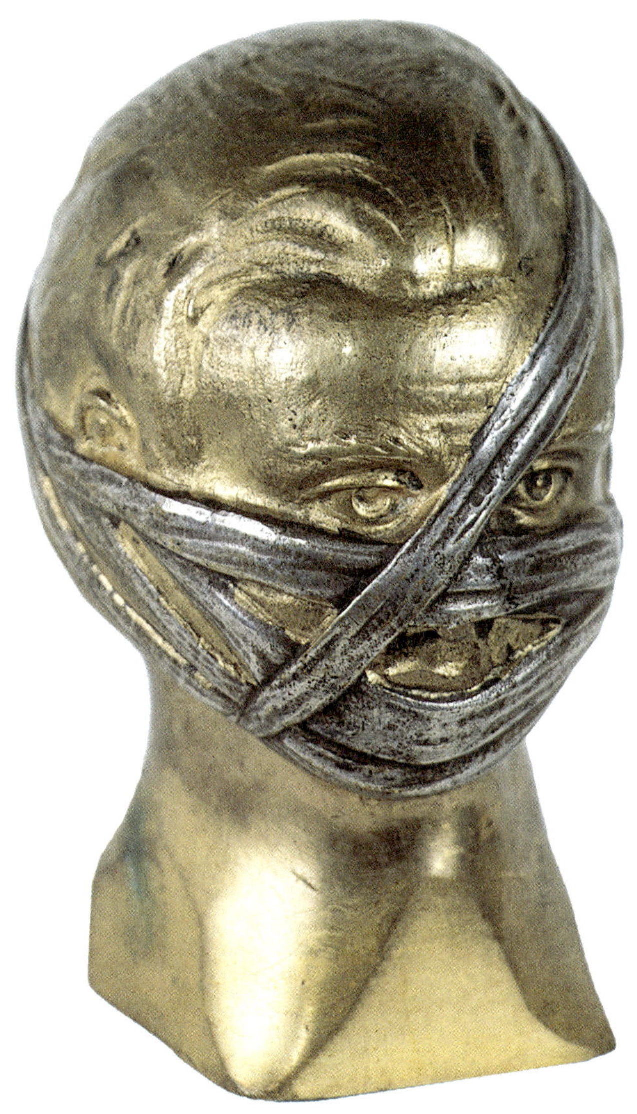

Car mascot in bronze depicting a bandaged *"gueule cassée"* (soldier with severe facial injuries). To be screwed on to a car radiator cap. Bears the inscription "Sold in aid of the Union of Soldiers with Facial Injuries", *c.* 1921
Bronze, 13 x 7 x 8 cm
Historial de la Grande Guerre, Péronne (Somme)

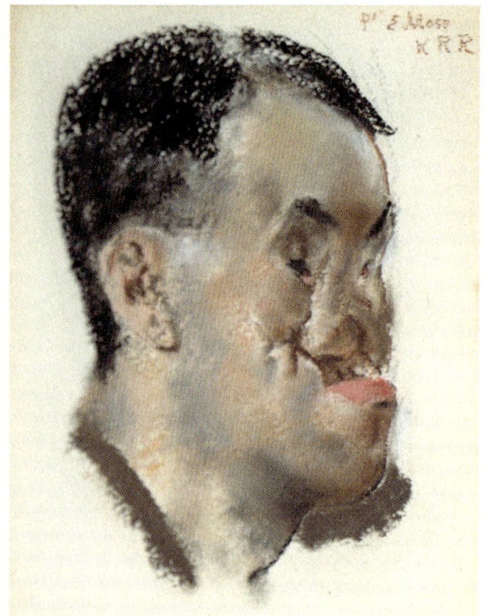

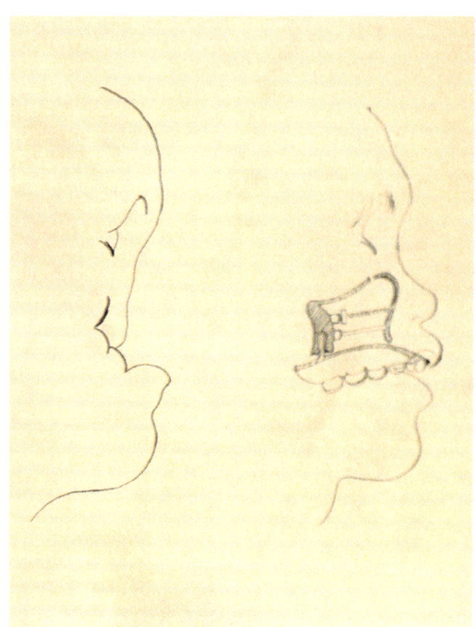

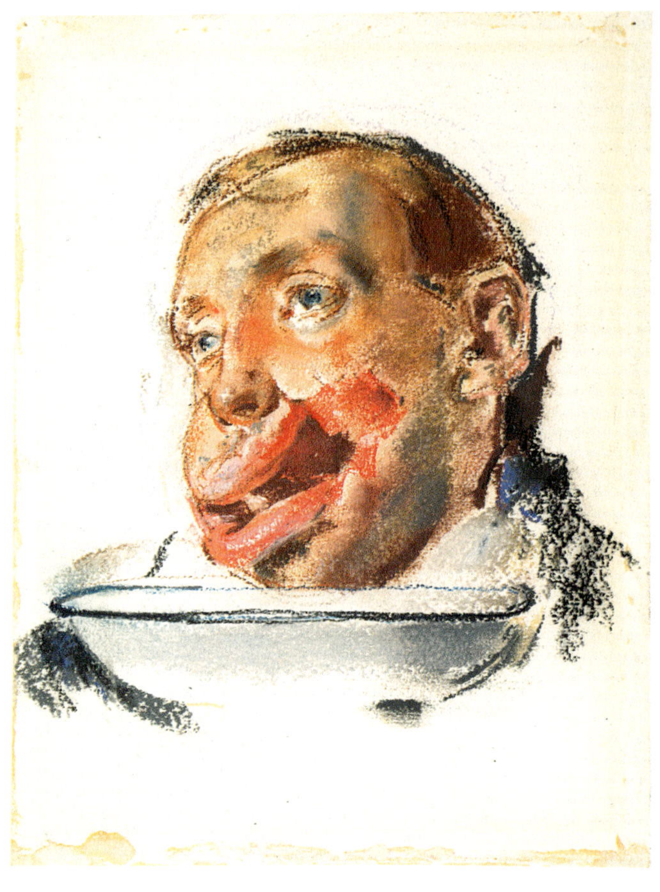

Another way of documenting the experience of war
through art are the studies which Tonks, a former surgeon,
made of the face wounds and the successive stages of
reconstructive surgery carried out by Sir Harold Gillies,
a pioneer of this technique.

HENRY TONKS, Soldier with facial injury no. 29, 1916
Pastel on paper, 27 x 20 cm
Royal College of Surgeons of England, London

HENRY TONKS, Soldier with facial injury no. 50, 1916
Pastel on paper, 27 x 20 cm
Royal College of Surgeons of England, London

HENRY TONKS, Soldier with facial injury no. 30, 1916
Pastel on paper, 27 x 20 cm
Royal College of Surgeons of England, London

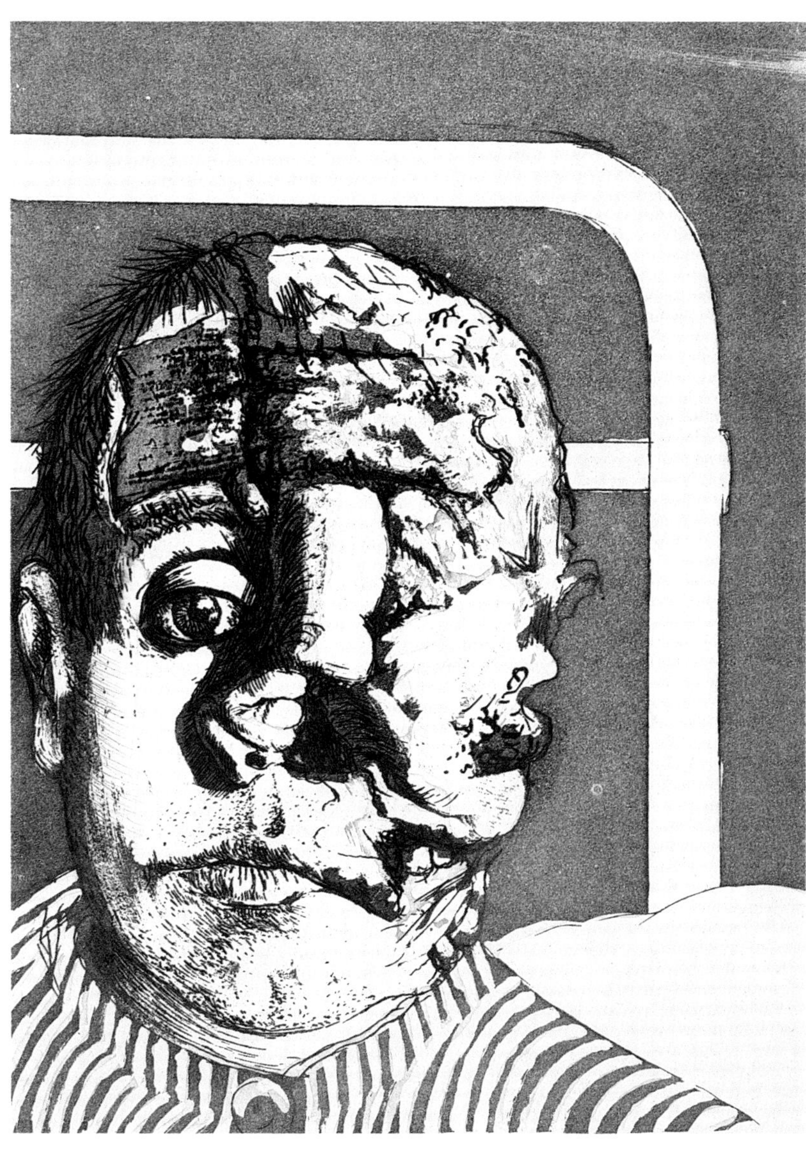

OTTO DIX, Transplant, from the portfolio "War", 1924
Etching, 19.3 x 14.3
The British Museum, London

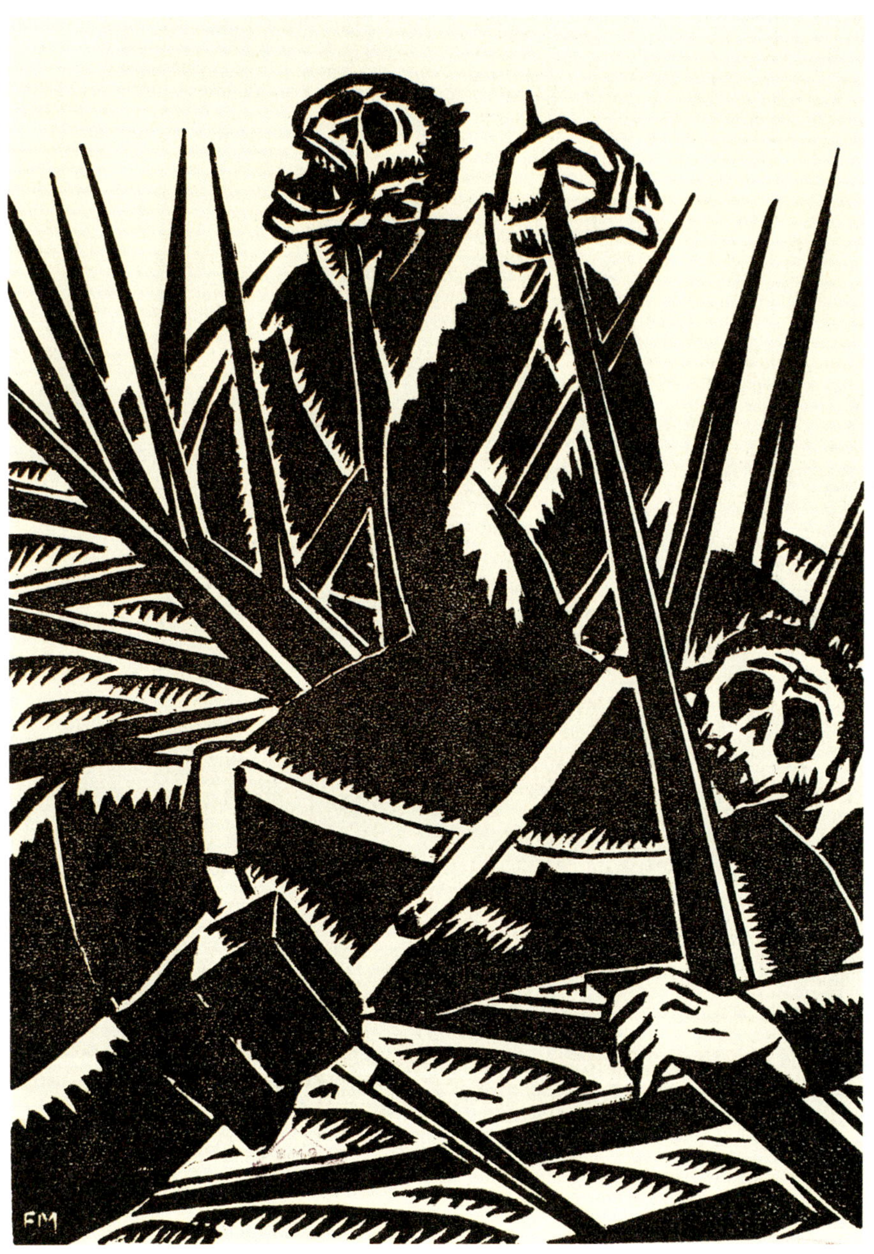

FRANS MASEREEL, The dead arise: infernal
resurrection, (engraving no. 3), 1917
Woodcut, 14 x 11 cm
Musée d'Histoire Contemporaine - BDIC, Paris

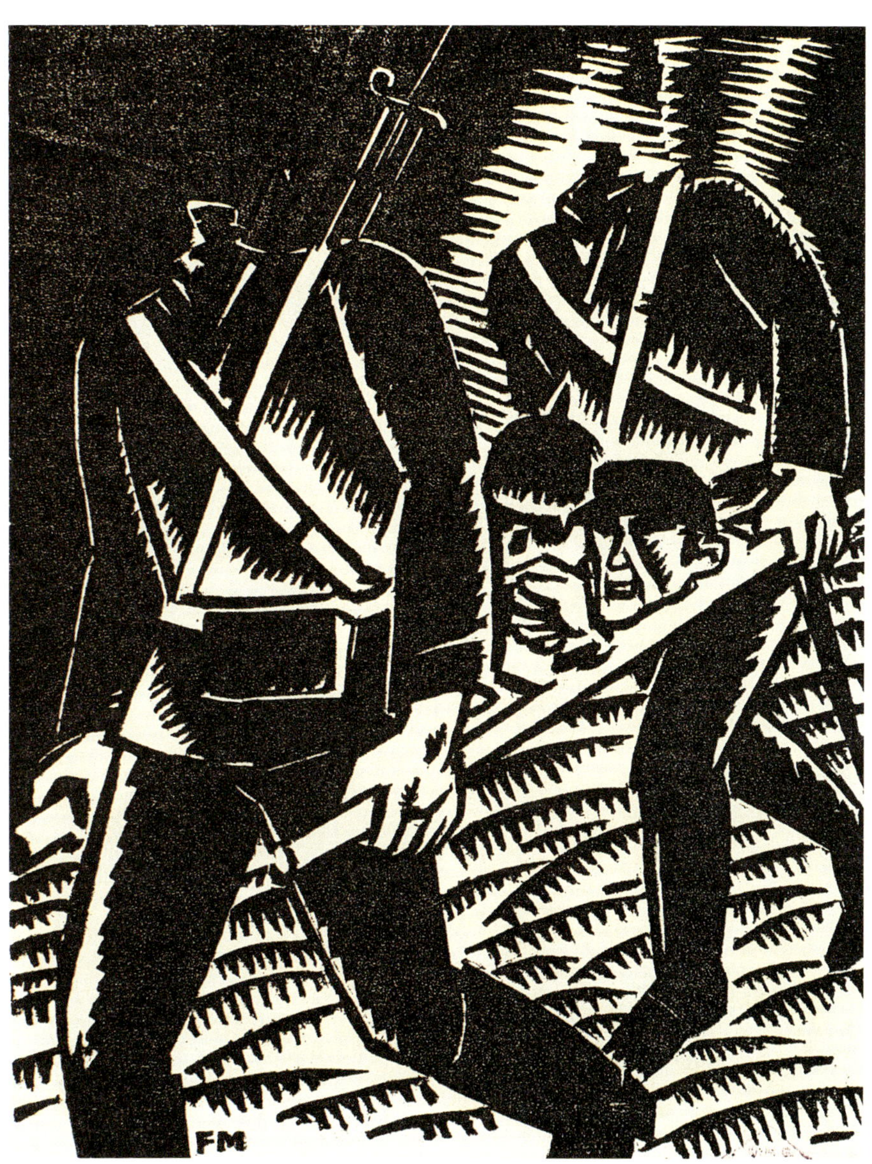

FRANS MASEREEL, The dead arise: infernal
resurrection (engraving no. 7), 1917
Woodcut, 14 x 11 cm
Musée d'Histoire Contemporaine - BDIC, Paris

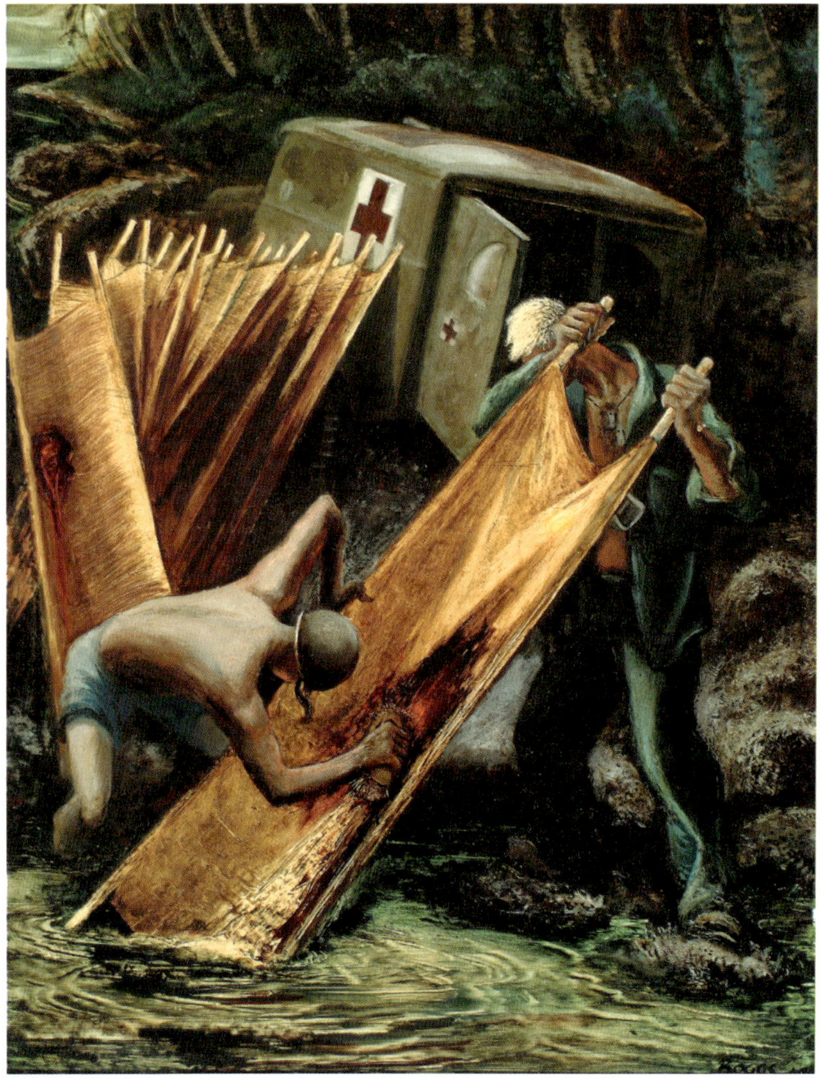

Abbot Laboratories was a pharmaceutical company which sponsored its own war artists' scheme during the Second World War, with commissions dealing particularly with the medical aspects of the conflict. Boggs was one of the civilian artists commissioned by Abbot and he recorded the everyday suffering of soldiers.

FRANKLIN BOGGS, End of a busy day, 1944
Oil on masonite, 84.4 x 66.9 cm
National Museum of the US Army, Army Art Collection, Washington

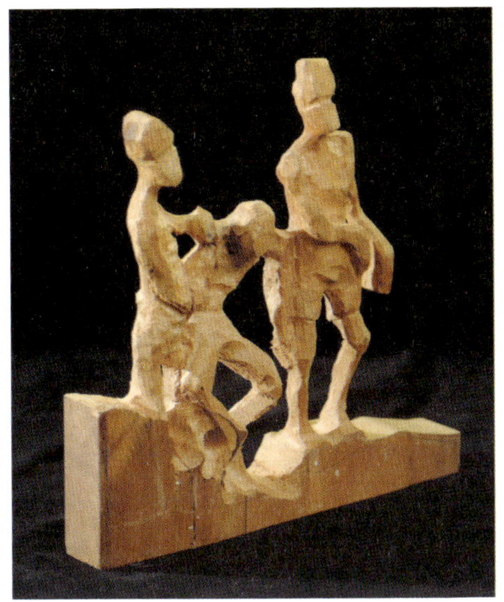
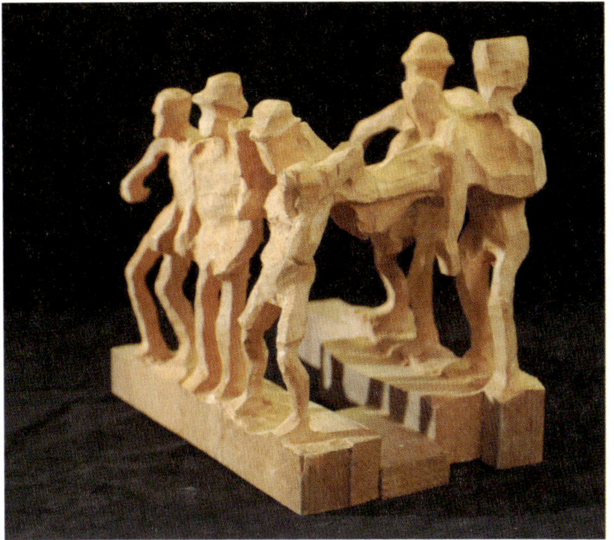
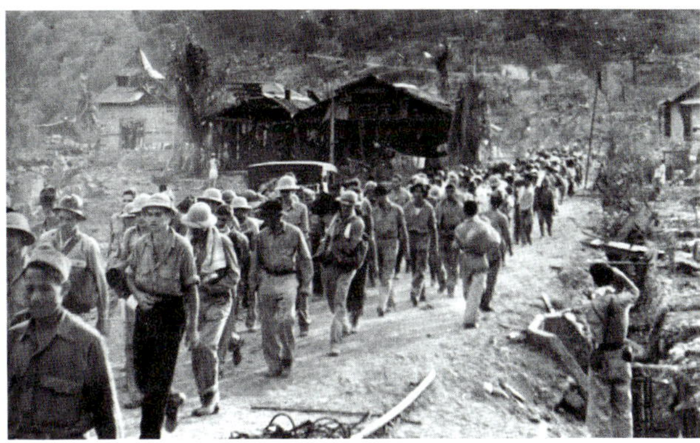

Figures carved by a survivor of the Bataan Death March. When
the Japanese occupied the Philippines in 1942, they forced the 70,000
American and Filipino soldiers who had surrendered on the Bataan
Peninsula, to go on a six-day march in extremely harsh conditions.
Nearly 10,000 prisoners died on the march but Clayton M. Rollins
escaped and joined the Filipino guerrilla fighters in the mountains.

CLAYTON M. ROLLINS, Bataan death march,
Second World War
Wood, 28 x 26 cm, 28 x 28 cm
National Museum of the US Army, Army Art
Collection, Washington

Bataan death march, Philippines, 1942
AP / Radial Press

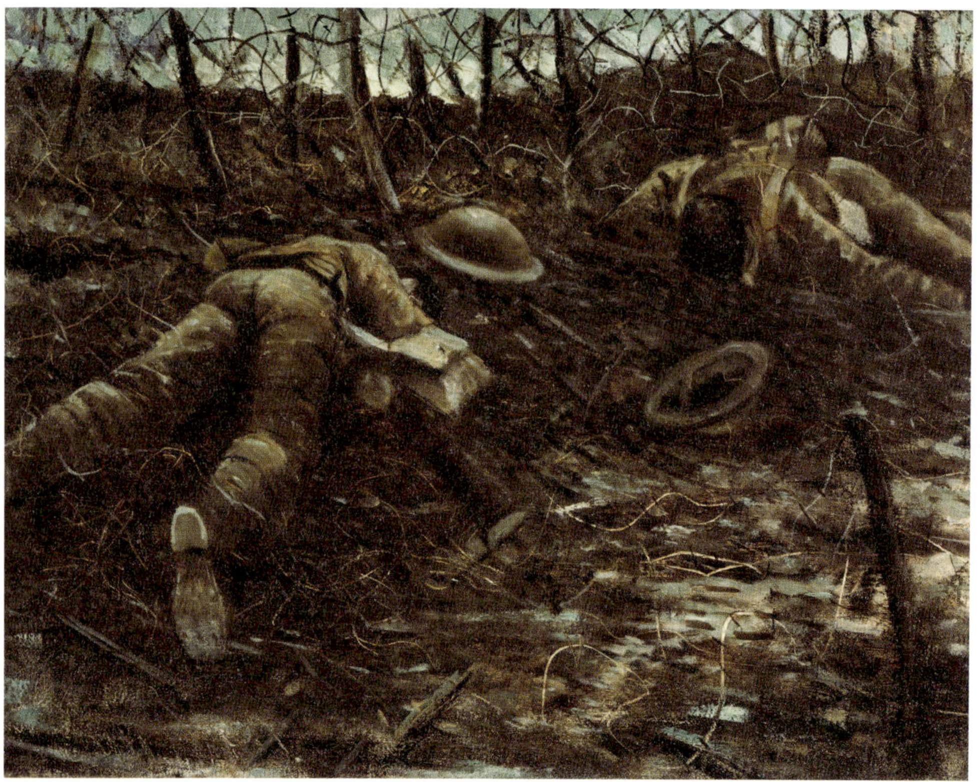

Keeping a check on the pictures of casualties from each side was already a cause for
concern during the First World War. When Nevinson was banned from exhibiting
this painting because it was considered bad for morale to show dead British soldiers,
he covered it with brown paper on which he wrote "Censored". The source of the ironic
title is a verse by Thomas Gray: " the paths of glory lead but to the grave".

CHRISTOPHER RICHARD WYNNE NEVINSON, Paths of glory, 1917
Oil on canvas, 45.7 x 60.9 cm
Imperial War Museum, London

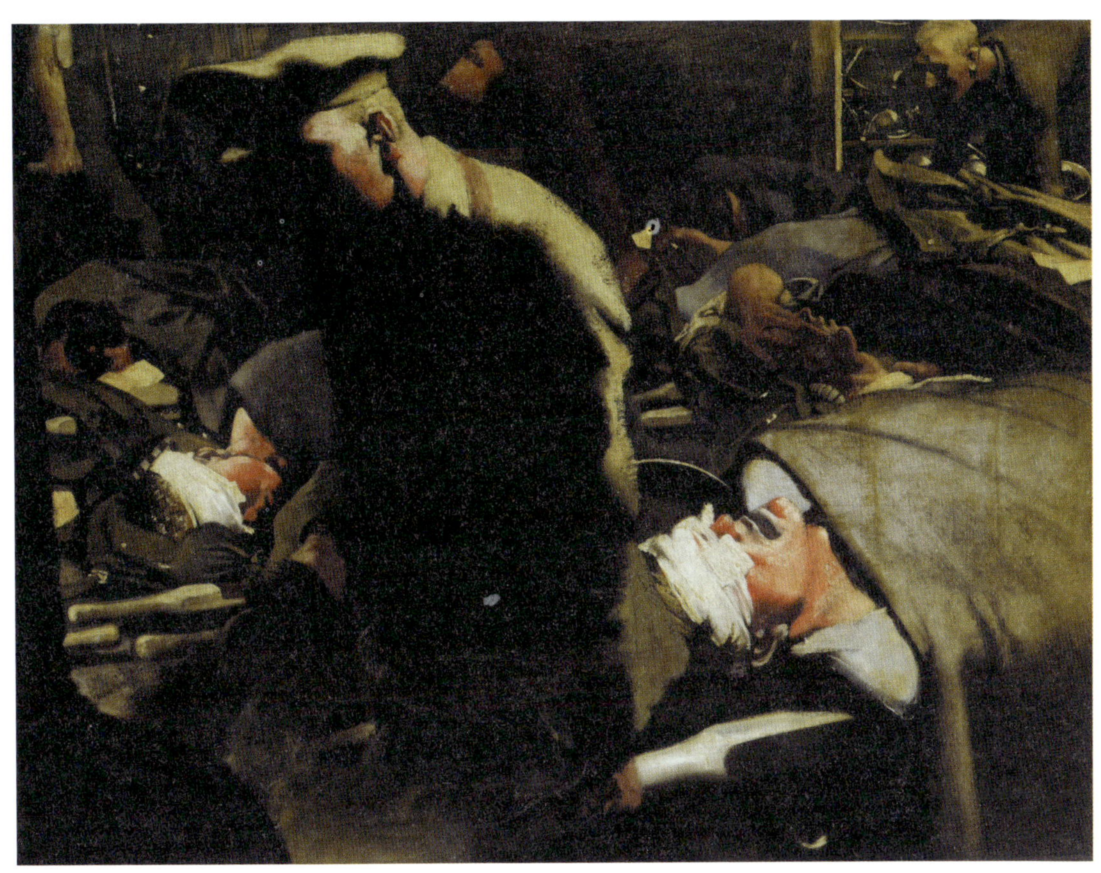

Kennington was named official war artist
following his experiences as a soldier at the front.
This picture shows the impression made on him
by the victims of gas attacks in the field hospitals
in France.

ERIC HENRI KENNINGTON, Gassed and wounded, 1918
Oil on canvas, 71.1 x 91.4 cm
Imperial War Museum, London. Gift of the artist, 1934

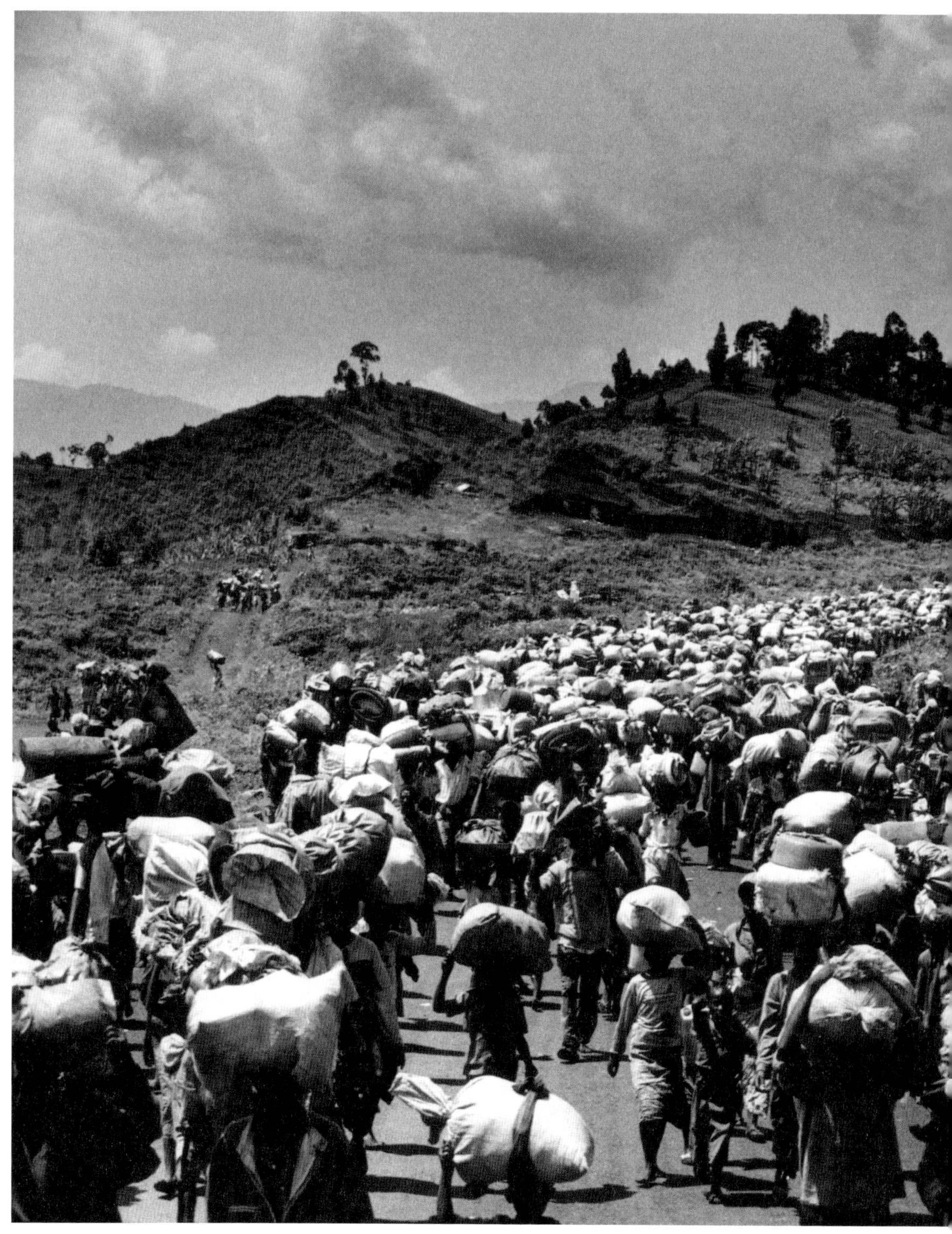

YUNGHI KIM, Hutu refugees fleeing Rwanda, 1997
Yunghi Kim / Contact Press Images / Contacto

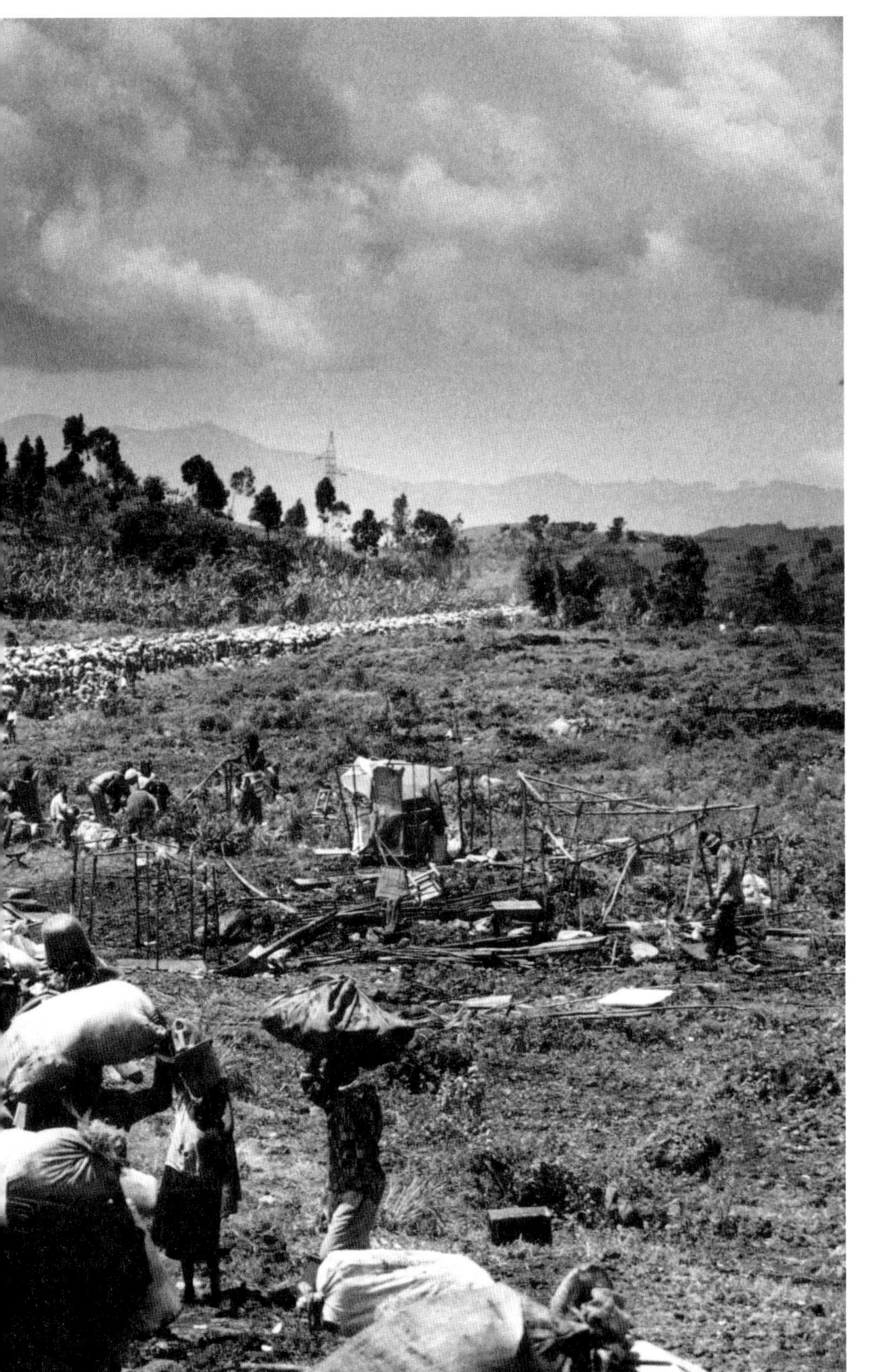

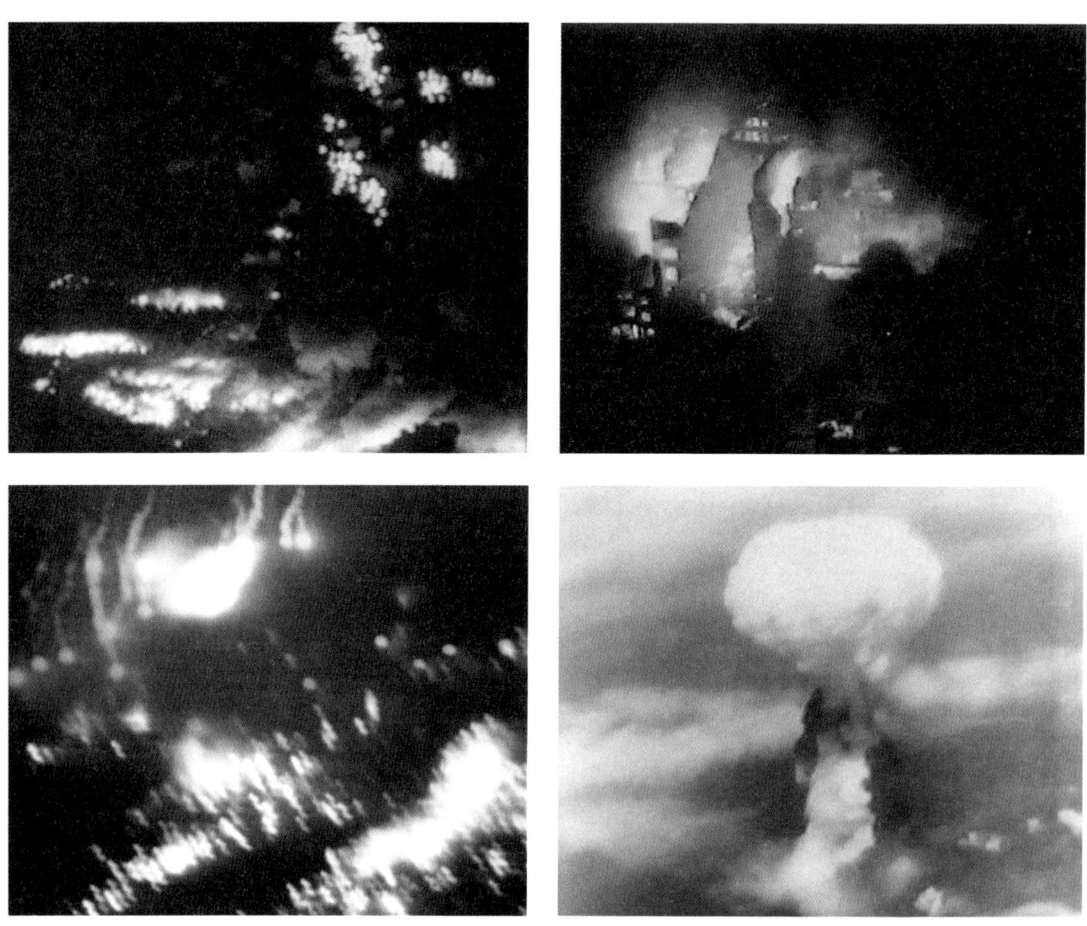

Bombing over Hamburg, Second World War

Bombing over London, Second World War
Footage Farm, London

Bombing over Hiroshima, Second World War

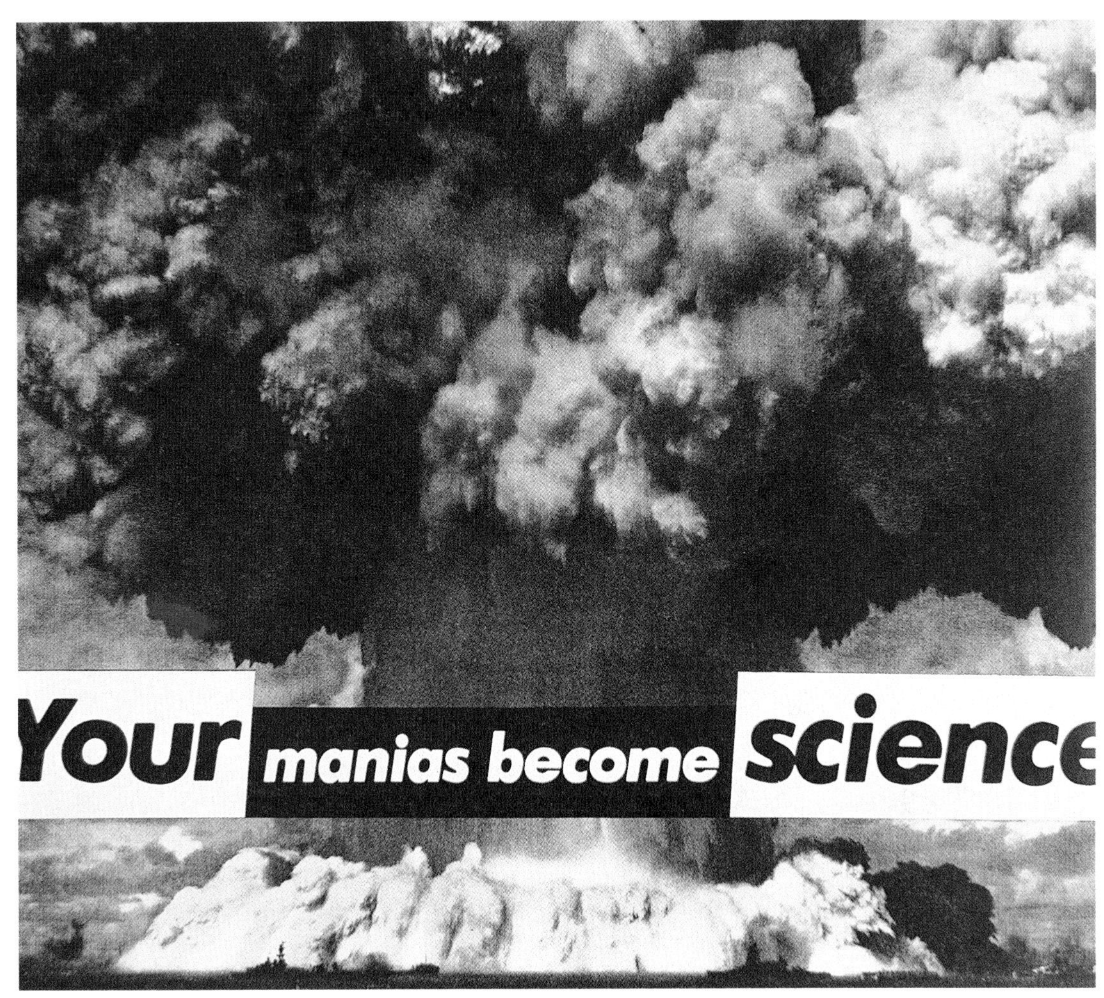

BARBARA KRUGER, Your manias become science, 1982
Gelatin silver mural print with print-painted artist's frame, 104 x 127 cm
Courtesy of The Broido Family Collection, Chicago

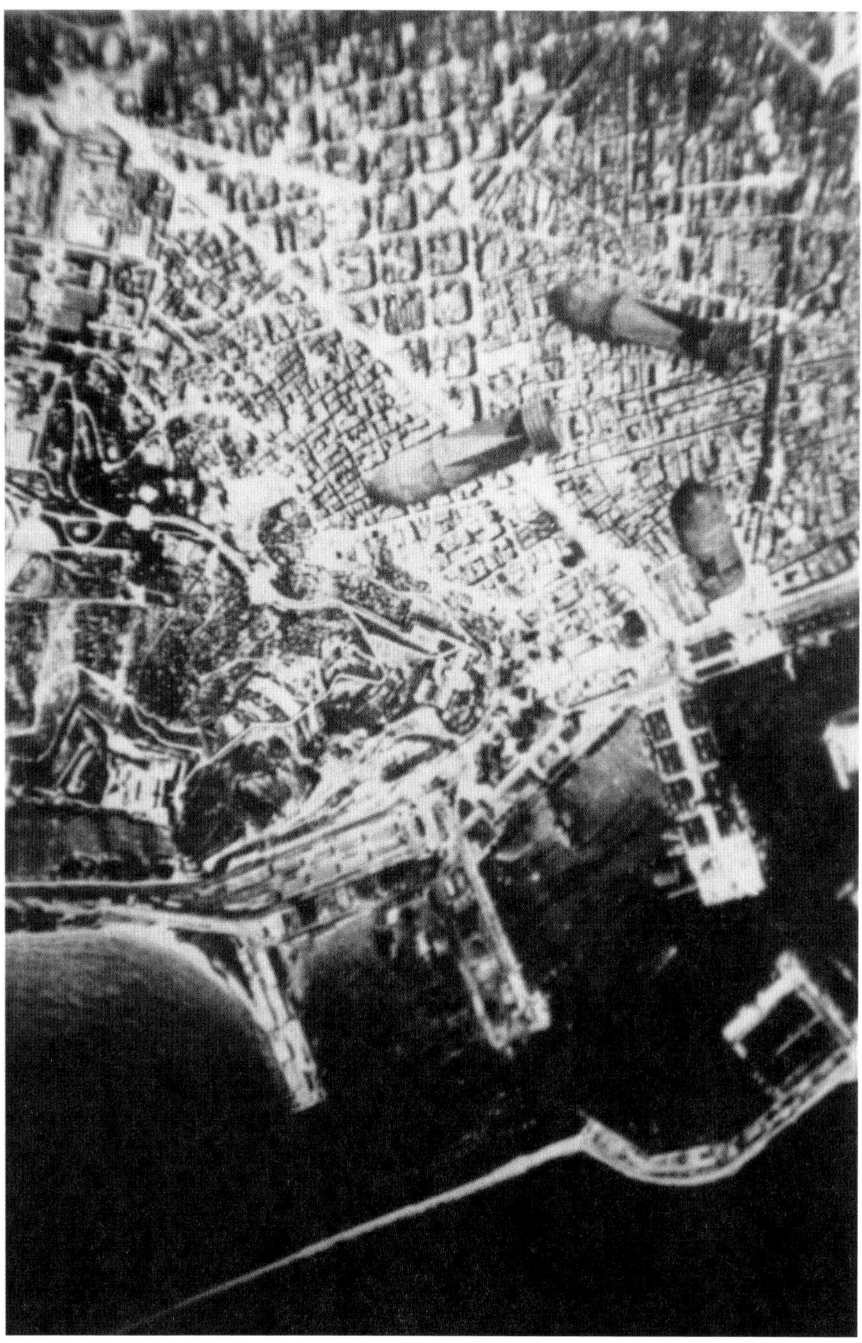

Bombs falling on Barcelona harbour, 17 March 1938
Arxiu Alcofar, Barcelona

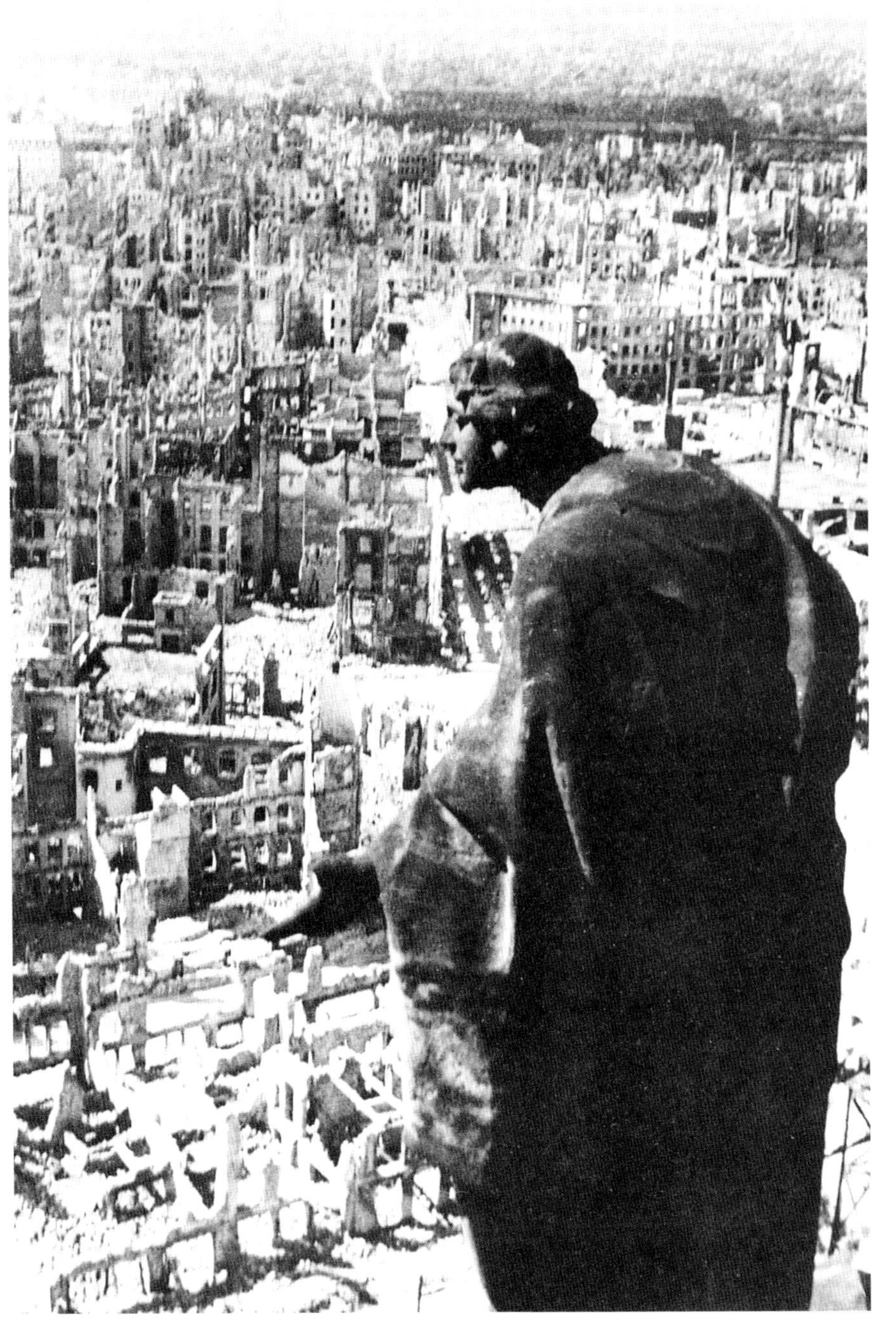

Dresden after the Allied raids, 1945
Deutsches Historisches Museum, Berlin

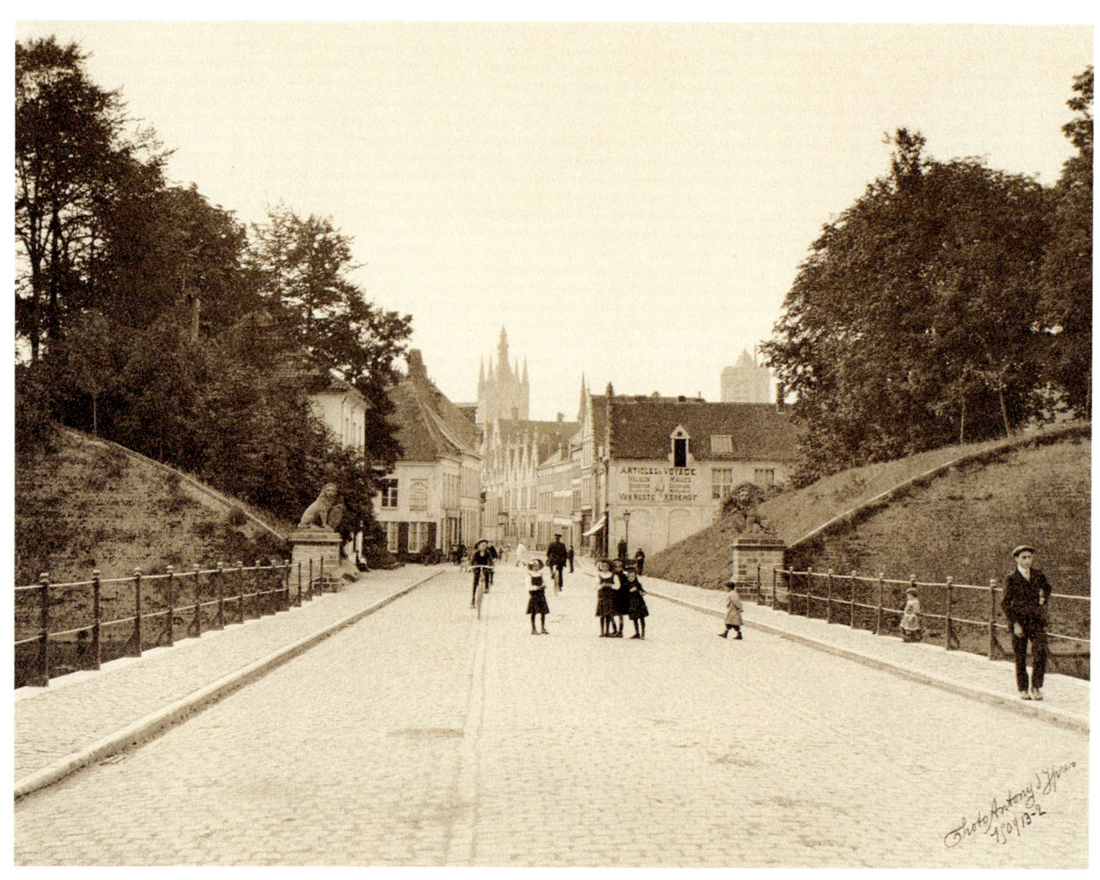

ANTHONY, Menin Gate, Ypres, Belgium, 1913
Musée d'Histoire Contemporaine - BDIC, Paris

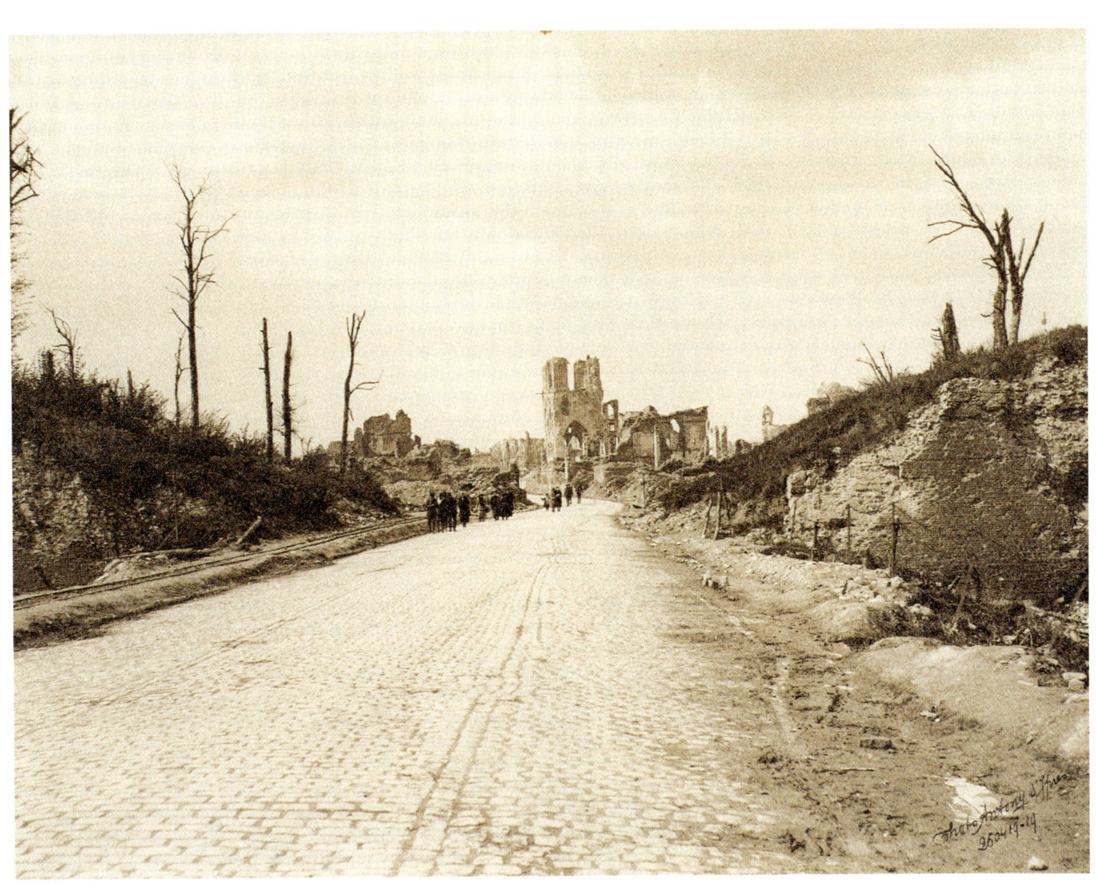

ANTHONY, Menin Gate, Ypres, Belgium, 1919
Musée d'Histoire Contemporaine - BDIC, Paris

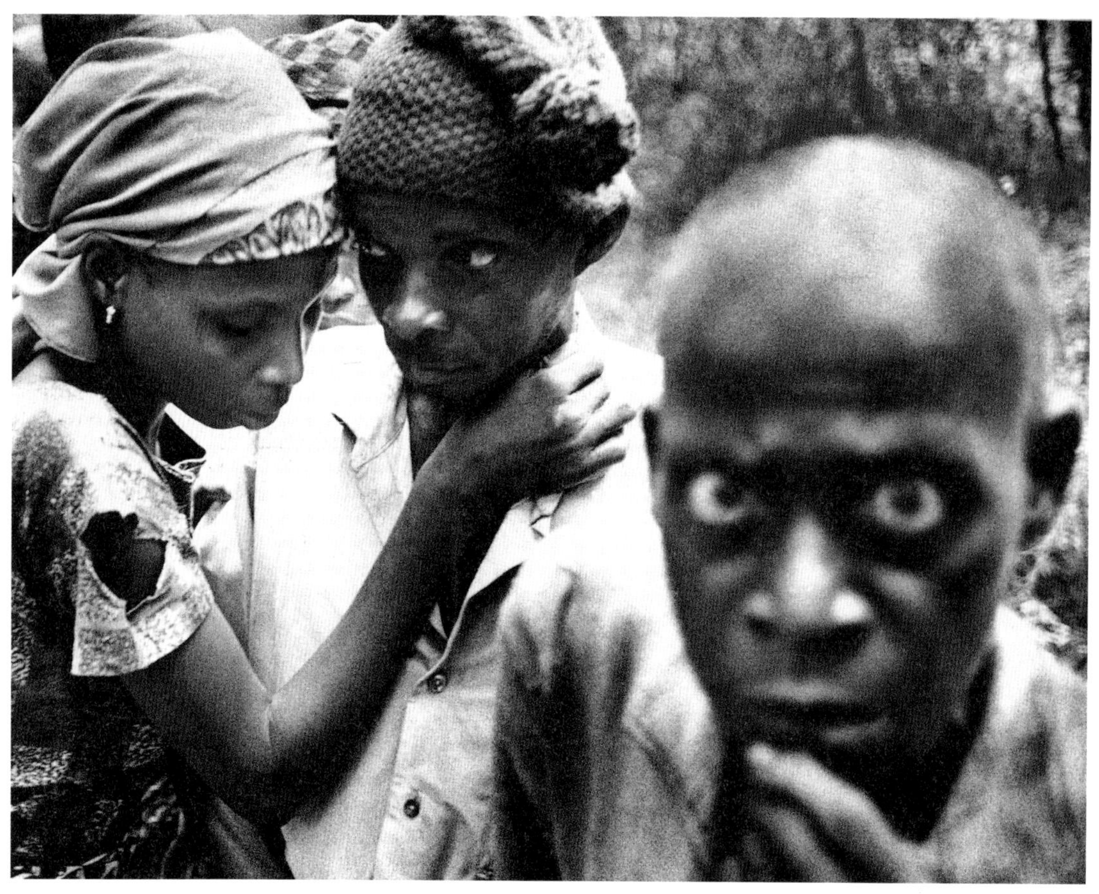

ROMANO CAGNONI, Terror of war, Biafra, *c.* 1970

GERVASIO SÁNCHEZ, Mined lives, 1995

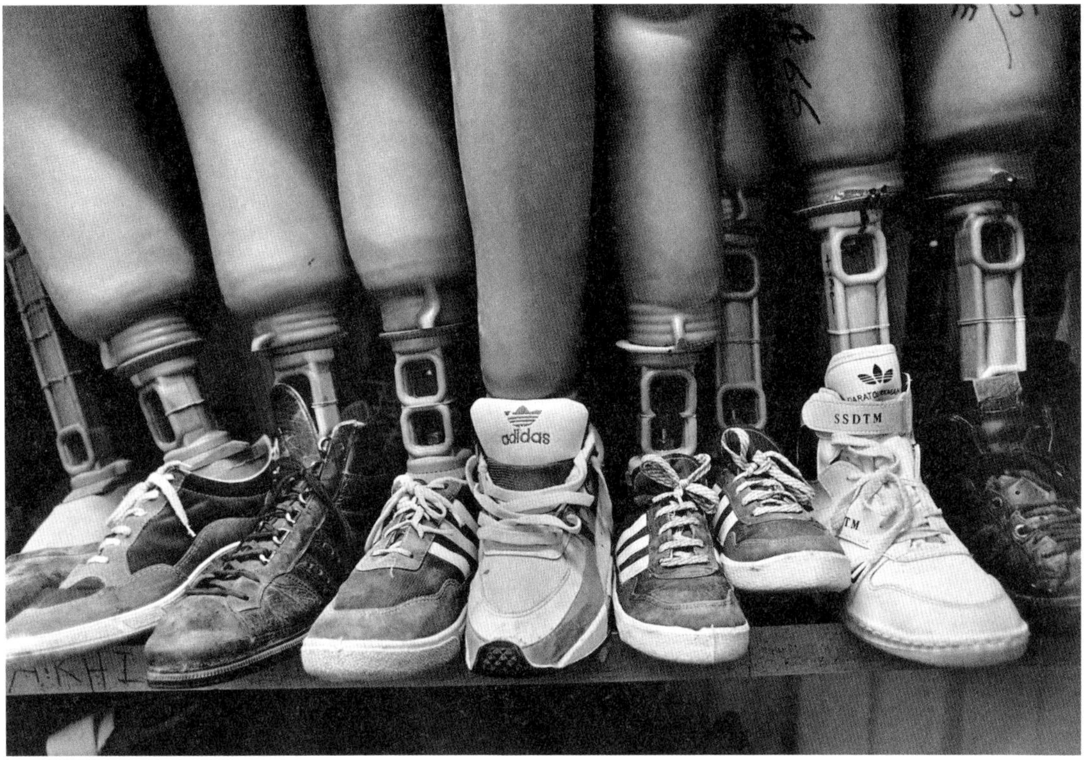

adidas
SSDTM
TM
MIKHI

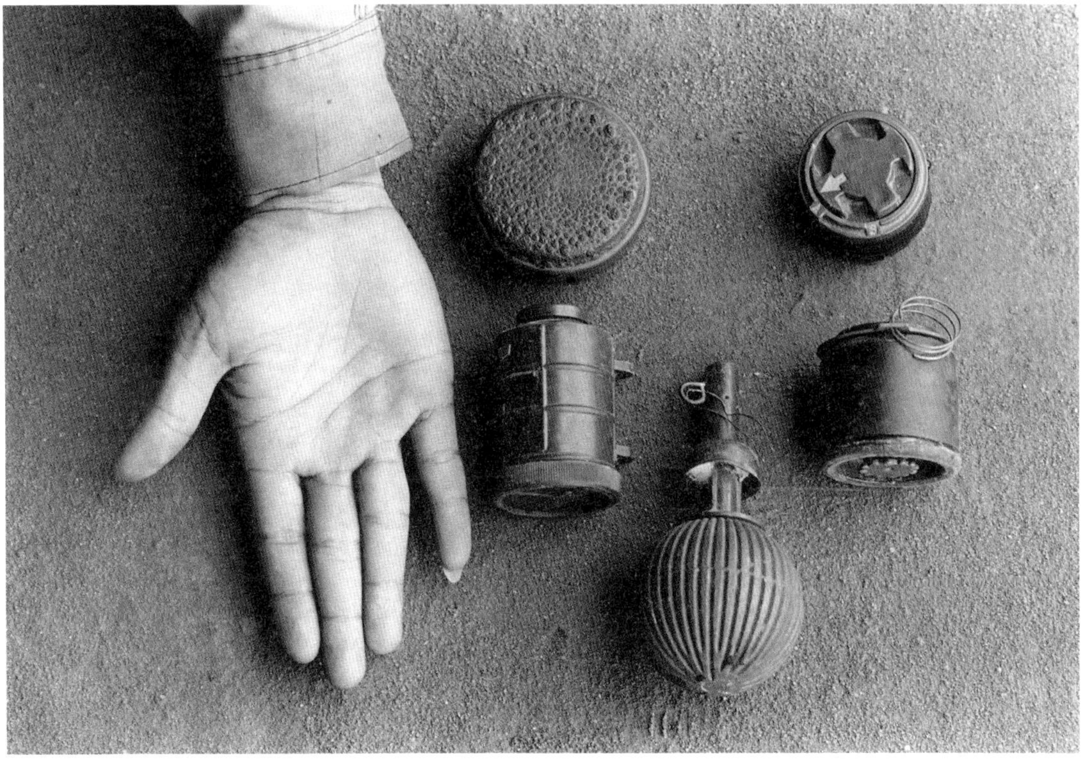

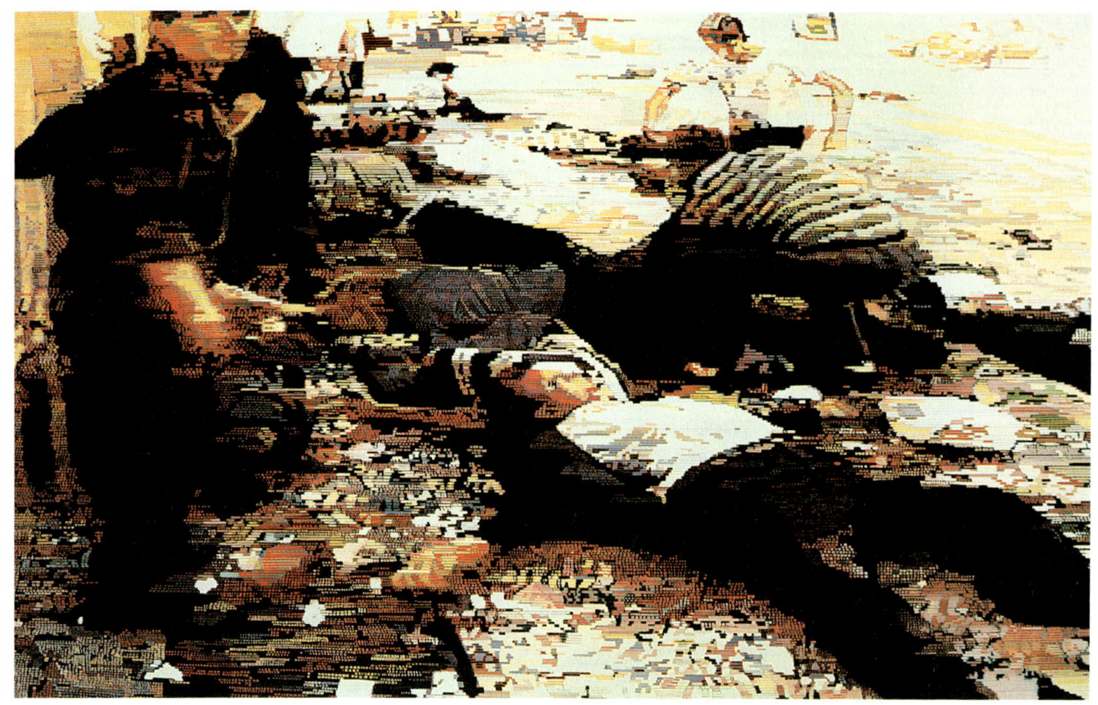

The siege of the city has become a symbol of barbarism at the end
of the twentieth century. It shows what ethnic confrontation
means during a civil war as well as its effects on non-combatants.
The key moment of the siege was the mortar attack on the people
in the bread queue on 28th August 1995.

SIMEÓN SAIZ RUIZ, Civilians in Sarajevo killed by missiles
which have fallen next to the main market, Monday 28
August 1995, 1999
Oil on canvas, 206.5 x 334 cm
C.A.C. - Museo Patio Herreriano, Valladolid

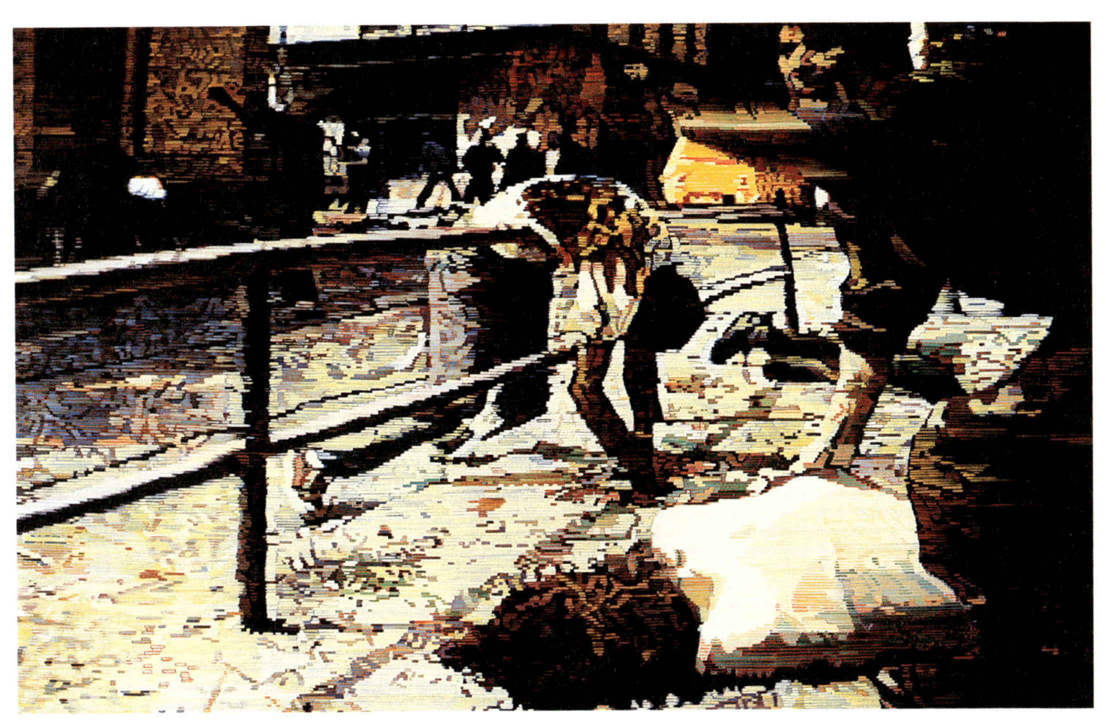

SIMEÓN SAIZ RUIZ, Civilians in Sarajevo killed by missiles which have
fallen next to the main market, Monday 28 August 1995. Body over a
railing, 1998
Oil on canvas, 171 x 277.5 cm
Universitat de València. Patronat Martínez Guerricabeitia, Valencia

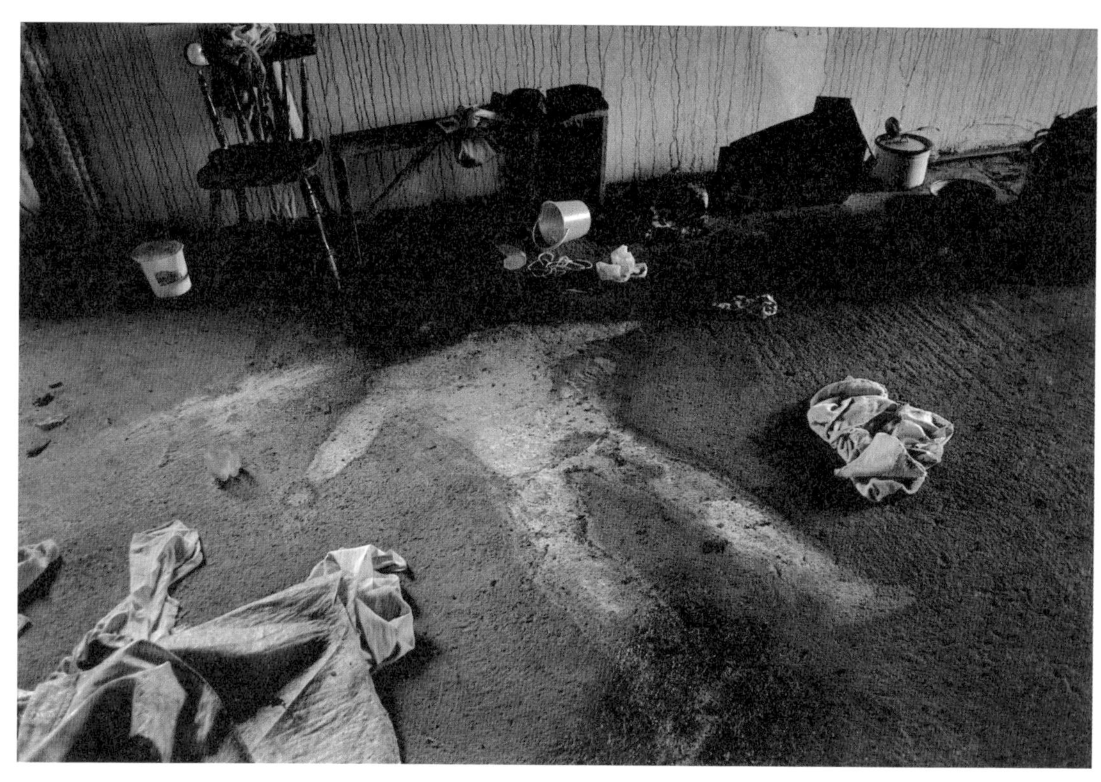

ANTHONY SUAU, Traces of an old man executed
by the Serbs in Kosovo, 1999
Courtesy of Anthony Suau, Paris

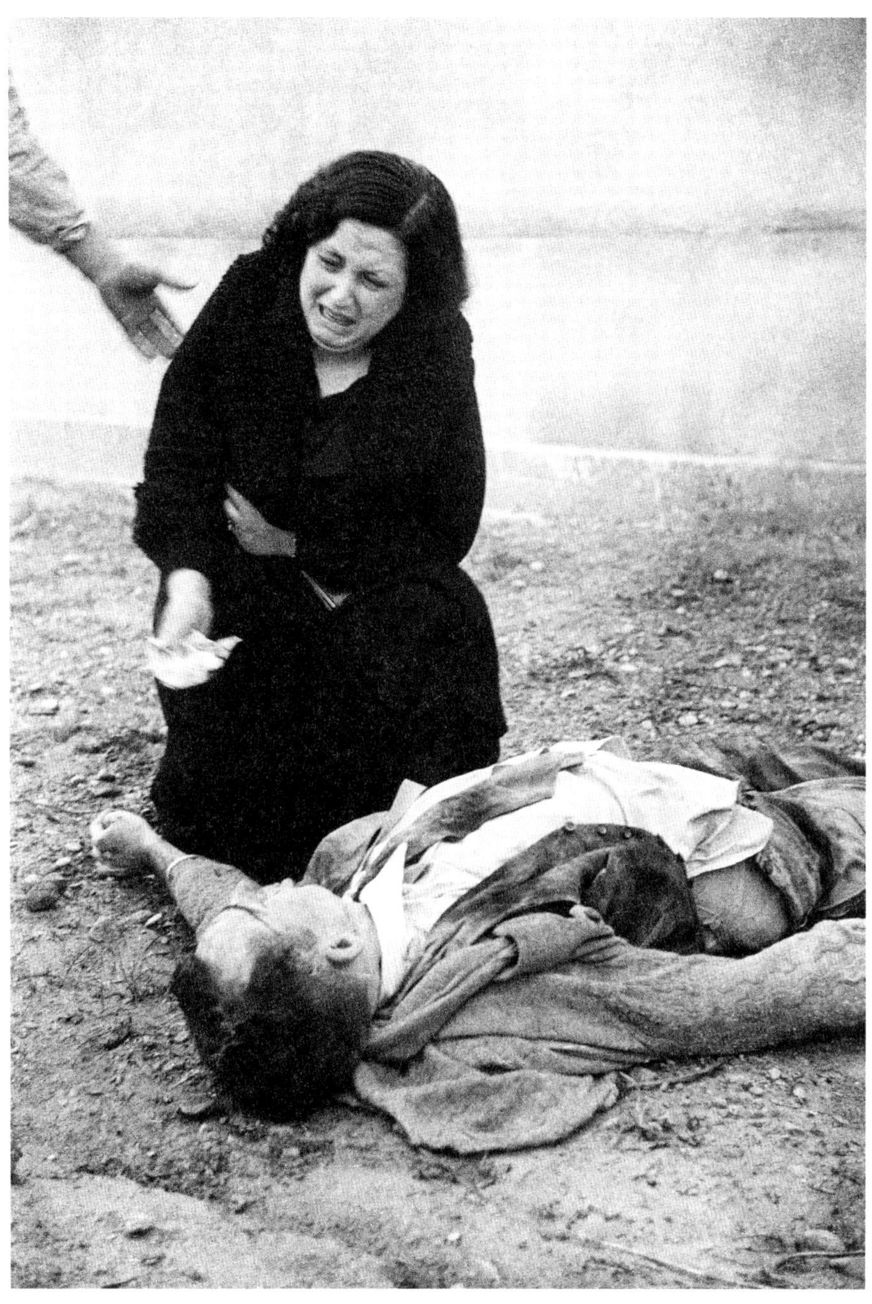

AGUSTÍ CENTELLES, Air raid over Lleida,
November 1937
Arxiu Agustí Centelles, Barcelona

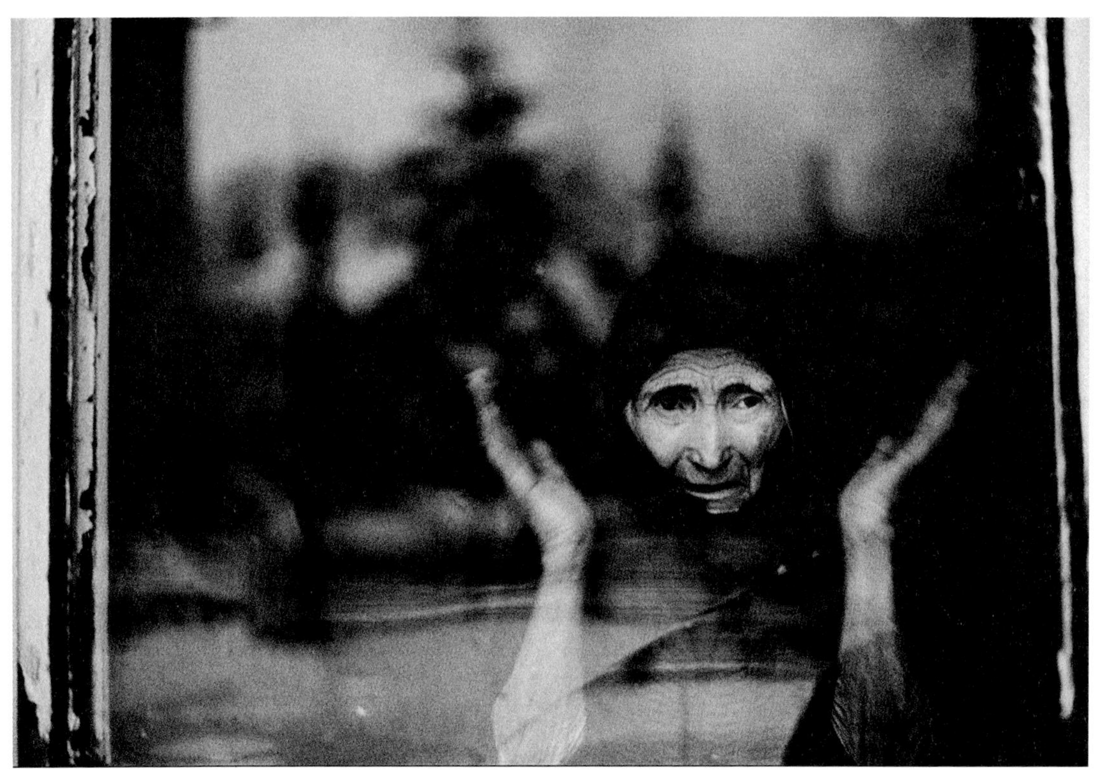

GILLES PERESS, An elderly woman watching the Bosnian police enter
the suburb of Vogosca, which was Serbian-held for most of the war,
and is now under Bosnian government control according to the Dayton
agreement, Vogosca-Sarajevo, Bosnia, 1996
Gilles Peress / Magnum Photos / Contacto

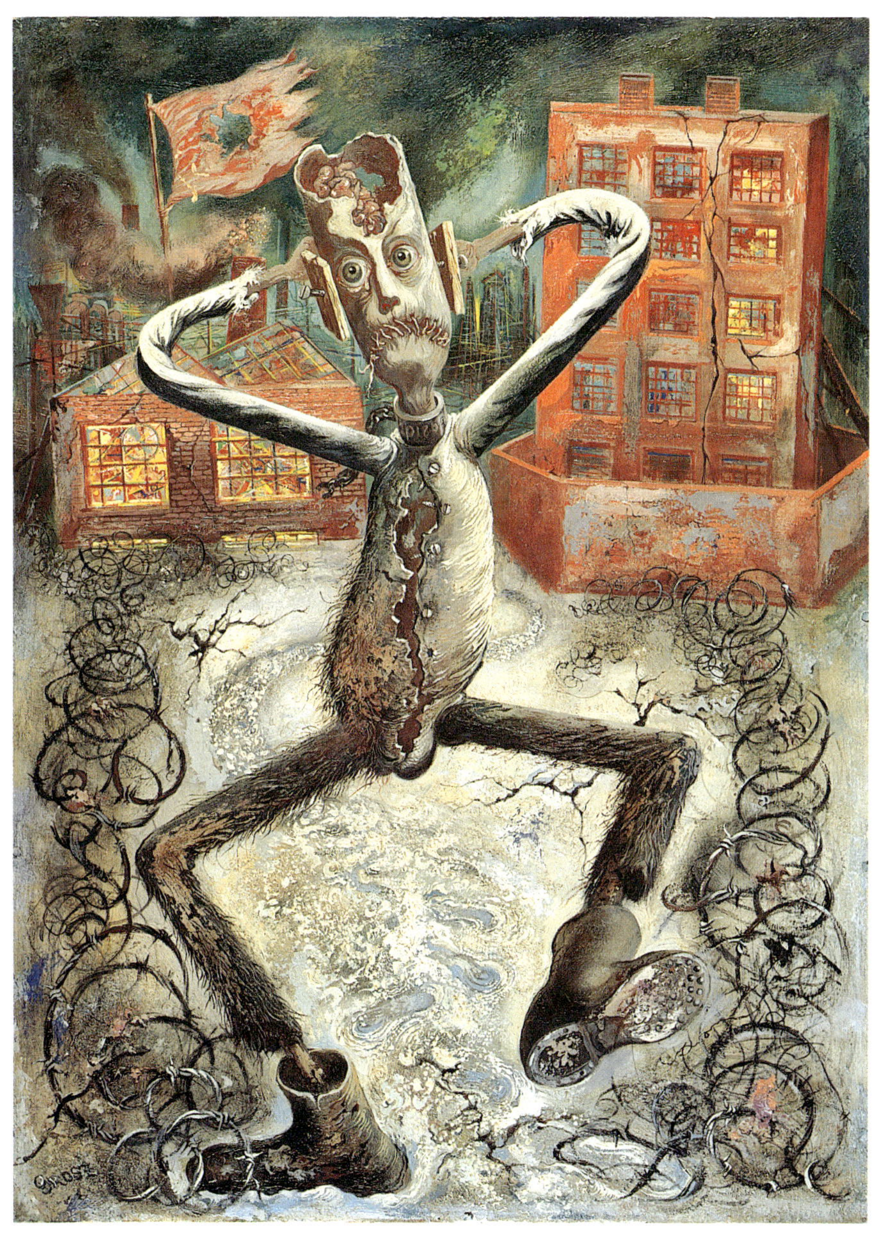

GEORGE GROSZ, The grey man dances, 1949
Oil on canvas, 76 x 55.6 cm
Private collection, Courtesy of Ralph Jentsch, Capri

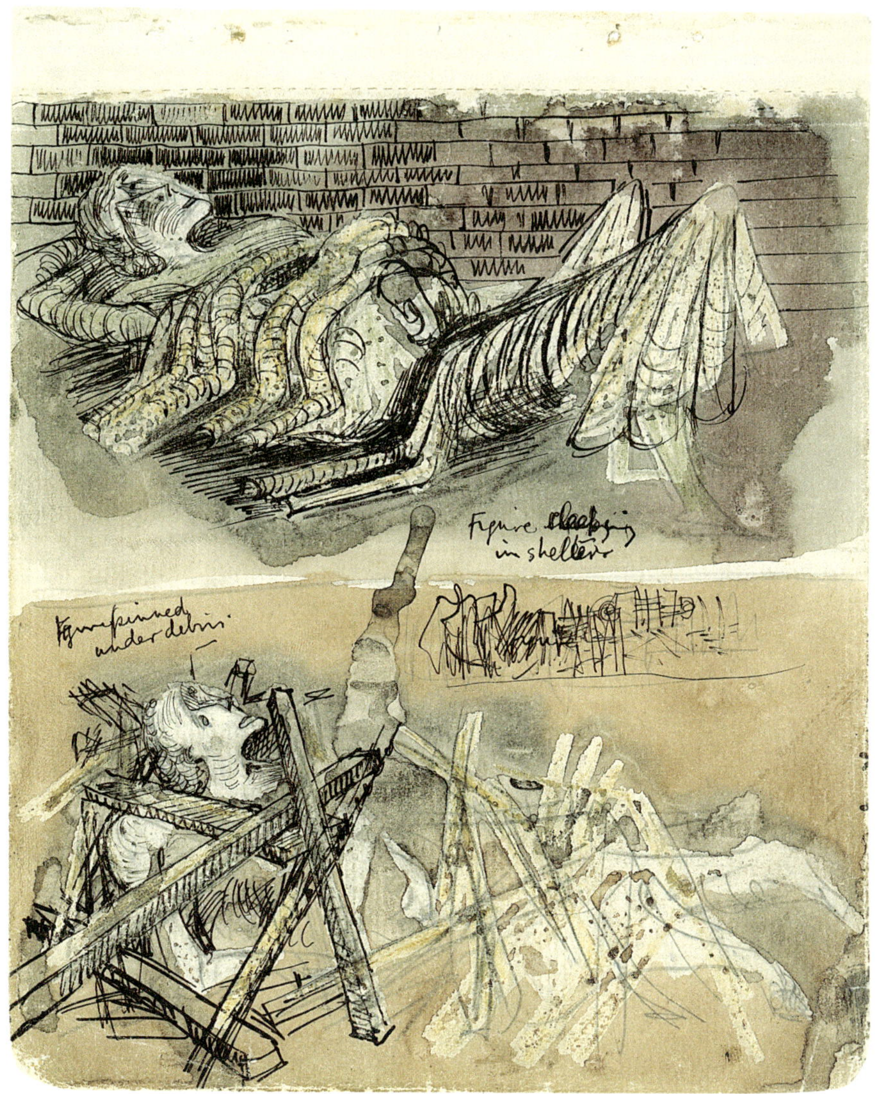

The city of London, which based its air-raid defences on the
experience of the bombing raids on Barcelona, is used as an example
to show the suffering of the civilian population under this form
of attack which has characterised contemporary warfare since the
time of the Spanish Civil War.

HENRY MOORE, Sleeping figure and figure pinned under debris, 1940-1941
Pencil, wax crayon, watercolour, wash, pen and ink, 20.4 x 16.5 cm
The Henry Moore Foundation: gift of Irina Moore, 1977, Hertfordshire

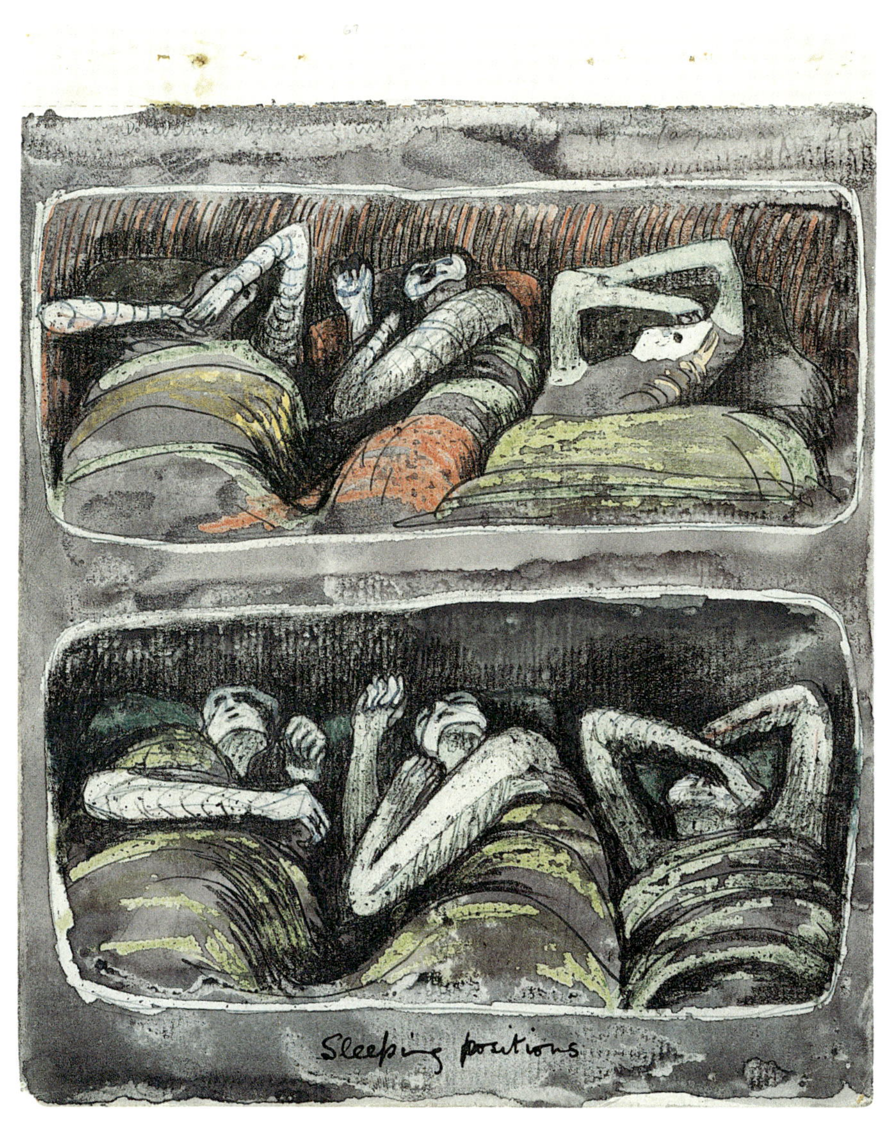

HENRY MOORE, Study for "Sleeping positions", 1940-1941
Pencil, wax crayon, coloured crayon, watercolour, wash,
pen and ink on off-white lightweight woven paper, 27.7 x 23.5 cm
The Henry Moore Foundation: gift of Irina Moore 1977, Hertfordshire

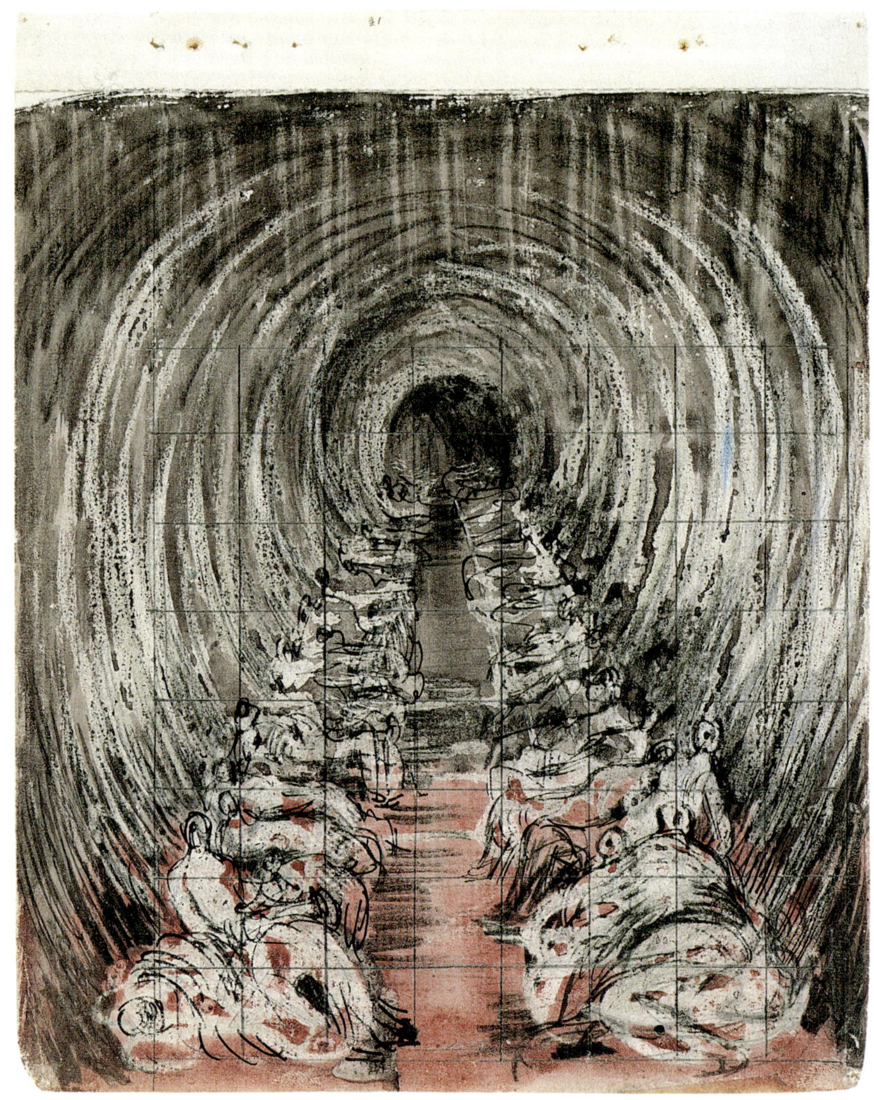

Moore's drawings of the air-raid shelters in the London Underground during
the bombings between autumn 1940 and summer 1941, are quite unlike
his other works. He began them as a personal exercise, which later became a
commission from the War Artists' Advisory Committee.

HENRY MOORE, Study for "Tube shelter perspective", 1940-1941
Pencil, wax crayon, coloured crayon, watercolour, wash,
pen and ink on off-white lightweight woven paper, 20.4 x 16.5 cm
The Henry Moore Foundation: gift of Irina Moore, 1977, Hertfordshire

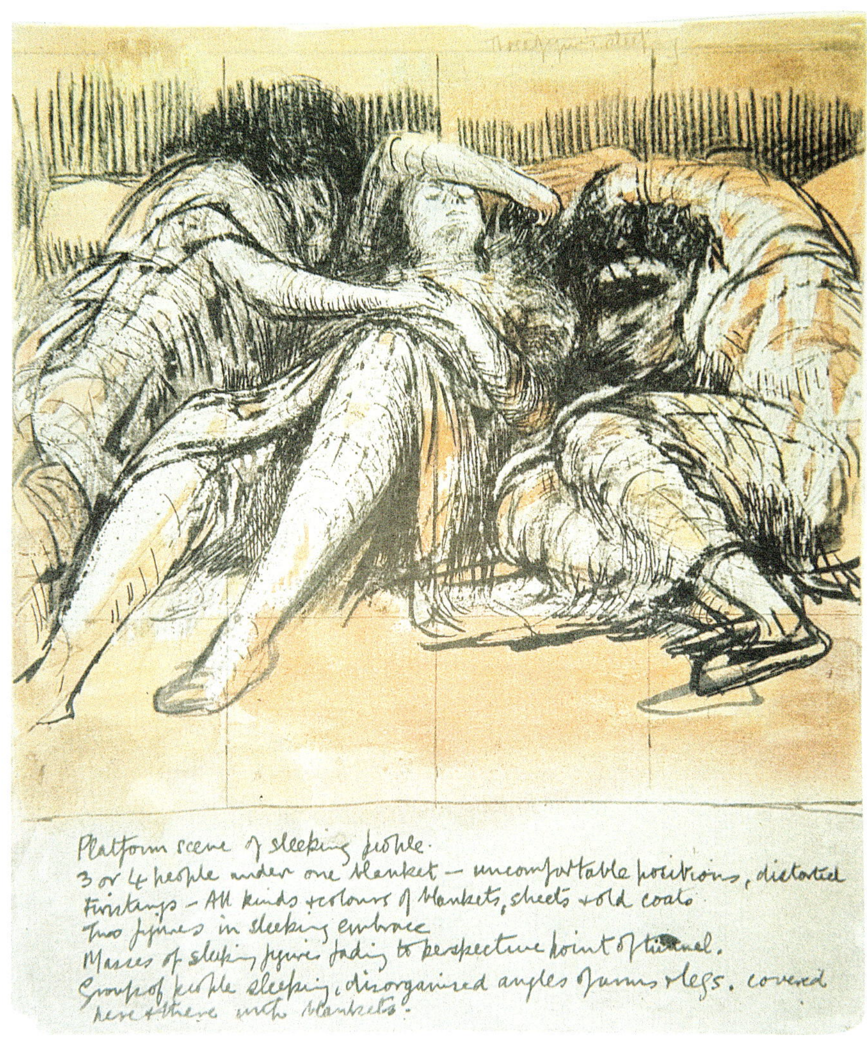

HENRY MOORE, Three figures sleeping: study for "Shelter drawing", 1940-1941
Pencil, wax crayon, watercolour wash, pen and ink
on off-white lightweight woven paper, 20.4 x 16.5 cm
The Henry Moore Foundation: gift of Irina Moore, 1977, Hertfordshire

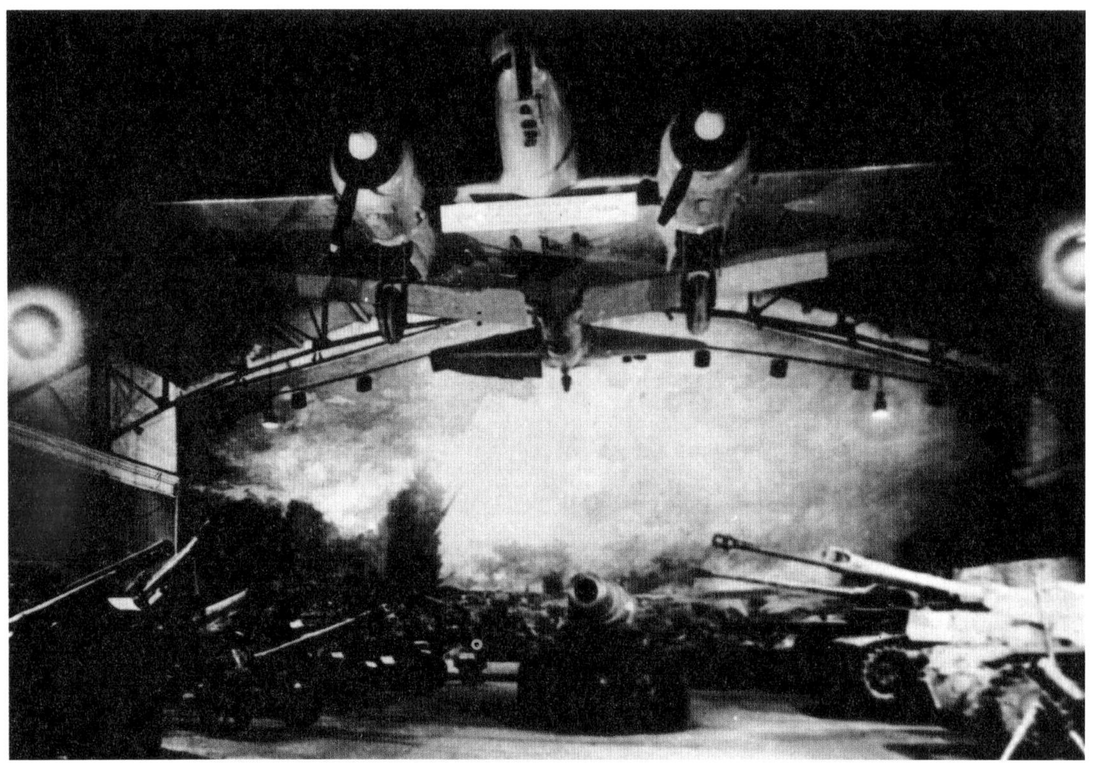

German troops laid siege to Leningrad for 872 days. A million people died. Hunger reached such extremes that the refugees in the Ermitage Museum had to eat carpenter's glue. The food ration per person was reduced to 125 grammes of bread made from flour mixed with sawdust. On 9th August 1942 a concert conducted by Shostakovich was held, and broadcast by radio across the country to show the morale of the community under siege. The Blockade Museum opened in 1944, just three months after the siege was lifted, and featured 37,000 exhibits, including tanks and aeroplanes. Three years later, Stalin ordered that the museum be dismantled and he had its director shot. It reopened in 1989.

View of the museum's trophy room, 1946-1949
The State Memorial Museum of Defence and Siege
of Leningrad, Saint Petersburg

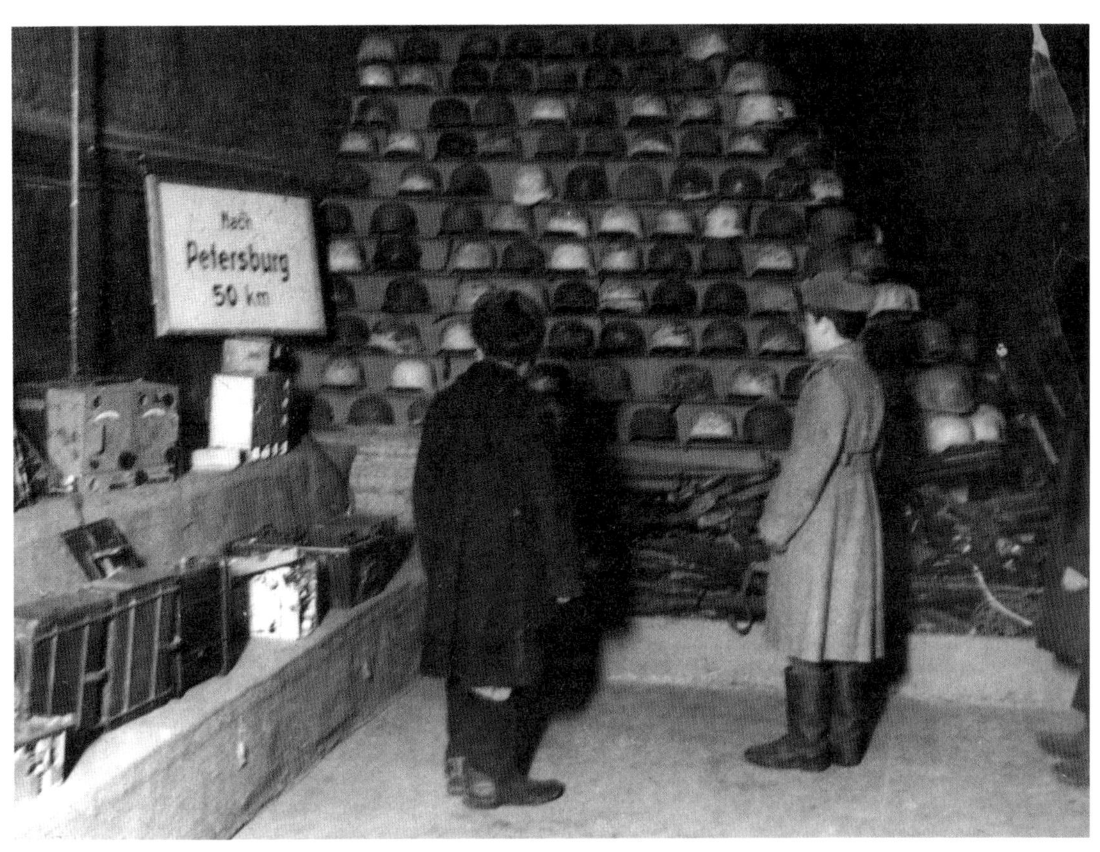

View of one of the museum's galleries, 1946-1949
The State Memorial Museum of Defence and Siege
of Leningrad, Saint Petersburg

STANDISH BACKUS, At the Red Cross hospital, Hiroshima, 1946
Watercolour, 76.8 x 56.5 cm
Navy Art Collection, Naval Historical Center, Washington

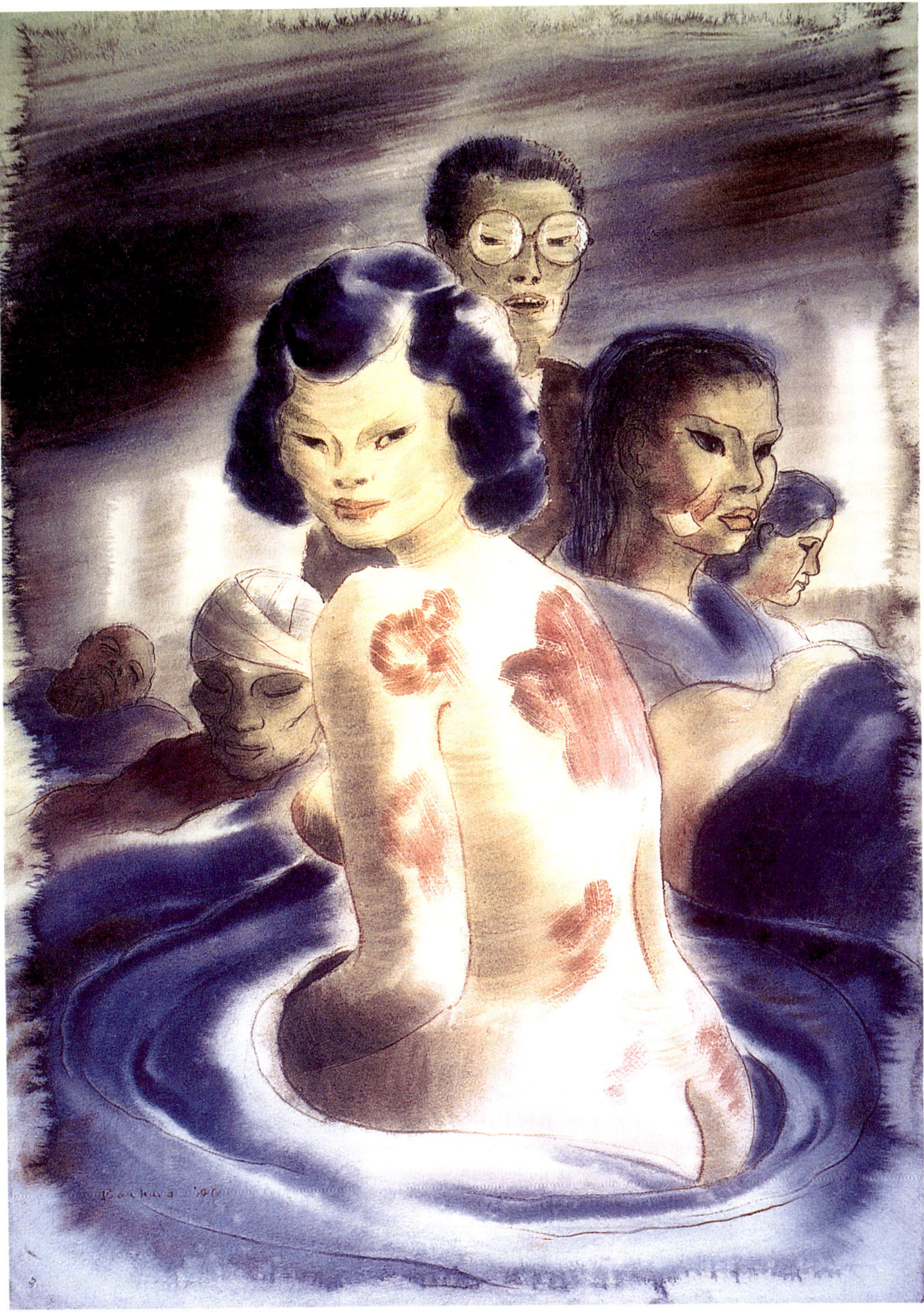

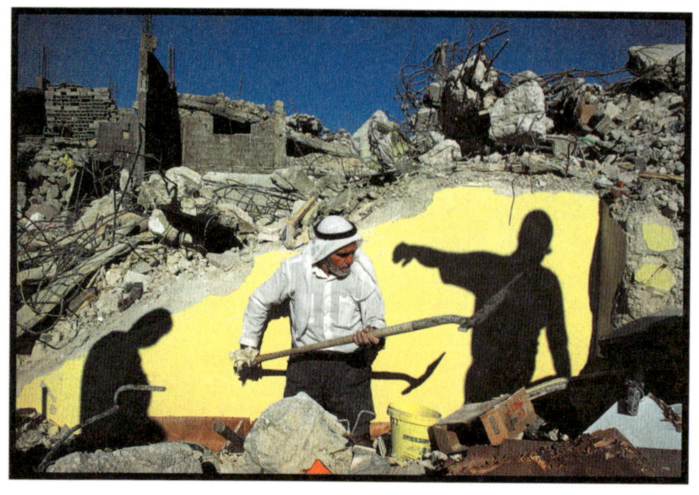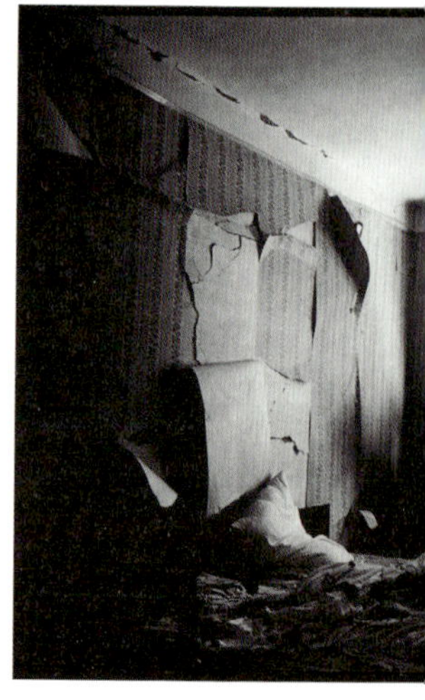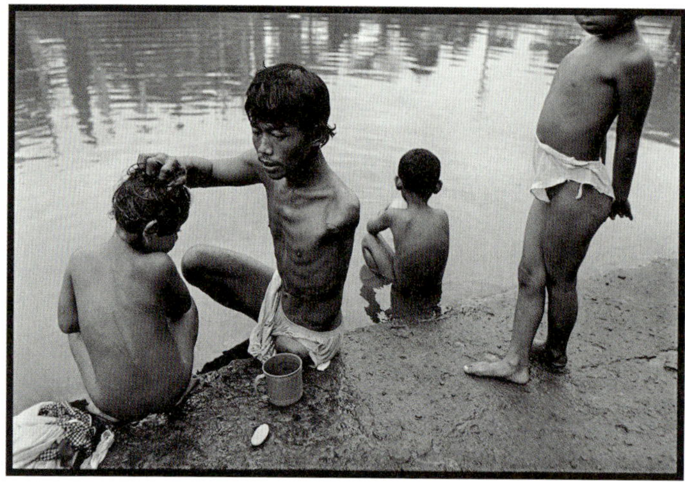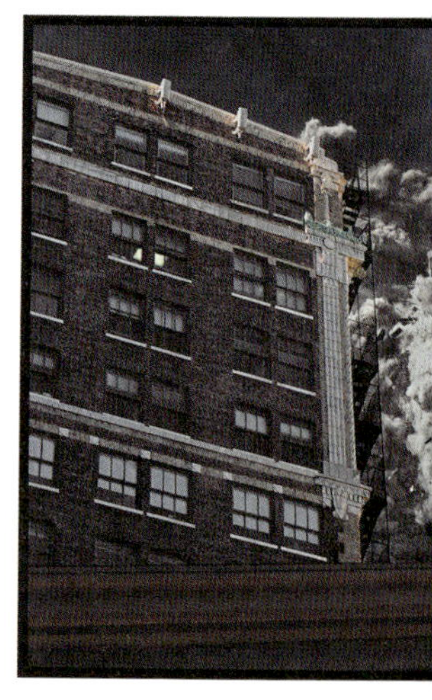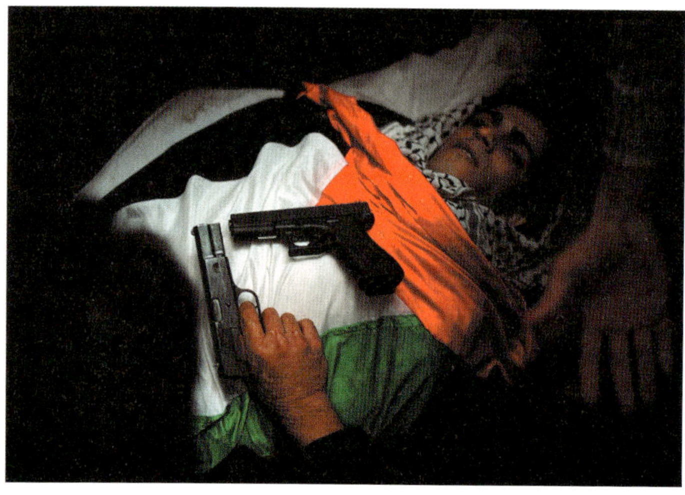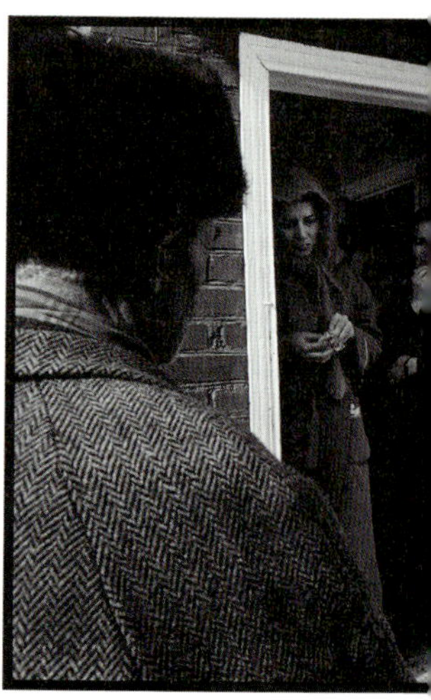

JAMES NACHTWEY, The passion of Islam, 2003
Inkjet on paper, 285.13 x 416.56 cm
Collection of the artist, New York

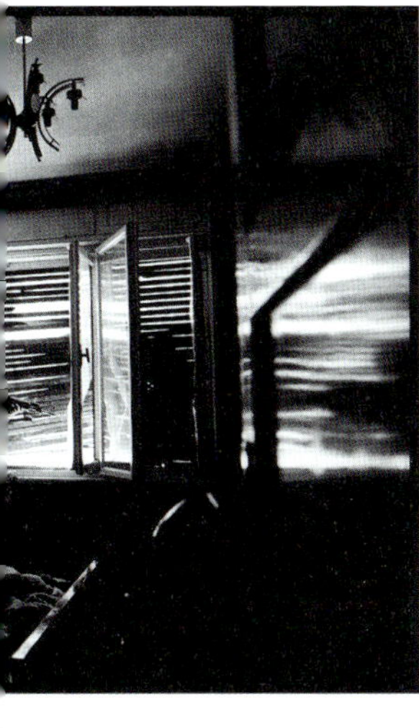
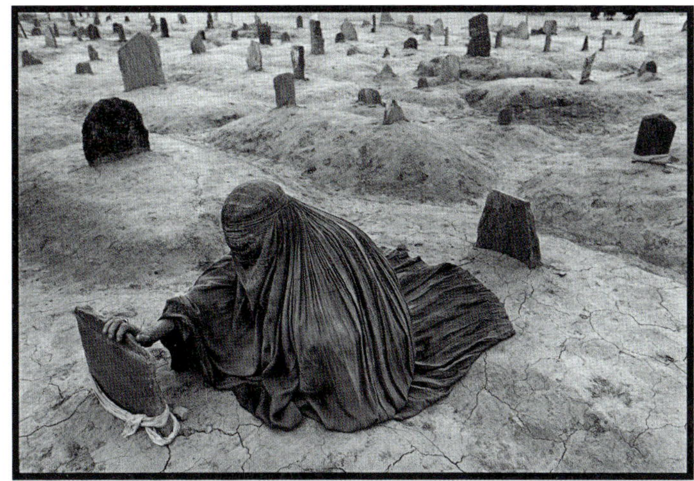
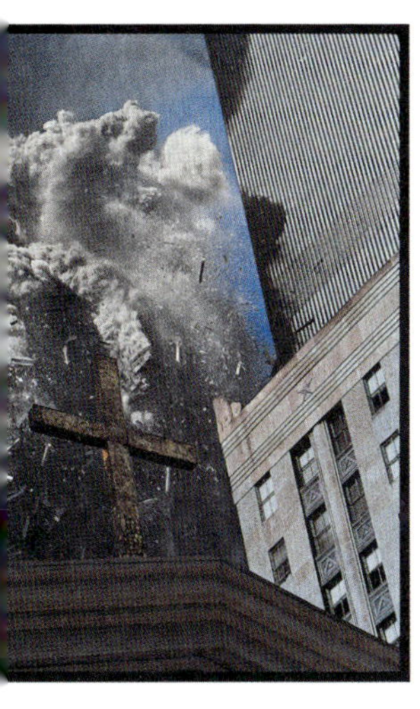
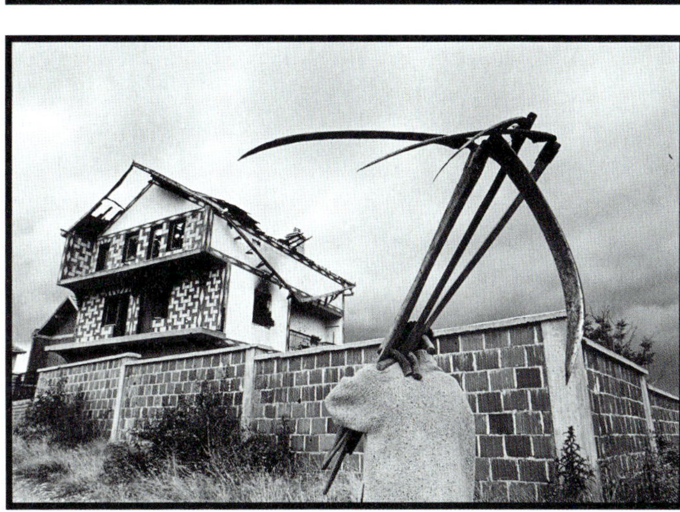
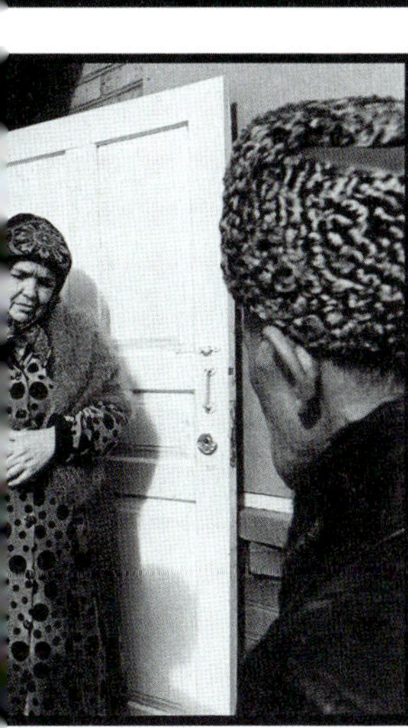
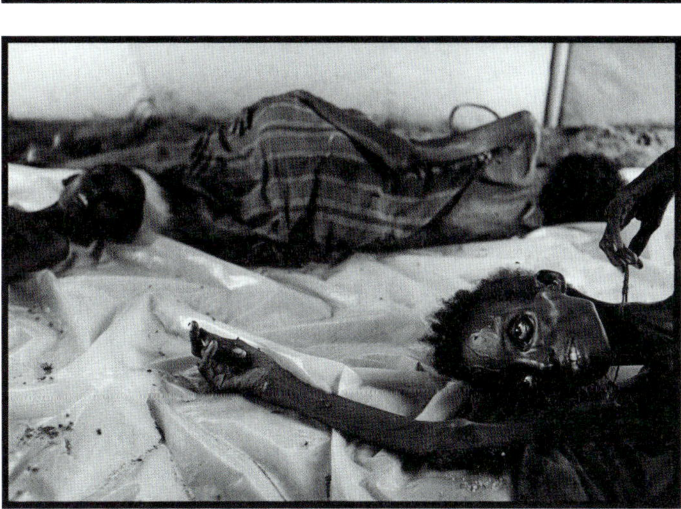

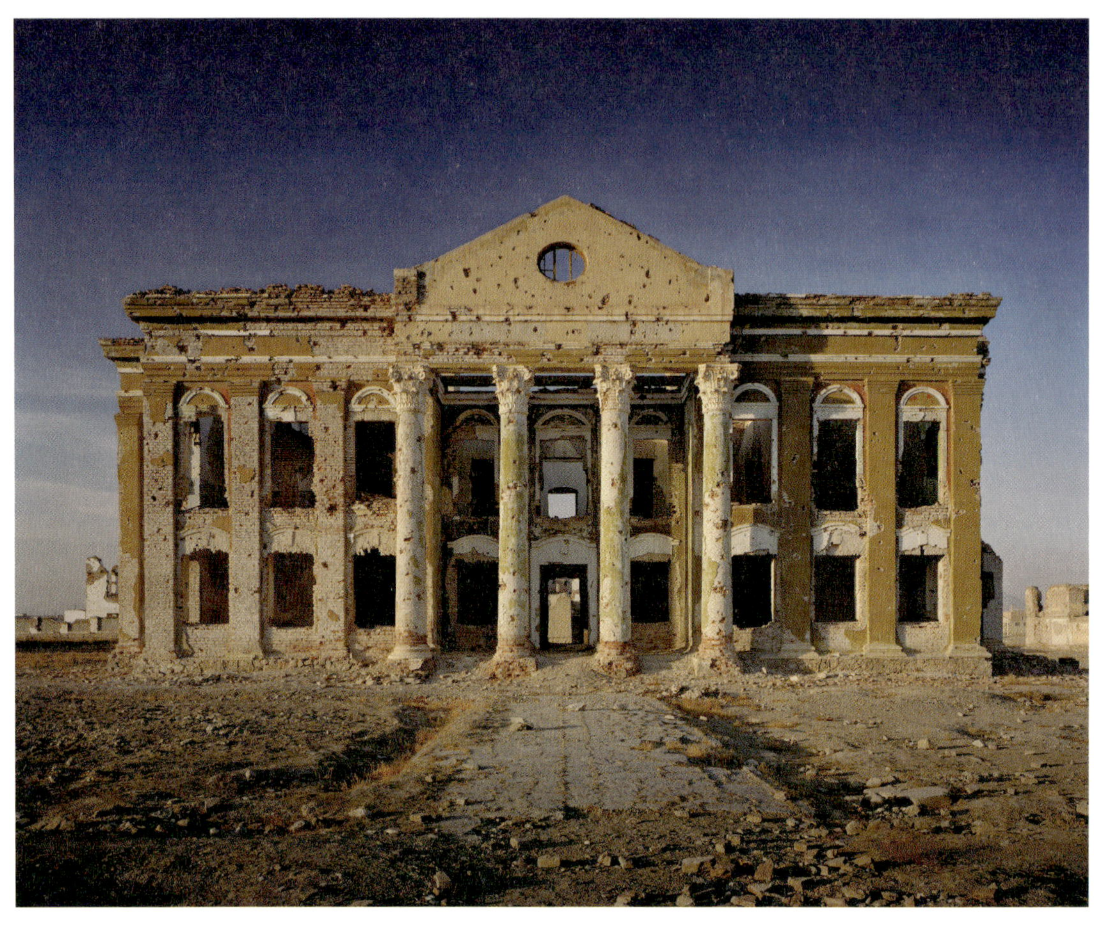

SIMON NORFOLK, A government building close to the former
Presidential palace at Darulaman, destroyed in fighting
between Rabbani and the Hazaras in the early nineties, 2001
Courtesy of Galerie Martin Kudlek, Cologne

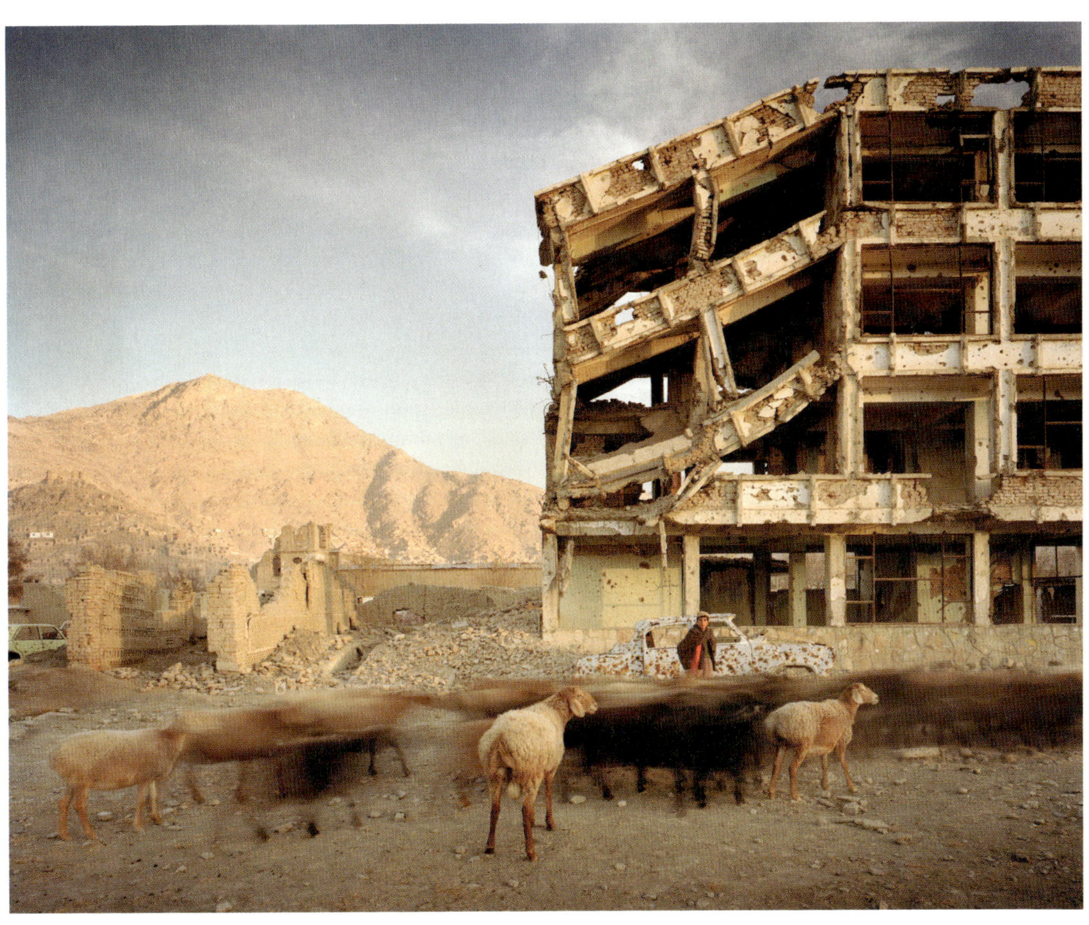

SIMON NORFOLK, Bullet-scarred apartment building
and shops in the Karte Char district of Kabul, 2001
Courtesy of Galerie Martin Kudlek, Cologne

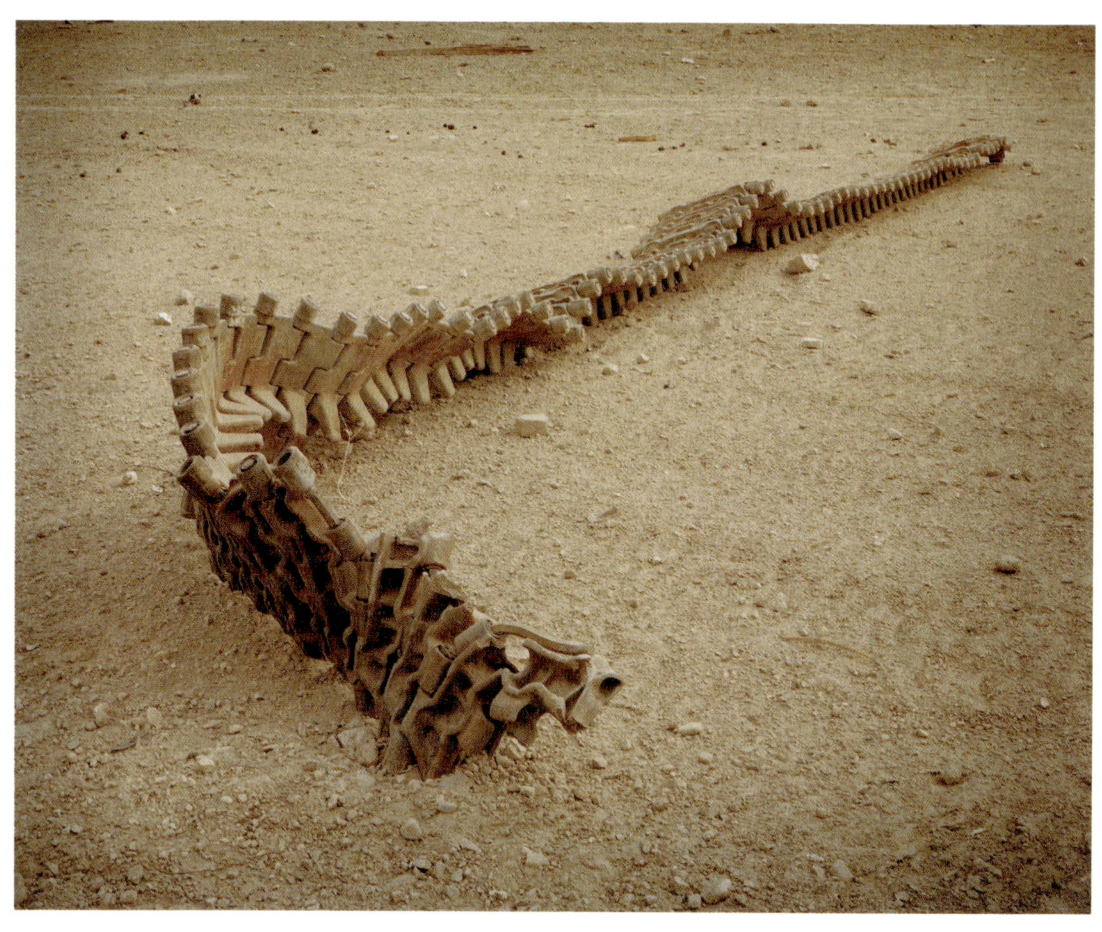

SIMON NORFOLK, Track of destroyed Taliban tank at Farm
Hada military base near Jalalabad, 2001
Courtesy of Galerie Martin Kudlek, Cologne

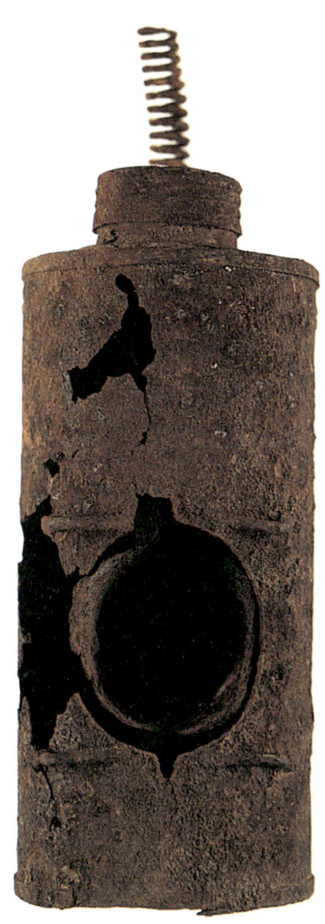

Grenade manufactured in France and used
by both sides during the Spanish Civil War,
1936-1939. Battle of the Ebro, 1938. Found
in 2002 near Gandesa.

Laffite hand grenade, 1921
Francesc Torres Collection, Barcelona

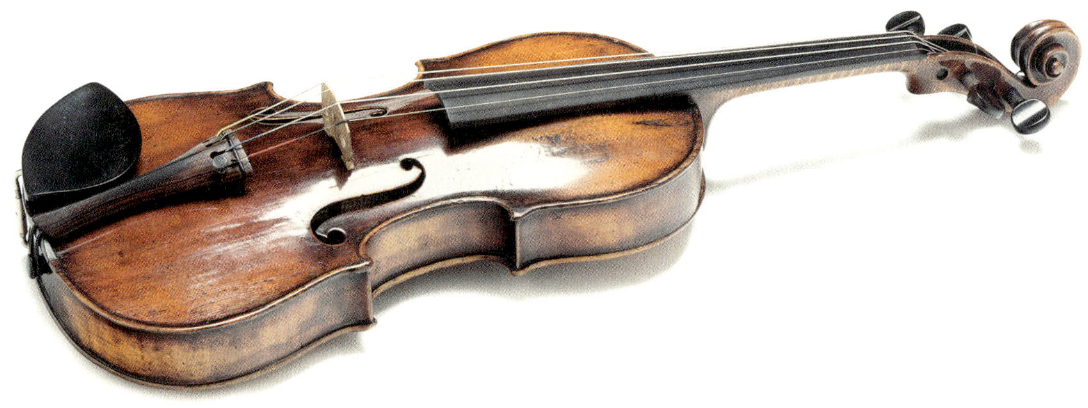

Rosner was a professional violinist who was interned in the Plaszow concentration camp, where he played for the camp commandant, Amon Goeth, and his guests. Among them was Oskar Schindler, who recruited Rosner and his family as part of the workforce at his factory. Schindler salvaged the violin from the camp and gave it to Rosner's wife when the musician was in Dachau. Both survived and, when they were reunited after the war, she took him his violin.

Nineteeth century Italian violin owned by Henry Rosner, a
professional Jewish violinist from Krakow who was saved by
Oskar Schindler during World War II, 1939-1945
Wood, metal, wire, 59 x 20.3 x 8.8 cm
Pantirer and Zuckerman Collection, United States Holocaust
Memorial Museum, Washington

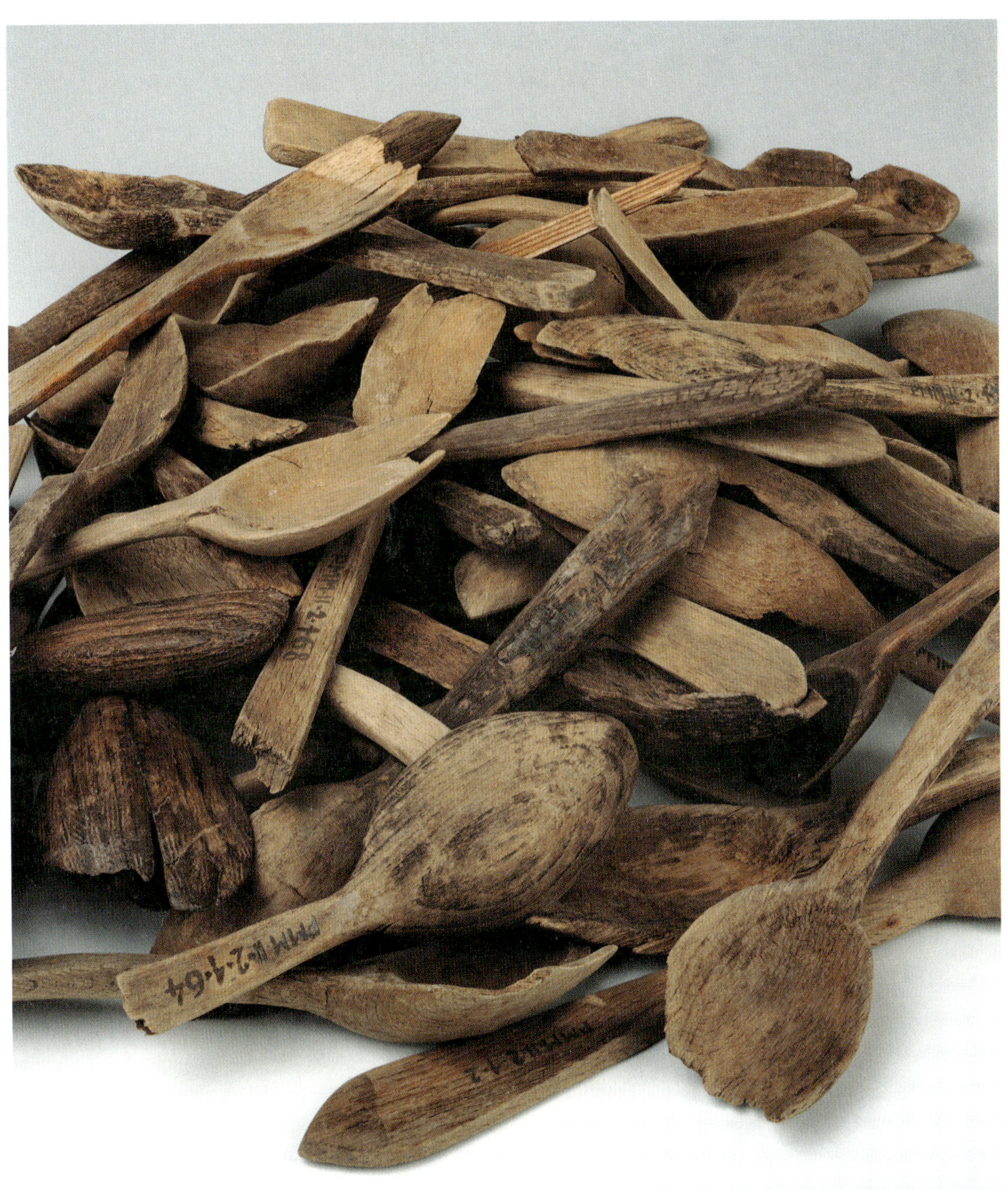

Spoons, item of camp equipment, Majdanek
concentration camp, 1942-1944
Carved wood, 15.4 x 4.2 x 1.4 cm
State Museum at Majdanek, Lublin, Poland

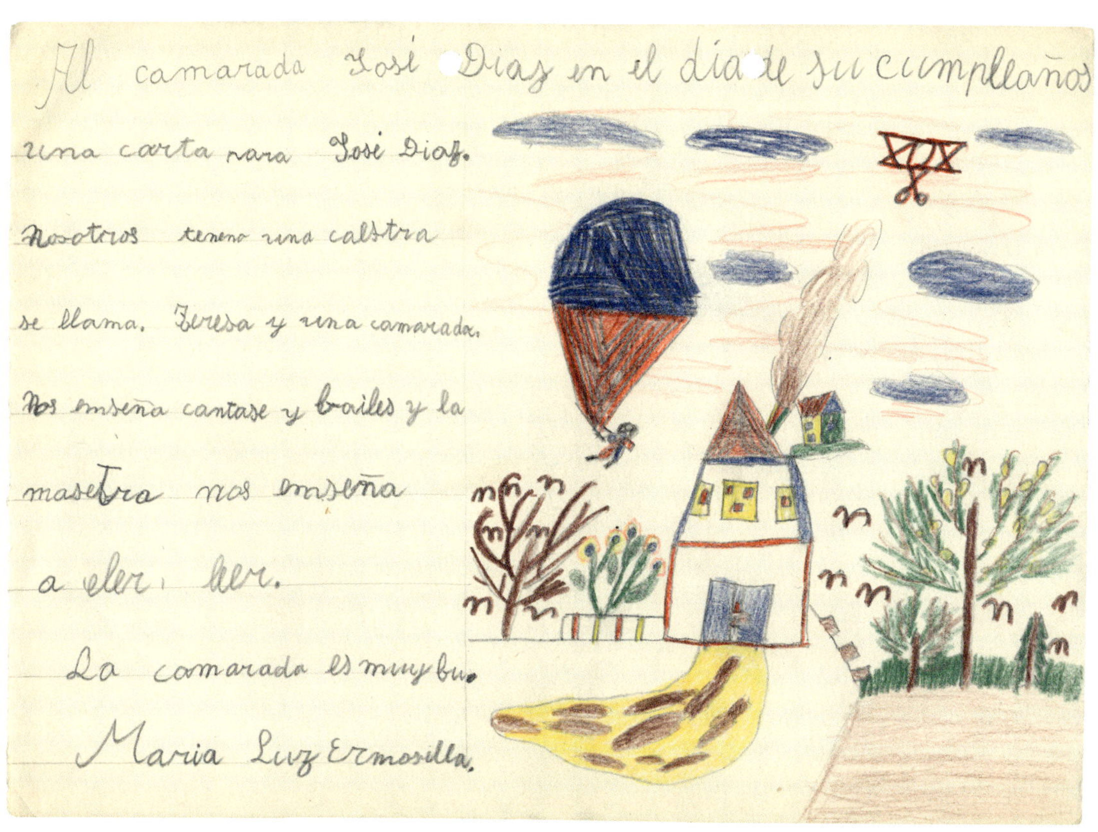

Direct testimony, comparable to the works from the
so-called literal avant-garde, is provided by the drawings
of children who have experienced war, at times as a way
of exorcising the horror and a form of trauma therapy.
The Spanish Civil War gave rise to an abundant legacy
of works, but this art form is a universal phenomenon.

MARIA LUZ ERMOSILLA, Letter from the child to comrade
José Díaz Morales (general secretary of the Spanish
Communist Party), USSR, between 1939-1941
Paper, pencil and colour pencils, 20.5 x 29 cm
ANC. Archivo Guerra y Exilio. Centro Español de Moscú,
Sant Cugat del Vallès

GREGORIO VARGAS, Letter from the child to comrade José
Díaz Morales (general secretary of the Spanish Communist
Party), USSR, between 1939-1941

Paper, pencil and colour pencils, 20.5 x 29 cm
ANC. Archivo Guerra y Exilio. Centro Español de Moscú,
Sant Cugat del Vallès

ALFONSO GUISASOLA, Letter from the child to comrade
José Díaz Morales (general secretary of the Spanish
Communist Party), USSR, between 1939-1941
Paper, pencil and colour pencils, 20.5 x 29 cm
ANC. Archivo Guerra y Exilio. Centro Español de Moscú,
Sant Cugat del Vallès

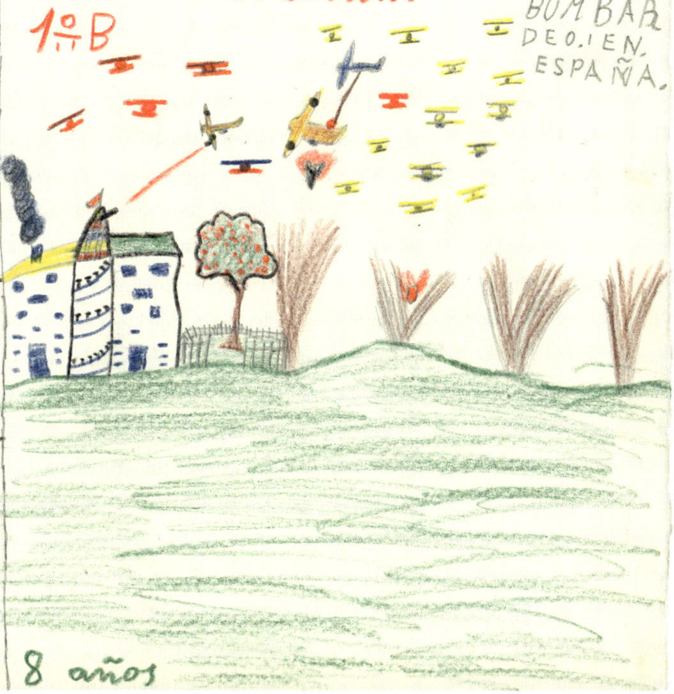

Querido padre
yo quiero que
ustez venga
pronto yo vivo
en la U.R.S.S.
Yo quiero mucho
a España y a
Madrid viva
Gregorio Vargas. de 8 años

Querido Jose.
Dia. Zenemenos.
fuena. distiplina
para. ser. pionero.
Y ub   Y marine
ro rojos. para luchar
contar los facistas.
para. salfar a todos
los niños. De España
1º B Alfonso Guisasola

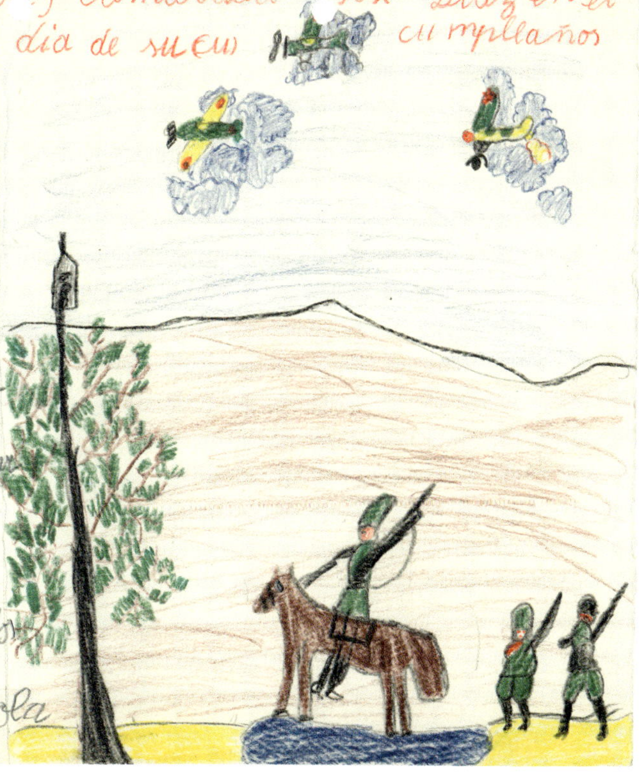

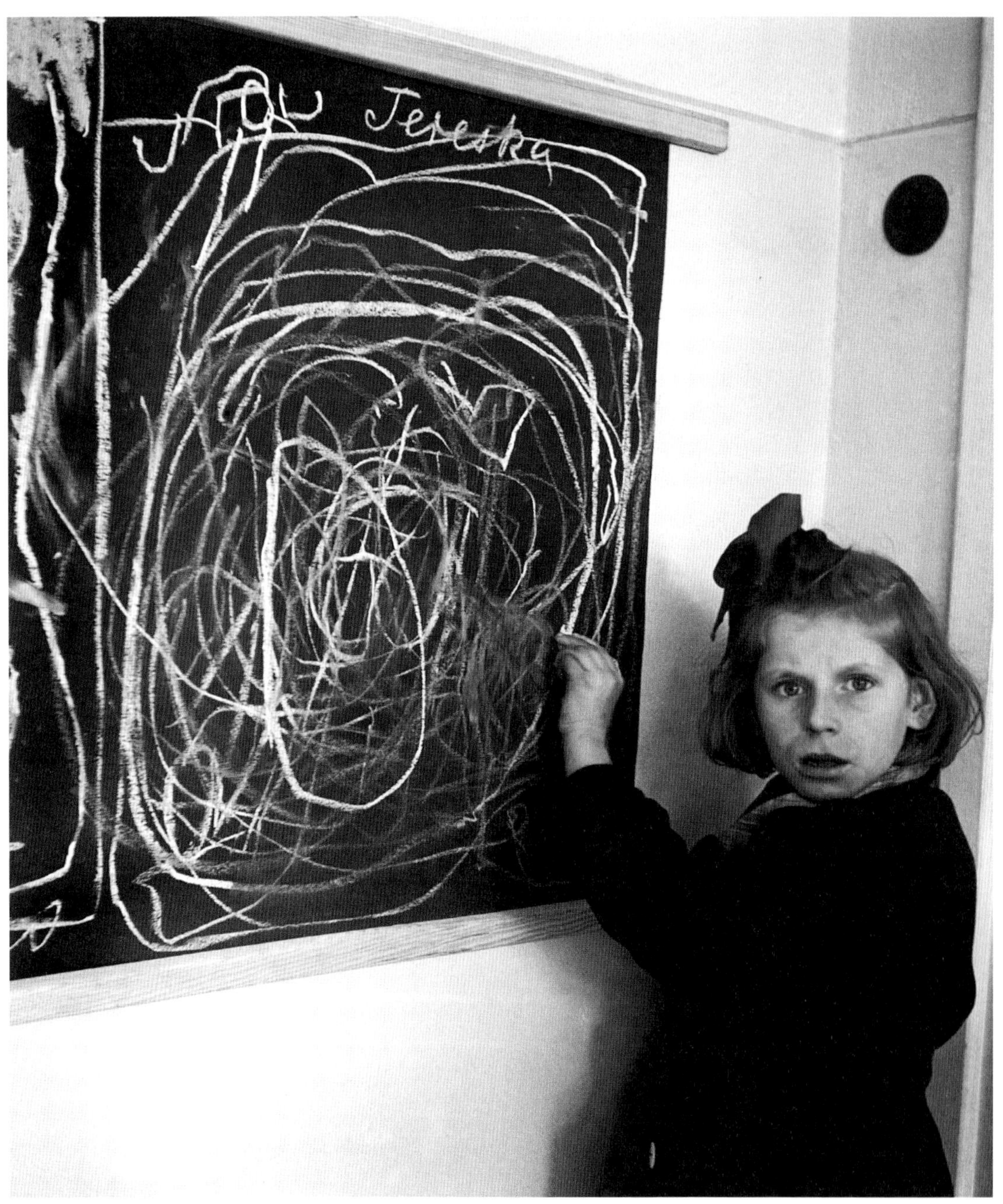

DAVID SEYMOUR, Teresa, a child in a residence for disturbed
children, grew up in a concentration camp.
She drew a picture of "Home" on the blackboard, Poland, 1948
David Seymour / Magnum Photos / Contacto

ŽTP-ERC SARAJEVO   PREKNJIŽENJA SA ZALII
                                          SITNOG INVENTARA
SKLADIŠTE: 40680   ZA MJESEC JU!

DOKUMENT PRIMA- BROJ IZ Z KOLIČINA V PREDAJNA VOZARINA
BROJ MJ. LAC   TMENIKA M CIJEL.DEC. U VRIJEDNOST DO OBRADE
****
00022 05 40603 3603101076 0   1,000 7

00023 05 40603 3603101076 0   1,000 7
00023 05 40603 3603111091 0   1,000 7

00025 06 40603 3420356036 0   1,000 7

SKLADIŠTE   40680 BROJ UPISANIH STAVKI   101
STOVARIŠTE 406   BROJ UPISANIH STAVKI   677

ALEN (4 year old), Drawing, Sarajevo, 1994
30.3 x 17.9 cm
Museu del Joguet de Catalunya, Figueres

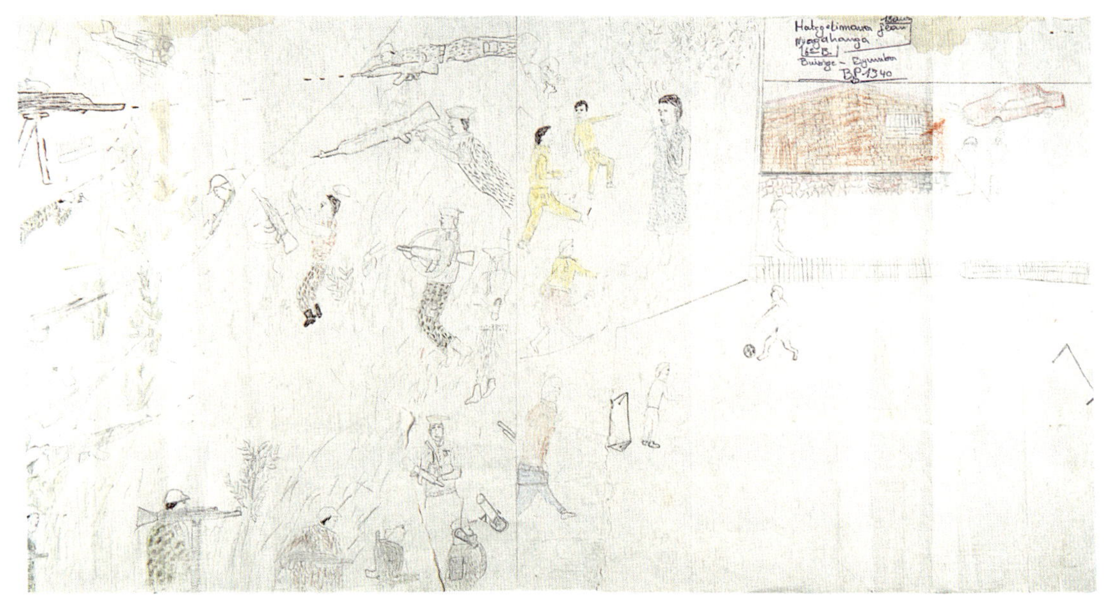

CHILD SURVIVOR OF GENOCIDE, A firefight between
the government forces and the Rwandese Patriotic Army,
1966-1967
Pencil, colour pencils, ink and paper, 30 x 61 cm
Richard Salem, Editor, *Witness to Genocide-The Children
of Rwanda,* New York, 2000

JANI (6 year old), Drawing, Sarajevo, 1994
Pencil, 21 x 31 cm
Museu del Joguet de Catalunya, Figueres

MASA MARCOVIC (6 year old), Drawing, Sarajevo, 1994
Pencil, 22.9 x 30.9 cm
Museu del Joguet de Catalunya, Figueres

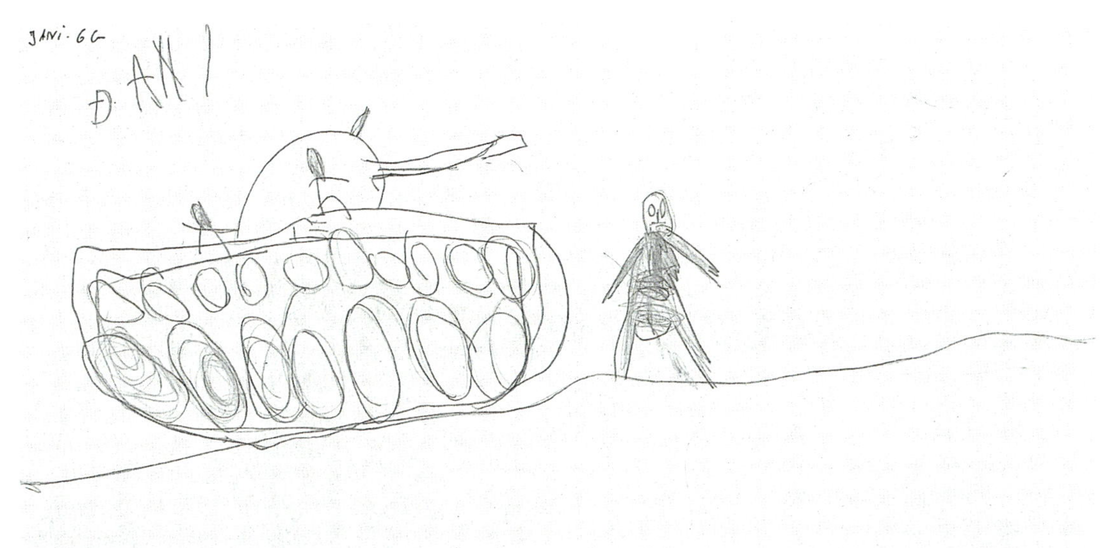

MAŠA

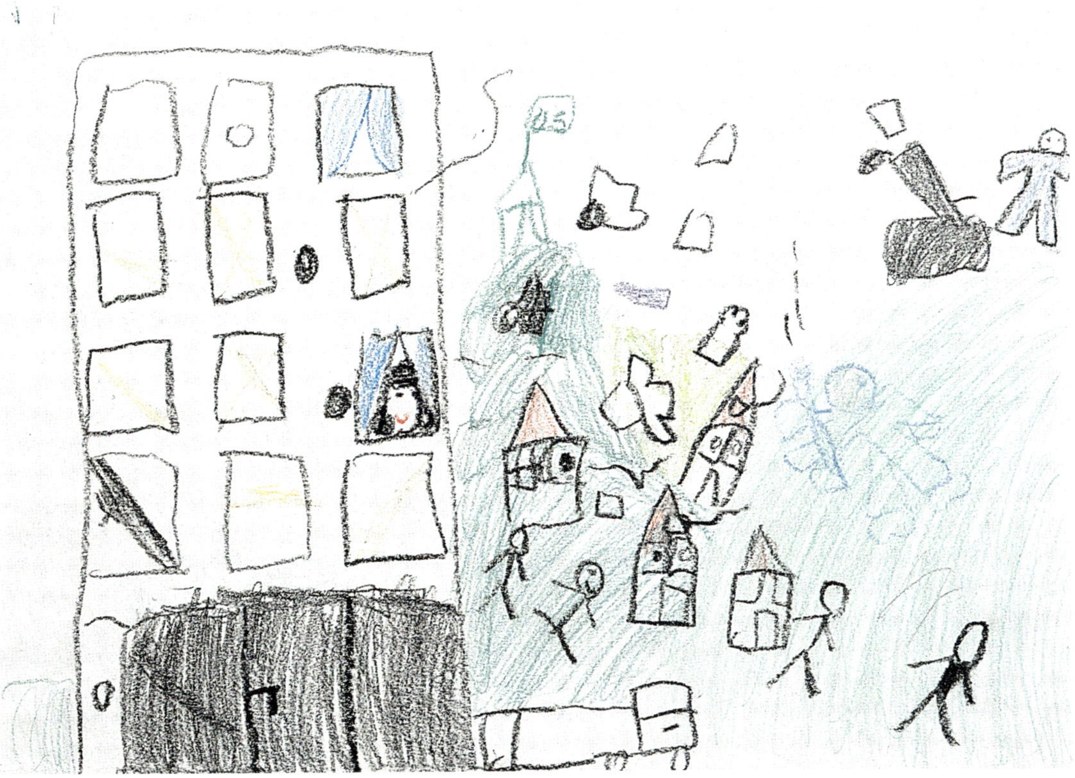

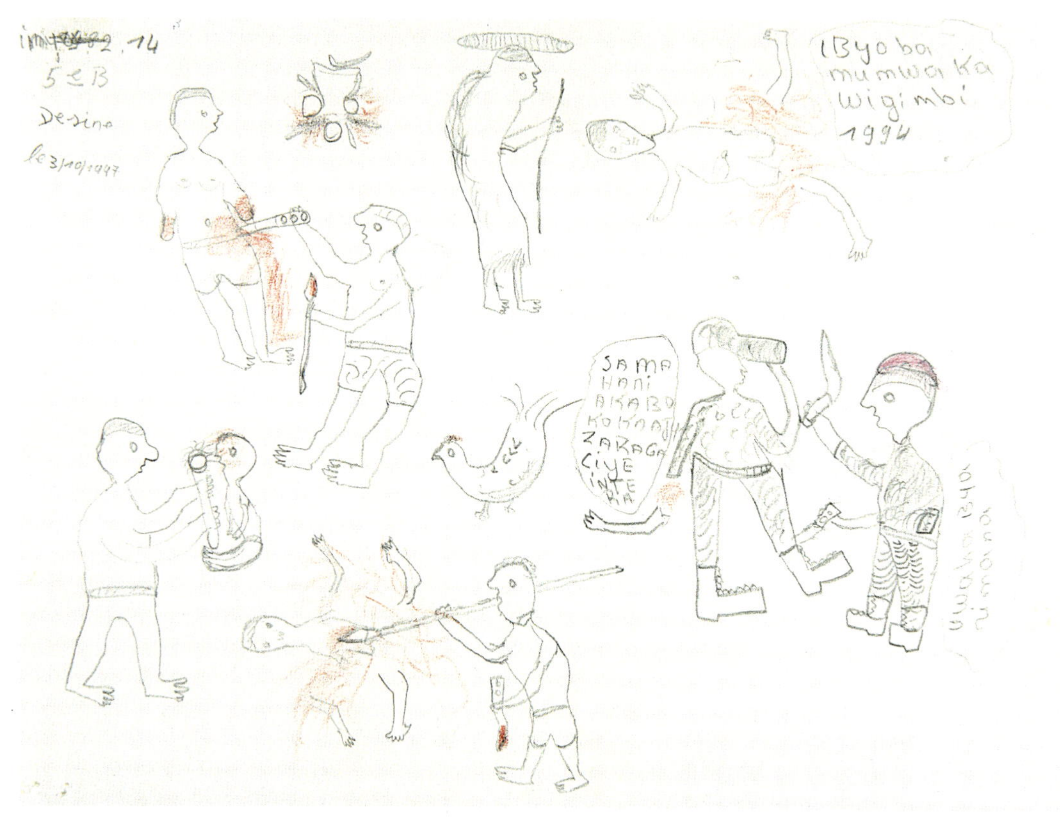

RWANDA CHILD, What happened with the Tutsis in 1994, 3 October 1997
Paper, pencil and colour pencils, 23 x 30 cm
Richard Salem, Editor, *Witness to Genocide-The Children of Rwanda*, New York, 2000

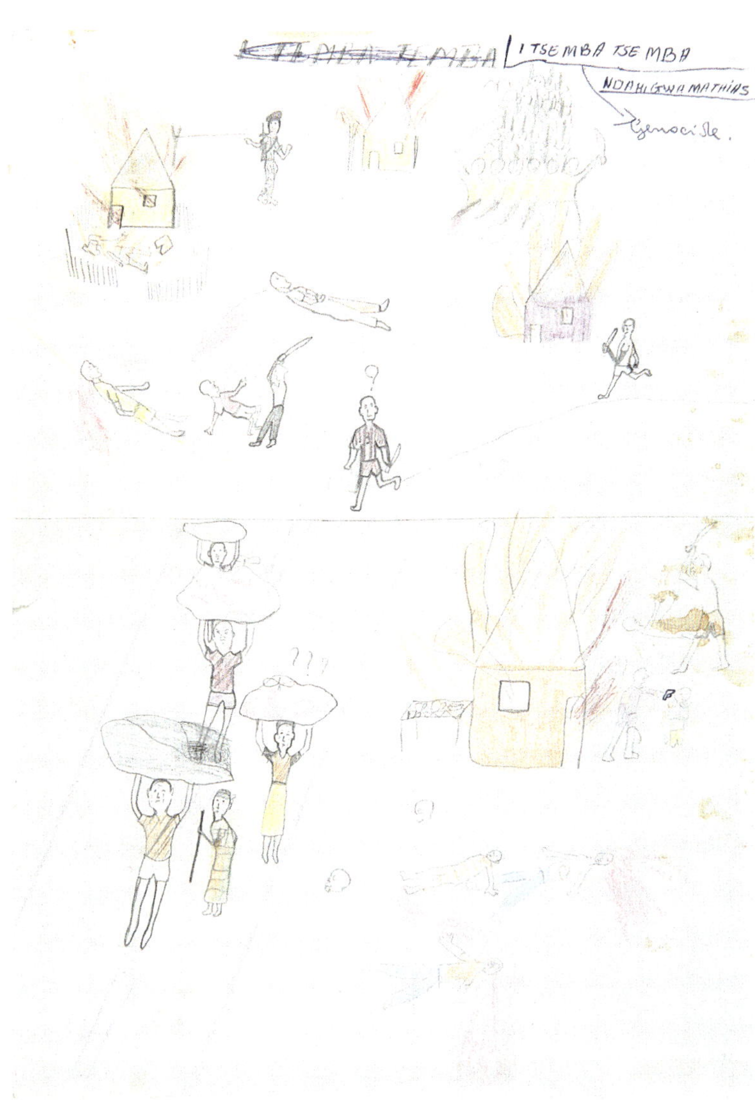

CHILD SURVIVOR OF GENOCIDE, Genocide, 1996-1998
Paper and colour pencils, 29.5 x 21 cm
Richard Salem, Editor, *Witness to Genocide-The Children of Rwanda*, New York, 2000

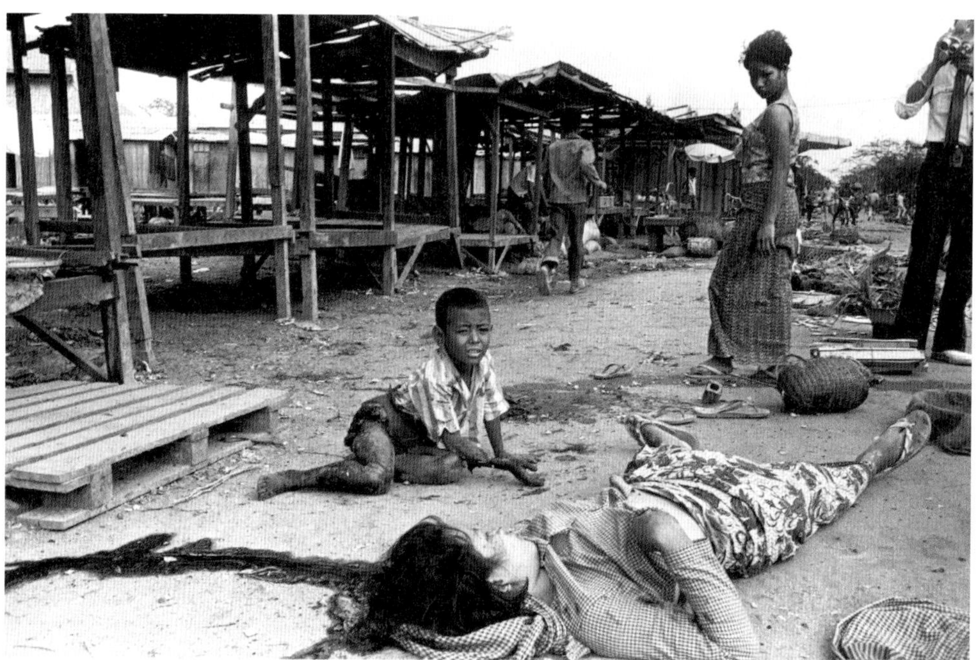

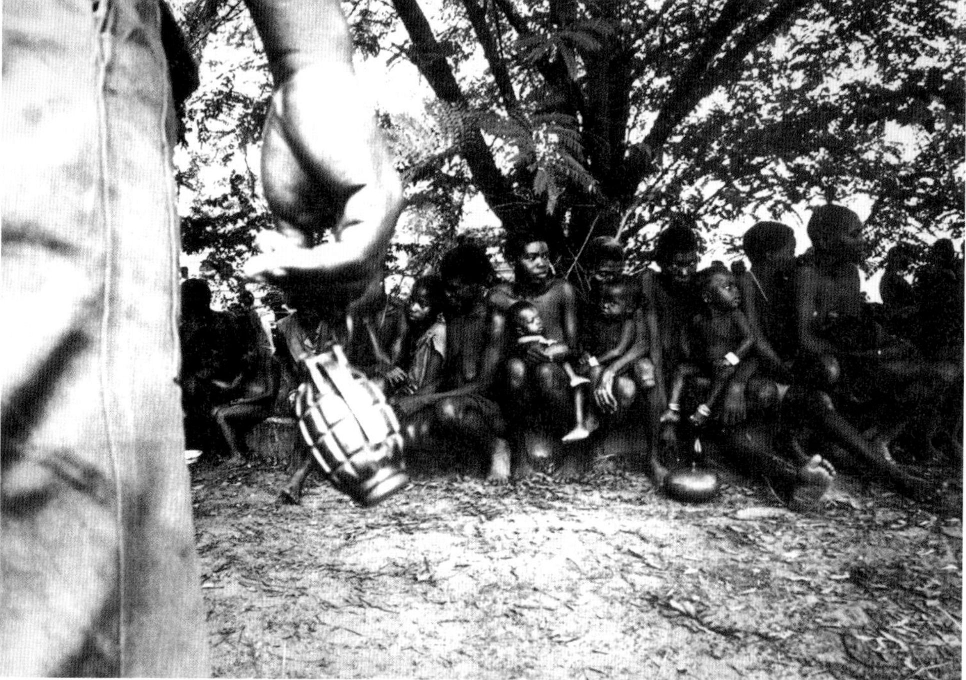

TEA KIM HEANG, After a rocket attack on the Pochentong central market, a boy with severe burns looks at his dead mother, Phnom Penh, Cambodia, 1975
AP / Radial Press

A federal soldier swings a hand grenade by its release pin while guarding Ibo women prisoners and their children in Nigeria, during the Biafran War, 19 July 1968
The Hulton Getty Picture Collection, London

The children killed in Madrid, photomontage used as the basis for the poster by the Ministry for Propaganda. "Murderers! Seeing this, who wouldn't pick up a rifle to end fascism's destruction", 1936
Musée d'Histoire Contemporaine - BDIC, Paris

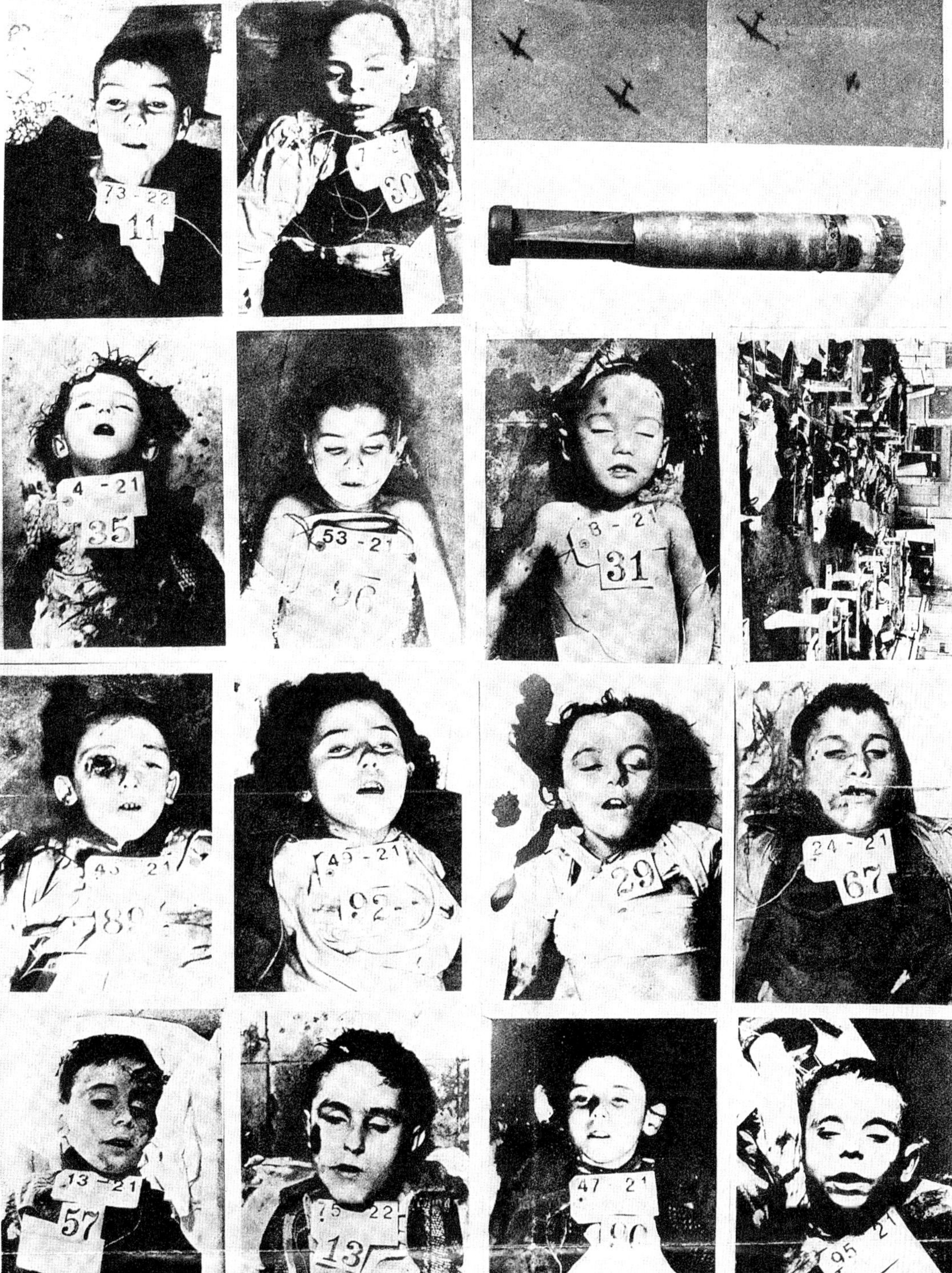

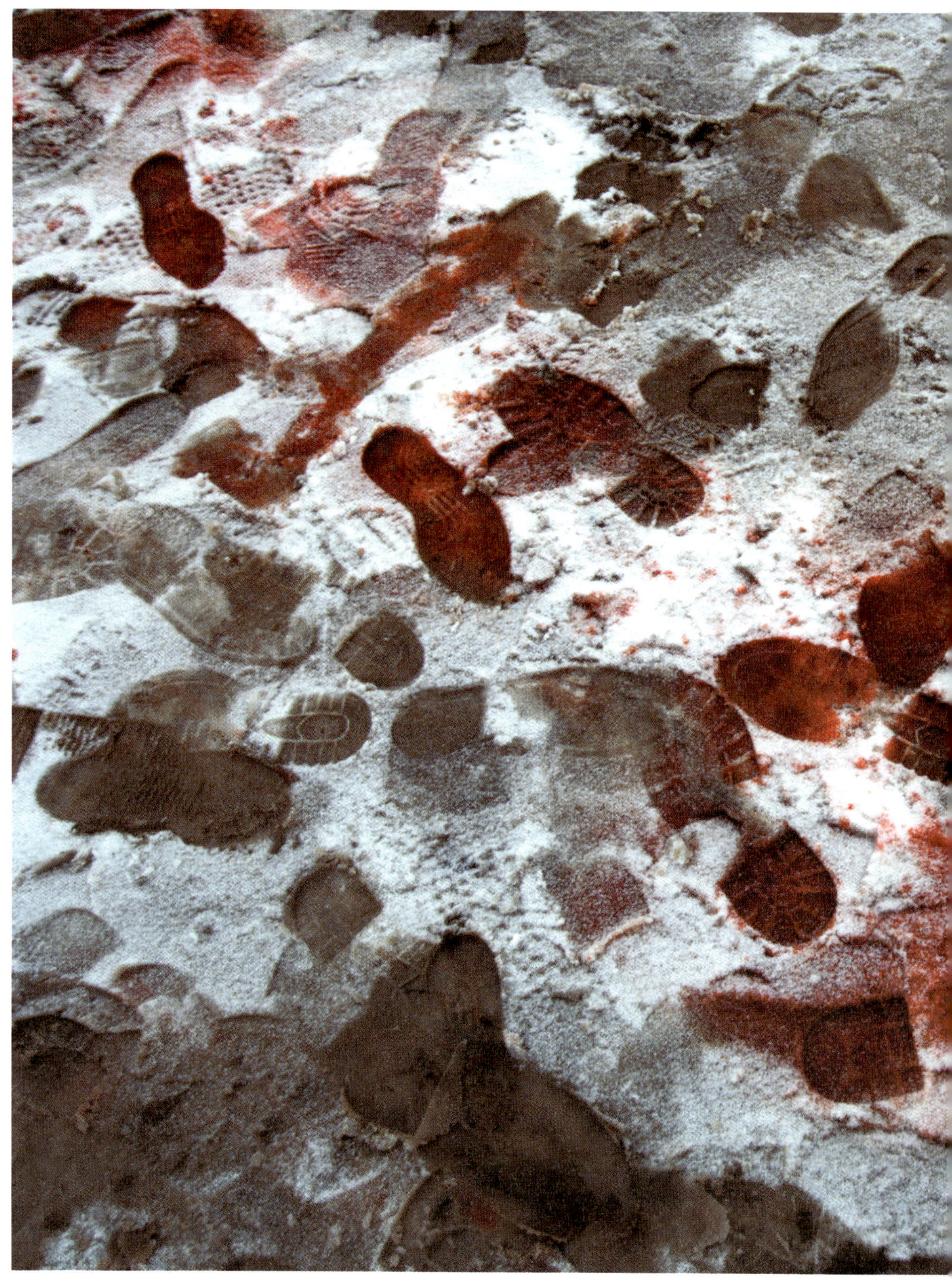

PAUL LOWE, Chechenia, 1994
Paul Lowe / Grazia Neri / Contacto

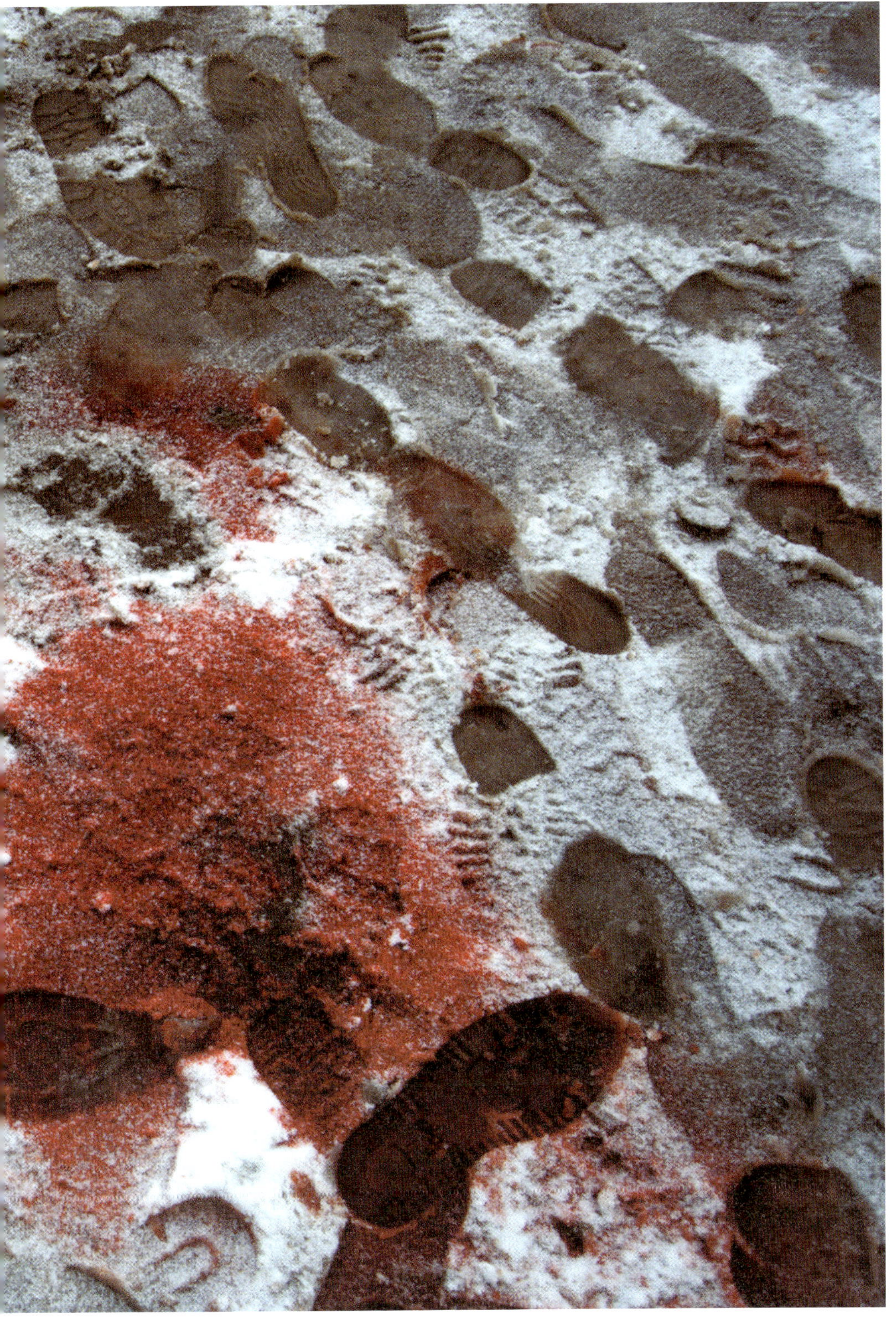

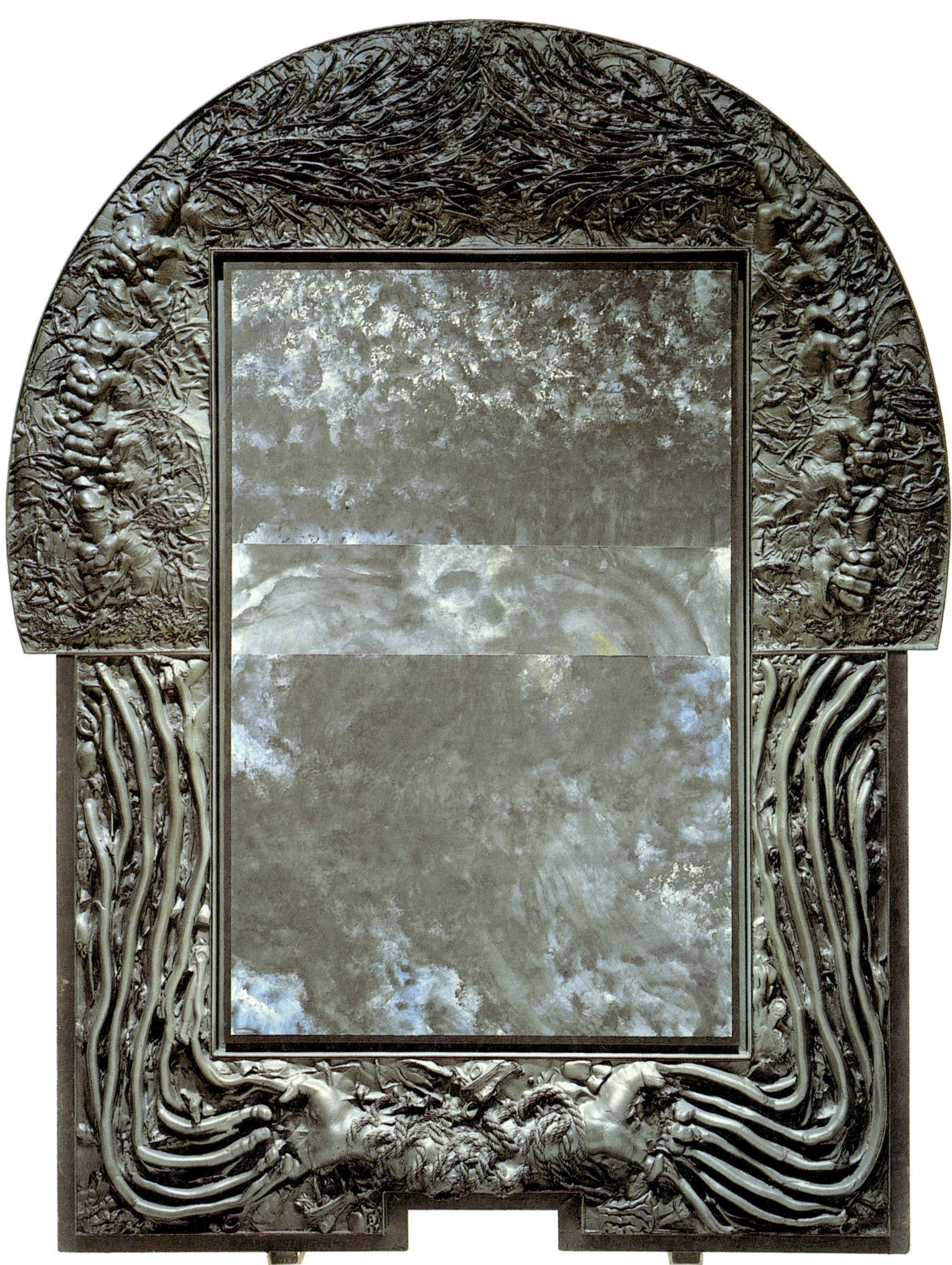

Victory and defeat

Arguing about war
Michael Walzer

Karl von Clausewitz's famous line, that war is the continuation of politics by other means, was probably meant to be provocative, but it seems to me obviously true. And the claim is equally obvious the other way around: politics is the continuation of war by other means. But it is very important that the means are different. Politics is a form of peaceful contention, and war is organized violence. All the participants, all the activists and militants, survive a political defeat (unless the victor is a tyrant, at war with his own people), whereas many participants, soldiers and civilians alike, do not survive a military defeat—or a victory either. War kills, and that is why the debates about whether to fight and how to fight are so important and so intense.

The theory of "just war" is first of all an argument about the status of warfare as a human activity. The argument is twofold: that war is sometimes justifiable and that the conduct of war is always subject to moral criticism. The first of these propositions is denied by pacifists, who believe that war is in every time and place a criminal act; and the second is denied by "realists," who have adopted the old Roman maxim, *inter arma silent leges* (in time of war, the laws are silent), and who deny the very possibility of moral critique. So just war theorists set themselves in opposition to pacifists and realists, of whom there are a great number, though some of the pacifists are selective in their opposition to war and some of the realists have been heard, in the heat of battle, to express moral sentiments.

But just war theory is not only an argument about war in general; it is also the ordinary language in which we argue about particular wars. This is the way most of us actually talk when we join the debates about whether to fight and how to fight. Ideas like self-defense and aggression, the view of war as a combat between combatants, the immunity of noncombatants, the crime of terrorism, the doctrine of proportionality, the rules of surrender, the rights of prisoners—all this is our common heritage, the product of many centuries of arguing about war. "Just war" is nothing more than a theoretical version of all this, designed to help us resolve, or at least to think clearly about, the problems of definition and application.

Still, bringing those two words together—"just" and "war"—seems odd to many people, and I want to address two common objections to the theory. The first is that those of us who defend and apply it are moralizing war, and by doing that we are making it easier to fight. We take away the stigma that should always be attached to the business of killing, which is what war necessarily is. When we define the criteria by which war and the conduct of war can be judged, we open the way for favorable judgments. Many of these judgments will be ideological, partisan or hypocritical in character and so subject to criticism, but some of them, given the theory, will be right: some wars and some acts of war will turn out to be "just." How can that be, when war is so terrible?

But "just" is a term of art here, a word used in a special sense; it means "justifiable," "defensible," even "morally necessary" *given the alternatives*—and that is all it means. All of us who argue about the rights and wrongs of war agree that justice in the strong sense, the sense that it has in domestic society and everyday life, is lost as soon as the fighting begins. War is a zone of radical coercion, in which justice is always under a cloud. Still, sometimes we are right to enter the zone. As someone who grew up during World War II, this seems to me another obvious point. There are acts of aggression and acts of cruelty that we ought to resist, by force if necessary. I would have thought that our experience with Nazism ended this particular argument, but the argument goes on: hence the current disagreements about "humanitarian intervention." The use of military force to stop the killing in Rwanda would have been, in my view, a just war. And if that judgment "moralizes" military force and makes it easier to use—well, I wish it had been easier to use in Africa in 1994.

The second criticism of just war theory is that it encourages us to think about wars in the wrong way. It focuses our attention on the immediate issues at stake in the months before the war begins—in the case of the recent Iraq War, for example, on inspections, disarmament, hidden weapons, and so on—and then on the conduct of the war, battle by battle, and so it avoids larger questions about imperial ambition and the global struggle for resources and power. It is as if citizens of the ancient world had focused narrowly on the conflict between Rome and some other Italian city-state over whether a treaty had been violated, as the Romans would always claim in the lead-up to their attack, and never discussed the long history of Roman expansion. But if critics can distinguish between concocted excuses for war and actual reasons, why can't the rest of us do the same thing? Just war theory has no fixed temporal limits; it can be used to analyze a long chain of events as readily as a short one. Indeed, how can imperial warfare be criticized if not in just war terms? What other language, what other theory, is available for such a critique? Aggressive wars, wars of conquest, wars to extend spheres of influence and establish satellite states, wars for economic aggrandizement—all these are unjust wars.

Just war is a critical theory. It singles out and justifies a very limited set of wars, which are, I think, intuitively justifiable: wars fought in self-defense against an invading army, wars fought in alliance with people defending themselves, and wars fought to rescue people from massacre and "ethnic cleansing." All other wars are denied justification; they are condemned as unjust. The theory is designed to help us make morally necessary distinctions. This point is often misunderstood. When I defended the American war in Afghanistan a couple of years ago, some European critics claimed that since I had opposed the war in Vietnam, and also many of the US Government's little wars and proxy wars in Central America, I was now being inconsistent. But that is like saying that a doctor who diagnoses one patient with cancer is then obliged to provide a similar diagnosis for every other patient. The same medical criteria yield different diagnoses in different cases. And the same moral criteria yield different judgments in different wars.

Still, the judgments are controversial, even when we agree on the criteria. We read a defense or a critique of this or that war, and then we look for a second opinion. There is always a second opinion, and a third, and a fourth. The fact that we disagree, however, doesn't distinguish "just war" from any other moral (or political) concept. We give different accounts of the same military action, but we also give different accounts of the same election. We disagree about corruption, discrimination and inequality, even when we talk about all three in the common language of democratic theory. The disagreements don't invalidate the theory; the theory, if it is a good one, makes the disagreements more coherent and comprehensible.

The ongoing disagreements, together with the rapid pace of political change, sometimes require revisions of the theory (any theory). Two revisions of just war theory have, in my view, become necessary in the last two decades. First, faced with the sheer number of recent horrors—with mass murder, systematic rape, and the harsh persecution of ethnic and religious minorities in Bosnia and Kosovo; in Rwanda, the Sudan, Sierra Leone, the Congo, and Liberia; in East Timor (and earlier on, in Cambodia and Bangladesh)—many of us who write about war have slowly become more willing to call for military intervention. We haven't dropped the presumption against intervention that is a standard part of just war theory, but we have found it easier and easier to override the presumption. And second, faced with the reiterated experience of state failure, the re-emergence of a form of politics that European historians call "bastard feudalism," dominated by warring gangs and would-be charismatic leaders, we have become more willing to defend long-term military occupations, in the form of protectorates and trusteeships, and to think of nation-building as a necessary part of post-war politics.

Both of these shifts also require us to recognize the need for an expansion of just war theory. *Jus ad bellum* (which deals with the decision to go to war) and *jus in bello* (which deals with the conduct of the battles) are its standard elements, first worked out by Catholic philosophers and jurists in the Middle Ages and the early modern period—the Spanish Dominicans, Suárez and Vitoria, were centrally important in their development. Now we have to add to those two an account of *jus post bellum* (justice after the war). The aftermath of the Iraq War demonstrates the need for a doctrine of just and unjust occupations. What sorts of rules and what international agencies ought to govern the settlement of wars? The stability of the settlement is likely to depend on its legitimacy, but we have only begun to think about what makes a war's ending legitimate.

Arguments about war are, as I have said, "ongoing." In fact, they are probably endless. There has been an effort to abolish war—it is reflected in the Charter of the United Nations—by treating aggression as a criminal act and describing any response as a "police action." This is what the Chinese call, or used to call, "the rectification of names." But it isn't possible to change reality by changing the way we talk about it. We can see this clearly in the original case: the UN's police action in Korea in 1950 is called by all its historians "the Korean War." Still, the impulse lingers. We saw it at work in the immediate aftermath of 11 September 2001, when many people in the United States and Europe insisted that the attack on the World Trade Towers was a crime and that we should not go to war (as we soon did in Afghanistan) but call the police. In the United States, the phone number for emergencies is 911, so I thought of this as the "dial 911" response to 9/11. It would have been a perfectly plausible response if anyone was answering the phone. In a global state with a monopoly on the legitimate use of force, calling the police would be the right response to violence. The criminal act, the pursuit of the criminal by police forces, and then his (or her) trial and punishment—these three would exhaust the field of action; we would read about war only in the history books. But that is not a description of the world we live in, and even if a global state ought to be our goal (I have some doubts about that, but they are not relevant here), it is a great mistake to pretend that we are already there.

So we are doomed to continue arguing about war; it is a necessary activity of democratic citizens. Some of the arguments will be purely political: is it prudent to fight here or there, in alliance with this country or that one? Is our own country really threatened by the military buildup of country X? Can we trust the intelligence agencies on which our government claims to rely? Skepticism is always necessary in responding to questions like these, though sometimes (despite the evidence of recent cases) dangers are real and sometimes intelligence reports will prove to be accurate. But many of the arguments will also be moral in character: is this a war that we ought to fight against aggression or murder? Can we fight it in a way that doesn't put

innocent people massively at risk? Are there options short of war that
we ought to explore?

There is no avoiding both these kinds of arguments. Realists claim
that only the political arguments are serious, but I do not know of any
national debate about whether or how to fight that was constrained
in this way. The moral argument comes naturally to all of us; it isn't
some philosophical imposition. Pacifists claim that the moral argument
has only one answer, but decent men and women have too often found
themselves in critical situations where they couldn't give that answer.
Faced with aggression, murder, terrorism and enslavement, they have
opted to resist forcefully. And surely sometimes they are right. Maybe
a collective and reiterated resistance, if we could organize it, would
eventually serve to deter criminal acts like these, and then we wouldn't
have to resist anymore. But just war theory isn't a utopian program.
All it tells us is that now, in this instance, it is right to fight. Or that now,
in that instance, it would be wrong to fight. That isn't by any means
all we need to know. Sometimes, however, it is necessary knowledge.

The culture of war: victory and defeat

Jeremy M. Black

Victory and defeat appear to be absolutes, measured by such readily apparent criteria as the defeat and capitulation of armies and the conquest of territory. Thus, in conventional accounts war seems to be a matter of how best to ensure these goals, and this is the basic narrative and analysis of military history and discussions. Indeed, the modern perception of conflict has been heavily shaped by the experience of World War II, by the Allies' insistence on the unconditional surrender of the Axis and by the cataclysmic fate of the latter in 1945 in the shape of the fall of Berlin and the use of atomic weaponry against Japan. This emphasis has led to a neglect of how atypical such war-endings are; and indeed, in the case of Japan in 1945, it surrendered with the main "home islands" uninvaded and with Japan in control of far more territory than it had occupied prior to the attack on the Western Allies in 1941. Most wars have ended with a far less complete victory, and this is certainly true of the situation since 1945; for example the Korea, Vietnam, Indo-Pakistan, Arab-Israeli and Iran-Iraq conflicts. Even the Israeli victory in the Six Day War of 1967, generally seen as a sweeping triumph, ended with the Israelis not in control of Cairo, Damascus or Amman and without the closure in terms of Arab surrender that they required, not least because with an army dependent on reservists Israel could not afford a high level of confrontation.

Whatever the result, in practice, however, the understanding of war in terms of campaigning, the operational approach to war, is far too narrow. Instead, it is more appropriate to understand war as a cultural process that focuses on the imposition of will. From this perspective it is necessary to appreciate that people are beaten when they understand that they have lost, and that in the absence of such an understanding victory in battle can simply lead to the need for an onerous occupation while much of the population continues to resist: the problem that Napoleonic forces faced in Spain or their Nazi counterparts in Yugoslavia; or with the defeated preparing to fight on, as with the Egyptians and Syrians after 1967, which led in 1973 to the outbreak of another full-scale conflict.

In many respects success in war has become more difficult from this perspective in recent decades due to profound social changes across much of the world. These can be summarised as democratisation, but the process is far more complex: as more of the world's population has become urban, literate and engaged in industrial or service activities, so political participation and expectations have increased and deference has declined.

Linked to these social changes, which greatly affect the possibility of consent to defeat, comes a transformation in the reporting and commemoration of war. The central feature in both democratic and authoritarian societies is its public character, and governments in each are as one in trying to elicit support to a degree that would have surprised regimes in the eighteenth century; although, even then, careful attempts were made to ensure that war enhanced the *gloire* of rulers.

This modern drive for support during conflict and for a public endorsement thereafter ensures, however, a degree of controversy over reporting and commemoration. In Britain the nature and content of the public acts held after the Falklands War of 1982 and the Gulf War of 2003 led to a controversy over praying for Argentinians during the commemoration service in St. Paul's Cathedral after the Falklands War, for example, and in each case this controversy was linked to differences over the morality of the conflicts or to such aspects of the conflicts as the sinking in 1982 of the Argentinian warship the *General Belgrano* (a serious threat to the British task force, but arguably not an immediate one when sunk) and in 2003 the decision to attack Iraq. Uneasiness over conflict per se or over a conflict in particular, which stems readily from the high rate of political awareness in democratised societies, is easily transferred into dissent over the assessment of victory and this in turn ensures that regimes feel it more necessary to influence, if not control, the reporting of war; which is an increasingly important aspect of its commemoration.

The democratisation in the reporting and commemoration of war has been taken a stage further with technology. The twentieth century brought radio, television and then e-mail. The first two took further the nineteenth-century innovation of the war correspondent, with all the attendant problems of news management that this posed for government. Indeed, as a positive public perception was important to a sense of victory, in fact increasingly a definition of it, so the immediacy that, first radio, and then television brought created important problems. The public, however, was still at a distance, as institutions were involved in the management of news and could be readily influenced by government and even more by their own sense of propriety.

The internet has changed this. Now soldiers in the field are able to communicate with family, friends and others at home and this creates serious issues for news management. These were made abundantly clear in 2003 when the problems that American occupation forces faced in Iraq were rapidly communicated, gravely undercutting the sense of victory that the government had sought to inculcate. This also suggested that in the future the views of the military will play a greater role in the perception of victory and, indeed, that the very process of conflict will be much more closely involved in this perception. Thus, rather than victory as a response to the result of war, will come victory as a response to the process of war; with all the problems that this entails for cultures or at least constituencies that have little idea of what to expect. In short, audiences as well as soldiers will have to be "blooded" to ensure success.

Earlier, the traumatic experience of World War I (1914-1918) had played a major role in the process by which public dissent over conflict developed, for what at the time was treated by Britain and France as a righteous struggle against German aggression became a conflict with a far more ambivalent position in public memory. As a consequence the victory, much applauded in and after 1918, appeared half a century later to be too hard-won, if not an ironic counterpoint to the horrors of trench warfare: thus, the very fact of war and the process of conflict itself appeared to be a defeat. The merits of the case were somewhat different—any attempt to resist German aggression against Belgium and France would have been very difficult—but the point at issue is that what became the dominant cultural trope of war in Western Europe was sufficiently anti-war to affect the understanding of victory.

World War II (1939-1945) was viewed less critically, being seen by the victors as a virtuous struggle and thus a necessary victory. Furthermore, the contrasting role of the USA in the two world wars—its far less central and far less costly part in World War I—helped ensure that the commemoration of war there was less anti-war than the case in Western Europe. Instead the Vietnam War was to be the cathartic experience for Americans and although this had a profound impact on a particular generation and on much of the American intelligentsia it did not suffuse American public culture as a whole with anti-war attitudes. The consequent results can be seen in the contrasting responses among the participants to victory in the Gulf Wars of 1991 and 2003; and this has led to discussion as to whether Americans and Europeans now have a contrasting civic militarism, with the shared reluctance to suffer casualties far more conditional in the case of the more bellicose Americans.

This serves to underline the degree to which the complex interaction of public culture and strategic culture produces, at any one moment, very specific understandings of war and victory which in turn shape responses to the prospect of conflict. This affects debates over decisions for war, not least as a presumption of success is the major cause of decisions. Thus, cultural assumptions emerge as crucial both before and after conflict. Indeed, the combat sits between these as part

of an ongoing process of warfare or at least as an accentuation of it.
In the absence of a cultural presumption of victory, this accentuation
is unlikely; but in turn a reading of other conflicts is required in order
to produce, or at least sustain, this presumption. The recent and remote
history of peoples and states is, then, scoured to provide evidence
of victory, while other wars are discussed in order to suggest that the
pattern of military history is clear. This entails a conceptualisation of
conflict that deliberately minimises risk and thus denies the nature
of war and of its consequences: in practice, even if victory is likely its
results are far less so.

Thus, for states considering war, an understanding or intellectual
grasping of victory serves an important utilitarian end, however much that
this is also presented in terms of the social or collective psychological
ends of commemoration. Such utilitarianism clearly varies by age and
society, but it serves as a reminder that victory has to be fought for in a
double sense: both on the battlefield and subsequently.

However, this utilitarianism is a matter not only of the politics
that encourage the resort to conflict but also of the wider value of an
intelligent scepticism that underlines the precariousness of victory and the
difficulties of translating it into lasting success. Indeed, this double sense
of utilitarianism captures much of the tension in the writing about war
and the practice of military history. It is not that scholarship is inherently
anti-war, but rather that the process of subjecting conflict to scrutiny
can make it harder to elicit the automatic consent that bellicose cultures
assume and require.

Modern Western militaries would accept this and suggest that their
requirement for trained soldiers, and even more for officers who have
volunteered for service, ensure that the situation has "moved on" and that
scholarly examination serves their purposes. While correct at one level,
this relates scholarship as an aspect of conditional social support to the
conditionality of military service in the modern volunteer age. The long-
term consequences of the latter are controversial, especially in terms of
support for expeditionary warfare.

The presentation of the wars in Afghanistan in 2001 and Iraq in 2003
as a response to the terrorist attacks in New York and Washington in 2001,
a form of retribution and thus exemplary commemoration, helped overcome
this problem, at least in the short term, but the wider issue of a rethinking
within the West of the ethics and practice of war is of great importance,
particularly in so far as Western states are militarily the most capable of
long-range power projection. The spread of missile and atomic technology,
though, may lessen this situation.

A theme of diversity also accords well with other aspects of the variety of war. For example, a focus on what is termed tasking is an important recent approach in the understanding of conflict and militaries. This focus draws attention to goals and to how they helped set the resulting force structures and doctrines of particular armies, which in turn contributed to the sustaining of goals. Thus, there is a major difference between an army which prepares essentially for state-to-state conflict and one that focuses instead on the maintenance of control within a state.

The latter purpose tends to be underrated, if not ignored, within the meta-narratives of military history, except in so far as civil conflict took the form, at least in large part, of large-scale conventional warfare between the conventional forces of rival states, as in the American, English and Spanish Civil Wars. While each were very important, these conflicts were in practice atypical as far as civil conflict is concerned. Instead, counter-insurgency warfare is more commonly on the pattern seen in Latin America over the last 150 years, with regular forces used against irregular opponents.

The dominant narrative and analysis of warfare devotes scant attention to such conflicts, but that reflects their intellectual limitation. There is no inherent reason why, say, the Wars of German Unification (1864-1871), which led in 1918 and 1945 to the military dead-end that was the German General Staff, with its lack of a strategic grasp to match its operational effectiveness, should be seen as so much more important than the Latin American warfare of the late nineteenth century. Much of this emphasis stems from a belief that a certain type of conflict defines modern warfare and that its development needs to be the focus of attention, therefore. This teleological perspective appeared credible in the aftermath of World War II and while a conflict between the USA and the Soviet Union seemed imminent, but appears less credible today. Instead, rebellions and counter-insurgency warfare appear more important.

This is linked to a geographical shift of attention from Europe to Africa and to a lesser extent to Latin America: the areas of greatest population growth will continue to be the most volatile, not least because resource pressures will be most acute while there will be a high percentage of the population under 25, the male cohort that it is easiest to persuade to risk death. The last is an essential precondition for conflict: it is relatively easy to get people to kill others, but far less so to lead them while sober, and over a long period, to risk death. Furthermore, in many such societies there was a political "impoverishment," in that the means to press for significant change peacefully within the political system were often absent. Again this affects the perception of conflict and thus of victory. The politics of

grievances over resources make it easy to elicit popular support, providing
a lightning-rod for regional, ethnic, religious and class tensions, and can
make it very difficult to secure compromise. The resulting clashes are then
remembered—in terms of victory or grievance—in collective memories
of these groups, as can be seen in the clashes between Hutu and Tutsi in
Burundi and Rwanda. Differences in the causes and protocols of wars and
in the conditions of engagement will affect outcomes and aftermaths.

The extent to which a focus on where wars are more common entails a
re-examination of norms of conflict, including the understanding of victory
and its commemoration, has not yet been sufficiently appreciated, and this
re-examination should extend to military history. As far as the wide sphere
of modern and recent conflict from Israel to India is concerned, Western
commentators appear happier discussing this in terms of regular rather
than irregular warfare; and this creates problems in assessment, as well
as reflecting the more genuine problems of the militaries involved as their
forces and doctrines respond to insurrections. This is readily apparent in
the treatment of conflict in Palestine/Israel, Iraq and Kashmir; let alone in
the disorder that is Afghanistan where, it is crucial to remember, the most
important combatants are not the Americans.

In recent decades insurrectionary conflicts have often had a guerrilla
dimension and sometimes a terrorist one as well, in so far as the two
can be distinguished. The understanding of victory and defeat in such
contexts and, more generally, in civil conflict is far from easy; indeed,
part of the strategy for both guerrilla forces and terrorist movements is
to remain sufficiently active to prevent closure on any terms acceptable
to the government. From the opposite perspective, despite the terrible
hardships for individuals and communities, it is possible for governments
to sustain high levels of disruption without accepting any sense of defeat.
This again is a reminder of the culturally specific character of warfare.
The level of killing seen in Kashmir, let alone Afghanistan, would, if
repeated in Denmark, lead to a sense of total breakdown, whereas in India
attitudes are different. This can be taken further by considering general
societal levels of individual and communal violence. Where these are
high, for instance in today's Brazil or South Africa, the degree to which
political violence represents a defeat for the state tends to be different to
where they are low, although banditry can become rebellion in particular
circumstances, while attacks on police stations in Brazil represent a major
challenge to the state. This argument has to be handled with care, as in
the USA a highly armed population with a relatively high rate of person-to-
person violence, especially in some communities, is nevertheless intolerant
of political violence and apt to see it as a challenge to the community.

In the case of civil conflict we therefore need to consider the view that war, in the shape of large-scale organised violence, is itself a defeat, akin to the breakdown of international order seen with the outbreak of hostilities between states. This provides a very different approach to victory and defeat than the conventional one, and again it is an approach that is more valid in some cultures than others. If victory is seen as the maintenance of peace and order, rather than the forcing of peace and order on others, and defeat is presented as a failure to sustain this situation, then we also approach a position in which war, understood as conflict, can be set alongside the other current usage of war as a serious struggle by the state against pernicious forces, as in the "war on crime," "war on drugs," "war on pollution," "war on poverty" and so on.

This linguistic usage reflects the extent to which our Western culture, while less bellicist than in the past (not least as seen with the end of compulsory military service), has nevertheless taken the language of warfare and applied it widely. Indeed, this can be taken further by noting the extent to which the language of conflict is used to describe not simply social relationships between groups, whether in terms of class, gender or ethnicity, but also the relationship of ideas: knowledge is widely seen as a power system, both about struggle and itself the product of struggle. Thus, the language used encompasses ideas of hegemony, spheres of contention and contested boundaries. In short, alongside the culture of war we have culture (and society and politics) as war and this contributes to a psychological state in which conflict is socialised as part of the human process.

This is a long way from the consideration of particular victories and defeats, but it serves to underline the link between the process in which the commemoration and memorialisation of individual wars shapes collective memories and that in which the use of the vocabulary and imagery of conflict helps make war a key social experience even for those who have not seen fighting. The latter is not new, nor simply a matter of the visualisation of war on film and television. Instead, the use of bellicist language to discuss religious faith, both on the individual level (the battle with Satan and sin) and collectively (religious identity as opposed to other confessional groups), ensures that this is a continuing, albeit globally very varied, process. The Iraq conflict of 2003 has suggested that the conflation of bellicism and a sense of religious struggle is important to influential American views and experiences, but the same is true of other cultures as well. Thus, war in the shape of images of violence answers to something deep in the human psyche, at least in so far as framing identities are concerned. It helps define groups and provides them with an apparent coherence and purpose driven by need.

This creates problems in advocating the alternative: the nuanced meaning and interpenetrating identities and interests that are more conducive to war avoidance. The culture of war avoidance is a subject that has received insufficient attention, and this is a challenge for modern scholars. It is also an aspect of the education of modern publics about the nature of war and its relationship with social pressures and concepts.

Bibliography
BLACK, Jeremy M., *War: Past, Present and Future,* Sutton, Stroud 2000.
BLACK, Jeremy M., *War: An Illustrated History,* Stroud 2003.

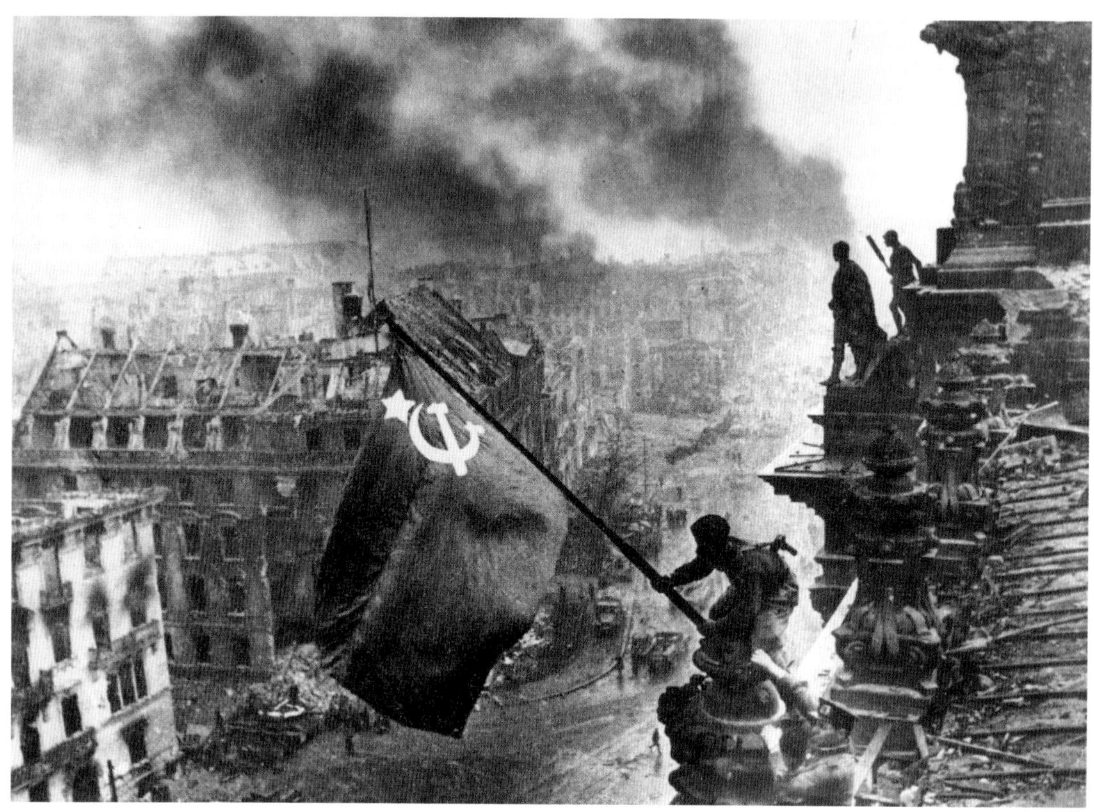

This photograph has been seen worldwide, yet, just like Rosenthal's
photograph of the flag being raised by the marines on Iwo Jima two months
earlier, it depicts a staged event. Khaldei arrived at the Reichstag after
it had been taken. He was determined to capture the moment of the conquest
and, as there were no real flags available, he used a tablecloth he had brought
with him as a flag, and pictured two soldiers raising it over the building.

EVGUENI KHALDEI, Soviet fighters raise the victory flag
over the Reichstag, Berlin, 2 May 1945
AKG Images, Berlin

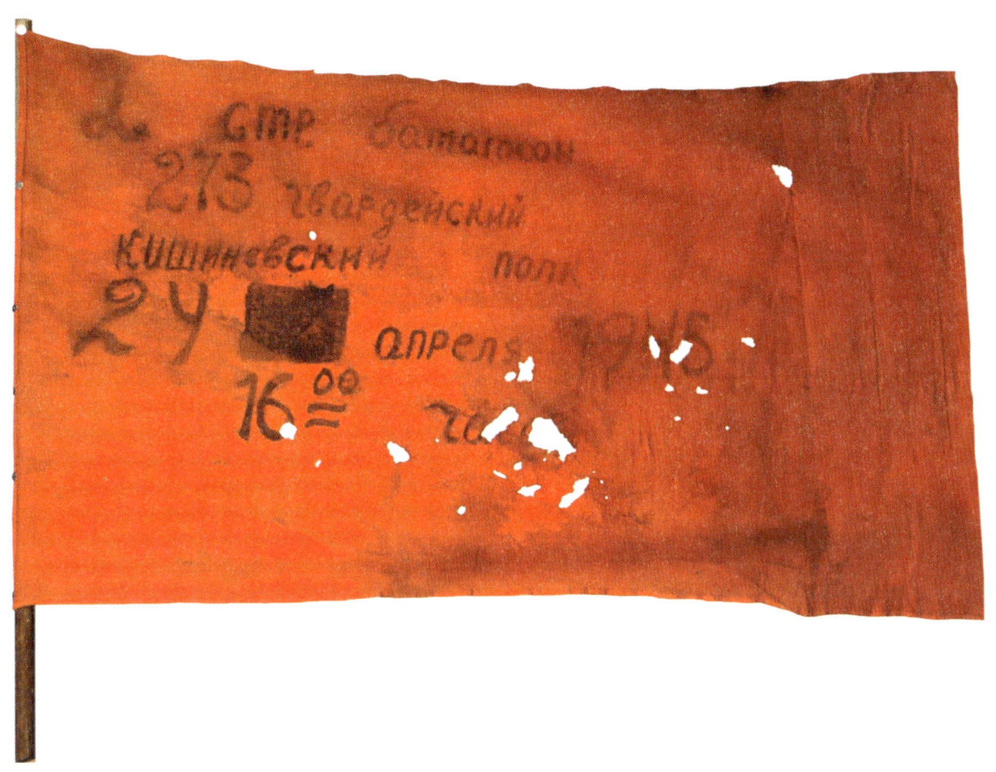

When the Soviet troops took Berlin, their final
objective was the Reichstag. A number of red flags,
raised by soldiers from the different units taking
part in the battle, flew over the building, but the
one pictured in the famous photograph by Evgueni
Khaldei is not among them.

Flag which flew over one of the houses in Berlin, 1945
Cotton fabric and ink, 132 x 76 cm
Central Armed Forces Museum, Moscow

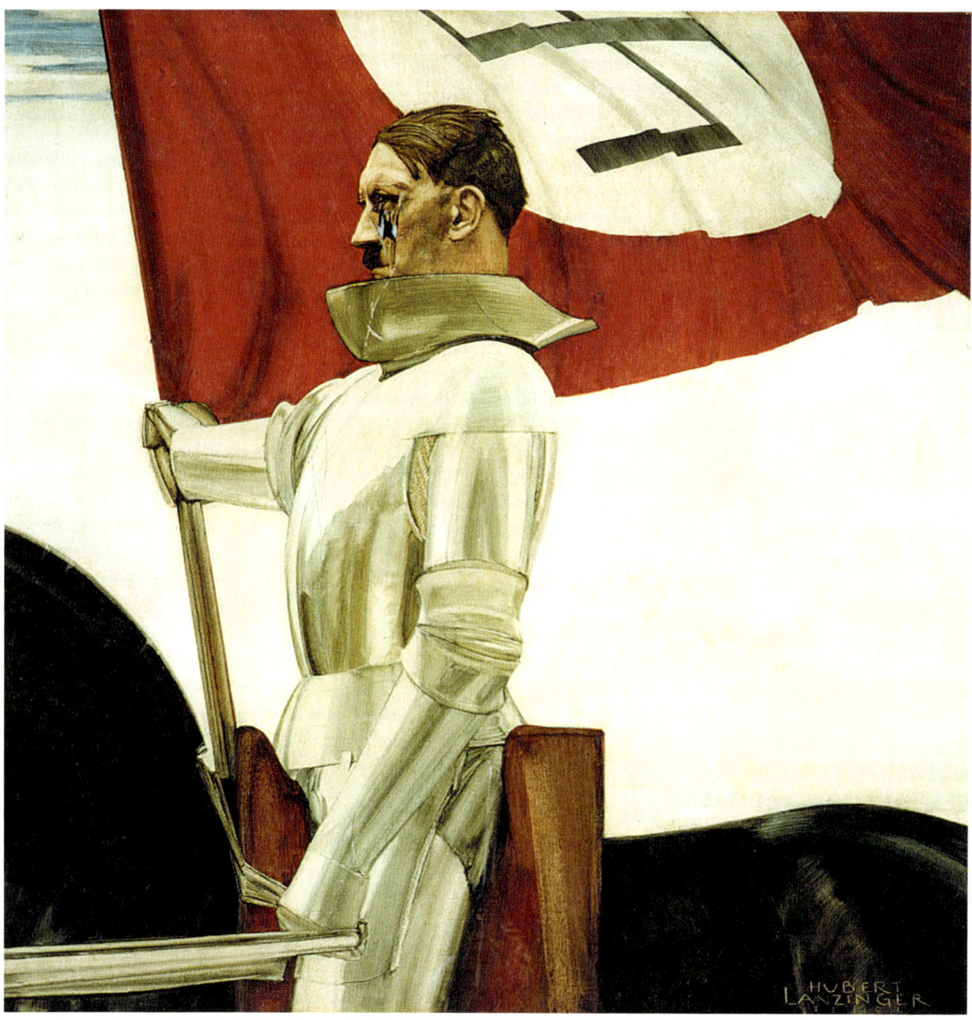

This painting by Hubert Lanzinger is part of the German National Socialist Art Collection seized at the end of the Second World War and is still part of the US Army's art holdings in Washington. The cut on Hitler's face is a trace of history, the result of a bayonet thrust made by a US soldier when he came across the portrait in an official building.

HUBERT LANZINGER, The flag bearer-Hitler in armor, 1934
Oil on plywood, 152.4 x 152.4 cm
National Museum of the US Army, Army Art Collection, Washington

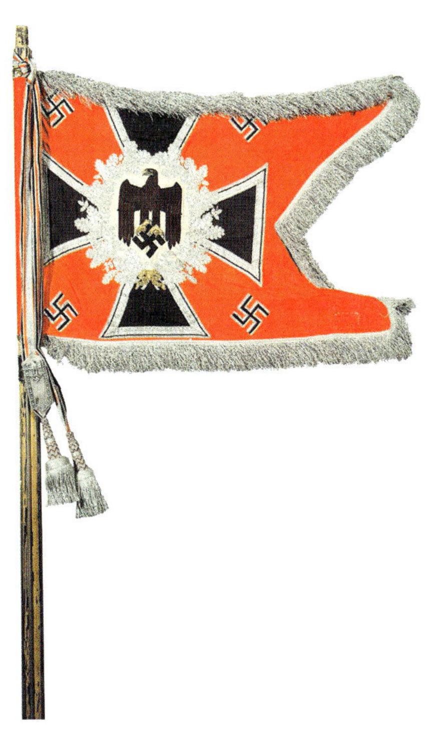

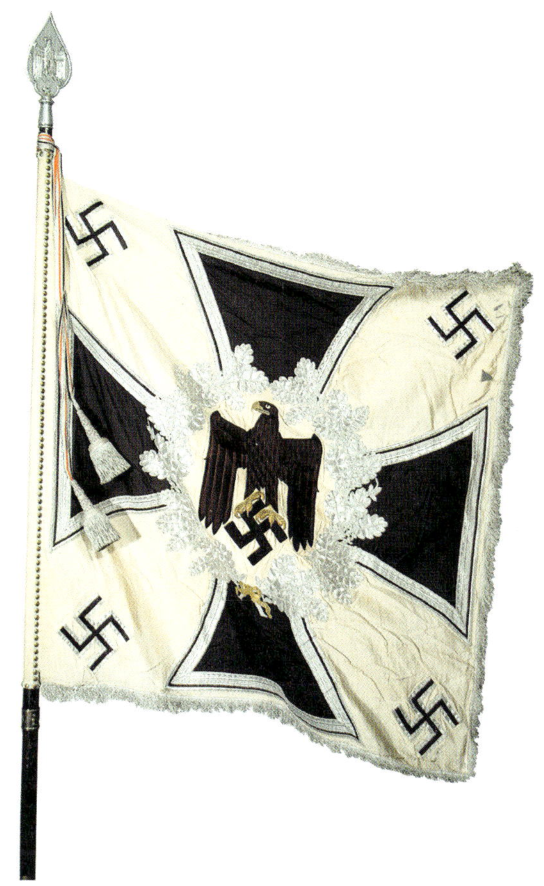

After the German defeat at Stalingrad, the Soviet army collected
large quantities of enemy flags up until the end of the Second
World War. Many of them were taken to Moscow and presented in
Red Square in front of the Kremlin, in a ceremony which marked
the culminating point of victory.

German standard from the second division of the 37th
artillery regiment, 1941-1945
Silk, 76 x 51 cm, 217 cm (flagpole)
Central Armed Forces Museum, Moscow

German standard from the first battalion of the 28th
infantry regiment, 1941-1945
Silk, 125 x 125 cm, 222 cm (flagpole)
Central Armed Forces Museum, Moscow

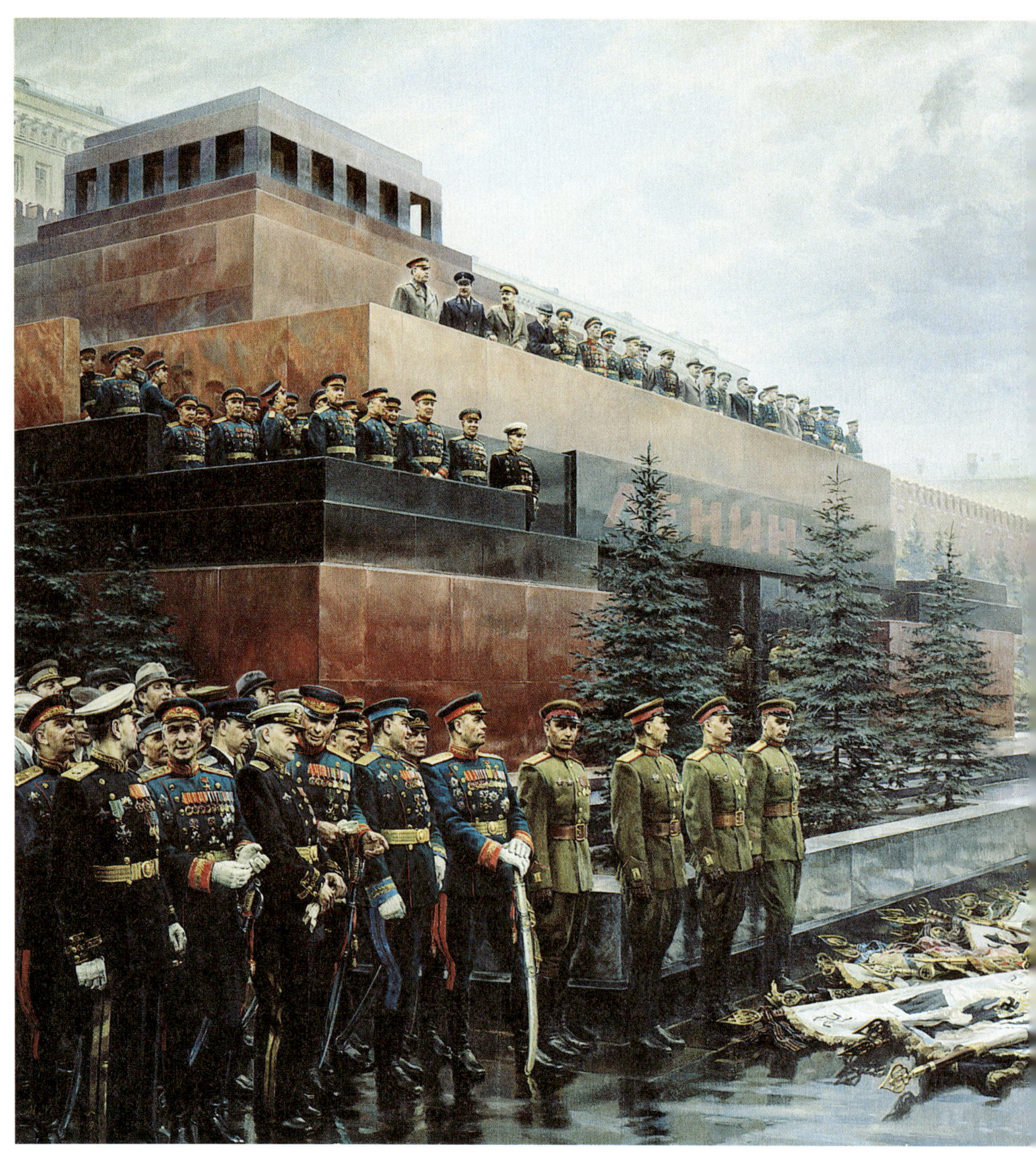

MIKHAIL KHMELKO, The triumph of the conquering people, 1949
Oil on canvas, 291 x 560 cm
Tretyakov Gallery, Moscow

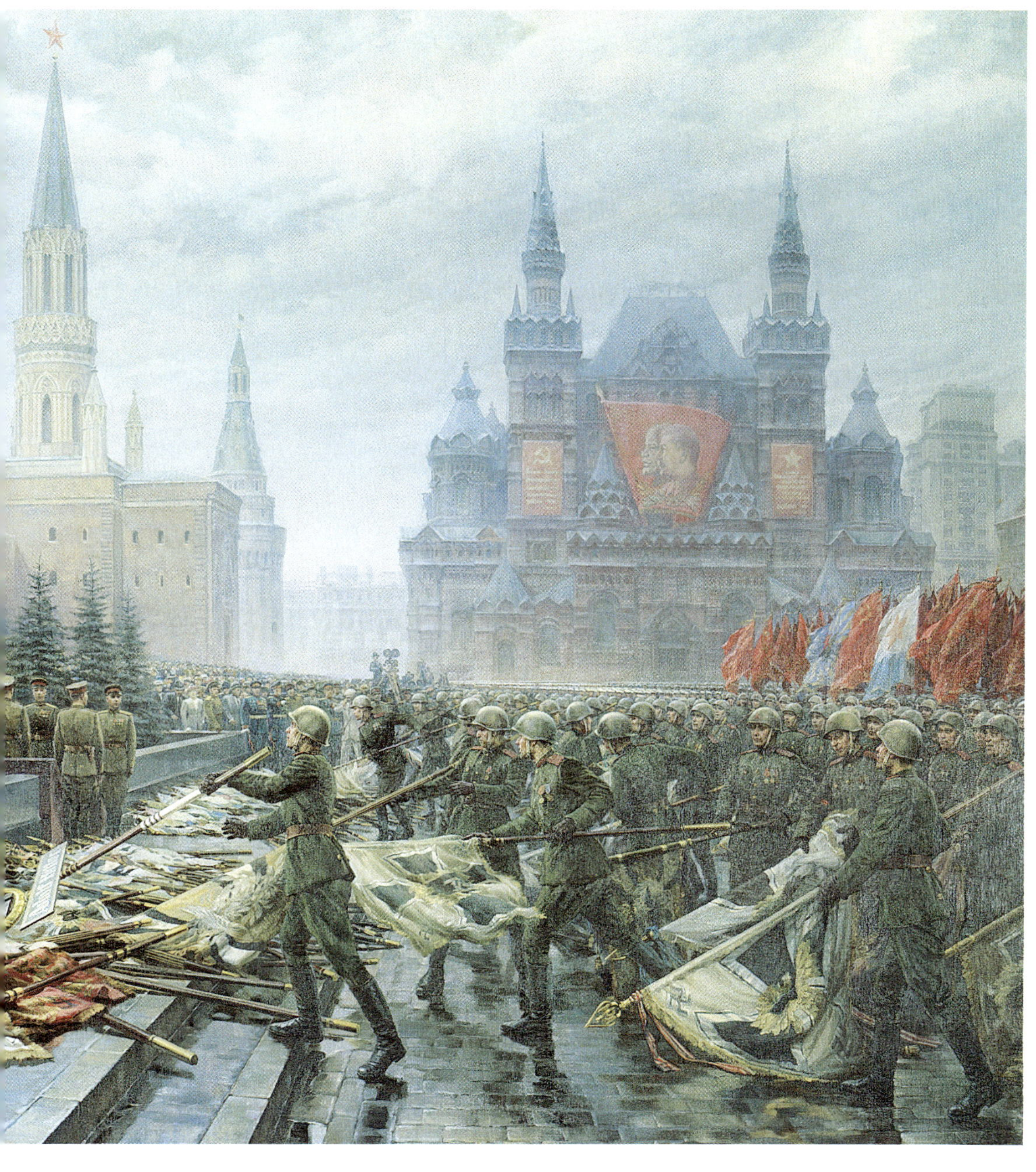

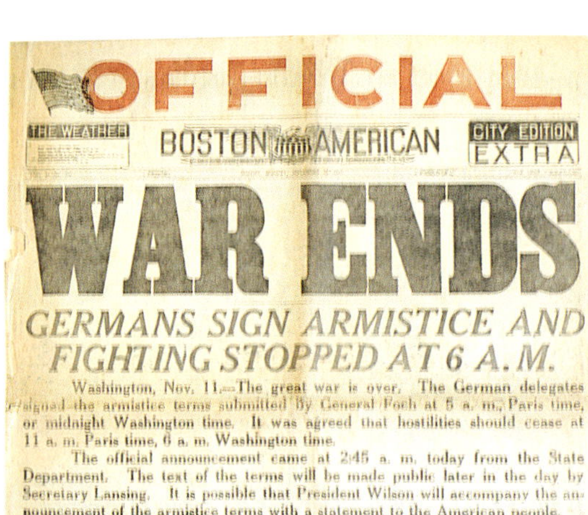

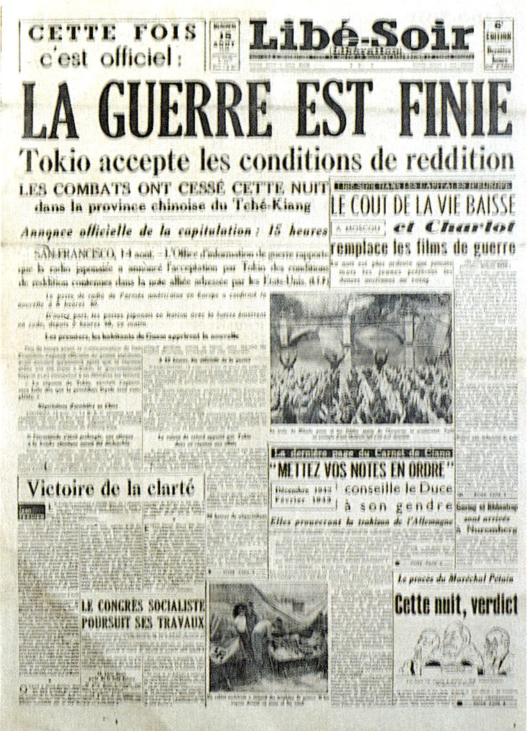

"War ends", *Boston American,* 11 November 1918
Printed paper, 55 x 46.5 cm
Josep Bosch Collection, Geneva

"The war is over. Tokyo accepts the conditions of surrender, fighting ended tonight", *Libé-Soir*, 15 August 1945
Printed paper d, 60 x 42.5 cm
Josep Bosch Collection, Geneva

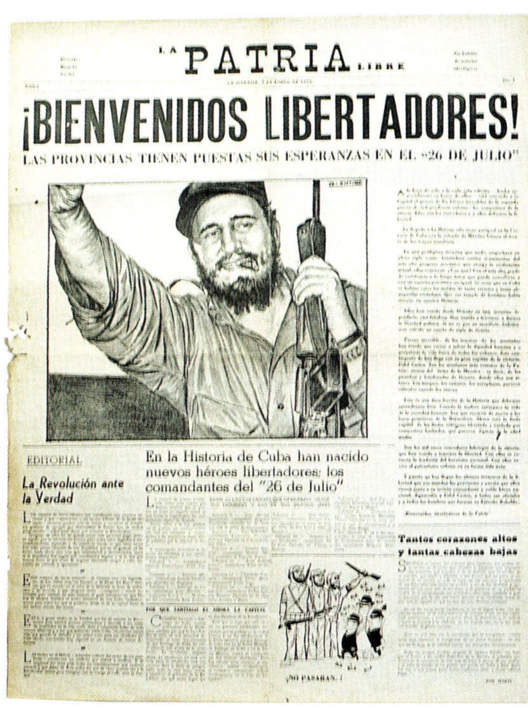

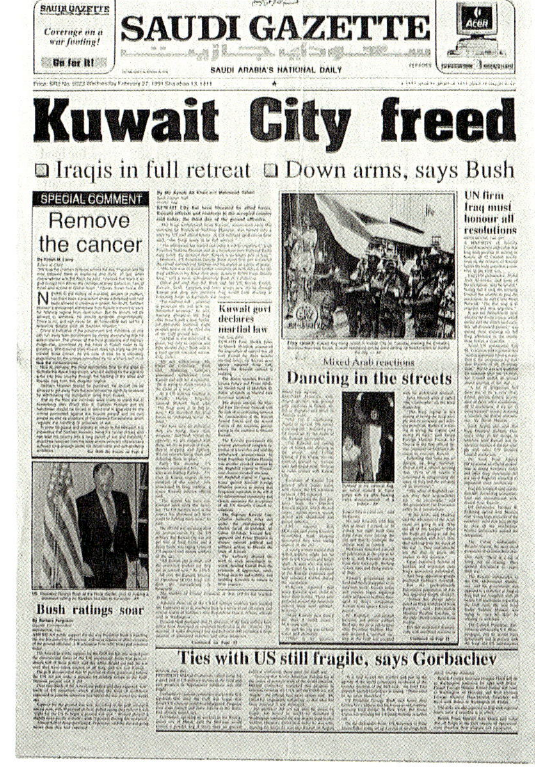

"Welcome liberators", *La patria libre,* 7 January 1959
Printed paper, 60 x 46.5 cm
Josep Bosch Collection, Geneva

"Kuwait City Freed", *The Saudi Gazette*, 2 February 1991
Printed paper, 58 x 38.5 cm
Josep Bosch Collection , Geneva

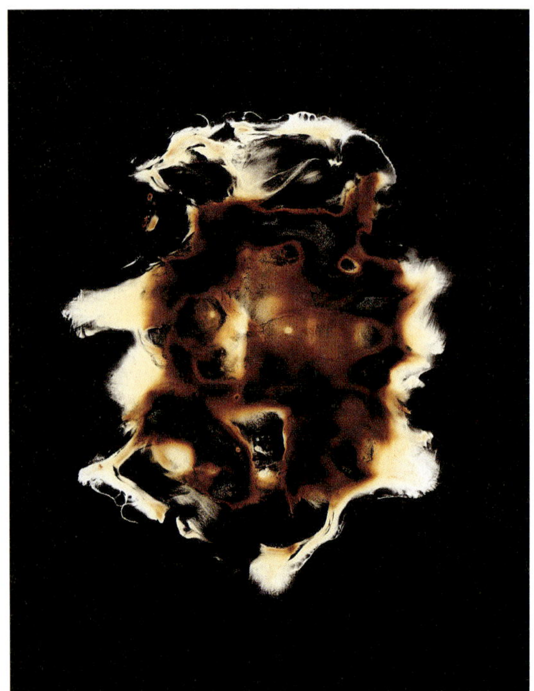 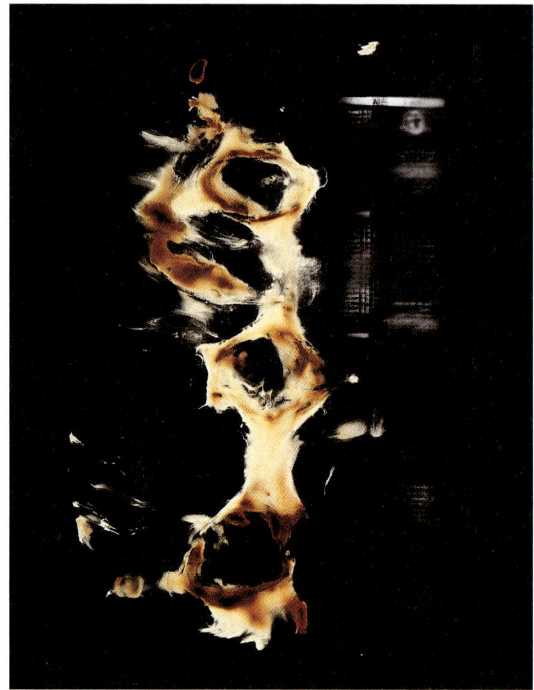

During the Kosovo War, the artist Gusi i Las burnt the
front pages of the newspaper *Avui* directly onto
photographic paper. The results are these frozen moments
of warfare which illustrate a virtual war which was
mainly fought in the media.

ALBERT GUSI I LAS, "Solana orders the bombing of
Yugoslavia to commence", Kosovo, 24 March 1999
Photographic image obtained by burning the newspaper
Avui onto photographic paper, 50 x 40 cm
Collection of the artist

ALBERT GUSI I LAS, "NATO threatens Milosevic with the
destruction of the entire Serbian army", Kosovo, 26 March 1999
Photographic image obtained by burning the newspaper
Avui onto photographic paper, 50 x 40 cm
Collection of the artist

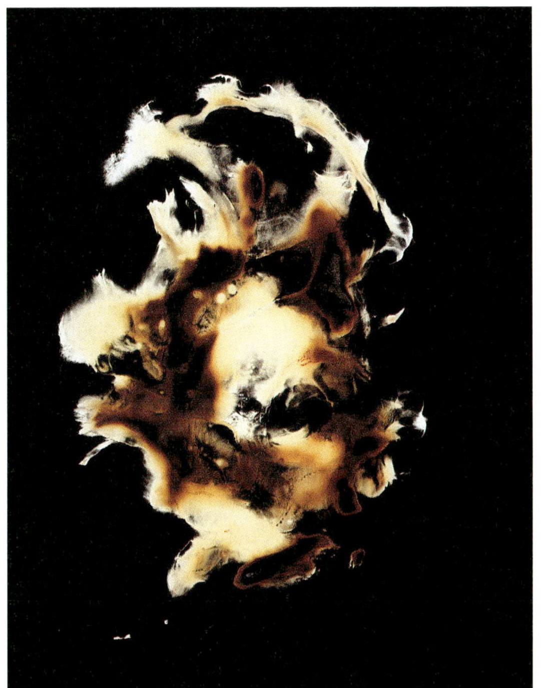 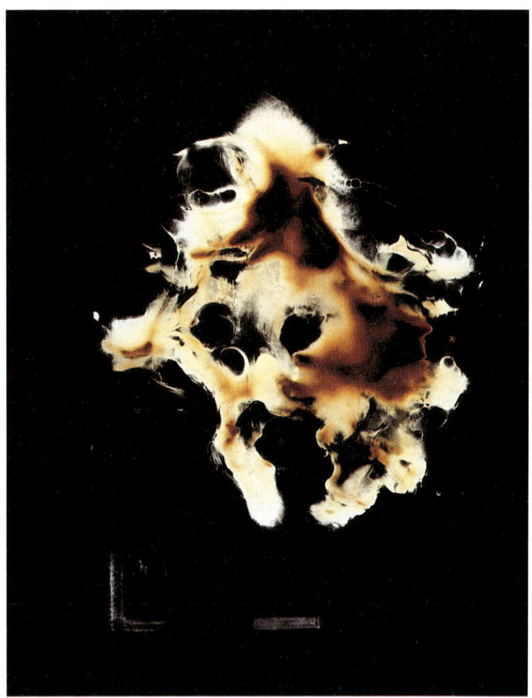

ALBERT GUSI I LAS, "Milosevic's indiscriminate repression
of civilians in Kosovo increases", Kosovo, 27 March 1999
Photographic image obtained by burning the newspaper
Avui onto photographic paper, 50 x 40 cm
Collection of the artist

ALBERT GUSI I LAS, "Milosevic murders two Kosovan
peace negotiators at the height of the ethnic cleansing
programme ", Kosovo, 30 March 1999
Photographic image obtained by burning the newspaper
Avui onto photographic paper, 50 x 40 cm
Collection of the artist

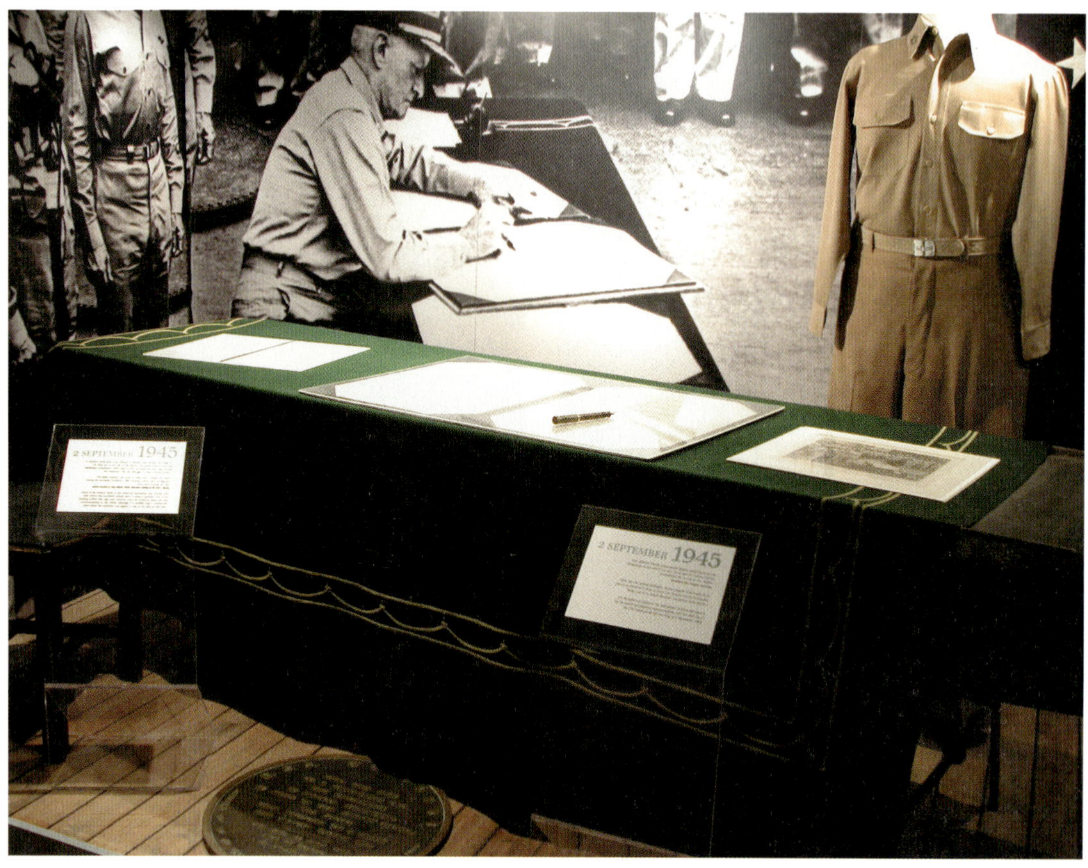

The Japanese surrender in the Second World War was signed in Tokyo Bay on 2nd September 1945, aboard the battleship *Missouri*, on a simple table taken from the officers' mess. The only chair used was taken from the British battleship the *Duke of York*. General MacArthur, accompanied by Admirals Nimintz and Halsey, presided over the ceremony.

Mess table from the USS Missouri (BB-63)
76 x 244 x 68.7 cm
US Naval Academy Museum, Annapolis Maryland

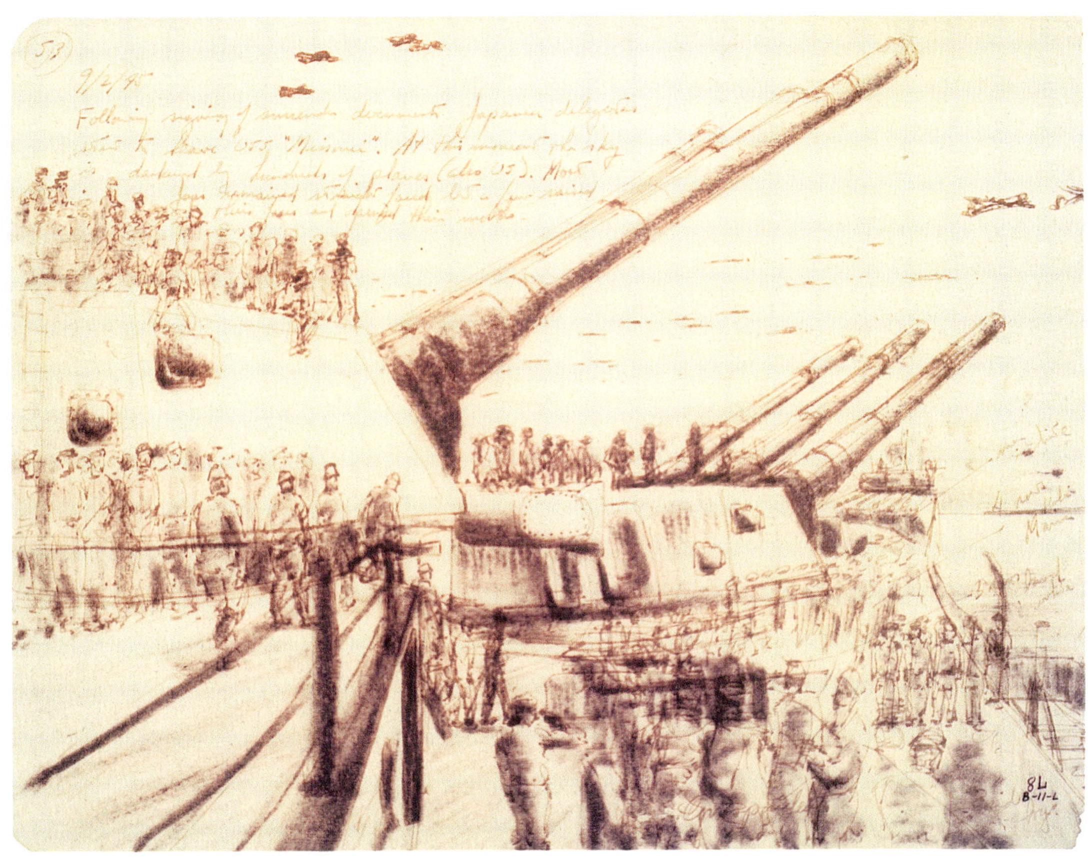

This drawing records the moments just
after the Japanese surrender was signed,
the first instants of declared peace.

STANDISH BACKUS, Following the signing of surrender documents, 1945
Pen and ink, 22.2 x 29.2 cm
Navy Art Collection, Naval Historical Center, Washington

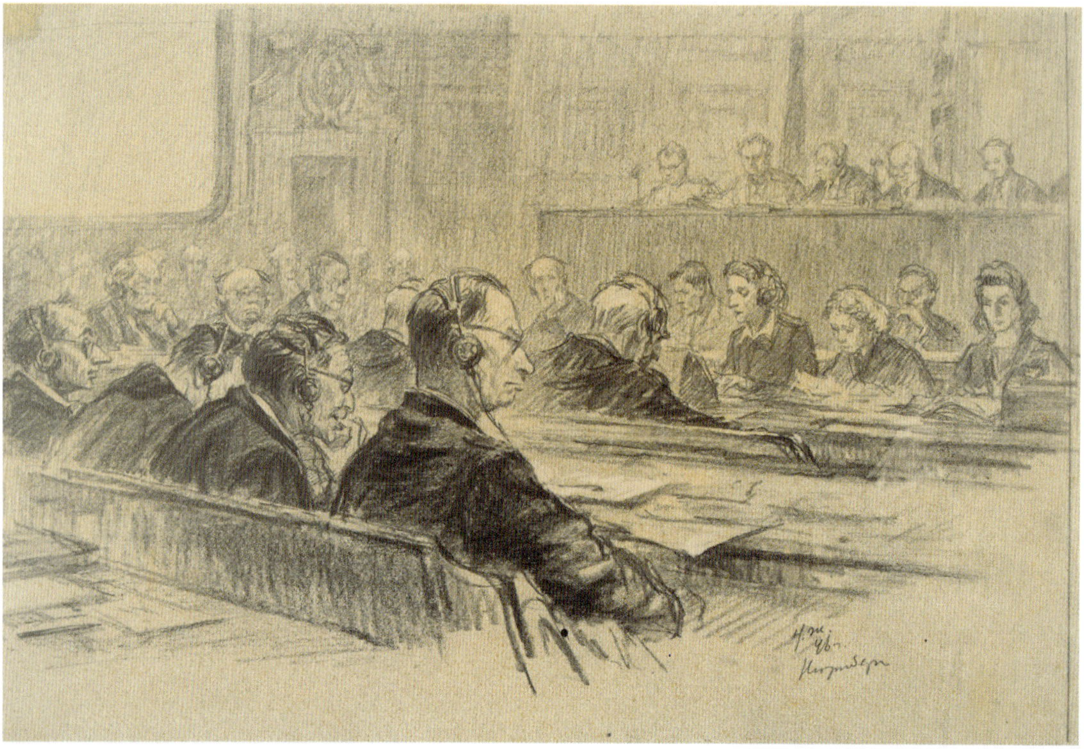

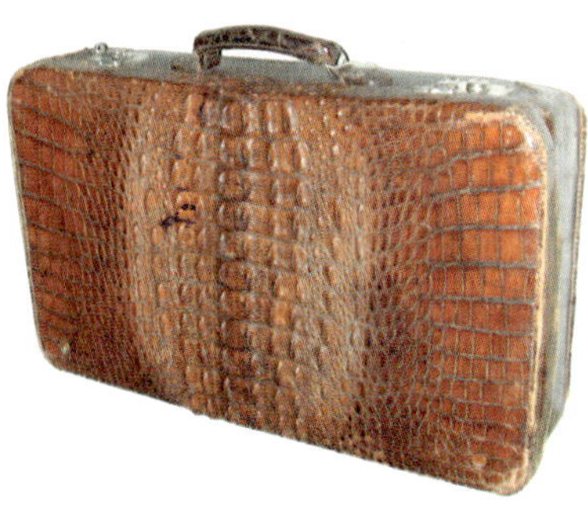

This is the medical case where Magda Goebbels kept the poison
used to kill her children, with the exception of the eldest child.
She then committed suicide in Hitler's bunker with her husband,
the Propaganda Minister Joseph Goebbels, while the Soviet troops
took control of the capital of the Reich in April 1945.

Magda Goebbels' medical case, 1945
Crocodile skin and steel, 70 x 40 x 20 cm
Military Historical Museum, Saint Petersburg

ZHÚKOV N.N, The defence is listening, from
the series "Drawings of the Nuremberg trials", 1946
Paper and pencil, 33 x 41 cm
Central Armed Forces Museum, Moscow

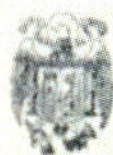

En el día de hoy, cautivo y desarmado el Ejército Rojo, han alcanzado las tropas nacionales sus últimos objetivos militares. La guerra ha terminado.

El Generalísimo
Franco

Burgos 1º Abril 1939.

Document marking the end of the Civil War, 1st April 1939
Paper, writing ink and printer's ink, 27.3 x 21.3 cm
Museo del Ejército, Madrid

Memory

Commemorating war

Jay Winter

Public commemoration is a matrix of activity, through which social groups express "a collective shared knowledge [...] of the past, on which a group's sense of unity and individuality is based."[1] In the twentieth century much of this commemorative work is inspired by war and the need to acknowledge the victims of war.

The group that organizes the commemoration inherits earlier meanings attached to the event being remembered, as well as adding new meanings. Their activity is crucial to the presentation and preservation of commemorative forms. When such groups disperse or disappear, commemoration loses its initial force and may fade away entirely.

Public commemoration of war is therefore a process with a life history. It has an initial, creative phase followed by a period of institutionalization and routinization. Such markings of the calendar can last for decades, or be abruptly halted. In most instances the date and place of commemoration fade away with the passing of the social groups which initiated the practice.

Commemoration operates on many levels of aggregation and touches many facets of associative life. While commemorative forms were familiar in the ancient world, the subject of remembrance in the modern period has attracted much discussion in the social scientific literature. I therefore concentrate on public commemoration in the epoch of the nation state, primarily in the nineteenth and twentieth centuries, and privilege the commemoration of war in this wider sphere of collective activity.

In the modern period most commemorative events surrounding war were marked distinctively and separately from the religious calendar. There has been, though, some overlap. Armistice Day, 11 November, in countries remembering the end of the 1914-1918 war, is close enough to the Catholic feast of All Saints on 1 November; in some countries with a large Catholic population, the two days occupy a semi-sacred space of public commemoration. The day marking the end of the Second World War in Europe, 8 May, is also the saint's day of Joan of Arc. Those engaging in commemorative acts on that day may be addressing the secular celebration or the Catholic one; some celebrate the two together.

Commemoration is an act arising out of a conviction, shared by a broad community, that the moment recalled is both significant and informed by a moral message; wars fulfill both requirements. Moments of national humiliation are rarely commemorated, though here too there are exceptions of a hortatory kind. "Never again" is the hallmark of public commemoration on the Israeli Day of Remembrance for victims of the Nazi persecution of the Jews. Where moral doubts persist about a war or public policy,

commemorative moments are hard to fix. That is why there is no one date
commemorating the end of the Algerian War in France, or the end of
the Vietnam War in the United States. There was no moral consensus
about the nature of the conflict; hence there was no moral consensus about
what was being remembered in public, and when was the appropriate
time to remember it.

Commemoration and political power

Much of the scholarly debate about commemoration concerns the extent
to which it is an instrument of the dominant political elements in a society.
One school of opinion emphasizes the usefulness to political elites of
public events establishing the legitimacy of their rule. Some such events
are observed whoever is in power—witness Bastille Day in France or
Independence Day in the United States. But other events are closely tied
to the establishment of a new regime and the overthrow of an older one:
7 November was the date in the calendar marking the Bolshevik revolution
and establishing the Communist regime in power in Russia. That date
symbolized the new order and its challenge to its world-wide enemies.
May Day similarly was a moment when labour movements, and Labour
parties in power, publicly demonstrated their place in history.

This top-down approach proclaims the significance of commemoration
as a grammar of national, imperial or political identity. This is particularly
evident in the commemoration of war. Anzac Day, 25 April, is celebrated
as the moment when the Australian nation was born. It commemorates the
landing of Australian and New Zealand troops as part of the British-led
expeditionary force sent to Turkey in 1915. The fact that the landing was a
failure does not diminish the iconic character of the date to Australians.
It is the day, they hold, when their nation came of age.

By no means are all commemorative activities associated with
warfare. The birthdates of monarchs or deceased presidents are marked
in similar ways. Queen Victoria's birthday, 24 May, was Empire Day in
Britain; now (1999) it is celebrated as Commonwealth Day. The creation of
such commemorative dates was part of a wider movement of what some
scholars have termed "the invention of tradition." That is, at the end of the
nineteenth century new nation states and pre-eminent imperial powers
deepened the repertoire of their ceremonial activity. Such flourishes of the
majesty of power were then immediately sanctified by a spurious pedigree.
To display ceremonies with a supposed link to ancient habits or forms
located in a foggy and distant past created an effective cover for political
innovation, instability or insecurity.

This functionalist interpretation of commemoration has been
challenged. A second school of scholarship emphasizes the ways that
public commemoration has the potential for dominated groups to contest

their subordinate status. However much political leaders or their agents try to choreograph commemorative activity, there is much space for subversion or creative interpretation of the official commemorative script. Armistice Day, 11 November, was, for different groups, a moment for both the celebration and the denigration of military values. Pacifists announced their message of "Never again" through their presence at commemorative ceremonies; military men used these moments to glorify the profession of arms, and to demonstrate the duty of citizens, if necessary, to give their lives for their country in a future war. The contradictions in these forms of expression on the same day were never resolved.

This alternative interpretation of the political meaning of commemorative activity emphasizes the multi-vocal character of remembrance. From this point of view, there is always a chorus of voices in commemorations; some are louder than others, but they never sound alone. De-centering the history of commemoration ensures that we recognize the regional, local, and idiosyncratic character of such activities.

Very occasionally, these dissonant voices come together. Between 1919 and 1938 in Britain, there was a two-minute silence observed throughout the country. Telephonists pulled the plugs on all conversations. Traffic stopped. The normal flow of life was arrested. Then the Second World War intervened, and such disruption to war production was not in the national interest. Thereafter the two-minute silence was moved to the Sunday nearest 11 November. But in the two decades between the wars, it was a moment of national reflection. Mass-Observation, a pioneering social-survey organization, asked hundreds of ordinary people in Britain what they thought about during the silence. The answer was that they thought not of the nation or of victory or of armies, but of the men who weren't there. This silence was a meditation about absence. As such it moved away from political orchestration into the realm of family history. To be sure, families commemorated their own within a wider social and political framework. But the richest texture of remembrance was always within family life. This intersection of the public and the private, the macro-historical and the micro-historical, is what has given commemoration in the twentieth century its power and its rich repertoire of forms.

The business of remembering
Commemoration is and always has been a business. It costs money; it requires specialists' services; it needs funding and over time, re-funding. There are two kinds of expenditure we can trace in the history of commemoration. The first is capital expenditure; the second is recurrent expenditure.

The land for such sites must be purchased; and an appropriate symbolic form must be designed and then constructed to focus remembrance activities. The first step may require substantial sums of public money. Private land, especially in urban areas, comes at a premium. Then there are the costs of architects' fees, especially when a public competitive tender is offered inviting proposals from professionals. Finally, once the symbolic form is chosen it must be constructed out of selected materials and finished according to the architect's or artist's designs.

When these projects are national in character, the process of production is in the public eye. National art schools and bodies of "experts" have to have their say. Standards of "taste" and "decorum" are proclaimed. Professional interests and conflicts come into play. Much of this professional infighting is confined to national commemorative projects, but the same complex step-wise procedure occurs on the local level too, this time without the same level of attendant publicity. Local authorities usually take charge of these projects, and local notables can deflect plans towards their own particular visions, whatever public opinion may think about the subject.

Most of the time public funding covers only part of the costs of commemorative objects. Public subscriptions are critical, especially in Protestant countries where the concept of utilitarian memorials is dominant. In Catholic countries the notion of a "useful" memorial is a contradiction in terms; symbolic language and utilitarian language are deemed mutually exclusive. But the Protestant voluntary tradition has it otherwise. In Protestant countries commemorative projects took many forms, from the sacred to the mundane: in Britain there are memorial wards in hospitals, memorial scholarships in schools and universities, alongside memorial cricket pitches and memorial water troughs for horses. In the United States and in Australia there are memorial highways. The rule of thumb is that private citizens pick up most of the tab for these memorial forms. The state provides subsidies and occasional matching grants, but the money comes out of the pockets of ordinary people. The same is true in Britain with respect to a very widely shared form of public commemoration: the purchase of paper poppies, the symbol of the Lost Generation of the First World War. These poppies are worn on the lapel, and the proceeds of the sale go to aid disabled veterans and their families.

Recurrent expenditure on commemorative sites is almost always paid for by taxpayers. War cemeteries require masons and gardeners. The Imperial (now Commonwealth) War Graves Commission looks after hundreds of such cemeteries all over the world. The cost of their maintenance is a public charge. Private charities, in particular Christian groups, maintain German war cemeteries. Once constructed, memorial statues, cemeteries or highways also become public property, and require public support to prevent them from decomposing. They are preserved as sites of commemorative activity.

Much of this activity is directed towards inviting the public to remember in public. This means guiding people towards particular sites of remembrance. Some of them are nearby their homes. In Britain and France there are war memorials in every city, in every town, and in virtually every village; it is there that Armistice Day ceremonies are held annually. Churches throughout Europe of all denominations have memorial plaques to those who died in war. Special prayers were added to the Jewish prayer book to commemorate the victims of the Nazis in the Second World War, and later those who died on active service in the Israeli army.

Remembrance in local houses of worship or at war memorials meant that the public need travel but a short distance from their homes to sites of remembrance. But given the scale of losses in the two World Wars, and the widely dispersed cemeteries around the world in which lie the remains of millions of such men and women, the business of remembrance also entails international travel. Such voyages start as pilgrimage; many are mixed with tourism. But in either case, there are train and boat journeys to take; hotel rooms to reserve; guides to hire; flowers to lay at graves; trinkets and mementos to purchase. In some places museums have arisen to tell more of the story the pilgrims have come to hear and to share. There too money is exchanged along with the narratives and the symbols of remembrance.

This mixture of the sacred and the profane is hardly an innovation. It is merely a secular form of pilgrimage, some of which cover substantial distances. Today thousands of Australians make the journey to Gallipoli, to be there for the dawn service on 25 April, (as we have already noted) the day of the Anzac landing in 1915. Where does pilgrimage stop and tourism take over? It is impossible to say, but in all cases the business of remembrance remains just that—a business.

Aesthetic redemption

Public commemoration is not only a set of political gestures and material tasks. It is also an art form, the art of arranging and interpreting signifying practices. This field of action can be analysed on two different levels: the first is aesthetic; the second is semiotic. The two are intimately related.

Some national commemorative forms are distinctive. Others are shared by populations in many countries. The figure of Marianne as the national symbol of the French Republic could not be used in Germany or Britain. The German Iron Cross, on commemorative plaques, denotes the location and the tradition in which commemoration is expressed. Germany's heroes' forests or fortresses are also imbricated in Teutonic history.

At times the repertoire of one country's symbols overlap with that of others, even when they were adversaries. After the First World War, the first industrialized war fought among fully industrialized nations, many commemorative forms adopted medieval notation. Throughout Europe, the revolutionary character of warfare was marked by a notation of a backward-looking kind. Medieval images of heroic and saintly warriors recaptured a time when combat was between individuals, rather than the impersonal and unbalanced duel between artillery and human flesh. The war in the air took on the form and romance of chivalry. On the losing and the winning sides, medievalism flourished.

On war memorials, the human form survived. In some instances, classical images of male beauty were chosen to mark the "lost generation"; others adopted more stoical and emphatically un-triumphalist poses of men in uniform. In most cases, victory was either partially or totally eclipsed by a sense of overwhelming loss. Within this aesthetic landscape, traditional Christian motifs were commonplace. The form of the grieving mother—*Stabat Mater*—brought women into the local and national constellation of grief.

In Protestant countries the aesthetic debate took on a quasi-religious character. War memorials with crosses on them offended some Protestants, who believed that the Reformation of the sixteenth century precluded such "Catholic" notation. Obelisks were preferable. In France war memorials were by law restricted to public and not church grounds, though many local groups found a way around this proscription. In schools and universities the location of such memorials touched on such issues. Some were placed in sacred space— in chapels—semi-sacred space—around chapels—or in secular space. Public thoroughfares and train stations also housed such lists of men who had died in war.

Twentieth-century warfare democratized bereavement. Previously armies were composed of mercenaries, volunteers and professionals. After 1914, Everyman went to war. The social incidence of war losses was thereby transformed. In Britain, France and Germany virtually every household had lost someone—a father, a son, a brother, a cousin, a friend. Given the nature of static warfare on the Western front, many—perhaps half—of those killed had no known grave. Consequently commemorative forms highlighted names above all. The names of the dead were all that remained of them and, chiseled in stone or etched on plaques, these names were the foci of public commemoration both on the local and the national scale.

This essential practice of naming set the pattern for commemorative forms after the Second World War and beyond. After 1945 names were simply added to Great War memorials. This was partly in recognition of the links between the two twentieth-century conflicts; partly it was a matter of economy. After the Vietnam war naming still mattered, and First World War forms inspired memorials, most notably Maya Lin's Vietnam Veterans' Memorial in Washington. Her work clearly drew on Sir Edwin Lutyens's memorial to the missing on the River Somme at Thiepval, inaugurated in 1932.

By the latter decades of the twentieth century artistic opinion and aesthetic tastes had changed sufficiently to make abstraction the key language of commemorative expression. Statues and installations thereby escaped from specific national notation and moved away from the earlier emphasis upon the human figure. In many instances, but by no means all, forms which suggested absence or nothingness replaced classical, religious or romantic notions in commemorative art.

This aesthetic shift had important social and political implications. Great War commemorative forms had sought out some meaning, some significance in the enormous loss of life attending that conflict. There was an implicit warning in many of these monuments. "Never again" was their ultimate meaning. But "never" had lasted a bare 20 years. Thus, after the Second World War the search for meaning became infinitely more complex. And the fact that more civilians died than soldiers in the Second World War made matters even more difficult to configure in art.

Finally, the extreme character of two elements of the Second World War challenged the capacity of art—any art—to express a sense of loss when it is linked to genocidal murder or thermonuclear destruction. Both Auschwitz and Hiroshima defied conventional notations of "meaning," though some individuals continue to try to rescue redemptive elements from them both. The construction of a national Holocaust memorial at the Brandenburg Gate in Berlin, the construction of which began in 1999, is a case in point. The debate over this and similar projects does not abate, since such events seem to force all participants—public officials, the public, survivors, architects, artists—to the limits of representation and beyond.

Ritual

Public commemoration is an activity defined by the gestures and words of those who come together to remember the past. It is rarely the simple reflection of a fixed text, a script rigidly prepared by political leaders determined to fortify their position of power. Inevitably, commemoration overlaps with political conflicts, but it can never be reduced to a simple reflection of power relationships.

There are at least three stages in the history of rituals surrounding public commemoration. The first we have already dealt with: the construction of a commemorative form. But there are two other levels in the life history of monuments which need attention. The second is the grounding of ritual action in the calendar, and the routinization of such activities; the third is their transformation or their disappearance as active sites of memory.

One case in point may illustrate this trajectory. The date of 1 July 1916 is not a national holiday in Britain; but it marks the date of the opening of the British offensive on the river Somme, an offensive which symbolized the terrible character of industrial warfare. On that day the British army suffered the highest casualty totals in its history; on that day a volunteer army, and the society that had created it, were introduced to the full terrors of twentieth-century warfare. To this day groups of people come to the Somme battlefields to mark this day, without national legislation to enable them to do so. Theirs are locally defined rituals. In France 11 November is a national holiday, but not in Britain. Legislation codifies activities the origins and force of which lie on the local level.

Public commemoration flourishes within the orbit of civil society. This is not true in countries where dictatorships rule; Stalinist Russia smashed civil society to a point that it could not sustain commemorative activity independent of the party and the state. But elsewhere local associations matter.

And so do families. Commemorative ritual survives when it is inscribed within the rhythms of community and in particular family life. Public commemoration lasts when it draws about overlaps between national history and family history. Most of those who take the time to engage in the rituals of remembrance bring with them memories of family members touched by these vast events. This is what enables people born long after wars and revolutions to commemorate them as essential parts of their own lives. For example, children born in the aftermath of the First World War told the story of their family upbringing to grandchildren born 60 or 70 years later. This transmission of childhood memories over two or sometimes three generations gives family stories a power which is translated at times into activity—the activity of remembrance.

This framework of family transmission of narratives about the past is an essential part of public commemoration. It also helps us understand why some commemorative forms are changed or simply fade away. When the link between family life and public commemoration is broken, a powerful prop of remembrance is removed. Then, in a short time, remembrance atrophies and fades away. Public reinforcements may help keep alive the ritual and practice of commemoration. But the event becomes hollow when removed from the myriad small-scale social units that breathed life into it in the first place.

At that moment commemorative sites and practices can be revived and re-appropriated. The same sites used for one purpose can be used for another. But most of the time, commemorative forms live through their life cycle and, like the rest of us, inevitably fade away.

This natural process of dissolution closes the circle on public commemoration. And rightly so, since it arises out of the needs of a very large number of small groups of people to link their lives with salient events in the past. When that need vanishes, so does the glue that holds together the social practice of commemoration. Then memories fade away.

We have reached, therefore, a quixotic conclusion. Public commemoration of war is both irresistible and unsustainable. People seek meaning in these vast and murderous events and try to relate them to their own smaller networks of social life. These are bound to dissolve, to be replaced by other forms with other needs, and other histories. At that point, the trajectory of creation, institutionalization and decomposition comes to an end. The initial effort to remember the victims of war collectively is therefore one which is bound to fail. At that point, literature, painting, music, story-telling take over and place the tale in a wider, more diffuse and more unpredictable cultural framework. When commemoration enters normal language, it is everybody's business, and therefore the business of no one in particular. The faces of those who die in war fade away, and so do the commemorative practices of those who mourn their loss.

Note

1. ASSMANN, Jan, "Collective memory and social identity," *New German Critique*, no. 65 (1995), p. 130, translation by the author.

War burnout:
memories of the air war

Andreas Huyssen

War burnout has been the dominant mindset in Europe since 1945, and for good reason. After centuries of internecine conflict and after two world wars, often described as having begun as European civil wars, the desire for peace took hold and provided a major impetus for European unification. To a large extent memories of war have lost their former function supporting heroic narratives of the past in European nations and conditioning the young for future warfare. Already after World War I, even victory felt like defeat and fuelled a powerful "never again war" campaign in England, France and elsewhere. The memory of defeat on the other hand was exploited by the Nazis to create a campaign of resentment and victimization that was then mobilized to drive Germany into the next war. No doubt the war against Hitler was a just war. But even the hard-won victory of the Allies over Hitler's Reich no longer carries the kind of triumphalism of resistance that shaped its memories in the immediate postwar decades in France or Italy. Too many painful compromises and collaborations have come to light in the then-occupied nations for the heroic narrative to stand uncontaminated and unchallenged. This does not take away from the achievements of the Allies in bringing down the Third Reich. It may, however, mark the major difference between memories of World War II in Europe as opposed to the United States where—after years of self-questioning over the Vietnam War—the narrative of the "greatest generation" still captures hearts and minds, and since 9/11 theories of a just war have been articulated by intellectuals from a broad political spectrum. It may also explain the huge demonstrations against the looming Iraq War all across Europe on 15 February 2003, while majority support for Bush's preemptive war policy carried the day in the United States.

Like all memories, memories of war are always of the present, susceptible to present-day events and interests. The distinct memories of World War II helped shape attitudes toward Iraq on both sides of the Atlantic and in Europe led to a widespread pacifism. As the mere reversal of militarism, pacifism can itself be deeply problematic: in the interwar years it fed the politics of appeasement; in the recent conflicts on the Balkans it strengthened the public reluctance in the West to intervene in a timely fashion; and in the first Iraq war it became one with a powerful and simplistic anti-Americanism. To be sure, when and how to confront murderous and threatening dictators like Milosevic or Saddam Hussein militarily will always be a contentious issue with many contingencies, but pacifism cannot serve as an absolute guide in making such decisions. Yet to understand the culture of war and peace today and to get beyond the simplistic pacifism/bellicism paradigm we must pay attention to differing national codifications of war memories. In Germany after 1945 it was the memory of Auschwitz and the acknowledgment of war guilt that shaped pacifism, factors that give German war memories their specific slant to this day.

Thus the history of post-fascist anti-militarism and of the various peace movements from the anti-Nato and anti-nuke movements of the fifties through the protests against the current Iraq war demonstrates a good deal of continuity. This continuity was challenged only briefly during the Bosnia and Kosovo campaigns, and it has come back full force in Germany over the past year in the unique unanimity of government, intellectuals and populace East and West regarding George Bush's war against Saddam Hussein, a kind of German unification by other means. All of these peace movements since 1945—including the protests against the Vietnam War, the Nato missile decision of the early eighties and the first Iraq war—were always also part of European-wide popular anti-war activities. But each one had its unmistakable German inflection, depending on how German memory culture was coded at any given time. This is no different for the German peace movement of 2002-2003 which for the first time drew extensively and explicitly on the German trauma of the carpet bombings of World War II. Baghdad equals Dresden: thus claimed a number of implausible posters in the big 15 February demonstrations.

Something, however, has changed in German memoryscapes. Critics have attempted to pinpoint the change in certain texts such as Martin Walser's peace prize speech of 1998, in which he chastised the relentlessness of Holocaust memory in the media, W.G. Sebald's *On the Natural History of Destruction* of 1999, in which he claimed that postwar German writers had repressed the experience of the air war, and Günter Grass's novella *Crabwalk* of 2002, in which he turned his attention to the fate that befell German refugees from the East at and after the end of the war. Others have pointed to political factors such as unification and the rise of a new national discourse in the nineties, or to the bombing of Belgrade and the images of trains filled with Kosovo refugees fleeing into Albania as a crucial factor in rekindling German war memories. Yet others point to generational aspects as, for instance, the waning of a political discourse of the 68ers for whom any mention of the firestorms of Hamburg or Dresden implied a denial of the Holocaust and asserted a reactionary claim to German victimhood. Clearly, the altered German memoryscape that now includes public recognition of German suffering both in the air war and the expulsion is overdetermined from the beginning and has been many years in the making. Indeed, the notion of German suffering and victimhood has always been latently or overtly present in public discourse. And yet there is something new in the current conjuncture. That which is new came to a head with the publication in the fall of 2002 of historian Jörg Friedrich's hugely successful book *Der Brand. Deutschland im Bombenkrieg 1940-1945* (The Burning: Germany in the Bombing War 1940-1945).

What interests me in the current debate about Friedrich is the literary and rhetorical dimension of his success and its political relationship to the current peace movement. I begin with a simple thesis: the experience of the bombings was publicly "forgotten" at the national (though not at the local) level in West Germany for several decades, while Dresden and "Anglo-American bombing terror" were always part of East German state propaganda. Memory and forgetting are of course always engaged in a frantic pas de deux, and the very notion of a "public forgetting" of the air war could itself be debated in more detail. Nevertheless, I would argue that a certain kind of public forgetting of the air war, a forgetting of German victimhood, was a necessary and enabling condition for the emergence of a strong discourse of German Holocaust memory beginning in the sixties.

This kind of public forgetting held up until recently. Then the topic emerged forcefully, though only briefly, in the debate on W.G. Sebald's book-length essay *On the Natural History of Destruction* in 1999. And it was catapulted into the center of public attention in the fall of 2002 with the publication of Jörg Friedrich's bestseller and a wave of documentaries in print and on television. In both cases an earlier forgetting of the bombing experience was challenged, though in significantly different ways and at significantly different moments. But they should be read together, not least because Sebald's claim that the air war had not left a *Schmerzensspur* (a trace of pain) in the collective German psyche reoccurs and is challenged in Friedrich's claim that he wants to document the *Leideform* (form of suffering) of the bombing war. Taken together, these two books and their public effects have indeed been central in altering German memorial culture in irreversible ways.

Sebald had become known in the early nineties as a writer of memory narratives in a new mode. *The Emigrants*, a collection of four stories about German-Jewish emigrants, quickly became an international success, and his 2001 novel *Austerlitz* received one of the most prestigious literary prizes in the United States. Sebald's essay about the air war is interesting for a discussion of the dialectic of forgetting and memory, since it implicitly questions the relationship between public memory of the Holocaust and public forgetting of the bombings. Of course, the Holocaust stands dead-center in many contemporary trauma studies in Germany as elsewhere, and it is the historical event that has shaped Sebald's literary and ethical imagination. But if there ever was a trauma for the Germans during World War II, it surely was not the Holocaust, but rather

the experience of the carpet bombings of German cities, however contro-
versially they may have been interpreted already at that time—as vicious
revenge, just punishment, or simply fate.

Sebald starts from the paradox that this traumatic experience does
not seem to have left a *Schmerzensspur* in the collective consciousness
of the Germans, and that it never played an important role in debates
about the inner constitution of the Federal Republic. He attributes this fact
to an extremely efficient and successful collective psychic repression.
He argues that postwar Germans (and he seems to have primarily the FRG
in mind) are bound together by the secret of the hundreds of thousands
of corpses in the basement of the new state, as it were, a kind of family
secret that fed the stream of psychic energy making reconstruction and
the economic miracle possible in the fifties. Forgetting, in other words,
appears as yet another German repression—repression hypothesis number
two, as it were: after the repression of the Holocaust, in which Germans
figured as perpetrators, comes the repression of the bombings, in which
German civilians figured as victims.

However questionable the value of Sebald's repression hypothesis
may be, it is rather the public reception of Sebald's book that becomes
interesting for an argument about a politics of public forgetting. Several
reviews attacked *On the Natural History of Destruction* as if it were part
of the right-wing discourse indulging the Germans as victims of the
Allies, and as if Sebald aimed at relativizing or even denying the role of
Germans as perpetrators. This attack on Sebald reflected and reproduced
an earlier political taboo on the *Luftkrieg* (aerial warfare) that had first
emerged in the fifties and gathered strength in the generational conflicts
of the sixties. In those times, speaking about the air war publicly, or
even privately in the family, was inescapably tied to the discourse of
German victimization (Germans as victims of the Nazis first, then of the
bombings, and finally of the Allied occupation). More often than not, talk
of the air war meant relativizing the crimes of the Holocaust. And then the
suffering of the air war was invariably linked to the stories of expulsion
from the East that played an important role in right-wing West German
politics, at least until the late sixties. The Right spoke of Dresden and the
expulsion, the Left of Auschwitz. Both sides displayed resistance to the
other memory, and this reciprocal resistance fed the generational conflict
that was to erupt fully only in the sixties with the rise of the New Left
and the protest generation. But it is important to remember, contrary to
what Sebald suggests, that it was ubiquitous talk about the bombings and
about the expulsion, familiar to anyone who grew up in West Germany in
the fifties, that produced the taboo on discussing the air war in the first
place. In this political debate the arguments of the Left were politically
legitimate. The notion of German victimhood, tied to a longstanding

nationalist discourse, was fundamentally reactionary and it had to be fought for the country to arrive at a new consensus regarding the German past. The price paid for this victory was the forgetting of the *Luftkrieg*, the forgetting of a traumatic national experience. Today, however, in the presence of a well-established Holocaust memory discourse in Germany, I see no justification for the continued unwillingness to discuss the experience of the bombings, their legitimacy or their military usefulness.

Enter Jörg Friedrich and his bestseller in the fall of 2002. Within a few months several hundred thousand copies were sold. The book was reviewed everywhere, and its publication was followed by a flood of documentary television programs, talk-shows, special issues of *Der Spiegel* (*Als das Feuer vom Himmel fiel*, When fire came down from heaven), *Geo* (*Verbrechen gegen die Deutschen?*, Crime against the Germans?), and other mass-circulation magazines. Friedrich, a freelance historian known for his critical work on the Nazi war machine and on postwar trials, kept appearing on television. At the high point of this media frenzy one could hardly get through an evening of television without seeing bombs falling on German cities, firestorms raging and survivors describing their harrowing experiences. Guido Knopp's ZDF memory machine was running at full capacity, and others followed suit. Sebald's 1999 book *On the Natural History of Destruction,* which first broke through the public silence about the air war and clearly serves as a hidden reference and inspiration for Friedrich, now appears only as a prelude to this new wave of public memorial discourse in which the experience of an older vanishing generation of Germans is being transmitted to their children and grandchildren. As with Sebald, some critics have mobilized the old taboos against Friedrich's powerful narrative of the bombings, but clearly not with much success and perhaps not even with much conviction. Memory of the *Luftkrieg* is no longer a public taboo, nor should it be. Its potential to feed a revival of national conservatism is nil, I think, because Germany has been sufficiently denationalized since the sixties. But it does raise thorny issues and it remains to be seen what public purposes it will serve in the long run.

Clearly some of Friedrich's narrative strategies are susceptible to criticism. He was taken to task for his emphatic tone, the lack of clarity regarding the issue of the bombings as war crimes, the occasional and calculated use of language usually reserved for the Holocaust (air-raid shelters as crematoria, bomber crews as *Einsatzgruppen* (task forces), the very title of the book *Der Brand* approximating to a German translation of Holocaust). But overall there is wide agreement that this is not a revisionist book about Germans as victims as much as it is a book about the suffering of German civilians whose experiences need to be acknowledged and taken into the national narrative about the war and postwar years.

Even such a differentiation goes only so far, however. It does not fully explain the fascination. The enormous resonance of the book in Germany only makes sense in light of the fact that it appeared midway between New York's 9/11 and the bombing of Baghdad. Of course the book itself mentions neither, and from interviews we know that Friedrich actually supported the war, just as he never leaves much doubt that the Allies were justified in fighting the Nazi war machine with everything they had. But the public reception of historical scholarship is a tricky business. The book fuelled the peace movement precisely through its strategies of discussing the air war in terms of a contemporary anti-war and anti-bombing sensibility, thus expanding the present backwards rather than insisting on the difference between then and now. Friedrich thus offered the growing opposition to the Iraq war a decontextualized and experiential take on German history that could make Baghdad look like Dresden, the firestorms of the forties like the "shock and awe" campaign of the American and British Air Force.

Friedrich does not give us new facts about history. Most of what he tells is known from the work of British, American and German historians and, I would want to add, from the literary writings of authors such as Hans Erich Nossack, Alexander Kluge and Hubert Fichte. The book's power lies, rather, in the force of its narration, which distinguishes it from a more distanced and contextual historiography. The lack of emphasis on political context has indeed been one of the major criticisms. In its focus on the experience of the bombings and the firestorms, its mix of obsessively detailed anatomical description of horror with an emphatic reconstruction of the subjective experience of suffering, Friedrich takes the reader directly to the place of destruction, making Germans into voyeurs of unimaginable horrors visited on the very sites they now inhabit. The accompanying photo book, *Brandstätten* (Places of Fire), published in the fall of 2003, exacerbates the problem by featuring horror images without much commentary. As the borders between past and present become fluid, it is as if one shared the experience itself. Certainly it becomes imaginable in ways not found in earlier historiographic work on the Allies' strategic air command and its campaign of "moral bombing." The reader is caught in an imaginary in which the firestorms of Hamburg and Dresden are immediately present, ready to be linked to other sets of images soon to explode on television screens once the bombing of Baghdad began. The near-simultaneity on German television screens of bombing runs on Hamburg or Cologne with image sequences of the fireballs from Baghdad did the rest. The experientially focused proximity of Friedrich's kind of writing of history, combined with the visually generated false sense of simultaneity, corresponds to the notion of an expanded present that no longer allows for sober comparison and differentiating evaluation.

Instead we get a newly mediated form of experiencing other times and spaces in which the imagined past is projected onto the screen of the present, a phenomenon of contemporary memorial culture that is by no means limited to Germany. The effect of Friedrich's book—intended or not-— is to close the gap between past and present by collapsing fundamental political differences: America and England bomb and civilians suffer—a facile and fallacious historical analogy between the German past and the Iraqi present, all the more questionable since the peace movement simultaneously covered the political nature of Saddam's regime with gracious silence or with references to the fact that Saddam was the fault of the Americans in the first place.

The former taboo against publicly discussing the *Luftkrieg* against German civilians had an explicit political dimension in that it countered a widespread nationalist discourse of German victimhood. By contrast, the German peace movement's embrace of what Friedrich calls the *Leideform* of the carpet bombings operates primarily today on an experiential emotional level, and practises its own politics of forgetting politics, which in turn leads to rising levels of anti-Americanism. Chancellor Schröder's refusal to participate even if the UN had sanctioned the campaign against Saddam's Iraq, however calculated his stance may have been in the election of 2002, is thus symptomatic of a much broader German mindset. Whether or not Friedrich's work puts Germans back onto the road of self-indulgent victimhood or simply permits a legitimately expanded view of a national trauma outside of the confining victim/perpetrator paradigm remains to be seen. A revival of rabid nationalism is not on the horizon. There is no doubt, however, that the embrace of the *Leideform* by so many in Germany today has a very powerful contemporary fear to prop it up. The name of that fear is globalization rather than carpet bombings, and globalization is predominantly understood in Germany as elsewhere in Europe as Americanization. This is where war memories do indeed become political in the present.

Memorial was presented at the Hirshhorn
Museum in Washington in 1992, tying
in with the first anniversary of the Gulf
War. This military cemetery, with its
eternal flame supplied by a Kuwaiti oil
well which had been set alight, refers
to the responsibility of democratic civil
society in the wars waged in their name.
It also alludes to the fact that the truth
is often the first victim of war and,
consequently, one of the most emblematic
images of that war was the televised
"snow" seen at the end of every smart
missile launch. The wall lights remind
us that history unfolds as a tragedy and
repeats itself as a farce, although in
this case perhaps the opposite was true.

FRANCESC TORRES, Memorial, 1992
24 M16 assault guns, 24 hats, 1 wooden shelf unit,
2 wall lights, books, television and video, 60 m²
Collection of the artist, Barcelona

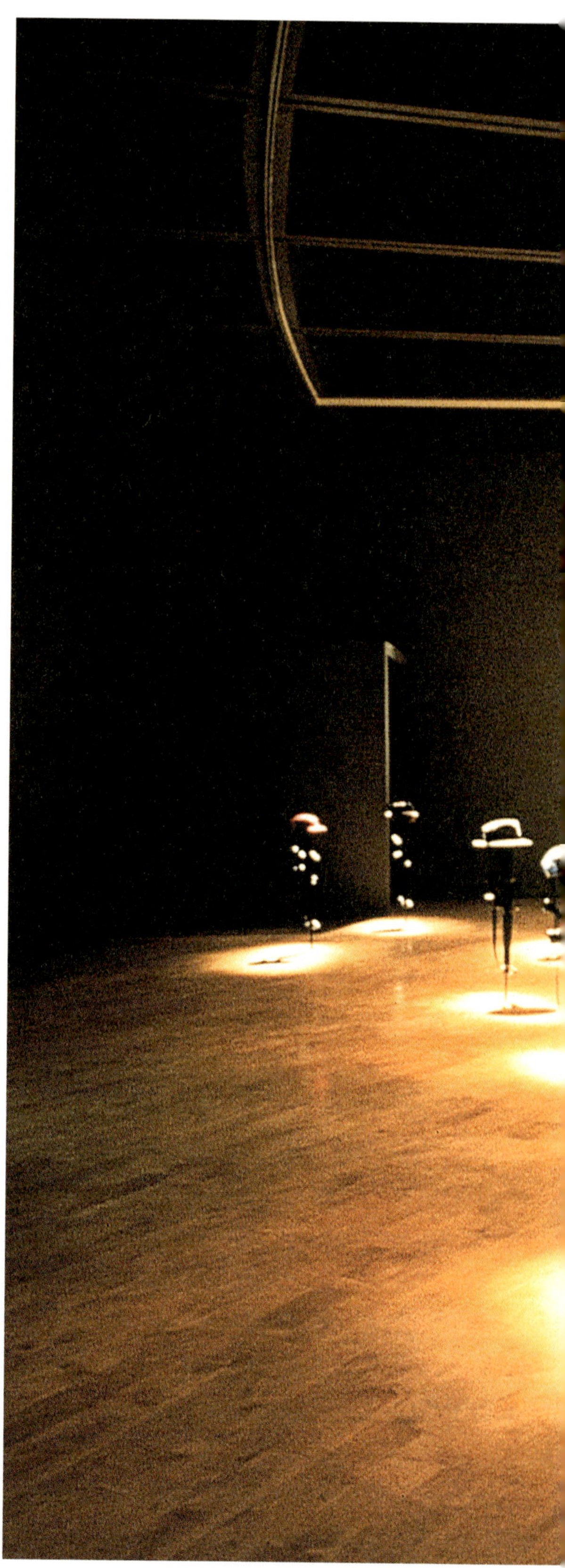

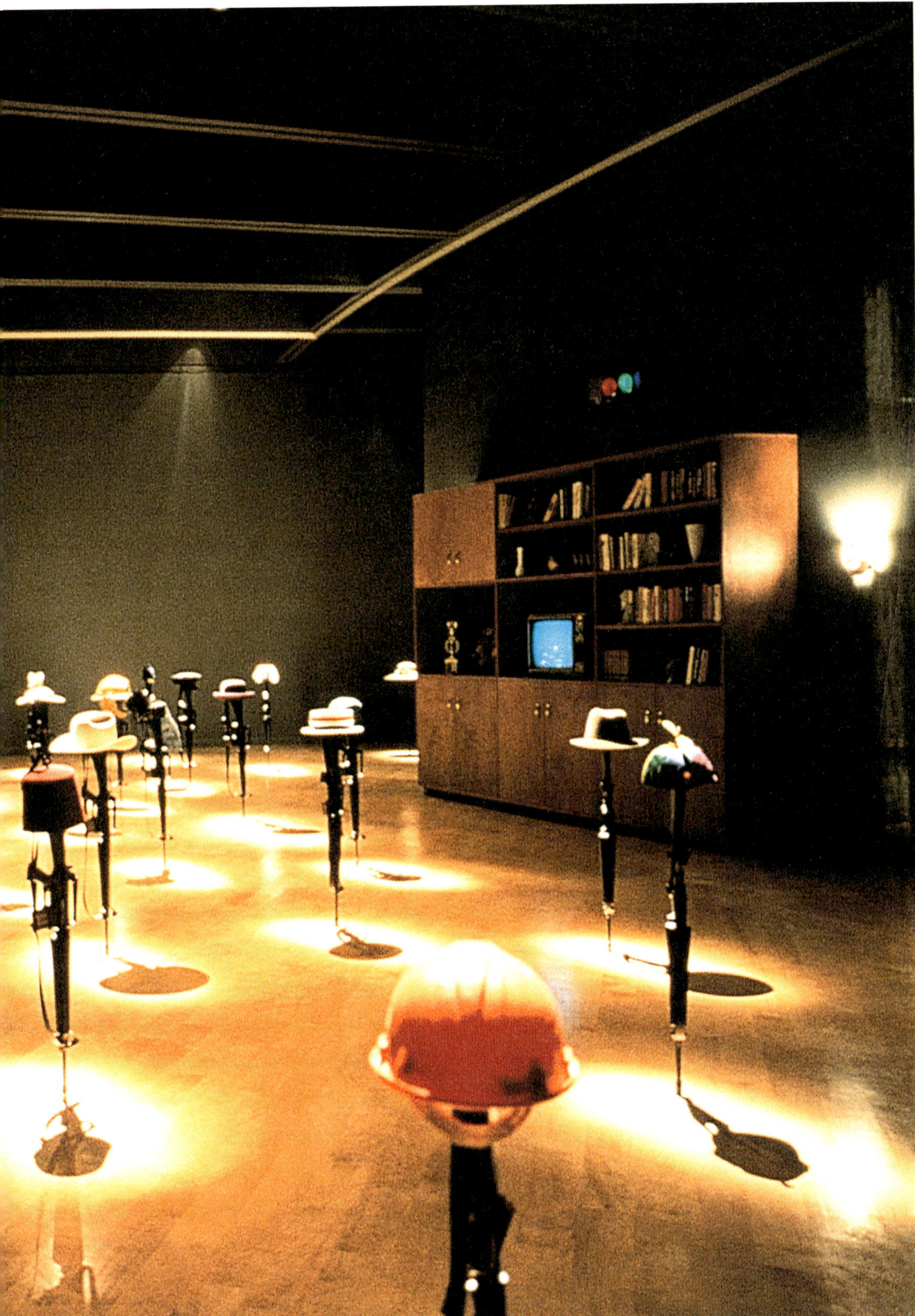

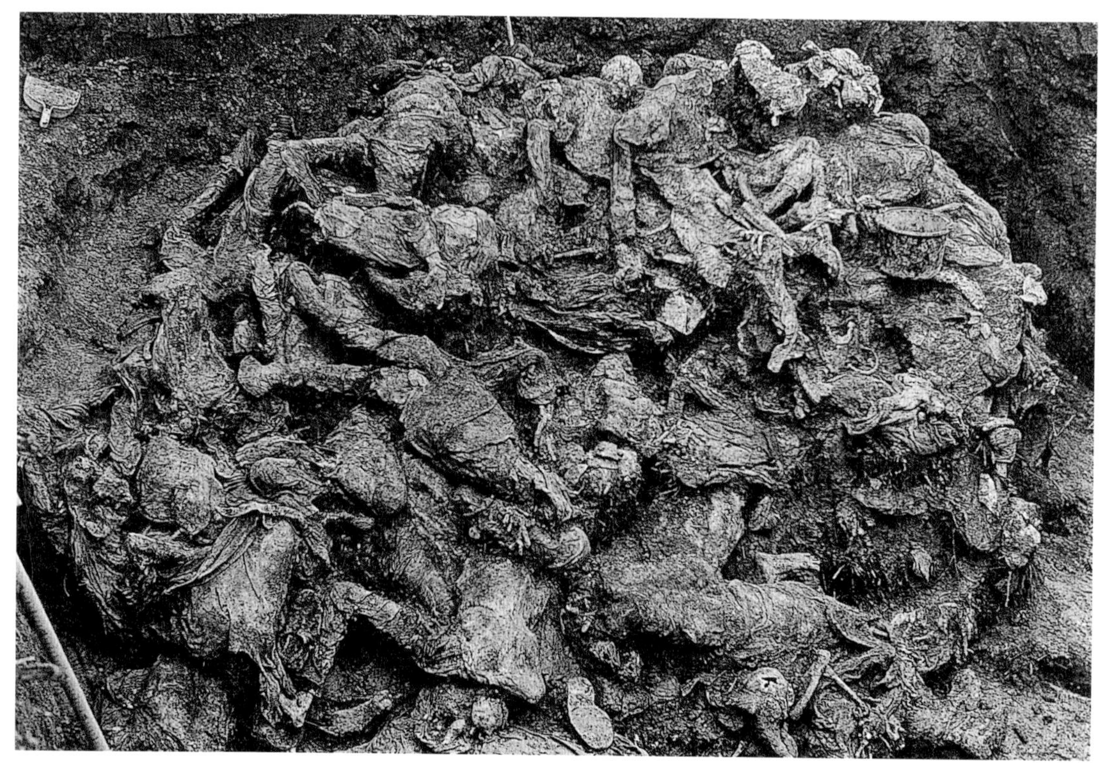

In 1996, Gilles Peress photographed the exhumation of the mass graves
of the thousands of victims of the massacre carried out in Srebrenica, Bosnia,
by the Serbo-Bosnian militias led by General Ratko Mladic. The exhumation
programme was supervised by William Haglund, a forensic anthropologist
at the War Crimes Tribunal in the Hague.

    In July 1995, thousands of Muslim men and boys were killed along the
"Trail of Life and Death" which stretches from Srebrenica to Tuzla.
"How long do you think it will take to gather all the remains from the trail?"
I asked Masovic. He thought for a minute. "My grandchildren could be doing
this, decades from now.", Gilles Peress, *The Graves*, 1998.

GILLES PERESS, Mass grave on collective farm
in Pilica, near Srebrenica, 1996
Photomontage, 270 x 480 cm
Gilles Peress / Magnum Photos / Contacto

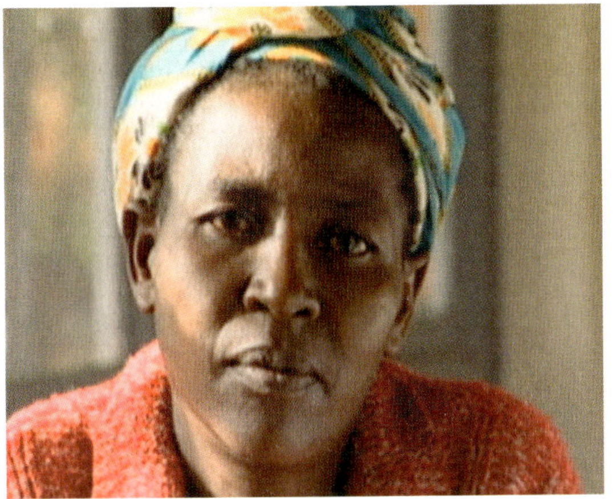

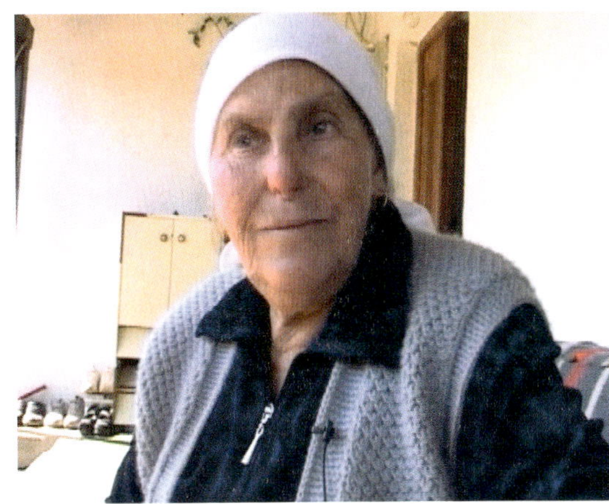

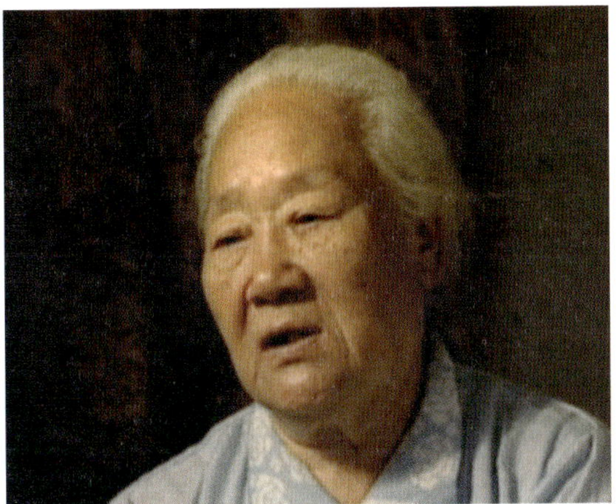

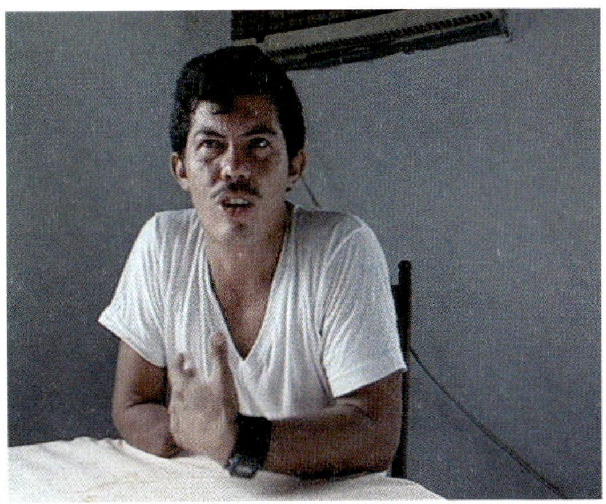

TESTIMONY FROM SEVERA MUKAKANAMI, Civil War,
Rwanda, 1994
Raymonde Provencher, *War babies, Nés de la haine*,
Canada, 2002
Video, 92'

TESTIMONY FROM CHUNG YUN-HONG, a Korean woman used
as a sex slave by the Japanese army in China, 1941-1944
Raymonde Provencher, *War babies, Nés de la haine*,
Canada, 2002
Video, 92'

TESTIMONY FROM KADA, Kosovo
Susan Muska and Greta Olafsdottir, *Women, the forgotten
face of war*, USA, *c.* 2002
Video, 84'

TESTIMONY FROM LUIS MORENO, lieutenant in Somoza's
guard and later a member of the Contras in Nicaragua,
1979-1984
Susan Meiselas, Alfred Guzzetti, Richard P. Rogers,
Pictures from a revolution, USA, 1991
Video, 88'10"

Jaar was in Rwanda in August 1994, after the massacres, and took over
3,000 photographs. On returning to New York he did not even want to look
at them or exhibit them, to avoid lapsing into the pornography of violence.
For this installation, first exhibited at the Chicago Museum of Contemporary
Photography in January 1995, he chose 60 photographs showing different
aspects of the genocide. In order to consider whether it is possible to depict
horror, he builds a "cemetery of images" which evidences a dual loss and
burial: the loss of the image which we cannot see, and the event buried in the
photograph. Each description written on the box, in the style of an epitaph,
speaks of both these absences.

ALFREDO JAAR, Real pictures. Rwanda project, 1995
Photographic boxes with texts, Cibachrome photographs
Courtesy of the artist

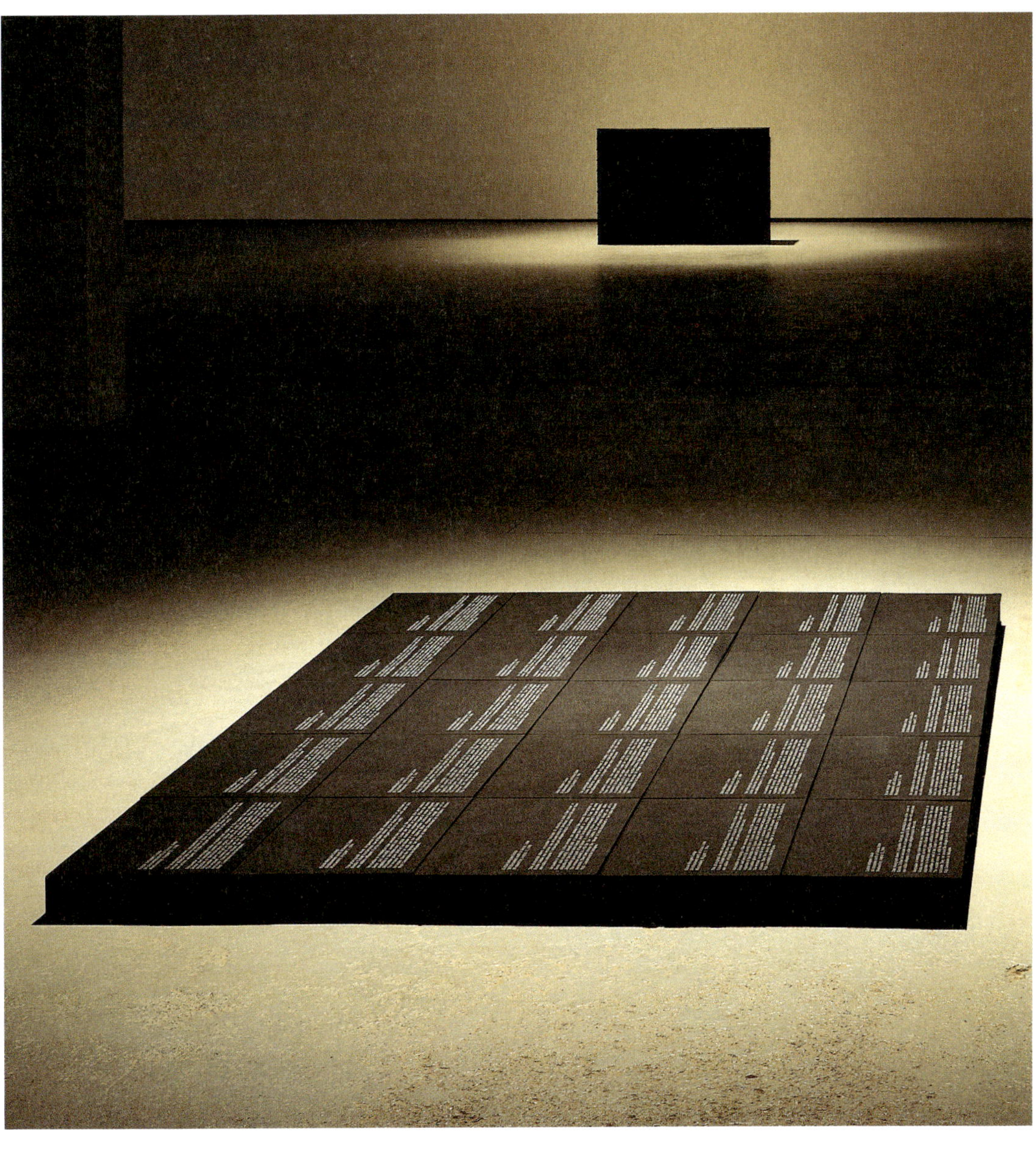

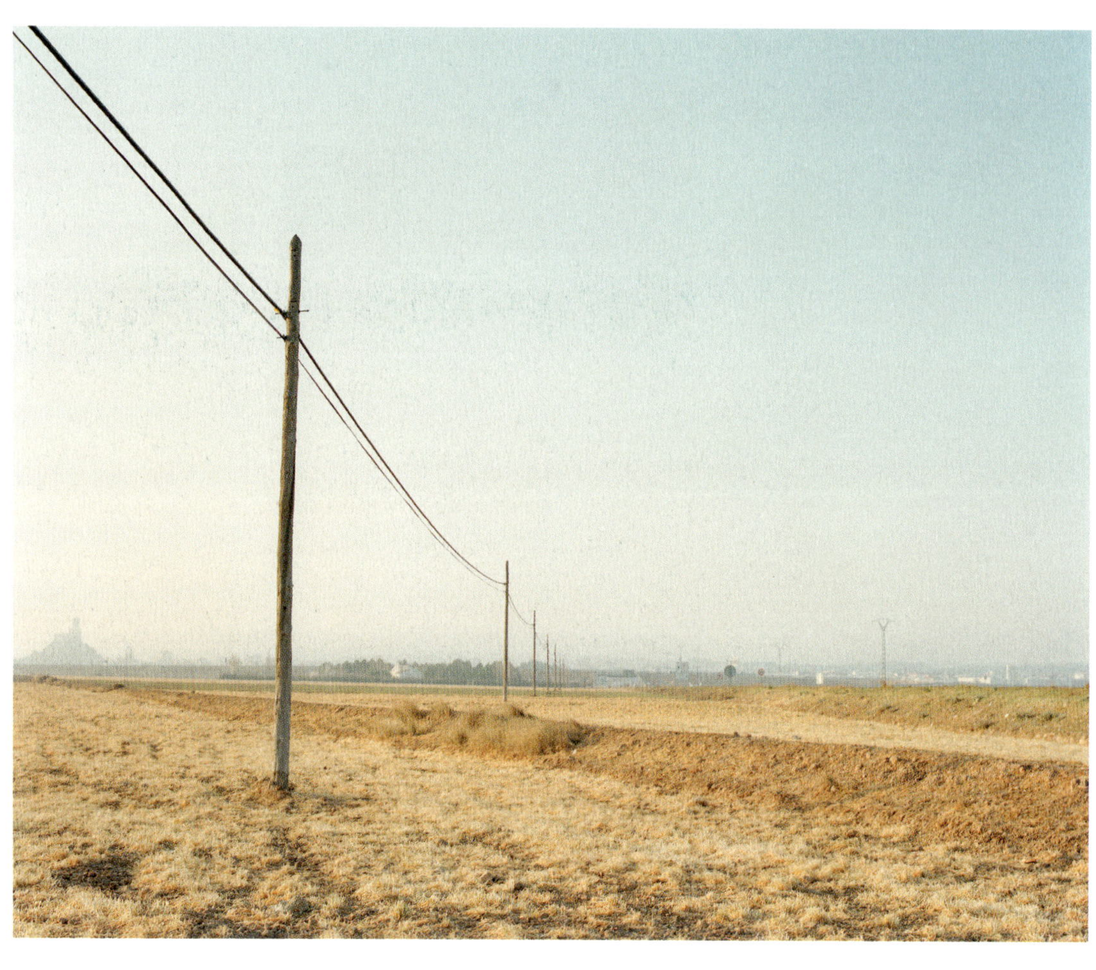

JOSÉ MARÍA ROSA AND MARÍA BLEDA, Covadonga, year 718, 1996
Colour photograph on aluminium, rigid cotton base and screenprinted text, 85 x 150 cm
Collection of the artists

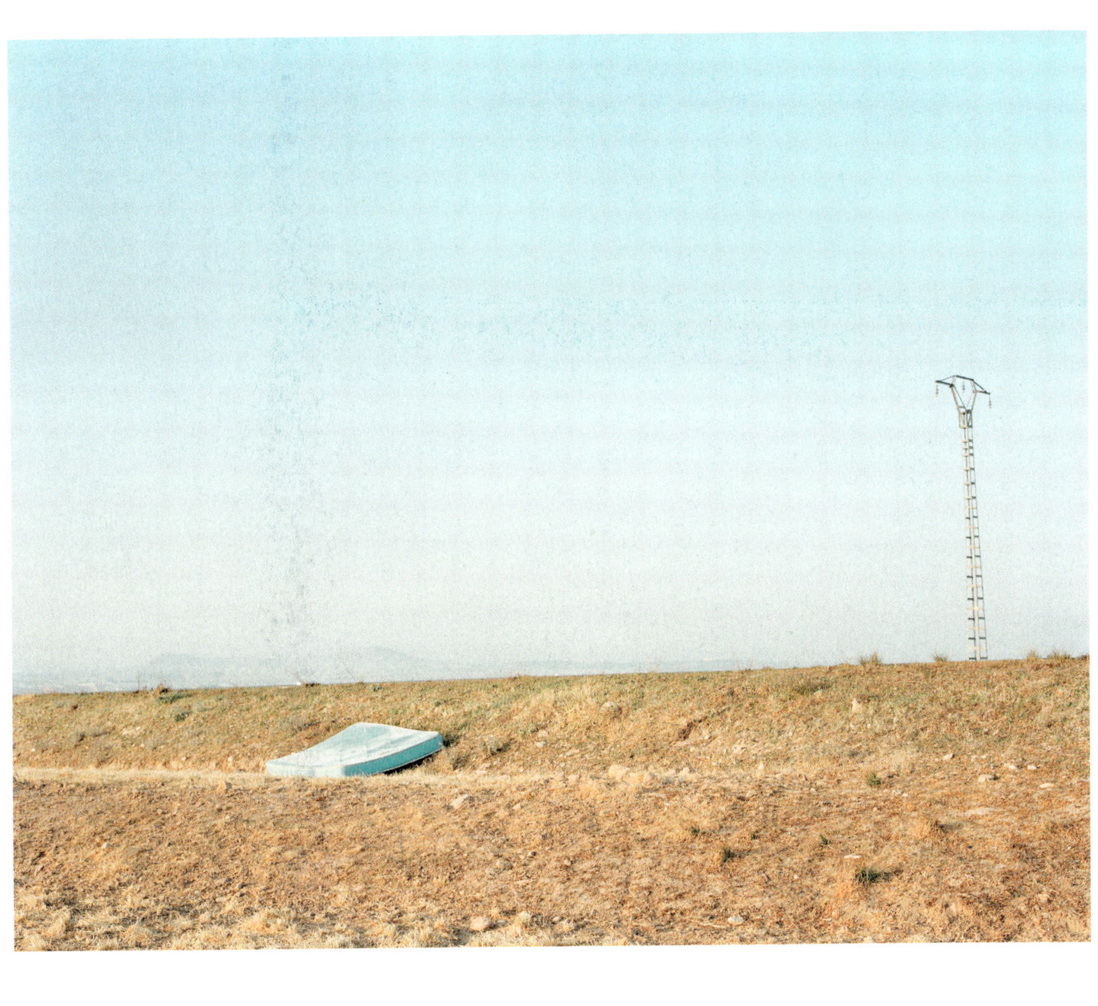

JOSÉ MARÍA ROSA AND MARÍA BLEDA, Near Almansa, 25 April 1707, 1994
Colour photograph on aluminium, rigid cotton base and screenprinted text, 85 x 150 cm
Collection of the artists

The future of war

War is plastic:
possible futures of combat and peace

Chris Hables Gray

"War is the arena of chance, furthermore, nothing in war is simple."
JOHN KEEGAN (2003, p. 326)

"Our job is to predict the future–and the best way to predict the future is to invent it."
Evil member of the Syndicate on the *X-Files* TV show

Futurology

Predicting the future is as important as it is difficult, and this is particularly true of war. Of course, shaping the future is one of the best ways to predict it, but this approach is limited by its complexity. Besides, it begs a key question: how does one shape the future unless one knows how it is determined, and therefore what it might possibly be? We can't even know the now very well, and we're supposed to predict the future? Yes, the answer must be, as much as we can. And it has to start with being clear on epistemology—what we can, and cannot, know.

War is one of the most complex of all human actions. It is shrouded in fog and uncertainty (according to Karl von Clausewitz); it is twisted by the goddess Fortune (in Niccolo Machiavelli's view). Still, understanding what war might become is not magic or augury nor is it art or science. It is a bit of all of these.

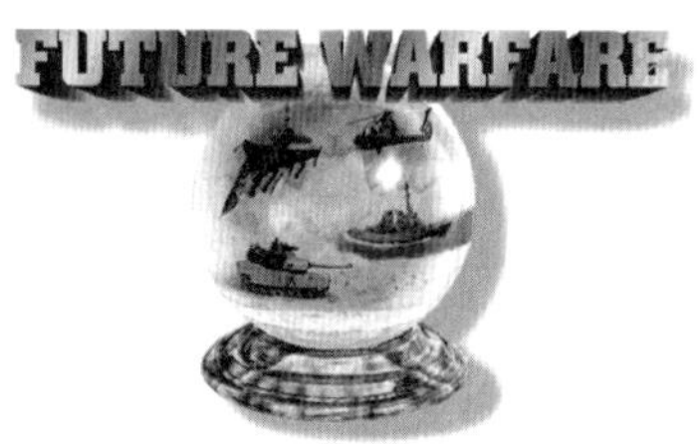

This is the introductory image for the latest major report on future war from the US Department of Defense. The image of a crystal ball was not innocently chosen. Military practitioners know that the only certainly in war is that chance and confusion will lay waste to all predictions and plans. Information will never be perfect and no technology will assure victory, for the goddess Victory blesses those with the most courage, the strongest will to sacrifice and therefore to win, and especially those with the greatest luck.

Crystal Ball, from the 2003 Department of Defense report on the future of war (Joint Chiefs of Staff, *Joint Vision 2020: Future Warfare*)

Most accurate predictions come from extrapolation—figure out what has happened and what is happening and go on from there. Unfortunately this misses the most important developments: the new. Even though most new things almost always follow old patterns, there are those extraordinary breaks from the past that are new in every sense. In physics and complexity theory these are called singularities. Sometimes there are branches (choices if we are lucky) between two possibilities, which are termed bifurcations, but usually potential outcomes are multiple. Sometimes they might depend on the slightest variation of a single event (the butterfly effect); in other instances it is a growing wave of occurrences until some tipping point is reached. Of course often nothing fundamentally new is on offer. A number of military historians have pointed out that Alexander the Great's army could have fought Napoleon's troops of over 2,000 years later. Despite some differences they were surprisingly similar in weapon power, tactics and strategies. This is certainly not the case today.

War is changing very quickly now, and not just technologically—although that is crucial and cannot be denied. It is changing strategically with the perfection of asymmetric war doctrines that allow militarily inferior forces to defeat superior ones through attrition and adroit politics. And philosophically the very legitimacy of war has never been challenged as it is being challenged here at the beginning of the twenty-first century. So there is every reason to think that war is on the verge of a fundamental transformation, because it is crystal clear that it cannot go on as it has been for the last four or five thousand years. How it will change (or even end) is certainly not even decided yet, but the possibilities can be laid out. But first, in order to chart the next developments of war, we must be clear about the war system of today.

War at the start of the twenty-first century

Predictive heuristics depend on having a good understanding of the present. Here we must resist the simplistic ideological schemas put forward by politicians, as well as those seductive academic meta-theories that promise much and deliver little. The analysis must start with the concrete realities of war today and a real engagement with the history and dynamics of war since its beginning.

Although Ancient War was technologically conservative, new technologies did play a significant role in changing it, eventually producing the ideology, and later practices, of Modern War starting roughly 500 years ago. In the last 100 years Late Modern War developed into a system of continual military innovation (Van Creveld 1989) producing, at the end of World War II, Postmodern War (Gray 1997). Because many of the new weapons (nuclear and biological in particular) were not really usable to full effect, Postmodern War (as I call it; there are many other labels) continues the institutions of Modern War without the catharsis of total war and decisive battle. It is framed by perpetual revolutions in military affairs (Gray 2003), a Cold War structure, and the convergence of terror and war, which are no longer distinguishable, into Terror War (Gray 2004).

In concrete terms war is now a bricolage of operations-other-than-war (peacemaking, peacekeeping), low-intensity conflicts (also called small, dirty or guerrilla war), the militarizing of space (US Army 2003), various preemptive war doctrines (from People's War to the current US policy), continued efforts to make so-called weapons of mass destruction usable (chemical weapons by Saddam Hussein; biological weapons by many; small nuclear weapons by the US) and their proliferation, and always, the threat of Apocalyptic War. All co-existing in the context of a permanent war mobilization within and between the nation-states of the world (Gray 1997).

Since 1940 the US has been on a war footing, culminating in the present situation where its raw military power (and expenditure) is greater than the next 15 countries'. However, this does not translate into usable force, as the conquest of Iraq shows. The low US tolerance for casualties and the realities of asymmetric war mean that vast as US military potential is, the US is profoundly limited in terms of what military power it can actually use.

The current international system has remained basically the same since World War II. It is a nation-state system with various regional and international networks, forums and alliances, all in the context of a US-defined Cold War. The so-called capitalist-communist Cold War has become McWorld vs. Jihad (BARBER 1995), but the structure remains surprisingly consistent. Because of the rules of Postmodern War, full-scale combat is impossible; instead it is a struggle of invasions of Third World countries, guerrilla wars, and acts of Terror War by both nation-states and non-governmental groups.

But there have been some ongoing changes in the last 50 years that show that the whole Postmodern War system is becoming increasingly unstable. These include:

• The decline of many nation-states in the face of growing corporate, regional (such as the EU) and international (WTO, UN, World Court) institutions. This includes the growing power of corporations over the US Government and other post-industrial countries.

• What has ironically been termed the democratization of weapons, especially WMDs, but including effective small and medium arms as well. This is not related to real democracy of course. In general, the countries (and non-governmental military groups) that pursue improved armaments are hardly democratic, but it is true that the relentless improvements in technology and science make it easier for more and more political actors to access increasingly greater amounts of firepower.

• The privatization of war. In the US this has meant turning over many logistical and even security operations of the Empire to corporations. But it also includes the improved armaments and power of various criminal associations, from US street gangs to Chinese pirates, the growing number of governmental kleptocracies (Chechnya; Georgia before the 2003 Rose

Revolution; Nigeria under Gen. Abacha; Haiti), various criminal-political alliances (war lords in Somalia; the so-called narco-terrorists in Latin America; the Diamond War combatants in Africa; the role of organized crime in Serbia, Bulgaria and other former Communist states), and the incredible growth of corporate security forces everywhere.
• The shift in some militaries from preparation for and actual war-fighting to peacemaking, peacekeeping and other operations-other-than-war.
• An incredible number of attempted genocides and successful ethnic cleansings, in the Balkans (Croatia of Serbs, Serbia of Croats and Bosnians, Bosnia of everyone; Kosovo of first Albanians then Serbs), in Africa (Sudan, Rwanda), East Timor, and in the Caucasus (Chechnya, Georgia, Armenia).
• The strongest peace movement in history, as was evidenced in 2003 before the US invasion of Iraq. This "second superpower" will seriously constrain aggressive war by the US and NATO.
• Potential battlefields can be anywhere. Any corner of the globe and any point in the atmosphere or near space can be a site of conflict. The most important part of this is the militarization of space, but systems for improved military operations in the deepest parts of the ocean and in the cold Arctic regions are also significant, as are attempts to make fighting in jungles, deserts, mountains and urban areas.

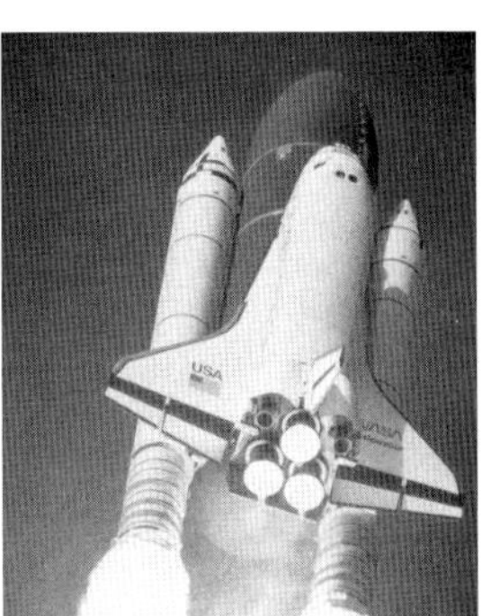

This image of NASA's space shuttle could have been used to illustrate the militarization of space, a key component of future US war plans which include a new branch of service, a Space Corp. However, it actually was used in a section on Interagency Operations, emphasizing how militarization permeates every aspect of US technoculture, in particular the "peaceful" exploration of space.

Space Shuttle image, from the 2003 Department of Defense report on the future of war (Joint Chiefs of Staff, *Joint Vision 2020: Future Warfare)*

These geopolitical developments are often, but not always, related to the technical developments of new weapons and logistical systems. Clearly, one of the main reasons war has changed over the last 500 years is new technologies and the strategies and tactics developed to accommodate them. Culture certainly was the main shaper of war when war was ritual, and it was recognized as extremely important for millennia. But in the last few centuries a belief in technological determinism has spread in Western military circles, so that now, despite of evidence to the contrary, it is preeminent. War remains personal, cultural, political most of all.

While the importance of invention and innovation cannot be denied,
it is not determinant.

In modern war carnage was industrialized. Force of fire, metal on
targets of flesh and machine, was the measure of military power. But that
has changed. Information is now the main "force multiplier" and that is
because of the ubiquity, and seemingly magical properties, of information
technology (IT). Fear, which always threatens to be the dominant emotion
in war fighting and even war preparation, looks for certainty wherever
it may. IT promises (but cannot deliver) control of war. Instead, it has
actually increased the uncertainty of war by facilitating the development
of complex new weapons and the means to deliver them, especially
nuclear and other super weapons. IT continues to drive the development
of new weapons, each generation of which it is hoped will render war more
controllable. Technologically, in the near future, we can expect:

• The continued proliferation of precision weapons (also known as
autonomous or smart munitions) and some improvements in their
performance. However, these weapons have never performed as well as
advertised, since they are dependent on excellent intelligence for their
targeting. In any event they are very susceptible to duping and other
counter-measures.

• Armed drones, such as the system that destroyed a car (perhaps full of
Al-Queda operatives) in Yemen in 2002, will be used more often, as they
help limit casualties to some extent, at least of the attackers.

• In a trend closely related to improved machine intelligence we will see
more sophisticated and more invasive human-machine interfaces
(cyborgization). Direct connections between human brains and weapon
control systems have been under development for decades and will
certainly be operational soon.

• While both machine intelligence and cyborgization have some use as
weapon platforms, it is as surveillance systems that they will be more
widely deployed. In a doomed quest for "total battlefield awareness" more
and more data will be collected from actual and potential combat sites.
Since this data will come from every part of the electromagnetic spectrum,
and since in Postmodern War almost anywhere is a potential three-
dimensional battle space, the problem won't be a lack of data, but rather
too much. The efficacy of panoptic solutions is severely limited
by the inability of machine or human intelligence to process more than a
small amount of what can be monitored, especially once one goes outside
prisons, inherently limited by definition, and seeks to turn the world
into a panopticon.

• Cyborgization will also continue to focus directly on the soldier's body.
Current research to modify humans for combat includes real advances
in producing sleeplessness, fearlessness, and consciencelessness in an

ongoing quest to develop a psychopathic cyborg fighting system that
has minimal-to-zero human requirements for eating, eliminating, sleeping,
comfort or morality.

• Because of cyborgization, technical needs and cultural factors, the role
of women in war will continue to grow. That Islamic fundamentalists even
use women as suicide bombers reveals how powerful this trend is.

• Information processing approaches won't solve the basic problems of
battle, but systems such as data mining will continue to be incredibly
oversold while not offering any real solutions in the next few decades, if
ever. But that doesn't mean that information technology in general hasn't
become a panacea for the militaries of the industrial and post-industrial
countries (Gray 1998).

• Myths of info/net/cyber war and related doctrines ("Shock and Awe")
will continue to shape military and political policy. This will encourage
more attempts to use simple military force to solve complex political
problems. The most dangerous illusion is that technology wins wars,
either in the form of greater force of fire as in the twentieth century or
through information management, as we often hear today. As John Keegan
concludes in his analysis of the role of intelligence in warfare, "it is force
that counts...intelligence may be usually necessary but is not a sufficient
condition of victory." (2003, p. 334; see also Gray 2004)

Postmodern War extends from peacekeeping to peacemaking to low-
intensity conflict to traditional war to Apocalyptic War. It is a continuum,
a slippery slope leading down, or up. Time will tell in which direction
it will flow.

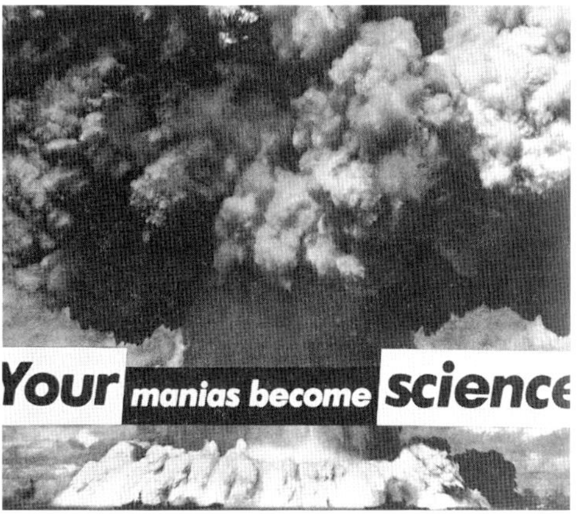

Relentless innovations in technoscience have made the problem of war an issue of human survival. Science is quite complicit in the current crisis. As J. Robert Oppenheimer said of his work leading to the development of nuclear weapons, "When you see something that is technically sweet you go ahead and do it and you argue about what to do about it only after you have your technical success. That is the way it was with the atomic bomb." He also admitted that because of this, he and the other scientists who made the first bombs "have known sin." They are not alone, for many scientists sinned before them and many since. (Hijiya 2000). [See p. 255]

Future war / Fantasy war

The best way to contemplate possible forms of future war is through scenarios, the little narratives that are widely used by military practitioners to think through various possible forms wars might take so as to prepare for them. These story-telling exercises draw on the long history of war gaming (going back further than chess) and can be on tactical, strategic or geostrategic levels. They can look to the near future or further on into what might be considered science fiction. Some of those "far-out" fantasies will be discussed below, but there is a good chance that the distant future of war will actually be decided in the next few decades, so that is where we shall begin.

On 28 September 2001, 17 days after 9/11, students and faculty from New York University gathered to create some possible scenarios for the next four years of the War on Terror. Their efforts are remarkably similar to many similar exercises since, and they nicely lay out the main possibilities (Kleiner 2003). Now that we are more than halfway through their predictive framework we can analyze their results and draw some conclusions about the assumptions behind the different scenarios.

Their five most likely futures are:

• An Empire Stretched Too Thin: US caught in never-ending quagmire.
• International McCarthyism: US wins, and becomes a social-control-oriented corporate state.
• Black-Market World: War leads to fragmentation, "gated nations," a war between rich and poor nations, and increased reliance on underground economies.
• Gloom and Boom: Pakistan goes radical-Islamic, leading to nuclear attacks and Chernobyls everywhere.
• Blooming World: The only optimistic future of the five, in which the war's imperatives change the culture for the better.

Major elements of the first three scenarios have already come to pass: US invasions of Iraq and Afghanistan, guerrilla war, US alienation of their allies, rise of corporate power, loss of civil liberties in the US and Europe. Other elements from them, especially more successful attacks on the US, have yet to materialize. What is most interesting is that the only positive scenario, and the worst, have proven to have very little predictive power so far. This highlights that the situation remains incredibly uncertain, a hallmark of Postmodern War.

In the long run it is hard to be optimistic about the outcome of US operations in the Middle East. As General Wesley Clark has emphasized, the US military is designed for war fighting, not for peacekeeping and certainly not for nation building (Clark 2003). Despite great faith being placed in US information superiority, the bloody reality on the ground is that all wars are won through fighting, and most, especially low-intensity conflicts, through attrition that is both moral and physical. As John Keegan puts it,

Official US military thinking for the short run (see Department of Defense 2003, for example) emphasizes continued reliance on improving technologies, especially information systems to ameliorate the danger of weapons of mass destruction. This is echoed in Russian (Baumann 1997) and Chinese (Pillsbury 2003) doctrines. Technically the focus is on lethality, precision of fire, integration of technologies, invisibility and detectability, the collapse of spatial limits, invading decision cycles, automatic target recognition, real-time battlespace data and full spectrum dominance. (DoD 2003; US Army 2003; Pillsbury 2003; Baumann 1997)

In the long run, there is talk of the War on Terror lasting 40 to 50 years and of the inevitable Chinese threat to US hegemony. There are also fantasies of nanospies and nanoweapons, of nonlethal munitions that conquer without killing, and of bloodless conflicts (at least to one side) thanks to intelligent weapons or the absolute dominance of the battle space through IT or some version of netwar/psychwar/cyberwar. There is no fundamental critique of the war system itself, nor should we expect one from within the official military.

From outside the world of military practitioners we can see that war is tending toward two different poles—peace or apocalypse. As more and more powerful military technologies proliferate within the current international system the chances of Apocalyptic War only increase. The mere danger of weapons of mass destruction has become the main reason to go to war and to further degrade democracy and citizenship. New military technologies of violence and control (from psychopharmacological interventions to brain implants) carry dark promises of transforming human culture and humans themselves.

Ironically, some of the same principles and technologies the military looks to for future war have some promise for helping foster real peace. After all, it was the mobilization of international civil society through the Internet by the Zapatistas that spawned theories of information war (Gray 1998.) Today, as the military plays with ideas such as swarming and decentralized networks it is the international peace movement that actually uses them. The role of high-technology surveillance has been at least as valuable to human rights activists, trained and equipped with video cameras by Witness (www.witness.org) and similar groups as it has

been to the military. Even nanobots, a favorite fantasy for the Chinese
and US armies, could just as effectively be used to enforce disarmament
in a totally open fashion (on the web), as Patrick Farley makes clear in
his charming story (2003) about pacifist hackers mobilized by the UN
preventing Iraqi bioweapons manufacturing with remote-controlled
nanobots as millions of people watch live on the net.

Fantasies often come true, especially those about new technologies,
because in the final analysis it is people trying to actualize their fantasies
who make them. But political fantasies can also come true, for we craft
the political world just as surely as the technical. While some technologies
seem to favor war and others not, few are inherently warlike or peaceful.
It is how they are used that is the decisive factor. This is certainly true
of the future of war, due to its very nature.

The morphological ontology of war

War has never been fixed; it has always been plastic. Its basic ontology
is that it is malleable, changeable. Or you could say that as a discourse
system, it has few meta-rules and one of them is that war can take many
forms. Weapons, codes, strategies and tactics have developed relentlessly.
War has always changed and the pace of change has never been greater
than it is today. The institutionalization of innovation (Van Creveld 1989)
and the linking of military technologies to the modern and postmodern
geometrical expansion of science and technology means that weapons,
strategies, tactics and soldiers are constantly morphing into new forms.

In this mad rush to invent new weapons and new kinds of war we must
be careful of the metaphors we deploy when trying to understand what
is happening. The facile use of information as an analogy for operational
intelligence and of complexity and other new theories of order as
metaphors is particularly dangerous.

For example, to point out that Postmodern War is a bricolage of many
different types of war should not obscure the reality that very seldom
has actual war limited itself to one pure form of combat. And that even if
many types of war co-exist, that doesn't mean that they are all of equal
importance. In today's case, so-called unthinkable war (using weapons of
mass destruction) might be the most important type of war of all. And low-
intensity conflict, with its confusing rules and asymmetrical patterns, is
much more of a reality than the "normal" types of battle that have seldom
been seen since World War II. Nation-building is more important militarily
than tank battles, but try convincing any self-respecting military of this.

That war can indeed change incredibly, to "morph" one might readily
say, is not to say that it is infinitely changeable. If it changes beyond a
social system that bases its power on the killing and maiming of humans
it won't be war.

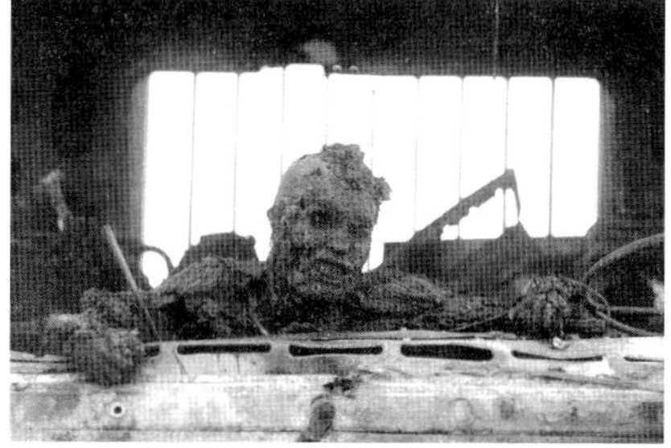

For all the talk of precision munitions and autonomous weapons, the very ground of war remains human bodies—killing them, wounding them. Otherwise it is not war. If humans continue to wage war bodies will continue to bleed, to suffocate, to burn, to die. The bodies may be intimately linked to machines or even modified to their very DNA core. The killers may be machines or other modified humans. But there will be death and probably on a massive scale or it will not be war.

KENNETH JARECKE, Charred body, Gulf War, 1992
Kenneth Jarecke / Contact Press Images / Contacto

We need to look at the forces that shape war in order to accurately predict, and then change, what is happening. In particular there are many lessons to be drawn from past attempts to predict the future of war. Robert Baumann has brought many of these together in his article "Historical Perspectives on Future War" (1997). He begins by pointing out that the "march of science suggests the next war will employ many new means. In contrast history suggests that by its very nature, war exhibits many continuities amid change." This leads him to emphasize the importance of social, political, economic, cultural and intellectual factors in war. New technologies open up new possibilities, but they are invented and produced and used because of decisions made by humans. They may have momentum, but they do not have a life of their own.

This means we must pay particularly close attention to the dance of fantasy and reality that makes up war culture today. Paul Virilio is one of the best interpreters of this danse macabre. He pointed out in 1983 how "pure" war was colonizing politics even in "peacetime." Lately, he has focused much of his analysis on the implications of what he calls the "computer bomb."

The atom bomb gave rise to the computer bomb [...] During the Cold War, the prevention of nuclear war meant that information structures related to the conquest of space had to be developed [...] The computer bomb is a result of both the atom bomb and the need for deterrence [...] the computer bomb and the power of information are assuming considerable proportions. The problem then arises of a deterrence by computer science, wisdom, and knowledge. As Goebbels, propaganda leader of the Third Reich, said, "He who knows everything fears nothing." So the power of information can be an absolute power. (1999, p. 103)

The computer bomb (also called the information bomb and the cyberbomb by Virilio) shows how technophilic policies and such illusions as infowar are degrading, indeed attacking, culture as a whole. It is an absolute weapon not of war, but of militarization. It is fueled by the increasing and inevitable fear that more and more powerful weapons provoke in us all, but especially in those charged with producing security in a world that is less and less secure because of their very efforts. It is the return of the repressed with a vengeance; war is out of control and denying this breeds more horrible weapons and more war.

The future of war will determine the future of humanity. This is not only true in the most obvious and important issue of human survival. If war does not end civilization, or even the human race, it will still shape the politics, and indeed the bodies, of us all. If we let it.

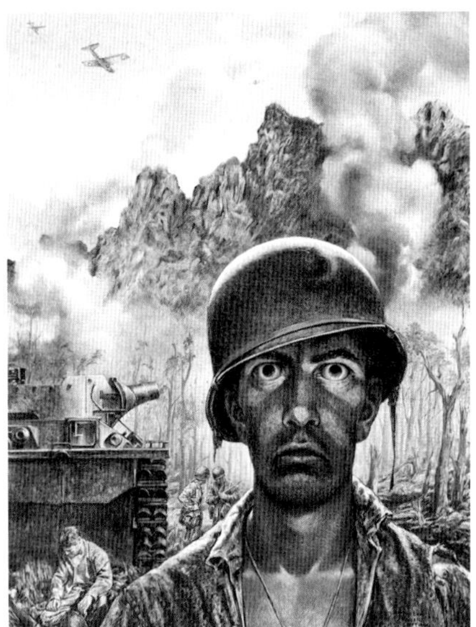

Combat does something to soldiers, as Tom Lea's painting from the Pacific Campaign in World War II makes horribly clear. One can die without ceasing to breathe. As Barbara Ehrenreich observed, not only do men make wars, but wars make men. So it follows that not only do societies make wars, wars make societies. And as with the men wars create, war societies are patriarchal, brutal, often psychopathic. Wars breed wars and this is the worst news for the future. For unless this cycle can be broken, our ever-improving technosciences mean that the wars of the future will be even more horrific than those of the present. Our view of the future is no more comforting than whatever nightmare this soldier sees. [See p.228]

Bibliography

BARBER, Benjamin R., *Jihad Vs. McWorld: How Globalism and Tribalism are Reshaping the World*, Ballantine Books, New York 1995.

BAUMANN, Robert, "Historical Perspectives on Future War," *Military Review*, March-April 1997.

CLARK, Wesley K., *Winning Modern Wars: Iraq, Terrorism, and the American Empire*, PublicAffairs, New York 2003.

DEPARTMENT OF DEFENSE, Joint Chiefs of Staff, *Joint Vision 2020: Future Warfare*, Washington, D.C. 2003, http://www.dtic.mil/jointvision.

DER DERIAN, James, *Virtuous War: Mapping the Military-Industrial-Media-Entertainment Network*, Westview Press, Boulder (CO) 2001.

FARLEY, Patrick, "The Spiders: Surprise Inspection," *Wired*, January 2003, pp. 124-129.

GRAY, Chris Hables, *Terror or Peace: Information, Globalization, and Power*, Routledge, New York / London 2004.

______"The Perpetual Revolution in Military Affairs," in Latham, Robert (ed.), *Information Technology and International Security*, The New Press, New York 2003, pp. 199-214.

______ "The Crisis of Infowar," in Stocker, Gerfield and Schopf, Christine (eds.) *Infowar*, Springer, Vienna / New York 1998, pp. 130-137.

______ *Postmodern War: The New Politics of Conflict*, Routledge, London 1997.

HIJIYA, James A., "The Gita of J. Robert Oppenheimer," *Proceedings of the American Philosophical Society*, vol. 144, no. 2, June 2000, pp. 123-168.

KEEGAN, John, *Intelligence in War: Knowledge of the Enemy From Napoleon to Al-Qaeda*, Knopf, New York 2003.

KLEINER, Art, "Scenarios for the New War", in http://stage.itp.nyu.edu/scenario/WTCscenarios.html #alternatives, 2003.

PILLSBURY, Michael (ed.), *Chinese Views of Future Warfare*, Institute for National Strategic Studies, Washington D.C. 2003.

US Army, "Army Space Future Operational Capabilities", http://www-tradoc.army.mil/dcscd/spaceweb/ foctitle2.htm, 2003.

VAN CREVELD, Martin, *Technology and War: From 2000 B.C. to the Present*, The Free Press, New York 1989.

VIRILIO, Paul, *Politics of the Very Worst*, Semiotext(e), New York 1999.

______ and LOTRINGER, Sylvère, *Pure War*, Semiotext(e), New York 1983.

Biographies

Jon Lee Anderson is a staff writer for *The New Yorker* magazine and the author of several books, including *Inside the League* (with Scott Anderson, 1986), *War Zones* (with Scott Anderson, 1988), *Guerrillas: Journeys in the Insurgent World* (1992), *Che Guevara: A Revolutionary Life* (1997) and *The Lion's Grave: Dispatches from Afghanistan* (2002). Anderson has covered numerous conflicts, including the recent wars in Iraq and Afghanistan. He is currently writing a book about the fall of Baghdad. Anderson is an American citizen but has spent much of his life in Latin America, Africa and Asia. He currently lives with his wife and three children in Dorset, England, and in Andalusia, Spain.

Jeremy M. Black is Professor of History at the University of Exeter, UK. His 57 books include: *War: Past, Present and Future* (2001), *European Warfare, 1494-1660* (2002), *World War Two: A Military History* (2003).

Joanna Bourke is Professor of History at Birkbeck College, University of London. She has published seven books on Irish history, gender and "the body", the history of psychological thought, and modern warfare. Her books have been translated into Chinese, Italian, Portuguese, Spanish and Turkish. *An Intimate History of Killing: Face-to-Face Killing in Twentieth-Century Warfare* (1999) won the Fraenkel Prize in Contemporary History for 1998 and the Wolfson History Prize for 2000. She has just completed a book entitled *Fear: A Cultural History of the Twentieth-Century* (2004) and is writing a history of rapists in the nineteenth and twentieth centuries.

Eudald Carbonell i Roura received his Ph.D. in Quaternary Geology from the Pierre et Marie Curie University (1986) and his Ph.D. in History from Barcelona University (1988). He is currently Professor of Prehistory at Rovira i Virgili University in Tarragona and Senior Researcher in Human Autoecology of the Quaternary Group at the same university. His areas of research include the technological systems of ancient prehistory and social behaviour in human evolution. Since 1991, he has co-directed a multidisciplinary research programme at the Sierra de Atapuerca (Burgos) and, in 1997, the entire research team from Atapuerca received the Prince of Asturias Prize for Scientific and Technological Research.

He is the author of numerous specialised articles, and the books he has published include: *Els somnis de l'evolució* (with Cinta S. Bellmunt, 2003), *Encara no som humans* (with Robert Sala, 2002) and *Planeta humà* (with Robert Sala, 2000).

Manuel Delgado is Resident Professor of Religious Anthropology at Barcelona University. His work has focused particularly on themes of ritual violence in urban contexts. He has undertaken part of his research on this theme in Medellín (Colombia) and has published articles in specialist magazines, as well as the books *De la muerte de un dios* (1986), *La ira sagrada* (1991), *Las palabras de otro hombre* (1992) and *Luces iconoclastas* (2001). He is also the author of *Diversitat i integració* (1998) and *Disoluciones urbanas* (2002). In 1999 he won the Anagrama Essay Prize for *El animal público*.

Joan Esteban has a Ph.D. from the Autonomous University of Barcelona and a Ph.D. from Oxford University. He is Research Professor and Director of the Institute for Economic Analysis at the Higher Council for Scientific Research. He was Institutional Coordinator in Catalonia for the Higher Council for Scientific Research (1993-1996). He was also a representative of the Spanish government at the Higher Council of the European University Institute in Florence (1988-1996). His research combines applied and theoretical work.

He has been published in *American Political Science Review, Econometrica, Economics of Governance, Economics Letters, European Economic Review, International Economic Review, Journal of Economic Behaviour and Organization, Journal of Economic Theory, Regional Science and Urban Economics, Social Choice and Welfare and Theory and Decision.* He is currently working on the modelling of conflict.

Chris Hables Gray, Ph.D., is the author of *Postmodern War* (1997, also available in Chinese and Turkish editions), *Cyborg Citizen* (2001; also in a German edition, 2002, and Spanish edition, 2004) and the forthcoming *Terror or Peace: Information, Globalization, and Power* (2004). He is an Associate Professor of Cultural Studies of Science and Technology and of Computer Science at the University of Great Falls, Montana, and is also Professor at Goddard College and the Graduate College of the Union Institute and University.

Andreas Huyssen is the Villard Professor of German and Comparative Literature at Columbia University in New York and editor of *New German Critique.*

He was educated in Europe and has taught in the United States since 1969. He is the author of *En busca del futuro perdido: Cultura y memoria en tiempos de globalización* (2002), *After the Great Divide: Modernism, Mass Culture, Postmodernism* (1986) and *Twilight Memories: Marking Time in a Culture of Amnesia* (1996). His most recent book is *Present Pasts: Urban Palimpsests and the Politics of Memory* (2003).

Antonio Monegal teaches literary theory, comparative literature and film at Pompeu Fabra University in Barcelona, Spain.

He received his Ph.D. in Romance Languages and Literature from Harvard University in 1989 and was a member of the Department of Romance Studies at Cornell University. Among other publications, he is the author of *Luis Buñuel de la literatura al cine: Una poética del objeto* (1993) and *En los límites de la diferencia: Poesía e imagen en las vanguardias hispánicas* (1998). He has edited *Literatura y pintura* (2000), and García Lorca's *El público y El sueño de la vida* (2000) and *Viaje a la luna* (1994). At present, he is writing a theoretical examination of the representation of wars in literature and the visual arts, which is the focus of a research project he directs at Pompeu Fabra University.

David D. Perlmutter is an Associate Professor of Mass Communication at Louisiana State University and a Senior Fellow at the Reilly Center for Media & Public Affairs. He is author of *Photojournalism and Foreign Policy* (1998), *Visions of War* (1999) and *Policing the Media* (2000).

Hélène Puiseux is a historian specialising in film analysis. Her history thesis was on *German newsreels during the Weimar Republic, 1918-1932, Inventory and analysis* (1978). She is Director of Studies at the École pratique des Hautes Études in Paris, where she directed a research seminar *"Cinema, television and contemporary mythology"* from 1978 to 2001. She uses a method of comparative analysis of films centring on a specific theme to show they comprise a network which brings the problems of our society into the domain of the media and puts into place a geography of the social imagination.

She has written numerous articles on the representation of war, and two books: *L'apocalypse nucléaire et son cinéma* (1988) and *Les Figures de la Guerre, représentations et sensibilités, 1839-1996* (1997). She also works on the representations of the scientific world and the savage world.

José María Ridao holds a degree in Arabic Philology and Law. He joined the Diplomatic Corps in 1987. He was in charge of the Department for the Near East at the Directorate General for the Middle East at the Ministry of Foreign Affairs (1987-1988); adviser to the Secretary of State for International Cooperation and Latin America (1988-1989); counsellor at the Spanish Embassy in Angola (1989-1991); Spanish Consul in Moscow (1991-1992); counsellor at the Spanish Embassy in Equatorial Guinea (1992-1994); counsellor at the Spanish Embassy responsible for dealing with the OECD and a board member of the Development Assistance Committee of the OECD (1994-1998); Head of Studies at the Diplomatic School (1998-2000). In October 2000, he requested voluntary leave of absence in order to devote himself to his intellectual pursuits. He is a regular contributor to newspapers such as *El País* and the broadcasting company Cadena Ser. He has published two novels, *Agosto en el Paraíso* (1998) and *El mundo a media voz* (2001), as well as a book of stories, *Excusas para el doctor Huarte* (1999). He is the author of the essays *Contra la Historia* (2000), *La desilusión permanente* (2000), *La elección de la barbarie* (2002), *El pasajero de Montauban* (2003) and *Weimar entre nosotros* (2004).

Robert Sala i Ramos received his Ph.D. in History from Rovira i Virgili University, he is Resident Professor of Prehistory at the same university and a member of the research team at Atapuerca and L'Abric Romaní (Capellades, Anoia). His areas of professional research include the evolution of the behaviour and lifestyles of Europe's early inhabitants, particularly the technological systems they developed, and the socialisation of science: research which has focused largely on the dissemination of knowledge of human evolution and the importance of technology in this process. Since 2003, he has been working on a research project on the Spanish Civil War in association with Barcelona University, which comprises the excavation and

analysis of the sites where traces
of the Civil War are still to be found, and
their subsequent social appraisal.
He is the author of numerous specialised
articles, and his books include: *Planeta
humà* (with Eudald Carbonell, 2000),
Sapiens (with Josep Corbella, Eudald
Carbonell and Salvador Moyà, 2000) and
Encara no som humans (with Eudald
Carbonell, 2002).

In 1997, he received the Prince of
Asturias Prize for Scientific and
Technological Research with the entire
research team from Atapuerca.

Francesc Torres is a plastic artist.
He lived in Paris from 1967 to 1969.
In 1972 he moved to the United States
(Chicago). In 1974 he settled in New York.
He lived in Berlin between 1986
and 1988 and has been in Barcelona
since October 2001.
He has exhibited at the Whitney
Museum of American Art (New York),
the Museum of Modern Art (New York),
the Carnegie Institute (Pittsburgh), the
Los Angeles Museum of Contemporary
Art, the Nationalgalerie (Berlin),
the State Russian Museum (Saint
Petersburg), the Massachusetts Institute
of Technology (Cambridge, Mass.),
the Museo Nacional Centro de Arte Reina
Sofía (Madrid, retrospective).

His work can be found in many
public and corporate collections around
the world. The awards he has received
include the National Endowment for the
Arts Individual Artist's Fellowship on four
occasions, the D.A.A.D. from the German
Federal Government and the Fulbright
Fellowship for academic exchange.
He has been awarded the National Plastic
Arts Prize by the Catalan government.

Michael Walzer is Professor of Social
Science at the Institute for Advanced
Study in Princeton, New Jersey and
co-editor of *Dissent* (a magazine of the
democratic left). He graduated from
Brandeis University, received his Ph.D.
from Harvard, taught at Princeton and
Harvard Universities before coming to
the Institute. He writes about war,
politics, and social justice. His books
include *Just and Unjust Wars* (1977),
Spheres of Justice (1983), *Interpretation
and Social Criticism* (1987), *The Company
of Critics* (1988), *On Toleration* (1997),
and the forthcoming *Arguing about War.*

Jay Winter is Professor of History
at Yale University. From 1979-2000, he
was Reader in Modern History at the
University of Cambridge and Fellow
of Pembroke College, Cambridge.
He is the author of many books on the
First World War, including *Sites of
memory, sites of mourning: the place of
the Great War in European cultural history*
(1995) and, with Jean-Louis Robert,
*Capital cities at war: Paris, London, Berlin
1914-1919* (1997). He was chief historian
and co-producer of the Emmy-award-
winning television series *The Great War
and the shaping of the twentieth century,*
first screened on PBS and the BBC in
1996, and subsequently broadcast in 27
countries. He is also a director of the
research centre of the Historial de la
Grande Guerre, an international museum
of the First World War at Péronne,
Somme, France.

Photographic credits

Naval Historical Center, Washington DC
p. 222: Imperial War Museum, London. © Artist's Estate
p. 223, 250, 251: Imperial War Museum, London.
© The Art Archive, London
p. 229: Don McCullin / Contact Press Images / Contacto
p. 231, 233: Courtesy of Another Vietnam (National
Geographic), Washington DC. © Doug Niven and Tim Page
p. 236, 237, 238, 239: Life © 1965 Time Inc., Courtesy
of James and Sarah Burrows
p. 240: © BHVP / Gérard Leyris
p. 241: Succession Picasso. Photograph: RMN - R. G. Ojeda.
© Pablo Picasso, Vegap, Barcelona, 2004
p. 244: Reproduced by kind permission of The Royal
College of Surgeons of England, London
p. 249 (below): © AP / Radial Press
p. 252, 253: Yunghi Kim / Contact Press Images / Contacto
p. 254 (above right): Footage Farm, London
p. 255: Courtesy of The Broido Family Collection, Chicago
p. 256: Arxiu Alcofar, Barcelona
p. 257: Bildarchiv – Deutsches Historisches Museum,
Berlin (unknown photographer)
p. 260: © Romano Cagnoni, Camaiore, Italy
p. 261: © Gervasio Sánchez. These photographs belong to
the photographic project "Mined lives", led and financed by
Metges Sense Fronteres, Intermón-Oxfam and Mans Unides
p. 262: Archivo Fotográfico C.A.C.- Museo Patio
Herreriano, Valladolid
p. 263: Universitat de València. Patronat Martínez
Guerricabeitia
p. 264: © Anthony Suau
p. 265: © Agustí Centelles, Vegap, Barcelona, 2004
p. 266: Gilles Peress / Magnum Photos / Contacto
p. 268, 269, 270, 271: Reproduced by permission of the
Henry Moore Foundation, Hertfordshire
p. 272, 273: The State Memorial Museum of Defence and
Siege of Leningrad, Saint Petersburg
p. 275: Navy Art Collection, Naval Historical Center,
Washington DC
p. 276, 277: © James Nachtwey
p. 278, 279, 280: Courtesy of Galerie Martin Kudlek,
Cologne. © Simon Norfolk
p. 282: © USHMM, Washington DC
p. 283: State Museum at Majdanek, Lublin, Poland.
Photograph: Tomasz Samek
p. 284, 285: ANC. Archivo Guerra y Exilio. Centro Español
de Moscú, Sant Cugat del Vallès
p. 286: David Seymour / Magnum Photos / Contacto
p. 287, 289: © Museu del Joguet de Catalunya, Figueres
p. 288, 290, 291: Richard Salem, Editor, *Witness to
Genocide-The Children of Rwanda*, New York, 2000
Published by Friendship Press with support from the
NCC's Church World Service, Conflict Management
Initiatives and W.K. Kellogg Foundation
p. 292: (above): © Tea Kim Heang / AP / Radial Press /
(below): © The Hulton Getty Picture Collection, London
p. 294, 295: Paul Lowe / Grazia Neri / Contacto.
p. 297: Courtesy of Sonnabend Gallery, New York

Victory and defeat
p. 314: © AKG Images Berlin
p. 315, 317, 326 (above): Central Armed Forces Museum,
Moscow
p. 316: Courtesy of the National Museum of the US Army,
Army Art Collection
p. 318, 319: © Tretyakov Gallery, Moscow
p. 320, 321: Collection Josep Bosch, Geneva
p. 322, 323: © Albert Gusi i Las, Vegap, Barcelona, 2004
p. 324: Courtesy of the US Naval Academy Museum,
Annapolis, Maryland
p. 325: Navy Art Collection, Naval Historical Center,
Washington DC
p. 326 (below): Military Historical Museum, Saint Petersburg
p. 327: © Archivo fotográfico del Museo del Ejército, Madrid
p. 346, 347: Francesc Torres Collection, Barcelona

Memory
p. 348: Gilles Peress / Magnum Photos / Contacto.
p. 349 (above left and below left): Raymonde Provencher /
(above right): Susan Muska and Greta Olafsdottir / (below
right): Susan Meiselas, Alfred Guzzetti, Richard P. Rogers
p. 350, 351: Alfredo Jaar
p. 352, 353, 354, 355, 380 © José María Rosa and
María Bleda, Vegap, Barcelona, 2004

The future of war
p. 367: © Kenneth Jarecke / Contact Press Images

Acknowledgements

The Centre de Cultura Contemporània de Barcelona would like to
thank the following institutions, collectors and artists for their
invaluable help in putting together this exhibition and catalogue.

Loaners:
Archives nationales, Centre historique, Paris
Arxiu Nacional de Catalunya, Fons Franch-Clapers and
Archivo Guerra y Exilio – Fondo Centro Español de Moscú,
Sant Cugat del Vallès
Bibliothèque historique de la Ville de Paris, Fonds
Apollinaire, Paris
Bleda and Rosa
British Museum, Departement of Oriental Antiquities, London
British Museum, Department of Prints and Drawings, London
James and Sarah Burrows
Romano Cagnoni
Carl H. Scheele Collection, Arlington
Colección Arte Contemporáneo - Museo Patio Herreriano,
Valladolid
Durand-Ruel Collection, Paris
Dvir Gallery, Tel Aviv
Thomas Dworzak
Galerie Albstadt, Städtische Kunstsammlungen,
Sammlung Walther Groz, Albstadt
Galerie Anne de Villepoix, Paris
Galerie Martin Kudlek, Cologne
Galerie Xippas, Paris
Plàcid Garcia-Planas
George Grosz Estate, courtesy of Ralph Jentsch, Capri
Albert Gusi i Las
Historial de la Grande Guerre, Péronne, Somme
Eros Hoagland
Alfredo Jaar
Josep Bosch Collection, Geneva
David Levinthal
Military Historical Museum, Saint Petersburg
Musée de l'Armée, Paris
Musée d'Histoire Contemporaine – BDIC, Paris
Musée National d'Art Moderne, Centre d'Art Pompidou, Paris
Musée Picasso, Paris
Museo Central de las Fuerzas Armadas, Moscow
Museo del Ejército, Madrid
Museo di Arte Moderna e Contemporanea di Trento e
Rovereto, VAF Foundation, Rovereto
Museu del Joguet de Catalunya, Figueres
Museum of Contemporary Art Antwerp (MUHKA), Antwerp
James Natchwey
National Museum of the US Army, Army Art Collection,
Washington DC
Navy Art Collection, Naval Historical Center, Washington DC
Doug Niven
Pedro Parra Calderón Collection, Barcelona
Gilles Peress / Magnum Photos / Contacto
Private collection, New York
Private collection, courtesy of Ralph Jentsch, Capri
Private collection, courtesy of Sonnabend Gallery, New York
Josep Maria Pueyo
Ronald Feldman Fine Arts, New York
Royal College of Surgeons of England, London
Richard Salem
Gervasio Sánchez
Smithsonian Institution, National Museum of American
History, Behring Center, Washington DC
Christine Spengler
State Museum at Majdanek, Lublin
Stiftung Haus der Geschichte der Bundesrepublik
Deutschland, Bonn
Anthony Suau
Tate, London
The Andy Warhol Museum, Pittsburgh
The Board of Trustees of the Royal Armouries, Leeds
The Broilo Family Collection, Chicago
The Henry Moore Foundation, Hertfordshire
The State Russian Museum, Saint Petersburg
The Trustees of the Imperial War Museum, London
Francesc Torres
Tretyakov National Gallery, Moscow
United States Holocaust Memorial Museum, donation
by Abraham Zuckerman, Murray Pantirer and Isak
Levenstein, Washington DC
US Marine Corps History and Museums Division,
Washington DC
US Naval Academy Museum, Annapolis, Maryland
US Naval Sea Systems Command, Washington DC
White Cube, courtesy of Jake & Dinos Chapman, Jay
Jopling and White Cube, London
Wiener Städtische Allgemeine Versicherung
Aktiengesellschaft der Stadt Wien, Vienna

**The CCCB would also like to thank the following for
their collaboration:**
Montse Armengou and Ricard Belis
Australian War Memorial, Canberra
Barcelona Plató Film Commission, Barcelona
Montse Bartuí
Miquel Berga
Ike Bertels
Peter S. Briggs
Marc Antoni Broggi
Mercè Camins
Carmen Claudín
Montserrat Codina
Lurdes Cortès and Marisol Soto
Jordi Costa

Avery Chenoweth
Michel Decaudin
Docúpolis, Hugo Salinas, Barcelona
John T. (Jack) Dyer
Sergei V. Esipov
Filmoteca de Catalunya, Ramon Font, Barcelona
FOCAL, London
Enric Folch
Péter Forgács
Véronique Foucault
Lucie Fougeron
Kimiyo Foujita
Josep Franch-Clapers
Galeria dels Àngels, Barcelona
Galeria Elba Benítez, Madrid
Galería Fúcares, Madrid
Leonor García
Anthony L. Geist
Leon Golub
Hans Haacke
Handicap International, Lyon
Jessica Harrison-Hall
Hiroshima Peace Memorial Museum, Hiroshima
Antonio Homem
Reiko Imai
Yuri Khashchavatsky
Renée Klish
Mapasonor, Sàgar Malé, Mataró
Leanne Mella
Antoni Miralda
Gale Munro
Museu de Zoologia, Barcelona
Museum of Contemporary Art in Chicago
Susan Muska and Greta Olafsdottir
National Gallery of Canada, Ottawa
Patronato Martínez Gurricabeitia, Valencia
Anand Patwardhan
Yevgenia Petrova
Tatiana Pigariova
Daniel Pitarch
Marie-Pascale Prevost-Bault
Llum Quiñonero
Radio Belgrade, Zorica Pribic, Belgrade
RENFE, Barcelona
Michael Rooks
Martha Rosler
Bonnie Rowan
Sala Parés, Barcelona
Rocío San Claudio Santa Cruz
José Luis Sancho Gaspar
Steven Seidenberg
Luis Alejandre Sintes
Smithsonian Institution,
Hirshhorn Museum and Sculpture Garden,
Washington DC
Sombrerería Mil, Barcelona
Stefilm, Stefano Toaldi, Turin

Joel Suttles
The National Museum of Modern Art, Tokyo
The State Memorial Museum of Defence and Siege
of Leningrad, Saint Petersburg
Vicente Todolí
Tokyo Contemporary Art Museum, Tokyo
UPF – Arxiu Miniput, Barcelona
François Verster
Albert Vidal
Anita Weber
Angela Weight
Whitney Museum of American History, New York
Christine Whittaker
Heimo Zobernig
Masha Zrncic

Source of photographs and audiovisual images:
AKG Images, Berlin
AP / RADIAL PRESS, Madrid
Archivo Histórico NO-DO, Madrid
Arxiu Centelles, Barcelona
Arxius de l'Observatori – OVNI, Barcelona
Associated Press Television News, London
Barcelona Televisió, Barcelona
BBC Worldwide, London
Biblioteca Nacional de España, Madrid
Bildarchiv Preussischer Kulturbesitz, Berlin
Bless Bless Productions, New York
British Movietonews, Denham
Brooks Kraft, New York
Buyout Footage, Los Angeles CNN, Atlanta
Corbis / Cover, Barcelona Cosmo Film, Copenhagen
Deckert Distribution, Leipzig
Electronic Arts Intermix, New York
Filmoteca Española, Madrid
Footage Farm, London
Gaumont-Pathé Archives, Saint Ouen
GMR Films, Susan Meiselas, Alfred Guzzetti and Richard
P. Rogers, Boston
Harun Farocki Filmproduktion, Berlin
Historic Films Archive, Greenport, New York
Independent Television News Ltd, London
Japanese Devils Production Committee, Tokyo
Macumba International, Montreal
Magnum Photo / Contacto, Madrid
Musée d'Histoire Contemporaine – BDIC, Paris
National Air and Space Museum, Smithsonian Institution,
Archives Division, Washington DC
National Archives and Records Administration, Maryland
Radio Nacional de España, Madrid
RTVE Delegació de Catalunya, Sant Cugat del Vallès
SIPA Press, Paris
Televisió de Catalunya, Sant Joan Despí
The Archives Project, New York
The Hulton Getty Picture Collection, London
TV3, Programa "30 Minuts", Sant Joan Despí
UNICEF, Madrid

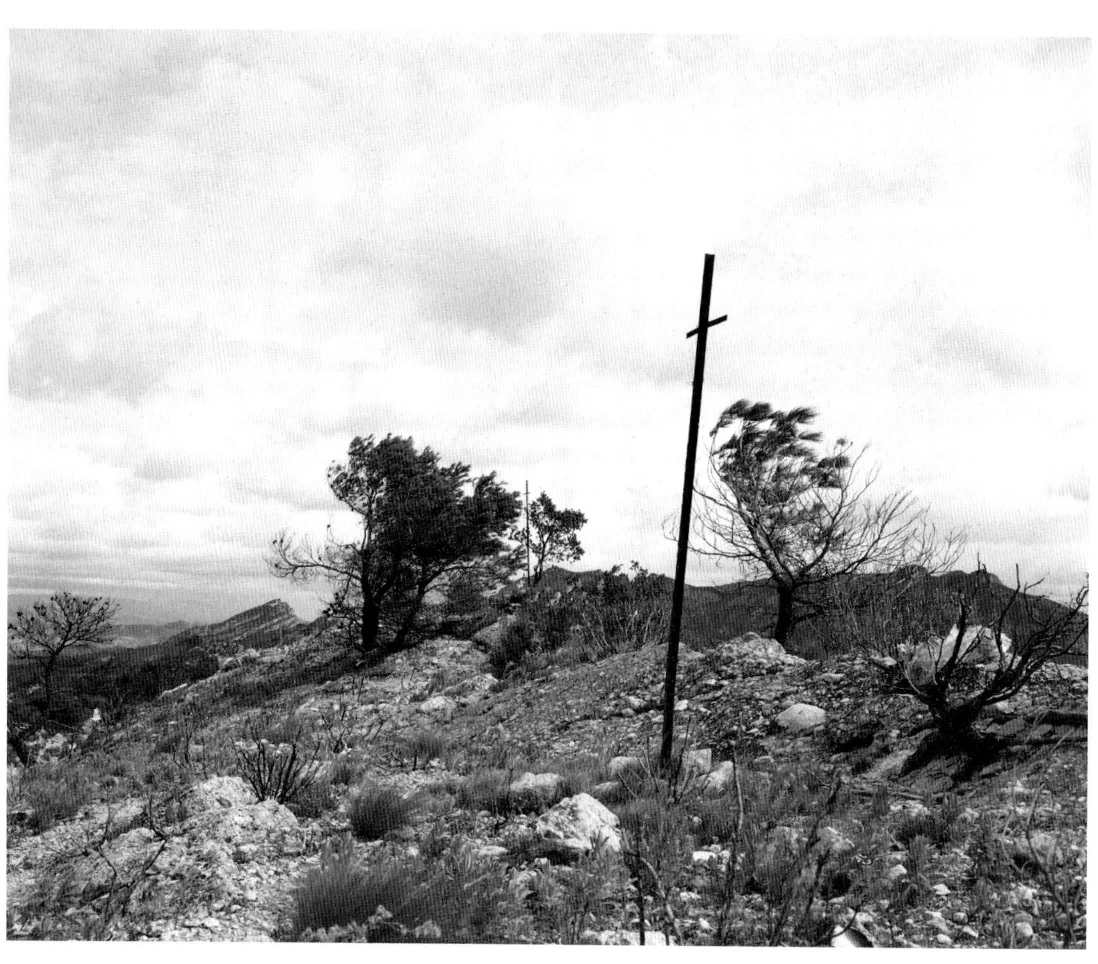

JOSÉ MARÍA ROSA AND MARÍA BLEDA, Death peak, 1995
Colour photograph on aluminium, rigid cotton base with text and wooden frame, 85 x 90 cm
Collection of the artists